SOCIAL RESEARCH METHODS

Sara Miller McCune founded SAGE Publishing in 1965 to support the dissemination of usable knowledge and educate a global community. SAGE publishes more than 1000 journals and over 800 new books each year, spanning a wide range of subject areas. Our growing selection of library products includes archives, data, case studies and video. SAGE remains majority owned by our founder and after her lifetime will become owned by a charitable trust that secures the company's continued independence.

Los Angeles | London | New Delhi | Singapore | Washington DC | Melbourne

SOCIAL RESEARCH METHODS

Qualitative, Quantitative and Mixed Methods Approaches

Sigmund Grønmo

Los Angeles | London | New Delhi
Singapore | Washington DC | Melbourne

Los Angeles | London | New Delhi
Singapore | Washington DC | Melbourne

SAGE Publications Ltd
1 Oliver's Yard
55 City Road
London EC1Y 1SP

SAGE Publications Inc.
2455 Teller Road
Thousand Oaks, California 91320

SAGE Publications India Pvt Ltd
B 1/I 1 Mohan Cooperative Industrial Area
Mathura Road
New Delhi 110 044

SAGE Publications Asia-Pacific Pte Ltd
3 Church Street
#10-04 Samsung Hub
Singapore 049483

Editor: Aly Owen
Assistant editor: Charlotte Bush
Assistant editor, digital: Sunita Patel
Production editor: Ian Antcliff
Marketing manager: Susheel Gokarakonda
Cover design: Shaun Mercier
Typeset by: C&M Digitals (P) Ltd, Chennai, India
Printed in the UK

Originally published as Samfunnsvitenskapelige metoder. First edition © 2004. Second edition © 2016. Bergen: Fagbokforlaget

Library of Congress Control Number: 2019936648

British Library Cataloguing in Publication data

A catalogue record for this book is available from the British Library

ISBN 978-1-5264-4123-2
ISBN 978-1-5264-4124-9 (pbk)

At SAGE we take sustainability seriously. Most of our products are printed in the UK using responsibly sourced papers and boards. When we print overseas we ensure sustainable papers are used as measured by the PREPS grading system. We undertake an annual audit to monitor our sustainability.

CONTENTS

PREFACE

This book provides an introduction to social research methods for university and college students. The purpose is to describe and discuss methods that are used in different social science disciplines and in multidisciplinary fields based on social research methods. The book contains a number of examples of how various methods are used in different disciplines and fields. In addition to examples from actual research, each chapter presents learning objectives, chapter highlights, student exercises and questions, as well as recommended literature for further reading.

Methodological and ethical issues in social science are discussed, and methods for designing and implementing social science studies are examined. The book presents methods and methodological concerns related to the main elements of the research process, from formulation of research questions and construction of research designs through collection and analysis of data to interpretation of findings and presentation of results. Throughout the book, qualitative and quantitative approaches in social research are described and compared, and reasons and strategies for combining the two approaches in mixed methods research are presented.

The book is based on my experiences from social research and teaching of social research methods at several universities in different countries since the early 1970s. Contact, communication, and interaction with colleagues and students at these universities have been extremely valuable. During the work on this book, I have been affiliated with the University of Bergen, Sámi University of Applied Sciences, and Institute for Social Research in Norway, James Cook University and Charles Darwin University in Australia, as well as the University of Cambridge in the UK. I am very grateful to these inspiring academic environments.

Most of the chapters in the book are based on the second edition of a similar book, which I published in Norwegian in 2016 (*Samfunnsvitenskapelige metoder*). I want to thank the Norwegian publisher, Fagbokforlaget, for permission to publish this book in English. Although these chapters have been partly rewritten, and some new chapters have been added in this book, English translations of most chapters from the Norwegian edition have been very useful in my work on the book. Many thanks to the translator, Diarmuid Kennan.

I have received support or comments from several colleagues. In particular, I want to thank Maria Iacovou, Trond Petersen, and John Scott. Several anonymous reviewers have given very valuable comments at different stages of my work on the manuscript. The Sage editorial team in London has been very helpful and supportive during the whole process, from the first ideas to the final manuscript.

Finally, I am very grateful to Eirun, for her patience and support.

Sigmund Grønmo

ABOUT THE AUTHOR

Photo Thor Brødreskift/
The Holberg Prize

Sigmund Grønmo is Emeritus Professor of Sociology and former Rector (Vice-Chancellor) of the University of Bergen, Norway. He is affiliated with the Institute for Social Research in Oslo, Norway, and he is an Honorary University Professorial Fellow at Charles Darwin University in Darwin, Australia, and a Life Member of Clare Hall at the University of Cambridge in the UK.

Previously, he was Professor at the Norwegian Business School, Adjunct Professor at the University of Oslo and Sámi University of Applied Sciences, and Research Director and Executive Director at the Norwegian Fund for Market and Distribution Research.

He is an elected member of the Norwegian Academy of Science and Letters, and Academiae Europaea, as well as a Fellow of the World Academy of Art and Science.

He has been a Visiting Professor at Dalhousie University, Halifax, Nova Scotia, Canada; Illinois State University, USA; University of California, Berkeley, USA; University of Queensland, Brisbane, Australia; James Cook University, Cairns, Australia; and University of Cambridge, UK.

He has published numerous books and a large number of journal articles, book chapters and papers, especially within economic sociology, the sociology of time, social network analysis, and social science methodology. He has extensive experience in teaching social research methods at universities and colleges in Norway and several other countries.

DISCOVER YOUR TEXTBOOK'S ONLINE RESOURCES!

Organised around the different stages of the research process, from theoretical foundations to writing up and presenting research, you can find the support you need to successfully complete your research course or project at: **https://study.sagepub.com/gronmo**.

Watch and learn! **Videos** selected by author Sigmund Grønmo give you deeper insight into key concepts.

Case studies help bring theory to life and show you how social research works in the real world.

Sigmund takes you on a **guided reading tour** of **journal articles**, helping you build your confidence when reading and understanding academic sources.

Practice your skills at your own pace with downloadable **datasets** that help you master data analysis.

Critical thinking exercises help you think more deeply about concepts and ideas.

With examples from qualitative and quantitative studies, Sigmund explains step-by-step how to **move from idea to design** in your research project.

Broaden your knowledge of important concepts and ideas in research methods with **encyclopaedia definitions**.

A **citation toolkit** offers a host of weblinks that help you take the hassle out of citing and referencing sources.

Web links directing you to relevant resources form a **software refresher guide** for IBM SPSS and NVivo.

Get up to speed with key terms and master social science vocabulary with **glossary flashcards**.

PART I

RESEARCHING SOCIETY

The online resources are here to help with the basics of researching society!

Visit https://study.sagepub.com/gronmo to access videos, case studies, key term definitions, and critical thinking exercises that will help you learn more about the foundations of social research methods and establishing ethical research.

HOW AND WHY WE STUDY SOCIETY

This chapter provides knowledge about the essential features of social science and its relationship to society, as well as some fundamental methodological issues and principles in social science.

The chapter will teach you about

- how social phenomena can be examined by means of different methods
- the difference between qualitative and quantitative data
- the researcher's roles as participant and observer

- the relationship between facts and values in social science
- debates on fundamental issues in social science, including positivism and postmodernism
- basic principles for social science, including the principle of truth as a primary value.

Science on society

Social science is based on systematic research about phenomena and conditions in society. Social science consists of the methods that are developed and applied in this research, as well as the knowledge and theories that are the results of the research. This book is focused on social research methods. Different methods will be presented and discussed, and in order to show how these methods have been used, the book will also provide examples of knowledge and theories about society that are based on various research designs.

The selection of methods in social research is related to knowledge development and theoretical perspectives. In order to develop interesting knowledge and theories, it is necessary to use appropriate and adequate research methods. The selection of methods for a particular study depends on the kinds of social phenomena that are examined and the kinds of social theories that are emphasized in the study.

This introductory chapter starts with discussions of why social research is important, and why it is useful to study social research methods. Then, an example of a social science study is presented. The example shows how different methods can be used to examine dynamic processes in bureaucracies. The next section presents a more general clarification of what social science is. Then, after a discussion of the

relationship between social science and society, and the distinction between qualitative and quantitative data, the relationship between facts and values is examined. Finally, the chapter presents an overview of how the book is organized.

Why is social research important?

Like other scientific fields, social science is valuable in itself, as a part of the total culture in society, and it is important in a more instrumental sense, for the development of different social activities and for society at large.

Social science has been important for our identity and self-understanding, and for our understanding of interpersonal relations and society as a whole. Cultural, social, political and economic conditions are described and discussed by means of concepts and ways of thinking that have been developed within social science. Policies, strategies and decisions in different areas are often based on knowledge and theories from social science.

On the other hand, there are many policies, strategies and decisions in business, administration and politics that are not based on insight and understanding from social science. Social science also presents critical perspectives on many conditions and trends in society. Moreover, social science analyses and theories may be ambiguous and unclear as a basis for decisions in specific cases. Such studies will often problematize conditions in society, rather than suggesting simple advice for actions or interventions. Typically, this reflects the fact that social conditions are both complex and complicated. Thus, social science is not always able to present clear and definitive conclusions. In any event, however, it may contribute to more insight and knowledge regarding different aspects of specific cases as well as social life in general.

Furthermore, different social science studies may present quite different analyses and interpretations of the same social phenomena. Different studies may emphasize different research questions, refer to different theories, apply different methods and end up with different conclusions. These differences are related to the great diversity in social science perspectives. However, even such differences between studies may be important and useful, since they demonstrate how social phenomena and conditions can be understood and interpreted in different ways, depending on the viewpoints of the researchers, the perspectives in the studies, and the premises for the conclusions. Thus, social science may contribute to informed, knowledge-based and rational public debates on various issues.

For example, perspectives, insights and knowledge from social science are very important for understanding and coping with the major global challenges in our time. One of these challenges refers to environmental issues, sustainable development and climate change. Whereas natural science examines such phenomena as global warming and how it is affected by emissions of carbon dioxide and other gases, social science provides knowledge about the human behaviour, social structures, economic conditions and political processes that lead to gas emissions and create other environmental problems. Social research can also describe and explain the consequences of climate change for people's living conditions in various parts of the world. Furthermore,

social science is an important basis for discussing what kinds of action would be needed to reduce or prevent environmental problems that lead to global warming and global changes.

Why is it useful to study social research methods?

There are a number of reasons for studying social research methods. The most obvious reason is that such methods are used in all kinds of social science studies, and that knowledge about methods is necessary for doing social research.

Social science students have to carry out their own research. In the early stages of their studies, students have to do small and simple research tasks in different types of exercises, and later they have to write a master's thesis and perhaps a PhD dissertation. Many university candidates with a social science degree will develop a career in research at a university or a research institute. In addition, social science graduates who work in non-academic institutions, such as business or public agencies, are often asked to write reports or carry out various types of studies on social phenomena.

In all these types of studies, it is necessary to use social research methods. Thus, it is important to study social research methods:

- Learning about the whole repertoire of available methods, the main features of each method, and the major differences between methods, is an important basis for choosing the most adequate method for a particular research task or a specific research question.
- Knowledge about the wide variety of methods for collecting and analysing data is essential for understanding the whole research process in different types of studies.
- Skills in using different methods are necessary for ensuring the quality and ethical basis of the research that is carried out.

Learning about social research methods is not only necessary for carrying out research. It is also very useful for assessing the quality and significance of social research that has been conducted by other students or researchers. Knowledge about different methods is important for understanding the content of a research report or information about a study that is presented in the media or at conferences. Our methodological insight enables us to

- assess the quality of the research
- understand the limitations of the study and its findings and conclusions
- compare the study with other relevant studies based on different methods.

Furthermore, studying social research methods is not only useful for social scientists in their professional roles, when they use their social science skills in their work. Knowing about different methods may also be very valuable for all citizens, and for our non-professional participation in social life. Insight into social research methods may be useful if we participate in public debates, in political work, or in other voluntary activities. Learning about social research methods is useful for

- knowing how to seek and find information about phenomena and conditions in society
- developing a systematic way of comparing information from different sources
- making critical evaluations of different types of information.

Dynamics of bureaucracy: Example of a social science study

A very good example of a social science study is Peter M. Blau's study of bureaucracies (Blau, 1963). The purpose of presenting this example is to show how particular phenomena in society can be examined by means of different social research methods, how different methods can shed light on different aspects of the phenomena, and how combinations of different methods can provide holistic insight or comprehensive knowledge about the phenomena that are examined. This example will be referred to in several chapters in this book.

Background and purpose of the study

Bureaucracies are a central and well-known feature of modern society. Bureaucratic organizations are common in both public administration and private business. Research about bureaucratic systems and bureaucratic activity is important within several disciplines in social science. Modern bureaucracies were analysed by Max Weber (1864–1920), who was one of the founders of social science. In particular, he was interested in how typical bureaucracies are structured and organized, and he focused on the characteristic features of bureaucratic activity in its most pure form, as an 'ideal type' (Weber, 2013).

With reference to Weber's analysis, Peter M. Blau (1963) carried out a study of activities and relations in public bureaucracies in the USA in the late 1940s. The report from his studies was presented in 1952, as Blau's PhD dissertation at Columbia University in New York, where he worked together with the well-known sociologist Robert Merton (1910–2003).

Weber emphasized studies of the stable structural features of bureaucracies as well as the general and enduring characteristics of bureaucratic activity. Blau was more interested in the dynamic aspects of bureaucracies. His purpose was to examine processes, developments and organizational change within public bureaucracies.

Blau focused on the daily activities of two selected government agencies, as well as the interpersonal relations among the employees of these agencies. One of the selected agencies was a public employment agency in an eastern US state.

The other was a department in a US federal enforcement agency, which was responsible for the implementation of two particular federal laws. Blau referred to each agency as a case in his study, and he described his study as a case study of the two agencies.

How the study was implemented

In both agencies, Blau conducted informal conversations, or unstructured interviews, with the administrative leaders of the agency, and he reviewed instructions, rules and other important documents in the agency. Based on this material, he selected one of the departments in each agency for more thorough investigations. Blau worked as an employee in the department for three months. In this fieldwork period, he observed officials in the office, joined them on their field visits and had lunch with them, and took part in informal interaction and social gatherings with the officials. At the same time he carried out more systematic collection of information, based on observation of activities in the department, interviews with colleagues and studies of documents and other available materials. All this information was described in field notes. Thus, in his fieldwork, Blau was both a participant in the department and an observer of the actors and activities within the department. This approach of combining participation and observation is called participant observation.

In addition to the participant observation, a structured questionnaire was used for interviewing each employee in the department. The interview focused on attitudes and assessments regarding work, career, clients and colleagues.

Results and importance of the study

Blau's study is an example of how social science studies can be based on different types of information, or data, and how different methods can be applied for collecting these data. Some data were recorded as numbers. These are called quantitative data. For example, Blau observed and counted how many times, or how often, the employees of the agencies were in contact with each other. The structured interviews provided large amounts of quantitative data, for example the number of employees who expressed different attitudes and assessments. The review of files, statistical reports and other available documents provided information about, for example, how many cases or clients had been handled, how long the handling of the cases had taken, and how many employees had been involved in these activities.

Some data could not be expressed as numbers, but were systematized and registered as text. These data, which mainly consisted of the field notes that Blau wrote in the evenings during his fieldwork periods, are called qualitative data. In his field notes, he could register, for example, what types of contacts he observed between the employees, what kinds of collaboration he received information about in informal conversations or unstructured interviews, and what types of administrative procedures and processes he learned about by reading files or other documents.

Blau used different methods for analysing his large and complex data sets. The field notes were already systematically reviewed and analysed during the fieldwork. More extensive analyses were carried out after the completion of the data collection. The qualitative and quantitative data were processed and analysed in different ways.

The different data and methods provided insight into different aspects of the bureaucratic organizations and their activities. Based on the combination of all data and methods, Blau could develop a comprehensive overview and a holistic understanding of the dynamics of these organizations. Thus, the variety of data and methods made it possible for Blau to examine his research questions. Whereas Weber had focused on stable structural features and general characteristics of bureaucracies, Blau's study showed that bureaucratic structures continuously create conditions that modify or change these structures. Blau's study documented important dynamic features of bureaucracies. He showed that the capacity of bureaucracies to adapt to environmental changes was greater than previously assumed. Inspired by his colleague and supervisor, Robert Merton, Blau interpreted these findings within the general social science perspective that is called functionalism. This perspective implies that organizations or other actors or elements in society will adapt to each other, to their environments and to society as a whole, in ways that function best for the interplay between the different elements of society as well as for the society at large. Since these adaptation processes are regarded as functional, the perspective is described as functionalism.

Thus, the general contribution of Blau's study of bureaucracies was that it resulted in new knowledge and new insight that made it possible to understand bureaucratic organizations and their activities in a new way.

What is social science?

After this example of a particular social science study, it is reasonable to clarify more generally what social science is. There is a wide variety of studies within social science, and many studies are different from Blau's study of bureaucracies. Nevertheless, it is possible to point out some common features of social science studies and some general characteristics of social science activity.

Social science deals with human beings in different types of societies. It is not limited to studies of individuals or groups of individuals. It also includes research on society as a whole. Major subject areas within social science are people's social background, attitudes and activities, characteristics of individuals and groups, individuals' and groups' relations to one another and to the society, as well as features of the society at large.

Social science is based on systematic research on such topics and includes the knowledge, theories and methods that are developed and used in this research. The historical development of social science is characterized by increasing specialization and differentiation, in several social science disciplines, such as sociology, political science, social anthropology, economics, psychology, and social geography. These disciplines may be referred to as the social sciences (plural). However, it seems reasonable to distinguish between the social science disciplines (plural) and social science (singular). Thus, social science consists of the totality of all social science disciplines. In addition, social science includes various research fields or programmes of study, such as media studies, which are based on combinations of elements from different disciplines.

Each discipline in social science may define its distinctive features and identity with reference to its most typical subject areas, its most important theoretical perspectives, or its most common methods. The topics, theories and methods of different social science disciplines will be further discussed in Chapter 2.

However, the distinctions between different disciplines in social science are complicated. First, there are different views on what topics, theories and methods should be most central in each discipline. Within each discipline there are different or competing perspectives on what should be examined, how studies should be conducted, and how social phenomena should be understood.

Second, the boundaries between different disciplines may be unclear and difficult to define. To some extent, different disciplines may include the same topics. For example, there are many overlapping topics between sociology and other social science disciplines. Some theories are emphasized in several disciplines, such as theories on social networks. The most important social research methods are also common for different disciplines. This methodological overlap between disciplines is particularly important here, because it is an important purpose of this book to present and discuss methods that should be regarded as a common methodological foundation for all social science disciplines. In this discussion, examples and illustrations of the application of different methods are drawn from research in different disciplines.

Another reason why the boundaries between social science disciplines are unclear is that the development of some new disciplines, programmes of study or research fields is based on combinations of perspectives and contributions from several traditional and basic social science disciplines. An example of this is media studies, which is often described as a separate discipline, although it consists of elements from several other disciplines, such as sociology, political science and economics. In general, when elements from different social science disciplines are combined or merged in various multidisciplinary study programmes or research fields it becomes more difficult to define the boundaries between the different disciplines.

Not only the distinctions between social science disciplines, but also the boundaries between these disciplines and other disciplines may sometimes be unclear and unstable. For example, there are different views regarding such disciplines as history and philosophy. Although these disciplines are usually included in the humanities, it is sometimes argued that they should be regarded as social science disciplines. Moreover, a number of disciplines combine social science elements with elements from other fields. For example, the discipline of media studies combines elements from social science with elements from the humanities, geography includes perspectives and topics from both social science and natural science, and psychology combines contributions from both social science and medicine.

Such ambiguities and variations regarding disciplinary boundaries are reflected in the organization of departments and faculties at universities and colleges. There are differences between institutions and changes over time as to what disciplines are included in the social science faculties, and how the disciplines are organized in different departments within the social science faculties.

These organizational variations and changes illustrate that there are different views on what social science is. The differences in definitions of social science may be related to the diversity of competing theoretical perspectives within social science. Moreover, the organization of social science faculties at universities and colleges does not only reflect different academic perspectives. It may also depend on the allocation of resources and the availability of competent academic staff, in addition to more general university policies or research strategies.

The fact that social science may be defined and organized in different ways is also important for the reading, understanding and use of this book. Since one of the purposes of the book is to present a common methodological foundation for all social science disciplines, the content and organization of the book must be based on a particular view on what this methodological foundation should include. This view reflects a particular perspective on what social science is. Hopefully, the book will stimulate discussion and reflection, not only about different methodological issues, but also about the nature and content of social science.

Social science and society

Since social science deals with human beings in different types of societies, the relationship between social science and society is an important topic in the theory of science.

Participants and observers

One feature of the relationship between social science and society is that social science is itself a part of the society that it studies. For example, social scientists may contribute to public debates by providing knowledge and information for other participants in the debates. However, the social scientists may also participate in the debates themselves, with their own views and arguments. As participants in public debates, they may present knowledge and insights from their research, but they may also, just like other participants in the debate, argue in favour of special values or interests that are not necessarily based on scientific knowledge or theories.

Thus, social scientists are not only observers of the society. They are also participants in the society. In this sense, social science may be regarded as quite different from natural science.

The relationship between social science and natural science has been an important topic in theory of science debates. There are different views on the significance and implications of the differences between the two fields of science. However, it is reasonable to argue that the special relationship between researchers and society has different and more challenging implications in social science than it has in other scientific fields. Two major implications of this relationship should be emphasized.

First, the research process may affect individuals or groups that are examined, so that their behaviour during the study is different from their usual behaviour. Thus, the knowledge of the behaviour that is obtained by the researchers may not be accurate and reliable. The knowledge may be biased because of the participants' reactions to being involved in the research process. This methodological problem is called *reactivity*. It is also referred to as a *control effect*.

Second, the researchers' social background and social experiences may affect their perceptions and interpretations of the phenomena that are examined. The knowledge developed by the researchers may not only be a result of how these phenomena 'really' are, but also reflect the researchers' frame of reference and way of thinking. This type of methodological problems is described as *reflexivity*.

Reactivity (control effect) and reflexivity are important challenges in social research, which will be further discussed in several chapters in this book.

The potential effects of reactivity and reflexivity on the results of social science studies have to be considered carefully in each study.

Debate about positivism

The relationship between social science and society is a central topic in the debate about *positivism*. In social science, the concept of positivism is associated mainly with Auguste Comte (1798–1857). He is regarded as the founder of sociology as a scientific discipline.

Positivism is a position in the theory of science which assumes that social scientific knowledge is developed through systematic studies of 'positively given' empirical facts about existing phenomena in society. It is argued that these phenomena exist as observable and objective facts, and that they cannot be influenced or changed by being observed and examined. The main task for social scientists is to discover or reveal the universal laws or regularities of social life and conditions in society. Theories in social science can be constructed as systems of such universal laws. This understanding of social science is based on the assumption that it is possible to establish an absolute boundary between facts and values, and that social scientific studies of social facts are completely independent of both the researchers' and other persons' evaluations of these facts. In this connection, it is important that the researcher is not a participant in the activities or processes that are examined, but only an observer of these activities or processes. Social life and society is observed from outside. The positivist position means that social science can relate to facts in society in the same way as natural science relates to facts in nature. Thus, positivism implies that there is no essential difference between social science and natural science.

In the 1960s, an intense debate about positivism arose in social science. The background for the debate was that the positivistic position at that time was central among leading social scientists, especially in the USA (Gorton, 2010). A debate about positivism was raised, in particular, by Jürgen Habermas and other sociologists and social philosophers at the University of Frankfurt in West Germany. In their academic environment, which was called the Frankfurt School, critical theory was emphasized, and positivism was criticized and rejected as a basis for social science.

One of the arguments against positivism is that phenomena and conditions in society cannot be regarded as objective and observable facts. Human beings in society are independent subjects who, within certain limits, can choose how they want to act and interact. How they really act or interact depends on their intentions and their context. Thus, it is not possible to predict how people will behave, and social conditions may at any time change in unexpected ways. Consequently, it is not possible to identify universal laws and regularities in society. The main task of social science is to interpret and understand particular social phenomena with reference to people's own intentions and the specific contextual conditions. People's actions must be understood in terms of the meaning the actions have for the people themselves. Society cannot be observed from outside. Intentional and contextual interpretation and understanding require involvement and empathy with people's lives and activities. Such involvement and empathy are not obtained if the researchers are only observers. They must also be participants.

Furthermore, it is not possible for social science to be outside society. Research on society can affect and interfere in people's actions and society's development. Thus, social science will be a part of the context in which people's actions have to be understood. Since social scientists cannot be only observers of the social life they study, they must consider consciously and systematically the implications of the fact that they are also participants in this social life. Social scientists cannot study society in the same way as natural scientists study nature. Thus, the fundamental critique of positivism means that there are considerable and essential differences between social science and natural science.

Qualitative and quantitative studies

The relationship between qualitative and quantitative studies in social science is another issue in the debate about positivism. However, this relationship is also discussed more generally, independent of positivism.

Although this discussion sometimes refers to qualitative and quantitative *methods* in social science, the distinction between qualitative and quantitative is primarily based on different characteristics of the *data* that are collected and analysed. Simply defined, *quantitative data* are expressed as numbers or in other quantity terms (for example, many–few, more–less, or high–low), whereas data are qualitative if they are not expressed in this way. Typically, *qualitative data* are expressed as text. Information on how long (in years) a person has spent in full-time education is an example of quantitative data. Information on what type of education the person has is an example of qualitative data. Based on this, social science studies are quantitative if they are mainly based on quantitative data, while qualitative studies are mainly based on qualitative data.

According to a positivistic understanding of science, social science should be based on the same types of research designs as other scientific fields. Based on this understanding, it may be argued that social science should apply research designs and methods that have been developed in natural science. More specifically, this means that social science should use experimental research designs and mathematical or statistical methods for analysing quantitative data. It is argued that use of quantitative data is the only scientific basis for examining facts about society. A well-known slogan for this position is that 'if you can't count it, it doesn't count' (Holsti, 1969: 11).

On the other hand, critics of positivism have maintained that, since social science is essentially different from natural science, social science has to use data and methods that are different from those used in natural science. Sometimes it is argued that quantitative data and statistical methods can be used in natural science but not in social science, and that meaningful, non-positivistic studies of social conditions can only be based on qualitative data. This argument implies that any use of quantitative data and statistical methods is regarded as positivistic research. The slogan for this position is that 'if you can count it, that ain't it' (Holsti, 1969: 11).

However, in this book it is maintained that it is not reasonable to make a fundamental choice of either quantitative data or qualitative data for all social science studies. Such a definitive choice between data types should not be justified by reference to theory of science or any other principles. There is no absolute connection between positivistic research and quantitative data, or between non-positivistic research and qualitative data. As pointed out above, Blau (1963) used both qualitative and quantitative data in his study of bureaucracies. It would not be meaningful to characterize the quantitative parts of his study as positivistic and the qualitative parts as non-positivistic. The most important features of positivistic research refer to the researchers' relationship to society, as well as their interpretation and understanding of phenomena and conditions in society. In other words, what is important in this connection is not the type of data that is used in a study, but how the results of the study are interpreted. Not only quantitative but also qualitative data can be interpreted within a positivistic perspective of social science. Similarly, both qualitative and quantitative data can be used and interpreted in non-positivistic or critical research.

The distinction between qualitative and quantitative data is not a pure dichotomy, but refers to a scale, as shown in Figure 1.1. The figure illustrates how different types of data may be placed along the scale, from the most quantitative data to the most qualitative data. The most precise quantitative data type is placed at one of the extreme positions on the scale. These data are called *metric data*. An example of metric data is data about a person's age, expressed as a number of years. The next data type on the scale is *non-metric data* expressed as numbers, which are somewhat less precise than metric data. Non-metric data are, for example, data on a person's education, not in years, but in two (numbered) categories, low education (1) and high education (2). The third data type is even less precise, since data are not expressed as numbers but may still be regarded as quantitative, since they refer to quantity terms. Examples of quantity terms are long (distance), strong (support), or few (members). Finally, the most qualitative type of data, expressed as text, is placed at the other extreme position of the scale. An example of text data is data on a person's argument in a debate on Brexit, expressed as a statement: 'I support Brexit because the UK should be independent'.

A differentiation between qualitative and quantitative data may refer to different points on the scale. In this book, the main distinction between qualitative and quantitative data is defined with reference to point (B) on the scale, as

(A) Quantitative data		(B) Qualitative data	
Metric data	Non-metric data expressed as numbers	Data expressed in quantity terms	Data expressed as texts
(Age, in years)	(Education, in numbered categories: 1 Low education 2 High education)	(Distance between home and work: A long distance)	(Argument: 'I support Brexit because the UK should be independent')

Figure 1.1 Overview of different types of data (examples in parentheses)

shown in Figure 1.1. This means, as pointed out above, that data are regarded as quantitative if they are expressed as numbers or in quantity terms, whereas data expressed as text are regarded as qualitative data. However, some researchers define the quality–quantity distinction with reference to point (A) on the scale in Figure 1.1. According to this definition, only metric data are regarded as quantitative data, while all other data types are regarded as qualitative data. This definition is preferred mainly by researchers who emphasize advanced statistical analyses in their studies.

Different types of data will be further described and discussed in Chapters 6 and 7.

The study by Blau (1963), which was presented above, shows that quantitative data are most adequate for studying certain phenomena in society, whereas qualitative data are more adequate for examining other social phenomena. Thus, qualitative and quantitative data are not competing, but complementary data types. Furthermore, in practical research, many research designs that are mainly qualitative may include some quantitative data, and many designs that are mainly quantitative may also include some qualitative data.

As exemplified by Blau's study, social phenomena may have both qualitative and quantitative aspects and may, therefore, be examined by means of both qualitative and quantitative data. Such studies are referred to as *mixed methods research.*

As there are different views on how fundamental the difference between qualitative and quantitative approaches is, there are also different views on how meaningful it is to combine qualitative and quantitative data in mixed methods research. One view is that the two approaches reflect so fundamentally different ways of regarding the nature of society and social phenomena that they are too incoherent to be combined in the same studies. The view presented in this book, however, is that mixed methods research is both meaningful and valuable in social science. Compared to strictly qualitative or strictly quantitative studies, research based on combinations of qualitative and quantitative data can

contribute to a more extensive analysis and a more comprehensive insight. However, in each mixed methods study, the challenge related to incoherence between qualitative and quantitative approaches should be considered, and how the qualitative and quantitative data are combined should be based on these considerations.

Nevertheless, when planning and designing a particular study, researchers often make a choice between qualitative and quantitative data. This choice is not based on principles, but on strategies. As pointed out above, in principle, neither of the two data types is better than the other, and neither is more scientific than the other. However, in a particular study, one of the data types may be strategically more adequate than the other for examining the specific research questions of the study and the specific kinds of phenomena the study is focused on. *Research questions,* and their importance for choosing adequate methods in social science studies, are discussed in Chapter 4.

An example of a qualitative study is found in an article by Balderrama and Molina (2009). The study is based on participant observation in three North Carolina farm labour camps in the summer of 2004. One of the researchers participated in the life and work of male farm workers, who were involved in moving plants in a nursery, picking cucumbers and harvesting tobacco. He observed the daily activities of the workers and listened to their conversations in the camps and in the work fields. Two weeks were spent in each of three camps. The observation focused on 'the complexity of farmworkers' survival strategies, their adaptation to life in the camps, and the usefulness of network ties in the adaptation process' (Balderrama and Molina, 2009: 199). Based on field notes from this observation, the article presents quite detailed descriptions of the workers' life and work, as well as 'job seeking, relocation, and survival strategies developed by the distinctive group of farmworking families settled in and near by the camps' (Balderrama and Molina, 2009: 199). The researchers were particularly interested in the importance of network ties, and they concluded that, whereas such ties are useful for finding temporary jobs, the farmworkers are not able to use networks for sharing resources and improving their long-term socioeconomic prospects.

An article by Yates and Warde (2015) represents an example of a quantitative study. This study is based on data from a survey in Great Britain in 2012, which are compared with results of a similar study in the 1950s. A total of 2784 persons participated in the survey on the web, answering questions about their pattern of eating for the most recent weekday and weekend day before completing the questionnaire. They also answered questions on their gender, age, education, household structure, employment and occupational status. The analysis focused on the percentages of the respondents who had different rhythms of eating (number of meals per day), and different combinations of food as the content of each meal. Furthermore, the analysis revealed variations in these percentages between different groups of respondents. In the article, the results are presented in tables and figures, or referred to (as numbers) in the text. The findings indicate that, in spite of some variations between groups, the main pattern of three meals per day, as well as the typical contents of the meals, are common to a large majority of the respondents. Compared to the 1950s, the study shows significant changes in the contents of the meals, and somewhat less change in the rhythms of regular eating.

Facts and values

The relationship between facts and values is a classical and fundamental issue in the theory of science, and it has been widely and intensely discussed among social scientists. Understanding this relationship is necessary for doing social research in a meaningful way.

Empirical and normative studies

Both facts and values may be examined in social science studies. Depending on whether facts or values are examined, we distinguish between *empirical* and *normative* studies. Empirical studies emphasize questions about facts (empirical questions). The purpose of such studies is to examine or clarify what the facts in society *are*, for example how the tax system is constructed and how it works. Studies of what values are most important for different groups in society (as a fact) are also regarded as empirical studies.

On the other hand, normative studies refer to specific values and examine how different conditions in society *should be* (normative questions). Such studies may, for example, refer to justice as a value and examine how the tax system should be constructed in order to obtain justice for different groups. Discussions of what should be the content and meaning of specific values, as well as what should be the relationship between different values, are also normative studies.

Although we distinguish between empirical studies, with emphasis on facts, and normative values, focusing on values, the relationship between facts and values may be problematic. In empirical studies, the clarification of particular facts may be influenced by different values, and in normative studies, different perceptions of facts may influence the analyses of particular values and their implications.

Do facts exist?

As pointed out above, the relationship between facts and values has been a topic in the debate about positivism. In positivism, it is assumed that social phenomena can be studied as a set of objective and observable facts, independent of the researchers' values and evaluations of these facts. On the other hand, the critics of positivism maintain that it is not possible to separate facts from values in such a rigid and absolute way.

In addition to the relationship between facts and values, the concept of fact in itself is an important issue in theory of science. This concept has been problematized. For example, among *postmodernists* or poststructuralists it is argued that social reality is fragmented, heterogeneous and diverse, and that individuals in society are irrational and confused, characterized by ambiguous and conflicting instincts and wishes. Consequently, there are no consistent, comprehensive or holistic patterns that can be defined unanimously as reality or social facts, and social scientists' description of reality isn't more objective or truer than any other way of describing reality. In other words, there is not one, but many realities. These realities are defined and constituted by those texts, stories or narratives that describe reality in different ways, and none of these descriptions can claim to be more correct than any other description. Apart from the descriptions of reality, there is no reality. In other words, social facts exist only as descriptions of phenomena in society (cf. Callinicos, 1989; Gorton, 2010).

An implication of this postmodernist view on facts and reality seems to be that the scientific foundation of social research is threatened or abandoned. Postmodernism is based on a relativistic view of social reality and denies that human beings are able to describe and understand society in a rational way. The ultimate consequence of this would be that it is not possible to establish those types of empirical knowledge and theoretical understanding that are central in social science. Then it would also be meaningless to develop and discuss different methods for systematic social science studies.

The perspective of this book is that these postmodernist views on facts and reality are not valid or tenable. Historical experience shows that, even though reality always has been described in different ways, all descriptions are not equally correct. For example, both the claim that there were no Nazi concentration camps during World War II and the numerous descriptions of such camps in several places cannot be equally correct. Based on the well-documented historical knowledge of World War II, it seems strange to assume that concentration camps did not exist as a reality apart from the descriptions

of them. This discussion seems to be relevant also for discussions of 'fake news' or 'alternative news' in politics, traditional media and social media.

The history of social science shows that it is possible to develop rational approaches and criteria for distinguishing between valid and invalid descriptions of social phenomena and conditions, that it is possible to develop more and more reliable knowledge about social reality, and that the validity of different research results can be discussed rationally and critically. Hopefully, this will be demonstrated and elaborated in the presentation of different social science methods in this book. Apart from this clarification of the perspective of the book, postmodernism and its methodological implications will not be further discussed here.

Classical discussions of the relationship between facts and values

Although postmodernist relativism is rejected, postmodernism reminds us that fact is not an uncomplicated concept, and that the relationship between facts and values is not always very clear. Furthermore, due to power structures in society, certain values may be more dominant than others, and dominant values may be more influential than others on how facts are defined and discussed. Powerful groups and their dominant values may also influence the choice of research topics and thus determine what types of facts to be emphasized in social research. Different aspects of the relationship between fact and values have been the topics of classical discussions in social science.

In his book on the rules of sociological method, Émile Durkheim (1858–1917) emphasized that society should be studied as a set of social facts, and that these social facts should be treated and analysed as things. Social facts are regarded as existing and observable phenomena in society. As an observer of society, the social scientist cannot avoid detecting the existing phenomena. When the observed social facts are treated and analysed as things, they are regarded in an objective way: social phenomena are assumed to exist independently of the researchers' or other people's individual consciousness. Furthermore, considering social facts as things means treating them as data, which are the basis for social science (Durkheim, 1964).

Thus, Durkheim argues that there is a sharp distinction between facts and values. He maintains that facts exist independently of the individuals' consciousness, and that they can be observed independently of the individual researcher's evaluations. However, Durkheim also emphasizes that social science should contribute to the improvement of society. He points out that a sound society is a primary value for social science. Thus, social science is not without values. However, whether or not a society functions in a sound way is not determined on the basis of the individual researcher's own personal values. The soundness or sickness of social phenomena can be regarded as an objective characteristic of the social phenomena themselves. Just as physicians, independently of their own values, diagnose the patients they examine, social scientists can, also independently of their values, diagnose the society they study.

Like Durkheim, Max Weber was also concerned with the relationship between facts and values in social science. In a discussion of the objectivity of science, Weber (2013) maintained that there is a fundamental difference between ideals and realities, or between values and facts. Like all other activity in society, research on society is, directly or indirectly, oriented towards values. However, social science must be based on truth, knowledge and logical principles as primary values. Thus, social science studies must mainly deal with facts. Choice or priorities between values cannot be made on a scientific basis. However, Weber realized that social science will be influenced by values in society, and that social scientists must relate to such values. This may create problems for the objectivity of social science, but such problems can be reduced by distinguishing between ends and means in social action. According

to Weber, the primary purpose of social science is to show how different means can be used for obtaining various ends in society. Priorities between different ends, or goals, are not determined by social science, but through competition or conflict between different values in society.

Weber argues that the implementation of social science studies should be oriented towards facts, but he also points out that the choice of research questions and methodological approaches may be affected by different values. This may influence the direction and development of social science. What is important is that the researchers themselves are aware of this, and that they present, in their scientific reports, the personal values that may have had an impact on the design and implementation of the research. Researchers should be familiar with value debates in society and clarify their own values through participation in these debates. However, each researcher should distinguish clearly between their role as researcher and their role as participant in the debate. Social scientists may express value positions in their research reports, as long as they clarify what are facts and what are values.

Basic principles for social science: Ontology, epistemology and methodology

Even though the relationship between facts and values in social science is complicated, it is possible to formulate a few simple but fundamental principles for social science activity. Just because the relationship between facts and values is complicated, it is also necessary to establish such a foundation for social science. In this connection, it is reasonable to emphasize three major principles, which are based on long traditions and generally accepted views. An overview of the three basic principles is presented in Table 1.1.

The first principle is that *social science is based on truth as a primary value*. This is an ontological

Table 1.1 Basic principles for social science

Philosophical basis	Principle
Ontology	Social science is based on truth as a primary value
Epistemology	Perceptions of truth in social science are theoretically, methodologically and contextually founded
Methodology	Evaluations of truth in social science are based on rational and logical criteria

principle, focusing on the existence of particular social phenomena. *Ontology* is the study of being, existence and reality. In social science, ontological discussions include considerations on the existence of different social phenomena. The aims and ambitions of social scientists are that the information they use in their analyses and the knowledge they provide in their analyses are as true as possible. This does not mean that the researchers at any time can be sure that they have reached the final or definitive truth. Other studies, based on different methods, referring to other perspectives, related to different insights, and implemented in other contexts, may lead to a revision of the established perception of truth. Previous perceptions of truth may be replaced by new perceptions. By constantly seeking the truth, researchers challenge established knowledge and develop new knowledge.

Perceptions of truth in social science may also be controversial. There may be both uncertainty and disagreement regarding what is true and what is false. It is important for social scientists to be open to criticism and self-criticism, to emphasize different perspectives and interpretations, and to consider alternative views and insights, in order to reach the best possible perception of what is true.

What is true information and knowledge is continuously considered and reconsidered, based on new studies and critical discussions. This leads to the development of truer knowledge. The credibility of the researchers' perceptions of truth is increasingly strengthened. The knowledge that is developed in this way is not necessarily objective, but may become more and more intersubjective.

The second principle is that *perceptions of truth in social science are theoretically, methodologically and*

contextually founded. This is an epistemological principle, emphasizing the development of knowledge about existing social phenomena. *Epistemology* is the study of knowledge, focusing on how knowledge is developed, the sources of knowledge and the conditions for the development of knowledge. What information researchers use in their analyses, and what knowledge their analyses lead to, do not only depend on how these phenomena 'really' are. This may also be a result of the researchers' particular point of view in their studies of the phenomena. Thus, the truth about social conditions that is established by social scientists is theoretically founded.

How particular social conditions are understood by researchers may also depend on the researchers' approaches for collecting and analysing information about these conditions. Thus, the truth about social conditions that is established by social scientists is methodologically founded.

In addition, particular social conditions may be perceived in different ways, depending on when and where they are observed. For example, in some countries and in some periods of time it is a truth that people's social background is the main explanation for their party preferences. However, this relationship is not true always or everywhere. Thus, the truth about social conditions that is established by social scientists is contextually founded.

The principle of truth as theoretically, methodologically and contextually founded is consistent with the understanding of people's perception of reality as socially constructed. This understanding has been thoroughly discussed by the sociologists Peter L. Berger and Thomas

Luckmann (1967). For social science this means that the foundations of truth should be described explicitly, rather than remaining implicit. Research reports in social science cannot be limited to presentation of the knowledge provided by the research, but must also describe the theoretical perspectives, methodological approaches and contextual conditions of the research. With reference to the discussion of facts and values, it should be added that it is also important to describe those values that might have influenced the choice of research questions and perspectives. Such explicit descriptions of the foundations of truth are necessary as a basis for continuous reconsiderations of what is true.

The third principle to be emphasized here is that *evaluations of truth in social science are based on rational and logical criteria*. This is a methodological principle, focusing on procedures for discussing and assessing knowledge about existing social phenomena. *Methodology* is the theoretical analysis of the methods applied in a research field, focusing on the fundamental ways of thinking and understanding that determine the development and application of different methods. Since the truth is continuously reconsidered based on new studies and critical discussion, it is necessary to have clear criteria for these reconsiderations. It is important to have a common understanding of how to examine if something is true, how to determine what is true, and how to discuss and assess such questions. In this connection, rationality and logic are primary values for social science.

This does not imply that human activities or social processes examined by researchers are assumed to be rational or logical. However, rationality and logic are the basis for the scientific methods that are applied in social science studies, and for scientific argumentation that is used in critical discussion of such studies.

Although methods and approaches may differ and change, the rational and logical foundation of these methods and approaches is common and stable. For example, this means that evaluation of truth in social science is not based on majority opinions, public authorities or historical traditions. Opinions, authorities and traditions can be examined empirically, but cannot be the basis for evaluating the truth of research results. Moreover, such evaluations cannot be based on the researchers' or other individuals' personal experiences, emotions, beliefs or fantasies. All this may be important for the researchers' ability to find relevant information on social phenomena, but cannot be the basis for evaluating the truth of information or knowledge.

Social science as a process: The organization of this book

Researching society

This chapter has provided examples of social science studies that show how important phenomena and conditions in society can be studied by means of different methods and different types of data. Furthermore, the chapter has described some essential features of social science and its relationship to society, and some fundamental methodological principles and issues in social science have been introduced. Thus, the chapter has demonstrated and discussed how and why we study society.

Fundamental principles and problems in social science will be further discussed in the next two chapters. Chapter 2 is focused on research methods and methodologies in social science. Essential features of scientific methods are described, followed by a presentation of some fundamental issues related to the use of scientific methods in studies of society, and a discussion of how methods are related to theory as well as empirical evidence in social science. Furthermore, methodological differences between six basic disciplines and five broad theoretical traditions in social science are discussed. Finally, it is pointed out how social science can be based on combinations of disciplines, theories and methods.

Chapter 3 is devoted to the ethics and politics of research. The most important ethical norms in social science are pointed out, and some examples of unethical conduct are presented. Ethics related to the rights of participants are discussed. Furthermore, it is described how technological developments create new ethical challenges for social science. It is discussed how assessment and control of the ethical standards of social research are organized and carried out, and the distinction between ethical norms and legal requirements is emphasized. As to the politics of social research, it is discussed how political dimensions are related to analytical, critical and constructive purposes of social science, as well as to action research, critical research, applied research and basic research.

As demonstrated by Blau's study of bureaucracy, which was presented above (Blau, 1963), social science research is a process. The research process can be regarded from a short-term perspective as well as from a long-term perspective. Each study is carried out as a short-term process, which examines a limited part of society. Blau's study represents a short-term research process, although it lasted for several years, from the planning and first fieldwork in 1948 until the completion of Blau's PhD dissertation in 1952. Many studies are carried out within shorter time periods, but other studies may take even longer than Blau's study.

Together, the large number of social science studies over time are included in the long-term process of social research. This process leads to an increasing amount of empirical knowledge and more and more theoretical understanding of society as a whole. Most often, this process is characterized by a gradual and cumulative scientific development, but sometimes one single study may create a completely new understanding, so that previous approaches and research results must be abandoned. Such sudden and big changes, or revolutions, are called paradigm shifts (Kuhn, 1970). Blau's study is a part of a long-term process of social research on features and activities of bureaucracies in society. This process started with Weber's analyses in the early twentieth century and is still continuing. This extensive

scientific process increases our insight into the activities, structures and functions of bureaucracies in different social contexts, in addition to renewing and improving the methods for doing research on bureaucracies.

Thus, in addition to focusing on social processes as central topics for its studies, social research is itself an important social process. This first part of the book is focused on the societal, scientific, methodological and ethical foundations of this research process. The rest of the book is organized mainly with reference to the different elements of the social research process. The purpose is to discuss methods and methodological challenges related to the major elements of the research process.

Designing social research

Part II of the book deals with formulation of research questions and selection of approaches and designs for empirical studies. This part includes Chapters 4–8.

Chapter 4 is focused on research questions. The features of research questions are outlined, different types of research questions are presented, and the relationship between research questions and models is pointed out. The formulation of research questions is described as a systematic process of reviewing literature from previous research, developing the research questions, specifying them and making them more precise. The importance of research questions in the research process is discussed.

Chapter 5 presents an overview of the importance and features of literature reviews in the research process. Different purposes and types of literature reviews are described, and different steps in reviewing literature are outlined. It is shown how the literature review provides a necessary basis for developing and specifying the research questions as well as for commenting on and discussing the findings and results in the report. Furthermore, the chapter presents advice on where and how to find the literature, and how to select the most relevant literature.

Chapter 6 examines how an empirical study can be designed and organized in order to investigate the research questions of the study. The designs for empirical studies are classified according to the types of sources and types of data that are used in the study. We distinguish three types of data sources: actors, respondents and documents. Each of these can be used for providing qualitative or quantitative data. Based on different combinations of the three types of sources and the two types of data, six major designs for empirical studies are described. The differences between qualitative and quantitative designs are examined, and the possibilities for combining qualitative and quantitative data in mixed methods designs are discussed.

Chapter 7 is focused on sources and data in social science. Different types of sources are described, and it is argued that sources should be critically examined. Furthermore, different units of analysis are discussed, and different types of information are examined. Then it is discussed how the research questions are used to specify and select the types of information that should be collected in a study. It is pointed out that there are many opportunities for social scientists to do secondary analyses, and the use and reuse of available data are discussed. Finally, it is emphasized how big data and social media represent new sources of available data, and how new computer software creates new possibilities for finding and utilizing available sources and data.

Chapter 8 deals with selection and sampling of units for empirical studies. The chapter starts with a description of the relationship between universe (population) and sample. Then the differences between population studies, case studies and studies based on samples of units are outlined. It is shown how different samples of units are used in different types of studies, and the features of population studies, case studies, as well as different types of samples are described. The main methods for probability sampling and strategic sampling are presented and compared.

Data collection and data quality

Part III deals with the collection of data for empirical studies as well as the quality of the data. This part consists of Chapters 9–15. Chapters 9–11 explain designs for collecting qualitative data, and Chapters 12–14 present designs for collecting quantitative data. The description of each design is focused on how the data collection is prepared, and how it is implemented, as well as typical problems related to the data collection. In addition to the chapters on specific research designs, one chapter (Chapter 15) presents a discussion of data quality, with emphasis on reliability and validity.

Chapter 9 presents ethnography and participant observation, which is a design for qualitative data collection based on observation of actors. It is shown how the researcher combines the observation of actions and relations with involvement in these actions and relations, and the challenges of this combination of roles are described. Furthermore, the chapter presents a discussion of online fieldwork in ethnography and participant observation.

Chapter 10 deals with unstructured interviews and focus groups, which is a design for qualitative data collection by asking individual respondents or groups of respondents questions. The similarities and differences between personal interviews and focus groups are pointed out, and the use of focus groups for data collection is explained. Finally, the chapter presents new possibilities and challenges related to online interviews and focus groups.

Chapter 11 is devoted to the use of documentary sources and qualitative content analysis. First, the chapter describes qualitative content analysis of text, which is the most common documentary source. Furthermore, the chapter presents discussions of computer-based qualitative content analysis, and qualitative content analysis of visual materials, as well as holistic studies and discourse analysis based on documents.

Chapter 12 deals with structured observation, which is a design for quantitative data collection based on observation of actors. It is pointed out how structured observation can be used in field observation, field experiments and laboratory experiments.

Chapter 13 presents questionnaires and surveys, as a design for quantitative data collection by asking respondents questions. The construction of the questionnaire and different ways of collecting the data are described, including respondent completion of the questionnaire, such as in mail surveys, e-mail surveys or web surveys, and use of interviewers, either in telephone interviewing, including computer-assisted telephone interviewing, or in personal interviewing, such as computer-assisted personal interviewing. Special features of survey experiments are also explained.

Chapter 14 describes quantitative content analysis, based on different types of documents as sources. First, quantitative content analysis of text is presented. Furthermore, the chapter explains the special features of quantitative content analysis of visual materials, and the possibilities and challenges related to automated content analysis, based on new computer software.

Chapter 15 is devoted to data quality, with emphasis on reliability and validity as the main criteria for quality assessments. Reliability and validity are defined, and the relationship between the two quality criteria is discussed. Various types of reliability and validity are explained, and different strategies for improving reliability and validity are suggested, for quantitative as well as for qualitative studies.

Data analysis

Part IV deals with data analysis. This part includes Chapters 16–20. In the explanation of data analysis it is not necessary to distinguish between different data sources, but the difference between qualitative and quantitative data is very important for the choice of methods of analysis. Thus, Part IV contains one chapter on analysis of qualitative data and three chapters on analysis of quantitative data. Furthermore, it includes a chapter on collection and analysis of data in mixed methods research, based on combinations of qualitative and quantitative data.

Chapter 16 deals with analysis of qualitative data. The chapter presents specific methods for organizing, processing and analysing qualitative data. The coding of qualitative data is described, followed by a description of the constant comparative method. It is explained how types and typologies, as well as matrices and figures, may be used as tools in qualitative analyses. Moreover, different purposes of qualitative analysis are discussed: holistic understanding of specific contexts, development of hypotheses and theories, and theoretical generalization. Finally, it is explained how qualitative data can be processed and analysed by means of computers and various types of software.

Chapter 17 is focused on indexes and distributions, as forms of statistical analyses of quantitative data. The chapter starts with a description of how the recorded data are organized in a data matrix, and it is explained how processing and analysis of quantitative data typically are based on various types of software packages. Then the possibilities for recoding of variables as well as construction of indexes are described and exemplified. The rest of the chapter is devoted to distributions of units on variables or indexes, as the main form of univariate analysis.

Chapter 18 presents analysis of bivariate and multivariate relationships, focusing on three types of methods: cross-table analysis, correlation analysis, and regression analysis. First, an overview of the differences between these types of methods is presented. Then several methods for analysing quantitative data are explained in more detail.

Chapter 19 is concerned with statistical generalization. The meaning of statistical generalization is explained, and the distinction between random and systematic errors is described. Furthermore, sampling distribution and sampling errors are explained, as basic concepts in statistical generalization. Different types of generalization methods are described and explained.

Chapter 20 presents different strategies for collection and analysis of data combinations. First, the main differences between collection of qualitative data and collection of quantitative data are examined. Based on these differences between the two data types, four strategies for combining qualitative and quantitative data collection are presented and discussed. Then the chapter discusses strategies for data analysis based on data combinations. Qualitative and quantitative data are compared, and different strategies and challenges for analysing combinations of qualitative and quantitative data are discussed.

Asking and answering questions in social science

Part V presents approaches to and perspectives for asking and answering typical questions in social science. This part consists of Chapters 21–24. Three of the chapters refer to the most common types of research questions, which were outlined in Chapter 4. Some of these questions refer to the types of knowledge that are developed in the analyses. Such questions are examined in Chapter 21. Other questions are related to the types of social phenomena that are emphasized in the analyses. These questions are discussed in Chapters 22 and 23. Furthermore, Part V includes a chapter on big data and computational social science, which provide new possibilities as well as new challenges regarding asking and answering research questions.

Chapter 21 deals with description, explanation and understanding. The discussion of descriptive qualitative studies is focused on ethnographic description. Various types of descriptive quantitative studies are identified, including description of distributions, relationships or structural patterns as well as differences or changes. The section on explanation discusses different types of explanations, how qualitative studies may be used in explanatory research, as well as how quantitative data are used in multivariate causal analysis and experimental studies. The last part of the chapter presents research focusing on understanding, which is typically based on qualitative data.

Chapter 22 is focused on questions related to time, space and level, as they appear in longitudinal, comparative and multi-level studies. Various types of qualitative and quantitative longitudinal studies are explained, and the risk of fallacies related to the time perspective is pointed out. The main features of qualitative and quantitative comparative studies are described, and problems related to linguistic, contextual, conceptual and methodological equivalence are explained. In the section on multi-level studies, contextual analysis is described as a typical example of qualitative studies and it is explained how quantitative multi-level studies combine variables with reference to different levels. The risks of ecological and atomistic fallacies are discussed. The last part of the chapter explains how questions regarding time, space and level may be combined in more comprehensive studies, for example in historical-comparative research.

Chapter 23 is devoted to questions concerning relations, networks and structures. It is explained how relations may be described and classified. Analysis of social networks is described, and the most important network concepts and measures are explained. It is described how social networks can be interpreted as social structures. Finally, the differences between quantitative and qualitative network analyses are discussed, and the advantages of combining qualitative and quantitative data in such analyses are pointed out.

Chapter 24 deals with big data and computational social science. Essential features of big data are described, and distinctions between different types and sources of big data are presented. The development of computational social science is explained, and it is pointed out how computers and computer software make it possible to collect and analyse various types of big data. Finally, it is discussed how big data and computational social science create new possibilities as well as new challenges regarding asking and answering questions in social science.

Writing and presenting research

The sixth and last part of the book deals with issues related to presenting and publishing research. This part consists of Chapter 25, which is focused on visualization of data and research results, and Chapter 26, which is concerned with the writing of papers, articles, books and other kinds of research reports.

Chapter 25 examines how we can work with data visualization. Such visualization may include presentation of just data as such or research results based on data that are more or less analysed. The purposes of data visualization are pointed out. Similarities and differences between qualitative and quantitative data visualizations are discussed. Furthermore, it is discussed how the technological development and the emergence of more and more complex big data lead to new challenges for data visualization. Finally, the need to avoid deceptive visualization is discussed, and examples of deceptive visualizations are presented.

Chapter 26 is focused on writing about research. While various types of visualizations are typically included in research publications, the emphasis in this chapter is on the writing of the text in publications. The chapter describes different purposes of academic writing and distinguishes between two main formats of such writing, the major report and the article. General features of the writing process and the style of academic texts are presented, and the structure and content of theses and articles are described and compared. Finally, some advice for publishing academic texts is provided.

Major elements in the research process

The main basis for the organization of this book is the typical distinction between four major elements in the research process:

- formulation of research questions and choice of research design (Parts I–II)
- collection of data (Part III)
- data analysis and interpretation (Parts IV–V)
- presentation of the research results (Part VI).

All these elements are important in the long-term development of social science in general. Also, a typical empirical study includes the four elements listed here. However, this is not the case for all social science studies. For example, in some theoretical studies, there is no collection or analysis of empirical data. Moreover, in some empirical studies, there is no collection of new data, because they utilize available data, which have been collected before the study.

The chronological order between the elements of the research process is not necessarily the same in all studies. In this book the elements are presented in an order that is common in many empirical studies. First, one or more research questions are formulated on the basis of previous research and established theory. Then a research design and a methodological approach are selected, the data are collected and analysed, and the findings are interpreted and discussed in relation to theoretical perspectives. Finally, the results of the research are presented and published. However, in several research processes, the chronological order between the elements is different. For example, the research process may start with collection of data, without any clear research question, and the analysis of these data may lead to the formulation of new research questions, rather than final conclusions.

Furthermore, it is not always easy to identify a clear chronological order between the elements of a research process. This may be more difficult in qualitative studies than it is in quantitative studies. In typical quantitative studies, each element of the research appears as a separate stage in the process. The research questions are formulated before the selection of design and approach. After this selection, the data collection starts, and it is completed before the analysis and interpretation commence. The presentation of the results is the last separate stage in the process. In typical qualitative studies, the elements of the research process are not so much separated from each other in different stages. This is illustrated by the qualitative parts of Blau's (1963) study of bureaucracies presented above. The various elements of this research are not sharply separated from each other in the process. Some elements occurred in parallel and simultaneously, and the researcher switched between different elements at the same time. Furthermore, qualitative studies may start the data collection based on only preliminary research questions and research designs. The data are analysed and interpreted as they are collected and may lead to

reformulation of the research questions and collection of additional data, in addition to creating more insight into the phenomena that are examined.

In this book, different methods and methodological issues will be discussed in connection with the main elements of the research process. The differences and relationship between qualitative and quantitative research will be emphasized through the book. Thus, at the outset, it is important to note that the differences between the two types of studies are related both to each element of the research process and to the process as a whole.

CHAPTER HIGHLIGHTS

- Social science deals with human beings in different types of societies – not only individuals and groups in the society, but also society as a whole.
- Social science is based on systematic research on society and includes the knowledge, theories and methods that are developed and used in this research.
- There are different social science disciplines and different perspectives, theories and methods within each discipline. The purpose of the book is to present a common methodological foundation for social science as whole. Differences and relationships between qualitative and quantitative research are treated throughout the entire book.
- Qualitative and quantitative data are complementary and can be combined in mixed methods research.

- Social scientists are both participants in society and observers of society.
- The relationship between facts and values is an important issue in debates about social science methodology.
- Three basic principles for social science activity are emphasized:
  1 An ontological principle: social science is based on truth as a primary value.
  2 An epistemological principle: perceptions of truth are theoretically, methodologically and contextually founded.
  3 A methodological principle: evaluations of truth in social science are based on rational and logical criteria.

RESEARCH EXAMPLES

I recommend that you read the publications used as research examples in this chapter. The main example is Peter M. Blau's book on bureaucracies:

Blau, Peter M. (1963) *The Dynamics of Bureaucracy: A Study of Interpersonal Relationships in Two Government Agencies* (rev. edn). Chicago: University of Chicago Press.

The book presents a study of two government agencies in USA, which was carried out in 1948–1949. The study is based on a combination of different types of data and methods and may be regarded as mixed methods research. Compared to Weber's earlier studies of stable characteristics and structures of bureaucracies, Blau focused on changes and functions of such organizations. Originally, the book was published in

1955, but a revised edition was published in 1963. The revised edition of the book includes an epilogue with descriptions and discussions of methodological considerations and experiences during the research process. This methodological epilogue is of particular interest here.

Balderrama, Rafael, and Hilario Molina II (2009) 'How good are networks for migrant job seekers? Ethnographic evidence from North Carolina farm labor camps', *Sociological Inquiry* 79(2), 190–218.

This article provides an example of a qualitative study, based on participant observation in three North Carolina farm labour camps in the summer of 2004. Two weeks were spent in each of three camps. The daily life and work of the farm workers, as well as their families' job-seeking, relocation and survival strategies, were observed. The article presents quite detailed descriptions of these conditions. The researchers were particularly interested in the importance of network ties, and they concluded that, whereas such ties are useful for finding temporary jobs, the farm workers are not able to use networks for sharing resources and improving their long-term socioeconomic prospects.

Yates, Luke, and Alan Warde (2015) 'The evolving content of meals in Great Britain. Results of a survey in 2012 in comparison with the 1950s', *Appetite* 84, 299–308.

This article is an example of a quantitative study, based on a survey in Great Britain in 2012, which is compared with the results of a similar study in the 1950s. A total of 2784 persons participated in the survey on the web, answering questions about their pattern of eating and the food content of their meals, as well as their gender, age, education, household structure, employment and occupational status. The results are presented in tables and figures, or referred to (as numbers) in the text. The findings indicate that, in spite of some variations between groups, the main pattern of three meals per day, as well as the typical contents of the meals, are common to a large majority of the respondents. Compared to the 1950s, the study shows significant changes in the contents of the meals, and somewhat less change in the rhythms of regular eating.

STUDENT EXERCISES AND QUESTIONS

1 What are the main topics in social science?
2 Why is social science important for society?
3 What is the meaning of
  a reactivity (control effect)?
  b reflexivity?
4 Why are social scientists both participants in society and observers of society?
5 Describe the differences between empirical and normative studies.

6 Discuss the principle of truth as a primary value in social science, with particular emphasis on how this principle can be understood in light of the distinction between facts and values.
7 Why is truth in social science theoretically, methodologically and contextually founded?

RECOMMENDED LITERATURE

Delanty, Gerard (2005) *Social Science: Philosophical and Methodological Foundations* (2nd edn). Maidenhead: Open University Press.

This book provides a critical discussion and comprehensive overview of the major debates on the methodological foundations of social science. The book deals with such questions as what social science is, whether social science differs from natural sciences and common sense, and what the relation is between method and knowledge. Developments in the philosophy of social science are described and discussed.

Gorton, William A. (2010) 'The philosophy of social science', *Internet Encyclopedia of Philosophy* (http:// www.iep.utm.edu/soc-sci/).

This article examines several questions and issues in the philosophy of social science, such as the relationship between social science and natural science, the possibility of a value-free social science, how social phenomena can be explained, and the relationship between different social science methods.

Wagner, Peter (2001) *A History and Theory of the Social Sciences: Not All that Is Solid Melts into Air*. London: Sage.

This book has been described as a major contribution to contemporary social theory, which provides essential insights into the task of social science today. The development of social theory since the nineteenth century is presented, and major concepts in social science are explained.

METHODS AND METHODOLOGIES
IN SOCIAL SCIENCE

This chapter provides knowledge about basic assumptions and principles underlying social research methods, as well as insight into important debates about these assumptions and principles.

The chapter will teach you to understand

- the distinction and relationship between methods and methodology
- how methods are related to theories and empirical evidence
- why methods are important for developing new and better knowledge about society

- methodological differences between disciplines and theoretical traditions in social science
- how different methods can be combined in mixed methods research.

Scientific methods

The purpose of Part I of this book is to discuss some basic assumptions, principles and problems related to social research. In particular, the discussion is focused on assumptions, principles and problems that are important for developing and using social science methods. The previous chapter considered the relationship between social science and society. The theme of the present chapter is the role of methods in social science. First, some characteristic features of scientific methods are presented. The next section deals with some fundamental methodological questions that arise when we use scientific methods to study society. Then the special role of methods in the development of knowledge about social conditions is examined, with particular emphasis on how methods are related to social science theory and empirical evidence. Furthermore, it is discussed whether there are methodological variations between different disciplines and different theoretical traditions in social science. Finally, the chapter points out how different disciplines, theories and methods can be combined in social research, emphasizing in particular the value of mixed methods approaches.

Scientific methods may be described as a set of guidelines to ensure that scientific activities are technically sound and carried out with sufficient quality. In general, a method is a planned approach to achieving a particular goal. In scientific activities,

the goal is to gather knowledge on particular phenomena and to develop a theoretical understanding of this knowledge. In line with this, the scientific methods in a particular field of study can be regarded as systematic and planned procedures to produce reliable knowledge and sound theories within this field. The methods specify how to gather the knowledge and develop the theories, and how to ensure that the knowledge and theories meet the requirements for scientific quality and relevance in the subject area in question.

The procedure for studying certain phenomena depends to some extent on the nature of the specific phenomena. For example, it is obvious that studies of the configuration and movements of celestial bodies require different procedures than studies of patterns of interaction and change in social networks. Different disciplines study different phenomena or subjects, so there will therefore be varying degrees of difference between the disciplines with regard to the methods they utilize, although there are also certain common features shared by all scientific methods.

We have mentioned that the social sciences include the methods that are developed and utilized in research about people in different societies, as well as the knowledge and theories produced in this research. Social science methods therefore consist of systematic and planned approaches to generating knowledge and theories about different aspects of peoples' societal life and activities. These methods provide guidelines for how to gather reliable knowledge and construct sustainable theories about society. The methods also include criteria and procedures for assessing the knowledge and theories in relation to the general principles of social science's commitment to truth, as highlighted in Chapter 1.

Scientific methods include principles and rules for scientific discussion and reasoning on a purely theoretical basis, as well as procedures and techniques for the organization and implementation of empirical investigations.

Theoretical discussion and reasoning

Systematic methods for theoretical discussion and reasoning should be based on general principles of logic and language use. Three such methodological principles may be emphasized. The first concerns *precision* in the use of terms and linguistic formulations. The discussion of theoretical issues in the field of social science entails that we relate to the usual terminology of the social science subjects, that we clarify and possibly define the concepts that are central to the discussion, and that the logic of these concepts and the relationships between them are formulated as clearly as possible.

The second principle refers to the *validity* of the reasoning. Such validity assumes that the reasoning is based on sound assumptions, and that there is a logical coherence between these assumptions and the implications or conclusions that the reasoning leads to. The question of the coherence between assumptions and conclusions must primarily be assessed on the basis of purely logical criteria. The question of the soundness of the assumptions may be more complex. An assumption for a theoretical argument could, for example, be a presumption of actual relationships in society. To be sustainable as an assumption, such a presumption must be correct, based on previous research and established knowledge of these actual

circumstances, or be reasonable, based on a relevant theoretical understanding of societal conditions. In other cases, especially in areas that are neither empirically nor theoretically explored, theoretical discussions may be based on other types of assumptions, such as intuitive understanding or self-explanatory statements. Clarifying this is a prerequisite for making a concrete assessment of the sustainability of these specific assumptions.

The third methodological principle for theoretical discussion emphasizes the importance of *completeness* in the reasoning. This means that all relevant factors must be taken into consideration. The reasoning must be clear, but not one-sided. A theoretical discussion of particular circumstances in society must consider all important assumptions and arguments that are relevant for these social conditions. When we discuss how changes in interest rates affect the economic conditions in society, we should not rely solely on the assumptions and reasoning related to investment behaviour in business. We should also consider, for example, relationships between interest rates, exchange rates and foreign economic conditions, and relationships between interest rates, housing prices and consumer-economy conditions. Furthermore, such a discussion should not be based solely on hypothetical or speculative considerations, but should also take into account the results of previous research on these issues.

Empirical studies

The principles for theoretical discussion and argumentation apply not only to purely theoretical studies. These principles are also relevant in empirical studies. In social science research, empirical studies of societal relationships are usually linked to theoretical understandings of these social conditions, albeit to varying degrees and in different ways. This link between theory and empirical evidence is particularly prominent when the research questions for the empirical studies are formulated and when the results of the empirical analyses are interpreted. It is particularly in connection with these elements of empirical social science research that it is important to use systematic methods for theoretical discussion and reasoning.

In addition to the principles for theoretical discussion of the research questions and the results of the analysis, there are a number of systematic methods for the organization and implementation of empirical investigations. Altogether, the social science methods for empirical research comprise a comprehensive set of principles and guidelines, procedures and techniques for the various elements of the research process. Thus, there are specific principles and procedures for formulating research questions, selecting units of analysis and types of information, constructing research designs, collecting and analysing data, and interpreting results of data analyses. These principles and procedures will be elaborated on through the discussion of the various social science methods in this book. It is primarily methods for empirical social science research that will be discussed.

Methodological issues

In scientific terminology, we often distinguish between 'method' and 'methodology'. The term *method* refers to the specific procedures for the planning and implementation of specific scientific studies. The term *methodology* is applied to the more fundamental approaches or ways of thinking and understanding that underlie the development and utilization of different methods. Methodology is the part of the logic that deals with the general principles for developing knowledge.

The relationship between method and methodology can be compared to the relationship between empirical evidence and theory. While social science theory refers to various ways of understanding social phenomena, social science methodology deals with various ways of understanding how

knowledge about such phenomena can be generated. Theory is based on the interpretation and understanding of empirical evidence, while methodology is about the interpretation and understanding of methods.

In other words, the methods that are developed and utilized in social science research are based on more fundamental methodological principles. The choice of specific methods for particular investigations is linked to more fundamental methodological issues. An example of such a methodological issue is the relationship between qualitative and quantitative data, as discussed in Chapter 1. This issue concerns what types of data can and should be used in social science studies. Should information about social phenomena be expressed in the form of text or numbers? As mentioned above, this question has been the subject of much debate. The point of departure for this book is that the two types of data are complementary, that they can shed light on different aspects of social life, and that it can therefore be an advantage to combine them in social science studies.

While the relationship between qualitative and quantitative data was discussed in Chapter 1, two other methodological questions will be emphasized here. These questions concern the *basis* for social science knowledge and the *scope* of such knowledge.

The basis for knowledge

The question of what can and should be the basis for the knowledge and theories that are developed in social science studies is central to the relationship between methodological individualism and methodological collectivism. *Methodological individualism* entails that all social science knowledge must be based on information about the individual and about the situations, actions and attitudes that can be associated with each individual. It is assumed not only that this basis for knowledge must apply to studies of individuals and their relationship to their specific environments, but also that information about individuals is a necessary basis for analyses of larger groups, institutions or structures in society. Knowledge about social contexts or about society as a whole must be based on data about each individual within this context or society. Knowledge of society as a whole is established through the aggregation of information about the individual elements in society.

Methodological collectivism, also known as methodological holism, assumes that information about individuals is not sufficient as a basis for knowledge about social contexts or society at large. The point of departure for this approach is that the entirety that comprises society is different and more than the sum of the parts that make up that society. Although groups, institutions and structures in society are comprised of individuals and individual actions, these larger social entities have their own distinctive features that cannot be understood simply by studying the affected individuals and their actions. Based on this assumption, it is impossible, for example, to understand a prison community simply by observing and aggregating the behaviour of each of the inmates and employees. In addition, it is essential to observe the overall pattern of interaction between individuals and groups, primarily within the prison walls, but to some extent also in relation to society outside. Patterns of interaction must also be viewed in light of circumstances such as traditions, norms and rules, physical structures, infrastructure and time rhythms, which together constitute certain disciplinary relationships, authority relationships and hierarchical arrangements. These collective features of the prison community are not the result of the behaviour of each individual prisoner or guard and cannot be understood on the basis of only data about individuals and their actions.

The classic works of social science contain different views on this methodological question regarding the basis for social science knowledge.

For example, Émile Durkheim (1964) is a proponent of methodological collectivism. On the other hand, Max Weber is usually considered to be a methodological individualist (Giddens, 2013).

Although these views are clearly highlighted in general programmatic statements and fundamental methodological discussions, they are not always expressed equally clearly in empirical or theoretical studies of specific societal conditions. It is not easy in practice to operate with a sharp distinction between methodological individualism and methodological collectivism. The benefit or appropriateness of such a dichotomy has also been disputed, and various intermediate positions have been argued concerning this methodological question.

One example of such an intermediate position is *methodological situationalism* (Knorr-Cetina, 1981). This position differs from methodological individualism in two ways. Firstly, methodological situationalism is based on the assumption that social action cannot be regarded as individual actions performed by separate individuals, but rather as interactions between several individuals. Both the interaction and the intentions behind it are characterized by each individual constantly relating to the other individuals involved. Secondly, the interaction between specific individuals must be understood in the context of the situation in which these individuals and their interaction are located. This situation in itself constitutes a social reality with its own dynamics and its own organization, which cannot be analysed solely based on information about the individuals involved in the situation. Therefore, methodological situationalism emphasizes that the relevant methodological units are not single individuals and their individual actions, but rather the interaction between individuals in certain social situations. This assumption is also different from methodological collectivism, because it means that broader social conditions, such as social institutions and structures, cannot be observed in isolation from situational interaction. Broader institutional and structural patterns in society cannot be understood only by examining individuals' actions or only by observing the institutions or structures as separate units of analysis. Knowledge of such patterns should be based on information about the specific interaction involved in the patterns and the specific social situations in which the interaction takes place.

Methodological relationism is another example of an intermediate standpoint, which also seeks to bridge the sharp distinction between methodological individualism and methodological collectivism (Elias, 1978; Bourdieu and Wacquant, 1992). Compared to methodological situationalism, methodological relationism emphasizes the importance of relationships in a broader sense. While situationalism focuses on relations in the form of concrete interaction between specific individuals or actors in given situations, relationism also emphasizes the importance of relations between actors and structures. Thus, methodological relationism differs from both methodological individualism and methodological collectivism: the point of departure is that knowledge about social conditions cannot be based solely on the characteristics of individuals or of structures, but must also consider the relations between these levels and their distinctive characteristics.

The methodological question concerning the basis for social science knowledge (individualism, collectivism, situationalism or relationism) is about which level in society we should focus on when we study societal conditions and develop knowledge about society. We can distinguish between three distinct levels in this connection. The *micro* level refers to the smallest and simplest units or elements in society, such as individuals, families and other small groups. The *macro* level, on the other hand, comprises the largest and most complex social units, such as the major institutions in society, the national state and society as a whole. The *meso* level is located between the micro and macro levels and includes, for example, social networks, organizations and local communities.

Simply put, methodological individualism entails that social science studies should focus on the micro level, while methodological collectivism entails that such studies should be based on information about the macro level. Both methodological situationalism and methodological relationism place greater emphasis on the meso level as a basis for social science knowledge.

A summary and overview of the characteristics of the four different positions is presented in Table 2.1.

The scope of the knowledge

The methodological question regarding the scope of social science knowledge is emphasized in the relationship between idiographic and nomothetic studies. *Idiographic* studies focus on individual phenomena or social conditions that are clearly

Table 2.1 Overview of different positions regarding the basis for knowledge in social science

Methodological position	Types of information as basis for knowledge about society	Main level of empirical studies
Methodological individualism	Individuals and their specific actions	Micro
Methodological collectivism	Larger patterns of action and interaction, norms and structures	Macro
Methodological situationalism	Interaction between individuals in specific situations	Meso
Methodological relationism	Relations between actors and structures	Meso

defined in time and space, such as the Irish banking crisis in 2008–2009 or the presidential election campaign in the USA in 2016. The purpose is to identify and understand the distinctive and unique characteristics of the specific conditions studied. This knowledge is believed to be valid only for the circumstances that are actually studied. *Nomothetic* studies are intended to reveal more general relationships and patterns that are not limited to specific historical periods or specific geographical areas. Nomothetic studies of banking crises, for example, can focus attention on the general relationship between international economic cycles and national banks' economic freedom of action. Similarly, nomothetic studies of election campaigns can focus on general characteristics of the relationship between mass media, social media and social networks in terms of the dissemination of political messages. In other words, the purpose of such studies is to develop general theories about the characteristics and relationships that are common to larger classes or categories of phenomena in society. Although such theories are developed on the basis of empirical studies of particular societal conditions or relationships, it is assumed that the theories can be generalized in both time and space. They are not limited to the particular circumstances investigated, but also have a more general character.

An overview of the difference between idiographic and nomothetic studies is presented in Table 2.2.

The distinction between idiographic and nomothetic studies was originally defined by the German philosopher Wilhelm Windelband (1904). He argued that history and other 'cultural sciences' must be based on idiographic approaches, while economics

and sociology will include nomothetic studies. However, this was a controversial opinion, and the relationship between ideographic and nomothetic studies was one of the central issues in a more comprehensive methodology debate (*Methodenstreit*) in Germany and Austria in the late 1800s.

There is still considerable disagreement in the social sciences about whether knowledge about social conditions should be based on idiographic or nomothetic studies. This disagreement exists not only between different social sciences, but also between different schools of thought within each discipline. For example, in psychology, there is a distinction between idiographic and nomothetic perspectives in research on individuals' characteristics, attitudes and behaviour. The idiographic perspective emphasizes what is unique and meaningful for each individual, whereas the nomothetic perspective refers to what is common for many or all individuals, as laws or generalizations. The two perspectives are compared in a study of psychological well-being (McDaniel and Grice, 2008). Based on quantitative data, the study examines how various measures of well-being can be predicted by nomothetic as well as idiographic measures of self-discrepancies. In this particular study, nomothetic measures seemed to be better predictors than idiographic predictors.

Methods, empirical evidence and theory

As mentioned above, social science includes not only methods, but also empirical evidence and theoretical understanding. Thus, the next

Table 2.2 Difference between idiographic and nomothetic studies

Type of studies	Scope of knowledge based on the study
Idiographic studies	Knowledge valid only for the specific phenomena that are studied, limited in time and space
Nomothetic studies	Knowledge from specific studies generalized to larger patterns and relationships, not limited in time and space

questions are: what is meant by empirical evidence and theory in social science, and what is the relationship between methods, empirical evidence and theory?

What is empirical evidence?

Empirical evidence is information, facts or data about actual conditions in society. The evidence is based on our experiences of these social conditions. We obtain this experience-based evidence using different senses, such as sight, hearing, taste or smell. More precisely, empirical evidence is information about actual conditions based on sensory experience. Empirical evidence in social science is primarily based on the senses of sight and hearing. For example, we see how people migrate between different geographical areas, and we hear what those migrants tell us about their reasons for migrating. We see how jobs are established and eliminated, and we hear about how business leaders and politicians explain these changes.

When empirical evidence is based on sensory experience, it is characterized by the human senses used in the experience. Specific societal conditions can be experienced and perceived in different ways by different observers, depending on how their senses are developed and used. The development and use of the senses can be linked to the personality, social background and life story of the observer. Our different forms of understanding and frames of reference affect what we see and hear, and also how we perceive audio and visual impressions. In other words, the information about the actual conditions in the form of empirical evidence is filtered through people's sensory organs. This filtration process is part of the reflexivity problem that was mentioned in Chapter 1.

This means that it is not always easy to interpret the results of an empirical study. When we decide what the empirical evidence shows about the social conditions studied, we must consider how this empirical evidence can be influenced by the sensory impressions upon which it is based.

Scientific studies are characterized by the empirical evidence being processed in a systematic manner. Emphasis is placed on obtaining all the empirical evidence relevant to the issues being investigated. We rely on certain rules and procedures to ensure that this empirical evidence is as reliable as possible and that it is recorded as accurately as possible. The empirical evidence collected and recorded in such a systematic manner constitutes empirical *data*. In other words, *data* consist of empirical evidence that is systematically collected and recorded. As pointed out above, such data may be qualitative or quantitative. Qualitative data are expressed in the form of text or images, while quantitative data are in the form of numbers or other units of quantity.

Empirical data are subjected to systematic analysis. The analysis can provide an overview of complex circumstances or insights into complicated societal relationships. Through such *empirical analysis*, we can reveal or discover social patterns that could not otherwise be readily observed through direct sensory experience.

The social science methods that will be reviewed in this book refer to different systematic procedures for collecting, recording and analysing empirical data about social conditions.

What is theory?

Compared with empirical evidence, *theory* is a more ambiguous term. While empirical evidence in social science is based on experience of conditions in society, social science theory is based on reflection on social conditions. However, not all reflection can be characterized as theory. Just as social science empirical evidence is based on systematic procedures, social science theory is also characterized by a specific, systematic form of reflection.

Basically, social science *theory* can be defined as a set or system of concepts and relationships that are in a mutual relationship with each other, and which summarize and arrange preconditions, assumptions and knowledge about society.

We will now discuss the various elements of this definition. Concepts constitute the basic components of a theory. A *concept* such as *class consciousness* or *party identification* is a more or less abstract term for certain clearly defined phenomena.

Theories consist not only of different concepts, but also of *relationships* between the different concepts. Such a relationship could be, for example, that there is a positive correlation between class consciousness and party identification, so that the greater people's feelings of belonging to a particular social class, the more strongly they identify with a particular party.

A theory constitutes a system of such relationships between concepts, in the sense that the various relationships that are part of the theory have a mutual relationship to each other. In other words, theories are made up of relationships at multiple levels, not just relationships between concepts, but also relationships between these relationships. For example, the positive correlation between class consciousness and party identification can be related to a positive relationship between class consciousness and political interest, as well as a positive correlation between political interest and party identification. One could also add that both political interest and party identification correlate positively with voter turnout. We thus obtain a theory about how people's participation in elections is directly and indirectly influenced by class consciousness, political interest and party identification.

The last element in the definition of social science theory is that this system of concepts and relationships summarizes and arranges preconditions, assumptions and knowledge about society. Firstly, traits of certain societal phenomena are summarized by each concept. Secondly, the relationships between the different concepts are an expression of what one presupposes, assumes or knows about the relationships between different social phenomena. Thirdly, the overall system of relationships in a theory contributes to a more comprehensive representation of a larger set of phenomena in society.

This systematic, theoretical reflection on societal relationships may be more or less empirically rooted. Social science theory may include both reflection on actual conditions in society based on empirical research, and reflection on reasoned assumptions about societal relationships that can be studied empirically. The reflection can also be based on assumptions regarding conditions in society that cannot be studied empirically.

A social science theory should thus be based on all relevant facts established through previous research. The theory should be tested, further developed and possibly revised through empirical investigations of the assumptions it contains or implies. The theory should also be based on assumptions that are reasonable. In this regard, emphasis is placed on the methodological principles for theoretical discussion and argumentation outlined above: precision, validity and completeness.

Later in this chapter, a number of different types of theories will be presented in relation to five major theoretical traditions in social science. For an overview of these typical theories, see Table 2.5.

Social science theories can be produced and described in different ways. The components and structure of the theories are not always clearly expressed. The concepts, the relationships and the overall system that they together constitute are not always explicitly formulated in theoretical reasoning and discussion. On the one hand, a theory may be more or less implicitly interwoven into a more comprehensive text. The concepts and relationships that are included in this implicit theoretical system may then be evident more or less indirectly from this presentation. In order to discuss, evaluate and possibly test such theoretical reasoning, it may be necessary to identify and clarify the individual concepts and relationships, as well as the relationships between them.

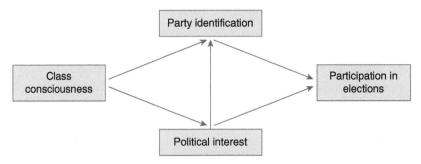

Figure 2.1 Example of a social science model: relationships between class consciousness, political interest, party identification and participation in elections

On the other hand, a theory may be presented in a highly formalized manner, so that both the individual components of the theory and the relationships between them are clearly and explicitly expressed. This applies in particular if the theory is presented in the form of a *model*. For example, the simple theoretical example outlined above can be expressed in the model presented in Figure 2.1.

In the figure, each concept is formulated in simple terms and is illustrated with boxes, and the various relationships between the concepts are symbolized by arrows between the boxes. In this case, the arrows express positive correlations. The model also provides a clear overview of how the different concepts and relationships are arranged in relation to each other, and how together they form an overall system. However, such a model contains fewer details and nuances than a more textual or verbal presentation of the theory. The purpose of a social science model is simply to provide a simplified and streamlined presentation of selected societal phenomena, highlighting the key features of these phenomena, while omitting other aspects of the phenomena.

Models of the type illustrated here are usually termed *conceptual* models or *theoretical* models, because they contain concepts with a clear substantive content and with reference to particular social conditions. In other types of models, the theories can be presented in even more formalized ways. The most formalized presentations of all are found

in various *mathematical models*. These are not just more formal, they are also more abstract, in the sense that they are not necessarily limited to a specific, concrete phenomenon. While the conceptual model in Figure 2.1 focuses on consciousness of social class and participation in political activity, a corresponding mathematical model could address, for example, more general and more abstract relationships between consciousness, interest and action. Mathematical models often express their concepts in the form of symbols, while the relationships are presented as mathematical formulas or functions, and these relationships are arranged in relation to each other in such a way that together they constitute a very precise, logical system, where the existing relationships in the system provide a basis for formulating or deriving new relationships.

Models are important in connection with both formulation of research questions for new studies, and interpretation of the results of analyses. Different types of models will therefore be discussed in more detail later in the book, especially in Chapters 4 and 21.

The relationship between methods, empirical evidence and theory

As mentioned above, social science theory may be more or less based on empirical evidence. On the

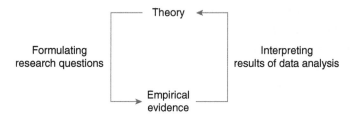

Figure 2.2 Switching between theory and empirical evidence by formulating research questions and interpreting results of data analysis

other hand, social science empirical evidence may be theoretically interpreted to a greater or lesser degree. In other words, social science research is characterized by an interaction between theory and empirical evidence about social conditions. The social science methods provide the basis for a systematic and fruitful design and development of the interaction between theory and empirical evidence.

Research is often characterized by a switching back and forth between theory and empirical evidence. In doing so, the researcher uses different methods to make links between theory and empirical evidence, depending on whether they are moving from theory to empirical evidence or vice versa. This is illustrated in Figure 2.2.

As the figure illustrates, the movement from theory to empirical evidence is based on methods for *formulation of research questions*. Based on theory, one or more *research questions* for empirical studies are formulated. The prerequisite is that a relevant theoretical basis exists for the phenomena to be studied. The purpose of the empirical study is usually to test whether the current theory is valid.

The movement in the opposite direction, from empirical evidence to theory, is based on methods of *interpretation*. The results of empirical studies are summarized and discussed from theoretical perspectives. Although this may be about understanding the new empirical evidence in light of current theories, the purpose of the empirical studies is often to generate new theory.

A social science study usually includes both formulation of research questions and interpretation of results. A fairly common design for a study is to start with a research question based on current theory, conduct an empirical study of the research question and conclude with a theoretical interpretation of the results of the study. However, there are also other types of design. Whether a study starts with a theoretical discussion or an empirical investigation may vary, and it is also possible to switch back and forth between theory and empirical investigation several times in the same study.

Some studies are mainly focused on formulation of research questions in order to test a current theory empirically, and some studies are primarily

Table 2.3 Overview of the relationship between method, empirical evidence and theory in deductive and inductive research designs

Typical research design	Relationship between theory and empirical evidence	Method of linking theory and empirical evidence	Theoretical purpose of the empirical study
Deductive design	From theory to empirical evidence	Formulating research questions	Theory testing
Inductive design	From empirical evidence to theory	Interpreting results of empirical analysis	Theory development

designed to interpret empirical analyses in order to develop new theory. Table 2.3 provides a schematic overview of the differences between these two types of study, with particular emphasis on the relationship between method, empirical evidence and theory.

Studies focusing on formulation of research questions and theory testing are based on *deductive* designs, because they are designed to deduce or derive certain research questions from the theory to be tested. In many cases, these research questions are formulated as hypotheses. Then the design is considered to be *hypothetico-deductive*. A hypothetico-deductive design is used in a study of political discussion in online forums (Karlsson, 2012). The analysis is focused on hypotheses about the intensity of the discussions, which are formulated on the basis of previous research on online political discussion and deliberative democratic theory.

Studies with particular emphasis on interpretation and theory development are based on *inductive* designs, because they are intended to induce or construct a particular theoretical understanding based on the empirical analyses that are conducted. An inductive theory building approach is used by Turcan and Fraser (2016) in an ethnographic study focused on the creation and legitimation of a new industry in an emerging economy. A selected international new venture in Moldova was examined in the period 2000–2011. The study is based on qualitative data from in-depth interviews, participant observation, and various types of documentary sources. The analysis and theory building based on these data 'led to the emergence of a process model of the industry and new venture legitimation' (Turcan and Fraser, 2016: 81). This is a conceptual model, which is described and discussed through further theoretical reflections.

While deductive designs may work well in areas that have already been widely investigated, inductive designs may be more appropriate when investigating phenomena that have not been the subject of prior research.

Social science disciplines and methodological specialization

As pointed out in Chapter 1, social science consists of many different *disciplines*, and there are different research traditions or theory traditions within each discipline. However, there are differences between the disciplines with regard to which theoretical traditions and methodological approaches are most central, as well as how various methodological issues are assessed and emphasized.

The way in which the social science disciplines are demarcated relative to each other and to other disciplines may vary between both institutions and countries, as well as over time. Based on which disciplines are well established today at most social science university faculties, we can highlight the following six disciplines as core social science *disciplines*: psychology, social geography, social anthropology, economics, political science and sociology. In addition, there are several social science research fields and programmes of study, for example media studies, which are combining elements from different core disciplines. However, the discussion here will focus on a comparison of the core disciplines.

Each discipline is characterized by different traditions and thus also by different perceptions of the discipline's academic profile. Different perceptions of the *theoretical characteristics* of each discipline will not be presented in this brief overview. In the next section, however, a general overview of various theoretical traditions and their methodological implications will be provided.

This presentation of each discipline will identify major *empirical areas* that are central to the discipline. Furthermore, it is particularly interesting in our context to emphasize the particular *methodological characteristics* of the individual disciplines. We can thus clarify the extent to which the differentiation between disciplines also involves some form of

Table 2.4 Overview of important thematic areas and methods in various social science disciplines

Discipline	Important thematic areas	Important methods
Psychology	The individual's relationship to society	Both qualitative studies based on informal interviews, and quantitative studies based on experiments or surveys
Social geography	Spatial aspects of society	Cartographic methods, geographic information systems
Social anthropology	Cultural conditions in society	Mainly qualitative studies based on field research
Economics	Economic conditions in society	Mainly quantitative studies with emphasis on mathematical models and statistical analyses
Political science	Political conditions in society	Both qualitative and quantitative studies based on different methods
Sociology	Society in general and different types of social conditions	Both qualitative and quantitative studies based on different methods

methodological specialization. We can also clarify what constitutes a common methodological basis for social science as a whole. It is precisely the common methodological basis of social science that will be presented in this book.

Different core disciplines

Table 2.4 presents an overview of important thematic areas and methods in the six core social science disciplines. With reference to this overview, each discipline will now be briefly described.

Psychology

Psychology is more individual-oriented than the other social science disciplines. Therefore, it is sometimes doubted whether the discipline can really be regarded as social science. This applies especially to the most clinical or therapeutic aspects of psychological practice, which focuses on the treatment of individuals' mental problems. These parts of the discipline may have a stronger connection to biology and medicine than to social science. However, psychology is included in the social sciences because the discipline rarely regards individuals as completely isolated from their social

environment. As a rule, the individual's relationship with society appears to be an important perspective in the field of psychology. It is partly about understanding how the individual's personality, attitudes and actions are shaped and influenced by social conditions, and partly about investigating the individual's scope of action and development potential in interaction with the social environment. In social-psychological studies, such relationships between individuals and society are particularly prominent. Studies of interactions in small groups are also common in social-psychological research. Psychological research has few decidedly discipline-specific methods, but procedures for analysing personality traits, motives and other individual characteristics are usually given greater emphasis in this discipline than in other social sciences. Typical approaches are qualitative studies, usually based on informal interviewing, as well as quantitative studies, which are often conducted on the basis of experiments or surveys.

Social geography

While psychology focuses on the individual in society, social geography is concerned with spatial aspects of society and focuses on its spatial constitution. The spatial localization, dispersion, distribution and patterns of various social phenomena are key topics. Spatial expression is understood as larger or smaller parts of the world, such as places or regions. Social geography aims to understand relationships and connections between different societal conditions in specific locations or within specific regions. Different places and regions can then be compared with regard to patterns of such relationships and connections. Accordingly, various cartographic methods are the most important methodological aspects of social geography. This means that empirical data are recorded, processed and analysed using different types of maps. Applying newer information technology, these methods have been developed to utilize digitized maps and larger geographic information systems. The discipline is also based on both qualitative and quantitative studies. Direct observation through field visits is a common procedure in geographic investigations.

Social anthropology

Social anthropology places particular emphasis on cultural conditions in society. The concept of culture has a very broad definition in this context and refers to all the values, norms, knowledge and traditions common to a society. Social anthropology aims to understand how different forms of life and social patterns reflect and are characterized by such cultural conditions. The discipline regards societal conditions and social life from a cultural perspective. Comparing societal conditions in different cultures is a central perspective in social anthropology. Such comparisons are based on descriptions of social life and social patterns within each of the cultures compared. These descriptions should be as complete and comprehensive as possible, and they are designed and developed through relatively long-term field visits in the society that is studied, where the researcher participates in community life while observing, describing and interpreting the social conditions. This procedure is a typical methodological feature of social anthropology. Overall,

social anthropology is the most qualitatively oriented discipline within the social sciences.

Economics

Economics focuses on economic conditions in society. The discipline's main topics refer to the allocation and management of scarce resources in order to satisfy human needs. Economics attaches great importance to studies of how markets act as mechanisms for allocating and managing resources, how different actors act in different markets and how this is related to the overall economic activities in society as a whole. Economic research deals with the relationships between economic processes and other conditions in society, partly how various social conditions constitute a framework for market transactions and other economic activities, and partly how the economy affects conditions in society more generally. Economic studies are often based on very precise formulations of conceptual relationships and theoretical reasoning, often in the form of mathematical models. Empirical analyses are usually based on advanced statistical methods. While social anthropology is the most qualitatively oriented social science discipline, economics is the most quantitative of all the social science disciplines.

Political science

Political science is concerned with political conditions in society. In political science the concept of politics is used in a very broad sense. In line with this, political science attaches importance to studying a variety of actors, institutions, processes and conflicts in society's political life. Power, democracy and governance are key topics in political science. Research in political science focuses on issues related, for example, to political activities among individuals and organizations, the design and functioning of political institutions, and political decision-making in local, national and international communities. Despite the fact that the discipline assigns such a broad definition to the politics concept as the basis for its activities, the thematic focus on political conditions represents a *substantive* delineation of political science from other social science disciplines. On the other hand, it is difficult to identify any particular *methodological* features that are distinctive for the discipline. Instead, research in the field of political science is characterized by a high level of methodological diversity. The discipline utilizes both qualitative and quantitative studies based on different approaches, methods and techniques.

Sociology

Sociology is regarded as the most general social science discipline. Sociology is not confined to specific social conditions or to specific areas of society, but aims to investigate both various types of social conditions, and society in general or as a whole. In terms of general studies of society, sociological research focuses on various themes associated with the relationship between individuals or between larger and smaller groups of individuals, such as social relations and networks between different types of actors, interaction processes and conflict patterns, as well as institutional arrangements and structural conditions. The discipline's delimitation or distinctive character in relation to other social sciences can be a little unclear with regard to sociology's interest in more special conditions in society. It can therefore be difficult to draw clear boundaries between cultural sociology and social anthropology, between economic sociology and economics, and between political sociology and political science. In this context, one could say generally that sociology seeks to investigate the same thematic areas as its neighbouring disciplines, and that it is the use of particular sociological concepts, theories and perspectives that distinguishes sociological analyses of such themes from corresponding analyses in other social sciences. Although it is difficult

to highlight any particular *thematic* characteristics of sociology, it is even more difficult to identify any particular *methodological* focus in the discipline. Like political science, sociology is also characterized by a great deal of methodological diversity. The discipline builds on both qualitative and quantitative studies and makes use of the majority of available approaches, methods and techniques in social science.

A common methodological basis

Following this description of each social science discipline, it is possible to return to the question of whether the differentiation between disciplines involves a methodological specialization. In other words, to what extent are there important methodological differences between the disciplines, and to what extent is there a general methodology in social science, a methodology that is common to the various social science disciplines?

This brief overview indicates that there is actually little methodological specialization among the different disciplines. It is only to a small extent that each discipline has its own distinctive methods that differ from the methods employed in other disciplines. The methodological differences that exist between the disciplines are mostly about what methods are *most central* to the different disciplines. The most important of these differences can be summarized as follows:

- Social geography makes more use of cartographic methods than other disciplines.
- Social anthropology places more emphasis on qualitative studies and less emphasis on quantitative studies than other disciplines.
- Economics places more emphasis on quantitative studies and less emphasis on qualitative studies than other disciplines.

Such distinct methodological features cannot be identified for each of the other three disciplines.

There are no essential methodological differences between psychology, political science and sociology.

This means that there is largely a *common* social science methodology. The disciplines of sociology, political science and psychology generally employ the full range of methods and techniques that are part of this common methodology. The disciplines of social anthropology and economics each use their chosen parts of the social science methodology. It is only the discipline of social geography that uses certain methods that *cannot* be said to be part of a common social science methodology.

Theoretical traditions and methodological implications

After the discussion of methodological differences between different *disciplines*, the question is whether there are special methodological characteristics associated with different *theoretical traditions* in the social sciences. Is there a clear connection between theory and method, so that research within a particular theory tradition requires or implies the choice of special methods?

The term *theoretical tradition* is not very clearly defined, and it is usually used more or less synonymously with expressions such as 'theoretical perspective', 'paradigm', 'school of thought' and 'research tradition'. A theoretical tradition or a theory tradition comprises a collection of theories about various conditions in society. The different theories that form a particular theory tradition have in common that they are based on the same basic assumptions about the nature of society or the members of society, and the same general perceptions of how social conditions can be investigated and understood. It is these basic ideas and general perceptions that make up the differences between different theoretical traditions. For example, some theory traditions emphasize that social conditions must be understood based on the actions of individual people (methodological

individualism), while other traditions emphasize more holistic studies of relationships, networks, systems or structures as a basis for understanding society (methodological collectivism). Such fundamental differences in perceptions and assumptions of society will now be explored further, as key theoretical traditions in the social sciences are described.

Different theory traditions

The intention is not to provide a complete overview of all perspectives in the social science disciplines, but to highlight some important features of some selected traditions. These theory traditions have been selected with the intention that they should each be relevant within several different disciplines or subjects, that together they illustrate the breadth of perspectives in social science, that they are different from each other, and that they all play key roles in social science research today. Based on these criteria, the following theory traditions will be examined:

- rational choice theories
- interpretive theories
- structuralist theories
- functionalist theories
- conflict theories.

There are no sharp boundaries between these perspectives and, in practice, a particular study can be based on theories from several different traditions. The social science literature also contains many different classifications of theoretical perspectives. For example, Ritzer (1980) distinguishes between three fundamental perspectives or paradigms in sociology: the social behaviour paradigm, the social definition paradigm, and the social facts paradigm. The five theory traditions reviewed here can be related to the Ritzer's categories. Rational choice theories can be regarded as a part of the *behaviour paradigm*, interpretive theories correspond to the

Table 2.5 Overview of important theoretical traditions and their methodological implications

Theory tradition	General features of the theory tradition	Typical theories	Disciplines where the tradition is particularly important	Methodological implications
Rational choice theories	Focus on individual actors and actions Actions are assumed to be based on the actors' rational choice, often with a view to utility maximization (utilitarianism)	Neoclassical economic theory Exchange theory Decision theory Game theory	Economics Political science Sociology	Methodological individualism Nomothetic studies Formal models Often experimental designs Mainly quantitative approaches
Interpretive theories	Focus on individual actors and actions Action and interaction are interpreted based on the meaning they have for the actors themselves in the current context	Action theory Hermeneutical theory Phenomenology Symbolic interactionism	Social anthropology Sociology	Idiographic studies Inductive designs Mainly qualitative approaches, with emphasis on participant observation or field research
Structuralist theories	Focus on larger patterns of relations (structure) The individual element in society is understood from the perspective of the element's relationship to other elements and to the structure as a whole	Structural linguistic theory Role theory Structural Marxist theory Network theory	Psychology Social geography Social anthropology Sociology	Historical and comparative studies Both qualitative and quantitative approaches based on different methods
Functionalist theories	Focus on the consequences (functions) of various social conditions for each other and for society as a whole The individual element in society is understood from the perspective of the element's function for other elements and for society as a whole	Structural functionalism Systems theory Neofunctionalism	Social geography Social anthropology Political science Sociology	Historical and comparative studies Both qualitative and quantitative approaches based on different methods
Conflict theories	Focus on contradictions and changes Assumes that society is characterized by contradictions related to the historical development of inequalities in people's fundamental living conditions and interests	Marxism Feminism Critical theory	Political science Sociology	Historical and comparative studies Both qualitative and quantitative approaches based on different methods

definition paradigm, and structuralist, functionalist and conflict theories are parts of the *facts paradigm*.

It is not intended to provide an in-depth presentation of the different perspectives here. Such presentations can be found, for example, in general introductory books in various social science disciplines. Here the focus will be on some general features of the five theory traditions, the types of theories each tradition encompasses, the disciplines in which each tradition is particularly important, and the methodological implications that follow from the different theory traditions.

In this context the methodological implications are particularly important. An overview of this presentation is provided in Table 2.5.

Rational choice theories

Rational choice theories focus on the actions of the individual actors in society. It is assumed that these actions are rational, that is, that the actors choose to perform the actions that are most likely to contribute to fulfilling their own objectives or preferences. This theory tradition is linked to utilitarianism and is often based on an assumption that the actors' objectives or preferences refer to pure egoism and self-interest. However, the perspective may also be extended to include other objectives. The point is that, in all cases, the actors are assumed to act rationally and instrumentally with a view to achieving their objectives, no matter what these objectives are. The point of departure for the study of society is first and foremost the individual person and their individual actions, but it is also relevant to study other types of actors, such as organizations. Social conditions are considered as overall results of the individual actors' specific actions.

The typical theories in this tradition include neoclassical economic theory, exchange theory, decision theory and game theory. These are theories that are particularly important in economics, political science and sociology. There is also research in the fields of psychology and social anthropology that is linked to rational choice theories, especially exchange theory perspectives.

Social science studies based on rational choice theories attach major importance to methodological individualism, in line with the assumption that social conditions can be regarded as aggregated results of the individual actions of individual actors. It is the individual actors and the individual actions that are subject to empirical investigations at the micro level. More comprehensive conditions in society and relationships at the macro level are analysed using aggregated data about a larger number of individual actors and their actions. These studies usually have a generalizing perspective and can therefore be characterized as nomothetic. The studies are often based on experimental designs. The analyses are based largely on formal mathematical models, quantitative data and statistical analysis.

Interpretive theories

Interpretive theories also focus on the actions of the individual actors in society. However, this theory tradition is not based on the premise that these actions are rational in any particular sense. The extent to which an action is rational, or what kind of rationality it expresses, depends on the actor's own intention and the meaning that the action has for the actor in the particular situation or context in which the action takes place. The social scientist's task is to understand or interpret the subjective meaning behind the individual action, viewed in the context in which the action occurs. Social conditions are understood based on the meaning associated with the actions of each actor and their interaction with other actors in various contexts. Organizations, institutions and other social systems are regarded as the results of this kind of intentional and meaningful action and interaction. The social importance of different conditions in society is based on the understanding and interpretation of these social conditions that the individual actors develop through concrete action and interaction.

Typical theories within this tradition include action theory, hermeneutical theory, phenomenology and symbolic interactionism. This theory tradition is particularly important in the fields of social anthropology and sociology. With its emphasis on contextual understanding of subjective meaning associated with the actions of individuals in society, interpretive theories also have some importance in psychological research, especially in some social psychology studies.

Since interpretive theories emphasize that action and interaction may have different meanings for different actors and in different contexts, social science studies within this tradition focus on distinctive features of the specific actors, actions and contexts being studied. This means that research based on interpretive theories mainly involves idiographic studies. These studies are usually based on inductive designs, where the approach is not to test hypotheses derived from existing theories, but rather to formulate new hypotheses and develop new theoretical insights. Overall, interpretive social research is based mainly on qualitative approaches. Participant observation and field research are particularly important methods, but interpretive theories can also be developed through other methods, such as qualitative content analysis of texts.

Structuralist theories

Structuralist theories focus on structural conditions, understood as larger patterns of relatively stable conditions in society. While both rational choice theory and interpretive theories are micro-oriented and actor-oriented perspectives, structuralist theories are macro-oriented and relationship-oriented. Unlike the first two theory traditions, structuralist theories attach greater importance to social structures than to social actions. Structuralist theories also have in common that the individual elements of society are perceived on the basis of their position in relation to other elements and as parts of the overall structure of which the element is a part. However, the types of elements and relationships that are emphasized in structural studies vary between different structuralist theories. Some theories focus on the relationship between idea-based elements, such as text units, abstract concepts, ideas and concepts, norms and values. Other structuralist theories emphasize relationships between substantive elements of society, such as specific actors at different levels.

In other words, this theory tradition contains a number of different theories about social structures. For example, structural linguistic theory is concerned with relationships between elements in texts, while role theory emphasizes relationships between the sets of norms and expectations associated with different positions. Structural Marxist theory and recent network theory are among the theories that focus on relationships between more substantive elements. This theory tradition is part of most social science disciplines, but it is particularly prominent in psychology, social geography, social anthropology and sociology.

Since this theory tradition encompasses so many different theories, focuses on so many different types of social structures and is part of so many different disciplines, structuralist social research can be based on several types of methodological designs. The macro-oriented approach suggests that historical and comparative studies may be important, focusing on comparisons of structural conditions over time and between different societies. However, such comparisons can be based on different types of data and methods. Consequently, it is not possible to identify any particular methodological implications of structuralist theories as a general tradition, although more specific choices of theoretical approach and structural perspective within this tradition may indicate that certain methodological approaches are more adequate than others. Overall, structuralist research includes both qualitative and quantitative approaches based on different methods.

Functionalist theories

Functionalist theories focus on the consequences of different social conditions, both the consequences for other social conditions and the consequences for society as a whole. Like structuralist theories, the functionalist tradition is macro-oriented and focuses on how different parts of society are related to each other and to the overall society to which they all belong. But there are also important differences between the two traditions. While structuralist theories can deal with different types of relationships, functionalist theories are concerned with a particular type of relationship, namely positive (functional) or negative (dysfunctional) consequences of social conditions. While the structuralist theory tradition is concerned with overviews of different features of the patterns formed by the relationships, the functionalist tradition aims to clarify how different patterns of behaviour, institutions and other circumstances in society contribute to maintaining each other and society as a whole. In some functionalist theories, society is considered to be a unified organism, where the various parts have specific functions in relation to each other and to the whole society. Consequently, each element or each relationship cannot be understood independently of the whole organized society in which the elements and relationships are integrated.

Among the typical functionalist theories, we find structural functionalism, systems theory and neofunctionalism. These are theories that are particularly important in social geography, social anthropology, political science and sociology.

The functionalist and the structuralist theory traditions have in common that they do not seem to have any particular methodological implications. The importance of a comprehensive understanding of society means that comparisons over time and between different societies are emphasized. Historical and comparative studies will thus be key components of functionalist social research, but in the same way as for structuralist research, such comparisons can be based on very different data and methods. Structuralist and functionalist research also have in common that the theoretical tradition primarily is focused on how social conditions should be understood, and what features of society should be studied.

However, it does not follow from the theory tradition in itself how these studies should be conducted and what kind of empirical data should be analysed. Within the framework of functionalist theories, there is a large diversity of both qualitative and quantitative approaches based on several different methods.

Conflict theories

Conflict theories focus on contradictions and changes in society. This theory tradition assumes that society is characterized by fundamental antagonisms that have developed historically in connection with social inequality. These conflict conditions entail that coercion and the exercise of power are more important than consensus as the basis for social order in a society. The fundamental conflicts in society are also regarded as the main driving force for social change processes. Although Collins (1975) has emphasized a conflict theory perspective that is micro-oriented and concerned with conflicts between individuals, the conflict theory tradition is mainly focused on conflicts between collective actors. Like the functionalist and structuralist tradition, therefore, this tradition is mainly macro-oriented. However, conflict theory differs markedly from the other two macro-oriented traditions. The emphasis on social conflicts is in contrast to the functionalist tradition's emphasis on social integration and consensus in society. Conflict theory's emphasis on the argument that conflict leads to social change is in contrast to the focus of the structuralist theory tradition on the stable characteristics of social structures.

Marxism, feminism and critical theory constitute examples of typical theories in the conflict theory tradition. Although such theories are included in research related to many of the social science disciplines, the theory tradition is strongest in the fields of political science and sociology.

Methodological implications

With regard to methodological implications, there are no particular differences between conflict theory and the two other macro-oriented theory traditions. The macro orientation indicates that it may be important to carry out historical and comparative studies in order to make comparisons over time and between different societies, but such studies can be based on different methods associated with both qualitative and quantitative approaches.

Stated briefly and in simplified terms, we can say that two of the five theory traditions that we have referred to here mainly include micro-oriented theories, while the other three place more emphasis on macro-oriented theories. While rational choice theories and interpretive theories are based on action and interaction among the individual actors in society, the majority of structuralist, functionalist and conflict theories are focused on more general conditions in society or on society as a whole.

The antagonistic relationship between micro-oriented and macro-oriented theories is a classical theme in social sciences. Many attempts have been made to develop theories that traverse this divide by placing greater emphasis on the mutual dependence between the micro level and the macro level, and between actors and structures in society. An example of such a theory is structuration theory, developed by British sociologist Anthony Giddens (2013). We will not explore this theme in more detail here.

In this context, we are particularly concerned with the methodological implications that follow from the various theory traditions. In connection with the three macro-oriented traditions, it is particularly important to emphasize historical and comparative studies, but these studies can be based on different data types and methods. In other words, there are few special methodological implications of the theory traditions that focus on society's macro conditions. On the other hand, we find clear methodological implications of the two micro-oriented traditions. These not only differ from the macro-oriented theory traditions but also are clearly different from each other. While rational choice theories are primarily associated with quantitative approaches, interpretive theories are strongly associated with qualitative approaches.

Multidisciplinarity, theoretical diversity and mixed methods research

So far, the distinctive characteristics of each discipline and each theory tradition have been emphasized, and the most prominent differences between the various disciplines and traditions have been highlighted. The discipline specialization and the theoretical and methodological differentiation in social science have been discussed. Some theoretical and methodological differentiation is found both between and within disciplines, and there is no clear connection between theoretical tradition and methodological approach.

A social science study is not necessarily conducted within the framework of just one discipline, rooted in just one theory tradition or based on just one type of method. On the contrary, social science studies can combine perspectives from different disciplines and theories, and they can be based on combinations of different methods. The disciplines, theories and methods are not necessarily mutually contradictory, competing or incompatible. The differences between them usually mean that they can shed light on different aspects or dimensions of society. Thus, they often complement each other. Combining several different academic insights, theoretical perspectives and methodological approaches can help to develop an understanding of social conditions that is more comprehensive and more in-depth than the understanding we can achieve through the individual disciplines, theories and methods separately.

Combinations of disciplines

Research studies based on combinations of different disciplines or subjects are referred to as *multidisciplinary* or *interdisciplinary* studies. One of the most obvious advantages of such studies is that combinations of perspectives, expertise and insights from different disciplines can provide a more comprehensive picture of complex social conditions than can be achieved by contributions from each discipline separately. For example, studies of fiscal policy matters may combine contributions from both economics and political science. If the theme is clarified to apply to the post-war fiscal policy, it may also be fruitful to include contributions from a discipline such as history, so that the multidisciplinary design combines both social science disciplines and other disciplines. Similarly, studies of environmental policy issues can combine perspectives from social science and biology, and research into health issues can be based on combinations of input from social science and medicine.

Multidisciplinary research can be important for the academic development of social science. The development of new theoretical perspectives and methodological approaches often occurs at the interface between different disciplines, arising from the interaction and the tension that occur when different academic perspectives are brought together and confronted with each other. Continued academic development and innovation are often stimulated when researchers from different disciplines can collaborate, discuss and mutually challenge each other's perspectives in joint projects. Thus, multidisciplinary studies are important in terms of the additional insight that is achieved through the combination of disciplines, but they are also important for the further development of the individual disciplines that are involved in the combination.

Combinations of disciplines in a single study are often based on collaboration between researchers with different academic backgrounds and competencies. In other words, multidisciplinary research based on combinations of input from psychology, economics and sociology will be conducted as a collaboration between psychologists, economists and sociologists. In such contexts, it is an advantage if the researchers in each of the disciplines also have some knowledge of the other disciplines involved in the collaboration. Although it is quite common for those who have research expertise in one particular discipline to also have some knowledge of other disciplines, it is very rare for the same person to have expertise as a researcher in several different disciplines or subjects. One of the most important challenges for multidisciplinary and interdisciplinary social research is to ensure that the input from all the disciplines involved is of satisfactory academic quality. The combination of disciplines cannot be valuable unless each of the disciplines in the combination is utilized in a professional and academically appropriate manner. In other words, one of the prerequisites for successful multidisciplinary or interdisciplinary research cooperation is that the researchers participating in the collaboration have a good level of expertise in their own disciplines. If this prerequisite is not fulfilled, the research process may be adversely affected by some researchers dabbling in other researchers' disciplines, and the result of the research may then be amateurish, superficial and uninteresting.

Another challenge is to ensure equivalence between the disciplines that are part of multidisciplinary or interdisciplinary research projects. In order to ensure academic quality, it is important that each discipline can contribute on its own terms and based on its own preconditions. It is also important that each discipline has its contributions assessed based on the discipline's own criteria and academic standards. In other words, a successful combination of different disciplines requires that none of the disciplines involved is dominated by other disciplines. If any of the combined disciplines acts in a 'discipline imperialist' manner with regard to the other disciplines in the combination, it will have unfortunate consequences for both the individual disciplines that are dominated and for the entire combination design.

Overall, multidisciplinary social research can be of great importance under certain conditions, both for the investigation of complex social conditions and for the theoretical and methodological development of social science. However, multidisciplinary research cannot replace discipline-oriented research. Good discipline-oriented research is a prerequisite for successful multidisciplinary or interdisciplinary studies.

Combinations of theories

Both discipline-oriented and multidisciplinary studies may be characterized by *theoretical diversity*. This term means that a particular study refers to several different theoretical perspectives. The most comprehensive is the combination not only of theories from a single theory tradition, but also of theory perspectives from different traditions.

While multidisciplinary studies are usually based on collaboration between researchers who are each expert in their own disciplines, it is not uncommon to find theory combinations in studies conducted by a single researcher. The multiplicity of theoretical perspectives is prominent in several of the social science classics, such as Marx, Durkheim and Weber. It is true that the classical works originate from a period when there was little differentiation between different social science disciplines. But even with the academic specialization that we see today, it is a common requirement that the individual researchers in each discipline must be familiar with the different theory traditions in their discipline. Knowledge of the discipline's

different schools of theory is an essential part of mastering one's discipline. Thus, it is easier for a single researcher to work with different theoretical perspectives than to combine different disciplines.

The researchers' choice of theoretical perspectives for their studies of society can be justified in various ways. On the one hand, the justification may be on *principle*. The choice of theoretical perspective is then based on theory of science principles or arguments for how the society should be understood and what types of approaches should be used to obtain an insight into social conditions. This may entail that a particular theory tradition or some particular types of theories will be emphasized as more adequate in principle than all the others. It has been argued, for example, that social conditions can be understood best based on individual actors' specific actions, and that these actions must be regarded as rational, so that rational choice theories should be a common theoretical basis for all social research (cf. Coleman, 1990).

On the other hand, social scientists' choice of theoretical perspective may be justified from a *strategic* perspective. Based on such research strategy considerations, the choice of perspective will depend on the specific social conditions to be studied and what specifically characterizes these particular social conditions. The researcher emphasizes the theories that are most relevant or most fruitful for the particular issues to be investigated. This means that no theory or theory tradition should be regarded as more fruitful in principle than others. For example, certain aspects of society can be described using interpretive theories, while other aspects of society can be better explained using structuralist theories.

Typically, it is such strategic considerations that form the basis for *combinations* of different theoretical perspectives in the same study. The social conditions that are studied are often complex and varied, so it can be useful to employ different theories to understand different aspects of these social conditions. For example, in a particular study of economic power, it may be relevant to use interpretive theories to describe individual actions among business leaders and the meaning that the actions have for the leaders themselves, structuralist theories to understand patterns of relationships between these business leaders, and conflict theories to discuss how the actions and the relationship patterns reflect antagonisms and power relationships in the economic life of society. In general, the more complex the social phenomena we study, and the more comprehensive an understanding we wish to obtain of these phenomena, the more appropriate it may be to combine different theories and theory traditions. Overall, the combination of the different theoretical perspectives can contribute to more and better social understanding than each of the individual perspectives could do separately.

By contributing to an ever better understanding of various social conditions and relationships, studies based on combinations of theories can also have an impact on the development of the general theoretical basis for social science. This usually happens in two different ways. Firstly, theory development can take place through the *integration* of the theoretical perspectives that are combined. This means that the theories are not simply used and discussed separately, but are viewed in context and assessed in relation to each other. It may then be found that there are grounds for integrating elements from different theories or theory traditions, so that in combination they form more general theoretical syntheses or completely new theoretical perspectives.

Secondly, the combination of theories in social science studies can contribute to theory development through *critical testing* of established theories. While the integration of elements from different theories assumes that the theories are mutually compatible or complementary, theory development through critical testing is based on the fact that the different theories are incompatible and competing. The critical test is designed so that two theories are contrasted with each other as contradictory explanations for particular phenomena in society, and that at least one of the two theories must be rejected as a result of the empirical analysis of these phenomena. If only one of the theories has to be rejected as a result of the empirical analysis, the credibility of the alternative theory is enhanced. If both of the competing theories have to be rejected, the critical test will reveal a need for other theoretical alternatives and will form the basis for new perspectives or explanations.

Overall, this means that the combination of theories in social science studies can be beneficial for the understanding of society and social development, as well as for theory development in the social sciences.

Combinations of methods and data

Social science studies can also be based on *mixed methods approaches*. This means that a particular study is based on a combination of different data and methods. Typically, mixed methods research combines qualitative and quantitative data. Such combinations have also been called *methodological triangulation*. The term 'triangulation' is taken from navigation and land surveying, where triangulation involves mapping an area by dividing it into a network of triangles, so that positions, distances and directions can be calculated from the corners and angles of the triangles. In social science, triangulation means that certain social phenomena are studied from different views and different perspectives. Methodological triangulation, or mixed methods research, entails exploring the same problem using different data and methods.

The study of online political discussion by Karlsson (2012), which was referred to above, is an example of mixed-method research. In addition to a quantitative analysis of all 28 online forums initiated by the European Commission, as part of the 2009 European Citizens' Consultations, the study also includes a qualitative analysis based on a case study of two of the 28 forums. It is argued that the qualitative data from the case study 'create the basis for a more in-depth analysis of the factors under investigation in the broad comparative analysis' (Karlsson, 2012: 72).

A mixed methods approach is also used by Van Der Wildt et al. (2015) in a study on language as a tool for changing social homophily in primary schools in Flanders, Belgium. Social homophily means that people select similar people as their friends. This study refers to homophily in terms of similarity in language, focusing on the importance of language for friendship. The study combines quantitative data based on a survey among teachers and pupils in 67 primary schools in three diverse regions in Flanders, and qualitative data from two focus groups, with 24 pupils at one school with an ethnically mixed pupil population. The quantitative data were used to examine how same-language friendship patterns are affected by the linguistic composition of the school and the teachers' attitudes towards multilingualism. The qualitative data provided insight into the linguistic culture among the pupils and the atmosphere for friendships between pupils. Thus, the qualitative analysis was 'mainly used to frame the quantitative results and to better understand how these quantitative results can be explained' (Van Der Wildt et al., 2015: 172).

Mixed methods approaches can be used in both multidisciplinary and discipline-orientated studies, and regardless of whether or not the studies are based on theoretical diversity. Like theory combination, mixed methods research can be carried out by several researchers in collaboration or by a single researcher. Researchers who master their discipline not only have good knowledge of its different theoretical traditions, but are also well qualified to use the different methods of the discipline.

A particular researcher may well be more familiar with some theories and methods than with others. Nevertheless, the choice of both theories and methods should generally be academically justified and not dependent on the theories and methods that the researcher is most familiar with.

As mentioned above, academic reasons for choosing a theoretical perspective may be based on principle or strategy. The justification of methodological choices can also be based on both principles and strategies. *Principle* reasons are usually rooted in theory of science considerations or perceptions of the nature of society and the nature of social research. On this basis, some methods are considered to be generally more suitable than others in studies of social conditions. For example, only quantitative approaches may be regarded as scientific, or only qualitative approaches may be considered suitable for revealing the essential features of interactions between people.

Strategic reasons for selection of methods are based on concrete assessments of the specific social conditions to be studied. The starting point is that social science methods differ in terms of which social conditions they are suitable to investigate. The methods that are most fruitful in connection with a particular study will therefore depend on the particular issue to be investigated. No methods should be considered as better in principle or more scientific than others.

Like theory combinations, mixed methods research is also primarily based on strategic reasons. The fact that social conditions are complex and multifarious suggests not only that it is fruitful to combine different theoretical perspectives, but also that it is appropriate to combine different methods. The combination of methods can provide a more comprehensive description of the phenomena studied than the individual methods can provide separately. For example, in a study of social interaction in a workplace, it may be relevant to combine observations of the employees' action and interaction patterns, interviews about what the interaction means for the employees themselves, and content analyses of documents in order to obtain an overview of organizational, institutional and other contextual preconditions for the social interaction.

Mixed methods research is fruitful and valuable in different ways (Jick, 1979; Greene et al., 1989):

- The validity and credibility of the research results are increased. If analyses based on different data and methods provide similar results, we can have a high level of confidence that the methods are relevant and adequate, and that the results are reliable and valid.
- The complementarity of qualitative and quantitative approaches is utilized in the research. The two approaches have different strengths and weaknesses. Results based on one approach may be illustrated and clarified by findings based on the other approach.
- The research results are more complete and provide more comprehensive knowledge about the phenomena that are examined. Qualitative and quantitative approaches can be used to analyse different types of research questions and to study different aspects of social life. Thus, the combination of the approaches expands the breadth and scope of the research.
- The potential for unexpected discoveries and the basis for explanations are strengthened. The difference between qualitative and quantitative approaches means that more variations of social life can be captured in the research, and findings based on one approach can be explained by means of the other approach.

- The basis for methodological and theoretical development is improved. Findings based on one approach can be useful for the methodological development of the other approach in a particular study. If there are deviations between results based on different methods, this may stimulate new interpretations and lead to theoretical integration or critical testing of competing theories. More generally, this can provide a basis for further development and renewal of social science disciplines.

Philosophical justifications for combining qualitative and quantitative approaches have been discussed by Onwuegbusie et al. (2009). They conclude that a pragmatist paradigm in social research represents an epistemological justification and logic for combining different approaches and methods. However, they point out that both qualitative and quantitative data are used also within other research paradigms, including post-positivism, constructivism, the critical theory paradigm, and the participatory paradigm.

Overall, it is often advisable to combine different data and methods in social sciences studies. This can be done in many different ways (Mason, 2006). Mixed methods approaches, with particular emphasis on combinations of qualitative and quantitative data, will be further discussed in several chapters in this book. In particular, strategies for such data combinations will be discussed in connection with different types of research designs (Chapter 6), and with reference to the collection and analysis of different combinations of data (Chapter 20).

CHAPTER HIGHLIGHTS

- Scientific methods specify how to gather knowledge and develop theories in a particular field or discipline, and how to ensure that the knowledge and theories meet the requirements for scientific quality and relevance.

1 Methods for theoretical discussion and reasoning are based on general principles for logic and language use:
   - precision

- validity
- completeness.

2 Methods for empirical studies include principles and guidelines, procedures and techniques for formulating research questions, selecting units of analysis and types of information, constructing study designs, collecting and analysing data, and interpreting results of data analyses.

- Methodology covers the basic and fundamental approaches or ways of understanding that underlie the development and utilization of different methods. Methodology is about interpretation and understanding of methods.
- The choice of specific methods for specific investigations is linked to more fundamental methodological issues:

    1 The relationship between qualitative and quantitative data
    2 The relationship between methodological individualism and methodological collectivism
    3 The relationship between idiographic and nomothetic studies.

- Empirical evidence is information or facts about actual conditions in society. Data consist of empirical evidence that is systematically collected and recorded.
- Theory is based on systematic reflection on social conditions. Theory covers a set of concepts and relationships that are in a mutual relationship with each other, and which summarize and arrange preconditions, assumptions and knowledge about society.

- Social science research is characterized by an interaction between theory and empirical evidence about social conditions, especially through formulation of research questions and interpretation of results from data analyses. We distinguish between deductive and inductive designs.
- The different disciplines are based on a common social science methodological basis.

    o Sociology, political science and psychology generally employ the full range of methods and techniques that are part of this common methodology.
    o Social anthropology and economics each use their chosen parts of the social science methodology.
    o Social geography uses some methods that are not as common in other social science disciplines.

- Rational choice theories are primarily associated with quantitative approaches. Interpretive theories are strongly associated with qualitative approaches. Other theory traditions are less associated with particular data types or methods.
- Multidisciplinarity, theoretical diversity and mixed methods approaches can be important for understanding society and for the development of social science.

RESEARCH EXAMPLES

I recommend that you read the publications used as research examples in this chapter.

Karlsson, Martin (2012) 'Understanding divergent patterns of political discussion in online forums – Evidence from the European Citizens' Consultations', *Journal of Information Technology & Politics* 9, 64–81.

This article shows how a deductive design is used in a political science study of political discussions in online forums. The article is also an example of mixed methods research, combining quantitative data on the discussion in 28 forums and qualitative data from a case study of two of the forums.

McDaniel, Brenda L., and James W. Grice (2008) 'Predicting psychological well-being from self-discrepancies: A comparison of idiographic and nomothetic measures', *Self and Identity* 7, 243–261.

This quantitative study is an example of how idiographic and nomothetic perspectives are used in psychological research. The two perspectives are compared in an analysis of relationships between self-discrepancies and well-being.

Turcan, Romeo V., and Norman M. Fraser (2016) 'An ethnographic study of new venture and new sector legitimation. Evidence from Moldova', *International Journal of Emerging Markets*, 11(1), 72–88.

This article exemplifies an inductive theory building design in an ethnographic study, where qualitative data are used to examine the development and legitimation of a new venture in an emerging economy.

Van Der Wildt, Anouk, Piet Van Avermaet, and Mieke Van Houtte (2015) 'Do birds singing the same song flock together? A mixed-method study on language as a tool for changing social homophily in primary schools in Flanders (Belgium)', *International Journal of Intercultural Relations* 49, 168–182.

This article is another example of mixed methods research, where quantitative survey data and qualitative focus group data are combined in a sociological study of the importance of language for friendship between pupils in primary school.

STUDENT EXERCISES AND QUESTIONS

1 What methodological principles are important for theoretical discussion and reasoning?
2 What is empirical evidence?
3 What are the characteristic features of theories in social science?
4 What are the main differences between nomothetic and idiographic studies?
5 Why are both theory and empirical evidence important in social research?

6 How could relations between male and female employees in a hospital be empirically examined on the basis of

   a methodological individualism?
   b methodological collectivism?

7 Why would it be useful to combine different data and methods in an empirical study of immigration and integration of immigrants?

RECOMMENDED LITERATURE

Blaikie, Norman (2007) *Approaches to Social Enquiry* (2nd edn). Cambridge: Polity Press.

This book presents a critical discussion of major research paradigms in the social sciences, and logics and strategies for research that are associated with these paradigms. A number of themes from the philosophy of social science, social theory and research methodology are covered.

Creswell, John W. (2015) *A Concise Introduction to Mixed Methods Research*. London: Sage.

This brief overview of mixed methods research presents the important steps in the process of planning and designing a mixed methods study. The book emphasizes the methodological foundations of mixed methods research.

Risjord, Mark W. (2014) *The Philosophy of Social Science: A Contemporary Introduction*. London: Routledge.

This book presents an introductory and a comprehensive overview of issues and debates within the philosophy of social science. The presentation includes a number of examples from empirical research in social science.

3

THE ETHICS AND POLITICS OF RESEARCH

This chapter provides knowledge about typical ethical issues and various political considerations that are involved in social research.

The chapter will teach you about

- the implications of different ethical norms
- the importance of informed consent from participants in a study
- the types of ethical issues in big data research
- the use of ethical guidelines and advice

- the political aspects of different purposes of social science
- the researchers' relationships to different groups and interests and to society at large in various types of social research.

Ethics of research

The purpose of this chapter is to discuss ethical foundations and political aspects of social research. These topics refer to the researchers' rights and duties in relation to individuals, groups and society at large: how should researchers deal with different interests in society, and how should they relate to national policies? What are the researchers' rights, obligations and responsibilities in relation to sources and participants in their studies, to sponsors and public agencies, and to weak groups and powerful actors in society?

The ethics of research will be discussed in the first part of the chapter, and the politics of research will be the topic of the last part of the chapter. The discussion of ethics starts with a presentation of the most important and most general ethical norms in social science, followed by descriptions of plagiarism and data fabrication, as two examples of unethical conduct in research. The next section is focused on specific ethical issues involved in the researchers' relationships to individual participants in a study. Then some new ethical challenges related to big data and online research are pointed out. In the further discussion of ethics, it is shown how ethical guidelines and ethics committees have been set up to advise researchers on ethical issues, and to oversee researchers' ethical conduct. Finally, since serious cases of unethical conduct in research may be taken to court, some reflections on the relationship between ethics and law are presented.

Research ethical norms

The three principles regarding truth in social research that were discussed in Chapter 1 may be regarded as a normative basis for the interpretation of facts and for the understanding of how facts are related to values. Social research is also regulated and guided by a number of *ethical norms*. The most important norms, which constitute the research ethical basis for social science, will be described here.

The research ethical norms have been developed gradually, as a part of the development of social science itself, and as a consequence of changes in the society at large. In the early 1940s, Merton (1973) formulated four important research ethical norms:

1 *Communalism.* All researchers should have common ownership of the research. Research should be transparent and conducted in full openness. Reports on the background, approaches and results of the research should be published and made available to everyone.
2 *Universalism.* Scientific activity should be evaluated in terms of purely academic criteria. The value of the research and the merits of the researchers are independent of the researchers' social background and personal characteristics.
3 *Disinterestedness.* Research should be conducted for the benefit of a common scientific enterprise. It should not be influenced by special interests or groups in society or by personal or non-scientific motives among the researchers.

4 *Organized scepticism.* This is consistent with the principle of continuous reconsideration of truth in social science. Research results should be critically discussed before they are accepted.

These early formulations of research ethical norms have been elaborated and further discussed, and several other norms have been added to the research ethics in social science (Alver et al., 2007). Thus, the ethical basis for social research also includes norms regarding originality, humility and honesty:

5 *Originality* refers to the duty of contributing to new and innovative knowledge, insights and understanding. Above all, researchers must avoid plagiarism.
6 *Humility* means that researchers should be conscious of limitations regarding their competence and their studies. Such limitations should be explicitly clarified and discussed in relation to the presentation of results.
7 *Honesty* is a general moral requirement, which is closely related to the principles of truth in social science. In cases regarding unethical research conduct, it is often referred to dishonesty in some sense.

Some of the research ethical norms are included in formal rules, and, to some extent, in national laws and regulations. Other research ethical norms are more informal, but most of them are described and discussed in various types of guidelines. All types of research ethical norms are emphasized in the education of students and in the training and socialization of new researchers. Research ethics are included in researchers' qualifications and competence, as internalized guidelines for scientific activity. Research ethics constitute a generally accepted and important basis for the legitimacy and credibility of science in society.

In practical research activity, it is not always easy to follow all the ethical norms. These norms are mainly statements of ideal requirements and demands. Sometimes the practical implications of the norms for the activities in specific studies may be unclear and difficult to determine. Different norms may even have different or conflicting practical implications. Thus, in social science there are many ethical dilemmas, where there is no 'correct' decision. Different concerns may have to be considered and balanced in relation to each other, and final decisions in such ethical dilemmas may have to be compromises between conflicting interests and concerns.

Unethical conduct in research

Typical examples of unethical conduct in research are plagiarism and data fabrication, which violate several of the ethical norms, for example communalism, originality and honesty.

Plagiarism means that students or researchers copy texts written by other authors and publish these texts as their own contributions, without sufficient references to the original authors. When we present a quotation from another author, we have an ethical obligation to show that it is a quotation, and to give an exact reference to the original author and the publication or site where the quotation has been found. Moreover, it is not allowed to use long quotations from other sources without asking for, and receiving, permission from the original authors and publishers. Another form of plagiarism is self-plagiarism, which occurs if researchers reuse their own texts without sufficient reference to the original publication, or if they reuse too much of a previously published text.

Plagiarism has received increased attention in recent years. Among both students and well-established researchers, the risk of plagiarism increases as more and more texts become easily available online. This availability on the web makes it easier for all of us to find texts and to copy them into our own writing. On the other hand, this may be counteracted by the increased attention towards plagiarism as an ethical problem. Furthermore, developments in technology have made it easier to discover plagiarism, and different types of new computer software have been introduced for detecting similarities between a particular text and previously published texts.

Many efforts to detect plagiarism are made by universities, in order to ensure that their students' degrees and their professors' publications are based on the ethical norms. Furthermore, such efforts are also made by academic journals, which want to secure both the academic quality and the ethical standards of the articles they publish. Stitzel et al. (2018) present a survey of journal editors, focusing on the editors' definitions of plagiarism and their reactions to suspected plagiarism. The findings are compared with the results of a similar survey carried out a decade earlier (Enders and Hoover, 2004). Whereas the first study focused on economic journals, the last study also included journals in sociology, political science and other social science disciplines. Stitzel et al. (2018) show that more and more journal editors see the need for a formal policy against plagiarism, and that more and more journals have such a policy. Furthermore, as to how plagiarism should be defined and punished, the study shows great variation within disciplines, but more agreement across disciplines.

The problem of plagiarism will be further discussed in Chapter 5, on doing literature reviews, and in Chapter 26, on writing about research.

Fabrication of data is another typical example of unethical conduct in social research. Whereas data fabrication may be more common in other fields than social science, false data may be produced in different ways also in social research. For example, questionnaires in a survey may be completed by the researcher or the interviewer instead of respondents, and field notes in participant observation may be constructed by the researcher without real empirical foundation. Furthermore, real data may be changed by the researcher, so that the analysis is based on false data. The researchers' motivation for such unethical behaviour may be to reduce the costs of the data collection, or to produce data that provide research results that are more expected or more exciting than real data would provide.

However, fabrication of data will most likely lead to various kinds of anomalies in the data set, which may be detected by means of special analytic techniques. Different types of computer programs have been developed for examining data sets, in order to detect fabricated or false data. In an article on data fabrication in business research, Stacey (2016) reviews the motivations for fabricating false data and discusses different techniques for revealing such unethical behaviour. It is shown how various statistical tests may be used for discovering anomalies that may be caused by data fabrication, and a special strategy or protocol for preventing fabrication of data is suggested. It is emphasized that it is the researchers' responsibility to ensure that no fabricated or false data are used in their research, and that researchers should be held more accountable in this regard.

It has been maintained that data fabrication and plagiarism are 'the most troubling of the problems we have found in research' (Produthase et al., 2018: 86). However, there are also many other kinds of unethical conduct in research, including use of inadequate or inappropriate research designs, the exclusion of particular observations or data points from the analysis, inadequate recording of data, and inappropriate assigning of authorship credit (Martinson et al., 2005: 737; Produthase et al., 2018: 86). Inappropriate assigning of authorship credit means either that persons with no contributions to the publication are included as authors, or that persons who have contributed are not included as authors. Principles and rules regarding who should, and who should not, be included as authors in social science publications are found in various ethical guidelines.

Protecting the rights of participants

A separate set of research ethical norms has been formulated to regulate the relationship between researchers and the participants or data sources in their studies. The purpose is to protect the rights of those persons, groups, organizations and institutions that are examined or provide information to the researchers. These norms are relevant for all scientific fields, but they are particularly important in social research, which is focused on studies of people in different societies, based on collection of data from, and about, large numbers of persons.

The main ethical principles for the researchers' relations to these people are that

- those who are asked to participate in a study must be informed about the purpose, design and implementation of the study
- those who are willing to participate must give their consent explicitly based on the information about the study
- those who are asked to participate are free to determine whether or not they will be participants, and they are free to end their participation whenever they wish
- participation in the study does not involve any risk of physical or emotional harm to the participants
- individuals who participate in a study will be anonymous, and information about individuals will be treated confidentially by the researchers.

These norms regarding *informed consent*, harms, anonymity and confidentiality are always used in relation to individuals who are participants in a study. If these individuals participate in the study as representatives of an organization or institution, it may also be necessary to obtain permission for the participation from the leadership of the organization or institution. For example, such permission may be necessary for studies of soldiers in a military camp, students at a school, employees in a company, or patients at a hospital. In *indigenous research*, or studies of indigenous peoples, it is a particular challenge to take into consideration that indigenous peoples typically regard their knowledge and information as common or collective goods. In such research, the researcher will have to agree a contract with those representatives of the

indigenous people who have a mandate to deal with the collective knowledge on behalf of their people.

In addition to protecting the rights of the participants in research, research ethics also include norms for protecting researchers' safety. Sometimes, conducting research might involve personal risks and dangers, for example if fieldwork takes place in communities with much criminality or in groups involved in violence. In all research involving such risks or dangers, it is an ethical requirement to secure the researchers' safety.

Big data and online research: New ethical challenges

Recent developments in information technology have created new challenges for research ethics. More powerful computers, more complex network systems, and more advanced computer software have made it possible to collect, store, process and analyse enormous amounts of data. Such data are called *big data*, and the use of computers and software packages for finding and analysing data that are available on the web is called *online research*.

For example, people's use of the Internet or social media can be recorded and included in various types of data registers. Registers on individuals can also be based on the use of credit cards, telephone conversations, or pictures and videos from surveillance cameras. Such data may provide information on network relations, economic transactions, opinion statements, shopping patterns and many other activities. In addition, there are a large number of public registers, which contain information on individuals' health conditions, income, consumption, education, employment and other conditions. Moreover, different registers may be combined or merged, providing a wide variety of information on each individual. Establishing and combining such registers is becoming more and more common, and such data are used for different purposes in politics, public administration, business and marketing, as well as in different kinds of surveillance. The establishment, combination and practical use of many of these registers may be ethically problematic, mainly because the individuals included in the registers do not know that the registers exist or how they are used. Some use of such data may even be a threat to the privacy, freedom and other human rights of the individuals involved. There is a lot of discussion about the ethical problems associated with such registers, and the need for more regulation and control of the use of data from these registers.

Obviously, such big data may be very useful, valuable and interesting for social research. However, from a research ethical point of view, it is a special challenge to use such data in social science studies. In particular, it may be very difficult to protect the rights of the participants or data sources in the studies. The individuals who are selected for the study may not know that they are included in the registers from which they are selected, and in many cases they do not even know about the existence of these registers. Even if they do know about the existence of the registers, and about their inclusion in them, they still might not know that they are selected for a particular study. Thus, it is common that participants selected from registers for a study have never given informed consent to be included in the registers in the first place, and it may be very difficult to ask each individual for informed consent to be included in the study based on the registers. Typically, the number of individuals is so large that it is very resource intensive to locate and get in contact with them all, and often each individual in the registers is anonymized.

Nevertheless, whenever it is possible, each individual selected from a register for a study should be informed about the study and asked for informed consent. If it is not possible to contact each respondent, the researcher should find out if there are any guidelines, rules or conditions for using the specific registers in social research. It may also be necessary to contact relevant ethics committees at universities or research institutions, or national agencies for research ethics, and ask for advice and perhaps special ethical clearance or permission to use data from these registers. In some cases, such ethical problems make it unjustifiable or impossible to use particular register data on individuals for social research.

Online research does not always involve big data. Computers and special software may also be used to collect and analyse primary qualitative or quantitative data, such as in online interviews, surveys or observation. E-mails, the Internet or social media may then be used to contact each participant in the online study. In connection with this contact, it is possible, and advisable, to give information about the study and receive informed consent from the participants. Thus, in principle, such online studies may be based on the ethical norms and rules that have been developed for social research in general. However, a number of ethical standards have been suggested for all online communication. These standards are focused on etiquette for the web, called *netiquette* (Mann and Stewart, 2000). In online research it is an ethical responsibility for researchers to use netiquette in their communication on the web.

Even though advice, clearance and permission can be received from committees or agencies, it is the responsibility of researchers to make sure that their studies, including big data analyses, are carried out on the basis of all adequate ethical norms and rules. Big data studies and online research require particular attention regarding researchers' ethical consciousness and responsibility.

Ethical guidelines and ethics committees

There are different types of resources available for researchers who need advice or support regarding ethical issues in their research. In addition, these resources are important for ensuring that social research in general is based on ethical norms and principles. Thus, these ethical resources are valuable for securing the legitimacy and credibility of social research in the whole research community as well as in society at large.

One type of ethical resource is *ethical guidelines*, which specify in detail the ethical norms, principles and rules that are relevant for social research. Ethical guidelines may be issued by different organizations or institutions, including:

- Professional organizations, such as the Social Research Association in the UK, which published its 'Ethical Guidelines' in December 2003 (http://the-sra.org.uk/wp-content/uploads/ethics03.pdf), or the American Sociological Association, which adopted its Code of Ethics in 1999 (http://www.asanet.org/sites/default/files/savvy/images/asa/docs/pdf/Ethics%20Code.pdf)
- National research councils, such as the Economic and Social Research Council in the UK, which presents a Framework for Research Ethics, along with other information on ethics on its website (https://esrc.ukri.org/funding/guidance-for-applicants/research-ethics/)
- National ethics committees, such as the National Committee for Research Ethics in the Social Sciences and the Humanities in Norway, which has issued Guidelines for Research Ethics in the Social Sciences, Law and the Humanities (https://www.etikkom.no/en/ethical-guidelines-for-research/guidelines-for-research-ethics-in-the-social-sciences--humanities-law-and-theology)
- International organizations, such as the European Union, which describes research ethics on the Science With and For Society website (https://ec.europa.eu/research/swafs/index.cfm?pg=policy&lib=ethics).

Although most of the ethical norms and principles are common for social science across disciplinary, institutional and national boundaries, different versions of ethical guidelines have been published for different disciplines, at different universities and in different countries. The main differences between these versions refer to rules and procedures regarding how suspicions or accusations of unethical research conduct should be assessed and handled. It is advisable for researchers to familiarize themselves with the ethical guidelines that are most relevant to their own discipline, institution and country.

Another type of ethical resource is *ethics committees*. Such committees may work at an institutional level, and ethics committees are appointed by many universities, for example

- The University of Cambridge in the UK, which has appointed a Humanities and Social Sciences Research Ethics Committee, or
- York University in Canada, which has appointed a Research Ethics Committee.

In some countries, there are ethics committees for social science also at the national level, for example,

- The National Committee for Research Ethics in the Social Sciences and the Humanities in Norway, appointed by the Ministry of Education, Research and Church Affairs, or
- The National Ethics Council for Social and Behavioural Sciences in the Netherlands, which is a network of ethics committees at universities in the country.

In addition to developing ethical guidelines, such committees may disseminate information on research ethics, in order to advance ethically sound research behaviour and prevent unethical conduct in research. Furthermore, ethics committees may provide ethical advice to particular researchers regarding their specific research projects or programmes. Typically, ethics committees also have responsibility for assessing specific behaviour to determine whether it is ethical or unethical. The purpose may be to provide ethical clearance or approval for planned research projects, or even permission to carry out a planned project.

Students who are planning a study for a master's thesis or a PhD, or researchers who are planning a new research project, should be familiar with ethical guidelines that are relevant to their research. They should also familiarize themselves with ethical advisors, agencies and committees that could be used for advice and support in ethical issues involved in their studies. An overview of some important ethical issues in social research, and how they are handled, is presented in Table 3.1.

Typically, ethics committees are also responsible for investigating and making decisions in cases of accusations or suspicions of unethical research conduct. Ethics committees may be authorized to determine how researchers involved in unethical behaviour should be sanctioned.

There are different types of sanctions for unethical conduct in research. Researchers who have acted unethically may get a warning, and they may be ordered to withdraw publications that are based on or involved in the unethical research behaviour. They may also forfeit exams or degrees that are based on unethical behaviour, and they may lose their jobs as researchers or their positions as university professors. Students who have acted unethically, for example by cheating or plagiarizing, may forfeit their exams, and they may also lose the right to continue their studies for a certain period of time.

Ethical norms and legal requirements

Cases regarding accusations or suspicions of unethical conduct in research may be taken to court, where they are reviewed and adjudicated by judges on a purely legal basis. Then it is ensured that the legal rights of the accused researcher are protected. The researcher can be defended by a lawyer, and all aspects of the case can be considered in terms of the relevant laws and rules. For example, in Europe, the General Data Protection Regulation (GDPR) is a very important set of rules for protecting

Table 3.1 Overview of important ethical issues and considerations involved in social science studies

Questions	Actions
Are there any ethical issues involved in the study?	• Make a list of potential ethical issues • Ask for advice from supervisor or colleagues
Is ethical clearance or permission needed for doing the study?	• Ask for advice from local ethical support (advisor, agency or committee at the university) • Read relevant local and national ethical guidelines • Apply for clearance or permission if necessary

Is it necessary to obtain informed consent from participants?	• Ask for advice from ethical advisor or agency whether this is needed
	• If necessary:
	   o Ask for forms that are used for informing participants and adapt them by including information about the study'
	   o Consider how and when the participants should be approached for informed consent
	• Consider whether it is necessary to obtain permission or consent from organizations or institutions, in addition to individual participants, and, if necessary, consider how and when such permissions should be obtained

Are (some of) the participants in the study particularly weak or vulnerable?	• Ask for ethical advice and consider whether special forms of protection of these participants are needed
Are there any risks to the researcher involved in the study?	• Ask for advice from supervisor, colleagues or ethical advisors • Make sure that the researcher's safety is secured

individuals in the processing of personal data, and for regulating the free movement of personal data.

However, when unethical conduct goes to court, the distinction between law and ethics is illustrated and illuminated. When the arguments and assessments are transferred from research ethics committees within the research community itself to lawyers and judges outside the research community, attention may be overly concentrated on purely formal laws and rules. The case may be more or less confined to legal arguments, and more informal but nonetheless important and fundamental ethical norms may be overlooked or neglected. Although it is important and necessary to bring the most serious cases of unethical research conduct to court, an increasing juridification of research ethics may have problematic consequences, especially if the purely legal aspects of ethical concerns also dominate in the public debate on research ethics outside the courts. If research ethical issues are confined to strictly legal considerations, it may become more difficult to prevent research conduct that is problematic or unacceptable in a wider ethical sense.

Politics of research

The ethical norms in social science regulate the relationship between researchers and society. In addition to ethical norms, there are different political dimensions involved in this relationship. The political dimensions of research do not refer to party politics, but more generally to various government policies as well as differences or conflicts between groups and interests in society. The following discussion of the politics of research focuses on researchers' relationships to different groups, conflicting interests and various policies. These relationships will be discussed with reference to different purposes of social science and different types of social research.

Analytical, critical and constructive purposes of social science

We may distinguish between three major purposes of social science:

- Analytical purpose. Various types of social phenomena and conditions should be analysed. The phenomena and conditions that are examined are not only described but should also be discussed with reference to more general concepts, theories and insights from social science.
- Critical purpose. Established arrangements and patterns in society should be challenged, problematized and critically discussed, with reference to different values and models for social interaction and organization of social life and society.
- Constructive purpose. The insight into social phenomena, conditions and problems that is developed through social science activity provides a good basis for suggesting certain solutions of these problems.

In other words, social science can contribute to understanding, criticizing or changing different phenomena and conditions in society. These three purposes may be conflicting, and among social scientists there are different views and different practices regarding how much they emphasize each of the purposes, and how much the different purposes are followed up in their research. However, the three purposes may also be regarded as complementary. Analysis is a necessary basis for criticism as well as for problem-solving, and solving problems for certain groups or interests in society may require criticism of other social groups or interests.

Thus, social science must realize that there are conflicts between different interests and groups in society. Contradictions and conflicts are in themselves important topics for analysis. Moreover, when social scientists get involved in critical or constructive research, they may have to clarify how the criticism or solutions of problems are related to different interests and values. In any event, social science itself may become involved in conflicts and debates. There may be conflicting views between researchers within social science, and social science may be regarded as being more positive towards some interests than it is towards other interests in society. The results of a study may strengthen the position of certain groups and weaken the position of other groups in society. Typically, this study will be disliked by the latter groups and more accepted by the former groups. Thus, social science may be controversial. In such situations, it is particularly important that the academic quality of the research is high, based on a well-founded selection and application of research methods.

Action research and critical research

There are many examples of social research that is consciously based on the interests of certain groups or deliberately sets out to solve specific problems for particular groups. A number of studies have been conducted to improve the conditions for various weak groups in society, such as patients, prisoners, consumers, or low-income groups. Such studies may focus, for example, on critical discussions of established structures or systems that create problems for the weak groups.

Several of these studies are designed and implemented as *action research*. This means that the researchers, in collaboration with the weak groups' own organizations or representatives, use the research results as a basis for actions to improve the problematic conditions for the groups. The researchers themselves participate in the actions, and the experiences from the actions are used in turn as a basis for further research. Through this continuous shifting between research and actions,

the action research is in several steps gradually developed and improved, based on the researchers' collaboration with the groups involved and the researchers' solidarity with the groups' interests.

Some of the social research that is based on solidarity with weak groups refers to more fundamental or general conflicts in society, related to, for example, class or gender. This research explicitly intends to advance the interests of weak groups that are considered to be suppressed. Dominant interests and power structures maintaining such suppression are critically examined and discussed. The purpose of this *critical research* is to contribute to the liberation of the suppressed groups. Examples of research based on such perspectives are Marxist studies and feminist studies. Marxist studies emphasize critical analysis of the class structure and the power of the capitalist class, or the bourgeoisie, with the liberation of the working class, or the proletariat, as their purpose. Feminist studies focus on patriarchal structures and gender discrimination, with the liberation of women as their aim.

In many countries, different indigenous peoples have long been the victims of colonization, discrimination and suppression. Indigenous peoples include, for example, the Aborigines in Australia, the Inuit and Native Americans in North America, and the Sámi people in the Nordic countries. The suppression of indigenous peoples has been examined and critically discussed in several social science studies. In indigenous research, it is necessary for the researchers to interact closely with the indigenous people themselves, not only to improve the conditions of the people, but also to collect information and data. Traditionally, indigenous peoples consider their knowledge as a collective good owned by themselves. To obtain access to this knowledge, researchers have to collaborate with the indigenous peoples or their representatives, and this collaboration must be developed on the indigenous peoples' own terms.

Applied and basic research

In action research and research for suppressed groups, the researchers combine critical and constructive purposes in their studies. In *applied research*, constructive purposes are involved, but usually not in combination with critical purposes. Applied research, which also may be called *contract research*, is not carried out for weak or suppressed groups, but for resourceful and powerful organizations or institutions in public administration, business or other sectors in society. Such actors may order and pay for particular studies, projects or even larger research programmes. Thus, they become sponsors of research that they want to use for their own interests. The typical intention is to obtain knowledge that can be used to improve the sponsors' decisions or practical activities. Although the results of the research are used by the sponsors to advance their own interests, the research process itself is not necessarily based on specific interests, and the researchers do not participate in the application of their research.

Nevertheless, an implication of applied research may be that researchers become 'social therapists', who are paid to reveal weaknesses in the functionality of established arrangements in society and to suggest measures to improve these arrangements. This type of research may also imply that the researchers become 'social constructors', who develop and construct new systems and arrangements for established organizations or institutions. In many countries, economists have been active in constructing and reconstructing economic systems and economic policies. These economists may be examples of both 'social therapists' and 'social constructors'.

A special form of applied research is *evaluation research*. The purpose of evaluation research is to examine and assess the implementation and effects of special interventions, such as a pedagogical reform in primary school, a reorganization of health institutions, or a merger of different business companies. The evaluation research may include studies of the process of planning, designing and implementing the intervention. Results and effects of the intervention may be examined by comparing selected phenomena and conditions before and after the implementation of the intervention. Furthermore, these results and effects may be discussed in relation to the intentions and purpose of the intervention.

Sponsors of evaluation research or other applied research may order a study in a specific area, on specific topics, and even with some specified research questions. However, sponsors should not be allowed to interfere in the research process in ways that might have negative effects on the quality of the research. Moreover, sponsors should not be allowed to have any influence on the findings and conclusions of the study.

In general, sponsors of applied research should not threaten the academic freedom of the researchers or the independence of the research. However, the fact that a large amount of the total social research in society is funded by wealthy and resourceful sponsors means that these actors have considerable influence on the selection of research areas and research topics within social science as a whole. Sponsors can afford to order research in areas that are important for themselves and their own interests. These areas are favoured in the development of the social research, whereas other topics, which might be important for other groups, for society at large, or for the theoretical and methodological development of social research itself, may be neglected due to lack of funding.

In *basic research*, on the other hand, the priorities of research areas and research strategies are based on assessments of how the academic disciplines in social research should be further developed. Improvements in the quality of the research and the competence of the researchers are emphasized as criteria for research priorities. Since assessments based on these criteria require research competence and insight into the research fields, the priorities of basic research are determined by researchers and research institutions. Usually, basic research is based on public funding, typically administered by national and international research councils, such as the European Research Council (ERC). Based on peer reviews of applications, it is ensured that the programmes and projects of the highest academic quality are funded. The researchers' academic curiosity is an important driving force in this process, and priorities of research programmes are based on assessments of research quality and research strategy within social science itself, rather than on assumptions regarding research needs in society.

However, in practical research activity, this distinction between basic and applied research is not very sharp. It is common for research projects and research programmes in social science to contribute to both academic development of disciplines and new knowledge that is relevant and important for society at large. The best studies in applied research may contribute to theoretical discussion as well as methodological reflection, and in basic research it is not possible to isolate assessments of the academic development of social science completely from considerations regarding the development of society. The quality of research is often related to the relevance of the research. In their overall evaluation of academic quality and relevance for society, researchers themselves may emphasize that it is a research responsibility to address grand challenges of our time, such as war and peace, environmental and climate issues, health problems, poverty, migration, and ethnic conflicts.

Moreover, basic research is not at all useless. Although basic research is not planned, designed and implemented for specific applications in society, many findings and results from basic research have turned out to be enormously useful for business activity as well as for the development of society. Numerous new products and innovations have come about as results of unforeseen and often surprising findings in basic research. With its long-term development of theories, methods and knowledge, basic research is also a necessary basis for all other types of research, including applied research.

CHAPTER HIGHLIGHTS

- Research ethics refer to the researchers' rights and duties in relation to individuals, groups and society at large.
- Research ethics are based on general ethical norms. Seven norms are emphasized:

  1 Communalism
  2 Universalism
  3 Disinterestedness
  4 Organized scepticism
  5 Originality
  6 Humility
  7 Honesty.

- Plagiarism and data fabrication are typical examples of unethical conduct in research.
- A separate set of research ethical norms has been formulated for protecting the rights of participants or sources in social research:

  o The participation should be based on informed consent
  o Individual participants should be anonymous
  o The information about each individual participants should be confidential
  o The participation should not involve any risk of physical or emotional harm.

- The development of big data and online research creates new ethical challenges, especially regarding the rights of individuals who are selected for a study from one or more large registers. For such studies, it may be necessary to get advice and perhaps clearance or permission from the relevant ethics committee or agency.

- In general, online research should be based on the same ethical norms as offline research. In addition, online research should be adapted to the 'netiquette' behaviour that is relevant to all online communication.
- Ethical guidelines, which specify ethical norms, principles and rules in social science, have been issued by professional organizations, national research councils, national ethics committees, and international organizations.
- University ethics committees and national ethics committees have been appointed, with a number of responsibilities, such as:
  - Developing ethical guidelines
  - Preventing unethical research conduct in general
  - Advising individual researchers
  - Providing ethical clearance or permission for planned studies
  - Investigating and concluding cases of accusations or suspicions of unethical conduct
  - Determining sanctions for unethical conduct.
- Serious cases of unethical conduct may be taken to court, but, due to important differences between law and ethics, research ethical issues should not be limited to strictly legal considerations.
- The politics of social research refers to researchers' relationships to different groups, conflicting interests and various policies in society.
- There are different political dimensions involved in social research, depending on the purpose of the research (analytical, critical or constructive), and the type of research (action research, critical research, applied research and basic research).

RESEARCH EXAMPLES

I recommend that you read the publications used as research examples in this chapter.

Produthase, Henry, Lisa Garza, and Jennifer Wood (2018) 'Scientific research misconduct in social science research: What is it and how can we address it?' *Sociology International Journal* 2(2), 85–86.

This article discusses what is meant by research misconduct in social science, and it describes different types of such misconduct, focusing on fabrication of data and plagiarism as the most serious problems. Furthermore, the article presents possible strategies for addressing common unethical practice, as well as suggestions for how to avoid or prevent such practice.

Stacey, Anthony (2016) 'Mitigating against data fabrication and falsification: A protocol of trias politica for business research', *Electronic Journal of Business Research Methods* 14(2), 72–82.

This article on data fabrication in business research reviews the motivations for fabricating or falsifying data and discusses different techniques for revealing such unethical behaviour. It is shown how various statistical tests may be used to discover anomalies that may be caused by data fabrication, and a special strategy or protocol for preventing fabrication of data is suggested. It is emphasized that it is the researchers' responsibility to ensure that no fabricated or false data are used in their research, and that researchers should be held more accountable in this regard.

Stitzel, Brandli, Gary A. Hoover, and William Clark (2018) 'More on plagiarism in the social sciences', *Social Science Quarterly* 99(3), 1075–1088.

This article on plagiarism presents a survey of journal editors, focusing on the editors' definitions of plagiarism and their reactions to suspected plagiarism. The findings are compared with the results of a similar survey carried out a decade earlier (Enders and Hoover, 2004). Whereas the earlier study focused on economic journals, Stitzel et al. also included journals in sociology, political science and other social science disciplines. Stitzel et al. show that more and more journal editors see the need for a formal policy against plagiarism, and that more and more journals have such a policy. Furthermore, as to how plagiarism should be defined and punished, the study shows great variation within disciplines, but more agreement across disciplines.

STUDENT EXERCISES AND QUESTIONS

1 What are the most important ethical norms for social research?
2 What do we mean by informed consent?
3 Why are there special ethical challenges involved in big data research?
4 What are the typical responsibilities of ethics committees?

5 Discuss the relationship between law and ethics in research.
6 Why are plagiarism and data fabrication especially important as ethical challenges for social research?
7 Why are there political dimensions involved in
   a action research?
   b applied research?

RECOMMENDED LITERATURE

Alver, Bente Gullveig, Tove Ingebjørg Fjell, and Ørjar Øyen (eds) (2007) *Research Ethics in Studies of Culture and Social Life*. Helsinki: Suomalainen tiedeakatemia.

The book presents discussions of a number of ethical challenges and dilemmas, such as the issues of privacy, intimacy and consent. Ethical concerns are considered in relation to a number of areas and approaches in research on culture and social life.

Israel, Mark (2015) *Research Ethics and Integrity for Social Scientists: Beyond Regulatory Compliance*. London: Sage.

This book presents recent developments and debates regarding research ethics. It covers ethical issues related to international, indigenous, interdisciplinary and Internet research. Ethical concerns are exemplified by means of case studies from all continents and from across the social science disciplines.

Richards, Neil M., and Jonathan King (2014) 'Big data ethics', *Wake Forest Law Review* 49, 393–432.

This article describes the rapid growth of the information revolution and the use of big data, and it discusses the need for a 'big data ethics'. The discussion is focused on 'a set of four high-level principles that we should recognize as governing data flows in our information society, and which should inform the establishment of legal and ethical big data norms'.

PART II

DESIGNING SOCIAL RESEARCH

The online resources are here to help with exploring literature and designing research projects!

Visit https://study.sagepub.com/gronmo to access a mapping exercise to take your research from idea to design, links to reference management tools, a guided reading tour of journal articles, examples of published student dissertations, and videos, exercises, and key term definitions.

CREATING RESEARCH QUESTIONS

This chapter provides the knowledge of research questions that is necessary for reading and assessing research reports as well as for formulating research questions for master's theses, doctoral dissertations or other new studies.

The chapter will teach you how to

- create good research questions for obtaining new knowledge and insight
- relate research questions to previous research
- formulate a research question as a topic, question or hypothesis
- improve a research question in terms of generality, complexity and precision

- clarify research questions by means of models
- find appropriate research questions for studying different kinds of social phenomena and studies focused on different kinds of knowledge about these phenomena
- develop research questions for both qualitative and quantitative studies.

What is a research question?

In research, good questions may be more important than correct answers. This statement refers to two fundamental insights. First, even though answers are correct they may be trivial, irrelevant and uninteresting. Correct answers may contain only information that is already well known, without providing any new knowledge. In research such answers are of little value. Whether answers will be not only correct but also relevant, important and original depends on the questions which are asked. The questions determine what the answers should deal with, and what type of information they should contain. Without asking good questions, we cannot obtain valuable answers.

Second, there may be a contradiction between correct answers and important answers. Sometimes the most interesting and least well-known conditions in society are highly complex. Studies of such conditions may not necessarily lead to clear and unambiguous results. However, the studies may be a good basis for formulating new and more challenging questions about the conditions that are examined. This may be more fruitful and more innovative than concentrating on only those answers that are correct. Thus, good questions may be more important than correct answers, both for our understanding of those conditions that are

studied, and for further research on those social conditions.

Questions to be examined

Research questions are questions to be examined and answered in scientific studies. A study may include one or more research questions (Merton, 1959). The research questions define the problems that are to be illuminated, discussed and perhaps solved in the study. Although a research question often is formulated grammatically as a *question*, followed by a question mark, it may also be formulated in other ways. Sometimes research questions are formulated as *topics*, describing what the aim of the study is, or what the study deals with. Research questions may also be formulated as *hypotheses*, which are statements about expected answers to the research questions or expected outcomes of the research. The study will then show whether these expected answers are supported or rejected.

Regardless of how it is formulated, a research question in social science will always imply one or more questions about how certain selected phenomena in society should be perceived or understood. In a quantitative study of leadership behaviour and organizational performance in German and Austrian companies, the general research question was initially formulated as follows (Steyrer et al., 2008: 364):

This paper investigates the effect of executive leadership behaviors on the organizational commitment of subordinate managers and the influence of the latter on measures of company performance.

This is a description of the topic of the research, but implicit in this formulation are the questions about how organizational commitment is affected by leadership behaviours, and how the commitment affects company performance. After a brief overview of previous research in this area, the researchers develop their research questions further, with the following formulation of the two specific questions (Steyrer et al., 2008: 365):

The preceding brief overview leads us to the two questions this study addresses: (1) How does senior leadership behavior influence followers' organizational commitment? (2) What relationship, if any, exists between organizational commitment and measurements of corporate performance?

Based on a more thorough review of the literature from previous research on leadership and organizational effectiveness, the research questions are further specified, in the following hypotheses (Steyrer et al., 2008: 366–367):

H1. Charismatic/value-based leadership is positively related to subordinates' organizational commitment.

H1a. Charismatic/value-based leadership has a stronger relationship with subordinates' organizational commitment than the other leadership dimensions examined.

H2. Team-oriented leadership is positively related to subordinates' organizational commitment.

H3. Participative leadership is positively related to subordinates' organizational commitment.

H4. Humane-oriented leadership is positively related to subordinates' organizational commitment.

H5. Self-protective leadership is negatively related to subordinates' organizational commitment.

H6. Organizational commitment has a positive influence on company performance.

The first six of these hypotheses are related to research question 1. Hypotheses H1 and H2–H5 specify how various aspects or dimensions of senior leadership behaviour may be expected to influence followers' or subordinates' organizational commitment. Hypothesis H1a states that the influence of charismatic/value-based leadership is expected to be stronger than the influence of the other dimensions of leadership behaviour. The selection of behaviour dimensions, as well as the specific expectations, are based on the results from previous research, mainly from a research program on 'Global leadership and organizational effectiveness' (GLOBE).

The seventh hypothesis (H6) refers to research question 2, specifying that organizational commitment is expected to be positively related to corporate performance. This expectation is also based on results from previous research.

Typically, hypotheses are developed from previous research in a *deductive* design, and they are tested through analyses of quantitative data, which show whether each of the hypotheses is supported or rejected. *Hypothesis testing*, based on statistical methods, is described in Chapter 19.

In qualitative studies, research questions are usually not specified as hypotheses to be tested. In such studies research questions are typically formulated in a more general way, as topics or questions to be explored or examined. Moreover, in contrast to quantitative studies, qualitative studies are not necessarily based on final formulations of the research questions before the collection and analysis of data start.

The research questions of a qualitative study may be further refined and specified during the study, in an *inductive* design.

In a qualitative study of housework among lesbian couples in Japan, the research question was initially formulated in the following way (Kamano, 2009: 130):

this study explores various aspects of housework division of lesbian couples in Japan.

After reviewing the literature from previous research on housework division, mainly among heterosexual families in North America, western Europe and Japan, the researcher specifies the research question as follows (Kamano, 2009: 131):

This article will explore the effects of factors that have been shown to affect heterosexual domestic arrangements in both the Anglo-American contexts and Japan, such as [how] relative resources, time availability, and gender role attitudes, affect housework division, and also pay attention to whether there is the egalitarianism that authors ... have found for lesbian couples in the UK and USA.

It is common for researchers in both qualitative and quantitative studies to point out some research questions for further research, based on the results of their own study. This was done by Steyrer et al. (2008: 370–371) in their study of leadership behaviour. In the study of housework among lesbian couples, generating research questions for future research was an important aim of the study (Kamano, 2009: 130):

given the paucity of published studies on lesbians in Japan, I hope to draw useful implications and generate specific questions for future research on both heterosexual and lesbigay families by examining how these couples manage and interpret housework division.

The nature of research questions

It is important to note that not all questions are research questions. Only certain types of questions

may be regarded as research questions (Merton, 1959). In social science, research questions are questions which

- focus on interesting and important phenomena in society
- lead to new studies of these social phenomena
- point to fruitful approaches for such studies
- contribute to further development of the relevant research fields for these studies.

This means that research questions are developed on the basis of previous research and formulated as a starting point for new studies. Typically such new studies will result in answers to the research questions which confirm, strengthen or revise existing knowledge in the relevant research fields (Merton, 1959). The answers should also add to the existing knowledge and bring to light new insights and understanding. In other words, a research question is a formulation of the gap, or distance, between what we know and what we want to know. The research question should guide us from the knowledge that is established in previous research to the new knowledge that we aim to develop through the new study.

A research question defines the field of research to be examined in the new study. By formulating the research question with reference to previous research in this field we can avoid the new study dealing with topics which has been investigated before. We can make sure that the study will result in new knowledge and further development of the research in this field. Furthermore, in this way we are also able to make use of methodological experiences from previous research. As pointed out above, the research questions of both the study of leadership and the study of housework were developed with reference to results and experiences from previous research in the relevant research fields.

As a starting point for new empirical research, the research question must be formulated in such a way that it can be examined empirically. Referring to the examples discussed above, the research questions in the two studies are based on the assumption that it would be possible to find data and carry out meaningful empirical investigations of leadership behaviour, organizational commitment and company performance, as well as the division of housework.

Research questions are guidelines for designing and conducting the new study. The research question of a study clarifies what actors or units in society the study should include, and what features or characteristics of these units the study should examine. In the housework study discussed above, the research question is limited to lesbian couples and various aspects of their division of housework. In the leadership study, the research questions deal with company leaders and their leadership behaviour, the leaders' subordinates and their organizational commitment, as well as the leaders' companies and their performance.

Furthermore, in the leadership study the research questions are focused on the *relationships* between leadership behaviour, organizational commitment and company performance. Some social scientists maintain that *only* questions about relationships between two or more concepts or social phenomena may be regarded as research questions (Kerlinger, 1999). The main argument for this position is that various types of relationships are more interesting and important than anything else in society, and that such relationships are the most meaningful and fruitful topics for social research. However, there is no consensus among social scientists that research questions must include relationships. There are many examples of research questions about characteristics, frequencies or distributions of certain phenomena in society.

An even more restrictive view is that only *hypotheses* should be regarded as research questions. The main argument is that hypotheses will lead to more precise conclusions than formulations of topics or questions. This view is also controversial.

It is found mainly among researchers who prefer quantitative approaches in their research, and among researchers who argue that quantitative studies are more scientific than qualitative studies. As pointed out above, hypotheses are not so common in qualitative studies, and good research questions formulated as topics or questions are widespread in both qualitative and quantitative research.

The importance of research questions

Although there are many different types of research questions, the process of formulating and reformulating research questions is a necessary part of all research in social science. Regardless of how this process is organized, and regardless of how the questions are formulated, research questions are very important for the development of social research, both for the design and conduct of each study and for the long-term accumulation of theory, knowledge and methods in wider research fields and thus in social science in general.

In each study the research question *delimits* and *specifies* those phenomena and conditions in society which are included in the study. The research question focuses on a limited area and clarifies why this area is an interesting and important topic for further research. Furthermore, the research question is a *guideline* for designing and developing the study. Even though the development of the study may lead to revision and reformulation of the research question, especially in qualitative research, the research question is always the main basis for selection of the most adequate approaches, data, analyses and interpretations.

As to the long-term development of research fields and social science in general, research questions are important both backwards and forwards in time. On the one hand, the research question for a new study represents a connection between this study and *previous research*. By relating the research question to earlier research, the new study takes into account the state of the art of the wider research field and builds on the theoretical insights, empirical knowledge and methodological experiences that have been developed so far in this field. This reduces the risk that the study will only rediscover phenomena and patterns that have been shown before, or reuse approaches that previously have been tried and turned out to be inadequate.

On the other hand, the research question of a new study connects this particular study to the *future* development of the wider research field to which the study is related. The research question, formulated with reference to the state of the art of the field, makes sure that the new study will add further insights, knowledge and experiences to the research field. The new study may challenge established knowledge and perspectives, it may lead to a strengthening or revision of results and interpretations from previous research, or it may contribute to completely new insight and innovative perspectives in the research field.

Types of research questions

As pointed out above, research questions may be formulated in different ways, and they have various functions in the research process. More systematically, we may distinguish among different types of research questions. Such typologies of research questions may be based on different criteria. One set of criteria refers to formal characteristics of the research questions. Another set of criteria is related to the substantial content of the research questions, with emphasis on different kinds of knowledge about society as well as different kinds of phenomena in society.

Formal characteristics of research questions

The distinction among topics, questions and hypotheses is a typology of research questions based on formal characteristics. The three types differ in terms of how they are formulated.

Three other formal characteristics may be used to distinguish among different types of research

Table 4.1 Formal characteristics of research questions

Characteristics	Criteria	Variations	Examples of research questions
Generality	Number of units	Specific (idiographic)	How was the result of the UK general election in 2017 affected by the election campaign?
		General (nomothetic)	How are results of general elections affected by election campaigns?
Complexity	Number of features of each unit or number of relationships between features	Simple (univariate)	How has the income level changed during the past decade?
		More complex (bivariate)	What is the relationship between education and income?
		Most complex (multivariate)	What is the relationship between age, education and income?
Precision	Degree of accuracy in definitions of units, features and relationships (existence, direction, form or strength of relationship)	Less precise	Question: Is there a relationship between education and income?
		More precise	Hypothesis: There is a strong positive relationship between the level of education and the level of income.

questions. These characteristics are generality, complexity and precision. Table 4.1 presents an overview of differences between these characteristics.

In terms of *generality*, research questions are more or less general, or more or less specific. Generality refers to the research question's scope or range in time and space. A research question is more general the longer the time period it covers, and the larger the geographical area it is focused on. The research question is more specific the shorter the historical period and the more geographically limited the social phenomena it deals with. While a general research question covers many actors or units in society, a specific research question is limited to few actors or units.

Regarding the two studies discussed above, the housework study has a more specific research question than the leadership study. The housework study is based on data from interviews with 12 lesbian couples in Japan, and the researcher does not 'intend to generalize any of the "findings" in this research to "lesbian couples in Japan"' (Kamano, 2009: 130). In other words, the research question is limited to the 12 couples included in the data set. In the leadership study, on the other hand, the research questions are general, covering company leaders, their subordinates and their companies. The study is based on a sample of 78 companies from Germany and Austria, described by the researchers as the 'Germanic cultural area' (Steyrer et al., 2008: 364). Thus, the research question might have been formulated in a more specific way, referring to this cultural area in particular. Both studies are based on data from one point in time, but they do not specify their research questions in terms of any time period.

The generality of research questions relates to the distinction between idiographic and nomothetic studies, which was described in Chapter 2. Whereas idiographic studies are characterized by quite specific research questions, the research questions of nomothetic studies are much more general.

While generality refers to the number of units (in time and space) covered by the research question, *complexity* has to do with the number of aspects or features of these units which are included in the research question. Research questions are more or less complex, or more or less simple, depending on the number of concepts or relationships they include. In terms of complexity, it is common to distinguish among univariate, bivariate, and multivariate research questions, in particular when the research questions are formulated as hypotheses. *Univariate* research questions are simple, focusing on one single concept or variations in one single phenomenon in society. *Bivariate* research questions are more complex, dealing with a relationship between two concepts or phenomena. *Multivariate* research questions are even more complex, including relationships among more than two concepts or phenomena.

In the leadership study mentioned above, most of the hypotheses (H1 and H2–H6) are formulated as bivariate research questions, since each of them deals with only one relationship between two concepts. Hypothesis H1a, however, is a multivariate research question, because it is focused on differences in strength between one relationship and other relationships. The research question in the housework study is complex and multivariate, paying attention to relationships between housework division and several different factors that might affect the housework division.

The *precision* of the research question refers to how clearly and accurately the units, concepts and relationships in the research question are described or defined. Depending on the degree of clarity and accuracy in these descriptions, research questions are more or less precise, or more or less vague.

The precision of a research question may be increased in different ways. First, the units included may be better defined, in terms of the units to be examined in the study as well as the units for which the results of the study are assumed to be valid. Such clarifications may be made with reference to the distinction between populations and samples, which will be discussed in Chapter 8.

Second, the concepts in the research question may be defined more clearly. Usually this is done by clarifying which aspects or features of the units are covered by the research question. It might be appropriate to distinguish between the features which are included in the specific study, and the features of the units which are supposed to be involved in the more general interpretation of the results of the study.

Third, the relationships in the research questions may be described in a more detailed way. The least precise descriptions of relationships only refer to the *existence* of a relationship, whether there is or is not a relationship. More precise descriptions will clarify the relationship's *direction*, whether it is positive or negative, its *form*, for example whether it is linear or not, and its *strength*, whether it is *deterministic* or a strong or weak tendency. The direction, form and strength of relationships will be further discussed in Chapters 18 and 21.

In the leadership study presented earlier in this chapter, the hypotheses are more precise than the initial overall research questions in the study. The initial research questions include three concepts and the existence of two relationships, between leadership behaviour and organizational commitment, and between organizational commitment and company performance. Hypotheses H1 and H2–H5 define the concept of leadership behaviour more clearly, by distinguishing among five different dimensions of the behaviour, and they clarify the direction of the relationships, by expecting that organizational commitment is positively related to four of the dimensions and negatively related to the fifth dimension. Furthermore, Hypothesis H1a clarifies the relative strengths of the relationships, by formulating that one of the relationships is stronger than the other relationships. Finally, Hypothesis H6 clarifies that the relationship between commitment and company performance is expected to be positive.

The initial research question of the housework study presented above refers to the existence of relationships between each of three concepts (relative resources, time availability and gender role attitudes) and a fourth concept (housework division). The precision of this research question is not increased before the study, but during the study the concepts are further clarified, and it is described in more detail how the concept of housework division is affected by the three other concepts.

The content of research questions

In addition to formal features, substantial content can be used as a basis for distinguishing between different types of research questions. In terms of substantial content, research questions may focus on different kinds of knowledge, and they may deal with different kinds of social phenomena.

As to kinds of knowledge, research questions may be descriptive, explanatory or interpretive. *Descriptive* research questions ask how phenomena or conditions in society really are, and how widespread they are. Such research questions may also ask about variations in the selected phenomena or conditions, for example between different groups or different contexts, and about changes over time. Factual descriptions or discoveries regarding certain aspects of society are in focus. Descriptive research questions are sometimes called *exploratory* research questions. They are most common for new studies in areas where there is little or no previous research. Exploring and describing previously unknown facts about social conditions may be necessary before it is possible to formulate explanatory or interpretive research questions about these conditions. In the housework study presented above, the initial overall research question is descriptive, formulated as an intention to explore various aspects of housework division of lesbian couples in Japan.

Explanatory research questions emphasize why certain phenomena or conditions are as they are, or why they differ or change as they do. Specific explanations of social facts are in focus. Such research questions deal with relationships between various phenomena or concepts. In addition they specify those concepts or phenomena which are supposed to be explained, and those which are regarded as potential explanatory factors. Sometimes explanatory research questions are formulated as causal hypotheses, which are expectations of specific causal relationships between different phenomena. The research questions of the leadership study discussed above are explanatory, asking how organizational commitment can be explained by leadership behaviour, and how commitment can explain company performance.

Interpretive research questions ask how various social phenomena or conditions can be understood in a meaningful way, for example within a larger context or within a more complex system. Holistic understanding of social phenomena is emphasized. Interpretive research questions do not refer to specific relationships between selected concepts or phenomena. Typically, those phenomena or conditions which are examined, are interpreted and understood in relation to more general frames of reference. The housework study is not limited to a description of housework division among the lesbian couples that are interviewed. The study also examines how these couples interpret housework division, focusing on 'meanings of housework more deeply' (Kamano, 2009: 136). Moreover, the study formulates some questions for further research, including a question about 'how we can understand their housework division in the context of their families of origin, the local community and their work in a hetero-normative society' (Kamano, 2009: 140). All these research questions are interpretive.

These differences between descriptive, explanatory and interpretive research questions are summarized and exemplified in Table 4.2.

There are several typologies of research questions with reference to the kinds of social phenomena they deal with. One such typology distinguishes among research questions which are focused on time, space and levels. Research questions on *time* perspectives refer to stability, change and processes during a certain time period. Such questions, which are called *longitudinal* research questions, may refer to short-term processes or long-term trends. Examples of analyses with longitudinal research questions are studies of changes in the income distribution in a country during the twentieth century, studies of stability and change in voters' party preferences during an election campaign, and studies of specific features of a selected decision process in a large business company.

Research questions with reference to *space* are typically focused on similarities and differences between two or more social contexts, and they are

Table 4.2 Typology of research questions based on the kinds of knowledge that are emphasized

Types of research questions	Definitions	Examples of research questions
Descriptive (exploratory)	How social phenomena really are, how widespread they are, how they differ or how they change	What are the main patterns of urbanization (increase in the population of cities in relation to the rural population) since 1950 in the UK and Germany?
Explanatory	Why social phenomena are as they are, or why they differ or change as they do	What are the main factors leading to urbanization in western Europe?
Interpretive	How social phenomena can be understood in a meaningful way, within particular contexts	What does it mean for young families to move from a rural area to a city?

called *comparative* research questions. The contexts which are examined and compared may be geographically defined, such as small communities, regions, nations or even larger parts of the world. The contexts may also be different institutions or organizations. Examples of analyses based on comparative research questions are studies comparing three different countries as to the role of bureaucracy in society, studies comparing election campaigns in two small communities, and studies comparing four different business companies as to their leadership behaviours.

Research questions related to different *levels* deal with the relationship between social phenomena at the macro, meso and micro level. Such questions are called *multi-level* research questions. A classical study with a multi-level research question is Durkheim's study of suicide (Durkheim, 1897). He asks how suicide among individuals, at the micro level, can be explained by features of the individuals' social contexts or communities, at the macro level. Such multi-level research questions, focused on the effect of macro-level conditions on micro-level phenomena, are called *contextual* research questions.

Another typology with reference to the substantial content of the research questions is focused on relations, networks and structures. Such questions are not limited to characteristics of individual actors, but deal with *relations* between two or more actors. They may be called *relational* research questions. Actors may be individuals or different kinds of organizations or institutions, and the research questions may refer to any kind of relation between these actors, such as kinship, friendship or interaction between individuals, collaboration between organizations, or alliances between states. Some research questions deal with social *networks*, which are smaller or larger patterns of such relations, for example networks of friends in a community or networks of business organizations that are involved in trade with each other. Furthermore, some research questions refer to social *structures*, which may be defined as relatively stable patterns of relations among social positions. Thus, stable and long-lasting social

Table 4.3 Typology of research questions based on the kinds of social phenomena that are emphasized

Types of research questions	Definitions	Examples of research questions
Longitudinal	Long-term trends: Stability or change during a certain time period	How has the income distribution in the Netherlands changed since 1990?
	Short-term processes	How did the election campaign develop during the US presidential election in 2016?
Comparative	Similarities or differences between two or more social contexts	What are the major differences between the USA, UK and Scandinavia in people's use of public welfare services?
Multi-level	Relationship between social phenomena at different levels (micro, meso, macro)	How can parents' influence on their children's motivation for school be explained by features of the communities where the parents and children live?
Relational	Relations between two or more actors	What are the main features of the trade relations between Spain and France?
	Networks of relations	What are the similarities and differences between the networks among psychology students and the networks among anthropology students?
	Structures (stable patterns of relations and networks)	How are power structures in business affected by increasing numbers of interlocking directorates between companies in different countries?

networks can be examined and interpreted as social structures. Examples of research based on questions regarding structures are studies of networks of interlocking directorates among large companies. An interlocking directorate is defined as the relation between two companies that is created by a person who is a board member in both companies. Networks of interlocking directorates can be understood as power structures in business (see, for example, Mintz and Schwartz, 1985).

An overview of the types of research questions based on substantial content are presented in Table 4.3. These types are typical research questions in social science. In Part V of the book they will be further discussed with reference to more general analytical perspectives in such studies. Chapter 21 is focused on descriptive, explanatory and interpretive studies. Chapter 22 contains a further elaboration on longitudinal, comparative and multi-level analyses. Chapter 23 deals with studies on relations, networks and structures.

In sum, there are several different typologies of research questions. A particular research question may be classified according to one or more of these typologies, and it may be reformulated and developed from one type to another type within the same typology. Moreover, a particular study may be based on a set of different types of research questions.

Research questions and models

In the leadership study discussed above, all research questions are summarized, presented together, viewed in relation to one another, and visualized in a comprehensive figure, which is reproduced here in Figure 4.1. This figure is an example of a social science model, which was discussed in Chapter 2. A model is defined as a simplified image of the real world, which is an idealized representation of selected phenomena and relationships in society. The simplification and idealization are obtained by isolating and emphasizing those aspects of social life which are

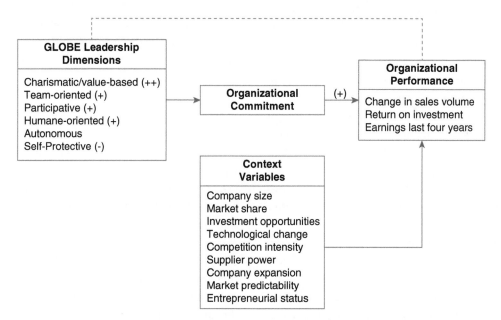

Figure 4.1 Model for relationships between leadership dimensions, organizational commitment, and organizational performance. Reproduced from Steyrer et al. (2008: 367)

of particular interest in the research to be carried out. Other aspects of social life are typically excluded.

The model in Figure 4.1 specifies six dimensions of leadership behaviour (GLOBE leadership dimensions) in the box on the upper left-hand side. The arrow between this box and the box in the upper middle part of the model shows that organizational commitment is influenced by leadership dimensions. The signs after each dimension indicate a positive relationship (+) or a negative relationship (–) between the dimension and organizational commitment. The (++) label denotes a particularly strong positive relationship. This is a summary and visualization of Hypotheses H1, H1a and H2–H5, listed above. The lack of a sign after one of the leadership dimensions (autonomous) means that this dimension is not expected to have any particular effect on commitment. Furthermore, the model lists three features of organizational performance in the box on the upper right-hand side of the figure. The arrow between this box and the box in the upper middle part of the model shows that the features of organizational performance are influenced by organizational commitment, and the (+) sign above the arrow shows that this relationship is positive, consistent with Hypothesis H6.

The three boxes in the upper part of the model and the two arrows between these boxes visualize the expectation of an indirect relationship between leadership and performance, through commitment. The dashed line in the model illustrates that there might also be a direct relationship between leadership and performance. Although no hypothesis is formulated about this relationship, it is 'briefly explored in the study' (Steyrer et al., 2008: 367).

Finally, the box in the lower part of the model specifies a number of context variables. The arrow between this box and the performance box indicates that performance is expected to be influenced by the context variables. Although no more specific hypotheses are formulated about these relationships, the context variables are incorporated in the analysis (Steyrer et al., 2008: 367).

Types of models

The type of model shown in Figure 4.1 is a *conceptual model*, which may also be called a *theoretical model*. Such models include relationships between specific social phenomena or conditions. The research question in this example is a typical research question when conceptual models are used. The model is used to clarify and specify the concepts and relationships involved in the research question. Conceptual models may also be used for clarification and specification of research questions about elements in activities, processes, debates or other social phenomena. The following research question is an example: 'What were the main arguments for different positions in the Brexit debate in the UK?'

Another type of model is the *formal model* or *mathematical model*. These consist of symbols and relationships which are expressed in mathematical form and linked together in a deductive system. For example, a formal model of the relationships between leadership behaviours and organizational commitment in Figure 4.1 could be formulated like this:

$$OC = CL + TL + PL + HL - SL.$$

The model indicates that organizational commitment (OC) is a result of charismatic/value-based leadership (CL), team-oriented leadership (TL), participative leadership (PL), humane-oriented leadership (HL) and self-protective leadership (SL). Organizational commitment is regarded as a function of the five leadership dimensions in the formal model. The model says that the organizational commitment (OC) is positively related to four of the leadership dimensions (CL, TL, PL, and HL) and negatively related to the fifth dimension (SL).

Formal models are used in *regression analysis* of quantitative data, which will be presented in Chapter 18. Then the model is formulated as a special type of equation. A simplified version of a regression equation would look like this:

$$y = b_1 x_1 + b_2 x_2 + b_3 x_3.$$

In this equation x_1, x_2 and x_3 are factors, for example gender, age and education, which have effects on y, for example income, whereas b_1, b_2 and b_3 show the direction and size of each effect. The direction and size of each effect are estimated in the regression analysis.

The research question could be formulated as follows: To what extent can income be explained by gender, age and education, and what is the effect of each of the three factors? This is a typical research question when formal models are used.

Whereas formal models are limited to quantitative studies, conceptual models are used in both qualitative and quantitative research. Compared to conceptual models, formal models may provide less concrete descriptions of the concepts or phenomena involved but more precise expressions of the relationships among these concepts or phenomena. Sometimes it may be problematic to use formal models in social science, because the relationships are formulated too precisely. The model expression of a relationship may be much more rigorous than the real empirical relationship. Thus, the model may be an unrealistic oversimplification, rather than a fruitful representation of the real world. The challenge is to find a good balance between theoretical rigour and empirical realism.

The importance of models

A model is an important connection between theoretical insights and empirical evidence. The model is founded on principles and arguments from theory, which are presented and expressed in the most fruitful and appropriate way as a basis for new empirical analyses. The reason for relating a research question to a model is to clarify and visualize how the research question connects the new empirical study to existing theory based on previous research. The model emphasizes the theoretical foundation of the research question and points to its potential for generating new empirical knowledge.

A model for a new study may cover exactly the same concepts and relationships as the research questions for the study. However, the conceptual model in Figure 4.1 is somewhat broader than the major set of research questions which were formulated for the leadership study. The six hypotheses for the study are visualized by the three boxes in the upper part of the model and the arrows between these boxes. In addition, the model includes a dashed line between two of these boxes, symbolizing a direct relationship between leadership and performance, as well as a fourth box with contextual variables and an arrow symbolizing a direct contextual influence on performance. Thus, in this case the model is not only clarifying and visualizing the research questions as such. The model is also important for showing the limitations of the research questions, and for demonstrating how the research questions are related to a wider context.

In other studies, models may cover only parts of the overall research question. Then the importance of the models may be to highlight those parts of the study which are most central. The models may also be used for those parts of the study where the connection to theory from previous research is particularly strong, for those parts of the study where it is particularly difficult to show how the new study is connected to earlier research and established theory, or simply for those parts of the study where it is easiest to clarify the research question by means of a model.

It is not always easy to use models to clarify the theoretical foundation of a research question before the study starts. Obviously, this is the case for studies in areas where there is little previous research. However, models are also useful during studies, for analysing data and interpreting the results of data analyses. Formal models are often used in analyses of quantitative data, for example in multiple regression analyses or other multivariate analyses. These types of analyses will be described and discussed in Chapter 18. Also in qualitative studies models may be useful for clarifying and visualizing patterns and relationships which are uncovered during the collection and analysis of the data. Thus the research questions can be clarified, either for further development of the ongoing study or for future research. In qualitative studies conceptual models are more common than formal models. The studies may lead to the development of new models, in order to show the meaning of key concepts and the existence of important relationships.

Development of research questions

Formulating good research questions is a process. Typically, the first formulation of a research question is not the final formulation. The question is further developed and reformulated several times, so that the connection between theoretical foundations and empirical evidence is gradually improved. The aim is to refine the formulation of the research question so that it is more founded on previous research and more adequate for the new study. During this process the researcher moves back and forth between theoretical discussions and empirical considerations, and between different steps related to the formulation of the research question. Reviewing the literature from previous research is a very important part of this process.

Review of literature and previous research

Knowing the literature from previous research is necessary for formulating good research questions.

The literature provides information on previous studies, with emphasis on research questions, methods and results. Moreover, in a typical research report, the particular study is discussed in relation to a wider research area, the selected methods are compared with other methods, and the results are interpreted with reference to more general theoretical perspectives. Most often the report also presents reflections on the limitations of the particular study and views on important research questions for future research. Thus, the literature contains the theoretical insights, the established empirical knowledge, and the methodological experiences within a research area which we need in order to ask the most interesting and most adequate questions for new research in this area.

It is challenging to find the existing research literature that is most relevant for a new study. The literature consists of different types of publications, including journal articles, books or book chapters, conference papers, and research reports from institutes or research centres. Previously these publications were available only in printed form, on paper, but more and more research publications are now accessible in digital form and can be read on the Internet. Increasingly, digital publications are available for everybody through 'open access', and both printed and digital publications are provided by university libraries or other research libraries, which have subscription agreements with the publishers.

Search engines and various bibliographical databases can be used to search for relevant literature, both printed and digital publications, which are available from libraries or on the Internet. It is important to select pertinent keywords for the search, focusing on the most central topics or researchers in the relevant research area. The selection of keywords should be adapted to the definition of the area which is relevant to the research questions of the new study. In the leadership study discussed above, the relevant area was defined as research on leadership and organizational effectiveness (Steyrer et al., 2008). In the housework study the literature review covered previous research on housework division, mainly among heterosexual families in North America, western Europe and Japan (Kamano, 2009).

It is a challenge to avoid too wide definitions of the relevant research area. For the literature search it is a good advice to follow a 'funnel' strategy, starting with a general definition of the research area, and then narrowing the definition to the more specific studies which are most relevant to the particular research questions for the new study. Furthermore, it is a good idea to start with those research reports which present the most general overviews of the relevant area. Another piece of advice is to start with the newest research reports in the area. These contributions provide the broadest and most updated descriptions of the development as well as the current status of the research in the relevant area, and they include the most central and most recent references to other literature. These references can be sources for finding older and more specific literature.

Based on the results of the literature search, it is important to select the most adequate literature for the final written review, which will become a part of the research report from the new study. It should be kept in mind that the purpose of the literature review is not to write a complete overview of the whole research area as such. The main aim is to present a description of the research area which is sufficient to show how the new research questions are founded on previous research, and how the specific new study is related to the more general research area. Thus, the selection of literature for the review should be based on the research question, and the final review should present those theories, concepts, empirical findings and methodological experiences which are most relevant to the particular research question. When describing contributions from previous research in the literature review, it is important to use the original references. Although a theory or an empirical finding presented in the literature review might have been found in a recent publication, the review should refer to those articles, books or reports where the theory or empirical finding was first presented.

Chapter 5 presents a more extensive discussion of literature reviews and how they are conducted.

Four steps to forming a research question

The process of formulating a research question includes four major steps. Figure 4.2 presents an overview of these steps.

The first step is to *identify the research question*. The researcher identifies or selects a topic or a problem to be examined, for example organizational commitment or housework among lesbian couples. The identification or selection of a research question may be a result of the researchers' theoretical and methodological competence, their research interests or concern for social issues, or their views on the development of the research field as well as changes in the society. In other words, the choice of research question depends on what the researchers *are able to* examine, what they *want to* examine, and what they think *should be* examined.

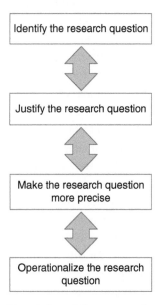

Figure 4.2 Steps in formulating a research question

In addition to the researchers' own competencies, interests and views, the selection of research questions may also depend on a number of other conditions in society, such as priorities in national research policies or availability of research funding. Thus, the researchers' freedom to choose their own research questions may be limited by political or administrative decisions on priority areas for public funding of social research. The researchers are dependent on funding and may have to select research questions for which funding is available rather than pursuing their own research interests. The researchers' freedom may be even more limited in contract research, where investigation of particular research questions is ordered and funded by companies, organizations, public agencies or other actors outside the research community. However, it is always the researchers' responsibility to consider whether a certain research question is acceptable or not, from an academic as well as an ethical point of view. Furthermore, even though research questions may be broadly defined by funding agencies, sponsors, or actors ordering contract research, the further development and final formulation of these research questions should be made by the researchers, who can make sure that the research project will be consistent with academic and ethical standards.

A second step involved in the process of formulating a research question is to *justify the research question*. The justification will refer to the research question's importance for society and for social science. As to the importance for society, it may be argued that investigation of the selected research question would be valuable for certain groups in society or for society at large. In a study of the policy effectiveness of US state governors, the research question was: 'why are some governors more successful in the policy arena than others? Specifically, what is the role of gender on a governor's legislative success?' (Dickes and Crouch, 2015: 90). One of the justifications for this research question was the changes in the demographic and cultural background of governors: 'As more women serve as high ranking policy executives, understanding the role of gender is both a timely and relevant research question' (Dickes and Crouch, 2015: 90). Thus, the research question is discussed with reference to the social context in which the research will take place, and it is shown how research on this question can provide new and important knowledge for increasing the understanding or solving special problems in the particular social context. The research question is legitimized in terms of its relevance for concrete and practical conditions in society. Such social justification of the research question may be more or less emphasized in research projects. Typically, it is more emphasized in contract research or applied research than it is in basic research.

In all kinds of research the research question should also be justified in terms of its importance for social science, and in particular for the further development of the research field. This scientific or research strategic justification relates the particular research question to the wider research field and shows how the new study will provide new contributions within this field. It is pointed out how investigation of the selected research question will lead to new empirical findings, new theoretical insights or new methodological experience. It is argued how research on the selected question is strategically important for the further development of the wider research field. In the study of gender roles and policy effectiveness mentioned above, the research question was also justified in relation to the research field: 'there is a paucity of research with regard to the policy influence of women executives on cities, states, and nations, and there is no research specifically addressing the role of gender on the policy success of governors. Clarifying the distinct roles that men and women may play in different policymaking environments is an important contribution to our understanding of the policymaking process' (Dickes and Crouch, 2015: 91).

A third step in formulating the research question is to *make the research question more precise*. As pointed out above, this means clarifying the description and definition of the units, concepts and relationships included in the research question. The aim is to formulate the research question as precisely as possible. Improving the precision makes the research question a better guideline as to how the new study should be designed and carried out, and how the results of the study should be interpreted.

On the other hand, it is also important that the research question is not formulated too precisely. The level of precision should not be higher than what is reasonable based on the results of previous research. If the research question is formulated in a very precise way, the new study may not be open enough for registering new discoveries, unforeseen findings and surprising results.

When the research questions are made more precise, the units, concepts and relationships are clarified by means of *theoretical* or *nominal definitions*. A fourth step in the formulation process is to *operationalize the research question*. Then the different elements of the research question are clarified by using *operational definitions*. These definitions specify clear criteria for how the units, concepts and relationships in the research question will be represented by empirical data. Operationalizing makes the research question even more useful as a guideline for designing and conducting the new study, in particular with respect to the collection of empirical data, but also when it comes to interpreting the results of the empirical analysis and understanding the limitations of the empirical study. Operationalization and operational definitions are further discussed in Chapter 7.

Balancing theoretical perspectives and empirical evidence

As pointed out above, the process of formulating and reformulating a research question is characterized by movements back and forth between the four different steps, as well as between theoretical perspectives and empirical evidence. There may be considerable variations among different studies as to how much each of the four steps is emphasized, and how the research question is developed in connection with each step. For example, it is easier to emphasize theoretical perspectives for justifying the research question, or for making it more precise, in research fields where there is much previous research and well-established theories than it is in fields where previous research is more limited. Another example is that the operationalization of the research question may lead to different kinds of definitions, depending on what types of data the study will be based on. In quantitative studies it is reasonable to use operational definitions in terms of quantities or degrees, such as size, length, age, or duration. In qualitative studies it is more appropriate to develop operational definitions with reference to qualities or types, such as characteristics, features, forms, or attributes.

Furthermore, there are variations among different studies as to the order in which the steps are carried out, and as to when in the research process the steps are dealt with. In quantitative studies with a deductive development of the research question, all four steps are usually completed before the data collection starts. In qualitative studies, and in studies with an inductive approach, those steps which are related to empirical evidence are often handled before those steps which are related to theoretical perspectives. In such studies the steps involved in formulation and reformulation of the research question may continue through the whole study. The collection and analysis of new data may be used as a basis for justifying and making the research question more precise. Thus the final formulation of the research question may be a result of the study and used mainly as a point of departure for further research.

However, all studies, including studies based on qualitative data and inductive approaches, should be related to previous research and start with a research question which is formulated as clearly as possible. Even when a new study is carried out in a field with very limited previous research, this scarcity of research should be explicitly pointed out, and the implications of this for the new study should be discussed. Even when it is considered important to revise and improve the research question during the collection and analysis of the new data, in order to be sufficiently open to new, unforeseen and surprising findings, it is advisable to start with a preliminary research question, formulated as precisely as possible, as an initial guideline for the development of the data collection and data analysis.

CHAPTER HIGHLIGHTS

- A research question is a formulation of the gap or distance between what we know and what we want to know. The research question
  1 is developed on the basis of previous research
  2 defines the field of research to be examined in a new study
  3 clarifies what social units the study includes, and what features of these units the study should examine.
- Research questions are formulated as topics, questions or hypotheses.
- Research questions may be different in their generality, complexity and precision.
- Research questions may focus on different kinds of knowledge. Thus, research questions may be descriptive, explanatory, or interpretive.
- Research questions may deal with different kinds of social phenomena, such as longitudinal, comparative, or multi-level research questions, and research questions on relations, network and structure.
- Research questions may be clarified by means of models. A model is an idealized representation of selected phenomena and relationships in society. We distinguish between conceptual and formal models.
- Literature reviews are important for ensuring that the research questions are based on previous research.

- Formulating a research question is a process involving four major steps:
  1 Identifying the research question
  2 Justifying the research question
  3 Making the research question more precise
  4 Operationalizing the research question.
- The process of formulating a research question is characterized by movements back and forth between the four different steps, as well as between theoretical perspectives and empirical evidence. There are differences between qualitative and quantitative studies as to the emphasis on each step and the order in which the steps are dealt with.
- In quantitative studies the research questions are formulated before the collection and analysis of data start. In qualitative studies formulation and reformulation of the research questions may continue through the whole study.
- Research questions are important
  1 for delimiting and defining the social phenomena and conditions to be included in a new study
  2 as guidelines for designing and developing new studies
  3 as connections between previous research and new studies
  4 for ensuring that new studies contribute to the long-term development of specific research fields and social science in general.

....**RESEARCH EXAMPLES**

I recommend that you read the publications used as research examples in this chapter.

Kamano, Saori (2009) 'Housework and lesbian couples in Japan: Division, negotiation and interpretation', *Women's Studies International Forum* 32, 130–141.

This article is an example of a qualitative study in which a general research question is further developed and specified through the process of collecting and analysing the data.

Steyrer, Johannes, Michael Schiffinger, and Reinhard Lang (2008) 'Organizational commitment – A missing link between leadership behavior and organizational performance?', *Scandinavian Journal of Management,* 24, 364–374.

This article is an example of a quantitative study where the research questions are developed, refined and specified as seven hypotheses before the collection of data starts.

A third example of the development of research questions is found in the following article, which presents a quantitative study of survey data:

Stier, Haga, and Meir Yaish (2014) 'Occupational segregation and gender inequality in job quality: A multi-level approach', *Work, Employment and Society* 28(2), 225–246.

The first presentation of the research question in this article is a formulation of a *topic*: 'This study focuses on gender differences in job attributes' (Stier and Yaish, 2014: 226). This is followed by the formulation of a *question*: 'to explore whether women's occupations offer conditions and characteristics that evidently compensate for the lack of high wages and good opportunities for advancement' (Stier and Yaish, 2014: 226). Furthermore, this question is *specified* in the following way: 'Specifically, the main interest is in the extent to which women's concentration in occupations embedded in specific national labour markets might explain gender differences in the subjective assessment of job quality' (Stier and Yaish, 2014: 226). Furthermore, based on a review of previous research, Stier and Yaish (2014: 227) specify their research question as four hypotheses.

A fourth example of the formulation of research questions can be found in the following article, which presents a qualitative study based on ethnographic fieldwork:

Jirata, Tadesse Jaleta (2012) 'Learning through play: An ethnographic study of children's riddling in Ethiopia', *Africa* 82(2), 272–286.

In this article on riddling among Guji children in Ethiopia, the first formulation of the research question is the *intention* 'to demonstrate how Guji children perform riddling and facilitate their own informal learning through it' (Jirata, 2012: 273). Based on the social constructivist epistemology, the central *objective* of the study is 'to document riddling as a sphere for children's autonomous entertainment and knowledge acquisition' (Jirata, 2012: 273). This objective is specified as two *questions* (Jirata, 2012: 273): 'First, how do children recreate their social world and share their play interactions through riddling? Second, how does riddling, as a child-centred practice, function as a context for children's informal knowledge acquisition?'

STUDENT EXERCISES AND QUESTIONS

1 What are the characteristic features of research questions?

2 Describe the typical differences between qualitative and quantitative studies in the process of formulating research questions.

3 Why are models useful in the formulation of research questions?

4 Why is the research question important in a new study?

5 Why are research questions important for the development of social science in general?

6 Formulate different types of research questions for a study of salaries and working conditions among male and female hotel employees.

7 Construct a conceptual model showing relationships between age, gender, level of education, and income.

RECOMMENDED LITERATURE

Alvesson, Mats, and Jörgen Sandberg (2013) *Constructing Research Questions: Doing Interesting Research*. London: Sage.

The book presents a methodology for generating research questions that can lead to more interesting and influential theories, with examples from social science.

Andrews, Richard (2005) *Research Questions*. London: Continuum.

This book is a less advanced guide to creating and formulating research questions.

Lave, Charles A., and James G. March (1993) *An Introduction to Models in the Social Sciences*. Lanham, MD: University Press of America.

This is an introductory book on constructing and applying models in social science. The book includes a number of examples from different research areas.

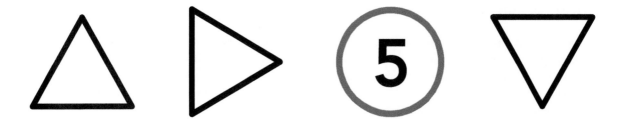

DOING A LITERATURE REVIEW

This chapter provides the necessary knowledge for reading and understanding literature reviews and for doing new literature reviews either as a separate stand-alone study (e.g. a term paper, research essay or master's thesis) or as a part of a larger study, for developing new research questions or discussing new findings (e.g. in a master's thesis or PhD dissertation).

The chapter will teach you how to

- decide what type of literature review is most appropriate for your purpose
- do different types of narrative and systematic literature reviews
- do literature reviews of both qualitative and quantitative studies

- follow up the major steps in the process of reviewing literature
- reference the sources in the literature review
- avoid plagiarism when writing about previous research.

What is a literature review?

In the previous chapter (Chapter 4) it was pointed out that literature reviews are important in the process of formulating research questions, and in this connection it was briefly discussed how the researchers can search for literature, select the relevant publications and organize the final review. The objective of this chapter is to present a more extensive discussion of literature reviews and how they are conducted.

A research literature review may be defined as a systematic way of identifying, evaluating and synthesizing the existing literature from previous research within a selected research field. The review process, including methods, procedures and criteria that are used, should be explicitly described, so that the literature review is reproducible. The review should be comprehensive, including all available literature from previous research in the field.

Although a literature review should be comprehensive, it is always limited to a selected and specified field of research, such as research on gender inequality, international conflicts, or networks among organizations. Thus, comprehensiveness means that the review should be based on all the available literature that is relevant for this specific field. The field may be specified as wide or narrow, depending on the research question of the study.

A literature review includes literature from previous research within the specified field. This means that the inclusion of relevant literature depends on the nature and content of this literature. In principle, it does not matter who are the authors of the literature that is reviewed. However, as argued by Fink (2014: 3), a good and accurate literature review bases its conclusions on high-quality original work by scholars and researchers. Typically, peer-reviewed books and journal articles are emphasized in literature reviews. The quality of such publications is assessed and ensured by referees or reviewers who are experts in the fields covered by the book or article.

A literature review is based on explicitly described methods, procedures and criteria, which are applied to identify the available and relevant literature, to evaluate the literature identified, and to synthesize the content of the literature. Since it might be difficult to find all the available literature, it is important to have reliable and efficient *search procedures* for discovering and locating publications within the specified field of research. It is also necessary to have clear *criteria for evaluating* these publications. The evaluation may refer to the publication's relevance for the particular review as well as its scientific quality and significance within the general development of the research field. Furthermore, it is valuable to have a *plan for synthesizing* the content of the literature. This is a plan for summarizing, discussing and presenting the different publications in relation to one another, in the context of the development of the research field, and with reference to the research question of the new study. The review is focused on those parts of the publications which are most relevant to the research question.

The literature review is a *systematic* way of identifying, evaluating and synthesizing the literature. As will be pointed out later in this chapter, there is a particular type of literature review that is called 'systematic review'. Nevertheless, as emphasized by Booth et al. (2016: 2), all types of reviews should be systematic. The systematic approach is a way of avoiding bias in the inclusion or evaluation of the literature.

Reporting the review process in an *explicit* way means that the search procedures, evaluation criteria and synthesizing plan are open and visible to everybody. Describing procedures, criteria and plans explicitly is also a way of ensuring that the researcher applies them consistently through the whole review. Moreover, when all this is explicitly recorded and written, it is possible for both the researcher to remember and others to know how the literature review has been done, and thus the review is *reproducible*. This is valuable for understanding the literature review and for assessing its quality and significance.

Reviewing the literature is a process, starting with the formulation of the research question for a new study and the specification of the research field to be reviewed, and ending with the final written literature review. The process consists of a number of different steps, which are related to the elements of the definition of the literature review. However, each step in the process, and each element in the definition, may be more or less important, depending on variations between different purposes of the literature review and different types of reviews.

The result of the reviewing process is the final literature review. This is a written text, which is published. How it is published depends on the purpose of the review. If the review is done as a part of a larger study, the literature review is included in the research report for the study. Although the identification and evaluation of the literature are comprehensive, the written review is usually focused on the literature that is most relevant for developing and justifying the specific research question of the study and for relating this research question to previous research. The literature review may also be produced as a stand-alone study, which means that the review is published as a separate research report. Stand-alone reviews are often more extensive than reviews included in reports from larger studies. Different purposes of the literature review and different types of literature reviews, as well as different steps in the reviewing process, are discussed below.

Purposes of literature reviews

Researchers may use literature reviews for three different purposes. One of these is to *develop research questions for a new study,* as discussed in Chapter 4. The literature review shows how the research question is founded on previous research. It presents the theoretical perspectives, empirical findings and methodological experiences from previous research that are important for formulating, refining and justifying the most interesting and most precise research question for the new study.

The second purpose of literature reviews is to *discuss findings from a new study*. In all types of studies, findings should be interpreted in relation to literature from previous research. When a literature review has been done in the process of formulating the research question, the same literature review is typically used also for discussing the findings. However, if a literature review has not been done in the process of developing the research question, it might be adequate to do a separate literature review for the purpose of relating the findings to previous research. Doing a separate literature review for discussing new findings is particularly important in studies where the research questions have not been very much developed before the collection and analysis of data. This might be the case in some exploratory studies, inductive studies, and qualitative studies. In such studies, the literature might be reviewed during the whole process of data collection and analysis.

Both these purposes of literature reviews refer to the use of the reviews as parts of a new and larger study, for formulating research questions and for interpreting research findings. In the studies discussed in Chapter 4, there are examples of literature reviews used for both these purposes. In her study of housework among lesbian couples, Kamano (2009) reviewed the literature on housework division in hetero-sexual families to develop her own research question on lesbian couples. In their study of organizational commitment, leadership behaviour and organizational performance, Steyrer et al. (2008) did a literature review to develop the research question towards specification of seven hypotheses. They also made use of the reviewed literature to discuss some of the findings in their study.

The third purpose is to *use literature reviews to answer research questions*. The literature review is not a part of a larger study. The review is in itself a separate study, which stands alone. A new research question is examined and discussed by finding new ways of summarizing, interpreting, integrating and synthesizing existing literature from previous research. Thus, new knowledge and new insights might be extracted and generated by combining and reinterpreting previous research results. Sometimes, a large body of literature within a field of research has not even been sufficiently summarized and synthesized before, so that the task of synthesizing will in itself provide an important basis for new insights. Typically, a literature review done as a separate stand-alone study is more extensive

and more thorough than literature reviews which are included in larger studies. The latter reviews are called *informative literature reviews*. Whereas the goal of an informative literature review is to inform primary research, the stand-alone review is an end in itself (Onwuegbuzie and Frels, 2016: 16).

An example of a literature review as a separate stand-alone study is a review on alumni loyalty carried out by Iskhakova et al. (2017). Their review summarizes key theoretical perspectives and empirical evidence in previous research on loyalty of alumni (former students) to their alma mater (the university where they studied). They specify four research questions (Iskhakova et al., 2017: 275):

1 Who is conducting alumni loyalty research?
2 Which theoretical perspectives (approaches) are most commonly employed in alumni loyalty research?
3 How does the research from different theoretical approaches measure (describe) the construct of alumni loyalty?
4 How can the term 'alumni loyalty' be defined in a more comprehensive way?

Stand-alone literature reviews may be important for social science as well as for society. As pointed out by Iskhakova et al. (2017: 274), the findings in their study of alumni loyalty 'can be used by academics as a framework to position new research activities appropriately and by practitioners as a roadmap to enhance alumni loyalty rate'. Thus, as to scientific importance, the review may be a basis for further research, and consequently an important part of the long-term development of the particular research field and social science in general. In terms of societal importance, such literature reviews may be valuable for various political, governmental, economic and other practical activities. Before making a decision about a new policy, politicians may want to know and understand the most recent research results that are relevant for this policy and its consequences.

Before implementing a new procedure, administrators may use literature reviews of relevant research as a guideline for the most successful implementation. Before business companies open a new shopping centre, they may be interested in the knowledge and insights they can get from literature reviews covering relevant areas of research. Iskhakova et al. (2017: 274–275) argue that their literature review on alumni loyalty is important because loyal alumni are willing to provide material and non-material support to their university, and because universities in many countries are increasingly dependent on such support.

In general, comprehensive reviews of research literature are often carried out as a basis for planning and performing practice in society. The idea is that updated knowledge from high-quality research is needed to obtain the best decisions and the most effective actions in various areas of practice in society. Practice based on literature reviews is called *evidence-based practice*. The increasing emphasis on evidence-based practice since the 1990s has been described as the evidence-based practice movement (Heyvaert et al., 2017: 3). For example, in the fields of health and medicine, evidence-based practice

has become more and more common. Decisions on the development of new medicines or new treatments are based on comprehensive literature reviews from relevant areas within medical and health research. Social science evaluation research is another example of research that may include literature reviews leading to evidence-based practice. In evaluation research, comprehensive literature reviews may be used in addition to other studies to obtain evidence on outcomes and impact of actions, interventions, programmes, or practices within for example health, education and welfare.

Types of literature reviews

It is common to distinguish between two major types of literature reviews. For each of these major types there are several subtypes. This classification of literature reviews is shown in Table 5.1. Each type and subtype will now be described.

Narrative reviews

One of the major types of literature reviews is narrative reviews, the other type being systematic

Table 5.1   Different types of literature reviews

MAJOR TYPES	SUBTYPES	
Narrative	General reviews	
	Theoretical reviews	
	Methodological reviews	
	Historical reviews	
Systematic	Full systematic reviews	Meta-analysis of quantitative studies
		Meta-synthesis of qualitative studies
		Mixed methods research synthesis of both quantitative and qualitative studies as well as studies based on combinations of qualitative and quantitative data
	Limited systematic reviews	Rapid reviews
		Scoping reviews

reviews. These terms may be somewhat misleading, since all literature reviews, including narrative reviews, should be based on systematic approaches and conducted in systematic ways. However, although the definition of literature reviews presented above is a useful guideline for all reviews, some of the elements in the definition are not so much emphasized in narrative reviews as they are in systematic reviews. Thus, in narrative reviews some elements of the definition may be less important in the process of reviewing or less visible in the final review. On the other hand, even though some elements are not explicitly described in the final review, they may have been important in the reviewing process.

As pointed out by Onwuegbusie and Frels (2016: 23), a *narrative review* is 'a written report that summarizes – and optimally critiques – the literature on a particular topic, without providing any integration of either quantitative findings or qualitative findings'. This has been the most common type of literature review, especially when the review is used as a part of a larger study, for developing research questions or for interpreting research findings. Typically, narrative reviews do not make a synthesis of the reviewed literature, and they do not provide answers to a specific research question. They present broad overviews of a special topic or a wider research area, so that the research question for a new study may be refined and theoretically founded, or that new findings may be discussed and understood in relation to previous research. A final narrative review does not necessarily include explicit information on how the reviewing process was conducted, or what decisions were made by the researcher during this process. Such reviews may not contain explicit description of the search procedure, selection process and evaluation criteria. Without this information, it is difficult to reproduce the narrative review.

An example of a narrative review is found in an article on class consciousness by Keefer et al. (2015). The objective of the article is to present a psychological model of class consciousness. In order to show how this model will 'enrich current social psychological understandings of social class' (Keefer et al., 2015: 254), they start with a narrative literature review of social psychological treatments of social class (Keefer et al., 2015: 254–255). Another example of a narrative review is presented in an article on bilingualism and geographical knowledge by Desforges and Jones (2001). The aim of their article is 'to show how the fact that different people speak different languages affects the ways in which they produce and consume geographical knowledges' (Desforges and Jones, 2001: 333). Their narrative review summarizes the literature within human geography on the circulation of geographical knowledge (Desforges and Jones, 2001: 334–335). In both examples of narrative reviews, the authors of the articles refer to reviewed publications that are relevant to their own studies, without describing the process of finding and selecting these particular publications.

Onwuegbusie and Frels (2016: 24) differentiate between four subtypes of narrative reviews. One of these is the *general* literature review. This examines and presents the literature within a research field that is most relevant to the particular research question in the new study. All aspects of the previous research covered in this literature are included in the literature review. Theoretical perspectives, major concepts, empirical findings and methodological experiences from earlier research are described and summarized, showing the development of the research field over time as well as the current state of the art within the field. Limitations of the previous research and challenges for further research may be emphasized. The purpose is to refine and justify the new research question in relation to previous research.

In contrast to general literature reviews, the three other subtypes of narrative reviews are focused on special aspects of previous research.

The *theoretical* literature review concentrates on theories and concepts that have been developed, used, discussed or tested within the relevant research field. This type of review is important for showing the theoretical foundation of the research question of a new study or for discussing the theoretical significance of the findings in a new study. Such literature reviews are also valuable for constructing a conceptual or formal model, or for formulating specific and precise hypotheses, which might be used in empirical testing of one or more theories. More generally, theoretical literature reviews are useful for establishing a theoretical framework for a new study.

The third subtype of narrative reviews is the *methodological* literature review, which is focused on approaches and methods that have been developed, discussed and applied in previous research within the relevant field. The review includes descriptions and summaries of the use of different approaches and methods as well as the experiences from using them. In addition, the review provides evaluation of these experiences, emphasizing both strengths and weaknesses, possibilities and limitations of various methodological contributions. The purpose is to learn from these experiences and thus choose the best possible approaches and methods for a new study. The methodological literature review is a good basis for discussing and justifying the methodological choices in the new study.

The fourth subtype of narrative reviews is the *historical* literature review, which presents an overview of the historical development of a given research field, as this is reflected in the body of literature within the field. Based on when the research reported in various publications was carried out, the review describes and summarizes the chronological and cumulative development of the research, and it discusses major changes and key turning points in theoretical perspectives, empirical insights or methodological approaches within the field. Furthermore, such reviews may contextualize the research, discussing and evaluating theories, findings or methods in the light of the particular scientific and societal context when and where the research was conducted and published. Historical literature reviews may be useful for discussing and developing various types of new research questions, for example, questions on how social phenomena or relationships are influenced by contextual conditions, or on how previously examined phenomena or relationships can be described and understood in a new contextual situation.

The most common type of narrative review for developing new research questions is the general literature review. This type is used by Keefer et al. (2015) in their article on class consciousness, and by Desforges and Jones (2001) in their article on bilingualism and geographical knowledge. Furthermore, the general literature review is also the most common type for students who are doing a literature review as a part of a master's thesis or a PhD dissertation. Students may use other types of narrative reviews for term papers or research essays, depending on the special assignment they are given.

Systematic reviews

As opposed to narrative reviews, a *systematic literature review* has been defined as 'a critical assessment and evaluation of all research studies that address a particular research question on a research topic' (Onwuegbusie and Frels, 2016: 25). This type of review is more common than narrative reviews when the purpose is to present a stand-alone literature review. The study of alumni loyalty (Iskhakova et al., 2017) is a systematic literature review. Typically, in systematic reviews, all elements of the definition of literature reviews presented above are included in the process of reviewing as well as in the final written review. The procedures for the review are transparent and visible, so that it is possible to reproduce the review. The criteria for including or excluding literature for the review are determined before the literature search and explicitly described in the final review. The strategy for searching the literature is also presented in the review. The studies chosen for inclusion are analysed and evaluated. The review integrates major findings from each selected study and presents a synthesis of the literature included in the review.

Referring to differences between qualitative, quantitative, and mixed methods studies, we may distinguish among three subtypes of systematic literature reviews (Heyvaert et al., 2017: 2–5). One of these is *meta-analysis of quantitative studies*. This type of review is focused on findings from studies based on quantitative data. It combines results from the studies that are included in the review. It is common to use statistical methods to analyse and aggregate these results. Typically, the meta-analysis deals with causal relationships that have been analysed in the selected literature, emphasizing findings from different studies on the effect of a specific action or programme. The aggregated results may show the mean size of the effect in all these studies, or may show variations in the effect sizes among different studies. The variations may be examined in relation to different designs of the studies in the review. This type of meta-analysis is used in research aimed at testing hypotheses or theories, but it is also useful for more practical purposes, especially in evidence-based practice. This is most common in medicine, where meta-analysis is used to examine effects of specific medicines or treatments. However, although meta-analysis is the most typical systematic literature review of quantitative studies, such studies may also be reviewed and synthesized without using a statistical meta-analysis. In social science, there are many examples of systematic literature reviews of quantitative studies presenting non-statistical syntheses.

The second subtype of systematic literature reviews is *meta-synthesis of qualitative studies*. Such reviews include literature from previous research based on qualitative data. The review summarizes, integrates and synthesizes findings from the selected studies. A meta-synthesis is an interpretive analysis of findings from several qualitative studies on a particular topic. The *synthesis* of these findings provides a more holistic understanding of particular social phenomena, or a deeper insight into the meaning of these phenomena within wider contexts in society. Meta-synthesis is useful for generating and developing new theories or models, especially in qualitative research. Like meta-analysis, meta-synthesis may also be used for practical purposes, as a scientific basis for decisions and implementations regarding new measures or programs. A meta-synthesis may provide valuable knowledge on the meaningfulness of a particular intervention and the contextual conditions for the effectiveness of the intervention.

The third subtype of systematic literature reviews is *mixed methods research synthesis* (Heyvaert et al., 2017). Reviews of this type have also been called *integrative* reviews (Boland et al., 2017: 13). Such literature reviews bring together and synthesize literature from both quantitative and qualitative studies, as well as studies based on combinations of the two types of data. Due to the methodological differences among the studies included in the review, different methods are used to summarize, interpret and integrate the results of these studies. As pointed out by Heyvaert et al. (2017: 5–6), a mixed methods research synthesis covering such a wide variety of previous studies is valuable for gaining insight and understanding on complex phenomena and topics in society. For example, this type of literature review may be used for evaluating complex interventions. The review makes it possible to examine the many different components of such interventions, as well as the relationships and interactions among these components. Thus, the intervention can be evaluated in terms of feasibility and appropriateness, in addition to effectiveness and meaningfulness. A mixed methods research synthesis provides a basis for discussing and understanding what works for whom, in what circumstances, in what respects, and why (Pawson et al., 2005; Heyvaert et al., 2017).

The systematic literature review on alumni loyalty (Iskhakova et al., 2017) is mainly a meta-synthesis. Their research questions are focused on theoretical perspectives, approaches and conceptual definitions, and they use qualitative methods for analysing the included literature. As they point out, since their review 'does not test or integrate the effectiveness of different factors, it would be reasonable to investigate this issue in future studies by running a quantitative meta-analysis' (Iskhakova et al., 2017: 304).

Systematic literature reviews may be conducted by students, for example as a stand-alone study for a research essay or a master's thesis. The essay or thesis may focus on one of the three types of systematic reviews, depending on the kind of research literature included in the review, whether this literature is based on quantitative, qualitative or mixed methods studies.

Doing literature reviews can be very resource-intensive. Typically, it takes a lot of time to identify, evaluate and synthesize all the relevant literature in a comprehensive, systematic, explicit and reproducible way, following all the procedures that are specified above. Therefore, literature reviews are sometimes less extensive, less ambitious, and carried out within a shorter time-frame than a full systematic review would require. One type of shorter literature review is the *rapid* review. As maintained by Boland et al. (2017:10), rapid reviews are 'primarily systematic reviews in which researchers take legitimate shortcuts in order to deliver findings rapidly'. Such shortcuts may be that the search is limited to only one database, the quality of the literature is not assessed, only limited data are extracted from the literature, or only a narrative synthesis is presented. All shortcuts should be explicitly described and justified in the final written review. Thus, all limitations of the review are visible, and the review is reproducible. Usually, rapid reviews are conducted for practical purposes, providing useful evidence for policy-makers, administrators, professionals or other practitioners (Onwuegbusie and Frels, 2016: 26).

Another type of literature review that is conducted within a short time-frame is the *scoping* review. Boland et al. (2017:10–13) point out that scoping reviews are similar to systematic reviews, although the approach may be more iterative and more often based on advice from consumers and stakeholders. In particular, the literature search and extraction of data from the selected literature are often based on iterative processes, repeating the search and data extraction several times to obtain the best results. Quality assessment of the literature is usually not conducted. Scoping reviews may be broader in focus than rapid reviews, but the breadth is balanced with the availability of resources. Although scoping reviews are based on iterative procedures and some of the criteria for inclusion and exclusion of literature may be defined during the reviewing process, the approach and methods should be explicitly described, so that the review is reproducible. A typical purpose of scoping reviews is to identify the types of literature that are relevant to a specific topic, and to describe the breadth of this literature. Scoping reviews are useful for finding possible gaps in previous research within a particular area, or for assessing how feasible it would be to conduct a full systematic review on a given topic. They may also be used as preliminary reviews in the planning of a more extensive review.

For students, who have limited resources, it may be reasonable to do such limited literature reviews, for example in connection with a research essay, a master's thesis or a PhD dissertation. In particular, scoping reviews may be very useful for this purpose, at least as a first step in developing a research question, or preparing a more comprehensive literature review.

Steps in reviewing literature

The process of reviewing literature consists of several steps. There are different ways of distinguishing among the steps and of defining each step. For our purpose, it is sufficient to describe five major steps in the reviewing process. An overview of these steps and the activities involved in each step is presented in Table 5.2.

However, the activities in each step are not equally important in all types of reviews. While all these five steps are emphasized in full systematic reviews, some of the steps may be less important or less detailed in narrative reviews, as well as in rapid reviews and scoping reviews. For example, narrative reviews do not necessarily include a review protocol (step 1), a quality assessment of the literature (step 3), a synthesis of the literature (step 4), or a description of methods in the final written review (step 5).

Planning the review

The first step is *planning the review*. It all starts with the *choice of a topic or a research area* for the literature review. This choice is based on the research question, either for the review as a

Table 5.2   Major steps and activities involved in the process of reviewing literature

Major steps	Activities involved in each step
Step 1 **Planning the review**	Choosing a topic or research area
	Scoping search
	Specifying criteria for including and excluding literature
	Identifying bibliographic sources or databases
	Indentifying key terms for the search
	Writing a review protocol
Step 2 **Searching and selecting the relevant literature**	Using the key terms and the selected databases
	Finding and collecting the literature
Step 3 **Assessing the selected literature**	Assessing relevance
	Assessing quality
Step 4 **Analysing and synthesizing the relevant content of the selected literature**	Extracting the relevant content
	Summarizing and comparing content from the publications
	Integrating and synthesizing the content from the publications
Step 5 **Writing the final review**	Introduction section
	Methods section
	Results section
	Discussion and conclusion section
	References section

separate stand-alone study, or for the larger study in which the review is included. The chosen topic or area must be relevant to the research question.

Sometimes it is advisable to conduct a *scoping search* before the final identification and definition of the search area. This is a preliminary search for and reading of important databases, key books and articles, or works by leading scholars. Although this is not a necessary part of the planning of the main literature review, a scoping review makes it easier to focus on a specific and well-defined search area, and to determine the scope of this area. The search area should not be too broad. It should only be broad enough to cover the literature that is relevant to the research question.

Another part of the planning process is to develop specific *criteria for including and excluding literature* in the search process. The criteria are adapted to the search area, and they are relevant to the research question. Sometimes the reflections on search criteria may be useful for clarifying or revising the research question. The search criteria may specify the types of literature that should be included in the search, for example published articles and books, and the types of literature that should be excluded, for example unpublished reports from research institutes and unpublished papers from research conferences. Iskhakova et al. (2017:291) included journal articles and conference papers in their study of alumni loyalty. Other criteria may define the publishing period, for example that only publications after World War II should be included and that earlier publications should be excluded. The search criteria may also refer to language, for example that only English-language publications should be included and publications in all other languages should be excluded (see, for example, Iskhakova et al., 2017: 304–305). All these criteria, as well as others, must be meaningful for the research question. Restricting the review to only English-language publications would not be very meaningful if the research question is focused on conditions in France that have

been important in previous French research. Thus, it is important to avoid criteria that would lead to a biased literature review.

Furthermore, the planning of the literature review includes different elements of the *search strategy*. One element is to determine where the relevant literature can be found. This means *identifying the bibliographic sources and databases* that can be used for the search. A search can be done at a library as well as on the Internet. It is advisable to start the search on the Internet, using Google, especially Google Scholar, or other search engines. Also a library search is usually done by means of databases. Through the library it is possible to get access to most available databases. In social science there are several general databases that are frequently used for literature search, for example *Social Sciences Index* or *CORDIS*, in addition to more discipline-specific databases, such as *Sociological Abstracts*. However, libraries typically have their books and journals available on open stacks, where it is possible to take a look at the publications. At most libraries books on the same topic or within the same area are placed together. Thus, if you locate one relevant book at the library, you will most likely find several other relevant books nearby. This procedure, which is called *hand searching*, might be useful, in addition to search in databases, for example in preliminary scoping reviews. A similar strategy is to find one of the most general and one of the most recent publications within your search area and then look at the list of references in these publications for other relevant and important contributions in the area. This is called *citation chaining*.

Furthermore, the search strategy involves *identification of the key terms* for the search. As the main search usually is done by using various kinds of bibliographical databases, it is important to select relevant and efficient key terms for the search. The key terms are adapted to the research question as well as the inclusion and exclusion criteria. Several key terms are usually necessary to cover the search area in an adequate and comprehensive way. Different combinations of terms may be used, for example "housework" AND "inequality", to find publications with both words, and "housework" OR "inequality", to identify publications with one or the other of the two words. Most journal articles include some keywords that are central to the content of the article. A good piece of advice is to find an article that is important within your search area and then use the keywords presented in that article for further search. Finding the most useful search terms is usually an iterative process. It is common to try several alternative key terms before identifying the best terms. Sometimes it might also be necessary to revise and improve the search terms during the search process.

In their study of alumni loyalty, Iskhakova et al. (2017:281) used the following keywords for their search in titles and abstracts of publications: 'alumni loyalty', 'student loyalty', 'alumni contribution', 'alumni giving', 'graduate loyalty', 'graduate contribution' and 'graduate giving'.

In the planning process, it might be valuable to contact experts in the relevant research area and ask for advice regarding the planning of the literature review. For students, the most important experts are their teachers and supervisors.

The plan for the review is usually described in a *review protocol*. Review protocols are less common in narrative reviews than they are in systematic reviews. The protocol presents the research question and describes the search area, the inclusion and exclusion criteria, and the search strategy, including bibliographic sources, and the most important key terms. In addition, the review protocol may include a brief description of the methods, criteria and procedures in the different steps in the further reviewing process, as well as the estimated time-frame for each step. The review protocol is important for the researcher in the reviewing process. The protocol ensures that the plan for the review is followed up, and that the criteria and strategy are applied consistently throughout the whole process. Moreover, the research protocol makes the reviewing process transparent and visible for the future and for everybody, which is necessary for the reproducibility of the review. Sometimes, especially in larger review projects, more than one reviewer is involved in the reviewing process. Then the review protocol is important for ensuring that the different reviewers apply the strategy and criteria in the same way. The review protocol is used for training reviewers and testing the consistency between different reviewers.

Searching and selecting literature

The second step in the reviewing process is *searching and selecting the relevant literature*. The selected bibliographic sources and databases are used, applying the specified key terms for searching the literature. All citations or references obtained in the search are noted and listed. It is necessary to examine the results of the search process carefully. On the one hand, if the result seems too limited in relation to the search area, it may be a good idea to change or extend the search strategy by improving the key terms or using additional databases. On the other hand, the search result may include literature that is outside the search area. This literature is not selected for the review.

Selecting the relevant literature also means finding or collecting the specific publications that will be included in the review. Traditionally such publications have been available in paper versions, as printed books and journal articles, or institute reports and conference papers. Many publications, especially older publications, are still available only in paper versions, as printed books or journal articles. These publications may be borrowed from libraries. However, more and more of the research literature is now published in digital form. Even older literature is digitized and made available for downloading and reading on various websites. Some of the digital literature can be accessed only on databases that require some form of subscription. Usually, access to such databases can be obtained through libraries. However, an increasing amount of the research literature is now made available via *open access* and free of charge.

Assessing the literature

The third step is *assessing the selected literature*. This step includes a critical reading and an assessment of each publication selected after the search. The assessment may focus on both relevance and quality. The relevance of each publication is evaluated with reference to the definition of the search area and the criteria for inclusion and exclusion of literature. Those publications that are found to be irrelevant are excluded from the review.

The relevant publications may then be assessed in terms of quality. This is a critical evaluation of each publication in relation to specific criteria, which have to be selected and defined before the evaluation. The criteria may, for example, refer to methodological quality in study design, data collection, data analysis, and interpretation of findings. The question is whether or not the findings of the study can be regarded as reliable and meaningful for the literature review. Only publications that are considered to be of sufficiently high quality are included in the further reviewing process. The selection of criteria for the quality assessment is related to the type and purpose of the review that is conducted. Furthermore, how the quality assessment is done depends on the type of studies that are reviewed. There are different tools available for assessing quantitative studies (Boland et al., 2017: 110–123), and there are different checklists that have been developed for assessment of qualitative studies (Boland et al., 2017: 212–214).

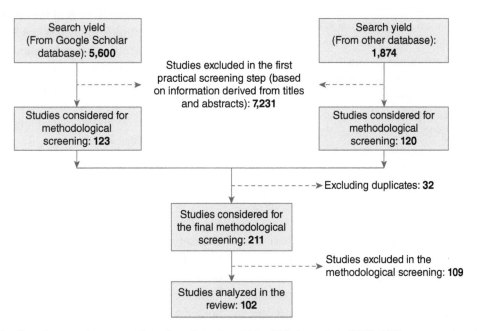

Figure 5.1   Flow diagram of a systematic review. Reproduced from Iskhakova et al. (2017: 285)

During steps 2 and 3 the number of publications to be included in the review may be considerably reduced. This is exemplified in Figure 5.1, which shows a flow diagram from the study of alumni loyalty by Iskhakova et al. (2017). In this study, the search resulted in 7231 studies. Relevance assessment with reference to the inclusion criteria (based on information derived from titles and abstracts), and removal of duplicates, reduced this number to 211 publications. Quality assessments (methodological screening) further reduced the number to 102 publications, and these were analysed in step 4 of the review.

Analysing and synthesizing

The fourth step in the reviewing process is *analysing and synthesizing the relevant content of the selected literature*. In this step the relevant content is extracted from the publications included in the review. In some of the publications only parts of the content may be relevant. What is relevant depends on the research question and the definition of the search area. It also depends on the type and purpose of the review. Typically, literature reviews are focused on substantial knowledge and insights established by previous research, which means that the findings reported in the publications should be extracted as the relevant content. However, it is often relevant to analyse the findings in relation to the theoretical perspectives, methodological approaches and contextual conditions of the studies. Consequently, these types of content of the literature may also be relevant, in addition to the research findings. Sometimes, information on theories, methods or contexts may be the most relevant content, instead of findings.

In the study of alumni loyalty, Iskhakova et al. (2017) carried out a content analysis for extracting the relevant information contained in each publication. For this purpose they developed a coding scheme and applied special data analysis software (MaxQDA). In this book, content analysis will be described in Chapters 11 and 14.

The extracted content of the publications is summarized with particular reference to the research question or to new findings, if the review is part of a larger study, or for answering and discussing the research question, if the review is a separate stand-alone study. In addition to summarizing the content of each publication, contributions from different publications are related to one another, compared, contrasted or integrated. This is particularly important in full systematic reviews, where previous research is synthesized. Publications from several studies are combined in the formulation of one or more syntheses, which integrate and transcend the results of each study. In the process of synthesizing it is important to consider the similarities and differences between the studies in the review, and to make sure that the development of a synthesis is based on studies that are sufficiently similar. The comparison of different studies shows the similarities and differences between the studies. Different findings can then be contrasted and possibly lead to alternative interpretations that are more specific than those presented in each of the original studies. Similar findings may be combined and integrated in a synthesis, which is more general than the separate findings from each study. As pointed out above, the synthesizing may be done as a meta-analysis, a meta-synthesis, or a mixed methods research synthesis, depending on the type of studies reviewed.

Writing the final review

The fifth and last step is *writing the final review*. The content, form and structure of the final written review may be very different, depending on the type and purpose of the review. Typically, a narrative review that is part of a larger study is limited to the results of the reviewing process, presenting summaries and comparisons of different contributions from previous research and discussion of these contributions with reference to the research question or the findings in the larger study. On the other hand, a full systematic review that is done as a stand-alone study is written like an ordinary research report, including presentation and discussion of the different steps in the reviewing process, in addition to the analysis and synthesis of the reviewed literature.

In its most comprehensive form, especially in full systematic reviews, the written review starts with an *introduction*, describing the starting point for the review and presenting the formulation and justification of the research question. The next section is focused on *methods*, where the review process is described and discussed. This includes reflections on the choices of strategies, procedures and criteria involved in each step of the process. The chosen approaches are discussed in relation to alternative approaches that could have been chosen. Strengths and weaknesses of the methods applied in the review are pointed out, with emphasis on how the results of the review may have been affected by the choice of methods. The section describes deviations from the initial review protocol during the reviewing process, as well as reasons for these deviations. The review protocol itself is referred to and sometimes included in the written review, for example as an appendix. The section on *results* presents the number of publications included in the review, and summaries, comparisons and analyses of the research contributions in these publications. Furthermore, this section shows how the contributions from previous research have been integrated and synthesized, and it presents the synthesis or syntheses that have been developed. The last section in the written review is focused on *discussion and conclusion*. The results of the literature are discussed in a wider scientific and societal context. This section contains discussion of the importance of the review for the development of the research field covered by the research, and for the understanding of the social phenomena examined in the reviewed literature.

Implications of the review for policy-making, professional work or other practical activities in society are also discussed. Furthermore, this section presents a conclusion of the literature review, with particular reference to the research question. Finally, the written review contains reflections on possible limitations of the literature review and recommendations for further research.

Referencing sources

The final written review refers explicitly to all publications that are used as sources or directly quoted.

When a direct quotation from a previous publication is used in the written literature review, it must be within quotation marks or formatted as a block quote (without quotation marks), and the reference must show exactly where the quotation is taken from, including information on author, title and year of publication, and page number in the publication. However, even when the quotation is presented with the proper use of quotation marks and references, there is a limit to the amount of text that can be quoted. This is regulated by laws of copyright. There are some variations in these laws between different countries, and there are no accurate definitions of the maximum amount of text that can be included in a quotation. For example, in the UK it is legal to use texts for the purpose of quotation when the use is fair and reasonable. It is allowed to use short quotations which are necessary and relevant, but long extracts cannot be used.

When describing a theory, an empirical finding or another contribution from previous research, the reference should be to the publication where this contribution was first presented. Although the contribution may be described and referred to in more recent publications, the rule is to use the original reference, or to refer to the original work in addition to more recent presentations.

As pointed out in Chapter 3, if you use ideas, thoughts, expressions, or quotations from other authors as your own original work, without referring to the original authors, it is regarded as *plagiarism*, which is a serious breach of research ethics.

Plagiarism may be intentional or accidental. It is intentional plagiarism when you consciously and deliberately use texts by other authors as your own, in spite of knowing that this is wrong. This includes borrowing or buying a paper from someone and submitting it as your own, or copying a text from the Internet and presenting it as your own contribution. Furthermore, it is intentional plagiarism if you take one of your own papers from a previous course and resubmit it for a new course. Reusing your own texts for new purposes without referring to the previous use is called *self-plagiarism*.

Accidental plagiarism means using a text written by another author as your own, without being aware or conscious of it, or without knowing or understanding that this is wrong. Such plagiarism is an accident or a mistake. It may occur if you do not distinguish clearly between your own ideas and ideas from other sources when you take notes from literature that you are reading, or if you do not mark clearly in your own text where you use or refer to thoughts from other texts. If you reuse a sentence or a paragraph from another text, with the same words as in the original text, without marking this as a *quotation*, it might also be an accidental plagiarism, even if you make an explicit *reference* to the original text.

It is the author's own responsibility to make sure that both intentional and accidental plagiarism are avoided. For the readers of the final text it is not easy to determine whether an instance of plagiarism is intentional or accidental. For the author of the text, it may be very difficult to show or prove that plagiarism is accidental rather than intentional. Plagiarism may be sanctioned as a breach of research ethics, regardless of the reasons for it. Whether it is intentional or accidental, the consequences of plagiarism may be equally serious.

The reference to a publication which is used as a source for a quotation or a description of a contribution from previous research is placed in the written literature review exactly where this quotation or description is presented. In addition, a list of all references is presented at the end of the written review, or at the end of the research report where the review is included.

There are different styles or systems of referencing. One system is to present references as footnotes on each page, or as endnotes at the end of the text, with the number of the footnote or endnote in the text where the referenced source is used. The other main system is to place references in parentheses in the text where the details are needed. The details given in the parentheses include the surname of the author, year of publication and page number within the publication. The complete reference to the publication is then included in the list of references at the end of the text. This author–date system is used in the Harvard style, which is one of the most common styles of referencing. A guide to the Harvard style can be found at http://www.citethisforme.com/harvard-referencing. A similar referencing style is the APA (American Psychological Association) style, which is called Academic Writer (https://www.apastyle.org/). Other styles include the MLA (Modern Language Association) style (https://www.mla.org/MLA-Style) and the Chicago style, used by the University of Chicago Press (https://www.chicagomanualofstyle.org/home.html).

There might be some variations between authors and publications in the practical use of each style, for example in terms of punctuation. It is important, however, that the referencing style is used consistently within the same publication.

In this book, the Harvard style is used for referencing. Some examples of referencing in this chapter are presented in Figure 5.4. The figure shows both correct and incorrect references within the text, as well as complete references at the end of the text.

Table 5.3 Examples from this chapter of Harvard style references to books and articles

Correct reference in the text	Incorrect reference in the text	Complete reference at the end of the text
Reference to a book with one author: As argued by Fink (2014: 3), a good and accurate literature review bases its conclusions on high-quality original work by scholars and researchers. *Surname of author, year of publication, page in book*	As argued by Fink, a good and accurate literature review bases its conclusions on high-quality original work by scholars and researchers. *Omitting the reference to the (year of) publication by Fink*	Fink, Arlene (2014) *Conducting Research Literature Reviews: From the Internet to Paper* (4th edn). London: Sage. *Surname of author, first name of author, year of publication, title of book, place of publication, publisher; title of book italicized*
Quotation from a book with two authors: A systematic literature review has been defined as 'a critical assessment and evaluation of all research studies that address a particular research question on a research topic' (Onwuegbusie and Frels, 2016: 25). *Surname of first author and surname of second author, year of publication, page in book* *Quotation within quotation marks*	A systematic literature review has been defined as 'a critical assessment and evaluation of all research studies that address a particular research question on a research topic' (Onwuegbusie and Frels, 2016). *Omitting the page number for the quotation*	Onwuegbusie, Anthony J., and Rebecca Frels (2016) *Seven Steps to a Comprehensive Literature Review: A Multimodal and Cultural Approach.* London: Sage. *Surname of first author, first name and middle initial of first author, and first and second name of second author, year of publication, title of book, place of publication, publisher; title of book italicized*
Reference to a book with three or more authors: As emphasized by Booth et al. (2016: 2), all types of reviews should be systematic. *Surname of first author et al., year of publication, page number; et al. used for the other authors*	As emphasized by Booth (2016: 2), all types of reviews should be systematic. *Omitting the other authors (et al.)*	Booth, Andrew, Anthea Sutton, and Diana Papaioannou (2016) *Systematic Approaches to a Successful Literature Review* (2nd edn). London: Sage. *Surname of first author, first name of first author, first and second name of other authors, year of publication, title of book, place of publication, publisher; title of book italicized*
Reference to a journal article: This type is used by Keefer et al. (2015) in their article on class consciousness. *Surname of first author et al., year of publication*	This type is used in an article on class consciousness. *Omitting the reference to the specific article*	Keefer, Lucas A., Chris Goode, and Laura Van Berkel (2015) 'Toward a psychological study of class consciousness: Development and validation of a social psychological model', *Journal of Social and Political Psychology* 3(2), 253–290. *Surname of first author, first name and middle initial of first author, first and second name of other authors, year of publication, title of article, title of journal, volume of journal, issue number, pages in journal; title of article within quotation marks, and title of journal italicized*
Quotation from a journal article: As they point out, since their review 'does not test or integrate the effectiveness of different factors, it would be reasonable to investigate this issue in future studies by running a quantitative meta-analysis' (Iskhakova et al., 2017: 304). *Surname of first author et al., year of publication, page in journal*	As they point out, since their review does not test or integrate the effectiveness of different factors, it would be reasonable to investigate this issue in future studies by running a quantitative meta-analysis (Iskhakova et al., 2017: 304). *Omitting the quotation marks for the quotation*	Iskhakova, Lilia, Stefan Hoffmann, and Andreas Hilbert (2017) 'Alumni loyalty: Systematic literature review', *Journal of Nonprofit & Public Sector Marketing* 29(3), 274–316. *Surname of first author, first name of first author, first and second name of other authors, year of publication, title of article, title of journal, volume of journal, issue number, pages in journal; title of article within quotation marks, and title of journal italicized*

A good piece of advice is to make notes on references to books, articles, reports or papers and keep records of the references in addition to the relevant content when you read the publications. This may be done manually, by writing notes and references in a book or on cards. It can also be done by means of computer software packages. There are several such tools available, such as EndNote and Reference Manager. When references are registered in one of these computer programs, the same program can be used for inserting the relevant references in the right place in the text, and for compiling a list of references at the end of the text.

These rules and systems for referencing sources in literature reviews are also used in other types of research reports and when writing any type of text about research. This will be further discussed in Chapter 26.

CHAPTER HIGHLIGHTS

- A research literature review is defined as a systematic way of identifying, evaluating and synthesizing the existing literature from previous research within a selected research field. The review process, including methods, procedures and criteria that are used, should be explicitly described, so that the literature review is reproducible.
- The review is focused on those parts of the literature which are most relevant to the research question.
- Each element of the definition may be more or less important, depending on variations between different purposes of the review and different types of reviews.
- There are three different purposes of literature reviews:
  1 Developing research questions for a new, larger study
  2 Discussing research findings from a new, larger study
  3 Answering research questions, with the literature review as a separate, stand-alone study.
- Typically, literature reviews as stand-alone studies are more extensive and more thorough than literature reviews that are parts of larger studies.
- Literature reviews are important for further development of social science, as well as for decisions and practice in society. Practice based on literature reviews is called evidence-based practice.

- There are two major types of literature reviews:
  1 Narrative reviews
  2 Systematic reviews.
- Both types of reviews are based on systematic approaches, but, in contrast to systematic reviews, narrative reviews do not necessarily provide a synthesis of the literature and do not always describe explicitly the methods used in the review process.
- Narrative reviews are most common as parts of larger studies, while systematic reviews are most common as stand-alone studies.
- There are four subtypes of narrative reviews, depending on the aspects of previous research emphasized in the review:
  1 General reviews
  2 Theoretical reviews
  3 Methodological reviews
  4 Historical reviews.
- There are three subtypes of systematic reviews, depending on the types of studies included in the review:
  1 Meta-analysis of quantitative studies
  2 Meta-synthesis of qualitative studies
  3 Mixed methods research synthesis of both qualitative and quantitative studies as well as mixed methods studies.
- Sometimes, less extensive and less expensive literature reviews are conducted within a limited time-frame, such as rapid reviews and scoping reviews

- There are five major steps in the reviewing process
  1 Planning of the review
  2 Searching and selecting the relevant literature
  3 Assessing the selected literature
  4 Analysing and synthesizing the relevant content of the selected literature
  5 Writing the final review.

- All publications that are quoted or used as sources in the written review are explicitly referred to.

RESEARCH EXAMPLES

I recommend that you read the publications used as research examples in this chapter.

Desforges, Luke, and Rhys Jones (2001) 'Bilingualism and geographical knowledge: A case study of students at the University of Wales, Aberystwyth', *Social & Cultural Geography* 2(3), 333–346.

Iskhakova, Lilia, Stefan Hoffmann, and Andreas Hilbert (2017) 'Alumni loyalty: Systematic literature review', *Journal of Nonprofit & Public Sector Marketing* 29(3), 274–316.

Keefer, Lucas A., Chris Goode, and Laura Van Berkel (2015) 'Toward a psychological study of class consciousness: Development and validation of a social psychological model', *Journal of Social and Political Psychology* 3(2), 253–290.

Both the qualitative geographical study by Deforges et al. (2001) and the quantitative psychological study by Keefer et al. (2015) are examples of research where a general narrative literature review is used as a part of a larger study, mainly for developing the research question, and to some extent also for discussing the findings. Iskhakova et al. (2017) is an example of a systematic literature review presenting a meta-synthesis as a separate stand-alone study.

Another example of a literature review is the following article:

Chan, Zenobya C. Y., Wun San Tam, Maggie K. Y. Lung, Wing Yan Wong, and Ching Wa Chau (2013) 'A systematic literature review of nurse shortage and the intention to leave', *Journal of Nursing Management* 21, 605–613.

The research question of this systematic literature review is 'to examine and describe the published empirical research on nurses' intention to leave their current employment or the profession' (Chan et al., 2013: 606). The literature review was conducted by four research students under the leadership of a research supervisor. Six electronic databases were used for the search of literature published in the period from January 2001 until January 2010. The search resulted in 8499 potentially relevant studies. This number was reduced to 31 studies through assessment of relevance and quality and by removing duplicates. The relevant content of these publications was extracted. Most of the studies included in the review were based on quantitative data, and the review was focused on factors related to the nurses' intention to leave their employment or profession. However, the review is not a typical meta-analysis. Data or findings from the reviewed studies are not analysed by means of statistical methods, but the review summarizes and categorizes different factors that are identified in previous research. It describes and compares characteristic features of each factor, and it concludes by pointing out that one of the identified factors is more important than other factors. The literature review presents a discussion of several practical implications of the findings, and it points out some limitations of the literature review.

STUDENT EXERCISES AND QUESTIONS

1 How can we define a literature review?
2 Why are literature reviews important in social research?
3 What are the similarities and differences between narrative reviews and systematic reviews?
4 Describe the different steps of a literature review.
5 Why is the review protocol emphasized in a systematic review?

6 Suggest a combination of keywords for a literature search on unemployment among immigrants.
7 Search for social science articles presenting systematic literature reviews, select two of the articles identified, and compare the reviewing processes described in the articles, with particular emphasis on different steps in the process.

RECOMMENDED LITERATURE

Booth, Andrew, Anthea Sutton, and Diana Papaioannou (2016) *Systematic Approaches to a Successful Literature Review* (2nd edn). London: Sage.

This book describes the different types of literature reviews and the different steps in doing literature reviews.

Fink, Arlene (2019) *Conducting Research Literature Reviews: From the Internet to Paper* (5th edn). London: Sage.

The book describes different types and purposes of literature reviews and the processes of searching, assessing and synthesizing literature.

Hart, Chris (2018) *Doing a Literature Review: Releasing the Research Imagination* (2nd edn). London: Sage.

The book explores the literature review process and describes different types of reviews. It combines a critical approach with a number of practical examples.

Heyvaert, Mieke, Karin Hannes, and Patrick Onghena (2017) *Using Mixed Methods Research Synthesis for Literature Reviews*. London: Sage.

This book is focused on a special approach for synthesizing literature based on mixed methods research.

CHOOSING A RESEARCH DESIGN

This chapter presents different research designs for empirical studies in social science and provides a basis for choosing a design that is adequate for the specific research questions of a study.

The chapter will teach you to understand

- the distinction between data sources and data
- how both qualitative and quantitative data can be collected from different types of sources
- the differences between actors, respondents and documents as data sources
- the essential features of six basic research designs

- similarities and differences between qualitative and quantitative research designs
- how various types of data sources and data can be combined in more comprehensive mixed methods research designs.

Types of data sources

This chapter deals with research designs. The research design of a social science study describes how the study will be organized or designed in order to gather and utilize the information that is needed to examine the study's research questions. The term 'research design' may be used in different ways, emphasizing different aspects of the research process. In this chapter, the term is used mainly with reference to the collection of data, focusing on strategies and methods for data collection.

The choice of an appropriate research design requires clarification of two questions. The first question concerns which types of *sources* we will rely on: where can we get the information we need, or who can provide us with this information? The second question relates to the types of *data* that will used in the study: how can the necessary information be recorded and organized for systematic analyses of the research questions?

First, differences between three types of data sources in social science studies are discussed. Then, characteristic features of different types of data are described, with particular emphasis on the distinction between qualitative and quantitative data. Next, six major types of research designs are discussed and exemplified, focusing on how the distinction between different designs is based on the types of sources and data in the studies. Furthermore, typical differences between qualitative

and quantitative research designs are discussed. Finally, it is pointed out how different types of sources and different types of data can be combined in mixed methods research designs.

The information that is needed to examine the research questions in a study can be obtained from different sources. Any basis for information about social conditions can be regarded as a *source*. For example, we can obtain valuable information by looking at different objects or images, by reading different kinds of written material, by listening to different oral presentations, or by observing people who act and interact. The sources used in a particular study depend on what type of information should be included in the study, what sources can provide this information, and what sources are available for the current study.

Although there is a large variety of possible sources of information, we can distinguish between three main types of sources in social science studies. One of these main types are *actors*, who can be observed when they express opinions, perform actions, participate in interactions or are involved in events. Through direct observation of different actors at different times, we can get information about what these actors say or do, how they appear or behave, where they are or who they are with. This information has to be obtained while the actors are in action. The information can be based on observations of individuals or groups of individuals, and those who are observed can act on behalf of themselves or as representatives of larger organizations.

Instead of observing people while they are in action as participants in community life, we can ask them about matters that are to be examined in the current study. Then the people represent another type of source. The information is not obtained from what they say or do as actors, but rather on the answers they give to the researcher's questions. The people respond to specific questions, and this response is the basis for the information that is used in the study. Persons who act as such sources are usually referred to as *respondents*. This is the second main type of source in social sciences.

Another term for this type of source is *informant*. The distinction between 'respondent' and 'informant' is not always used in a consistent manner in the academic literature. However, there may be good reasons for using the term 'respondent' when the persons being questioned provide information about themselves, their background and status, and their experiences, opinions and actions, while the term 'informant' is used when the persons being questioned provide information about other actors' background, status, actions and opinions or about other conditions in society. For the sake of simplicity, only the term 'respondent' will be used here.

Respondents can be questioned about opinions, actions, interaction processes, events or other matters about which they have knowledge. This information does not have to be obtained while the actions are being performed, while the opinions

are being expressed or while the events are taking place. Respondents can provide information about what has been done, said or happened previously, or what is usually done, said or happening. The precondition, however, is that we focus solely on matters that are so close in time and space that the people we ask are able to know about them or have an opinion on them.

The third main type of source is *documents*. These are different types of documentary material that can be examined in order to obtain relevant information about the social conditions we want to study.

Documents can be very different in terms of both form and content. With regard to form, the typical document is a written presentation, but documents can also be sound recordings of oral presentations or may be in the form of visual representations, such as images, graphics, videos or films.

With respect to the variations in content between different documents, there is one particular distinction that is important in connection with the utilization of documents as a source for social science studies. On the one hand, documents can contain statements of opinions and be expressions of perceptions, views or assessments by the person or persons behind the document. This is an important source when we focus on opinions as information about actors. On the other hand, the content of documents can be factual information about various conditions, which can be an important source in very many contexts. Table 6.1 presents some examples of different types of documents that may be relevant as sources.

Table 6.1 Examples of different types of documents as sources

Form of document	Content of document	
	Expression of opinion	Factual information
Written presentation	Editorial in a newspaper	Annual report from an organization
Oral presentation	Contribution to debate at a political meeting	News report on radio
Visual presentation	Commercial on TV	Documentary on TV

In this way, documents can contain both opinions and facts in the form of text and numbers, sounds and images. Documents are increasingly being drafted, communicated and processed in digital form, and an increasing number of them are available on the Internet. A special type of online document is Twitter, Facebook, Instagram and other social media, which include texts, images and videos, and which can express both facts and opinions. The content of these media can be analysed in different types of big data studies.

Documents can be utilized in many different ways as sources in social science studies. Systematic studies of the content in documents are called *content analysis*. This means that the documents are reviewed in a systematic manner in order to categorize, record and analyse the content. Content analysis is most appropriate when the documents have verbal content in the form of texts expressed in writing or orally, but the method is also used in connection with images and other visual forms of expressions.

Compared with actors and respondents as sources, documents can provide information about social conditions over far larger distances in time and space. Direct observations of the actors must take place simultaneously with and in the immediate vicinity of the actions, events or expressions of opinions to be studied. Respondents can recount such phenomena at other times and other locations. Documents can contain information about or traces of actions, opinions or events in distant places and further back in time. Documents are particularly valuable as sources in studies of developmental processes and change processes over extended periods of time.

Types of data

Information that we obtain or find in a source is not necessarily the same as data. The information is not data in itself, but forms the basis for data. The information must be systematized and recorded as data. The term *data* means information that has been processed, systematized and recorded in a specific form and for the purpose of a specific analysis. The systematization and registration of the information can be done in different ways, in order to obtain different types of data. The distinction between qualitative and quantitative data is particularly important in this context.

As mentioned in Chapter 1, this distinction does not constitute a dichotomy, but can be regarded as the extremes on a scale. We can place different types of data along this scale, from the most quantitative data at one extremity to the most qualitative data at the other extremity. Between these extremes, we find data that are more or less quantitative and data that are more or less qualitative.

With reference to this scale, we can distinguish between four types of data (see Figure 1.1):

1 *Metric data.* This is the most quantitative type of data, including such information as age (in years) and income (in euros or US dollars). These data can be analysed using advanced statistical methods.
2 *Categorical data.* This is non-metric data expressed in numbers. These data include such information as gender (male [1] or female [2]), and education (low [1], intermediate [2] or high [3]). Categorical data can also be analysed using statistical methods, but these analytical methods are less advanced than those that can be used for metric data.
3 *Data expressed in quantity terms other than numbers.* This is data that are available in the form of text, but which nevertheless refer to quantitative conditions, such as large–larger–largest, or many–more–most. These data cannot be analysed statistically, but they provide a basis for comparing the units based on certain quantitative criteria.
4 *Data expressed in text.* This is the most qualitative type of data. Such data provide a basis for identifying characteristic features of the various units, but they cannot be analysed statistically, and they do not provide a basis for quantitative comparisons between the units.

In Chapter 7, metric and categorical data will be further described and specified in relation to four different *levels of measurement* in quantitative studies.

There may be different perceptions of where the decisive distinction should be between qualitative and quantitative data. Based on a narrow definition of quantitative data, it can be argued that only metric data are quantitative and that analyses of all the other types of data must be regarded as qualitative analyses. However, in this book, the first three types of data are regarded as quantitative data, while the fourth type of data will be referred to as qualitative data. In practice, the third type of data is less common than the other three. Thus, the main distinction is between the first two types of data on the one hand, and the last type of data on the other. This means that quantitative data are expressed as numbers, and that qualitative data are presented as text.

Major types of research designs

Each of the three types of sources can be used for recording and processing both qualitative and quantitative data. Both types of data can be used in conjunction with observing actors, asking questions to respondents, or content analysing documents. On this basis, we can distinguish between six major types of research designs, as shown in Table 6.2. The table also shows in which chapter each of the designs will be further discussed.

Ethnography and participant observation

The most typical design for qualitative studies based on direct observations of actors is *participant observation*. This means that the researcher is a participant in the social processes being studied and that this participation is combined with observation of the other actors and the relationships between them. Such studies are typically called *ethnographic research*.

The term 'participant observation' is used here in a narrow sense, with particular emphasis on how especially the observation method is used in order to obtain qualitative data. However, the term is also used in a wider sense, almost synonymously with the term 'field research', which will be discussed later in this chapter. Used in this way, the term refers to more comprehensive designs, where the researcher's participation is combined with both observation and other methods, such as unstructured interviewing. This expanded meaning of the term 'participant observation' occurs especially in connection with field research designs, which are based mainly on qualitative data, and where observation is the most important method.

A classic example of participant observation is a study that was conducted in the 1930s by the American sociologist William Foot Whyte (1914–2000). He observed the social life among immigrants from Italy in a slum neighbourhood

Table 6.2 Typical research designs for the use of qualitative and quantitative data based on different types of sources (and chapters where the designs will be further discussed)

Source type	Data type	
	Qualitative data	Quantitative data
Actor	Ethnography and participant observation (Chapter 9)	Structured observation (Chapter 12)
Respondent	Unstructured interviews and focus groups (Chapter 10)	Questionnaires and surveys (Chapter 13)
Document	Qualitative content analysis (Chapter 11)	Quantitative content analysis (Chapter 14)

in Boston. Whyte carried out his observations while living in this environment for 3½ years. He spent 18 months of this period with an Italian family in the neighbourhood. Whyte studied the social structure of this environment, and he was particularly interested in the formation and organization of local boy gangs. He observed relationships and activities in these gangs, which were usually found on street corners. The study resulted in the book *Street Corner Society* (Whyte, 1943).

A more recent example of participant observation is a study of the election campaigns of two democratic candidates for the US congressional elections in 2008 (Nielsen, 2012). The study focused particularly on how the two candidates and their supporters in the election campaign developed and implemented direct contact and personal communication with the electorate in the local constituencies. The participant observation was carried out in parallel in the two constituencies. It started in February and continued until the elections in November. The researcher himself participated in the election campaign in both constituencies. He personally contacted many voters, partly by telephoning them, partly by visiting them where they lived. He collaborated and conversed with both professional and voluntary election campaigners. The interaction between the participants in the election campaign and their personal communication with the voters could thus be observed at first hand. He continuously wrote notes about what he observed, as well as various reflections about what he heard and saw. These field notes, which totalled more than 1000 pages, constituted the data of the study. These data formed the basis for a comprehensive and analytical description of the personal communication and its importance in the election campaign. This study will be referred to below as the 'election campaign study'.

This design will be further discussed in Chapter 9.

Structured observation

Structured observation is a typical design for direct observation of actors in order to obtain quantitative data. This observation focuses on selected types of actions, opinion statements or events. As these are observed, they are registered on a schedule that has been prepared in advance. This type of observation is rarely combined with participation in the processes that are observed, but it can be used both in natural situations and in experimental contexts. Structured observation may be used in *laboratory experiments*, which are carried out under strictly controlled conditions, or in *field experiments*, which are set up to experimentally examine the effects of an intervention in the real world. In both types of experiments the strategy is to examine the effect of an intervention by comparing individuals who have been exposed to this intervention (the experiment group) with individuals who have not been exposed to the intervention (the control group). The logic and implementation of experiments are systematically described and discussed in Chapter 21.

Among the best-known examples of structured observation under experimental conditions is a series of studies of communication and interaction in small groups, which was conducted by the American social psychologist Robert F. Bales (1916–2004) at the end of the 1940s (Bales, 1952). The people in the group were placed around a table and were asked to take part in a discussion to reach a solution to a particular task. This laboratory experiment was conducted by varying the conditions for communication between the group members, including how the people were positioned in relation to each other, who could speak directly to each other, and who had to communicate indirectly through a third party. The purpose was to see how different communication patterns affected the interaction and task resolution in the group as a whole. The group was observed through a so-called *one-way mirror*. For the group, this looked like a mirror on one of the walls in the room. From the other side, however, the one-way mirror was transparent, like a window pane. The observers could therefore sit in the room and watch the group during the experiment, without being visible to the group members. The structured observation entailed observing the development of the group conversations and placing statements from the group members into different categories, focusing on what was said, who said it, who the statement was addressed to and when it occurred. The categories for this registration were selected and designed in advance.

Bales's small-group studies gradually came to play an important role in the development of the structural functionalist theories of the American sociologist Talcott Parsons (Parsons and Bales, 1953).

Under more natural conditions, structured observation was used in a comprehensive study of activities among passengers on local buses and trains in Wellington, New Zealand, in 2008 (Russell et al., 2011). The observation study was part of a larger project about how passengers on public transport use and appreciate their travel time, and how this affects their health and welfare. Over 2 months, the observations were conducted by two people, based on strategically selected train and bus routes. The routes were divided between short and long distances, city centre and suburbs, as well as wealthy and deprived areas. On each of these routes, the passengers were observed at different times during the day, with particular emphasis on the morning and evening rush hours. The two observers placed themselves at different locations on the bus or train and observed the adult passengers closest to them. Each observer observed two passengers at the same time, and each passenger was observed for 4 minutes. During a 20-minute trip, they could observe up to 20 passengers. The entire study included 812 passengers. The observers completed a schedule for each of these passengers by crossing off the appropriate categories for means of transport (train or bus), the time of the observation, as well as the passenger's gender, age (young, middle aged or older) and activities. The activities were to be recorded for each minute during the 4-minute period. They were pre-divided into 11 specific categories (such as looking out of the window, reading, talking with fellow passengers, talking on the telephone or sending text messages), as well as an unspecified residual category (other activities). On the basis of these data, the researchers were able to analyse the proportion of the passengers who performed different activities during the trip, and they could analyse differences in the patterns of activity between modes of transport and times, between different age groups and between women and men. This study will be referred to below as the 'passenger study'.

Structured observation will be further discussed in Chapter 12.

Unstructured interviews and focus groups

Unstructured interviews is a typical design for using qualitative respondent data. This design consists of conversations between the interviewer and the various respondents. Neither the questions nor the options for answer are determined in advance. The interviewer usually uses an interview guide, which provides general guidelines for the implementation and management of the interviews. However, the interview guide may be more or less detailed and more or less elaborated. Depending on the degree of details and elaboration of the guide, this type of design is sometimes called *semi-structured interviews*.

Typically, unstructured or semi-structured interviews are used for interviewing one respondent at a time. However, the design may also be used for asking questions to a whole group of respondents and thereby stimulating conversations among the participants within this group. This group of respondents is called a *focus group*. The conversations within the focus group lead to a special group dynamics in addition to the interviewer–respondent interaction. This dynamics is often very efficient for gathering useful information.

Unstructured interviewing was used in a study of British nurses (Gould and Fontenla, 2006). The study concerned nurses' satisfaction with their job, their commitment to the nursing profession and their loyalty to the hospital where they were employed. The purpose was to investigate how satisfaction, commitment and loyalty were influenced by various factors, with particular emphasis on opportunities for further education, flexible and family-friendly working hours, and innovative work tasks. This problem was investigated and discussed on the basis of informal interviews with 27 nurses. About half of these were chosen from a small local hospital with patients from a deprived urban area. The rest were chosen from a major university hospital with a high level of specialization and internationally recognized education. The interview was conducted based on a guide that consisted of 15 very general and open questions. These questions concerned a number of aspects of the nurses' work, such as the content of the job, changes in the job content, the most positive and least positive aspects of the job, opportunities for improving the job content, and opportunities for further education. Furthermore, the guide included questions on previous jobs and career development, the nurse's professional values in relation to the hospital's values, assessments of whether the job has lived up to their expectations, and any thoughts about quitting the job. The interviews were recorded on audio tapes and later transcribed. These transcripts constituted the data of the study. The study will be referred to below as the 'nursing study'.

This design will be further discussed in Chapter 10.

Questionnaires and surveys

The typical design in connection with quantitative respondent data consists of *questionnaires and surveys*. The researcher collects the requested information from the various respondents using a questionnaire with fixed questions and mostly fixed response options. Since such studies primarily contribute to a general overview of different social conditions, they are often referred to as *survey studies* or *surveys*. The questionnaire may be completed by the respondents themselves. The questionnaire can be in paper form, so that it can be delivered and collected by the researcher or sent back and forth by post. However, it is becoming increasingly common for the questionnaire to be made available in digital form so that it can be distributed and answered by e-mail or on the Internet. The questionnaire can also be used by an interviewer, who asks the questions and records the answers, in an interview with the respondent. This can occur during a personal meeting between the interviewer and the respondent, but it is becoming more and more common to rely on interviews over the telephone. The interviewer can rely on a paper version of the questionnaire, but it has gradually become possible to rely on digital versions, also during the interview, so that the interviewer uses a computer, preferably a laptop, to complete the form while the interview is taking place.

Sometimes surveys are used in experimental contexts, examining various kinds of effects by asking different questions to different groups of respondents (experiment group and control group). This particular form of survey is called a *survey experiment*.

A good example of questionnaires and surveys is the European Quality of Life Survey, which is conducted by Eurofound at regular intervals. Eurofound is a body created by the EU to help improve living and working conditions. The first survey was conducted in 2003. The survey was conducted for the third time in 2011 (Eurofound, 2012). The data were based on personal interviews with a probability sample of the adult population in each of the 27 EU countries. The number of interviews in each country varied between 1000 and 3000. In total, 35,516 respondents were interviewed. The interview was based on a questionnaire with over 300 questions. The average duration of each interview was around 40 minutes. The questions concerned many aspects of the quality of life of the respondents and their households, such as subjective experience of welfare, economic living conditions, employment and household work, family situation and social life, belonging and involvement in society, housing situation and local environment, health services and public services, and trust in institutions and society. The answers were processed and analysed using computers and software programs for statistical analysis. The data are stored in digital form and are generally available to most of us for secondary analysis. The study will be referred to below as the 'quality of life study'.

This design will be further discussed in Chapter 13.

Qualitative content analysis

Documents can be used as data sources by means of qualitative or quantitative content analysis. In both cases, the typical documentary sources are written or oral texts, but they may also include various kinds of sounds, still pictures, videos or films.

Qualitative content analysis can include different types of source-critical methods or other types of documentary studies that are common among historians. Qualitative content analysis of texts in various documents is also an important procedure for discourse analysis. Through systematic and detailed studies of the content of a particular text, discourse analysis aims to reveal how this text as a whole is structured by larger thought patterns. Qualitative content analysis will generally involve systematization of selected text quotations, image sections or other content elements in order to highlight specific research questions. It could concern, for example, obtaining an insight into what narratives, arguments, opinions, attitudes or values are central to different texts.

This form of document analysis was used by Oosthuizen (2012) in connection with a study of how nurses are referred to in South African newspapers. The study was based on all newspaper articles containing the words 'nursing' or 'nurse' in the period 2005–2009. A pragmatic sample of 161 of these 1841 articles was included in the qualitative content analysis. Each newspaper article was carefully read in order to identify and record statements (words, sentences or paragraphs) about nurses or the nursing profession. The recorded statements constituted the data material of the study. These statements were divided into a number of different categories and marked with codes that indicated which category the individual statements belonged to. The coded statements in each category were then interpreted in a more systematic manner. Several of the original categories were then merged into more general categories. The analysis resulted in 18 such general categories of statements about the nursing profession. The categories were divided into four main themes: the need for more nurses, and drop-out rates for the profession; impairment of the health-care service and poor working conditions; deaths, suffering, abuse and incompetence; as well as praise of the profession. In the presentation of the results of the analysis, the different themes and categories were discussed and exemplified using typical quotes from the newspaper articles analysed. This analysis will be referred to as the 'newspaper study'.

This design will be further discussed in Chapter 11.

Quantitative content analysis

Like qualitative content analysis, *quantitative content analysis* also involves systematizing those parts of the content in the various documents that are relevant for given research questions. However, this systematization is not about comparing different quotes or other content elements. The content of the document, however, is assessed with reference to a structured coding schedule. In qualitative content analysis, the generation and development of categories may be a result of the analysis, as demonstrated by the newspaper study. In quantitative content analysis, however, the categories are specified, and the coding schedule is fully developed before the systematic review of the content of the documents commences. If the document contains text, the categories may include, for example, themes, arguments, values, attitudes or opinions. The analysis is then concerned with recording how many of the sampled text units can be placed in each category. The text units can be, for example, articles, notifications, paragraphs or statements. Similar procedures are followed if the documentary sources are images: various parts or aspects of the images are coded in different categories, and the number of image units in each category is counted.

Such a procedure was used in an analysis of tweets as a new social medium (Humphreys et al., 2013). The study was based on the English-language messages from a probability sample of people who had published publicly available tweets during a period of three weeks in January–February 2008. A random sample of these messages was included in the quantitative content analysis. The sample consisted of 2100 tweets. The content of each message was assessed, classified, registered and coded using a structured coding schedule. The purpose was to compare the content of the tweets with the content of diaries from the eighteenth and nineteenth centuries. Historical literature about the content of such diaries was therefore used as a basis for the

development of the category schedule in the content analysis of the tweets. The categories covered three dimensions: the subject of the message (I, he/she, they, you), the theme of the message (weather, family, media, food/drink, religion, health, sleep, activities, places) and the messages' style (description, comment, information search, content sharing, response). The coding of the contents of each tweet using this coding schedule resulted in a comprehensive data set in the form of numbers that could be analysed using statistical methods. The analyses showed how the 2100 messages were distributed across the different categories, and thus which subject, which theme and what style was most prominent in these tweets. We will refer to this study as the 'tweet study'.

Quantitative content analysis will be further discussed in Chapter 14.

Differences between qualitative and quantitative research designs

Following this description and the exemplification of different types of research designs, it is possible to compare qualitative and quantitative designs. This comparison will highlight some typical and common features of ethnography and participant observation, unstructured interviewing and focus

Table 6.3 Typical features of research designs based on qualitative and quantitative data

Aspect of the study	Data type	
	Qualitative data	Quantitative data
Types of research questions	Analytical descriptions	Statistical generalizations
Methodological design	Flexibility	Structuring
Relationship to sources	Proximity and sensitivity	Distance and selectivity
Interpretation of findings	Relevance	Precision

groups, and qualitative content analysis on the one hand, and structured observation and field experiments, questionnaires and surveys, and quantitative content analysis on the other. Table 6.3 outlines some key features of qualitative and quantitative research designs, with emphasis on four different aspects of the studies.

Analytical descriptions versus statistical generalizations

Let us first consider which main types of research questions are usually investigated using qualitative and quantitative data, respectively. The former type of data is usually best suited to various types of *analytical descriptions*. The purpose is usually to describe total situations or whole contexts. In some qualitative studies, the findings provide a basis for *theoretical generalization*. In other qualitative studies, the question of generalization is not relevant. The purpose of the election campaign study was to develop a comprehensive description of the personal political communication that was observed during the election campaign. In the nursing study, the purpose was to provide the most comprehensive description possible of the interviewed nurses' satisfaction, commitment and loyalty. Such holistic descriptions may be appropriate in studies of processes and social interaction. This can be said, for example, about the election campaign study, which is focused on the mutual interaction between the election campaigners and their communication and interaction with the voters. The fact that the descriptions are analytical means that they are systematically based on well-defined terms, categories or theories. Thus, the various categories in the newspaper study were systematically arranged in relation to clear concepts about the nursing profession's activities and the development of health-care service. Analytical descriptions and other types of qualitative data analysis will be explained in Chapter 16.

In this sense, quantitative studies are also analytical. What mostly characterizes quantitative approaches, however, is that the research questions typically concern different types of *statistical generalizations*. The purpose is often to provide an overview of larger populations or a more extensive universe. The quality of life study provides information about the quality of life for the entire adult population in the different EU countries. Quantitative research designs are focused on distributions and comparisons. The passenger study deals with the distribution of passengers across different types of activity and presents comparisons of such distributions between both passenger groups and means of transport. Such generalizing analyses are largely based on statistical techniques. One of the most important reasons why the data are expressed in the form of numbers is precisely so that it is possible to utilize different statistical techniques. Quantitative analysis will be discussed in Chapters 17–18, and statistical generalization will be explained in Chapter 19.

Major types of research questions in qualitative and quantitative research will be examined in Part V of the book.

Flexibility versus structuring

Another important difference between qualitative and quantitative studies is the *methodological design* of the studies. In qualitative studies, the design is characterized by *flexibility*. The methodological design may be altered during the data collection, so that it can gradually be adapted to new experiences as the study progresses. The design is usually flexible, also in the sense that it may be used in different ways *vis-à-vis* different units in the study. Quantitative studies, on the other hand, are based on designs characterized by strong *structuring*. The design is usually fully decided upon before data collection commences and it cannot be changed during the study.

The intention is that, in principle, all of the units should be approached in the same way, even though different types of filtering can be used to some extent, for example so that respondents who are different in terms of given properties can receive alternative question formulations. In the quality of life study, virtually the same question formulations were used for all the respondents. There were greater opportunities in the nursing study to adapt the questions to each of the nurses interviewed.

Both flexible and structured designs can be problematic, but in different ways. For example, it may become evident during the data collection that the design is not capturing all the relevant data. It may also emerge that some questions or categories do not work satisfactorily. This may disrupt the rest of the data collection process, especially in interview studies. These problems are greater for structured than for flexible designs. For flexible designs, however, we encounter another possible problem: if the design is altered to a large extent during the process, the researcher may lose sight of the original perspective for the study, and the logical reasons for the methodological design.

Proximity and sensitivity versus distance and selectivity

The third aspect of the study concerns the researcher's *relationship to the data sources*. Regardless of whether the sources are actors, respondents or documents, this relationship is characterized by *proximity* and *sensitivity* in qualitative approaches, while it is more likely to be characterized by *distance* and *selectivity* in quantitative studies. In qualitative studies researchers usually work directly with their sources or together with the sources. In the election campaign study, the researcher himself participated actively in the election campaign, especially in the personal communication he observed. The relationship with the sources was also close in the nursing study, where the same

researcher conducted all the interviews. She could then be sensitive to the nurses interviewed, in the sense that she could evaluate experiences with different question formulations and gradually formulate new questions as the interview developed. Thus, the relationship to the data sources determines to a great extent what data become central in the study.

In quantitative surveys, it is more likely to be determined in advance what data should be central. The fact that the relationship to the sources is selective means that only certain aspects of the sources will be explored and that these aspects have been selected before the data collection occurs. Generally, there is also a greater distance between researchers and sources in quantitative designs. In many cases, the researcher has no direct contact with the sources. Data collection is often performed by others. The passenger study was characterized by such a distance and selectivity. Although the physical distance between the observers and passengers was not large, there was no personal contact between the observers and the passengers, and the passengers were unaware that they were being observed. In the quality of life study, the researchers never met the respondents. After the researchers had prepared the questionnaire, the data collection was carried out by a number of different interviewers from commercial agencies.

Relevance versus precision

This difference between qualitative and quantitative studies regarding the relationship to the sources can have consequences for how the collected data can be understood, and how the results of the data analysis can be interpreted. Thus, *interpretation of findings* is a fourth general aspect of the studies. Qualitative approaches based on a flexible design and a close and sensitive relationship to the sources should provide particularly good opportunities for *relevant* interpretations. The data collection process can be managed so that it gathers information that is as appropriate as possible for both the study's research questions and the unique features of the specific data sources. However, this may lead to variations as to what data are collected from different sources. The more the design changes during the process in order to obtain relevant information about the individual units, the greater the risk of obtaining different types of information about the different units. The interpretations can thus be somewhat unclear, and they may have quite limited validity.

In quantitative studies, the interpretations of the collected data are often more *precise* in nature. A structured design and a distant and selective relationship to the sources result in a well-defined and unified data set. Since such data can be expressed in the form of numbers, they can be processed based on mathematical and statistical principles. Such analysis techniques do not only provide accurate answers. They can also form the basis for estimating *how* accurate the answers are. However, the risk is that the relevance of these accurate interpretations may be questionable in some cases. Quantitative research designs must generally be limited to the questions or categories that are appropriate for all the units in a study. Questions or categories that might be important or necessary in order to obtain relevant information from some units may need to be excluded because they do not work for other units. The result can be a measuring instrument that constitutes a kind of lowest common denominator for a large number of mutually very diverse units. The data may thus become relatively superficial. The interpretations may then be overly exact. In the worst-case scenario, therefore, the choice might be between imprecise answers to relevant questions, and precise answers to irrelevant questions.

The implications of this problem will naturally also depend on how well or how poorly the various studies are conducted. The situation is not particularly dramatic for the studies that have been referred to here. Nevertheless, it might be appropriate to question the relevance for people's quality of life of all the statistical measurements that can be calculated on the basis of the quality of life study. The nursing study, on the other hand, does not provide a very precise description, even though this description may be highly relevant for interpreting the situation of the nurses who were interviewed.

Mixed methods designs: Combining different sources and data

Each of the six main types of research designs has been described separately, and the three qualitative designs have been compared with the three quantitative designs. It is very often relevant in specific studies to use both different types of sources and different types of data, so that elements from two or more of the six main types of designs are combined within more comprehensive research designs. As mentioned in Chapter 2, such combinations are referred to as mixed methods research or methodological triangulation. The kind of data and sources that are combined in a particular design will depend on, among other things, the research question and which sources and data are available. Moreover, it is important to consider possible problems related to ontological or epistemological incoherence between different types of data (Onwuegbusie et al., 2009).

Field research is a common design for combinations of different sources and data. As mentioned above, field research is sometimes referred to as participant observation because this is one of the most important methods in field research designs. The most prominent feature of field research, however, is that participant observation is used in combination with other methods.

Peter M. Blau's study of the activities of two government agencies in the United States in the late 1940s, which was described in Chapter 1, is a good example of a field research design (Blau, 1963). Table 6.4 provides an overview of the sources and data used in this design. As the table shows, Blau used both qualitative and quantitative data based on all three types of sources. The main method was participant observation, which was carried out during the periods when Blau worked at each of the two agencies. He observed his colleagues while simultaneously participating in the daily work at the agency. These observations mainly resulted in qualitative data based on field notes. Blau also conducted structured observation in order to gather quantitative data concerning contact patterns among colleagues, such as how many times or how often different employees had contact with each other.

Both before and during the observation studies, Blau conducted informal interviews with strategically selected managers and employees at the agency. Minutes and notes from these interviews formed the basis for qualitative data. After the participant observation was completed, all the staff at the agency were interviewed based on a structured questionnaire in order to gather quantitative data about the employees' opinions and assessments, as well as a number of other matters related to the bureaucratic activities.

Blau also used many different documents as sources during the entire field research period. These documents were not subject to separate content analyses based on systematic categorization of different content elements, but the documents nevertheless formed the basis for different types of additional data. The review of instructions, rules and case files resulted in qualitative data, while quantitative data could be obtained from various statistical overviews of the activities at the agencies.

Thus, the six main types of research designs highlighted in this chapter can be combined in different ways within larger and more complex designs for social science studies. Each of the six designs will be further described and discussed in Part III of the book (Chapters 9–14), and different strategies for mixed methods research will be discussed in more detail in Chapter 20.

The choice of a research design for a particular study is based on the research question of the study. What the study intends to examine determines how the study should be designed. The research question is the main basis for selecting and combining different types of sources and data in the study. However, the choice of a design may also be influenced by a number of other factors, such as the availability of sources for the data and resources for the data collection. Thus, in practice, the final choice of a research

Table 6.4   Example of a field research design based on different types of sources and data: A study of two government agencies in the United States (Blau, 1963)

Source type	Data type	
	Qualitative data	Quantitative data
Actor	Participant observation of the activity at the two agencies	Structured observation of contact patterns among the employees
Respondent	Unstructured interviews with employees (strategic samples) before and during the observation studies	Structured questionnaires to all employees after the observation was completed
Document	Review of the content of rules and case files at the agencies	Review of the content of statistical overviews of the activity of the agencies

design may be pragmatic, emphasizing what it is possible to do, and what is satisfactory for examining the research question, rather than what is ideally the best selection. Sometimes, it may even be necessary to modify and adjust the formulation of the research question to the data that can be used in the study. This may be an iterative process, in which the research question and the research design are more and more adapted to each other.

Knowing the differences between the six types of research designs and how they can be combined is particularly important when new data are collected for a study. Such data are called *primary data*. However, many studies are based on available data, which have been collected by others, either for previous studies or for other purposes. Such available data are called *secondary data*, and a new study based on secondary data is referred to as a *secondary analysis*. Also when secondary data are used, it is important to know how they have been collected, and knowledge about different research designs for collecting data is important for considering the quality and limitations of the secondary data that are used. Use and reuse of available data for secondary analyses will be discussed in Chapter 7.

Research designs and analytical perspectives

In this chapter the term 'research design' is used in a very particular sense, focusing on strategies for data collection, with particular reference to the types of sources and data on which the study is based. However, the term 'research design' is often used in a more general and less precise sense, as an expression of how a study is planned, organized and implemented. Used in this manner, the term is not restricted to the data collection or the types of sources and data, but can also refer to other aspects of the study or to the study as a whole.

Similarly, it is quite common to distinguish between different research designs based on the analytical perspectives on which the study is based. Some examples can illustrate this. One analytical perspective is the time perspective, which emphasizes analyses of processes, changes or trends. Studies based on this perspective require the collection and analysis of comparable data at different times, or continuous observation of phenomena over a certain period of time. Studies of this type are usually referred to as *longitudinal research designs*.

Another analytical perspective is the space perspective, which emphasizes analyses of similarities and differences between societal conditions in different places or in different contexts, for example in two or more organizations, communities or countries. Studies from this perspective must be based on comparable data about the conditions in the different places or in the different contexts. Such studies are referred to as *comparative research designs*.

A third analytical perspective is the causal perspective, which focuses on analyses of causal relationships, to what extent and in what way certain conditions in society can be considered as reasons for other social conditions. There are a number of different approaches for analysing causal relationships. One of these approaches is based on *experimental research designs*. Experimental designs often include structured observation, but may also combine different combinations of sources and data. In their simplest form, experimental research designs involve distributing the persons participating in a study randomly into two different groups, exposing one of these groups to the impact of the causal factor we wish to study, and comparing the two groups both before and after this impact. If the two groups have become more different, this change can be regarded as an effect of the assumed causal factor.

These three research designs, as well as other designs for following up certain analytical perspectives, will be discussed in more detail in Part V of the book (Chapters 21–24). It is important to emphasize here that none of these designs are based on other types of sources or data than the six main types of research design described in this chapter. On the contrary, longitudinal, comparative and experimental studies are examples of large and complex research designs that often include different combinations of the six main types of design that are included in Table 6.2.

CHAPTER HIGHLIGHTS

- Any basis for information about social conditions can be regarded as a data source.
- We distinguish between three main types of data sources:
  1 Actors
  2 Respondents
  3 Documents.
- Data is information that has been processed, systematized and recorded in a specific form and for the purpose of a specific analysis.
- There is a key distinction between qualitative and quantitative data.
- There are six major types of research designs:
  1 Ethnography and participant observation
  2 Structured observation
  3 Unstructured interviews and focus groups
  4 Questionnaires and surveys
  5 Qualitative content analysis
  6 Quantitative content analysis
- Four differences between qualitative and quantitative research designs are highlighted:
  1 Types of research questions: Analytical descriptions versus statistical generalizations
  2 Methodological designs: Flexibility versus structuring
  3 Relationship to sources: Proximity and sensitivity versus distance and selectivity
  4 Interpretation of findings: Relevance versus precision.
- There are various mixed methods designs for combining different types of sources and data, such as field research.

RESEARCH EXAMPLES

I recommend that you read the publications used as research examples in this chapter.

Two of the texts are based on observation of actors:

Nielsen, Rasmus Kleis (2012) *Ground Wars: Personalized Communication in Political Campaigns*. Princeton, NJ: Princeton University Press.

Russell, Marie, Rachel Price, Louise Signal, James Stanley, Zachery Gerring, and Jacqueline Cumming (2011) 'What do passengers do during travel time? Structured observations on buses and trains', *Journal of Public Transportation* 14(3), 123–146.

The book by Nielsen (2012) presents a qualitative political science study using participant observation to investigate patterns of personal contact and communication in the election campaign of two candidates for the US congressional election in 2008. The researcher participated in the election campaign while he observed how the candidates and their supporters communicated with voters. The book referred to here is based on Nielsen's PhD dissertation at Columbia University in 2010.

The article by Russell et al. (2011) reports on a quantitative study where structured observation was used to examine activities among passengers on local buses and trains in Wellington, New Zealand in 2008. Each of 812 passengers was observed during a 4-minute period. The observers recorded the passengers' activities using a structured schedule consisting of predefined activity categories. The study was part of a larger research project on health and well-being.

Two research examples refer to respondents as data sources:

Gould, Dinah, and Marina Fontenla (2006) 'Commitment to nursing: Results of a qualitative interview study', *Journal of Nursing Management* 14, 213–221.

Eurofound (2012) *Third European Quality of Life Survey – Quality of Life in Europe: Impacts of the Crisis.* Luxembourg: Publications Office of the European Union.

The article by Gould and Fontenla (2006) presents a qualitative study within nursing where unstructured interviews were used to explore how nurses' job satisfaction, professional commitment and organizational loyalty are affected by various factors, including opportunities for continuing professional education. Twenty-seven nurses from two different hospitals were interviewed based on a guide with general and open questions.

The Eurofound (2012) research report presents a quantitative sociological survey study on quality of life, where structured questionnaires were used in personal interviews with more than 35,000 respondents in the European countries in 2011. The respondents answered more than 300 questions on various aspects of their quality of life. This particular study is the third quality of life survey presented by Eurofound. Such Eurofound studies of quality of life have been carried out at regular intervals since 2003.

Finally, two articles are based on content analysis of documents:

Oosthuizen, Martha J. (2012) 'The portrayal of nursing in South-African newspapers: A qualitative content analysis', *Africa Journal of Nursing and Midwifery* 14(1), 49–62.

Humphreys, Lee, Phillippa Gill, Balachander Krishnamurthy, and Elisabeth Newbury (2013) 'Historicizing new media: A content analysis of Twitter', *Journal of Communication* 63(3), 413–431.

The article by Oosthuizen (2012) is a qualitative content analysis within health studies, focusing on how nurses are referred to in South African newspapers. A pragmatic sample of articles in the period 2005–2009 were read in order to record statements about nurses or nursing. The statements were categorized, and the resulting specific categories were then merged into 18 more general categories. Thus the categories were generated from the empirical data.

The article by Humphreys et al. (2013) presents a quantitative content analysis of tweets. A probability sample of 2100 English-language tweets in 2 months in 2008 was included in the analysis, and the tweets were assessed, classified and coded according to a structured coding schedule. While referred to here as an example of quantitative content analysis, the study is also an example of how big data from social media can be collected, processed and analysed.

STUDENT EXERCISES AND QUESTIONS

1 What is the difference between data sources and data?
2 What are the strengths and weaknesses of documents as sources in social studies?
3 What are the differences between actors and respondents as data sources?

4 What are the similarities and differences between unstructured interviews and questionnaires?
5 Why are mixed methods designs useful in social research?
6 Discuss what aspects of people's quality of life might be examined by means of

a   qualitative data

b   quantitative data.

7   Discuss what types of research designs might be used for studying

a   relations among students on a university course

b   differences between parties in an election campaign.

RECOMMENDED LITERATURE

Bechhofer, Frank, and Lindsay Paterson (2000) *Principles of Research Design in the Social Sciences*. London: Routledge.

This book discusses research designs in various social science disciplines. It is focused on issues involved in choosing a research design for a study. The issues of research designs are related to philosophy of social science.

Blau, Peter M. (1963) *The Dynamics of Bureaucracy: A Study of Interpersonal Relationships in Two Government Agencies* (rev. edn). Chicago: University of Chicago Press.

This book is a research report from a study of two US governmental agencies in the late 1940s. This is a classical sociological study of bureaucracy based on mixed methods. The study is a good example of field research. Here it is especially recommended to read the methodological epilogue (Part IV, Chapters 14–15) in the revised edition of the book. In this addition to the original book, Blau presents a detailed description of the procedures and processes involved in his study, as well as reflections on the types of sources and data that were used.

Greener, Ian (2011) *Designing Social Research: A Guide for the Bewildered*. Los Angeles: Sage.

In this book the term 'research design' is used in a broad sense, referring to the planning and organization of the whole research process. However, the book provides an understanding of how different types of sources and data are related to other aspects of a study, and to more general methodological principles. The book is written as a guide for planning a research project.

Olsen, Wendy (2012) *Data Collection: Key Debates and Methods in Social Research*. London: Sage.

This book deals with important theoretical issues as well as practical methods for designing and implementing data collection in social science studies. Designs and methods for collecting qualitative, quantitative and mixed data sets are discussed and exemplified with reference to research in different disciplines and in different countries.

FINDING SOURCES AND DATA

This chapter provides knowledge about how to select and find sources and data for social science studies. The chapter will teach you how to understand

- what kinds of sources and data are adequate for examining the research questions of a study
- how to select different types of information about the units of analysis in the study, and how to assess this information critically

- how to find available data and data sources on the web
- how to make use of social media and other big data in social science studies.

Data sources and source-critical assessments

As pointed out in Chapter 4, the research question of a study clarifies what units in society the study should include, and what features or characteristics of these units the study should examine. In Chapter 6 it was discussed how a study can be organized or designed in order to gather and utilize the information that is needed to examine the study's research question. This discussion of research designs focused on what types of data and data sources are most appropriate for obtaining the necessary information on the units and their features which are included in the research question. The next step is to select more specifically those particular units and that particular information about these units that are to be included in the empirical data of the study. This chapter describes different types of units and different types of information, before outlining some systematic strategies for selecting information in a study. The selection, or sampling, of units for a study is discussed in Chapter 8.

This chapter starts with a discussion of the need for critical assessments of sources that could be used in a study. Then different types and levels of units are presented. Next, different types of information are described, emphasizing what types of information are relevant for different types of units. A distinction is also made between information about each unit and information about relations between the units. In the following section,

some strategies for the specific selection of information in different types of studies are discussed. Then new data sources, such as big data, are described, and new techniques for finding data, including data scraping, are presented. While most of this chapter is focused on primary data, which are collected particularly for a new study, the last section of the chapter deals with secondary data, which have been collected for previous studies or other purposes and are available for use or reuse in a new study.

Although there are a wide variety of potential or possible sources for social science studies, the choice of specific sources for a particular study must be based on careful consideration, and the use of these sources must occur in an academically sound manner. It is important that the sources are not used uncritically. Before we use specific sources in a study, we should conduct critical assessments of these sources (cf. Scott, 1990). Four types of such *source-critical assessments* are particularly important:

1 *Availability*. Sources that could be interesting, in principle, may not be available. This could be, for example, people who do not want to be observed or interviewed, organizations that do not want to give access to their archives or protocols, and correspondence or diaries that are not available to the public. This should be clarified before the study commences and the researcher should consider the consequences that it could have for the study that important

sources may not be available. It can be difficult to obtain the data necessary to investigate the problem. The data may be so limited that only certain aspects of the research question can be examined. The data can also be biased, so that the results of the analysis become incorrect or unreliable. In such cases, it may be necessary to reformulate the research question so that it only includes conditions that can be investigated using the sources that are available. In certain cases, the lack of available sources may mean that it is simply impossible to carry out the study.

2   *Relevance*. The sources available are not necessarily relevant to the problem to be addressed in the current study. For example, in informal interviewing, there may be many sociable or talkative people who would like to converse with the researcher, even though they do not have any relevant information to contribute. If we wish to study attitudes and positions among political actors, we will find a range of readily available sources, such as party programmes, election speeches, letters and voting in political bodies, as well as debates, articles and statements in various media. If the research question focuses on attitudes and positions expressed in various political parties' public programmes and resolutions, these available sources are very relevant. However, these sources may be less relevant if the research question focuses on personal attitudes and positions found among different party politicians. Then we would need other sources, such as personal diaries, letters, confidential notes or internal protocols and minutes from meetings. Such sources would be more relevant, but generally less available than those found in public documents, open meetings or different media. Thus, it is reasonable to consider availability and relevance in context: among the available sources, we choose those that can contribute the most relevant information for examining the research question.

3   *Authenticity*. Before a source is used, it must also be ensured that this source is authentic or genuine. It must be considered whether

a particular actor or respondent is really the person he or she claims to be. In interviews, for example, an interviewer may complete a questionnaire for a particular respondent, without having received the respondent's own answers to the questions in the form. The information in the questionnaire then appears to originate from the particular respondent, but this is a falsification. The source is not authentic. When we use documents as a source, we also need to consider whether the different documents really are what they appear to be. For example, written representations may have been prepared by someone other than those listed as authors. Clarifying this is particularly important in studies where documents are used as sources for analysing the opinions of specific actors. It may be uncertain what actors are really behind the opinions expressed in the documents. As a rule, it is more difficult to assess the authenticity of documents than the authenticity of actors or respondents as sources. This is especially true when we assess documents that are old, or which originate from distant societies.

4   *Credibility*. Even if the source is authentic, we must consider whether we can trust the information we receive from observing specific actors, asking questions of specific respondents or analysing the content of specific documents. The observed actors may act in a way that deviates from their usual behaviour, possibly because they want to appear to the observer in a particularly favourable light. Respondents may give incorrect answers, for example, because they wish to impress the interviewer. Documents may contain incorrect information, perhaps because they are designed to promote particular interests. Opinion statements may be ironically formulated, such as in a newspaper article or in social media. Such statements can be difficult to interpret without in-depth knowledge of the author's background and the context of the statement. It can often be difficult to assess the credibility of sources, but it is essential to consider whether, and possibly how, the data in a study may be affected by such credibility issues.

Units of analysis

The *units of analysis* in a social science study are the social units or elements in society which are emphasized in the research question, and which are focused on in the analysis of the data. The units of analysis may be different from the *units of observation*, which are the key elements in the collection of data. For example, if families are units of analysis in a study, the observation units may be the individual family members. In this case, information about each family member may be used to generate data on the whole family. Furthermore, units of analysis should be distinguished from data sources. For example, actors or respondents may be used as data sources in a study where the units of analysis are the actions or opinions of the individuals that are observed or interviewed. Then the actors provide information on their own actions or opinions.

Types of units

There are different types of units of analysis in social science. The most common type is *actors*. An actor can be a single individual or a group of individuals, such as a family, an organization, a business company, a municipality or a nation. In a study of cigarette access behaviour among Canadian youth, the unit of analysis is individuals, more specifically students in grades 9–12 attending public and private elementary school (Vu et al., 2011).

A study of social networks and firm performance in China is based on companies as a unit of analysis and it investigates the networks that arise between companies due to the fact that some people are members of multiple company boards. The analysis is focused on how the companies' economic performance is influenced by the centrality of the company in the network of interlocking directorates (Li et al., 2013). Although the centrality of the company is based on individuals as members of company boards, the company as an organization is referred to as the unit of analysis.

Thus, an organization may be regarded as an actor, although it is individuals that are acting on behalf of the organization. In general, the use of organizations, institutions or other groupings of individuals as units of analysis requires that these groups constitute unique actors or meaningful social units.

Another type of unit of analysis is *actions*. Then the study is not focused on actors but on the activities carried out by different actors. For example, it may be appropriate to study activities such as visits to friends, use of seat-belts, work trips, electoral participation, political decisions, financial investments or participation in international organizations. Actions as units of analysis include not only activities performed by a single actor, but also activities based on interaction between several actors. These can be, for example, conversations between colleagues, meetings between government leaders, transactions between sellers and their customers, negotiations between business leaders, or discussions between members of parliament.

Compared to actors, actions as a unit of analysis can be more difficult to identify and define in an unambiguous way. Complete lists of various types of actors can often be found in systematic registries. Most types of actions are not registered in this way. They must usually be tracked using different sources or identified and recorded while they are performed. Actions to be used as a unit of analysis must therefore be clearly defined.

A third type of unit of analysis is *opinions*. Opinions are found in statements from different actors. The units of analysis are then the content elements in these statements. The content can be opinions in a very broad sense, such as views, attitudes and arguments, thoughts, ideas and perceptions, considerations, values and assessments. The opinions may be expressed in different forms. They may be oral, such as speeches in the parliament or at the UN General Assembly, or they may be in writing, such as newspaper articles and party programmes.

The statements may be verbal, in the form of words, which is common, for example, in letters, lectures and contributions to debates, or visual in the form of images, such as cartoons and advertisements.

The unit of analysis can be defined as an identifiable opinion element, such as a statement, a point of view or an argument. Alternatively, the unit of analysis may be a limited element of the statement, as it exists in the form of a text or image, such as a sentence, a paragraph, an article, drawing or photograph. In a study of mission statements of international airlines, the statements are used as the unit of analysis (Kemp and Dwyer, 2003). The mission statement is regarded as 'the most generalized statement of organizational purposes and can be thought of as an expression of its raison d'être' (Kemp and Dwyer, 2003: 636).

In addition to actors, actions and opinions, *events* can also be used as units of analysis in social science studies. An event is something that occurs. It is something that happens to actors or to their surroundings. This may be planned, such as a protest meeting or a referendum, but it can also be both unintended and unforeseen, such as a traffic accident or a natural disaster. Unlike actions performed by actors and opinions expressed by actors, events are not necessarily initiated by specific actors. Events are of interest to social science only if they affect or are significant for one or more social actors. An earthquake in itself is a natural phenomenon and hence an event in nature, but because an earthquake can have major social consequences, this event also becomes a relevant object for social science research. Generally, events are an important type of unit of analysis in social science because they can have a major impact on various social actors, both for those directly involved in the event and for other actors.

Like actions, events can be difficult to identify and define as unique units of analysis. Sometimes it can also be difficult to distinguish between actions and events. An act performed by an actor may appear to be an event for another actor. A death is usually considered to be an event, but if the death is a murder, it is also an action performed by a murderer. The question of whether we use the event or the action as a unit of analysis in such cases will depend on the perspective and the research question to be addressed by the study. Death as an event is an important unit of analysis for demographic research, while murder as an action is a common unit of analysis associated with criminological studies. Regardless of whether the unit of analysis is an event or an action, it is important that the unit is well defined so that it can be clearly identified.

Units at different levels

No matter what type of unit of analysis we rely upon, we can distinguish between different levels of analysis. The units can be at different levels in society or within a hierarchy of categories and subcategories that the relevant type of unit can be divided into. The level of analysis corresponds to such characteristics of the unit of analysis as size, complexity and extent in time and space. Small and simple units of a very limited extent are at the *micro* level. Large and complex units with a very extensive scope are at the *macro* level. Between these extremes there are many different intermediate types of units of varying size, complexity and extent. It is also quite common to refer to the *meso* level as a third, intermediate level of analysis. Regardless of whether we distinguish between all three levels or rely on the simpler division, there are no sharp or well-defined boundaries between the levels.

Referring to the examples in Table 7.1, the distinction between units of analysis at different levels can be specified in more detail. The division into different levels of analysis is used primarily with reference to actors as units of analysis. Here, the individual is the smallest unit and is the most common example of a unit at the *micro* level. Small groups of individuals, such as families and households, are also units at the micro level.

The state, on the other hand, is a large and complex actor which is clearly a unit at the *macro* level. At this level there are even bigger actors that extend beyond the national society. This applies, for example, to the EU, NATO, UN and other international organizations. Various types of local, regional or national organizations, such as business companies, hospitals or voluntary organizations, are usually placed at the *meso* level.

Although the different levels of analysis are mainly associated with actors as a unit of analysis, the classification of levels may also be relevant and useful for other types of units. As Table 7.1 shows, relatively simple actions, such as attendance at a meeting, will be a unit of analysis at the micro level. Somewhat more comprehensive and complex actions, such as planning of a conference, can be placed at the meso level. Coordination of a general strike is an example of an even more comprehensive and complex action, which must therefore be regarded as a unit of analysis at the macro level.

In terms of opinions as units of analysis, an argument is an example of one of the smallest and simplest units at the micro level. A contribution to a debate usually consists of a set of arguments and is therefore more comprehensive and more complex as a unit of analysis. This is a good example of an opinion unit at the meso level. Even more comprehensive and complex is an overall debate, which consists of many different inputs. This applies, for example, to the debate on the Brexit referendum in the UK. Based on the individual arguments and the various inputs, it is reasonable

to place the overall debate at the macro level. Similarly, texts as expressions of opinions can be divided into analytical units at different levels, such as sentences or paragraphs at the micro level, articles at the meso level, and newspapers or magazines at the macro level.

Regarding events as units of analysis, the division into different levels of analysis can be illustrated by means of examples of different types of meetings. A meeting is an example of an event. Depending on the size, complexity and extent of the meeting, this event can be placed at different levels of analysis. A small local meeting, such as a local branch meeting in an organization or a political party, is an event at the micro level. An organization meeting or party meeting at regional level, such as a county branch meeting, is more comprehensive and more complex and would be a meso-level event. A national meeting is an even more extensive and complex event, which can thus be described as a unit of analysis at the macro level.

Such a classification of units with regard to different types and different levels is useful as a basis for delimiting, defining and identifying the specific units of analysis in specific studies. The distinction between different levels may also be important in connection with the data analysis, where both choice of methods and options for interpretation must be seen in relation to the particular level of the unit of analysis. For example, if we have studied organizations as units and we draw conclusions about the individual members of these organizations, we can easily

Table 7.1 Examples of units of analysis at different levels

Level of analysis	Unit of analysis			
	Actor	Action	Opinion	Event
Micro	Individual	Attendance at a trade union meeting	Argument	Local branch meeting
Meso	Organization	Planning a conference	Contribution to a debate	Regional branch meeting
Macro	State	Coordination of a general strike	Debate	National convention

make a wrong conclusion, a so-called *wrong-level fallacy* or *ecological fallacy*. This is especially important if we include units at different levels in the same study and conduct what is known as a *multi-level analysis*. Wrong-level fallacies and multi-level analyses will be further discussed in Chapter 22.

The relation between units at different levels is also central in connection with the more fundamental questions about methodological individualism, methodological collectivism, methodological situationalism and methodological relationism, which were discussed in Chapter 2.

Types of information

Different types of information about units can be classified in various ways, based on different principles. One important distinction is the difference between information about the individual units and information about relations between the units. These key types of information will be discussed with reference to the different types of unit of analysis.

An overview of this simple classification of information types is presented in Table 7.2. The further presentation will be based on this overview. First, information about the individual units is discussed, and then the information about relations between the units is clarified.

Information about the individual units

In social science, it is quite common to rely on information about each individual unit. Data collection usually involves finding and recording information about the individual units separately, while the data analysis aims to identify general patterns in the information about the various units. The types of information that will be relevant for studies focusing on the individual units will depend on the type of units to be studied. In this connection, there is an important distinction between information about actors on the one hand, and information about actions, opinions and events on the other hand.

In the case of actors as unit of analysis, social science studies will usually cover one or more of these four types of information:

Table 7.2 Different types of information about different types of unit of analysis

Types of unit of analysis	Types of information about the units	
	Information about the individual units	**Information about relations between units**
Actor	Background Status Actions Opinions	Formal characteristics (e.g. strength or direction of the relation) Substantial aspects (content of the relation)
Action	Formal characteristics (e.g. location, duration or frequency of the action) Substantial aspects (content of the action)	
Opinion	Formal characteristics (e.g. intensity, stability or consistency of the opinion) Substantial aspects (content of the opinion)	
Event	Formal characteristics (e.g. location, duration or frequency of the event) Substantial aspects (content of the event)	

1 Information about the actor's background. In essence, this will be historical information about the actor's development prior to the investigation date, such as the upbringing and career of a person, the establishment and development phases of an organization, or the creation and history of a state. This may be information that is relevant and interesting in itself for a study, but it may also be a type of information that forms a contextual background for understanding and interpreting more relevant information about what the actor is or has, does or believes.

2 Information about the actor's status. This is current information about what the actor is or has, or everything that characterizes the actor's situation, conditions and opportunities when the current study is conducted. This concerns a number of different circumstances related to actors at different levels, such as attributes, resources, positions, connections and recognition.

3 Information about the actor's actions. The emphasis here is on what the actor does. This may be information about general behaviour and common patterns of action that are typical of a person, an organization or an institution, or it could be information about special activities that the particular actor performs or has performed in certain situations.

4 Information about the actor's opinions. This type of information concerns what the actor believes, in a very broad sense. This category includes general values, principles, ideas and attitudes that the actor is fundamentally concerned with, as well as special perceptions, opinions and arguments regarding specific questions or issues. This could be, for example, individual persons' political perspectives or views on Brexit, political parties' ideological basis or position on the immigration debate, or the position of different states to the death penalty.

In studies where the unit of analysis is actors, we can thus emphasize information about these actors' actions and opinions. As we have pointed out, actions and opinions may themselves be separate units of analysis. In that case, the individual actions and the opinions are not necessarily linked to specific actors. If such studies place emphasis on which actors perform the various actions or represent the various opinions that constitute unit of analysis, the information about these actors will be a type of information about the action or opinion as a unit of analysis. While studies of actors as a unit of analysis may include information about the actors' actions and opinions, studies of actions or opinions as unit of analysis may include information about the actors to which the actions or the opinions are linked. What is defined as the unit of analysis and what is regarded as information about the unit of analysis will depend on the research question in the individual study.

In connection with actions, opinions and events as units of analysis, we can generally distinguish between two main types of information:

1 Information about formal properties of the unit. In terms of actions and events, these may be attributes such as location in time and space, duration and frequency: when and where the action or event takes place, how long it lasts and how often this action or event occurs. For opinions, it may be about features like intensity, stability and consistency: how strongly the opinion is expressed, how lasting or how changeable it is, and how much logical consistency exists between the various units in the opinion.

2 Information about substantial aspects of the unit. This is information about different aspects of the specific content of the unit of analysis, that is, what the particular action is about, what the particular opinion concerns, or what the individual event is about. Information about which actors the unit of analysis is associated with is usually included in this category. There will be concrete and specific information about who performs the action, who subscribes to the

opinion in question or who is involved in the event. For example, studies of certain actions such as grocery purchases may emphasize which particular activities are performed in connection with the trip to the shop, how these activities are performed, why they are performed, and who performs them. Studies of events, such as traffic accidents, can be based on information about which road users and vehicles are involved, what caused the accident, and the consequences of the accident. In the study of airline mission statements mentioned above, information was gathered for each unit of analysis (statement) as to whether the statement included different predefined components, such as customers, products/services, locations/markets, concern for public image, or concern for employees (Kemp and Dwyer, 2003: 637).

Just as different types of social units can be either the unit of analysis or the basis for important information about the unit of analysis, units at different levels can be either the unit of analysis or the basis for information. If we study national organizations as the unit of analysis, we can emphasize information about which persons are members of the organizations or in which international associations the organizations are members. If we study debate contributions as the unit of analysis, we can utilize information about which arguments are included in the individual contributions, or in what major debates the various contributions are included.

The purpose of collecting information about each unit may be to compare different units or different categories of units with regard to particular characteristics. For example, we can compare the level of education and annual income of women and men, or we can compare the types of argument and methods of reasoning in opinion statements for and against Brexit.

Another purpose for the information about the individual units can be to find possible relations between different properties or characteristics of

the units, such as correlations between education level and annual income, or correlations between argument types and methods of reasoning.

Whether the purpose is to make comparisons between units or to find correlations between the characteristics of the units, it is important that the information about the different units is comparable. In quantitative studies, such comparability is a major reason for the structuring of the data collection. However, the requirement for comparability is also important in qualitative studies that emphasize comparisons or relations.

Particularly in qualitative studies, there is also a third purpose of obtaining information about each unit of analysis. This purpose is to identify typical features of specific units or to develop a comprehensive understanding of these units. Getting the most exhaustive information about the relevant features of each unit of analysis may then be more important than gathering comparable information about the different units. Particularly in case studies, which are typically concentrated on just a single unit, the requirement for comparability may not be relevant. However, in some case studies, two or more units are included, and then it may be appropriate to gather comparable information about the different units, as Blau (1963) did in his bureaucracy study, which was described in Chapter 1.

Information about relations between units

Society is not just about the individual social units or about conditions related to each of these units. The most characteristic feature of a society is that it consists of relations between actors and other social units. In many situations, therefore, information about such relations can be as relevant and important as information about the individual units separately.

Information about each unit of analysis may include information about connections that this unit of analysis has to other social units. This could be links to other units of analysis in the current study or links to units that are not included in this study. In such cases, the information about connections is considered to be information about a characteristic of the actor. The actors can be compared with regard to how many or what connections they have, and we can identify possible relationships between the actors' connections and other characteristics of the actors.

When we obtain information about relations between all the units of analysis, it is not usually in order to make comparisons of units or to identify relationships between characteristics of the units. The purpose of obtaining information about relations between each unit and each of the other units in the study is rather to clarify how the units relate to each other, or how they are positioned in relation to each other. Such studies are intended to explore the larger patterns that are formed by all the relations between the units of analysis. These patterns represent different types of networks or structures. In Chapter 23 analyses of relations, networks and structures will be further discussed.

Structural patterns or networks of relations can be studied regardless of what types of units of analysis the studies are based upon, and irrespective of what levels the units of analysis refer to. The studies can also include many different types of relations. The types of units of analysis and the types of relations that are part of a particular study will depend on the types of structures or networks that the study is focusing on. In a specific study, the information about the relations between the units of analysis must conform to the network type to be studied and ensure that the different relations are comparable.

Regarding information about relations, there are no clear or unambiguous differences between different types of units. For all types of units of analysis, we can generally highlight two main types of information about relations between the units:

1   Information about *formal* properties of the relations. This may be information about how strong the relation is, whether it is formal or informal, whether the relation is positive or negative, whether it is characterized by reciprocity between the two units or is dominated by one unit and, if so, in which direction the relation goes, that is, which of the units dominates the relation. Particularly in connection with actors as a unit of analysis, the strength of the relation is of particular interest because the distinction between strong and weak ties is of major importance in recent social network theory. While strong ties are typical of small groups and cliques, it is primarily weak ties that form the links between different cliques, so that these are integrated into larger social structures (Granovetter, 1973).

2   Information about *substantial* aspects of the relations. This category includes specific information about specific content aspects of the relations. The information shows what the relation concerns. For example, it may be a friendship or acquaintanceship between individuals, interlocking board memberships or ownership relations between companies, links between various actions within the same interaction pattern, connections between events involving the same actors or associated with the same development process, or relations between different expressions of opinions that are rooted in a common value base.

Strategies for selecting information

Specification of the *type* of information to be used is one of the two main elements in a systematic clarification of the information requirements in a particular study. The other main element is the *selection* of the specific information.

The methods for information selection are less standardized than the selection, or sampling, of units, which will be described in Chapter 8. Nevertheless, we can highlight some common procedures for selecting information in different studies. First, however, some important differences between qualitative and quantitative studies with regard to selecting information will be pointed out.

Differences between qualitative and quantitative studies

In connection with information selection, there are four important differences between qualitative and quantitative studies. Firstly, the amount of information per unit of analysis is greater in qualitative studies than in quantitative studies. As mentioned, it may be more important in many qualitative studies to obtain exhaustive information about each unit of analysis than to obtain comparable information about all the units of analysis. The selection of information thus becomes considerably more *specific* in quantitative studies than in qualitative studies.

Secondly, the difference between comparable and exhaustive information means that quantitative studies are largely based on the same type of information about all units, while qualitative studies can often utilize different types of information about different units of analysis. The selection of information thus becomes considerably more *uniform* in quantitative studies than in qualitative studies.

Thirdly, qualitative and quantitative studies are different with regard to when the selection of information occurs. In quantitative studies, this selection, like the sampling of units, takes place prior to the data collection. The kind of information to be included in the study is fully determined before data collection begins. In qualitative studies,

the selection of both units and information will take place partly during the empirical study, in parallel to the collection and analysis of data. In other words, the selection of information becomes considerably more *concentrated* in quantitative studies than in qualitative studies.

Fourthly, it follows from the fundamental difference between qualitative and quantitative studies that the latter require information that is quantifiable. When the information in such studies is recorded as data, it is expressed as numbers that can be analysed quantitatively for the purpose of statistical generalization. In qualitative studies, data are usually expressed as text. The information is not quantified and therefore does not need to be quantifiable. The consequence of this is that the selection of information must be more *structured* in quantitative studies than in qualitative.

Overall, these differences mean that the selection of information will be less standardized and more flexible in qualitative studies than is the case in quantitative studies. A concrete expression of this difference is that the information selection in qualitative studies is based on dimensions and categories, while the selection of information in quantitative studies is organized in the form of more specific variables and values. In other words, both qualitative and quantitative studies are based on dimensions and categories, but only quantitative studies emphasize the further development of the dimensions into variables and the categories into values.

Information selection with emphasis on dimensions and categories is thus a general procedure that is common to all studies, while selecting information with reference to variables and values is a special procedure for quantitative studies. This difference is illustrated schematically in Table 7.3. The different procedures will be further described with reference to this table.

Table 7.3 Step-by-step systematic procedure for selecting information

General procedure (both qualitative and quantitative studies)	Special procedures for quantitative studies	
	Simple measures	Composite measures
Step 1: Specify and define each of the concepts in the study	Step 1: Specify and define each of the concepts in the study	Step 1: Specify and define each of the concepts in the study
Step 2: Decompose the concepts: specify and define different dimensions for each term	Step 2: Decompose the concepts: specify and define different variables for each concepts (one variable for each dimension)	Step 2a: Decompose the concepts: specify and define one or more indexes for each concept (as a rule, one index for each dimension)
		Step 2b: Specify and define different indicators for each index
Step 3: Specify and define a set of categories for each dimension	Step 3: Specify and define a set of values for each variable	Step 3: Specify and define a set of values for each indicator
Step 4: Clarify operational definitions	Step 4: Clarify operational definitions and measurement levels for the variables	Step 4: Clarify operational definitions and measurement levels for the indicators and indexes

General strategy

A good starting point for selecting information in a particular study is an overview of the different *concepts* included in this study. These concepts can be explicitly stated in the research question, or they may be derived as more implicit consequences of the research question.

One of the research questions in the study of airline mission statements by Kemp and Dwyer (2003) is to discuss 'the major components of a clear and comprehensive mission statement' (Kemp and Dwyer, 2003: 635). The empirical identification of components of the statements in the study referred to nine predefined components, based on previous research on mission statements.

In a survey study of factors explaining risky behaviour online in Israel, Sasson and Mesch (2016) focus on two research questions. The first question is 'whether there are gender differences in the contribution of the norms of the participants' parents and friends as well as perceived behaviour control and attitudes to risky online behaviour' (Sasson and Mesch, 2016: 974). The second

question is 'whether gender differences are related to the quality of the relationships within the family' (Sasson and Mesch, 2016: 974). Thus, in this comparison of females and males (aged 10–18), the following concepts are central:

- Risky online behaviour
- Norms of parents and friends
- Perceived behaviour control
- Attitudes to risky online behaviour
- Quality of family relationships.

The study is based on specific *theoretical definitions* of each of these concepts. These definitions clarify, for example, that risky online behaviour refers to 'posting personal details, sending an insulting message, or meeting face-to-face with a stranger met online' (Sasson and Mesch, 2016: 973). The plan for information selection can be further developed based on the theoretical definitions of the concepts. The next step will usually be to *decompose* the concepts so that we can differentiate between different components of each concept. For example, Sasson and Mesch (2016: 977) distinguish between the following components of the concept of attitudes to risky online behaviour:

- Attitude to posting personal details online
- Attitude to uploading an offensive clip
- Attitude to sending an offensive message
- Attitude to meeting face-to-face with persons first met online.

The components can be considered as different *dimensions* of the more general concept. A *dimension* is often an expression of a particular property of social units. General concepts are often multidimensional, and one of the challenges of empirical studies of such concepts is to identify useful dimensions of the concept so that the most relevant and most interesting aspects of the concept are investigated in the study. How a concept is decomposed may vary, depending on the purpose of the use of the concept in different studies. For example, in certain studies it could be useful to perform a further decomposition of each of the four components of attitudes that Sasson and Mesch (2016) distinguish between.

Each dimension is usually divided into different *categories* so that the various units of analysis can be positioned with reference to the dimension. A *category* includes all the units that have a particular position in the current dimension. As to the attitude dimensions listed above, Sasson and Mesch (2016: 977) divide each dimension into two categories:

- It is OK (to post, upload, send, or meet)
- It is not OK (to post, upload, send, or meet).

Alternatively, the dimensions could have been divided into more categories, for example:

- It is perfectly OK (to post, upload, send, or meet)
- It is OK (to post, upload, send, or meet)
- It is not OK (to post, upload, send, or meet)
- It is definitely not OK (to post, upload, send, or meet).

In any event, the categories are defined in such a way that they are mutually exclusive and that together they are exhaustive for the dimension. Specifically, this means that each unit of analysis can be placed in only a single category on each dimension and that all the units of analysis can be placed in one category on each dimension. The difference between dimensions and categories then becomes that any unit of analysis can be related to all the dimensions in a study, but each unit of analysis cannot be placed in more than one category of each dimension. The different categories of the same dimension should also be as equivalent as possible, either based on logical assessments of how we can achieve a balanced relation between the different parts of the dimension, or based on assumptions about how the units of analysis can be evenly distributed between the different categories.

This categorization in itself helps to elaborate and clarify the content of the individual dimensions. In addition, both the dimensions and the categories are *operationally defined* to clarify precisely what kind of specific information is required about the units of analysis for each dimension, and the specific criteria that will be used to determine how each unit of analysis is positioned in relation to the various categories.

As already mentioned, this step-by-step process, with an emphasis on an overview of the concepts in the study, decomposing the concepts into various dimensions, and dividing the individual dimensions into a set of categories, is a systematic procedure for selecting information that can be used in connection with both qualitative and quantitative studies. In qualitative studies, the procedure is often used in parallel with the collection and analysis of data and with the aim of developing concepts. On the other hand, it is typical of quantitative studies that this systematic selection process is carried out prior to data collection and is based on established concepts.

Special strategies for quantitative studies

Compared with qualitative studies, quantitative studies are based on a more standardized procedure for selecting information. The information about the units must be expressed in the form of numbers. The utilization of the information to position the units in relation to specific categories is then referred to as *measurement*. This measurement is organized using a particular system of variables and values, where each unit is given a specific value in the form of a number on each variable. When these variables and values are operationally defined, they become measurable.

Simply put, a *variable* corresponds to what has so far been called a dimension, and a *value* corresponds to what has so far been referred to as a category. In other words, a variable is divided into values in the same way as dimensions are divided into categories. Dimension and category are general terms that apply to the organization of both qualitative and quantitative data. Variable and value are special terms for a dimension and a category, respectively, which are used specifically in connection with quantitative data. Since the dimension 'attitude to sending an offensive message', which was mentioned above, was used as a variable in a quantitative study, the two categories were defined as values and each of them was given a specific number:

1 It is OK
2 It is not OK.

This variable can also be referred to as a *measurement* of the attitude. A measure that consists of just one variable with only these two values is a very simple measurement of the attitude to risky online behaviour. The study by Sasson and Mesch (2016), therefore, developed a more complex and nuanced measurement, using a composite measure based on all four attitude dimensions mentioned above. In general, such composite measures consist of several variables. The composite measure is called an *index*, and each of the variables included in an index is called an *indicator*. In this example, the index for attitudes to risky online behaviour is comprised of the four indicators specified above (attitudes to the four types of risky behaviour).

When we use composite measures, it is usually the index and not every single indicator that corresponds to a dimension. For each dimension, we can thus have several different variables. However, we try to avoid the same individual variable referring to several different dimensions, because it may cause confusion during the data collection and possibly problems with data quality. In Chapter 12 it is shown how data collection using a questionnaire can be designed in order to construct indexes, and Chapter 17 examines different methods for index construction during the data analysis.

Regardless of whether we use a simple measure based on just one variable, or a composite measure in the form of an index, these measures may have varying degrees of nuance and contain varying amounts of information. Based on this, we distinguish between four different *levels of measurement* for variables and indexes. An overview of these levels of measurement is presented in Table 7.4.

Table 7.4 Overview of different levels of measurement for variables

Measurement level	Characteristics	Example	Possible calculations
Nominal level	Inequality between values	Gender (female, male)	$\neq$
Ordinal level	Rank order between values	Education (low, medium, high)	$\neq < >$
Interval level	Distance between values	Temperature (degrees)	$\neq < > + -$
Ratio level	Proportion between values, with a meaningful or natural zero value	Age (number of years)	$\neq < > + - \times \div$

The simplest and broadest measurement consists of a variable at the *nominal level*. Here, the numbers for each of the values are used mainly as labels to show that the values are different and mutually exclusive. Gender is an example of such a variable, where the values will be female (1) and male (2). This is also an example of a dichotomous variable, or a *dichotomy*, because the variable consists of only two values. While the gender variable is a *natural* dichotomy, we can also *construct* dichotomies, for example by distinguishing between just two values for a variable such as income (low income and high income). The attitude variables mentioned above, with the values 'It is OK' (1), and 'It is not OK' (2), is a constructed dichotomy. If we used the alternative division of the variable into four values, perfectly OK (1), OK (2), not OK (3), and definitely not OK (4), the variable would be at the *ordinal level*. What characterizes such variables is that the values are not only different and mutually exclusive, but they are also arranged in a particular order, in this case from perfectly OK, through OK and not OK, to definitely not OK (from more positive to less positive attitude, or from less negative to more negative attitude). The values are both different and ranked. If we compare two values of a variable at the ordinal level, one value will be greater or less than the other.

Interval-level variables are characterized by providing information about the distances between values. When the variable 'performance' has three values (poor, average and good), we cannot know anything about the distances between the three values. The distance between poor and average performance can be as great as the distance between average and good, but the latter distance may also be larger or smaller than the former. This is not apparent from the variable because it is at the ordinal level. If the variable had been at the interval level, the distance between the values 1 and 2 would be as large as the distance between the values 2 and 3, because the difference between the two numbers in both cases is equal to 1. When the

variable is at the interval level, the values are not only different and ranked. They can also be added or subtracted. Instead of using the performance variable with three values, we could measure school performance by average grades based on the grade scale from 1 to 6. This could be an example of a variable at the interval level if we assume that the distance from one grade to the next is the same along the entire scale. But this would be a questionable assumption. The best examples of variables at the interval level are found outside the social sciences. Temperature scales, such as Celsius and Fahrenheit, are often mentioned in this connection.

Ratio-level variables have all the properties we find in variables at the interval level, and in addition they have a meaningful or natural zero point. Age and income are typical examples of such variables. Unlike the temperature scales mentioned above, where the zero point is based on a chosen definition that varies between different scales, both age and income have a zero value that is not arbitrarily chosen. What is unique about such variables is that they provide information about the ratio (proportion) between the values. An 80-year-old is twice as old as a forty-year-old, and an annual income of €50,000 is half as much as an annual income of €100,000. In addition to being different and rank-ordered, the values can be processed using all four types of arithmetical operation. As well as addition and subtraction, we can also perform multiplication and division.

The measurement level for a variable shows not only how much information the variable contains. It is also very important for selecting methods and techniques for quantitative data analysis. The higher the measurement level of the variables, the more advanced statistical methods can be used to analyse these variables. Some methods can be used only in connection with variables at the interval level or the ratio level. Such variables are also called *continuous variables*. The importance of measurement levels in quantitative data analysis will be further discussed in Chapters 17 and 18.

Secondary analyses: Use and reuse of available data

So far, this chapter has been focused on primary data, which are collected particularly for a new study. However, it is possible to carry out new empirical studies without collecting *new* data. In many fields of social sciences, there are good opportunities to conduct new studies based on secondary data, which have been collected for previous studies or other purposes and are available for use or re-use in a new study. These opportunities should always be considered before we collect new data.

New analyses based on available data have traditionally been limited to quantitative studies, because the collection of qualitative data is typically carried out by the researchers themselves, and because qualitative analyses take place partly in parallel with the data collection. Increasingly, however, field notes from qualitative studies may be analysed or reanalysed by other researchers. This requires that the field notes are very comprehensive and systematic, with in-depth and detailed descriptions of both the methods and observations.

Various organizations and institutions in society have large amounts of data that can be utilized in social science analyses, even though these data have not been collected for research purposes. This applies primarily to register data and statistical overviews.

Register data may be collected for administrative or commercial purposes. Some data of this kind can be found in private registers, but large public records are particularly interesting. In many countries, census data and a lot of other register data, for example on individuals' health, income, tax, expenditures, and family relations, are available from public agencies. Furthermore, register data are available on other types of units, such as organizations, institutions, business companies and municipalities.

Data collected for different purposes can also be used for statistical overviews. Both public institutions, companies and other private organizations have a number of statistical overviews that can be used in social science studies. In most countries, there are national statistical offices, which coordinate the production and dissemination of public statistics for the entire country. International and global statistical data are also available, coordinated by international statistical agencies, for example in the EU or the UN. Lists of national and international statistical services can be found on the Internet, for example at https://www.unece.org/stats/links.html.

As mentioned earlier, advances in computer technology have increased the ability to store, process and analyse large volumes of data. This applies not least to data from large registers. Linking data about the same people from different registers has also become easier than before. Thus, more and more available register data are big data, which will be further discussed in next section of this chapter.

Social scientists can also carry out new analyses of available data that have been collected for research purposes. These available data include general databases as well as data collected earlier for more specific studies.

General databases are built up and made available for research within a limited field of research. These databases are often based on extensive questionnaire surveys and repeated on a regular basis, so that comparable data are available for different time periods. Some databases are also multinational, so that comparable data are available from different countries. Examples of multinational databases include the European Quality of Life Survey, the European Social Survey and the International Social Survey Programme.

Access to general databases is typically organized by special national or international data service agencies, sometimes in collaboration with research councils or statistical agencies.

Data from *particular* previous studies have been collected for the investigation of *particular* research questions. However, most data sets can be used to analyse a number of other research questions, in addition to those included in the original study. This is especially true if the data set is extensive. The researcher responsible for the data collection in a particular study will often retain the sole right to use the data until this original study has been completed. Subsequently, however, the data are usually made available to other researchers who can carry out other analyses. Typically, when a data collection is based on public funding, for example from a research council, the data must be made available to other researchers and for new analyses after a certain period of time.

Before we conduct secondary analyses, reusing secondary data, we must carry out a critical assessment of the available data. This is not only an assessment of the *sources* of the data, which was discussed earlier in this chapter. It is also an assessment of the final *data*, especially with regard to relevance, quality and ethics. The assessment of relevance is intended to clarify whether the available data are pertinent for the new research questions to be investigated. The quality assessment focuses on the reliability of the data and the potential for the data to have been affected by various problems during data collection. The most important ethical question is whether it is appropriate to carry out new analyses of data that have been collected for other purposes. This question is especially important for reanalyses of data about individuals. It may be difficult or impossible to inform these people about the new analyses and to obtain their permission to reuse the data about them. Such projects may require approval from special research ethics committees. However, the researcher is personally responsible for ensuring that the research ethics issues are considered in a satisfactory manner.

These assessments of relevance, quality and ethics require that we familiarize ourselves with both the characteristics of the specific data and the implementation of the original data collection, and that we have good knowledge of the different research designs that were described in Chapter 6, as well as the procedures and problems associated with collection of social science data.

New data sources: Social media and other big data

Available data for secondary analyses may be found online, where they may be accessed by anyone or by those who can get permission to reuse them. A lot of information that can be used as sources for primary data can also be found online. Referring to the three types of data sources that were discussed in Chapter 6 (actors, respondents, and documents), the most common type of online source has been documents. Various kinds of textual, oral and visual documents have been stored and distributed online, where they have been accessible and ready for content analysis. However, the development of new communication technology makes it possible to observe specific actors and their activities as they are conducted, for example by means of CCTV cameras or other forms of surveillance that are linked to computer networks. Furthermore, online communication becomes more and more interactive, participative and dynamic, which means that specific respondents may answer questions immediately or quickly, for example in a chat or in different types of social media.

More and more online information is big data or can be used as sources for big data. This is information or data that are available in large amounts. Typically, the diversity and complexity of such data are high. Moreover, big data are frequently updated and changed. Thus, big data are characterized by 'the three Vs': volume, variety and velocity.

Social media, such as Facebook, Twitter and Instagram, are examples of sources of big data. These media contain enormous amounts of information about people all over the world, including their activities, opinions, locations and relations. These social media are rich sources of big data, which are increasingly being used in social science.

In general, the content of social media is information about individuals that is provided by the individuals themselves. Thus, in his classification of sources for big data, Kitchin (2014: 85–97) describes social media as an example of *volunteered information*, which is one of three main categories of big data sources. The information is regarded as volunteered because it is traded or gifted by individuals to a system. In addition to social media, there are several other examples of volunteered information as sources for big data. One of these examples is transaction information, which may be generated when credit cards or other payment systems are used, when personal data are requested from customers in connection with a purchase, or when consumers are reviewing or rating a service. Another example of volunteered information is sousveillance, which refers to people's use of digital technologies for monitoring and recording personal data on their own health and life, which is shared with service-providing companies. Furthermore, volunteered information includes crowdsourcing, which refers to collective production of information for a particular purpose, such as building a knowledge base like Wikipedia. Finally, volunteered information may be based on citizen science, which is a special form of crowdsourcing. Such information is obtained from communities or networks of citizens at different places, who contribute voluntarily to science by observing or measuring particular phenomena, for example traffic jams or children's use of public playgrounds.

Another main category in the classification of big data sources is *automated information*, which is generated automatically as a function of a device or a system (Kitchin, 2014: 88–91). The generation of information may be a primary purpose or a by-product of the system. An example of this is automated surveillance, such as automatic reading of meters regarding use of water or electricity, or systems for registering licence plates of cars passing through various traffic points. Another example is our use of digital devices, such as smart phones, which automatically generates a lot of data on our behaviour, such as where we are, whom we are communicating with, and what information we are searching for or using. Automated information is also generated by different kinds of sensors, which register various conditions, movements and changes in certain places, such as light, sounds, movements, or speed. Sensors can be connected in networks, which make it possible to monitor and register activities or events over time and in large areas. Furthermore, the amount of scan data is increasing. Barcodes are used in more and more connections, for example on products, in passports, on receipts, on luggage, on letters, and on prescriptions. The scanning of these barcodes provides a lot of big data on these things and our use of them, such as where the things are located at different times, and how they are moved around. A lot of interaction data are also generated automatically, for example when we use the Internet, or when we send or receive e-mails. There are data on what websites we connect to, where we connect to the websites from, and how we respond or react to these websites through further clicking on various alternatives. Moreover, data are generated about our relations and networks based on e-mails and other forms of online communication.

The third category of big data sources is *directed information*, which is focused on traditional forms of surveillance (Kitchin, 2014: 86–87).

This surveillance is directed towards specific persons or places and conducted by human operators. This may be done by the police and by means of, for example, CCTV cameras or drones, which are linked to computer networks. In addition, various systems of personal identification, such as fingerprints or social security numbers, can be used, in combination with cameras, for tracing specific persons. The increasing use of digital equipment and computer systems for such surveillance has made it easier to keep track of individuals or groups in large areas and over time. At the same time, this has made it possible to generate, process and store large amounts of data on human behaviour, which can be analysed for social science purposes.

This classification of big data sources is summarized in Table 7.5.

As pointed out in Chapter 3, the use of big data may involve ethical issues that are particularly important and sometimes quite serious. For example, different forms of surveillance data are collected or generated without informing those who are monitored, and, typically, it is not possible to ask for their consent to be included in a social science study. These ethical concerns should be considered very thoroughly before such data are used.

In summary, the development of new information and communication technology increases the possibilities for finding data and data sources online. It is possible to search online for secondary data that may be reanalysed in new studies, as well as information that may be used as sources for new primary data. Increasingly, this includes big data and sources for big data.

Table 7.5 Classification of sources for big data, based on Kitchin (2014: 85–97)

Type of source	Definition	Examples
Volunteered information	Information that is traded or gifted by people to a system	Social media
		Transactions
		Sousveillance
		Crowdsourcing
		Citizen science
Automated information	Information that is generated as an inherent automatic function of a device or a system	Automated surveillance
		Digital devices
		Sensors
		Scan data
		Interaction data
Directed information	Information that is based on traditional forms of surveillance, focused on a person or a place by a human operator	CCTV
		Drones
		Individual identification

New techniques for finding sources and data: Search engines and data scraping

Although the amount of online data and data sources, including big data and big data sources, is large and rapidly increasing, technological developments have made it possible to create new techniques for finding specific data or data sources among all the information that is available online.

The most common way of searching online for specific information is to use one or more search engines, such as Google, Bing, Yahoo!, or Ask. These are computer programs used to search for documents or other content on the World Wide Web that include a specified keyword or a combination of words. The programs provide a list of websites where the word or word combination is found. Almost everybody who has a computer, laptop, tablet or smart phone uses such search engines daily. These tools for searching online information are also very useful for social science purposes. As for ordinary users, it is important for researchers to specify the most appropriate and most efficient keywords for the search process. Thus, Google or other search engines can be used to identify and locate available secondary data as well as relevant sources for new primary data.

Data and data sources may also be identified or located by means of *data scraping* (Munzert et al., 2014). Compared to Google and other ordinary search engines, data scraping is a newer and more advanced technique, which is also more specialized for finding research data. The main purpose of data scraping is to extract data from various types of documents or other sources. This is done by means of data programs, which gather specific data from documents or other sources and copy these data into a database or spreadsheet, so that the data can be used and analysed in a social science study.

Typically, the sources for data scraping consist of readable text or numbers that are produced for various purposes. Most often these sources are found on the web. Data scraping for extracting data from websites is also called *web scraping*. Web scraping programs fetch and download the web pages to be scraped and then extract the relevant data from these pages. The data might be various types of text or numbers on the web page, for example names of persons or companies, telephone numbers, addresses, opinion statements, or occurrence of meetings. The extracted data are listed and copied to the database for the particular study.

Data scraping may also be based on sources other than web pages, such as written reports that are available in digital form (*report mining*), or various texts that are displayed on the computer screen (*screen scraping*). The purposes and procedures of the data scraping are the same for these sources as they are for web sources.

There are several programs available for data scraping, including Web Scraper, Spinn3r, ScraperWiki, and Dexi. For extracting qualitative data it is possible to use special software such as NVivo and NCapture.

Data scraping is related to *data mining*. The difference is that data scraping only extracts data from the web, a screen, or a document, whereas data mining also detects and identifies patterns in the data that are extracted. Some programs, such as SAS Text Miner, combine data scraping and data mining. Data mining may be particularly useful for content analysis of texts, which will be further discussed in Chapters 11 and 14. Data scraping and data mining are included in computational social science, which will be further discussed in Chapter 24.

Using online data and data sources requires thorough consideration of ethical and legal issues. Data or information found on the web may not be used or reused without permission from authors of texts, or owners of documents. It may be necessary to get such permissions from persons or institutions who have copyright or other legal rights regarding the use of the data or data sources. Even with the necessary permissions to use the data or information, it is important to make sure that plagiarism or other ethical violations are avoided.

- Data and data sources for social science studies should be thoroughly discussed, focusing on four types of source-critical assessments:
  1. Availability
  2. Relevance
  3. Authenticity
  4. Credibility.
- The research question of a study clarifies what units in society the study should include, and what features or characteristics of these units the study should examine.
- The unit of analysis in a social science study is the social unit or element in society on which the study is focused.
- There are different types of units of analysis: actors, actions, opinions and events.
- The units of analysis can refer to different levels of analysis: micro, meso or macro.
- We distinguish between information about each unit and information about relations between the units.
- Studies of actors usually include information about the actors' background, status, actions and opinions.
- We also distinguish between information about formal properties and information about substantive aspects of the units or the relations being studied.
- In quantitative studies, information selection is more selective, more uniform, more concentrated and more structured than in qualitative studies.
- Both qualitative and quantitative studies focus on dimensions and categories in information selection. In quantitative studies, the information selection is also organized with reference to variables and values.
- A dimension is a component of a general concept and is often an expression of a particular characteristic of social units. Dimensions are divided into categories, so that each category encompasses all the units with a particular position on the dimension. The categories of a particular dimension must be exhaustive, mutually exclusive and equivalent.
- If the categories of a dimension are expressed in the form of numbers, the dimension represents a variable, and the categories then represent the values of the variable.
- Measurement involves assigning each unit the number that corresponds to the unit's value on the variable in question.
- A variable is a simple measurement. A composite measurement is called an index and consists of several variables. The variables in the index are referred to as indicators.
- We distinguish between different measurement levels for variables: nominal level, ordinal level, interval level and ratio level.
- In many fields of social science, there are excellent opportunities to conduct new studies based on secondary data.
- More and more secondary data and sources for new primary data can be found online.
- Social media and other big data represent new data sources in social science.
- Search engines and programs for data scraping are increasingly used for finding online sources and data for social science studies.

I recommend that you read the publications used as research examples in this chapter.

Kemp, Sharon, and Larry Dwyer (2003) 'Mission statements of international airlines: A content analysis', *Tourism Management* 24, 635–653.

This article presents a study using opinion statements as the unit of analysis. A selection of 50 mission statements from the corporate websites of international airlines are examined. The content of the statements is analysed with reference to nine typical components of mission statements, which were identified and defined in previous research. The study shows that less than half of the statements include more than four of the nine predefined components. The three most important components seem to be references to the self-concept of the airline, the philosophy of the company, and the customers of the business.

Li, Liuchuang, Gaoliang Tian, and Wenjia Yan (2013) 'The network of interlocking directorates and firm performance in transition economies: Evidence from China', *Journal of Applied Business Research* 29(2), 607–620.

This is an article about network centrality and economic performance of Chinese companies, where the companies are used as the unit of analysis. The study is focused on networks of interlocking directorates, which are networks formed by persons who are board members of two or more companies. Although the networks are formed by individuals as representatives of their companies, the companies as organizations are regarded as the relevant unit of the analysis. A sample of 8727 companies were examined in the period 2006–2010. The study shows that companies that are central in the network have a higher economic performance than companies that are less central in the network. Furthermore, it is shown that this relationship between centrality and performance is stronger among non-state-owned enterprises than it is among state-owned enterprises.

Sasson, Hagit, and Gustavo Mesch (2016) 'Gender differences in the factors explaining risky behavior online', *Journal of Youth and Adolescence* 45(5), 973–985.

In this article, it is illustrated how concepts are defined and specified in terms of dimensions and categories, or variables and values. It is also shown how variables can be combined and used as indicators in a composite measure, which is called an index. The article presents a survey based on a representative sample of 495 students aged 10–18 in a large city in Israel. The study examines gender differences in how risky behaviour online can be explained by various factors, including attitudes, perceived behaviour control, and parents' norms. The results show that these factors can explain boys' risky online behaviour, whereas girls' risky online behaviour seems to be more dependent on the girls' family relationships. Compared to other girls, those girls who engage in risky behaviour 'have less cohesive and supportive relationships with their parents and friends' (Sasson and Mesch, 2016: 983).

Vu, Mary, Scott T. Leatherdale, and Rashid Ahmed (2011) 'Examining correlates of different cigarette access behaviours among Canadian youth: Data from the Canadian Youth Smoking Survey (2006)', *Addictive Behaviors*, 36(12), 1313–1316.

The article is based on individuals as the unit of analysis. It presents a survey based on a nationwide representative sample consisting of 41,886 students in grades 9–12 in Canada. The article is focused on the students' access to cigarettes, examining differences between those who get cigarettes from friends, family members or others (social sources), and those who buy cigarettes in stores (retailer sources). The analysis shows that 'youth can undermine retailer restrictions to obtain cigarettes through social sources' (Vu et al., 2011: 1316).

STUDENT EXERCISES AND QUESTIONS

1 Why is it important to make source-critical assessments?

2 What are the most important differences between qualitative and quantitative studies as to selection of information?

3 Why is it important to distinguish between different levels of measurement for variables?

4 What is an index?

5 Why are social media interesting and challenging as new sources for data in social research?

6 Specify some important dimensions for a qualitative study of working conditions among male and female employees at a hotel.

7 Specify some important variables for a quantitative study of working conditions among male and female employees at a hotel.

RECOMMENDED LITERATURE

Bishop, Libby, and Arja Kuula-Luumi (2017) 'Revisiting qualitative data reuse: A decade on', *Sage Open*, 7(1).

This article points out that secondary analysis of qualitative data has been increasing, and the authors discuss several factors that may explain this growth, including better infrastructure for data sharing in social science. The breadth and diversity of data reuse in qualitative studies are illustrated by research examples. The article is mainly focused on developments in the UK, but it also provides some discussion of the international environment.

Corti, Louise (2012) 'Recent developments in archiving social research', *International Journal of Social Research Methodology* 15(4), 281–290.

This is an article about the availability of data for secondary analyses in social science. It is focused on recent developments in archiving data for reuse, including archiving qualitative data, safe access to disclosive data (data where specific individuals may be identified), institutional data archives, and the emergence of 'new' types of data.

Lazer, David, and Jason Radford (2017) 'Data ex machina: Introduction to big data', *Annual Review of Sociology* 43, 19–39.

This article discusses the characteristics of big data and the potentials for using big data in social science, as well as some trends in the use of such data. Furthermore, potential problems in using big data for research are pointed out, the need for institutional clarification of ethical rules is emphasized, and some trends in the use of big data are described.

SAMPLING

This chapter provides the knowledge of sampling that is necessary for understanding and assessing how various types of samples are used in qualitative and quantitative studies, as well as for choosing adequate samples for new studies.

The chapter will teach you how to

- distinguish between population studies, sample studies and case studies
- use the research question to choose an adequate sample in a study
- determine the appropriate sample size in different types of studies

- use different types of samples for statistical or theoretical generalization
- combine elements from different sampling methods in multi-stage probability samples or in more flexible strategic samples.

Universe, samples and generalization

In Chapter 7 it was pointed out that the units of analysis in a study are the social units or elements in society which are emphasized in the research question and in the analysis of the data. Different types and levels of such units were discussed.

Furthermore, it was pointed out that the units of analysis may be different from the units of observation, which are the key elements in the collection of data. In some studies, it is not possible to conduct direct empirical examination of the units of analysis. If we wish to examine differences between hospitals regarding patient assessments of the treatment options, the units of analysis will be the individual hospitals, but the empirical investigation of the patients' assessments of the various hospitals must be based on the individual patients as units.

The units of observation are the units that are directly investigated. In this example, the unit of observation is different from the unit of analysis. The hospital as a whole is the unit of analysis, while the individual patients are units of observation. In many studies, however, the unit of analysis can be investigated directly. The two units will then coincide. The unit of analysis is also the unit of observation.

The specific selection of units for a particular empirical study is based on the unit of observation, regardless of whether it is different from the unit of analysis or whether the two units are identical. The term 'unit of observation' is used for all types of research designs, not only for observation of actors, but also for questioning respondents and analysing the content of documents.

The process of selecting units for a study is called *sampling*, and the final selection of units for the study is called a *sample*. This chapter deals with different types of samples and different methods for sampling in social science studies. First, the characteristic features of different types of samples are described, and it is pointed out what kinds of samples are used in different types of studies. Then different sampling methods will be reviewed, focusing on four methods for probability sampling and four methods for strategic sampling.

Universe and sample

The research question provides the basis for clarifying the types of units to be included in the study and the levels that these units refer to. In addition, the research question usually contains a more detailed description of which units the study should provide knowledge about. A research question concerning networks between Norwegian companies limits the units of observation to companies in Norway. The study will not aim to contribute to knowledge about, for example, other organizations in Norway or companies in other countries.

The set of all the units that the research question applies to is called the study's *universe*. Another term is *population*, which is used synonymously with universe, especially when the units are actors. In the example above, Norwegian companies are the universe of the study. This must be understood as the set of all Norwegian companies. By rewording the research question, this universe can be expanded to, say, Scandinavian companies, or narrowed to, say, large Norwegian companies.

The universe of a particular study consists of all the units covered by the study's research question. The purpose of the study is to investigate the research question in the best possible way. The study must therefore aim to obtain knowledge that applies to all the units in the universe specified by the research question. In other words, the universe includes all the units that may potentially be included in the study.

The development of computer technology has gradually made it possible to collect, store, process and analyse very large amounts of data. Such *big data* studies may include individual information about the entire population based on records of health, income, taxes, consumption, education, employment and other details. Big data studies could also include all posts in Facebook and other social media for different periods, or all the images and videos from surveillance cameras in different locations and during different time periods. In such studies it is technically possible to include all the units in the universe, even when the universe is very large.

Nevertheless, it is very common for social science research to include only some of the units that are part of the universe, especially when the universe is comprised of a large number of units. Even with the new technological capabilities for big data studies, it can be very complicated and challenging to handle empirical investigations of all the units in a large universe. Many important research questions in social science also require information about the units that cannot be generated from existing registers or media. Studies that cover the entire universe can therefore be very costly. Quite often, the study only includes a sample of units in the universe. Such studies are called *sample studies*.

In sample studies, we only obtain direct information about a portion of the units in the universe, but this information is usually assumed to be valid for the entire universe. Based on the information about the selected units, we draw conclusions about the entire universe. In other words, the information about the sample forms the basis for more general knowledge. Drawing conclusions from the sample to the universe is therefore called *generalization*.

There are different procedures for generalization, each of which requires a specific type of sample and a specific method of sampling. An overview of different *sample types* in social science studies is presented in Table 8.1. As the table shows, we distinguish between five types of samples. For each sample type, it will now be discussed what types of studies, data types and generalization methods are typical for the sample type, how many of the universe's units are investigated, how much information about each unit is included in the study, as well as how large the universe and the sample usually are.

Population studies

Some studies include all the units in the universe. The sample of units is then identical to the universe. Such studies are usually called *population studies*, especially when the studies are based on actors as units.

Table 8.1   Overview of different types of samples in social science studies

Characteristics of the use of the sample type	Sample type				
	The sample equals the universe	Pragmatic sample	Probability sample	Strategic sample	Strategic selection of case
Study type	Population studies	Exploratory studies (pilot studies)	Theory-testing sample studies	Sample studies for theory development or holistic understanding	Case studies for theory development or holistic understanding
Data type	Qualitative or quantitative data	Qualitative or quantitative data	Quantitative data	Qualitative data	Qualitative data or combination of qualitative and quantitative data
Generalization method	Generalization not relevant	No systematic generalization	Statistical generalization	Theoretical generalization	Theoretical generalization (or no generalization)
Units included in the study	Entire universe	Sample of units	Sample of units	Sample of units	Focus on one unit
Amount of information about each unit	Varies	Varies	Relatively little	Much	Much
Size of the universe	Varies	Varies	Large	Varies, but often small	Small (or equal to the focused unit)
Size of the sample	The sample equals the universe	Varies	Large	Small	One unit

A national census is an example of a population study, where certain types of information are collected for all citizens of a country. All the citizens receive a questionnaire with a number of questions on, for example, gender, age, education, occupation, income, family and housing situation. Although the amount of information about each citizen is very limited, such a census is very resource-intensive. It has therefore been unusual to carry out such extensive population studies, especially when it is necessary to collect new data about all the units. However, as mentioned above, advances in computer technology have made it possible to generate and analyse big data about a large universe based on information contained in various registers, social media or other sources.

Sometimes the universe is so small that it is relatively straightforward to study all the units. This is the case, for example, if the research question is about the lower secondary school pupils in a small municipality or about the arguments in a specific, time-limited series of debate programmes about the EU on a specific television channel.

Population censuses and other population studies of large universes are based on quantitative data and must usually be limited to relatively little information about each unit. Population studies of small universes, on the other hand, are usually based on qualitative data and may include relatively large amounts of information about each unit. In general, the greater the universe, the more limited the amount of information for each unit.

Since population studies cover the entire universe, it is not relevant to make generalizations of the results of the analysis.

Pragmatic samples

Some sample studies are conducted without the purpose being to draw conclusions about the universe as a whole. The study is not intended to achieve any systematic generalization. Therefore, the sample of units is not composed or constructed in such a way that it provides a basis for systematic generalization. The units are often chosen in a pragmatic or discretionary manner. This sample type can be termed a *pragmatic sample*.

The purpose of such studies may be to perform a simple and preliminary study of an area where there is little previous research. Such a study can provide new insights, which can then provide the basis for designing more precise research questions. The study can also provide methodological experience that can be used to develop better and more comprehensive designs for later studies. Such preliminary studies are called *exploratory studies* or *pilot studies*.

Exploratory studies are often based on qualitative approaches. Typically, such studies are based on relatively small samples, although the size of the universe may vary. Regardless of whether the universe is large or small, it may suffice to have a sample that is large enough for the study to reflect the breadth of the activity being studied and capture important variations in this activity. If the intention is, say, to conduct an exploratory study of new forms of organization for hospitals, the sample should be large enough to obtain experience and insight regarding, for example, different departments, different professions, different job categories and different patient groups.

Exploratory studies can also be based on quantitative designs. The purpose of quantitative exploratory studies could be, for example, to test different methods for collecting quantitative data.

Another purpose of such studies may be to provide a very broad overview of certain social conditions, such as the extent of the use of medicine in different groups in the population, which can provide a basis for more in-depth, but also more limited studies in the next round. Such exploratory studies are based on a large universe and are preferably based on a large pragmatic sample.

Probability samples

As mentioned above, generalization is a common purpose of sample studies. The purpose is to use the information about the sample to draw conclusions about the entire universe. We distinguish between two main types of generalization: statistical generalization and theoretical generalization. These two types of generalization are very different. They are based on different logical principles and have different consequences with regard to sample size.

Statistical generalization is based on probability theory and is used in quantitative studies, often with a view to testing hypotheses or theories. For such generalization, the differences between the sample and the universe will in principle be due to chance. Using probability calculations, we can estimate how large these random differences will be, given different assumptions about how accurate and how reliable we want this estimate to be. For example, we could think of a poll on attitudes regarding Norwegian membership of the EU, based on a sample of 1000 people in Norway. If we find that 51% of the sample are in favour of EU membership, we could estimate with 95% certainty that support for EU membership within the population would be somewhere between 47.9% and 54.1%. We could then be fairly sure that EU supporters represented about half of the population, but we could not know if they represented a small majority or a large minority.

The assumption for such calculations is that the sample is a *probability* sample of the population. A *probability sample* is defined as a sample where all the units in the universe have a known probability of being included in the sample, and where this probability is greater than 0 (no unit is excluded from the sample) and less than 1 (no unit is guaranteed to be included in the sample). If the 1000 units are drawn randomly from a population of 4 million, each unit will have a probability equal to 1000/4,000,000 (= 0.00025) of being included in the sample.

The statistical generalization from this sample to the population regarding support for EU membership is then based on the size of the purely random differences between the sample and the universe. Calculations of these random differences make it possible to estimate, with 95% certainty, that support among the population will be a maximum of 3.1% lower or a maximum of 3.1% higher than the support demonstrated by the sample. Statistically speaking, the support is 51% ± 3.1%. This interval (±3.1%) is called the *confidence interval* but is also referred to as the *statistical margin of error*. The 95% certainty entails that there is still a 5% probability, or *risk*, that we will be wrong when we operate with this confidence interval. There is a 5% probability that those in favour of the EU nevertheless account for less than 47.9% or more than 54.1% of the population. This probability is often expressed as $p < 0.05$ and is referred to as the *significance level*. The difference between those in favour of the EU (51%) and those opposed to the EU (49%) in the sample will not be statistically significant at this level, because it may be due to random differences between the sample and the population.

In this case, the sample size depends on the *precision* of the conclusions we want to draw about the universe from the sample, and how *certain* we want to be about our conclusions. If we want to increase the level of precision, such as reducing the confidence interval to ±2.5%, we must either reduce the certainty or increase the sample size. If we want to increase the certainty, for example to 99% ($p < 0.01$), we must either reduce the precision level (i.e. expand the confidence interval) or increase the sample size. The question of the size of the sample is usually settled before data collection starts.

Chapter 19 will present a more thorough discussion of various types of statistical generalization based on probability theory. What we have highlighted here illustrates the assessments that can be made in connection with the size of the sample.

Firstly, it is important to be aware that probability theory and probability calculations mainly apply to relatively large numbers. Probability samples are therefore comprised of relatively many units, usually at least 100, and often many thousands.

Secondly, the sample is still significantly smaller than the universe. Probability samples are used primarily when the universe is particularly large. If the universe itself is not much larger than the sample, there is little to gain from probability sampling and statistical generalization compared with a study of the entire universe.

Thirdly, we can increase the precision or certainty of the generalization by increasing the sample size, but the increase in size must be relatively large to achieve substantial gains in this way. At a given level of significance, we need to quadruple the sample size to halve the confidence interval.

Fourthly, it is primarily the size of the sample that affects how precise and certain are the generalizations that can be made. The size of the universe plays a smaller role, especially when the universe is large and when there is a large difference between the size of the universe and the size of the sample.

Strategic samples

Theoretical generalization is not based on statistical calculations but refers to theoretical understanding of the social conditions being studied. This type of generalization is used in qualitative studies. The purpose of studying a sample of the units referred to in the research question is not to draw conclusions about specific characteristics of the various units in the universe, or about the distribution of different characteristics of the individual units in the universe. Theoretical generalization is based on completely different purposes.

Two such purposes are particularly important. One purpose is to use the study of the sample to develop concepts, hypotheses and theories that, based on theoretical reasoning, are assumed to apply to the entire universe of units. Many important and well-known social science concepts, such as *social networks* and *street corner society*, have been developed on the basis of qualitative studies and theoretical generalization. This approach is often referred to as *analytical induction* and plays a central role in a type of empirically based theory known as *grounded theory*, which is discussed by Glaser and Strauss (1967). Generally, such qualitative studies can be characterized as theory-generating studies.

The second purpose of theoretical generalization is to study selected units in order to develop an overall or holistic understanding of the larger group or the context that these units form together. This holistic understanding is not limited to the collection of units included in the sample itself. Based on theoretical assessments, the holistic understanding is also assumed to apply to the overall context that encompasses the entire universe. This approach is common in anthropological studies and may be intended, for example, to obtain a comprehensive understanding of a narrowly defined local community.

Such theoretical generalizations are not based on probability samples but are based instead on *strategic samples*. Such samples are sometimes called *non-probability samples*, because the sampling is not based on the randomness principle. However, here these samples will be referred to as strategic samples, since the sampling is based on strategic and

systematic assessments of which units are most relevant and most interesting from a theoretical and analytical perspective. Thus, these samples are distinguished from other non-probability samples that are not strategic in the same sense, such as pragmatic samples.

To exemplify the kinds of systematic assessments involved in strategic sampling, we may think of a study of patterns of interaction in a hospital. Each interaction (between two or more persons) can be the unit, and the universe can be defined as all interactions (all interaction units) during a certain period of time, such as a month or a year. The interaction units that are studied can be divided into different types of interaction based on particular characteristics, such as how long the interaction lasts, where it takes place, what actors are involved, and what the interaction is about.

If the study is intended to develop a comprehensive understanding of the social interaction at the hospital, it is appropriate to conduct theoretical generalization based on strategic sampling of the interaction units to be studied. Based on theoretical insight, empirical knowledge and methodological experience from previous research, we can consider how to do the sampling, such as how to choose typical interaction situations and typical forms of interaction, and how to ensure that the sample covers the full range of different types of interaction. As we study more and more selected interaction units, we will also gain further insight and thus a better basis for strategic assessments of how the sample should be expanded and improved, constantly aiming to develop as comprehensive an understanding as possible. Such a comprehensive understanding is not limited to the characteristics of each single unit of interaction. We should also explore how different interaction situations develop in relation to each other and how together they form longer interaction processes. This requires a flexible sampling of units, in the sense that strategic assessments along the way lead to ongoing reviews of which units should be included in the sample.

If the purpose of the study is to develop more specific concepts, hypotheses or theories about specific aspects of this interaction, the sampling is done essentially in the same way, based on strategic assessments and with the aim of performing a theoretical generalization. However, in this case, the sampling is more concentrated on interaction situations that are particularly relevant to the theoretical concepts and the relationships to be developed. For example, the study may place particular emphasis on the relationship between status differences and forms of interaction. Eventually, the study could form the basis for two possible hypotheses – that the greater the status differences between the involved actors, the more conflictual the interaction will be, and that the lower the status of the involved actors, the more conflictual the interaction will be. The strategic sampling of units would then increasingly be targeted towards interaction situations that are relevant for these hypotheses. It is important to find a larger number of different interaction situations that support the hypotheses, but it will eventually also entail an increasingly intensive pursuit of situations and conditions that may deviate from the hypotheses, because this will provide a better basis for assessing the hypotheses and will clarify the range and limits of their validity.

In theoretical generalization and strategic sampling, there are no methods for calculating how large the sample should be in terms of precision and certainty for the conclusions we draw about the universe. The sample size is also determined on the basis of strategic assessments. An important criterion for these assessments is that the sampling can be terminated when the inclusion of new units in the sample does not provide significant information that is both relevant to the problem to be addressed and new compared to the information that the previously selected units have contributed.

This situation is usually referred to as a *theoretical saturation point* for the sampling of units (Glaser & Strauss, 1967). Just as the development of the specific study gradually provides a basis for new assessments of which units should be selected, it is experience from data collection and data analysis that shows when the theoretical saturation point has been reached. Unlike statistical generalization, theoretical generalization therefore implies that the sample size cannot be determined in advance before data collection takes place.

In a qualitative interview study of participants in a support programme for parents of preschool children in Sweden, Rahmqvist et al. (2014) initially recruited 18 parents, including 3 fathers and 15 mothers, for their strategic sample. During the study, three of the parents could not be reached by the researchers, and two of the parents declined to be interviewed, so that the sample size was reduced to 13. However, after interviewing only 10 parents, the researchers concluded that the data had reached saturation, so there was no need to contact the last three parents that had been recruited for the sample. Thus, the final sample used in the analysis consisted of the 10 respondents that were interviewed (Rahmqvist et al., 2014: 936).

Compared to probability samples, strategic samples are usually relatively small. While probability calculations and statistical generalization require large numbers, theoretical generalization is based on completely different assumptions. The universe may vary in size, but the universe is also usually smaller in studies based on strategic sampling than in studies with probability sampling.

Although strategic samples are usually relatively small, the size may vary greatly from study to study, from less than 10 units to several hundred or more. The size of the sample will depend on the type of conditions being studied. The more extensive and complex these conditions are, the larger the sample must be before the theoretical saturation point is reached. When the purpose is to develop an overall understanding of a particular context, it is the size and complexity of this context that will determine the sample size. When the study is intended to develop concepts, hypotheses and theories, the sample size must also be adapted to the complexities and variations in this conceptual or theoretical framework.

The fact that strategic samples are smaller than probability samples is also due to more practical and resource-related issues. How extensive a study can be before it becomes too difficult to handle or too costly depends not only on how many units the study includes, but also on how much information is gathered about each unit. As more units are included in a study, less information about each unit can be processed. The more information gathered about each unit, the fewer the units that can be included.

Case studies

As this review shows, social science studies can differ greatly in terms of how many units they include. A particular type of study restricts itself to just *one* unit. Such studies are referred to as *case studies*.

Like qualitative studies based on strategic samples, case studies can have different purposes. One such purpose is to develop a comprehensive or holistic understanding of the one unit being studied. This unit is considered to be unique and of scientific interest in itself, without necessarily being considered as part of a larger universe. In principle, the study's universe is limited to the unit, or case, being investigated.

Another purpose of case studies is to develop concepts, hypotheses or theories. These case studies are usually based on theoretical generalization to a larger universe. The single unit being studied is regarded as a very typical unit within this universe (Tight, 2017).

Theoretical generalization is especially common in comparative case studies, which are based on systematic comparison of two or more units within a larger research design. The sample of units is based on strategic assessments of which comparisons are particularly interesting and useful considering the conceptual and theoretical problems to be addressed in the study. Although the overall research design covers more than one unit, such designs are regarded as case studies because the individual units are initially studied separately. However, they are studied in such a way that the results of the analysis for the various units become comparable.

Peter M. Blau's bureaucracy study, which was presented in Chapter 1, is an example of a case study. Blau (1963) studied two units, a government agency at the state level and a government agency at the federal or national level. He used exactly the same methods in the studies of both offices. His intention was not primarily to compare the two units, but, by choosing two different types of offices, he obtained a broader empirical basis for the concepts and overall understanding he developed. Comparative studies based on comparison of different cases will be further discussed in Chapter 22.

Case studies are often based on qualitative approaches, but can also combine qualitative and quantitative data, as Blau did in his bureaucracy study. Case studies are usually very intensive studies that include a lot of information about the unit being studied.

The most common units in case studies are relatively complex but nevertheless clearly defined units at the meso level, such as different types of organizations or specific local communities. Within such a complex unit, there are often different types of subunits, such as actors, actions, opinions and events at the micro level. In principle, the case study's unit of analysis at the meso level (the case) can be considered a universe in relation to all of these subunits at the micro level. Thus, to some extent, the case study can be based on strategic samples of subunits, and theoretical generalization from these samples to the universe, which consists of all these subunits within the whole case.

Sample size: Considerations on methodology and resources

Based on Table 8.1, different aspects of five different types of samples have been discussed. Overall, there is a major difference between relatively large probability samples with relatively little information about each unit, and relatively small strategic samples with relatively large amounts of information about each unit. Probability samples are typically used in quantitative, theory-testing studies intended to perform statistical generalization for large universes. The typical use of strategic samples is in relation to qualitative, theory-generating or holistic studies intended to perform theoretical generalization for small universes.

The reason why probability samples must be larger than strategic samples is that there are fundamental differences between the two methods of generalization. Statistical generalization requires many units, while theoretical generalization requires a great deal of information about each unit. These methodological differences are usually considered in connection with considerations on resource constraints for social science studies. Due to such resource constraints, quantitative studies must be limited to relatively little information about each unit, because they, for methodological reasons, have to include many units, while qualitative studies must be limited to relatively few units, because they, for methodological reasons, have to include much information about each unit. Quantitative studies designed for statistical generalization are referred to as *extensive*, while qualitative studies aimed at theoretical generalization are described as *intensive*.

This trade-off between the number of units and the amount of information per unit not only affects the size differences between strategic and probability samples. It is also important for assessing how large a strategic sample we should have in a particular qualitative study, or how large a probability sample we should have in a given quantitative study.

Simply put, methodological assessments are critical for how large the sample must be, while resource considerations determine how large the sample can be. However, the methodological assessments are more important than the resource assessments. Methodological assessments determine how large the sample must be *as a minimum,* and which methodological benefits can be obtained with different increases in the sample size beyond the minimum limit. Resource considerations must be based on these assessments. If there are insufficient resources available for a sample that is large enough to be methodologically sound, there is no basis for conducting the study. If the available resources allow a larger sample than is methodologically necessary, the final sample size should be determined based on an overall assessment of the resource effort in light of possible methodological benefits.

Methods for probability sampling

Having discussed different types of samples, we will focus on how the specific sampling of units is done. Different sampling methods will now be reviewed, starting with methods for probability sampling, before moving on to methods for strategic sampling.

From universe to sample

All the methods for probability sampling require that the universe is defined, that the units in the universe can be identified, and that these units are available for sampling.

The definition of the universe is developed in connection with the clarification and operationalization of the research question. This was discussed in Chapter 4, as two of the four main tasks in the formulation of the research question. It was pointed out that we distinguish between theoretical and operational definitions of the various elements of the research question, including the universe of units covered by the research question.

The theoretical definition of the universe is a verbal or conceptual description of which units the universe comprises. This is a basic clarification of the types of units to be studied, the levels of the units, and the limits of the universe in time and space. The operational definition specifies how these units can be identified and located with regard to sampling and data collection. 'The adult Finnish population' is an example of a theoretical definition of a universe for a study, whereas an operational definition of this universe could be 'those persons aged 16–74 years who are registered at the Population Register Centre in Finland at the time of the study'. If we are to study networks and power structures in Swedish business, the universe can be theoretically defined as 'large Swedish companies'. An operational definition of this universe could be 'the 100 largest banks and the 200 largest companies in Sweden'. This operational definition can be further developed by specifying business-size criteria. The banks' size can be expressed in terms of total assets, and the size of the other companies can be determined based on annual sales. The operational definition can also specify that it is total assets and sales for the last year before the date of the study that will be used as the basis for defining the largest companies.

In addition to theoretical and operational definitions of the universe, we also need a more concrete overview of the units contained in the universe. Several of the sampling methods for probability sampling require lists of all the units, and in some cases it is also necessary to have an overview of location or other characteristics for each unit in the universe. This concrete basis for the specific sampling of the individual units is called the *sampling frame*. Based on the sampling frame, we can design a *sample plan* that describes the detailed procedures for the various stages in the sampling. If the universe is large Swedish companies, the sampling frame can be constructed from information available at the Companies Registration Office in Sweden. When the universe is the adult Finnish population, one of the best sampling frames will be the resident register, which is managed by the Population Register Centre. The sample plan will outline how this register should be used in the specific sampling process.

In recent years it has become increasingly common to conduct studies based on telephone interviews. These studies are usually based on the sampling of phone numbers, where the telephone directory is used as the sampling frame. In a study of lottery playing in Germany, Beckert and Lutter (2012) used landline telephone numbers for their sampling. This was taken into account in the definition of the universe of the study, which included 'every individual over 18 years of age residing in Germany and living in households with a landline telephone' (Beckert and Lutter, 2012: 1157–1158). Random digit dialling was used for the sampling of households, and within each sampled household the person who had the most recent birthday was selected for the final sample of individuals. The result was considered to be a probability sample of the individuals within the defined universe.

A few decades ago, using telephone numbers for sampling was a very problematic approach because there were many households without a phone. Although telephone ownership is now extremely high, the telephone directory can still be a problematic sampling frame. Many people have secret telephone numbers, and more and more people use mobile telephones rather than landline telephones, which is often the starting point for the sample. An increasing number of people have more than one telephone number and are therefore more likely than others to be included in the sample. The sample may also be biased because people who spend very little time at home have a smaller probability than others of being included in the sample of landline telephone numbers. Problems in distinguishing between telephone numbers of individuals and telephone numbers for companies and institutions can also lead to bias in the sample.

Even if telephone number sampling is targeted at mobile telephones instead of landlines, we still encounter many of the same issues. It is particularly important that many people may have multiple mobile telephones, that it is not easy to distinguish between private telephones and company telephones, and that a large number of telephone numbers are unregistered or secret. It is also increasingly common for children and young people to have mobile telephones, and they would be included in a sample based on telephone numbers, even though most such samples are limited to adults.

Although such conditions can create special problems when the telephone directory is used as a sampling frame, it is important to be aware that there are various problems and limitations associated with virtually any sampling frame. These issues may be large or small, and they may be of different natures, but regardless of the type of sampling frame used, it is necessary to assess what kinds of sampling bias such problems may lead to.

In probability sampling, the sampling of units is usually performed before data collection starts. It assumes that the universe of units can be identified independently of the current study, for example in the form of person registers or other lists, so that it is possible to establish a clear sampling frame. This is not always the case. For example, we may be interested in observing particular types of actions

while they take place. Then the universe and the sampling may be specified in terms of time and space. The universe may be defined as all actions of this type that take place within a limited time period and within a particular geographical area. Thus, the sample can be limited to, for example, all actions of this type that take place at randomly selected locations within the area and at randomly chosen times during the time period. The universe is predefined theoretically, and the sampling is based on a clear operational definition, but the units themselves are not identifiable before data collection commences. We cannot know exactly which actions will be performed. The units are identified at the same time as the data collection is performed. In this way, the final sampling can provide a basis for a more specific reconstruction of the universe after the data collection has been completed.

These assumptions regarding definition and clarification of the universe apply to all probability sampling. The specific sampling of units from the universe is usually done by computers and special sampling programs. However, there are different methods for probability sampling. Four such methods are described here. For each of these methods, the discussion is focused on the features of the sampling procedure, the assumptions upon which the method is based, as well as the particular possibilities and limitations associated with the method. A schematic overview of this is presented in Table 8.2.

Simple random sampling

One of the probability sampling methods is *simple random sampling*. This can be compared to a lottery. From a complete list of all the units in the universe, units are randomly selected one by one for the sample until the predetermined sample size is reached. If each unit is identified with a unique name, such as in a person register or in a

Table 8.2 Overview of different probability sampling methods

Sampling method	Procedure	Assumptions	Possibilities	Limitations
Simple random sampling	Random drawing from a list of all units in the universe	Unique sampling frame	Statistical generalization	Data collection costs
Systematic sampling	Sampling of every *n*th unit on a list of all units in the universe The first unit is drawn randomly from the *n* first on the list	Unique sampling frame No systematic cyclical patterns in the list of units	Statistical generalization	Data collection costs
Stratified sampling	The units in the universe are divided into categories (strata) according to their properties Random (proportional or disproportional) drawing of individual units within each category	Unique sampling frame Knowledge of certain characteristics of the units Weighting of findings for generalization from disproportionate sampling	Statistical generalization Increased precision or certainty Selecting enough units from small categories in the universe	Complexity of sampling Data collection costs
Cluster-sampling	The units in the universe are divided into clusters according to location Random drawing of entire clusters	Unique sampling frame Knowledge of units' location Large number of clusters	Statistical generalization Simplification of sampling Reduced costs	Reduced precision or certainty

list of businesses, the random draw can be made from among these names. When the universe is large, and the list of names is long, it will be easier to number the list from 1 up to the number corresponding to the total number of units in the universe list, and then draw random numbers from among these numbers so that the sample includes the units that correspond to the numbers drawn. In practice, this sampling is performed using computers and special programs for random sampling.

Simple random sampling assumes that we have a well-defined and well-operationalized universe, so that we can specify a unique sampling frame. In this case, this sampling method provides particularly good opportunities for statistical generalization, because the procedure ensures that there are only random deviations between the universe and the sample. On the other hand, simple random sampling may cause data collection costs to be high, because there may be large distances between the selected units. This is especially true if the universe has a large extent in space or time. A simple random sample of the population of a large country, for example, will result in a sample with a very wide spread of people from all parts of the country. If the data collection assumes that all these persons must be contacted where they live, travel and accommodation expenses could be very high.

Systematic sampling

Another sampling method for probability sampling is *systematic sampling*. This procedure assumes that the units in the universe can be listed or ordered in a clear sequence. For example, the sample may include every 10th unit on this list. In that case, the first unit of the sample will be randomly drawn from among the first 10 units on the list. If this randomly drawn unit is, say, no. 6 on the list, the sample will consist of the units 6, 16, 26, 36, 46 and so on. In general, we can say that a systematic sample includes every *n*th unit on a list of all the units in the universe and that the first unit is randomly drawn from among the first *n* units on the list. The number *n* is selected so that with a given size of the universe, we achieve a certain desired size of the sample.

This procedure assumes that the order between the units on the universe list is random, or at least that there are no systematic cyclical patterns in the order that can provide a systematically skewed sample. For example, if we select each seventh day from a calendar, the sample will consist of just one specific day of the week (e.g. only Sundays or only Wednesdays), no matter how many units we include. If we wish to study special actions on the selected days, such as work trips or purchasing activities, the results of the analysis can be greatly affected by the sample.

If the sampling frame is clear and the order between the units is random, systematic sampling will provide equally good opportunities for statistical generalization as provided by simple random sampling. On the other hand, the two sampling methods can also have similar constraints in the form of large data collection costs. The spread of the selected units can be equally large for both methods.

Stratified sampling

A third method for probability sampling is *stratified sampling*. The universe is then divided into several strata or categories based on particular characteristics of the units. If the units are individuals, for example, we can stratify based on gender, so that the universe is divided into one category consisting of women and another category consisting of men. From each of these categories, we can then draw a simple random or systematic sample of units. The total sample consists of the selected units from both categories. Stratification can also be based on combinations of different attributes, such as both gender and age, so the number of strata or categories may vary.

The stratified sample may be *proportional*. This means that the units from all categories in the universe have the same probability of being included in the sample, so that the distribution of units between the different categories is the same in the sample as in the universe. Alternatively, the stratified sample may be *disproportional*. In that case, the probability of being included in the sample is different for different categories, so the distribution of units between the categories is different in the sample than it is in the universe. Some of the categories are over-represented, while other categories are under-represented in the sample.

When we conduct a statistical generalization to the universe from such a disproportional sample, the results of the analysis for the individual categories must be *weighted*, so that the results for the under-represented categories are given greater weight in the generalization than the over-represented categories. The relationship between the weights for the different categories corresponds to the inverse relationship between the categories' probability of being included in the sample. If we have a disproportional sample stratified according to gender, where men have twice the probability of being included in the sample as women, then the analysis results for women should be weighted twice as high as the results for men when we generalize to the universe.

The purpose of stratification can be to increase the certainty or precision of the generalization. Through stratification, possibly in combination with weighting of the results, we ensure a good match between the sample and the universe. However, this only applies to the properties that form the basis for the stratification. For each of these attributes, the generalization will be based on the actual distribution of units in the universe. With regard to all other attributes of the units, the certainty or precision will not be affected by the stratification.

Another purpose of stratification can be to ensure that certain categories of units are sufficiently represented in the sample. If there are few units of a particular category in the universe, a simple random or systematic sampling may result in so few units from this category in the sample that it will not be possible to perform a meaningful analysis of these units. This can happen, for example, if we compare male and female nurses, or male and female board members in large companies. In such cases, it would be particularly useful to use a disproportional stratified sample, so that male nurses and female board members respectively are over-represented in the sample. We could thus obtain a large enough number of units from both genders to carry out comparisons, and the results of the analysis can be weighted when they are generalized to the universe. Stratified probability sampling assumes that we have an overview of how the units in the universe are distributed across the different categories on which the stratification is based, and that we know the position of each unit in relation to these categories. If we are to have a sample of people that is stratified according to age, we must have information about the age of each individual in the universe before the sampling is performed.

In the German study of lottery playing mentioned above (Beckert and Lutter, 2012), stratified sampling was used, distinguishing between persons who were lottery players and persons who did not play the lottery. The key category of lottery players was then over-represented in the sample, in order to make sure that the number of players would be sufficiently large in the analysis. There were approximately 66% more lottery players in the sample than in the universe. The proportion of players in the universe was estimated based on a separate pre-test, and the identification of lottery players in the sample was based on a question during the telephone sampling (Beckert and Lutter, 2012: 1158).

Stratified sampling can easily become quite complex, especially if we stratify based on multiple attributes or if we perform disproportional stratifications. The costs for data collection can also be as large as for simple random and systematic sampling.

Cluster sampling

The fourth main method of probability sampling is *cluster sampling*. Like stratification, this method involves grouping the units in the universe before performing the sampling itself. However, the grouping methods are different. In stratification, each stratum or category consists of units with the same attributes. In cluster sampling, the units are divided into clusters, where each cluster consists of units that are located physically or geographically close to each other. While stratified sampling is based on similarity between the units, cluster sampling is based on proximity between the units. If the universe is Canadian hospital patients, the patients at each hospital can be considered a cluster. If we wish to study the British Brexit debate in the major newspapers, the debate contributions in each newspaper could be a cluster.

In addition to the grouping methods being different, there is also another important difference between stratified sampling and cluster sampling. The two sampling methods are based on different approaches to selecting units after the universe has been stratified into categories or grouped into clusters. In connection with stratified sampling, we conduct simple random or systematic sampling of individual units within each category. For cluster sampling, however, entire clusters are selected in a simple random or systematic manner. The final sample may consist of all the units within the clusters selected, but it may also be restricted to units that are simple randomly or systematically selected within each of the selected clusters.

Cluster sampling is especially used when the universe is large and complex. The purpose may be to simplify the sampling process. The division into clusters reduces complexity and makes the universe more manageable. Another purpose of cluster sampling is to reduce the costs of data collection. The sampling of entire clusters reduces the physical or geographical spread of the units in the sample. Data collection can thus be concentrated into fewer areas. The cost-related benefits of such a concentration of data collection are particularly large and important in connection with interview surveys based on nationwide person sampling, where travel expenses for the interviews can be extreme.

On the other hand, the number of clusters must be relatively large, both in the universe and in the sample. This is a prerequisite in order to conduct statistical generalization based on probability calculations. Nevertheless, cluster sampling will still lead to a certain reduction in the certainty or precision of the statistical generalization, because we must expect that the random differences between the universe and the sample will be somewhat greater when sampling entire clusters than when sampling individual units.

Cluster sampling requires that we have an overview of where each unit is located in the universe, and how the units are located in relation to each other. If we wish to use municipalities as clusters in a cluster sample of the German population, we need to know how the population is distributed across the different municipalities, and we must have information about which municipality every individual in the population resides in. The number of residents in each municipality will form the basis for assessing both how many municipalities should be included in the sample, and how many people will be drawn from each of the selected municipalities. In order to carry out this person sampling, we need an overview of all the residents in each municipality, or at least in the municipalities that have been selected.

Multi-stage probability sampling

In practice, probability sampling can be based on various combinations of the four main methods. As we have mentioned, simple random or systematic sampling is an element or a separate stage in both stratified sampling and cluster sampling. We can also combine stratified sampling and cluster sampling, for example by carrying out stratification within each of the selected clusters. Such combinations, where different sampling methods are used in turn, are commonly referred to as *multi-stage probability sampling*.

Multi-stage probability sampling is often used when the universe is large and complex. When the sampling is divided into several different stages, the sampling in each stage becomes simpler and more manageable than a single sampling from the total universe would be. By combining different sampling methods, we can also take advantage of the various benefits and opportunities associated with the different methods. For example, a combination of stratified sampling and cluster sampling can *both* provide opportunities for specific categories of units to be sufficiently represented in the sample, *and* form the basis for cost-effective data collection.

Methods for strategic sampling

In qualitative studies based on strategic sampling and theoretical generalization, the sampling of units is not usually completed before the data collection, but during the study, in the course of the data collection and on the basis of preliminary analyses. The strategic or theoretical assessments underlying the sampling process are usually further developed through this process. As new units are selected for data collection and analysis, insights also develop regarding which additional new units would be strategically relevant and interesting to include in the sample.

This open process means that the sampling of units is more flexible than it is in probability sampling. Compared to probability sampling, strategic sampling cannot be planned as precisely before data collection begins, nor can it be based on such standardized methods and techniques. The sampling process is based on the approaches that gradually prove to be most appropriate based on the research question. This also means that it is common to combine different procedures in the same study.

Overall, the procedures for strategic sampling of units are less clear and less well defined than the methods for probability sampling. Nevertheless, we can identify some main types of procedures that are often used for strategic sampling. Four methods will be described and discussed in terms of procedures, assumptions, possibilities and limitations. Table 8.3 provides a schematic overview.

Quota sampling

One of the methods for strategic sampling is *quota sampling*. This procedure is based on specific categories of units to be included in the study, and it entails selecting a certain number of units (i.e. a certain quota) within each of these categories. The quotas could include, for example, five people in each of the four categories 'younger women', 'older women', 'younger men' and 'older men', or 10 interaction units in each of the three categories 'interaction between two doctors', 'interaction between a doctor and a nurse' and 'interaction between two nurses'.

The division of the units into categories means that quota sampling is similar to stratified sampling. In both cases, the category breakdown is based on strategic assessments. The difference between the two sampling methods is that quota sampling is not based on random sampling of units within each of the categories. Quota sampling of the individual units can be based on special strategic assessments, but may also be more pragmatic, for example depending on which units are the most accessible for the study.

Table 8.3 Overview of different methods for strategic sampling

Sampling method	Procedure	Assumptions	Possibilities	Limitations
Quota sampling	The units are divided into specific categories Selection of a certain number of units (quota) within each category	Strategic assessment of category divisions	Studies of typical features of different categories Development of typologies	The quotas are not based on theoretical saturation Limited insight into variations within each quota
Haphazard sampling	Sampling of the units that happen to be located in a particular place at a particular time	Strategic choice of time and place	Studies of range and limits for hypotheses or typologies	Possible bias due to special choice of time and place
Self-selection sampling	The sample consists of actors who volunteer to participate in the study	Strategic assessment of where and how the invitation to participate is disseminated, as well as who can be expected to volunteer	Sampling of actors who have a lot of information and a good ability to communicate it	Limited control over and information about who chooses to participate Possible over-representation of motivated, interested and outward-oriented actors
Snowball sampling	The first actor selected is requested to suggest other actors for the sample These are asked to propose additional actors, etc.	Strategic assessment of which criteria the actors' proposals should be based on	Studies of special network patterns Studies of areas where the researcher initially has limited insight	Limited insight into the actors' use of the criteria for proposals

The only fixed criterion for sampling is that the unit belongs to one of the defined categories. Whether the units within each category are similar or different in terms of other attributes may vary and is not necessarily subject to further consideration.

Quota sampling may be appropriate when we wish to study units that are thought to be typical in some context. It may then be appropriate to have relatively large quotas within relatively few categories, so that the typical attributes of these units are well developed. Quota sampling may also be relevant in studies intended to develop a typology, that is, a set of types that are systematically related to each other. We can then have more categories and perhaps fewer units in each category because it becomes important to capture the maximum variation between different types within the relevant typology.

In view of the theoretical saturation point criterion, which was discussed in connection with sample size, quota sampling may sometimes be a rather mechanical procedure. On the other hand, the size of the quotas can be changed during the process and adapted to new insights obtained by the researcher during the data collection and the first analyses. It can also be a problem that it is difficult to keep track of how the units vary within each category. It can therefore also be difficult to assess how the composition of the individual quotas can affect the analytical results. This problem is usually smaller when the researchers themselves select the units, than when the sampling is carried out by others.

Haphazard sampling

Strategic samples can also be based on *haphazard sampling*. This entails that we select the units that happen to be available in a particular place at a particular time. This could be, for example, those who are present at a special debate meeting on British membership of the EU, or it could be the arguments for and against British EU membership expressed at this special meeting.

For such sampling, we must take into account that it is not accidental who attends such meetings. Generally, those who are particularly interested in the theme of the meeting will be over-represented compared to other people. There could also be special circumstances associated with the meeting in question that affect who is present. If the meeting has only one speaker, and if this speaker is a significant and well-known EU supporter, there is reason to believe that EU supporters will be over-represented at the meeting compared to EU opponents. The same would be likely if the meeting took place in an area strongly dominated by EU supporters. This would also affect the meeting with regard to what arguments are presented. If the intention is to study the EU supporters and their arguments, these problems are naturally less than if the purpose is to study the EU debate in general or to compare supporters and opponents of British EU membership.

Thus, it is important that the choice of time and place for the haphazard sample is based on clear strategic assessments. By making such sampling at different locations and different times, we can systematically vary the conditions for which units are expected to be available. This can be done in order to obtain the most balanced sample overall. For example, we can carry out haphazard sampling of the participants at different meetings about the EU, so that some meetings can be expected to be dominated by opponents, while others can be assumed to be dominated by supporters. We can also try to find meetings where we can expect a more balanced distribution of supporters and opponents among the meeting participants.

However, haphazard sampling may also be used to establish strategic samples with a deliberately biased composition. The purpose may be, for example, to test the boundaries of a typology or the scope of a hypothesis. Then it may be necessary to select units that are extreme or marginal with respect to the particular typology, or which are deviating or peripheral with regard to the particular hypothesis. An example would be a hypothesis about a certain correlation between standpoint and argumentation in the EU debate, or, more specifically, that some ways of arguing are used only by EU *opponents*. It would then be especially interesting to study the argumentation among EU *supporters*. If we could find the same ways of arguing among them, we would have to reject or revise the hypothesis. Such a 'search for deviant cases' is a common procedure in qualitative analysis and will be discussed in more detail in Chapter 16.

Self-selection sampling

A third approach in strategic sampling is *sampling based on self-selection*. The starting point is that different actors receive information about the study to be conducted and that they are invited to participate in the study. The sample is established on the basis of the actors who volunteer to participate in the study. Since this sampling method assumes an active response from actors, it is usually these actors themselves who are the units in the sample. However, the units may also be actions, opinions or events that the volunteering actors choose to report.

Self-selection sampling is used, for example, for simple questionnaire studies. The questionnaire is made available in shops, schools or public offices, distributed on streets, published in newspapers or spread on the Internet. The questionnaire is accompanied by a request to complete it and deliver it or send it back to the researcher. Self-selection can also be used for more in-depth interviews or for participation in various types of experimental studies.

With this sampling method, the researcher has little control of who is included in the sample and also has little insight into who does not choose to participate in the study. It is important to decide strategically where and how the invitation to participate is distributed, and to consider who will be expected to be most motivated to participate. It may be people who are generally outward-oriented or who are seeking contact, people who are particularly interested in the theme of the study, or people who would like to present a particular message. This may lead to special biases in the sample, which may need to be offset by other sampling methods. However, in certain contexts and for individual purposes, self-selection sampling may be both relevant and effective as a basis for data collection. If we wish to study relationships and processes in a large company and we wish to obtain a first insight into the company's inner life as quickly as possible, it may be efficient to rely on self-selection. The most interested and most outspoken actors usually have a lot of interesting information to contribute and a great ability to communicate this information.

Snowball sampling

A fourth method for strategic sampling of units is *snowball sampling*. This is a form of sampling of actors that takes place in consultation with the actors themselves. The first actor selected is asked to propose a number of other actors who can also be included in the sample. These are in turn asked to propose additional actors for the sample. This process continues until the sample is considered large enough. From the one actor with whom the whole process starts, the number of actors increases rapidly, and the sample grows just like a small snowball that is rolled in wet snow. Like self-selection sampling, this sampling method assumes active involvement from actors, so that it is usually these actors who also constitute the sample of units. But here, too, the units can be actions, opinions or events that the actors provide information about.

It is important for the researcher to make strategic assessments of the criteria underlying the sampling of units. Therefore, as a rule, the actors will receive information about what they should emphasize when proposing new actors for the sample, even though the researcher has limited control and information regarding how the actors use these criteria. For example, the actors may be asked to propose their closest friends or others with whom they have a special relation. The sample will then consist of a specific network of actors, and if we select multiple start actors with different contact interfaces, the sample can be composed of different networks.

This procedure is especially appropriate if special network patterns are the subject of the study. But snowball sampling based on network connections can also be used efficiently for many other research purposes. Since such relations between the actors are a common starting point for this sampling method, the method is also called *network sampling*. Snowball sampling, however, is a more general and more suitable term because the actors' suggestions for new units for the sample are not always based on network relations. Instead, the actors may be asked to suggest people who they think would be particularly good informants for the study. Particularly in situations where the researcher has a limited overview or insight, it can be extremely valuable to utilize the actors' own assessments of who can contribute relevant and interesting information.

In general, sampling for qualitative studies may be very flexible, combining elements of different sampling methods. In the study of the Swedish support programme for parents, which was referred to above, the sample was based on a combination of self-selection and haphazard sampling (Rahmqvist et al., 2014). The first recruitment to the sample was done by means of fliers that teachers distributed at the participating preschools. Four parents responded to these fliers by signing up as volunteers for the study. This part of the sample is an example of self-selection sampling. Research assistants did the rest of the sampling by visiting the preschools and recruiting those parents who happened to be there at that time to pick up their children. This is an example of haphazard sampling (Rahmqvist et al., 2014: 936).

CHAPTER HIGHLIGHTS

- The set of all the units that the research question applies to is called the study's universe or population.
- In sample studies, we obtain direct information about only a portion of the units in the universe, but this information is usually assumed to be valid for the entire universe. Drawing conclusions from the sample to the universe is called generalization. We distinguish between statistical generalization and theoretical generalization.
- Studies can be based on different types of samples: we distinguish between samples that encompass the entire universe (population studies), pragmatic samples, probability samples, strategic samples, and a single unit (case studies).
- The sample size depends on methodological and resource-related assessments.
- There is a major difference between these types of samples:
  - large probability samples developed for quantitative data and statistical generalization
  - small strategic samples intended for qualitative data and theoretical generalization.
- Probability sampling requires a clear definition and delimitation of the universe, based on theoretical definition, operational definition and sampling frame.

- There are various methods for probability sampling:
  - simple random sampling
  - systematic sampling
  - stratified sampling
  - cluster sampling.

- There are various methods for strategic sampling:
  - quota sampling
  - haphazard sampling
  - self-selection sampling
  - snowball sampling.

RESEARCH EXAMPLES

I recommend that you read the publications used as research examples in this chapter.

Beckert, Jens, and Mark Lutter (2012) 'Why the poor play the lottery: Sociological approaches to explaining class-based lottery play', *Sociology* 47(6), 1152–1170.

The study presented in this article is based on a stratified probability sample, which was generated by random digit calling to landline telephone numbers. The stratification of players and non-players was established by means of a pretest and a question about lottery playing in the initial telephone call. The research question is focused on relationships between gambling and social stratification, and the analysis examines how lottery playing may be explained by socio-structural conditions, cultural values, and social networks.

Rahmqvist, Johanna, Michael B. Wells, and Anna Sarkadi (2014) Conscious parenting: A qualitative study on Swedish parents' motives to participate in a parenting program', *Journal of Child and Family Studies* 23, 934–944.

This article presents a qualitative study based on interviews with a small strategic sample of participants in a support programme for parents of preschool children in Sweden. Some of the parents were recruited by self-selection sampling, and the rest were recruited by haphazard sampling. The sample size was determined based on saturation of the data. The research question is focused on why the parents joined the support programme, what they thought about the programme, and how the programme related to their parenting philosophy.

Yang, Tingzhong, Ian R. H. Rockett, Qiaohong Lv, and Randall R. Cottrell (2012) 'Stress status and related characteristics among urban residents: A six-province capital cities study in China', *PLoS ONE* 7(1), e30521.

This article presents a quantitative interview study based on a five-stage probability sample of residents in large cities in China. In the first three stages, cluster sampling was conducted by selecting the capitals of six provinces, according to geographic location, followed by random selections of residential districts, neighbourhoods within each residential district, and blocks of buildings within each neighbourhood. In the last two stages, family households were randomly selected within each block, and one adult individual within each household was selected based on date of birth closest to the date of contact. The purpose of the study was to examine relationships between stress levels and sociodemographic characteristics. The analysis shows that the stress level in general is high, and that it is especially high among young people, as well as among the least educated and poorest people.

1 What is the difference between universe and sample?
2 What are the main differences between probability samples and strategic samples?
3 What are the differences between stratified sampling and cluster sampling?
4 What are the differences between stratified sampling and quota sampling?
5 Why do we distinguish between statistical generalization and theoretical generalization?

6 Discuss how the debate about climate change and global warming could be studied by using
   a different types of units
   b units at different levels.

7 Discuss how different types of samples could be used in a study of organizational activities among students at a university.

RECOMMENDED LITERATURE

Blair, Edward, and Johnny Blair (2015) *Applied Survey Sampling*. London: Sage.

This book presents a discussion of different sampling methods, mainly methods for probability sampling. Although it is focused on survey research, it is relevant to probability sampling in general.

Daniel, Johnnie (2012) *Sampling Essentials: Practical Guidelines for Making Sample Choices*. London: Sage.

The book presents principles of sampling and guidelines for choosing adequate samples for different studies. Samples are discussed in relation to censuses or universes, probability and non-probability samples are compared, and issues related to the selection of sample type and sample size are examined.

Marshall, Martin M. (1996) 'Sampling for qualitative research', *Family Practice* 13(6), 522–525.

This article compares sampling for quantitative research and for qualitative research, and it suggests different strategies for sampling in studies based on qualitative data.

PART III

DATA COLLECTION AND DATA QUALITY

The online resources are here to help with collecting data!

Visit https://study.sagepub.com/gronmo to access videos, case studies, key term definitions, and critical thinking exercises that will help you learn more about data collection and ensuring quality.

ETHNOGRAPHY AND PARTICIPANT OBSERVATION

This chapter provides the knowledge that is necessary for understanding how participant observation is used to collect qualitative data in social science. The chapter will enable you to carry out studies based on this type of data collection.

The chapter will teach you how to

- obtain access to the relevant field of the study
- find the most appropriate position and viewpoint for the observation
- get access and trust, and build good relations in the field
- develop a good balance between participation and observation

- handle typical problems during the data collection
- use online approaches in participant observation and ethnography.

Participant observation, field research and ethnography

As pointed out in Chapter 6, we may distinguish between six basic research designs, referring to collection of qualitative or quantitative data based on actors, respondents or documents as sources. In this chapter and the following five chapters, each of these research designs will be discussed. First, designs for collecting qualitative data are discussed in three chapters (9–11), followed by three chapters (12–14) on designs for collecting quantitative data. Then, in Chapter 15, which is the last chapter in this part of the book, it is discussed how we can assess the quality of the data used in various studies.

The purpose of this chapter is to discuss the typical design for collecting qualitative data based on actors as the source. The researcher collects data directly by observing actors, by looking at and listening to actors while they are acting or interacting, while they are expressing opinions, or while they are involved in various types of events. In order to be able to see and hear this, the researcher must be present in the actors' own context, where the actors are and when the relevant actions, expressions of opinion or events take place. Participating in the actors' own activities is often the best way to

be present. The researcher then becomes both a participant and an observer, and 'participant observation' is the most common term for this data collection design.

As pointed out in Chapter 6, this term may be used in both a narrow and a wider sense. In its narrow sense, the term refers strictly to the application of the observation method to collect qualitative data. This is the most common use of the term. In the wider sense, however, 'participant observation' refers to more comprehensive designs, in which observation is combined with other methods of data collection. Although observation is the main method, it may be combined, for example, with interviewing and content analysis of documents.

However, as suggested in Chapter 6, 'field research' is a better term for such comprehensive designs. Thus, in this book, the term 'participant observation' is used in its narrow sense, limited to the researcher's use of observation during the period of participation in the study context. This means that participant observation is the most important method of data collection in field research, which may be based on various combinations of data collection methods in addition to participant observation.

Also in ethnographic research, or ethnography, participant observation is the main method of data collection, although it is sometimes combined with other types. Whereas the term 'field research' is used in social science in general, ethnography refers more specifically to studies of cultures and cultural phenomena. Traditionally, ethnographic studies were conducted by Western anthropologists, focusing on more or less 'exotic' cultures far away. More and more, however, ethnography deals with cultures in all societies, including the researchers' own social environment, and the concept of culture is understood in a wide sense. Ethnography includes research on general patterns of action and interaction of participants in a particular context, as well as the meaning of these patterns for the participants themselves. Ethnographic research comprises holistic studies of social life in communities, institutions, organizations or other contexts. As a methodological approach, ethnography is a form of field research. Thus, ethnographic research is not only limited to anthropology. It is relevant to social science in general. Typically, research reports from ethnographic studies are comprehensive ethnographic descriptions, based on inductive and interpretive analyses of the whole variety of data collected in the study. Ethnographic descriptions will be discussed in Chapter 21.

This chapter deals with participant observation, as the basic design for using actors as the source in qualitative data collection, which is the methodological core of field research as well as ethnography. The discussion is focused on how to prepare and implement the data collection, and how to handle typical problems that may arise during the data collection. This discussion refers to Table 9.1, which presents an overview of the most important aspects of data collection in participant observation. After this presentation of the main elements of participant observation in general, some particular aspects of online approaches to this design are discussed.

Table 9.1   Overview of data collection in participant observation

Aspect of data collection	Characteristics of participant observation
Preparations for data collection	• Select field • Agree on access • Select position and viewpoint • Clarify the focus • Determine the degree of transparency • Ensure the safety of the researcher

Implementation of data collection	• Achieve acceptance and trust
	• Build field relations
	• Switch between
	  ○ different roles
	  ○ proximity and distance
	  ○ different perspectives
	  ○ data collection and data analysis
	• Use different types of field notes
	• Wind up the fieldwork

Typical problems during data collection	• The researcher may be completely or partially rejected • The perspective can be one-sided • The participation may affect the actors • The observation may affect the actors

Preparing the data collection

Since the researcher cannot predict what the actors will say or do, it is not possible to prepare detailed plans for the data collection before the participant observation starts. The study design is based on the researcher exhibiting a high degree of flexibility, openness and adaptability to new discoveries and experiences during the data collection itself. There are nevertheless some preparations that can and must be made before the observation is carried out.

Selection of the field

Firstly, the researcher must choose where the participant observation should be conducted. The area or place where the observation takes place is called the *field*, and the implementation of the participation and observation is therefore referred to as *fieldwork*. The field can be any context that is sufficiently demarcated and clear to allow participant observation to be carried out, such as a company or other organization, a hospital or other institution, a tribal society in Africa or a local community in Scotland.

In a specific study, the choice of field must be relevant to the research questions in the study. As highlighted in Chapter 6, Blau (1963) chose two government agencies as a field to observe the dynamics of bureaucracy, while Nielsen (2012) selected two local constituencies as an observation field in his study of a congressional election campaign in the USA.

Access to the field

Secondly, the researcher must obtain access to the field. This can involve both formal and informal access. It will usually be necessary to obtain authoritative permission to carry out the fieldwork in formal organizations or institutions. If participation in the field is to take place in the form of temporary employment, as was the case in the bureaucracy study conducted by Blau (1963), or through other participation in an organized business, this must also be performed in a formal or authoritative manner. In such cases, access to the field must be agreed with formal managers of the business to be observed. In other cases, access can be agreed more informally, but even then it may be necessary to contact leading actors within the field.

However, this is not always sufficient. Access to the field not only entails the researcher obtaining permission to be present as a participant. It must also be possible to get close to all the actors who will be observed. Therefore, it may be appropriate to gain entry and secure access to different groups of actors in the field. In organizations or contexts that are characterized by contradictions and conflicts, it may be particularly important to arrange access with different parties. When access is agreed with only one of the parties in a field characterized

by conflict, the researcher may be considered a representative of this party and may for that reason have problems obtaining access to other parties.

In general, access to the field must be agreed in different ways and with different actors, and such agreements will often require different types of negotiations. In a study of lawyers, Flood (1991) negotiated with different law firms about how to observe lawyers at work, before he was employed as a part-time associate in one elite law firm, where he could conduct a participant observation. In such negotiations, it may be useful to identify key individuals who have special opportunities to arrange access to different parts of the field and who can thus function as facilitators for the researcher.

Position and viewpoint

Thirdly, the researcher must choose their position as participant and thus their viewpoint as an observer. Within a selected observation area, it is usually possible to place oneself in different positions, for example in different departments in a hospital or among different groups of employees in an industrial operation. The perspective on what is to be observed will vary depending on the researcher's position as a participant. Operations in an industrial company can seem very different, depending on whether they are viewed from the workers' perspective on the shop floor or from the perspective of the officials or managers in the administration offices. The position and perspective that the researcher should choose in a specific study will depend partly on which positions are available, and partly on which perspectives are most relevant to the research questions in the study. After a period of time in the field, the researcher obtains a better basis for assessing which perspectives are most appropriate, and it may be relevant then to change the positioning that was initially chosen. As a rule, it is most fruitful to switch between different positions and perspectives during the observation period, if this is possible in practice.

Focus

Fourthly, the researcher must choose the focus for the observation. It is never possible to see and hear everything that occurs in the field at all times, no matter how delimited and clear the field, and no matter how centrally positioned the researcher. The researcher must therefore be selective with regard to what should be prioritized during the observation. It is essential to consider what is particularly important to observe.

On the other hand, the researcher must also be open and flexible in order to discover new, unforeseen circumstances as the observation develops. The focus of the study may therefore be both adapted, adjusted and sharpened during the fieldwork. Usually, the fieldwork starts out being relatively broad and general, and the focus of observation gradually sharpens during the observation period. However, it is important from the very start, during the preparations for the fieldwork, to focus especially on the conditions within the field that are most relevant to the research questions in the study.

Degree of transparency

Fifthly, the researcher must decide on the degree of transparency in the observation: how much information about the observation and the study to share with the actors observed. The degree of transparency in the study design can vary from complete openness to complete opaqueness. Those who are observed can get full information about both the observation and the purpose of the study, or they can be informed that the observation is taking place but without being informed of its purpose. However, both the observation and the purpose of the study can also be kept hidden for the actors in the field. The degree of transparency can also vary for different actors in the field, such that, for example, facilitators or other key people receive more information than other actors do.

In principle, there should be as much transparency as possible about both the implementation of the observation and its purposes. In the study of lawyers mentioned above, Flood (1991) gave full information to the law firm and its employees about his research as well as his roles as participant and observer. Also in the election campaign study, described in Chapter 6, Nielsen (2012) was open about his research and his roles. He studied personal communication in local election campaigns in the Democratic Party in the USA by observing campaign activities while participating in the campaigns.

The most common reasons for completely or partially concealing a participant observation are that full transparency could impair the researcher's ability to access the field, and that transparency could affect the behaviour of the actors who are being observed. These reasons apply especially to organizations keen to hide their operations from the outside world, such as Freemasons, and to illegitimate or illegal activities, such as economic crime. Participant observation that is wholly or partly hidden may breach important research ethics principles of transparency in research. It is particularly important, therefore, to consider how such studies can be conducted in an ethically sound manner.

The safety of the researcher

As pointed out in Chapter 3, research may sometimes involve personal risks and dangers for the researcher. In some studies based on participant observation there may be particular reasons for considering and ensuring the safety of the researcher. This depends on the type of field where the fieldwork takes place. For example, fieldwork in some criminal groups, extremist organizations, isolated communities, or hostile cultures may be dangerous, and the personal safety of the researcher may be threatened. In studies involving such potential risks, it is necessary to take precautions to ensure the safety of the researcher during the fieldwork. Thus, consideration of the researcher's safety is an important part of the preparations for the data collection in participant observation.

Implementing the data collection

As already mentioned, participant observation requires flexibility. Several of the choices and decisions made during the preparations will be re-evaluated and possibly revised during the fieldwork. This applies particularly to the early decisions regarding positioning and focus. Let us now take a closer look at what happens during the fieldwork and how the data collection is conducted.

Acceptance and trust

A prerequisite for performing fieldwork is that the researcher gains acceptance and trust among the actors to be observed. Becoming accepted and trusted will therefore be a key task in the initial part of the field visit. This work is based on the researcher's agreements regarding access to the field. Participation in the actors' activities means that the researcher comes into direct contact with the actors and that the researcher and the actors must interact in different ways.

Basically, the researcher will be an outsider who may also be regarded as an intruder. The researcher must reduce the actors' scepticism and suspicion. The researcher should try to stand out as little as possible from the environment and should choose clothing, behaviours and expressions that are as consistent as possible with the norms and practices of the actors to be observed. On the other hand, this imitation of the actors can go too far, so that the researcher acts in an obviously affected manner in relation to their own identity and may therefore appear to be insincere.

A question that often requires special attention is how the researcher's gender affects the ability to be accepted and gain trust. This will depend on the type of actors and the kind of activities to be observed, and it must be assessed specifically in each study. In some cases, it may be advantageous for the researcher to have the same gender as (the majority of) the actors, but there are also examples that certain male-dominated environments accept female researchers more easily than male researchers, and that some female-dominated environments find it easier to accept male researchers than female researchers.

The key to gaining acceptance and trust is often that the researcher emphasizes understanding the actors' own perspectives and relating to the actors' activities with humility and open interest. As a participant, the researcher is a beginner in the actors' activity, which is a reason to highlight the need to learn from the actors. On the other hand, as an observer, the researcher is an expert who may seem intimidating to the actors, because they have less knowledge of research or because they fear that the particular study could be used against them in some way. Another key to gaining acceptance and trust among the actors is therefore to explain to them what the research is about, and not least to explain the ethical foundation upon which the current study is based.

Building field relations

The effort to gain acceptance and trust is part of the more general development of field relations. The researcher enters into different relations with the actors in the field, both as a participant and as an observer. It is the development of such relations that forms the basis for acceptance and trust. The fieldwork, however, is a complex interaction with many different actors, where the relations with different actors can vary in both form and content. Fieldwork is also a dynamic process in which relations develop and change. Relations are not only developed. They can also break down. Maintaining and further developing the different field relations is therefore an important challenge throughout the data collection process. It will usually be necessary to relate in different ways to different actors, depending on the actors' backgrounds and characteristics, as well as their positions in the environment that is being observed. As a participant in this environment, the researcher will be located close to some actors, but at a greater distance from other actors. This will characterize the social relations with the actors. During the fieldwork, the researcher will become better acquainted with many of the actors and will also become more familiar with the social conventions and inner life in the environment as a whole. Relations will then become stronger, more intense and perhaps more intimate and emotional.

It is important that the researcher conducts a continuous and systematic assessment of such differences and changes in the field relations. A continuous and systematic assessment should also be conducted of how the field relations and their development could influence the data recorded during the participant observation. Based on such assessments, the researcher should control the development of the field relations so that they provide a good basis for observation, and so that they do not lead to emotional problems, stress, conflict or other difficulties for the actors or for the researcher. The strategies and tools that can be used to manage and develop the field relations with different actors will vary between different studies and different environments. As a rule, the long-term development of field relations can be based on the same approaches as the initial effort to gain acceptance and trust.

Switching between different roles, between proximity and distance and between different perspectives

In the development of different field relations, researchers must constantly evaluate their field

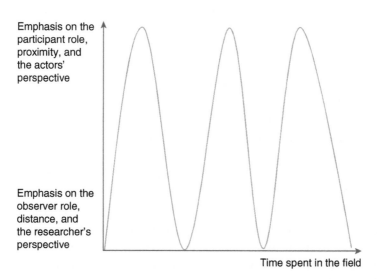

Figure 9.1 The relationship between the participant role and the observer role, between proximity and distance, and between actor perspectives and researcher perspectives in participant observation: switching back and forth during the fieldwork

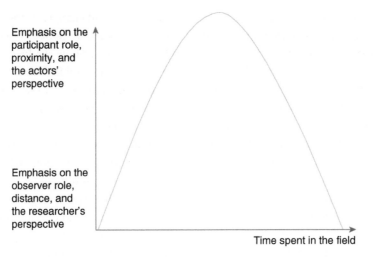

Emphasis on the
participant role,
proximity, and
the actors'
perspective

Emphasis on the
observer role,
distance, and
the researcher's
perspective

Time spent in the field

Figure 9.2 The relationship between the participant role and the observer role, between proximity and distance, and between actor perspectives and researcher perspectives in participant observation: typical development of the fieldwork as a whole

roles. Essentially, this will involve finding the right balance between the role of participant and the role of observer: how much emphasis should be placed on the role of the participant, compared with the role of observer? The balance that is most appropriate can vary from situation to situation. The balance between the two roles may also vary for different actors in the field. In typical fieldwork, the researcher will constantly combine the two roles, yet still switch between emphasizing the observer role and emphasizing the participant role. This is illustrated in Figure 9.1.

Furthermore, there is a typical long-term pattern in the development of the relationship between the participant role and the observer role during the fieldwork period as a whole. In the beginning, the researcher will be mainly an outsider and an observer, since it will take some time to become a full participant. As the researcher gets more involved in the participation, gets closer to the various actors, and learns more about the social life and the context, the role as participant becomes more and more important or dominant. Then, when the researcher obtains more experience and insight into the field, it will become necessary to

re-establish a more distant and analytical relationship to the environment, with emphasis on systematic and focused observation of selected phenomena. Thus, the participant role will be less important, and the observer role will be strengthened. This is illustrated in Figure 9.2.

As shown in Figures 9.1 and 9.2, the relationship between different field roles is associated with two other factors in fieldwork. This concerns the relationship between proximity and distance and the relationship between different perspectives. The fact that the observer role is more prominent in comparison with the participant role means that the researcher keeps a certain distance to the actors being observed. The actors are considered from the outside, from the researcher's point of view. This means that it is primarily the researcher's perspective that underlies the consideration and understanding of what is being observed. Placing the main emphasis on the participant role entails that the researcher's relations with the actors are characterized by greater proximity. The researcher relates to the participants through the interaction with them in a joint activity. The researcher and the actors share the same viewpoint. The actors are observed from within, from their own point of view. The researcher thus gets more opportunities to understand the actors' own perspective and to use this as a basis for interpreting what is observed.

Participant observation attaches great importance to both proximity and distance, as well as to the perspective of both the actors and the researcher. Proximity and the actors' perspective are often a prerequisite for discovering relevant conditions and, not least, for understanding the meaning and significance of different circumstances for the actors themselves. The researcher gains insights through empathy. The distance and the researcher's perspective are necessary in order to analyse and interpret the actors and their activities in a larger research context. Using a critical distance and an analytical perspective, the researcher reveals major empirical patterns and theoretical connections.

It is always a challenge in fieldwork to find the most fruitful balance between proximity and distance and between the actors' perspective and the researcher's perspective. The fieldwork will therefore often develop as shown in Figures 9.1 and 9.2. The researchers will constantly alternate between the observer role, distance, and their own perspective on the one hand, and the role of participant, proximity, and the actors' perspective on the other hand. At the same time, the fieldwork as a whole

will usually evolve as explained in connection with the various field roles. The first part of the fieldwork will gradually develop from major emphasis on the observer role, distance and the researcher's perspective, to steadily increasing emphasis on the participant role, proximity and the actors' perspective, while the final part of the fieldwork is characterized by the opposite trend.

Switching between data collection and data analysis

Data collection during participant observation occurs largely in parallel with data analysis. The researcher analyses the data as they are collected. Thus, the researcher develops insight into and understanding of the conditions observed. At the same time, the researcher also obtains better prerequisites for assessing how the data collection should be further developed, and what the observation should focus on in the fieldwork going forward. This results in a constant alternation between data collection and data analysis.

However, the relationship between the two tasks changes during the time spent in the field. There will be relatively little data to analyse in the early stages of the fieldwork, so that most of the time

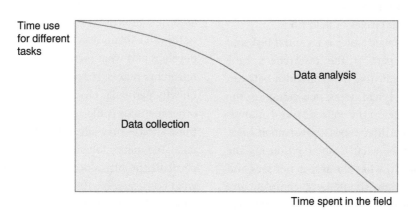

Figure 9.3 Typical development of the time distribution between data collection and data analysis during fieldwork in participant observation

will be used for data collection. As the fieldwork gradually develops and the data collection continues, the amount of data will increase, and the ongoing analyses of these data will become increasingly time-consuming. Therefore, the researcher will gradually use an increasing part of their time on analysis and a correspondingly smaller part of their time on data collection. In the final part of the fieldwork, the data analysis will take up most of the researcher's time, and the analyses will continue after the fieldwork is completed. During a typical piece of fieldwork, the distribution of the researcher's time between data collection and data analysis will therefore develop as illustrated in Figure 9.3.

Strategies and methods for analysing qualitative data, including data collected in participant observation, are explained in Chapter 16.

Field notes

Data recording during participant observation takes place by means of notes prepared by the researcher during the fieldwork. These notes are called *field notes*. Data can also be recorded in the form of audio or video recordings. Such recordings can be a useful supplement to the field notes, but they can never replace the researcher's written notes. The field notes constitute the study's data. In his study of election campaigns, Nielsen (2012) produced about 1000 pages of field notes.

The work on the field notes is a central task and occupies a large part of the researcher's time throughout the fieldwork. We distinguish between three main types of field notes, depending on the function of the notes in the collection and analysis of data. One of the three types is *observation notes*. These notes describe what is observed during the observation, that is, what the researcher sees and hears. The descriptions should be as complete and exhaustive as possible, with the most detailed account possible of what is happening, including details and nuances that the researcher notices.

In addition to the presentation of what actually occurred during a particular observation, the observation notes will also explain when and where the observation took place, which actors were present, how they were positioned in relation to each other, and what context or setting the actors and their activities were a part of. The notes will also provide a description of the researcher's position and viewpoint during the observation. The presentation in the observation notes is strictly descriptive, without comments, assessments, discussions or reflections by the researcher.

However, the researcher's discussions and reflections are expressed in the other two types of field notes. *Analytical notes* are used to explain the researcher's substantive analyses during the fieldwork. This may include assessments and interpretations of conditions observed during observation, a description of patterns or relationships revealed on the basis of the observation notes, a description of concepts or typologies developed during the fieldwork, or theoretical perspectives that can throw light on the conditions observed. During the fieldwork, as the data analysis gradually becomes more extensive, the analytical notes will become more extensive, more complex and more significant.

The third type of field notes, *methodological notes*, contains the researcher's discussions and assessments of the methods, practices or strategies used in connection with the data collection. The notes can explain how the participant observation develops and what methodological choices the researcher makes. Here, the researcher can reflect on why particular procedures were used, what other methods could have been used, and how these choices may affect the observation and the data. The methodological notes can show which particular problems occur during the fieldwork and what consequences this may have for the collected data. In these notes, the researchers can also reflect on the importance of their own role in the field and their relations with the actors observed.

The field notes should be written as close to the time of observation as possible, while the observations are still fresh. This applies to all types of notes, but it is particularly important for the observation notes, which should provide the most complete, accurate and detailed description possible of the actual circumstances observed. Based on this, it is best to work with the observation notes while the observation is ongoing. However, in many cases, this will not be possible. The researcher's note-taking may interfere with the activity observed and with the researcher's own participation in this activity. Working with notes may also cause the researcher to concentrate less on the actual observation and therefore reduce their ability to see and hear what is happening. Although it is possible for the researcher to take notes during the observation, this will usually be limited to preliminary, keyword-type notes that must be processed later or used as a basis for more comprehensive observation notes. During the fieldwork, therefore, the researcher must withdraw from the observation at regular intervals to work on the field notes. Particularly in connection with the observation notes, this must be done often enough so that the researcher remembers as much as possible of what has been observed since the previous notes were written.

Leaving the field

The last important task during the researcher's fieldwork is to wind up the field visit. Typically, the fieldwork lasts quite a long time. It often takes place over several months, and sometimes over many years. In the study of lawyers mentioned above, Flood (1991) was a participant observer for a year, working as a part-time associate in the selected law firm. In his study of election campaigns, Nielsen (2012) spent about 9 months in the field as a campaign worker and an observer. During such a long period, the researcher will develop many field relations. These may be strong and quite emotional relations with different actors in the environment being observed. For the sake of both the researcher and the observed actors, it is important that the field relations are scaled down or wound up carefully and in a proper manner. The researchers must prepare the actors for their withdrawal from the various relations and from participation in the actors' activities. In this connection, the actors must be informed of the researchers' further work so that they are not left with unrealistic expectations about the results and significance of the study or about how the findings will be followed up by the researchers.

Typical problems during the data collection

Fieldwork is a lengthy and complex process. Many problems can arise during such a process. Typical problems may be that the researcher is completely or partially rejected, that the perspective of the observation becomes too one-sided, or that the actors and their activities are affected by the researcher's participation or observation.

The researcher can be rejected in various ways. In a worst-case scenario, this may entail a complete exclusion from the environment. Access may be formally or informally withdrawn. The rejection can also be more limited. The researcher may be systematically kept out of certain types of activities in the environment or frozen out by individual actors. One reason why the researcher is completely or partially excluded is that the fieldwork develops differently than the actors or their managers expected.

The researcher's ability to prevent or possibly resolve problems in the form of exclusion is primarily related to the efforts to obtain access to the field, to be accepted and to win trust, and to maintain and further develop the various field relations.

Problems in the form of a one-sided perspective entail either that the observation becomes too strongly influenced by the researcher's academic and research perspective, or that the actors' perspectives become too dominant in the observation of the environment. The first possibility is called *ethnocentrism*, because the mode of observation is overly centred around the researcher's own culture. The second possibility is referred to as *going native*, which means that the researcher completely adapts to the culture of the environment's 'natives' in their understanding of the activities being observed.

Such problems can be prevented or solved by systematic and consistent switching between the roles of participant and observer, between proximity and distance, and between the actors' perspective and the researcher's perspective. It may also be important that the researcher switches between different positions and viewpoints during the fieldwork, and that the focus is sharpened as the fieldwork develops.

The actors can be affected by both the participation and the observation. They may react to the researcher's presence and the implementation of the study, and this may cause them to change their behaviour. Those who are studied are affected by the research taking place. As pointed out in Chapter 1, this is a general problem in social science studies and is referred to as *reactivity* or the control effect. A special feature of participant observation is that the researcher gets very close to the actors during the observation of their activities, and that this occurs while the activities are ongoing. The researcher and the research can therefore be particularly visible to the actors while they perform the activities that are being studied. As a participant in this activity, the researcher also becomes part of the environment being studied. All these factors can cause the actors to appear and act differently than they usually do.

Such problems can be counteracted by the researcher systematically developing their field relations in order to be as naturally integrated as possible into the actors' environment, and by providing the actors with good information about the research and the current study. It is important to emphasize the research ethics aspects of the study, with particular emphasis on privacy, such as ensuring the anonymity of the actors and the confidentiality of information about individuals. Generally, experience shows that the actors soon grow accustomed to the researcher and the participant observation, so that the control effect decreases gradually as the fieldwork progresses.

In general, the researcher must continuously assess how the data can be affected during the fieldwork, both by the conditions mentioned here and by other issues. These assessments must be taken into account when analysing and interpreting the data.

Online fieldwork in ethnography and participant observation

In conventional participant observation and ethnographic research, the researcher participates in face-to-face communication and interaction with the actors being observed. The field in which this communication and interaction occur, and where the actors' activities and interactions are observed, is a physical place or space. However, more and more interaction among actors are based on online communication rather than face-to-face communication. Such online communication is found in social media, in various discussion groups, or in other kinds of online forums. Some of this communication is developed in more or less stable networks of actors, and some of these communication networks may be regarded as online communities, where the participants share common interests, values, views or goals.

Increasingly, such communication networks or forums are active parts of society, with their own cultures and characteristics. As such, they are interesting fields for ethnography and participant observation. These fields are virtual, and the fieldwork is conducted online. The researcher may become a participant in the field by joining the online communication among the actors in the selected network or discussion forum, and this participation can be combined with observation of the ongoing communication in the network or forum.

Ethnographic research on online activity and communication has been called *netnography*. Kozinets (2015: 67) describes netnography as 'participant-observational research based in online hanging-out, download, reflection and connection. Netnographers use online and mobile data sources for social data to arrive at ethnographic understandings and representations of online social experience.'

Some online communication forums are open, which means that the researcher can join the forum like everybody else. Other forums are closed. Then the researcher may need special permission or membership of a group to be able to join the forum as a participant, and usually participation is necessary for observing the communication among the actors in a closed forum. If the selected forum is closed, the researcher may have to negotiate access to the forum as a participant.

Online participant observation may be overt or covert. In overt studies, the participation and observation are open and transparent. Typically, the researchers use the forum to introduce themselves as participants and observers, and to provide information on the study and its purpose. In covert research, there is no openness or transparency. The researchers join the forum and conduct their observation without introducing themselves and without providing any information about the study to the actors in the forum.

Typically, in open forums, covert participant observation is relatively easy to conduct, since the researcher can just join the communication in the forum. However, if the researcher deviates much from the actors in the forum, and if this deviation is revealed, the researcher's participation may be regarded as suspicious. In closed forums, where the researcher may have to apply for permission to participate, it is more difficult to conceal the identity as a researcher and the research intention of the participation. In any event, the researcher must usually give a plausible and credible reason to get access to the closed forum.

However, in order to conduct a covert study the researchers may hide their identities by constructing a fictitious person with characteristics that might be easily accepted as a participant in the selected forum, without having to give any further reasons for the participation. An example of covert participant observation is a study on the 'pro-ana' community by Brotsky and Giles (2007). This virtual community consists of a number of closed websites related to the eating disorder anorexia nervosa, often as non-judgemental environments or support sources for people with this eating disorder. The researchers created a fictitious person with characteristics that were identified as typical of members of the 'pro-ana' community. These characteristics referred to age, sex, height, eating disorder, and highest, current and lowest weight, as well as short-term and long-term goal weight. Using this fictitious person, the researchers gained access to 23 groups across 12 websites, 'including forums, chat rooms, blog sub-communities, online journal/diary sites, and e-mail group affiliations' (Brotsky and Giles, 2007: 98). Participant observation was conducted in all these groups.

Covert participant observation may be very controversial in terms of ethical considerations, including deception and lack of informed consent. These issues are thoroughly discussed by Brotsky and Giles (2007), whose justification for their covert approach is that the study is important and useful for the eating disorders clinical field, and that it could not have been implemented with an overt participant observation. Most likely, with an open approach the researchers would have been denied access to the 'pro-ana' websites.

The presence of the researcher as a participant and observer in a virtual online field is quite different from such a presence in a physical offline field. The researcher's presence may be less visible in an online field than it is in a physical field (Mann and Stewart, 2000: 89). Furthermore, whereas methodological and analytical field notes are important in both online and offline studies, empirical field notes may be less important and less challenging in online fieldwork, since the communication on the web is automatically recorded. In general, however, there are not many differences between physical and online fieldwork in participant observation. By and large, the characteristic features of participant observation, pointed out in Table 9.1, are relevant to both offline and online participant observation and ethnography. In principle, both types of studies are prepared and implemented in the same way, and the same types of problems may arise during the data collection.

.... CHAPTER HIGHLIGHTS

- Participant observation is the basic design for using actors as the source in qualitative data collection. This is the methodological core of field research and ethnography.
- In participant observation, the researcher is both a participant and an observer.
- Participant observation is a flexible design, but before gathering data, the researcher should select fields, arrange access, choose a position and perspective, clarify the focus and determine the degree of transparency.
- During data collection, it is important to gain acceptance and trust and to develop good field relations. The researcher alternates between different roles, between proximity and distance, between different perspectives, and between the collection and analysis of data.
- In participant observation, the researcher uses different types of field notes:
  1 Observation notes

  2 Analytical notes
  3 Methodological notes.
- When winding up the fieldwork and leaving the field, it is important to handle the field relations in a proper and careful way.
- The following problems are typical for data collection based on participant observation:
  1 The researcher may be rejected, completely or partially
  2 The perspective can be one-sided
  3 The participation may affect the actors
  4 The observation may affect the actors.
- Participant observation may be conducted online, for studies of communication and interaction in various online communities, which are found in social media, discussion groups or other open or closed online forums.
- Ethnographic research on online activity and communication is called netnography.

.... RESEARCH EXAMPLES

I recommend that you read the publications used as research examples in this chapter. One of these examples is a book about election campaigns in the USA, which was also referred to, and described as the *election campaign study*, in Chapter 6:

Nielsen, Rasmus Kleis (2012) *Ground Wars: Personalized Communication in Political Campaigns*. Princeton, NJ: Princeton University Press.

Another example is an article based on an ethnographic study of an American law firm:

Flood, John (1991) 'Doing business: The management of uncertainty in lawyers' work', *Law & Society Review* 25(1), 41–71.

This article refers to a study of an elite corporate law firm in Chicago, examining what the lawyers in the firm do. The researcher spent a year as a part-time associate in the firm. This participation in the firm was combined with observation of the lawyers' activities. The researcher collected data on more than 100 cases, based on his direct involvement and his access to files. Furthermore, he observed interactions among the lawyers in formal meetings as well as in informal discussions, and he observed discussions between lawyers and their clients in both meetings and telephone calls. The findings suggest that the main activity of business lawyers is to manage uncertainty for both their clients and themselves, and that this is done through interaction rather than appeals to the law.

A third example is an article on a covert online participant observation of a virtual community related to eating disorders:

Brotsky, Sarah R. and David Giles (2007) 'Inside the "pro-ana" community: A covert online participant observation', *Eating Disorders* 15(2), 93–109.

This article is based on a study of the 'pro-ana' community, which consists of several closed websites related to the eating disorder anorexia nervosa, often as non-judgemental environments or support sources for people with this eating disorder. By constructing and using a fictitious person with characteristics that were identified as typical for members of the 'pro-ana' community, the researchers gained access to several groups and forums on 'pro-ana' websites, in which they carried out participant observation. The article includes a discussion of ethical concerns with their covert participant observation, as well as a justification for implementing the study in spite of such ethical concerns. The research questions are focused on the meanings of interaction in this online community, and the findings suggest that 'the sites are best understood as local cliques offering temporary relief from offline hostility, but it is doubtful whether they can be said to possess any therapeutic value beyond the immediate online context' (Brotsky and Giles, 2007: 93).

STUDENT EXERCISES AND QUESTIONS

1 Describe the switching between different roles during a participant observation.
2 What kinds of field notes are used in participant observation?
3 Why is it important to avoid both *ethnocentrism* and *going native* in participant observation?
4 What is the meaning of netnography?
5 Why is reactivity (control effect) a problem in participant observation?
6 Discuss how participant observation could be used to study

    a interaction patterns in the editorial staff of a newspaper
    b collaboration and competition among students at a university.

7 Conduct a small study based on

    a participant observation in an organization where you are a member
    b online participant observation of an open discussion forum on the web.

RECOMMENDED LITERATURE

Angrosino, Michael V. (2007) *Doing Ethnographic and Observational Research*. Los Angeles: Sage.

This book presents an introductory overview of ethnographic research and participant observation. It includes practical advice for preparing and implementing the fieldwork in ethnographic studies, as well as for assessing ethical issues involved in this type of research.

DeWalt, Kathleen Musante, and Billie R. DeWalt (2011) *Participant Observation: A Guide for Fieldworkers* (2nd edn). Lanham, MD: AltaMira.

This book discusses participant observation as the foundation of ethnographic research. It is an introduction and a guide to doing participant observation, including discussions of online participant observation and ethics of participant observation.

Kozinets, Robert V. (2019) *Netnography: Redefined* (3rd edn). London: Sage.

This book is a guide to understanding and conducting online ethnography. In addition to step-by-step descriptions of how to do the online ethnographic research, the book presents ethical considerations in netnography, and includes examples from studies of social media and other types of big data.

UNSTRUCTURED INTERVIEWS
AND FOCUS GROUPS

This chapter provides the knowledge that is necessary for understanding how unstructured interviewing and focus groups are used to collect qualitative data in social science. The chapter will enable you to carry out studies based on this type of data collection.

The chapter will teach you how to

- construct a guide for the interviews or the focus group conversation
- use the guide in a flexible way during the data collection
- create good conditions for communication with respondents or focus group participants

- record the data obtained from respondents or focus groups
- handle typical problems during the data collection
- carry out online interviews or focus group conversations.

Personal interviews and focus groups

This chapter will consider the collection of qualitative data based on respondents as the source. The researcher asks the respondents questions about the conditions to be studied, and the respondents' answers constitute the data for the study. When this questioning is intended to produce qualitative data, the design is unstructured, informal and flexible. The design is referred to as *unstructured interviewing*. This type of data collection may also be called semi-structured, informal or qualitative interviewing, reflecting that the interviewing may be carried out in different ways.

Unstructured interviewing is a conversation between the researcher and the respondent, where the respondent is a single person. However, this type of data collection can also be based on conversations with several people at the same time. The researcher then asks questions and initiates discussions within a group of people. Since such group conversations typically are focused on specific topics, the group is referred to as a *focus group*.

Unstructured interviewing and focus group conversations are conducted by the researchers themselves. Prior to the data collection, the researcher selects a number of topics to be included in all the interviews or group conversations, but

the interviews or conversations are conducted in a flexible manner. How the data collection develops depends on what type of information the respondents or group participants contribute and how the communication develops. New questions may be formulated on the basis of the researcher's interpretation of the answers to the previous questions. Collection and analysis of data take place in parallel. The researcher is constantly open to unforeseen circumstances and is prepared to improve the design based on both empirical findings and methodological experience gained during the data collection. Since the data collection cannot be planned in a detailed manner, the researcher may have a very demanding role during the interview or focus group conversation.

Traditionally, both unstructured interviews and focus group conversations have been based on face-to-face communication in physical meetings between the researcher and the respondents or focus group participants. However, new information and communication technologies have made it possible to organize online interviews and focus group conversations.

This chapter starts with a discussion of personal interviews with individual respondents. Then, the particular features of focus group conversations will be examined, and, finally, some aspects of online interviews and focus groups will be presented.

Personal interviews

The discussion of unstructured personal interviews refers to Table 10.1, which provides a schematic overview of the main features of unstructured interviewing. The table shows how the data collection is prepared and implemented, and the kinds of problems that are typically involved.

Preparing the data collection

Although unstructured interviewing cannot be planned in a detailed manner, there are some tasks that should be performed before data collection commences. The most important of these tasks will be described here.

Constructing the interview guide

An important part of the preparation for data collection is to construct an interview guide. The interview guide describes in broad terms how the interview will be conducted, focusing on the topics that will be discussed with the respondent. The guide is the researcher's starting point and guideline for the interview. It should be sufficiently comprehensive and specific so that the researcher obtains the types of information that are relevant to the study, but it should also be so simple and general that each interview can be conducted in a flexible manner, adapted to the characteristic features of the particular respondent and the specific communication.

The researcher must assess the information requirement in connection with the design of the interview guide. It is essential to think through the kind of information that should be obtained from the interviews. This assessment is based on the research questions to be addressed in the study and can be based on the general approaches for selecting information described in Chapter 7 (Table 7.3). For unstructured interviewing, the information requirements cannot be finalized before data collection commences. The researcher can constantly review and possibly revise the requirements for information on the basis of new substantive insights and new methodological

Table 10.1 Overview of the data collection in unstructured interviewing

Aspect of data collection	Characteristics of unstructured interviewing

Preparations for data collection	• Construct interview guide
	  ○ Consider information requirements
	  ○ Specify topics
	  ○ Consider the form of communication
	• Determine the degree of transparency

Implementation of data collection	• Provide information to the respondents and agree on an interview
	• Conduct the interview
	  ○ Establish a good communication situation
	  ○ Use the guide as a basis
	  ○ Consider the sequence of topics and formulate questions based on the development of the interview
	  ○ Use audio recordings and/or notes
	• Make transcripts of audio recordings
	• Where appropriate, select additional respondents and interview them

Typical problems during data collection	• Communication between the researcher and the respondent may be poor • The researcher may influence the answers • The respondent's recall errors or self-presentation may affect the answers

experiences gained during the data collection process. Nevertheless, when designing the interview guide, it is important to make as thorough an assessment as possible of the information requirement before the data collection begins.

The researcher can specify the topics of the interview based on this first clarification of the information requirements. As mentioned above, the overview of the topics is the main content of the interview guide. The full list of topics provides an overview of the types of information that the researcher initially intends to obtain during the interview. At the same time, the specification of different topics gives an initial, preliminary breakdown of the information into different dimensions and perhaps also into different categories.

During the design of the interview guide it is recommended to evaluate what form of communication is most appropriate for the particular respondents who will be interviewed. The researcher should focus as much as possible on the respondents' background, environment and culture, their activities, their modes of expression and forms of communication, and how they relate to their environment. Knowledge of such circumstances reinforces the researchers' ability to express themselves to the respondents in an understandable way and to perceive and interpret the respondents' statements correctly. In the nursing study (Gould and Fontenla, 2006), mentioned in Chapter 6, it was important to understand the nurses' special forms of communication, as well as the issues that might be important to nurses at British hospitals at the time of the interview. The guide used in the nursing study is reproduced in Table 10.2.

Degree of transparency

Before starting the interview, the researcher must decide on the degree of transparency with regard to the respondents. Interviewing cannot be conducted entirely covertly. However, although the researcher cannot hide the fact that a study is being conducted, there can be varying degrees of transparency regarding the purpose of the study.

Table 10.2 Example of interview guide for unstructured interviewing, from Gould and Fontenla (2006: 221)

The interview guide
1 Tell me about your job (details of grade, duties, length of time in post)
2 Has your current role changed since you have been in post?
3 What are the most positive aspects of your role?
4 What are the least positive aspects of your role?
5 Tell me about the opportunities you have received for continuing professional education and education
6 Tell me about the types of job you have had in the past (details of career breaks, changes of direction)
7 How do you see your career progressing?
8 To what extent do your own professional values coincide with those of the trust (details of achievement, progression, independence, economic return)?
9 Thinking back to when you came into nursing, is it all you expected it to be?
10 Have you ever thought of leaving this post and taking another nursing post?
11 Why did you think of changing? What keeps you here?
12 Have you ever thought of leaving nursing for a non-nursing post? Why was this?
13 Could you identify the three things that are most important in making your current post attractive?
14 What, if anything, could be done to make your post better?
15 Is there anything else you would like to add?

The respondents may get very detailed information about the research purpose, or they may get only a general or vague information about the study. In principle, there should be as much transparency as possible.

In some cases, interview studies require permission from special agencies or public authorities. As pointed out in Chapter 3, there are differences between countries as to the rules and regulations governing whether permission is required, what type of permission might be required, how permission can be granted, and what agency can grant it. Typically, the purpose of such permission is to ensure that the study is based on all the ethical standards. The researcher must emphasize *confidentiality*, that all data about individuals should be treated confidentially, and *anonymity,* that it is not possible to identify the individual respondents in reports based on the interview data. In addition, the researcher must obtain *informed consent* from each respondent. In this regard, the respondents must be given information about the study and its purpose, as well as the emphasis on confidentiality and anonymity. The respondents should also be informed of their right to refuse to participate in the study or refuse to answer some of the questions.

Implementing the data collection

Unstructured interviewing is a flexible design. The implementation of data collection can therefore be demanding. Here it is described how the data collection is usually conducted.

Agreeing on the interview

The implementation of data collection begins with the researcher informing the respondents and agreeing to conduct an interview. The information must be in accordance with all ethical standards, any conditions that might have been specified for permission to do the study, and the researcher's decisions generally on the degree of transparency or openness of the study. At the same time, the information must be formulated and presented in such a way that the respondents are motivated to participate in the study, that they regard the study as important, and that they experience their own participation as interesting. Although this information may be provided orally at the start of the interviewing, the information should be available for the respondent in written form and preferably sent to the respondent in advance, before the interview takes place.

Interviewing

In unstructured interviewing, successful data collection depends on a good interaction and communication between the researcher and the respondent. Thus, it is important to establish good conditions for the communication. The choice of the time and venue for the interview should ensure that the interview can take place without interruptions or interference from family members, colleagues or others. The interview should take place at a venue where the respondent feels relaxed and at a time when the respondent is not too busy. The researcher should emphasize finding a good form of conversation and making the conversation as relaxed and normal as possible, so that the respondents feel they are on the same wavelength as the researcher. In an article on gender-based sibling roles in Iran, it is emphasized that the researchers 'worked to create a friendly and empathic atmosphere and attempted to be nondirective and non-judgmental' (Nasrabadi et al., 2016: 700).

The researcher must be open to initiatives from the respondent during the conversation, but must also direct the interview so that it concerns the topics that are relevant to the study. This steering of the interview is based on the interview guide. The guide is the researcher's point of reference and checklist for conducting the interview. In the study by Gould and Fontenla (2006) mentioned above, the researchers considered it 'important to allow the respondents themselves to identify factors which contributed to commitment to nursing and to their employing trust, and which encouraged them to remain in post, rather than suggesting possible reasons through the use of more focused questions' (Gould and Fontenla, 2006: 215). However, the researchers were especially interested in the importance of continuing professional education as a factor, so if this was not mentioned by the respondents, 'it was specifically introduced approximately half way through the interview to ensure that it was included' (Gould and Fontenla, 2006: 215).

Thus, the interview guide is used in a flexible manner. The researcher should ensure that all the topics are covered during the interview, but should also consider the sequence of the topics and formulate questions based on the development of the interview. The researcher listens to the respondent's answers, interprets the answers and follows up with new questions based on these interpretations. The interviewer may use various kinds of prompts to stimulate the respondent to talk about relevant topics, and different types of probes to clarify the content and meaning of answers from the respondent. In this way, the respondent's answers can be elaborated on and clarified. Thus, during the interview the researcher obtains an increasingly improved basis for addressing relevant topics and asking fruitful questions. The researcher is open to new topics that the respondents introduce into the conversation, but must also ensure that very talkative respondents do not take control and sidetrack the interview or take it in irrelevant or unhelpful directions. In the study of gender-based sibling roles in Iran mentioned above, the interviewers 'asked probing or complementary questions if there was a need to clarify the participants' perceptions or experiences' (Nasrabadi et al., 2016: 700).

It is important to ensure a good flow in the conversation and good transitions between the questions. The background to the conversation topics and the questions should be explained, and it is recommended to complete one topic before introducing a new topic, so that repetition can be avoided. The typical procedure for the interview is to start with easy, simple and interesting topics in order to find a good format and flow. It is often a good idea to start with questions like these: 'Could you describe a typical day at your work?' or 'Could you tell me about your family activities last weekend?' More serious, complicated but central topics can then be taken up, and these will usually form the main part of the interview. Sensitive or controversial questions are usually raised towards the end of the interview. In the event that such questions create emotional or other problems for further communication, it is recommended to refrain from raising them until most of the interview has been completed. However, the interview should be concluded with easy and uncomplicated questions, so that both the researcher and the respondent are left feeling good after the conversation and can round off their communication in a good atmosphere.

The interview may last for a relatively long time, sometimes several hours. For example, in the study of gender-based sibling roles by Nasrabadi et al. (2016), the interviews lasted between 60 and 75 minutes. However, it is important to assess the duration individually for each study, in view of not only the information requirements of the study, but also what is appropriate for the particular respondents in the study. If respondents become too tired, the useful information obtained from the interview may be limited. In long interviews, it may be necessary to take small breaks, so that both the researcher and the interviewer can relax, clear their minds and gather their thoughts.

Data recording

Data recording is usually based on audio recording. In some cases, a camera can also be used to video-record the interview. This assumes that the respondent approves the use of audio tapes and any video camera before the interview starts. Sometimes respondents may feel uncomfortable with devices such as microphones and cameras, but experience shows that most respondents quickly get used to them.

Instead of audio recordings, the data recording can be based on the researcher's notes from the interview. However, it is very difficult to take note of what is said by both the researcher and the respondent while also listening to the respondent, interpreting the answers, formulating new questions and managing the development of the interview along relevant and useful paths. As a rule, the researcher must settle for taking note of keywords during the interview. Complete notes or minutes should be prepared based on the keywords as soon as possible after the interview. Such notes are essential if the respondent refuses to agree to the use of audio recordings. However, even when using audio recording, it is recommended that the researcher takes supplementary notes during the interview, partly to maintain an overview of the steering and development of the interview, and partly to document circumstances that are not included in the audio tape. This could be observations of the respondent's body language, or it could be impressions, experiences, assessments and interpretations, which may be useful as background for subsequent interviews or analyses of the data.

Audio recordings cannot be used directly in data analyses, but must be transcribed. These transcriptions constitute the data. In both studies mentioned above, all interviews were audio-recorded and transcribed for the data analysis (Gould and Fontenla, 2006; Nasrabadi et al., 2016). It is recommended that each respondent receives a copy of the transcription of their interview for review, correction and approval. This is an additional assurance of the data quality. Respondents sometimes require an opportunity to correct and approve the transcription as a condition for conducting the interview.

This is especially common among respondents who belong to social elites.

Data analysis in parallel with data collection

The data analysis takes place partly in parallel with the data collection. The researcher's interpretation of the respondent's answers in order to formulate new questions during the interview is a form of analysis. In addition, notes, recordings and transcriptions from interviews are analysed as the data collection is developed. Not only does this provide an increasing degree of insight into the research questions to be addressed. It also provides methodological experiences that are important for further data collection. The interview guide and the interview process may be improved. In addition, the researcher obtains a better basis for strategic selection of new respondents. As the researcher gradually obtains an increased understanding of which respondents can contribute relevant and fruitful information, additional respondents may be selected, and the new respondents can be interviewed.

Strategies and methods for analysing qualitative data, including data collected in unstructured interviews and focus groups, are explained in Chapter 16.

Typical problems during data collection

Unstructured interviewing is based on interaction or communication between two parties in order for one party to receive information from the other. Typical problems during this data collection process may be related to each of the parties or the interaction between them.

A typical problem associated with the interaction process during data collection is poor communication between the researcher and the respondent. Most likely, this means that the information exchange will be limited. The researcher will not be able to access all of the relevant information that the respondent possesses. Poor communication can also mean that the two parties misunderstand each other, that the respondent does not understand the questions or does not understand what type of information the researcher wants, and that the researcher misinterprets the information provided by the respondent. This impairs the quality of the data.

Researchers may prevent or reduce these communication problems by assessing the form of communication prior to conducting the interview, by finding the most appropriate way of communicating with the particular respondents in the study, and by creating a good communication situation and a relaxed atmosphere during the interview.

Another typical problem is that the researcher may influence the answers provided by the respondent. The researcher may appear or act in a manner that stimulates or provokes the respondents to express themselves in certain ways. For example, the researcher may ask leading questions or otherwise give the impression that the respondent is expected to provide specific answers. The respondent's answers can also be influenced by the researcher's appearance or characteristics. Unstructured interviewing requires special assessments of how the researcher's gender may affect the respondents' responses. This may vary depending on both the type of topic the interview is about, and the type of respondents being interviewed.

These problems also show the importance of the researcher working systematically to find a neutral and appropriate form of communication and to develop a safe and reassuring atmosphere during the interview.

Some problems that occur during data collection are related to the respondent's characteristics. The most common of these problems is that the respondent's recall errors or self-presentation can affect the answers given. Respondents may provide incorrect information about factual matters because they do not remember properly or because they have repressed parts of what actually happened. The risk of such recall errors is particularly high if the respondents are asked about events that occurred a long time before the interview is conducted. Respondents may also provide false information about their own actions or opinions because they wish to present themselves in a particularly favourable light to the researcher. Such problems are especially important if the interview is about circumstances that are controversial, stressful or deviant in relation to dominant social norms.

It is a challenge for the researcher to detect such problems during the interview. Both recall errors and self-presentation can be detected and counteracted by interpreting different answers in relation to each other and by asking different follow-up questions, where the respondent is asked to clarify and elaborate on their answers.

No matter how much the researcher strives to avoid or reduce these problems during the data collection, it is important to consider how the final data material may be affected by different sources of error. Such assessments must be made during the analysis of the data and the interpretation of the findings.

Focus groups: Conversations and group dynamics

Focus groups are very similar to unstructured personal interviews. The main difference refers to the number of respondents that are involved in each conversation. Whereas a personal interview is a separate conversation with only one respondent, a focus group involves conversation with several respondents at the same time. Moreover, the communication in a focus group is not only limited to conversation between the interviewer and each of the respondents. It also includes conversations or discussions among all the respondents within the group.

In a focus group, the respondents are called group participants, and the researcher acts as a moderator of the discussion in the group. In addition to asking questions, the moderator also steers the discussion in the group. Although the discussion is unstructured and flexible, it is based on a discussion guide, which is similar to the interview guide in unstructured interviews. The construction of the guide is based on the same type of preparations as for personal interviews, including assessments of information requirements and specification of topics for the data collection.

The guide for the focus group lists the topics that should be covered in the group discussion. The moderator introduces each of these topics, typically as a question for responses from the participants and discussion in the group. The formulation of the topics or questions and the order in which they are introduced are adapted to the development of the conversation in the group. Furthermore, the moderator asks follow-up questions for clarification and may introduce additional topics for further discussion. The group discussion is recorded in the same ways as unstructured personal interviews, typically as audio or video recordings, which are transcribed for data analysis. The data analysis is conducted in parallel with the data collection.

Focus groups were used in a study of transport infrastructure in Sweden (Folkeson et al., 2013). The study was based on two focus groups, one group in each of the two major cities. The discussion guide consisted of only five questions, but additional questions and follow-up questions were asked by the group moderators. In addition to transcribed audio recording of the group discussions, the data analysis was based on notes made by the moderators during the discussions. One of the focus group meetings lasted 60 minutes, and the other group meeting lasted 80 minutes (Folkeson et al., 2013: 246).

Compared to personal interviews, the additional benefit of focus groups is that the group dynamics, in particular the discussion among the group participants, may provide more and different information on the topics in the study. The purpose is to obtain a variety of views, assessments and creative associations about specific relatively delimited topics. The interaction among the participants may stimulate the memory of each participant and motivate all participants to provide information about their experiences, ideas and attitudes. Expectations and reactions from other participants in the group may encourage each participant to contribute actively with responses, opinions and clarifications. It is a challenge for the moderator to be sensitive to the particular development of the discussion in the group, in order to ensure that new information and perspectives from participants are stimulated and followed up. However, it is also a challenge to avoid or prevent discussions that are irrelevant or of no use to the study and its research questions.

Successful use of focus groups requires that the group is of appropriate size, usually 5–10 participants. The two focus groups in the Swedish study mentioned above included nine women and five men (Folkeson et al., 2013: 246). If the group is too large, it will be difficult to activate all participants. If the group is too small, it will be difficult to obtain a creative and dynamic discussion. In addition to the group size, the composition of the focus group is also important. It is recommended to recruit group participants who are able and willing to communicate with one another on equal terms, although they may have different backgrounds, experiences and views. In any event, it is a challenge for the moderator during the focus group conversation to make sure that all participants are stimulated to respond to the questions and contribute to the discussion. Some participants may need special attention and motivation to be active in the group's communication, and no participant should be allowed to dominate the communication. The moderator has to find a good balance between various inputs from each participant in the group and the general discussion in the group as a whole.

The typical problems that were discussed in connection with unstructured interviewing are relevant also in focus group conversations, although in somewhat different ways. Communication problems may be more serious in focus groups than they are in interviews, since such problems may arise both between the moderator and the participants, and between the participants themselves. To avoid or handle such problems is a special challenge for the recruitment of group participants, and for the moderation of the group discussions.

Like respondents in personal interviews, focus group participants may be influenced by the researcher. In addition, they may be influenced by other participants in the group, especially by dominant participants. It may be more difficult to express controversial or deviant opinions, and participants may be tempted to give responses that they think are expected or desirable. On the other hand, the researcher's influence and the participants' influence may counteract each other. The presence of other participants may give each participant the strength to resist any possible influence from the researcher, and the researcher may use their position as moderator to ensure that each participant feels confident in relation to all other participants, and that all views are regarded as equally legitimate.

In focus groups, the risk of recall errors may be reduced by the fact that several participants provide responses to the same questions. The memory of each respondent may be stimulated and refreshed by the responses from other participants. On the other hand, participants may be influenced to harmonize their own memory with responses from other participants, especially responses provided by dominant participants in the group.

The problem of self-presentation is related to the risk that some focus group participants may become particularly dominant in the discussion. The reason for such dominance might be that these participants want to make an impression on the other participants in the group. On the other hand, the presence of the other participants may make it more difficult to stand out in a dominant way, especially if all or most of the group participants are actively engaged in the discussion.

Online interviews and focus groups

Traditionally, unstructured interviews and focus groups have been based on face-to-face conversations in physical meetings between the researcher and the respondents. Due to the development of new information and communication technologies, the web can now be used to organize online interviews and focus groups. The researcher does not meet the respondents or the focus group participants physically, and the focus group participants do not get together in physical meetings. All communication takes place on the web.

This communication can be synchronous or asynchronous. In a synchronous interview the researcher and the respondent communicate with each other simultaneously, and in a synchronous focus group both the researcher and all group participants interact at the same time. Such interviews or focus groups can be conducted by means of Skype or other software programs for chatting, conferences or simultaneous communication between two or more participants.

In an asynchronous interview the respondent answers the researcher's question after some time, and the next question is asked some time after the previous response. Similarly, in an asynchronous focus group the researcher's questions and the participants' responses and comments are pre-sented sequentially over a time period. For this purpose, it is possible to use e-mails as well as various types of online forums. If it is not possible to use an existing online forum, the researcher may create a new forum for the particular study.

Asynchronous online focus groups were used in a Dutch study of parents' reasons for refusing to vaccinate their children (Harmsen et al., 2013). The researchers created a special online forum for the study. A sample of parents who had refused to vaccinate their children received a letter about the study with an invitation to participate in a focus group. Those who wanted to participate received an e-mail with details about how they could join the forum as a focus group participant. Eight focus groups, including 60 participants in total, were organized. Each group was conducted over a period of 5 days. Each day the researcher presented one question from the discussion guide, and the participants could anonymously present their responses and comments. All questions, responses and comments remained open for all participants during the whole period of the focus group.

Apart from the virtual communication and the possibility of asynchronous communication in online interviews and focus groups, there are not many differences between online and traditional face-to-face use of this design for data collection. Online data collection is prepared in the same way as face-to-face data collection. The basic procedures for the implementation of the data collection are also the same in online and face-to-face use of interviews and focus groups. However, one particular advantage of interviews or focus groups based on chatting programs, e-mails or online forums is that transcripts of the data are generated automatically.

Online interviews and focus groups are easy and inexpensive to conduct, and they can be used with respondents or group participants from large geographic areas. However, it may be difficult to verify the identity of the respondents and group participants.

Asynchronous online interviews and focus groups can be used in studies that include respondents or participants from different time zones, since responses or comments can be given whenever it is most convenient. Furthermore, this means that the respondents can take time to think about their responses before giving them. Such planned responses may be more accurate and more founded than spontaneous responses, but the planning may also lead to responses that are believed to be politically correct or socially desirable. In asynchronous focus groups the participants can be anonymous in relation to the other participants, and the risk that some participants are dominated or influenced by other participants is relatively low. However, in such data collection, it may be difficult to keep the participants' attention over the duration of the focus group, and the drop-out risk may be high.

CHAPTER HIGHLIGHTS

- Unstructured interviewing is conducted by the researchers themselves in the form of conversations with the respondents.
- Unstructured interviewing is a flexible design, but the researcher prepares an interview guide and considers the degree of openness before carrying out the data collection process.

- During the data collection in unstructured interviewing, it is important to provide information to the respondents and to reach an agreement about the interview, to establish a good communication situation, to base the process on the guide and to tailor the interview to the individual respondent, to ensure good data recording and to analyse the material as the data collection proceeds.

- The following problems are typical for data collection based on unstructured interviews:

  1 The communication between the researcher and the respondent may be poor
  2 The researcher may influence the answers
  3 The respondent's recall errors or self-presentation may affect the answers.

- Focus group conversations are similar to unstructured personal interviews. The group typically includes 5–10 participants, with the researcher as moderator for the discussion in the group. The discussion is based on a guide, which is used in a flexible way.

- Compared to unstructured personal interviews, the additional benefit of focus groups is the information provided in the dynamic discussion among the participants.

- It is a challenge for the moderator to avoid irrelevant discussions and ensure that all participants are equally active in the group.

- Unstructured interviews and focus groups may be conducted online.

- Online interviews and focus groups may be synchronous or asynchronous.

RESEARCH EXAMPLES

I recommend that you read the publications used as research examples in this chapter. Two of the articles are examples of the use of unstructured personal interviews:

Gould, Dinah, and Marina Fontenla, (2006) 'Commitment to nursing: Results of a qualitative interview study', *Journal of Nursing Management* 14, 213–221.

This article presents a study of how different factors influence nurses' job satisfaction as well as their commitment to the nursing profession and to the organization or institution where they work. Unstructured interviews were carried out with 27 nurses from two different hospitals in the UK. The interviewing was based on a guide with open-ended questions, allowing the respondents themselves to identify factors that influenced their commitment to nursing and their employing hospital. The findings indicate that a family-friendly policy is the most important factor for ensuring commitment, and that professional autonomy also is important for the nurses' professional and organizational commitment.

Nasrabadi, Alireza Nikbakht, Ali Montazeri, Hasan Eftekhar Ardebili, Setareh Homami, Yousef Karimi, Saharnaz Nedjat, Mahdi Moshki, and Ali Akbar Mansourian (2016) 'Exploring gender-based sibling roles: A qualitative study on contemporary Iranian families', *Journal of Family Issues* 37(5), 692–716.

The study presented in this article examines perceptions of gender-based sibling roles in Iran. Semi-structured interviews were conducted with 21 Iranian married men and women between 21 and 66 years of age. The interview guide included only three general questions, but probing or complementary questions were asked for clarification of perceptions and experiences. The findings of the study show some role differences between men and women. Six role categories are found for sisters, and four role categories are described for brothers. Three of these categories are common to both brothers and sisters.

The third article exemplifies the use of focus groups:

Folkeson, Lennart, Hans Antonson, and J. O. Helldin (2013) 'Planners' views on cumulative effects: A focus-group study concerning transport infrastructure planning in Sweden', *Land Use Policy* 30(1), 243–253.

This article presents a study of views and experiences among Swedish transport infrastructure planners regarding the cumulative effects of various actions, especially the cumulative environmental effects of combinations of past, present and future actions. The study was based on two focus groups, one in Stockholm, and one in Malmö. The two groups included nine women and five men with different roles in transport infrastructure, spatial planning, and a non-governmental organization. Five questions were presented for discussion in the focus groups. The researchers, who were moderators of the group discussions, asked additional or follow-up questions. The discussions were audio-recorded, but the researchers also made notes on the conversation in the group and the reactions of the group participants. The findings show that there is only limited attention to cumulative effects among the planners, but the focus group discussions led to several suggestions as to how to increase this attention in the planning processes.

The fourth article exemplifies the use of online focus groups:

Harmsen, Irene A., Liesbeth Mollema, Robert A. C. Ruiter, Theo G. W. Paulussen, Hester E. de Melker, and Gerjo Kok (2013) 'Why parents refuse childhood vaccination: A qualitative study using online focus groups', *BMC Public Health* 13, 1183.

This article presents a study of parents who refuse vaccination of their children, with emphasis on the reasons for this refusal. Parents with children (0–4 years) only partially vaccinated or not vaccinated were selected for online focus groups. Eight asynchronous focus groups were included in the study. Each group was conducted over 5 days during a week. The participants could log in and respond to questions from the researcher as well as comment on responses from other participants. The findings show that there are multiple reasons for parents' refusal to vaccinate their children.

STUDENT EXERCISES AND QUESTIONS

1 What is an interview guide?
2 How is the interview guide used in unstructured interviewing?
3 What are the main differences between unstructured personal interviews and focus groups?
4 Why is the size of the group important in studies based on focus groups?
5 What are the differences between synchronous and asynchronous use of online focus groups?
6 Discuss how the study conditions for various groups of students at a university could be examined by means of focus groups.
7 Construct a guide for an unstructured interview about people's leisure activities. Select three other students as respondents and use the guide in unstructured interviews with each of the selected students.

RECOMMENDED LITERATURE

Barbour, Rosaline (2018) *Doing Focus Groups* (2nd edn). London: Sage.

This book presents a practical introduction to focus group research. In addition to describing how to plan and organize focus groups, the book discusses advantages and limitations of focus groups as a method in social science.

Brinkmann, Svend, and Steinar Kvale (2018) *Doing Interviews* (2nd edn). London: Sage.

This book provides an introduction to interviewing in qualitative research. The authors describe how to conduct interviews, and they discuss different ways of using and understanding qualitative data based on interviews.

James, Nalita, and Hugh Busher (2014) *Online Interviewing*. London: Sage.

This is a short and practical introduction to planning, organizing and conducting online interviews in qualitative research. Furthermore, the book deals with methodological and epistemological challenges as well as ethical issues involved in online interviewing.

King, Nigel, Christine Horrocks, and Joanna Brooks (2018) *Interviews in Qualitative Research* (2nd edn). London: Sage.

Using examples from previous research, this book shows how interviews can be designed, planned, conducted and analysed. In addition to practical guidance on data collection, the book also explains how to deal with ethical issues in interview-based qualitative research.

DOCUMENTARY SOURCES AND QUALITATIVE CONTENT ANALYSIS

This chapter provides the knowledge that is necessary for understanding and assessing how documentary sources and content analysis are used to collect qualitative data in social science. The chapter will enable you to carry out studies based on this type of data collection.

The chapter will teach you how to

- distinguish between different types of documentary sources in social science and different ways of examining them
- conduct source-critical and contextual assessments of documentary sources
- use qualitative content analysis for examining various types of texts and visual materials

- handle different problems that might arise in quantitative content analysis
- understand how documentary sources are used in discourse analysis and holistic qualitative studies.

Qualitative studies based on documentary sources

This chapter deals with qualitative data collection based on documents as sources. The content of various types of documents is systematically reviewed in order to find and analyse relevant information on the social phenomena and conditions that are emphasized in the research question of the study. The relevant parts of the content of the documents are systematized and registered as data in the study.

As pointed out in Chapter 6, there are many different types of documents that can be used as sources in social science. Documents may include

- written texts, such as books, newspapers, diaries and letters
- audio recordings of, for example, radio programmes, speeches, debates and conversations
- visual materials, such as photographs, graphics and other images
- audio-visual presentations, including TV programmes, videos and films
- digital texts, sounds, images or videos, which are available online or stored as data files. Social media, such as Facebook, Twitter and Instagram, are examples of new forms of online documentary sources for social science studies.

There are large differences between documents in terms of their content. An important distinction for researchers' use of documentary sources is between documents containing factual information, such as news reports in newspapers, and documents expressing values, evaluations, opinions or emotions, such as newspaper editorials.

Documents may have very different purposes. Typically, documents used as sources in research are produced for purposes other than the research. Sometimes, however, documents are solicited by the researcher, expressly for the purpose of a particular study. For example, participants in a study may be asked to write a brief note on critical events in their life histories, or a short essay on their opinions on environmental challenges. Even texts produced by the researchers themselves, such as field notes in participant observation, are documents that may be systematically reviewed and processed in the same way as other documentary sources.

Furthermore, there are considerable variations in the availability of documents as sources for research. Typically, public documents, such as government publications and press releases from organizations, are more available than private documents, such as personal diaries, photographs and letters. However, both public and private documents may be open or closed. Some closed documents are not accessible for research, since they are regarded as very sensitive or secret, such as various military documents. Other closed documents, for example personal diaries and some closed online groups, may be made available for research purposes after applications and negotiations. Even if documents are open, researchers may need permission to use them as sources, due to copyright or other restrictions.

The basic design for collecting qualitative data based on documentary sources is qualitative content analysis. Typically, the documents are reviewed in a systematic manner in order to categorize, record, analyse and interpret the content. The data collection is not based on a predefined set of categories, but often the analysis of the collected data will result in a categorization of the documents' content. The data analysis is conducted in parallel with the data collection, and, apart from revealing empirical patterns, the analysis may also provide a basis for including additional documents in the data collection. Thus, the data collection is so demanding that it has to be conducted by the researchers themselves. The data collection may be rather unpredictable, and it cannot be planned in great detail before it starts. If it is planned, the plans may be changed during the data collection.

In this chapter, some characteristic features of qualitative content analysis will be discussed. First, content analysis of texts is described, with emphasis on the major features of the data collection in such studies. Then, content analysis of visual materials is examined. Finally, it is discussed how content analysis of documentary sources can be used in holistic studies and in discourse analysis.

Qualitative content analysis of texts

The discussion of data collection in qualitative content analysis of texts is based on Table 11.1, which presents an overview of how the data collection is prepared and implemented, as well typical problems that may arise during data collection.

Preparing the data collection

Although data collection in qualitative content analysis cannot be planned in detail, it is important to make some preparations before the data collection starts. The most important

Table 11.1   Overview of data collection in qualitative content analysis

Aspect of data collection	Characteristics of qualitative content analysis
Preparations for data collection	• Clarify the focus • Select important topics • Select types of texts • Find texts • If necessary, agree on permission to use the texts, and determine the degree of transparency

Implementation of data collection	• Systematically review the selected texts:
	  ○ Conduct source-critical and contextual assessments
	  ○ Select and register relevant content
	  ○ Categorize the relevant content
	• Select additional relevant texts and review these systematically

Typical problems during data collection	• The researcher's perspective may affect the selection and interpretation of the texts • Limited source-critical understanding may affect the interpretation of the texts • Limited contextual understanding may affect the interpretation of the texts

preparation is to clarify the focus of the study. Since the implementation of the data collection is flexible, it is necessary to determine as clearly as possible at the outset what should be the aim and purpose of the analysis. This clarification is based on the research question of the study. The development of the data collection may lead to new insight regarding the availability of additional data and the need for new data, but the main basis for assessing the relevance of new and additional data is the research question and the focus of the study. The research question is a fixed and stable point in a design that otherwise is characterized by a lot of flexibility.

Already at the outset, the research question provides a basis for two types of clarifications regarding the focus of the study. One type of clarification refers to the topics that should be emphasized in the data collection, or, in other words, what the researcher should be looking for during the systematic review of the content of the texts. The other type of clarification concerns the kinds of texts that should be selected for the content analysis. The selection should focus on those texts that are most likely to provide relevant information on the research question of the study. Even though these early clarifications may be modified and adjusted during the data collection, they are important for bringing the data collection in the right direction right from the start. The early clarifications are useful as general guidelines for continuous assessments of the relevance of the data.

Another task in the preparations for the data collection is to find the texts for the content analysis. This is an easy task if the relevant texts are available and based on open access, such as contemporary newspaper articles or radio programmes. Finding the texts might be more difficult if they are private, closed, or old. Then the researcher has to locate the texts in archives or libraries. This search is similar to the search for literature in literature reviews and can increasingly be done online, by means of the Internet, or existing databases and networks for texts and data. In the newspaper study, described in Chapter 6, where the purpose was to examine statements about nurses in South African newspapers, relevant newspaper articles were identified through an online search based on the keywords "nurse" and "nursing" (Oosthuizen, 2012).

Some texts are not publicly available. They may be secret or confidential, and they may be personal and private, for example personal diaries, letters, e-mails or other private memos or manuscripts. Such texts may be valuable sources for social research. For example, the content of the diaries of politicians may provide interesting information in studies of political debates and decision-making processes. If it is decided to include these types of text in a content analysis, the researcher has to apply for access to them. It may be necessary to negotiate with those who own or control the texts, in order to obtain permission to use the texts for the research. This is another important task in the preparations for the data collection.

In this connection, the researchers have to consider how much information they will give regarding why they want to examine the texts, and about the study in general. As usual, there should be as much transparency as possible about the research and its purpose, and content analyses are based on the same ethical principles as research based on other designs. However, the issue of transparency is less relevant if the content analysis is based on texts that are generally available and open to anybody.

Implementing the data collection

The implementation of the data collection is based on a systematic review of the texts that are selected for the content analysis, as well as a continuous assessment of which texts could be relevant and useful for the study.

Source-critical and contextual assessments

An important activity in this connection is to conduct source-critical and contextual assessments of each text. As pointed out in Chapter 7, *source-critical assessments* should focus on the availability, relevance, authenticity and credibility of the sources. Such assessments are important in all types of research designs, often as a part of the preparations for the data collection. In qualitative content analysis source-critical considerations are *especially* important, and in such studies critical evaluations of the sources are involved in the *implementation* of the data collection. Assessments of the availability of texts have to be made before the data collection starts, but both needs and possibilities for including additional texts in the study may arise during the data collection. Thus, considerations regarding availability are important throughout the study. Relevance considerations are even more necessary during the text review process, since the major purpose of the data collection is to identify and register the content of various texts that are relevant for the research questions of the study. The assessment of relevance is an important part of the systematic and thorough review of the content of the texts. The review process also makes it possible to assess the authenticity and credibility of the texts as sources.

In source-critical assessments the texts are compared with other sources and evaluated in connection with other available knowledge and information, especially regarding the background of the texts and their authors, as well as the phenomena and conditions that are described in the texts. This means that the texts are critically assessed in the light of their context. By evaluating the content of the text in connection with its origin and context, it is possible to judge whether the text is authentic, and whether its content is credible. Thus, contextual assessments are closely connected to, and provide a basis for, source-critical assessments.

However, contextual assessments are not only important for the critical evaluation of the sources. They are also necessary for interpreting and understanding the content of the texts. One useful contextual assessment refers to the *representativity* of the texts: for whom or for what are the texts representative? Do the texts represent only the authors themselves, or are they written on behalf of other people as well? Does a text express the author's own message, or does it present a message from a larger group, an organization or an institution?

Another contextual assessment relates to the *meaning* of the texts. The meaning of a text is interpreted in the light of the context in which the text was produced and disseminated: what was the significance of the text, not only for the author, but also for the readers? What intentions did the author have for the text, and how did the readers understand the text? What message did the author want to disseminate, and how did the audience interpret the message?

In order to understand the representativity and meaning of the texts, the researcher has to consider a number of contextual conditions, including such questions as who authored the texts, who were the readers, what were the backgrounds of the authors and the readers, and in what situations the texts were formulated, distributed, received and read.

Selecting and registering relevant content

Based on the systematic review of the texts, the researcher can select and register the relevant content of these texts. The content selection refers to the research question and the prioritization of topics that was made in the preparations for the data collection. However, the criteria for the selection may be reconsidered, modified or revised as more and more texts are reviewed, and as more and more of the contents are registered, assessed and interpreted.

Typically, the selected text content, or part of the text, is copied, and each copy is marked with an accurate reference. For example, the marking shows which text the content is taken from, how the selected content is located or positioned within the larger text, as well as where and when this text is presented or published. The marking may also include descriptions of contextual conditions that are important for source-critical assessments and for evaluations of representativity and meaning of the text.

The marked text selections are filed or archived in a systematic way, for example chronologically (with reference to time of publication), geographically (with reference to place of publication), or thematically (with reference to topics covered in the text). These marked text selections constitute the data of the study.

Categorization

Typically, during the data collection, the relevant text content is *categorized* by the researcher. It is this part of the data collection that is most closely connected to the data analysis. The content of the texts is reviewed, assessed and interpreted with reference to the research question, and each part of the content is examined in relation to other parts of the content. This provides a basis for identifying common features between different text elements and for grouping these elements together in more general categories.

In some studies the categories may be selected and defined before the data collection starts. The specification of categories may be based on the research question or more general concepts and theories. Then the different parts of the text content are related to these predefined categories. In other studies new categories are generated and defined inductively, based on the content of the texts that are reviewed and analysed. Different elements of the texts are then compared, in order to generate a set of more general categories, and to relate each text element to one of these generated categories.

This procedure for inductive generation of categories was used by Oosthuizen (2012), in her study of South African newspapers, which was mentioned above. Statements about nurses in the selected newspaper articles were classified into different categories and marked with codes showing which category each statement was related to. Gradually, during the analysis, several of the original categories were merged into more general categories. Finally, the analysis resulted in 18 general categories, which were divided into four major groups, based on the themes covered in the articles. An overview of these four themes and 18 categories is presented in Table 11.2.

As more and more text content is related to the different categories, the categories may be modified or revised. For each category, the researcher is particularly interested in the most typical text elements, which define the major meaning of the category, and the text elements that do not fit in, which define the boundaries of the category.

Based on this categorization, the researcher can develop concepts and typologies, as well as theoretical generalizations or a holistic understanding of the text as a whole. Thus, the categorization is a part of the data analysis, which will be further explained in Chapter 16. However, the categorization process also provides more and more insight regarding additional texts that would be relevant and useful to include in the study. Therefore, the categorization starts already during the data collection and goes on in parallel with the selection of texts and the registration of the texts' content. This switching between data analysis and data collection is important for the theoretical development of categories and concepts as well as the strategic selection of texts for the qualitative data. Thus, additional texts may be added to the data as the data collection continues, and these additional texts are systematically reviewed, with emphasis on

Table 11.2 Categorization of the content of newspaper articles about nurses in South Africa, reproduced from Oosthuizen (2012: 54)

Theme	Category
Nursing shortage and emigration	• Decline in numbers of student nurses and young professionals • Exodus of nurses • Statistical evidence of nursing shortage • Human resources for health
Declining health-care system and poor working conditions	• Public hospitals in state of collapse • Occupational health and safety issues • Excessive workloads • Conditions of service • Negative relationships
Death, suffering, humiliation, misconduct and incompetence	• Industrial actions/strikes • Horror stories of alleged patient neglect • Nurse–patient ratio and patient mortality • Alleged misconduct • Lack of professional values
Celebration of a noble profession	• International Nurses Day • Nurses' role in South Africa • Positive patient experiences • Recognition of service excellence

source-critical and contextual assessments, selection and registration of the relevant content, as well as categorization of this content.

Computer-based data collection

The development of new information technologies has made it possible to use computers in qualitative content analysis. Computer programs may be used to search for, and select, texts that might be relevant for the research question. Furthermore, computer software may be used for marking, filing and categorizing relevant content in the selected texts.

Kaefer et al. (2015) shows how software packages can be used in qualitative content analysis of newspaper articles. The analysis includes 230 articles in Australian, British and American newspapers covering New Zealand's carbon emissions and environmental global positioning during the five-year period 2008–2012. Using keywords, computer programs were used to identify relevant articles in the newspapers, and these articles were imported into the software package NVivo. This software was used to locate the text content referring to specific search terms (words or combinations of words), which were selected and defined as relevant to the research question. In addition to identifying the occurrence of the words and word combinations used as search terms, the software also highlighted the text around each search term, typically the paragraph in which the search term was found. The text around the keywords was used by the researchers as a context for understanding the meaning of the keywords within the text. Based on this interpretation of the meaning of the words and word combinations, the identified text elements were marked and categorized in different ways by means of the software package.

Although Kaefer et al. (2015) used the computer program in the categorization process, this process was based on the researchers' involvement and assessments. They read through the texts and interpreted the contextual meaning of words and statements, and, with reference to the research question, they evaluated the relevance of the texts and the need for various categories. The categorization of texts in qualitative content analysis may also be more open and more inductive. Then the categorization may also be more computerized. For example, texts may be analysed by means of software for text mining. This is a special type of data mining, which was mentioned in Chapter 7. In text mining, computer programs are used to identify and select texts, and to cluster similar text elements together in more general categories. The only involvement of the researcher is to specify criteria for the identification and clustering process, before the texts are processed by the computer.

Whereas Kaefer et al. (2015), in their study of newspaper articles, used the software package NVivo, in combination with NCapture, there are several other computer programs available for qualitative content analysis and text mining, such as QCAmap.

The advantage of using computer programs for data collection in qualitative content analysis is that such programs make it possible to handle relatively large amounts of text. Even big data, such as texts from Facebook, Twitter or other social media, can be examined in qualitative content analysis if computer programs are used in the collection and processing of the data.

However, the major limitation of the use of computers in qualitative content analysis is that computers cannot manage the source-critical and contextual assessments, and the interpretation of the representativity and meaning of the texts, which are necessary in these studies. Therefore, Kaefer et al. (2015) switched between their own personal interpretations and assessments and the use of computers to identify, process and categorize the texts based on the researchers' interpretations and assessments. As pointed out by Mayring (2014), the computer 'serves as an *assistant* to the researcher. The researcher is still responsible for the interpretation of the text, but the computer helps to organize the materials, the

steps of analysis, the interpretation rules, and the results.' Computers can detect and process the *manifest* content of texts, specified explicitly as words or combinations of words, but cannot interpret the *latent* content, which refers to the particular and often implicit meaning of words and statements as they occur in a specific context. This distinction between manifest and latent content of texts will be further discussed in Chapter 14, on quantitative content analysis.

Typical problems during the data collection

In content analysis, reactivity is usually avoided. The sources are not influenced by the data collection. The texts are not changed because they are analysed. However, reactivity may occur if the sources are texts that are solicited by the researcher, such as life histories, diaries or essays. The formulation of such solicited texts may be affected by the participants' knowledge of the fact that their texts will be analysed by the researcher.

In order to reduce or control this influence, and to assess the extent and direction of the influence, the researchers should provide good information about how the texts will be used in the particular study, and they should ensure that all participants in the study receive the same information.

Reflexivity is a more important problem in qualitative content analysis. The selection and interpretation of the texts may be affected by the researcher's perspective. A narrow perspective may lead to a biased selection of texts and a one-sided interpretation of the selected texts. Texts that are relevant and meaningful for the research question may be neglected or left out because they do not fit into the researcher's perspective. Possible interpretations that are interesting and important may not be discovered or discussed because they are outside the perspective emphasized by the researcher.

Such problems may be reduced or avoided if the relevance and meaning of the texts are assessed from different perspectives, and if the researcher does not emphasize texts that are typical of established categories, but also pays attention to texts that deviate from these categories. Furthermore, in order to avoid problems related to a limited or narrow perspective, the researcher should discuss the content of the texts with reference to alternative possibilities of interpretation.

Another typical problem during the data collection is that the researcher may have a limited source-critical understanding, and that the interpretation of the texts is affected by this limitation. The risk is that the study includes texts that are not authentic or credible. It is obvious that this may lead to false interpretations of the content.

This problem may be prevented if each text is assessed in relation to other sources and available knowledge. This provides a basis for checking and controlling the background, origin and production of the text, as well as conditions that are described in the text.

Furthermore, the researcher's interpretation of the texts may be affected by a limited contextual understanding. The interpretation may be wrong if it is based on insufficient assessments of the representativity and meaning of the texts. For example, statements made by politicians during an election campaign are presented on behalf of their political parties, in order to profile and promote the politics of their parties. These messages may be misinterpreted if they are understood merely as expressions of the politicians' personal opinions.

To avoid such misinterpretations the researcher should ensure that the content of the texts is understood in the light of the specific situation in which they were formulated and presented, and in the light of the intentions of the author or speaker, the social functions of the texts, and the possible perceptions of the readers or listeners.

Qualitative content analysis of visual materials

In addition to texts, several types of visual materials can be used as documentary sources for social science. Visual materials include various kinds of images and pictures, photographs, graphics, drawings and paintings, as well as the visual parts of audio-visual presentations, such as videos and films.

Qualitative content analysis of images includes descriptions of what the images show, and interpretations of what the images mean. For example, in studies of photographs, descriptions of what is shown may focus on such aspects as the theme of the photograph, the actors in the picture, the clothes that are worn by the actors, the activities that are visible, the buildings that are included, the places that are shown, and the event that is photographed. Exactly what aspects are included in the description depends on the research question of the particular study. In some studies it is adequate to emphasize comprehensive descriptions of what the images show, but in other studies it may be relevant to concentrate on only a few selected features of the images that are examined.

The research question is also the basis for interpretations of the meaning of the images. Whereas describing what the image shows can be a rather straightforward task, based on what can be seen in the image itself, the interpretation of the meaning is more complicated. As for the meaning of texts, the meaning of images must be understood within a larger context. The meaning should be interpreted in light of the origin of the image, such as when, where, how, and by whom the image was created. Furthermore, contextual assessments should include consideration of the possible purpose of creating the image, for whom it was created, how it has been used or distributed, how it may have been perceived and understood by different people, and what social functions such images may have had. For example, there are many differences between private photographs of family life and newspaper photographs of public events. Awareness of such differences is important for understanding the meaning of a particular photograph.

Furthermore, source-critical assessments are as important for visual materials as they are for texts. Researchers should compare the images selected with other images and other types of sources, and they should critically evaluate the images in light of available knowledge and information regarding the images and their context. Thus, the authenticity and credibility of the images can be assessed. Were the images really created where and when they seem to have been or claim to have been? Are they really showing the persons or the buildings that we think they are? For example, as to newspaper photographs that are presented as illustrations of a mass meeting, we may ask whether they are true images of that meeting, or whether they are constructed or manipulated, as a form of fake news?

In a qualitative content analysis, the images selected may be categorized based on the descriptions of what the images show as well as the interpretations of what they mean. This was done in a study of images, mainly photographs, in Finnish textbooks in history (Hakoköngäs, and Sakki, 2016). The images were regarded as visualized collective memories, or social representations of history. With reference to the semiotic research developed by Roland Barthes (1977), it is argued that images work through a combination of three meanings: denotative, connotative and mythological meanings. The purpose of the qualitative content analysis was to examine the content and meaning of the images in the construction of Finnish history since the early nineteenth century. Three contemporary and comprehensive textbooks were selected for the study, and 541 images in these textbooks were categorized in terms of year and place of the image, as well as the themes and actors

in the image. Moreover, the researchers noted some categories that were not visible in the images. Based on this categorization, the analysis shows that politics, culture and war are the major contents of the visual collective memory in Finland, and that categories related to religion and minorities are less visible in this collective memory.

As to typical problems during the data collection in qualitative content analysis, there are no significant differences between texts and visual materials as sources. In both cases, the selection and interpretation of the sources may be affected by the researcher's perspective, and the interpretation of the sources may also be affected by limitations in the researcher's source-critical and contextual understanding.

Holistic studies and discourse analysis based on documents

So far in this chapter, the main focus of the presentation has been on the use of qualitative content analysis for categorization of texts or visual materials. However, the content of documentary sources may be examined in other ways as well. One alternative approach is to use various types of documents in more holistic studies. Then the purpose is to develop a comprehensive description and understanding of more or less complex social phenomena, conditions or processes, as they are unfolded in a larger context. Rather than dividing the content of the documents into different categories, the different parts of the documentary sources are continuously put together and increasingly integrated into one whole pattern or story. This is done early in the data collection, which is combined with more and more data analysis.

One systematic procedure for processing the data in such holistic studies is *condensation* of the documents. When texts are used as sources, this procedure is called *systematic text condensation* (Malterud, 2012). The content of relatively large amounts of texts or other documents is summarized or condensed into much briefer notes, in which the holistic description and understanding are built up in a simplified and crystallized form. The condensation may be conducted in several steps and at different levels. First, different parts of the sources may be condensed into several brief notes, and then different notes may be put together, further condensed and integrated into fewer, but more general and comprehensive notes.

Another systematic procedure for data processing in holistic studies of documentary sources is to organize the content of the documents into *narratives*. This procedure is particularly useful for examining processes or changes over time, for example decision processes in organizations or life histories of individuals. Different parts of the documentary sources are reorganized, put together, integrated and rewritten as an entire cohesive story about the processes or changes that are examined. Typically, in narratives the content of the document is organized chronologically. This type of data analysis is conducted gradually and increasingly in parallel with the data collection, and the data collection is adapted to the narrative perspective. Altogether, the sources may be used to create one overall and comprehensive narrative or several smaller or more limited narratives. In any event, the purpose is to use the narratives as a basis for a holistic description and understanding of the processes or events that are examined.

In addition to holistic studies, discourse analysis may be used as an alternative approach in qualitative content analysis, especially for texts as sources. Discourse analysis is focused on how language is used in particular contexts, and it examines discourses, which are communications or texts with specific information or knowledge that reflect or shape people's views of the world and reality. Discourse analysis is a *constructionist* approach, which is based on the assumption that reality is what people consider to be real. Reality is constructed by people's views, and since there are different views among people, there are also different realities. Thus, a typical purpose of discourse analysis is to study views that are expressed in various types of texts.

This was done by Chaiyapa et al. (2018), in a discourse analysis of motivations among oil and gas companies in Thailand to invest in renewable energy. They analysed discourses used by the companies to legitimize their 'green' investments. Three oil and gas companies were selected for the study, and their annual reports since the early 2000s, found on the companies' websites, were used as data sources. The analysis focused on views expressed in these online documents, especially the companies' rhetoric or reasons for investing in renewable energy. Based on keywords regarding different types of renewable energy, the software MaxQDA was used to identify and record relevant text content, which consisted of sentences or phrases as discourse fragments. The researchers conducted a thematic coding, and by systematically identifying keywords that occurred repeatedly, and by interpreting the meaning of those sentences, they grouped all related fragments under a theme or a discourse strand (Chaiyapa et al. 2018: 451). The discourse strands for the companies were illustrated in figures, which were created by means of MaxQDA. One of these figures is shown in Figure 11.1. The figure shows that this particular oil and gas company (PTT) uses several discourses for legitimizing its green investments. For example, the company refers to hydropower, arguing that this form of renewable energy is important for the national energy security, and for generating national income. In general, the study indicates that the discourses used to legitimize the companies' investments 'varied according to energy source and company' (Chaiyapa et al., 2018: 448).

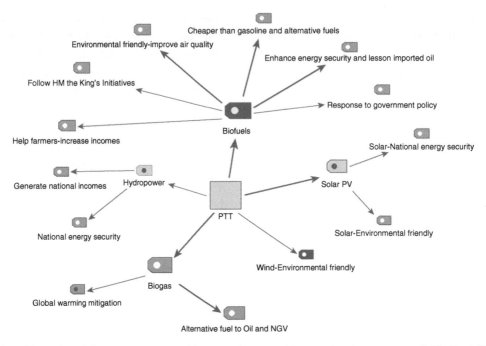

Figure 11.1 Illustration of discourses on renewable energy investment in one oil and gas company in Thailand (PTT), reproduced from Chaiyapa et al. (2018: 454)

The procedure used by Chaiyapa et al. (2018) in their data analysis was based on the *grounded theory* approach developed by Glaser and Strauss (1967), which will be further discussed in Chapter 16. It is emphasized by the authors that, although the software, MaxQDA, could not be used to analyse the data, it was very useful for facilitating (re)reading and rearranging of the texts that were used as data sources. Furthermore, the software was very efficient at creating the figures that were used as illustrations of the results of the analysis (Chaiyapa et al., 2018: 451).

Holistic analysis as well as discourse analysis will be further discussed in Chapters 16 and 21.

CHAPTER HIGHLIGHTS

- Qualitative content analysis is the basic design for collecting qualitative data based on documentary sources.
- Social research may be based on a wide variety of documentary sources, such as written texts, audio recordings, visual materials, audio-visual presentations and digital documents.
- Before conducting the data collection in qualitative content analysis of texts, the researcher must clarify the focus, select important topics and types of texts, find the texts, agree on permissions, and determine the degree of transparency.
- During the data collection, the selected texts are systematically reviewed, source-critical and contextual assessments are conducted, relevant content is selected, registered and categorized, and additional texts are selected and reviewed.
- The following problems are typical for data collection based on qualitative content analysis of texts:

1 The researcher's perspective may affect the selection and interpretation of the texts
2 Limited source-critical understanding may affect the interpretation of the texts
3 Limited contextual understanding may affect the interpretation of the texts.

- Qualitative content analysis may be used for examining visual materials, in addition to texts.
- Qualitative content analysis of images includes description of what the image shows and interpretation of what the image means.

- Computer programs may be useful in qualitative content analysis, not for analysing the data, but for identifying, recording and organizing relevant content of texts.
- Qualitative content analysis may be used in holistic studies of documentary sources, based on condensing the content of the documents or organizing the content in narratives.
- Discourse analysis is used for examining texts, in order to identify discourses, which shape or reflect people's views of the world and reality.

RESEARCH EXAMPLES

I recommend that you read the publications used as research examples in this chapter.

One of these articles was also referred to in Chapter 6. The study presented in this article is an example of a qualitative content analysis of South African newspaper articles on nursing:

Oosthuizen, Martha J. (2012) 'The portrayal of nursing in South-African newspapers: A qualitative content analysis', *Africa Journal of Nursing and Midwifery* 14(1), 49–62.

Three other articles are referred to as research examples in this chapter:

Kaefer, Florian, Juliet Roper and Paresha Sinha (2015) 'A software-assisted qualitative content analysis of news articles: Example and reflections', *Forum: Qualitative Social Research, 16*(2), art. 8.

This article shows how computers can be used in qualitative content analysis. It presents a study of Australian, British and American newspaper articles about New Zealand's carbon emissions and environmental global positioning. The main software used in this content analysis was NVivo. The authors provide a step-by-step description of how the software was used in their study. They conclude that, although the software cannot do the analysis for the researchers, it can make the analytical process more flexible, transparent and trustworthy.

Hakoköngäs, Eemeli, and Inari Sakki (2016) 'Visualized collective memories: Social representations of history in images found in Finnish history textbooks', *Journal of Community & Applied Social Psychology* 26(6), 496–517.

The study presented in this article is an example of a qualitative content analysis of visual materials. The research question is focused on the content and meanings of images, mainly photographs, in the construction of Finnish history. The study includes 541 images in three contemporary and comprehensive textbooks on Finnish history. The images are regarded as visual aspects of collective memory. In the content analysis, which covers the history since 1809, the images were categorized in terms of the year and location of the image, as well as the theme and actors shown in the image. In addition, the researchers noted some themes that were not included in the images in the study. The findings indicate that the main contents of Finnish visual collective memory are politics, culture and war, whereas topics such as religion and minorities are missing in the images.

Chaiyapa, Warathida, Miguel Esteban, and Yasuko Kameyama (2018) 'Why go green? Discourse analysis of motivations for Thailand's oil and gas companies to invest in renewable energy', *Energy Policy* 120, 448–459.

The study presented in this article is an example of a discourse analysis. The study examines discourses used by oil and gas companies in Thailand to legitimize their investments in renewable energy. Annual reports from three companies were used as data sources. Based on keywords regarding different types of renewable energy, the MaxQDA software was used to identify and record relevant fragments of text. The researchers conducted a thematic coding of the recorded text content and grouped all related fragments under a theme or a discourse strand. The software was used to create figures that illustrated the discourse strands for each company. The findings show that there are variations between energy sources and companies as to the discourses used to legitimize the companies' investments.

STUDENT EXERCISES AND QUESTIONS

1 Describe different types of documentary sources that can be used in social science.
2 What are the most important preparations for a qualitative content analysis?
3 Why are source-critical assessments important in qualitative content analysis?
4 What is the difference between categorization and condensation in studies of texts?

5 Why is contextual understanding important in qualitative content analysis?
6 Discuss advantages and limitations of using computer programs in qualitative content analysis.
7 Select a current debate in a newspaper, and discuss how this debate could be examined by means of qualitative content analysis.

RECOMMENDED LITERATURE

Ledin, Per, and David Machin (2018) *Doing Visual Analysis: From Theory to Practice*. London: Sage.

This book provides tools for examining a wide range of visual data, including photographs, videos, websites, data visualizations, branding of packaging, and designs of buildings and furniture. The authors present examples of the use of such tools, and they discuss what types of research questions are best suited to different tools and methods.

Schreier, Margrit (2012) *Qualitative Content Analysis in Practice*. London: Sage.

This book is a step-by-step guide to qualitative content analysis of various types of texts, including textual data collected through interviews or focus groups. The book provides detailed descriptions of each part of the research process, as well as advice on the use of software. Research examples are presented as illustrations of each step of the content analysis.

Scott, John P. (1990) *A Matter of Record: Documentary Sources in Social Research*. Cambridge: Polity Press.

This textbook provides an introduction to the use of documentary sources in social research. Documentary sources are discussed in relation to other data sources. Criteria for evaluating documentary sources are discussed, and these criteria are used in the presentation of a number of documentary sources that are available for social research, including census data, official statistics, government publications, directories, yearbooks, personal diaries, and letters.

Titscher, Stefan, Michael Meyer, Ruth Wodak, and Eva Vetter (2000) *Methods of Text and Discourse Analysis: In Search of Meaning*. London: Sage.

This book presents a comprehensive overview of social science approaches to text and discourse analysis. Each approach is described in the same way, and the different approaches are systematically compared. Furthermore, the social science approaches are discussed in relation to linguistic models for analysis of texts.

STRUCTURED OBSERVATION

This chapter provides the knowledge that is necessary for understanding and assessing how structured observation is used to collect quantitative data in social science. The chapter will enable you to carry out studies based on this type of data collection.

The chapter will teach you how to

- use structured observation in field observation, field experiments, and laboratory experiments
- construct a structured observation schedule

- use the schedule in the observation of selected phenomena
- handle different problems that might arise in structured observation.

Structured observation in different settings

After three chapters on designs for collecting qualitative data, designs for quantitative data collection will now be discussed in three chapters. The first of these is this chapter, which deals with the basic design for collecting quantitative data based on actors as the source type.

Like participant observation, structured observation involves observing the actors while they perform the activities that the researcher wants to study. However, structured observation differs in several ways from participant observation. Structured observation is not combined with participation in the actors' activity. The observation is not open and flexible regarding what should be observed. Instead it is limited to some pre-selected features of the actors and their activities. Data recording is not conducted by writing field notes, but by completing specific observation schedules, which are constructed before the data collection process. Data collection is not combined with data analysis. While participant observation is always performed in the actors' natural environment, structured observation can be carried out in both natural and artificial environments, such as laboratories. Moreover, unlike participant observation, structured observation is often combined with one or more interventions, in different types of *experiments*.

Referring to the setting of the observation, structured observation may be used for data collection in three major types of studies. An overview of these settings and types of studies is presented in Table 12.1.

First, structured observation of actors in their natural environment without any intervention from the researcher is called *field observation*. The purpose is to study selected activities without interfering in any way in these activities or the context in which they take place. The passenger study described in Chapter 6 is an example of field observation. The study focused on activities among passengers on local buses and trains in Wellington, New Zealand (Russell et al., 2011). Another example is a British study of interaction between nurses and patients during the administration of medication in a mental health unit (Duxbury et al., 2010).

Second, structured observation may also be used in *field experiments*, where observation of actors in their natural environment is combined with one

Table 12.1 Different settings for structured observation

Type of study	Setting of the structured observation
Field observation	Natural environment, without intervention
Field experiment	Natural environment, with intervention
Laboratory experiment	Laboratory, under controlled conditions, typically with intervention

or more interventions from the researcher. The purpose is to examine effects of the interventions on selected activities or interaction patterns. The intervention may, for example, be a special teaching programme in a school class, and effects of the programme may be identified by observing selected activities among the students in the class, and comparing their activities before and after the intervention, or observing and comparing activities in classes with and without the intervention. Hultén (2015) conducted a field experiment in a Swedish grocery store to examine the impact of sound experiences on the shopping behaviour of children and their parents.

Third, structured observation may be conducted in a laboratory, where the actors are observed under strictly controlled conditions in an artificial environment. This type of laboratory consists of special rooms that are designed and constructed for structured observation of actions and interaction, mainly in small groups of actors. The actors to be observed are gathered in one room, and the observers are usually placed in an adjacent room, where they can observe the actors through a one-way mirror or on a video screen. Typically, the observation is also combined with one or more inventions from the researcher, in addition to the researcher's control of the study conditions. As in field experiments,

the purpose is to analyse how the activities observed are influenced by the interventions, by comparing observations of the same actors before and after the invention, or by comparing actors who experience the invention and actors who are not exposed to the intervention. Therefore, such studies are called *laboratory experiments*. As pointed out in Chapter 6, a series of laboratory experiments was carried out by Bales (1952), who observed communication and interaction in small groups, examining how the groups' solution of particular tasks was influenced by different conditions for communication between the group members.

Experimental research will be explained in more detail in Chapter 21. In this chapter, the purpose is to look into the characteristic features of the data collection in structured observation. Most of these features are relevant for all the settings and types of studies in which the structured observation is used. The chapter is focused on the preparation and implementation of data collection, as well as the typical issues that may arise in connection with the data collection. The discussion is based on Table 12.2, which presents an overview of the most important aspects of data collection through structured observation.

Table 12.2 Overview of data collection through structured observation

Aspect of data collection	Characteristics of structured observation

Preparations for data collection	• Select field or laboratory
	• Decide on possible interventions
	• Construct the observation schedule
	   ○ Select focus
	   ○ Specify categories
	• Determine the degree of transparency
	• Instruct the observers

Implementation of data collection	• Provide information to the actors • Find position and viewpoint • Observe the selected phenomena • Complete the observation schedule
Typical problems during data collection	• Field observation may limit the perspective • Laboratory observation may affect the actors • The observation may vary between different observers

Preparing the data collection

Compared to participatory observation, structured observation requires more comprehensive preparations for data collection. The data collection itself is less flexible. It must therefore be prepared more thoroughly and in greater detail. Let us see what this entails.

Selection of field observation, field experiment or laboratory experiment

During the preparations for the data collection, the researcher must choose the setting where the observation is to take place. It must be decided whether the structured observation should be a field observation, a field experiment or a laboratory experiment. Based on the research questions of the study, the researcher decides whether the study should be conducted in the field or in a laboratory, and then it is decided more specifically which field or type of laboratory should be chosen for the observation.

The passenger study mentioned above is an example of a field observation, where the field consists of local buses and trains in Wellington (Russell et al., 2011). The study of interaction between nurses and patients is based on field observation, where the field is a mental hospital unit in England (Duxbury et al., 2010). In the field experiment conducted by Hultén (2015), the field is a grocery store in Sweden.

The small-group studies carried out by Bales (1952) are examples of laboratory experiments. The laboratory consisted of two rooms with a one-way mirror between them. In such studies, the laboratory can be designed in many different ways. For example, the observation can be conducted using a video camera instead of a one-way mirror. The main point is that the actors are observed in a researcher-controlled environment. How extensive or strong this control is may vary between different studies. In Bales's small-group studies, the control was relatively strong. The researcher controlled the composition and structure of the groups, the types of activities they should perform, and when and where these activities were to be performed.

Furthermore, the researcher decides whether the observation should be combined with one or more interventions, in an experiment. In experiments, it has to be decided which interventions should be chosen, and how they should be used in combination with the structured observation. In laboratory studies, it is typical to use various types of interventions. In the laboratory experiments conducted by Bales (1952), the interventions are different tasks that the small groups are asked to solve, combined with various structural conditions for communication within the groups.

In his field experiment, Hultén (2015) used an audio story track system as an intervention. Each family in the experiment in the store was offered an MP3 player with a story that was supposed to stimulate the knowledge about the merchandise and thus affect shopping behaviour.

Construction of the observation schedule

Constructing an observation schedule is another important task in the preparation for data collection. All the actors should be observed in the same way and with a view to obtaining the same types of information. The observation is therefore conducted based on the same schedule for all the actors, so that the schedule must be designed before the data collection begins. As an example, the observation schedule used in the study of shopping behaviour by Hultén (2015) is presented in Table 12.3.

Table 12.3 Observation schedule for structured observation of shopping behaviour, reproduced from Hultén (2015: 214–215)

Dependent variables

1. Voice behaviour of children in terms of screaming, bothering or general loudness
   - The child is quiet or saying something to the parent/parents
   - The child has a normal conversation with the parent/parents, or hassles them some of the time
   - The child is loud, constantly hassles, and/or screams

2. Movements of children, running, jumping or wandering around on parent/parents
   - The child is walking with or close to the parent/parents
   - The child is moving around close to the parent/parents or acting on its own initiative
   - The child is walking around on its own initiative, climbing around or rambling

3. Leaders of the shopping trip
   - The parent/parents is/are leading the family through the shopping process
   - The parent/parents decide about the walking directions, but also watch what the child is doing and occasionally give the child directions on where to go
   - The child is moving around on its own initiative and is the shopping leader, whilst the parent/parents is/are either following the child or constantly have to call for the child

4. Expressions of parental stress:
   - The parent/parents act calm and systematic
   - The parent/parents act not stressful but efficient in the section
   - The parent/parents act notably stressful

Independent variables

5. Time in section: _____
6. Age of children: 3–5 6–8
7. Number of children: _____
8. Walking/sitting children:
   - The child is walking
   - The child is sitting in the trolley
   - The child is sitting in the baby stroller
9. Type of shopping: Trolley or basket

The observation schedule must specify what factors should be focused on, and what the observer should look for or listen out for. The design of the schedule depends on the focus of the observation. Compared to participant observation, structured observation is more limited and is concentrated on fewer phenomena, and these phenomena are selected and clarified before the observation starts. This focus is based on the research question of the study, which is usually more delimited and specific in structured observation than it is in participant observation. The items in focus in the schedule presented in Table 12.3 are closely related to the research questions in Hultén's study of shopping behaviour. The research questions were formulated as five hypotheses on the activities of the children and the interaction between the children and their parents (Hultén, 2015: 201–202).

The schedule should also specify categories for the observation. While the focus, typically the list of items, is on what the observer should look out for or listen to, the categorization shows how the different actors can be described on each of the items. What is observed is not described in an exhaustive manner in field notes but is recorded by ticking off, or encircling, the relevant and appropriate categories in the observation schedule. For example, in the observation schedule in Table 12.3, regarding item 4 (expressions of parental stress), the observer has to choose between three categories (calm and systematic, not stressful but efficient, and notably stressful). In the observation schedule of the passenger study in Wellington (Russell et al., 2011), the observers had to cross off the appropriate categories for means of transport (train or bus), the time of observation, as well as the passenger's gender, age (young, middle aged or older) and activities. The activities were pre-divided into 11 specific categories (such as looking out of the window, reading, talking with fellow passengers, talking on the telephone or sending text messages), as well as an unspecified residual category (other activities).

The construction of the observation schedule is usually based on the step-by-step procedure for selecting information as described in Chapter 7 (see Table 7.3). The focus consists of specifying dimensions or variables for the different concepts in the study. The categorization involves explaining how each of the variables should be divided into different values. Through operational definitions of variables and values, the researcher must specify how different observations in the field or in the laboratory should be placed in relation to the different categories. For each category or value, a set of criteria is usually specified for the assessment of which observed phenomena should be included in the category. The observation schedule presented in Table 12.3 is very simple. The schedule includes only a few variables and categories, and the operational definitions are not very complicated. Other studies may require a more comprehensive and more complex observation schedule, but the schedule must always be simple enough for it to be handled properly while the observation is in progress.

Degree of transparency

Before the observation starts, the researcher must decide how much transparency there should be in relation to the actors that are observed. In laboratory experiments it is not possible to hide the fact that the observation is occurring, and also in field experiments it is difficult to hide the interventions that are going on. However, the researcher can choose whether to be open about the purpose of the study. In the field experiment in the Swedish grocery store, Hultén (2015: 205) informed the families that an experiment was taking place. However, he did not tell them that they would be observed during the experiment, because he feared that their behaviour might be affected if they were aware of the observation.

On the other hand, in some field observations, it may be difficult to be transparent in relation to the actors, with regard to not only the purpose of the study, but also the implementation of the observation. This is the case when the observation is carried out in public places, where there are many actors, where the researcher does not know in advance which actors will be observed, and where the distance between the observer and the actors is too large for the actors to be informed. The passenger study with structured observation on buses and trains in Wellington (Russell et al., 2011) is an example of this. In such studies, the researcher can provide general information through media about the observation and the purpose of the study, but it is impossible to contact each actor individually.

However, in the field observation of interaction between nurses and patients in a British mental hospital unit, there was full transparency about the study, and informed consent to participate was provided by the management of the unit as well as by each nurse and each patient observed (Duxbury et al., 2010: 2484).

Apart from some special circumstances, as mentioned here, the issue of transparency in relation to the actors is quite similar for participant and structured observation. In most cases, the researcher has the opportunity to choose the degree of transparency. In principle, there should be as much transparency as possible. If transparency is limited during the structured observation, the researcher should emphasize the same types of methodological and ethical considerations as highlighted for participant observation.

Instructing the observers

While participant observation is conducted by the researchers themselves, structured observation is often carried out with the help of several other observers. The observation of all actors can be so extensive that it cannot be conducted by the researcher alone, and the observation is so simple that it can be carried out by others. However, when researchers use observers other than themselves, it is important to instruct the observers. This is also part of the preparations for data collection. Part of this instruction is provided in writing. The researcher formulates written observation instructions that the observers read before the observation and bring with them into the field or the laboratory. These instructions describe as accurately as possible what the observer should do, what the observation should focus on and how the observation schedule should be completed. Based on the operational definitions of the various categories in the schedule, the observation instructions provide supplementary comments on the criteria specified, and describe examples of behaviour that should be placed in the different categories.

In addition to these written instructions, the observers should also be prepared through conversations, pretests of the observation schedule and other training. The purpose of all this is to ensure that all the observers carry out the observation and use the observation schedule in the same way, so that the data are affected as little as possible by which observers are used.

Implementing the data collection

Since structured observation requires such extensive and detailed *preparation* for data collection, the *implementation* of the data collection is less demanding in structured observation than it is in participant observation. The most important tasks during the data collection will now be described.

Providing information to the actors

The first task is to provide information to the actors who will be observed. Naturally, this task is irrelevant if the observation design is completely hidden. In any event, the information must be adapted to the researcher's choice with regard to the degree of transparency. The most extensive information will be provided for laboratory observation, which assumes that the actors perform researcher-initiated activities under conditions fully controlled by the researcher. In general, the information must be such that the participants are encouraged to participate in the study, but they must also be informed about their rights to refuse to participate.

Position and viewpoint

When the observation is to be carried out, the observer must find an appropriate position and viewpoint. In the laboratory experiments carried out by Bales (1952), the observers were in a separate room behind a one-way mirror, where they could easily see and hear the actors gathered in the adjacent room.

In the field observation of passengers in Wellington, the two observers placed themselves in different locations on the bus or train, and each of them observed the closest passengers so that they could record both the passengers' activities and their gender and age. At the same time, they had to place themselves in such a way that they could carry out the observation and registration in a discreet manner and without this being annoying for those who were observed or for the other passengers (Russell et al., 2011).

Generally, it is important to find a position and a viewpoint that combine two considerations: the observer must have as good a view as possible, while the actors' activities must not be disturbed more than necessary by the observation.

Observation and schedule completion

The main task during data collection is to observe the selected phenomena. The observer must concentrate on the phenomena specified in the observation schedule and the observation instructions. It may also be relevant to notice conditions that are not to be registered in the schedule, because these may be important for the assessment of which category is most appropriate for what is to be registered. Otherwise, the observer should be careful not to be distracted by activities that are not relevant to the structured observation.

The observer must complete the observation schedule at the same time as the observation is performed. One observation schedule is used for each unit of analysis, whether it be an actor, event, action, interaction or a statement of opinion. The unit of analysis in the passenger study by Russell et al. (2011) is an actor, namely each passenger. In the small-group studies by Bales (1952), the unit of analysis is an action, more specifically the interaction process linked to the group's solution to the assigned task. Each group was observed several

times, with different task solutions and varying communication structure within the group. An observation schedule was completed for each task solution and thus there were several schedules for each group. In the field experiment in the Swedish grocery store, Hultén (2015) used each shopping family as the unit of analysis.

As already mentioned, the implementation of the observation and completion of the schedule assume that the observation schedule is not too comprehensive or too complicated. The schedule must be simple enough for the observer to maintain an overview of all the phenomena to be observed and the schedule must be so easy to use that it can be completed at the same time as the observation is performed, without distracting the observer's attention from the observation.

Typical problems during the data collection

There are certain differences between structured observation in the field and structured observation in the laboratory with respect to typical problems experienced during data collection. During a structured observation in the field, the viewpoint may become too restricted, so that the perspective becomes too limited or one-sided. It can be difficult to place yourself close enough to the actors to be able to see or hear what is to be recorded during the observation. In this case, the observation will not be detailed enough. On the other hand, the location can also be too close, so that the observer only captures specific details and loses their overview of the observation area as a whole. Some phenomena may be difficult to observe and register, for example because they have a short duration, or because they occur very rarely. In the field observation of passengers in Wellington, the activities of each passenger were observed for a period of 4 minutes. It was sometimes difficult to see all the passengers' activities during this period. A passenger could do several things at the same time, move to another seat or get off at a stop before the observation period ended. Other passengers could also place themselves between the observer and the observed passenger (Russell et al., 2011).

Such problems are prevented primarily by careful consideration of the choice of position in the field and by ensuring that the scope and complexity of the observation schedule are sufficiently adapted to the observation conditions.

If the observation is conducted in a laboratory, under conditions controlled by the researcher, the viewpoint and perspective will rarely be a problem. On the other hand, laboratory experiments may affect the actors. The actors are brought into an artificial environment to perform specific tasks. The impact under such conditions can be even stronger than for participant observation. Nevertheless, this problem may be less serious than it is in participant observation, because laboratory experiments are not intended to study the actors' usual behaviour in their natural environment, as is the case in participatory observation. The researcher's control of the study conditions also provides a good basis for understanding what can be expected to affect the actors and their actions. The challenge

is to take sufficient account of this during the analysis of the data and the interpretation of the results of the analysis.

If the observation is conducted by several observers, there might be systematic variations between different observers in their collection and registration of data. Different observers may notice different phenomena, perceive the observed conditions differently or use the observation schedule in different ways. This problem can occur in both field observation and laboratory observation. The problem is that the data may be influenced by the observers.

This can be prevented by a careful construction of the observation schedule, with particular emphasis on specifying and defining the categories, providing good instructions for the implementation of the observation and ensuring good training of the observers. There are also methods for systematically comparing the observation schedules from different observers. Such comparisons can clarify how much the collected data are influenced by the observers. The *reliability* of the data is weakened if the observation varies between different observers. Investigations of these variations are called *reliability testing*. Reliability and reliability testing will be discussed in more detail in Chapter 15.

CHAPTER HIGHLIGHTS

- Structured observation is the basic design for collecting quantitative data using actors as the type of source.
- Structured observation may be conducted in natural or artificial environments, and may or may not be combined with one or more interventions. Thus, structured observation is used for collecting data in three main types of studies:
  1 Field observation
  2 Field experiments
  3 Laboratory experiments.

- Structured observation is not combined with participation. The preparations for data collection are more extensive and the implementation of the data collection is less demanding than in participant observation.
- Prior to conducting data collection in structured observation, the researcher must select the setting and decide on possible interventions, construct the observation schedule, determine the degree of transparency and instruct the observers.

- During the data collection process, the researcher must provide information to the actors (if appropriate and possible), find a position and viewpoint, observe the selected phenomena and complete the observation schedule.

- The following problems are typical for data collection based on structured observation:
  1. Field observation may limit the perspective
  2. Laboratory observation may affect the actors
  3. The observation may vary between different observers.

RESEARCH EXAMPLES

I recommend that you read the publications used as research examples in this chapter.

Two of these articles were also referred to in Chapter 6. The article by Bales (1952) is an example of a laboratory experiment, and the article by Russell et al. (2011) is exemplifying a field observation:

Bales, Robert F. (1952) 'Some uniformities of behavior in small social systems', in Guy E. Swanson, Theodore M. Newcomb, and Eugene L. Hartley (eds), *Readings in Social Psychology* (rev. edn). New York: Holt, Rinehart and Winston, pp. 146–159.

Russell, Marie, Rachel Price, Louise Signal, James Stanley, Zachery Gerring, and Jacqueline Cumming (2011) 'What do passengers do during travel time? Structured observations on buses and trains', *Journal of Public Transportation*, 14(3), 123–146.

Two other articles are referred to as research examples in this chapter:

Duxbury, Joy A., Karen Margaret Wright, Anna Hart, Diane Bradley, Pamela Roach, Neil Harris, and Bernie Carter (2010) 'A structured observation of the interaction between nurses and patients during the administration of medication in an acute mental health unit', *Journal of Clinical Nursing* 19(17–18), 2481–2492.

This article presents a study based on field observation. The purpose was to examine interaction between nurses and patients during the process of medication in a mental hospital. Three observers used an observation schedule in observation of practical aspects and interaction patterns during 20 rounds of medication. Fifty-seven patients and 24 nurses were included in the observation. The findings indicate that there is limited collaboration between nurses and patients, and that information exchange during the medication rounds could be improved.

Hultén, Bertil M. L. (2015) 'The impact of sound experiences on the shopping behavior of children and their parents', *Marketing Intelligence & Planning* 33(2), 197–215.

The study presented in this article is a field experiment in a Swedish grocery store. The purpose was to examine how family shopping behaviour is influenced by a sound track system containing stories for children. Structured observation of the children's activities and interaction between the children and their parents were conducted both in an experimental group of families, who experienced the new sound track system, and in a control group of other families, who did not experience the intervention. The findings show that the sound system does influence the shopping behaviour in a significant way.

STUDENT EXERCISES AND QUESTIONS

1 What are the main differences between structured observation and participant observation?
2 What are the most important differences between structured field observations and laboratory experiments?
3 Why is structured observation not combined with participation in the activities that are observed?
4 Why is it important to instruct the observers carefully before implementing a structured observation?
5 Describe the typical problems that may arise during a structured observation.
6 Discuss how activities and interaction patterns among students at a seminar could be examined by means of structured observation.
7 Construct an observation schedule and conduct a structured observation of selected activities in a student cafeteria.

RECOMMENDED LITERATURE

Gillham, Bill (2008) *Observation Techniques: Structured to Unstructured*. London: Continuum.

This book is an introductory text, providing an overview and a guide for both structured, semi-structured and unstructured observation techniques. Furthermore, it deals with the use of observation in experimental research, and it discusses various ethical dilemmas related to observation.

Mansell, Jim (2011) 'Structured observational research in services for people with learning disabilities', *SSCR Methods Review*, 10. NIHR School for Social Care Research, London (http://eprints.lse.ac.uk/43159/).

This paper is a literature review that presents examples of the use of structured observation to assess and improve the quality of services, especially when users of the services are unable to answer questions about their experiences. The review discusses the sampling, the practical steps of observations in services, and the analysis and presentation of observational data.

Wilson, T. D., and D. R. Streatfield (1981) 'Structured observation in the investigation of information needs', *Social Science Information Studies* 1(3), 173–184.

This article discusses how structured observation can be used in studies of information needs. Referring to a particular study, the article is focused on structured observation as a method. It describes the reasons for choosing this method, the preparations for data collection, the use of the method in the field, and the problems and effectiveness of structured observation.

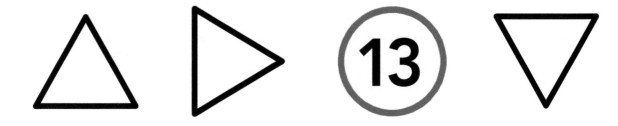

QUESTIONNAIRES AND SURVEYS

This chapter provides the knowledge that is necessary for understanding how questionnaires and surveys are used to collect quantitative data in social science. The chapter will enable you to carry out studies based on this type of data collection.

The chapter will teach you how to

- formulate various types of questions and various options for responses
- construct the questionnaire
- conduct a survey experiment

- use the questionnaire and collect the responses from the respondents
- handle typical problems during the data collection.

Quantitative data collection from respondents

The topic of this chapter is structured questioning, which is the basic design for collecting quantitative data from respondents as the source. This design is often referred to as a *survey*.

The key element of the structured questioning in a survey is the questionnaire, which consists of fixed questions in a particular order and predefined response options for most questions. The questionnaire can be used by the respondents themselves, who complete the questionnaire by ticking off their answers to each of the questions, or by an interviewer, who reads out the questions for the respondent and crosses off the respondent's answers to each question. The questionnaire may contain many questions, but the questions are nevertheless limited to specific conditions that are based on the research question of the study and selected before the data collection is conducted.

The implementation of the data collection is less demanding than is the case with unstructured interviewing. Therefore, the data collection is not necessarily done by the researchers themselves. Furthermore, as a rule, structured questioning involves so many respondents that it is impossible for the researcher to perform the data collection alone.

The data collection depends primarily on how well the questionnaire works. The construction of the questionnaire is completed before the data collection starts and it is used in the same way for all the respondents. Thus, the questionnaire cannot be altered during the data collection process. The preparations for the data collection are therefore very important.

This chapter deals with the characteristic features of data collection based on structured questionnaires. The preparation and implementation of the data collection are described, and typical problems associated with the data collection are discussed. The presentation refers to Table 13.1, which provides a schematic overview of the main features of the data collection in structured questioning.

Preparing the data collection

The main tasks during the preparation for data collection are to choose which method of questioning should be used, and to construct the questionnaire. The questionnaire must also be pretested, any interviewers must be instructed, and the respondents must be informed. Let us take a closer look at all these tasks.

The construction of the questionnaire is the most demanding task. It involves formulating the

Table 13.1 Overview of data collection through structured questioning

Aspect of data collection	Characteristics of questionnaires and surveys

Preparations for data collection	• Clarify the questioning method
	• Construct the questionnaire
	   ○ Formulate questions
	   ○ Formulate response options
	   ○ Determine the order of the questions
	   ○ Assess the length and layout
	• Pretest and possibly improve the questionnaire
	• Instruct interviewers
	• Determine the degree of transparency
	• Provide information to the respondents

Implementation of data collection	• Carry out the questioning:
	   ○ Structured personal interviews
	   ○ Self-administered questionnaires, received and returned through personal delivery, mail, e-mail or Internet
	• Send a reminder or visit again if necessary

Typical problems during data collection	• Drop-out or unreliable answers related to
	   ○ the respondents' willingness to respond
	   ○ the respondents' ability to respond
	   ○ the respondents' understanding of the questions

questions to be asked and the response options to be used, as well as determining the order of the questions and the layout of the questionnaire. These challenges will be discussed, with particular emphasis on the differences between different types of questions and different types of response options.

Selection of method of questioning

One of the first tasks during the preparations for data collection is to clarify the method of questioning. This clarification must occur at an early stage, because the method of questioning must be considered in connection with the questionnaire's design and length, or scope.

There are two main questioning methods. One method is that the respondents complete the questionnaire themselves, while the other entails that the respondent is interviewed based on the

questionnaire. Respondents who complete the questionnaire themselves can receive and return it by normal post, as an e-mail, via the Internet or by personal delivery. The interview can take place in the form of a personal interview, conducted in a face-to-face meeting between the interviewer and the respondent, or in the form of a telephone interview, carried out in a phone call between the interviewer and the respondent. The different methods of questioning can also be combined, for example such that the respondent is initially interviewed by telephone and then receives a questionnaire to be completed. The questionnaire can then be collected by an interviewer, who concludes the questioning with a personal interview. Statistics Norway regularly conducts extensive studies of people's consumption and people's time use. In both of these studies, the data collection is based on structured questioning, where personal interviewing is combined with the respondents completing structured questionnaires in the form of diaries.

A questionnaire to be completed by the respondents themselves must be relatively short and simple, so that all the respondents can understand and complete it. In a personal interview, the questionnaire may be more comprehensive and more complicated because it will be handled by an interviewer, who can motivate the respondents and explain difficult questions. For telephone interviews, the distance between the interviewer and the respondent is greater, so the questionnaire should be shorter and simpler than for a personal interview. During telephone interviews, however, the questionnaire can be more demanding than when it is completed by the respondents themselves.

The use of the telephone, e-mail or the Internet assumes that all the respondents can be contacted by these means. Telephone interviewing has become common in recent years, but the use of e-mail or the Internet remains problematic for some types of respondents, such as older or disadvantaged persons.

Personal interviewing has many advantages compared to other forms of questioning, although it is far more costly. The costs are least when the questionnaire is completed by the respondents themselves and sent back and forth in e-mails or web communication, but the greatest problem with this method of questioning is motivating the respondents to participate. The drop-out rate of respondents can therefore be high.

Open-ended or closed-ended questions

The main task when preparing for data collection is to construct the questionnaire. This entails formulating questions and response options, determining the sequence of the questions and evaluating the length and layout of the questionnaire.

Formulating questions entails both selecting which questions should be asked and writing each question. The selection of questions is based on the research questions to be addressed in the study and the procedure outlined in Chapter 7 (Table 7.3). As a rule, each question will refer to a particular variable or a specific indicator in an index. The formulation of the question is based on the operational definition of the variable or indicator.

We can distinguish between different types of questions, partly based on the form of the question (how we ask) and partly based on the content of the questions (what we ask). Regarding the form of the questions, there is an important distinction between open-ended and closed-ended questions. An *open-ended* question has no fixed response options. Only the question is formulated in advance and space is provided in the questionnaire to write down the answer as formulated by the respondents themselves. A *closed-ended* question has fixed response options so that the respondent's answer can be registered by ticking off the response option that is most appropriate. Figure 13.1 provides an example of an open-ended and a closed-ended question. In the closed-ended question the respondent is instructed to select only one of the response options. Such instructions are usually written in capital letters.

In structured questioning, the vast majority of questions are closed-ended, but the questionnaire may also include some open-ended questions. Closed-ended questions are easier to handle for both the respondents and any interviewers. This is especially true if the questions are difficult or sensitive and if the respondents have little experience of formulating clear answers or completing a form. The response options can also help explain and clarify the question for the respondents. For interviewing, this requires that the interviewer reads out both the question and the response options. When there are many response options, however, it may be difficult for the respondent to remember all the options or to obtain an adequate overview in order to choose

---

1 The issue of women's access to abortion is widely discussed in politics. What is your opinion in this issue?

_____

_____

_____

_____

2 The issue of women's access to abortion is widely discussed in politics. What is your opinion in this issue? SELECT ONLY ONE ANSWER

☐ Abortion should never be allowed.

☐ Abortion should be allowed only if the woman's life or health is at risk.

☐ Abortion should also be allowed if the woman cannot take care of her child because of personal circumstances.

☐ The individual woman may decide for herself whether she will give birth to her child or have an abortion.

Figure 13.1 Example of an open-ended question (1) and a closed-ended question (2)

the most appropriate option. In a personal interview, this problem can be reduced by allowing the respondent to view a card listing the response options. Other types of visual illustrations can also be used during a personal interview.

In some cases, however, fixed response options may be *leading*, implying, for example, that respondents who actually do not have any opinion about a particular question nevertheless choose one of the response options provided because it looks nice or convenient. During the interview, such an effect can be avoided if the response options are not read out. However, the fact that the interviewer still has the fixed response options to relate to is an advantage for the data entry. When a structured questionnaire is to be used for interviewing, the researcher must evaluate and clarify which response options should be read out, and which response options should be visible only to the interviewer. Figure 13.2 shows examples of

---

SELECT ONLY ONE ANSWER FOR EACH QUESTION

1 The issue of the extent of your country's aid to developing countries is widely discussed in politics. What is your opinion in this issue?
   ☐ The aid should be reduced
   ☐ The aid should be maintained at current levels
   ☐ The aid should be increased

2 The issue of the extent of your country's aid to developing countries is widely discussed in politics. What is your opinion in this issue? Do you think the aid should be reduced, that it should be maintained at current levels, or that it should be increased?
   ☐ The aid should be reduced
   ☐ The aid should be maintained at current levels
   ☐ The aid should be increased

3 The issue of the extent of your country's aid to developing countries is widely discussed in politics. What is your opinion in this issue? READ OUT THE RESPONSE OPTIONS!
   ☐ The aid should be reduced
   ☐ The aid should be maintained at current levels
   ☐ The aid should be increased

Figure 13.2 Example of different forms of a closed-ended question for interviewing

QUESTIONNAIRES AND SURVEYS

different forms of the same interview question with fixed response options. In version 1, the interviewer reads out the question, but not the response options. In version 2, the response options are included in the question itself, which is read out in its entirety. Version 3 provides instructions for the interviewer (in capital letters) that the response options should be read out.

When the respondents complete the questionnaire themselves, all the response options will be visible. If the response options are considered to be leading, then it may be appropriate to use an open-ended question. This may also be relevant during an interview if there is a risk that the response options could be leading with regard to the interviewer's registration of the responses. Open-ended questions can otherwise be an advantage if it is difficult to formulate response options that are adequate for all respondents, or if there is a risk that the respondents will feel uncomfortable choosing between a few categories or placing themselves in a general category. Open-ended questions may also be used if the researcher wishes to allow for more nuanced differences between the answers from different respondents.

In such cases, we can use a combination of open-ended and closed-ended format in the same question, for example by concluding the list of response options with a residual category, and inviting the respondents to specify this category in their own words if it is used. Figure 13.3 shows an

example of this. The residual category in this example is 'other reason', which includes all possible reasons other than those included in the three alternative categories above.

Single or composite questions

Regarding the form of the questions, we can also distinguish between single questions and composite questions. Single questions appear separately in the questionnaire. Each of these questions refers to a single theme and requires a single response, and each of these answers makes sense as an independent element in the data. The examples in Figures 13.1–13.3 show such single questions. Composite questions actually include a package or a battery of multiple question elements, where the respondent provides an answer for each element. Each of these answers has little value in itself, but becomes meaningful when viewed in conjunction with the answers to the other questions. Such composite questions are often used in connection with *indexes* in order to study attitudes towards specific phenomena. The entire question battery then corresponds to the index, and each question element refers to an *indicator*. In a study of workaholism among Norwegian employees, composite questions were used to examine work addiction as well as personality (Andreassen et al., 2014).

The formulation of composite questions must be based on the same assessments that form the basis for the wording of individual questions. We must also ensure that the different question elements (the indicators) fit well together, and that the battery of questions as a whole (the index) is comprehensive and relevant to what is to be measured. Procedures for examining and assessing the relationships between the indicators in an index and the index as a whole will be presented in Chapter 17.

The price increase in the country is less than before. What do you think is the main reason for this?

SELECT ONE ANSWER

☐ Government policy

☐ The National Bank's interest rate decisions

☐ International economic conditions

Other reason:

_____

Figure 13.3 Example of questions with combination of open-ended and closed-ended format

---

Over the last 12 months, have you done any of the following activities?		
	Yes	No
a Attended a meeting of a trade union, a political party or political action group	☐	☐
b Attended a protest or demonstration	☐	☐
c Signed a petition, including an e-mail or online petition.	☐	☐
d Contacted a politician or public official (other than routine contact arising from use of public services)	☐	☐
e Commented on a political or social issue online	☐	☐
f Boycotted certain products	☐	☐

Figure 13.4   Example of composite questions as a basis for an index: modified version of a question in Eurofound (2016: 15)

Figure 13.4 provides an example of a composite question that forms the basis for constructing an index. In this case, the six questions together can provide information about the respondent's involvement in political activities during the last year.

Questions about the respondents themselves or about other matters

As regards the content of the questions, we can distinguish between many different types of questions. Respondents can be asked about lots of different matters, but structured questioning is better suited to certain types of questions than to others. The starting point is that we should concentrate on questions that are meaningful to the respondents, so that they can provide meaningful and reliable responses. This means that the questions should preferably deal with topics that are close to and concrete for the respondents, or matters that the respondents are involved in. Respondents are usually poor sources of information regarding issues to which they do not have a close and specific relationship. If we ask questions about distant or abstract topics, we risk getting no answers or getting unreliable answers.

Three distinctions between questions with different content are of particular interest. Firstly, we can distinguish between questions about conditions linked to the respondents themselves and questions about other matters. Structured questioning is primarily suitable for clarifying matters linked to the respondents themselves. We can ask about the respondent's background and status, actions and opinions. We can also ask about the respondent's relationships with other actors and about events in which the respondent has been involved. The respondents have a good basis for answering such questions. These are issues with which they have an intimate and concrete relationship. If we ask questions about other matters or other actors, we must ensure that these are not too remote or too abstract. Questions about matters related to immediate family and close friends or colleagues may work well, especially if the questions concern specific observable conditions, such as specific features of family members' background and status, or particular colleagues' actions in a specific situation. Managers of organizations or institutions can also answer questions about the organization or institution as a whole. It would be more problematic to ask a respondent about other people's opinions or behaviour. On the other hand, we could ask about the respondent's own opinion or assessment of other actors' opinions or patterns of behaviour. Such assessments could also be the topic of questions about subjects that are even more distant from the respondent. For example, we do not use structured questioning of British respondents to examine what policies the EU has on environmental protection, but we can ask respondents about whether they are familiar with different aspects of EU environmental policy and what they think about this policy.

Cognitive or evaluative questions

Secondly, we can distinguish between *cognitive* questions that relate to actual circumstances, and *evaluative* questions that refer to values and assessments. Questions about what environmental policies are actually pursued by the EU are cognitive, while questions about the respondent's assessment of EU environmental policy are evaluative. In general, cognitive issues focus primarily on background, status and actions, while evaluative questions mainly concern opinions.

Questions about actions usually work best if they are specific. It is more effective to ask about what the respondent did in a particular situation or at a particular time, than to ask about what the respondent usually does, for example during holidays or on Sundays. Hypothetical questions about what the respondent would have done in an imaginary situation are particularly difficult, but they can work if they concern a type of situation with which the respondent has concrete experience. For example, in opinion polls, respondents are often asked about which party they would vote for 'if there was a parliamentary election tomorrow'.

Some questions about actions are particularly sensitive. These may be illegal or socially unacceptable actions, such as drink-driving, or actions that are intimate or very private, such as sexual behaviour. It is difficult to get reliable answers to such questions. When these types of actions are studied

using structured questioning, the scope of the actions is usually under-reported or underestimated. The opposite impact on the data may occur if we ask about actions that have high social prestige, such as going to the theatre. Then the respondent, consciously or subconsciously, may exaggerate their own activity so that these types of actions are over-reported or overestimated in our data. The specialist literature on survey research (see the recommended literature at the end of this chapter) contains more in-depth discussions of issues related to sensitive questions and a great deal of advice on question formulations that can be used to reduce such problems.

Questions about opinions are often less specific than questions about actions. Evaluative questions can therefore be more difficult to formulate than cognitive questions. Structured questioning, however, is the most important and most common research design for representative studies of people's attitudes and opinions. The development of methods and techniques for structured questioning has primarily occurred in connection with different types of opinion polls.

The way in which questions about opinions should be designed can vary from study to study, depending on both the types of opinions we are asking about and which respondents we ask. The formulation of such questions, however, can be based on some general experiences from research based on opinion polls. One of these experiences is that not only questions about actions, but also questions about opinions should be designed as specifically as possible and should ideally be linked to specific circumstances and specific relationships. General and abstract opinion questions may be understood in different ways by different respondents. Therefore, it also becomes difficult to interpret the answers clearly. A question about what the respondent thinks about fees on the banks' services, for example, provides the basis for more unambiguous answers than a question about what the respondent thinks about the banks. Even more unambiguous answers can be expected to a question about what the respondent thinks about the fact that the banks decided last week to increase the fees on ATM services. The questions can be further specified and clarified using the response options and through an initial explanation of the background to the question.

As these examples show, the specification of a question about opinions often entails a narrowing of the circumstances to which the opinions apply. In principle, the opinion on fees on the banks' services constitutes only part of the opinion about the banks' overall business activities or about the banks as a whole. The respondents' opinion about the banks' interest rate policy may be different from their opinion regarding fees on the banks' services. Therefore, composite questions and indexes are of major importance for investigating attitudes and opinions. Various question elements or indicators can refer to the respondent's opinion about different aspects of the banks and their business, and the battery of questions as a whole or the index can be an expression of the respondent's overall opinion about the banks. This will provide more reliable information about their overall opinion than can be obtained by a single general and stand-alone question.

Another experience is that the respondents' answers to questions about opinions can easily become superficial. Respondents can express a certain opinion, even if they do not really have a considered view of the circumstances covered by the question. This is especially true if the question has a general and abstract form, and if the respondent is given fixed response options. This problem can be reduced by using a *filter question*. In this filter question, respondents are asked whether they have an opinion about the particular matter, so that only those respondents who explicitly say that they have an opinion are asked what their opinion is. Another approach to mitigate the problem of superficial responses is to have a separate response option for 'no opinion', so that the respondent is made aware of this option. A respondent's answer that expresses a particular opinion can also be followed up with questions about how strong or intense this opinion is. Thus we have a certain basis to assess how extensive the problem of superficial responses may be. This opportunity to distinguish between strong and weak opinions can also contribute to a more nuanced analysis.

Questions about the past, present or future

The third distinction between questions with different content refers to the time dimension. The questions can apply to circumstances in the *past*, *present* or *future*. The main distinction is between questions about current matters and questions about previous matters. Current matters concern the respondent's current background, status, actions and opinions, or other matters that are current when the questioning takes place. As mentioned above, questions about the respondent's current actions can be formulated in different ways, by asking what the respondent usually does, or what the respondent did in a particular situation or at a particular time. The latter wording assumes that we are referring to a situation or a time that is recent, such as last week or the last time the respondent was in a shop.

If we refer to situations or times that are further back in time, the question will no longer be concerned with current matters, but with past matters. Questions about matters in the past are called *retrospective questions*. Such questions are used to obtain information about developments or changes over time: how has the respondent's status changed? Has the respondent changed their behavioural pattern or opinions? By asking questions about the same circumstances with reference to multiple instances, both current and previous, we can reconstruct such development processes. Such approaches can be used in, for example, studies of life-cycle or occupational mobility.

Retrospective questions are more difficult to answer than questions about current circumstances. When we ask about matters far back in time, it may be difficult for the respondent to remember the circumstances, and the circumstances may be remembered differently than how they actually occurred. Such recall problems and *recall errors* increase with time, and they are usually greater for questions about actions than they are for questions about status. The greatest problems occur in connection with questions about opinions. Experience shows that the respondents will, either consciously or subconsciously, tend to exaggerate the accordance between past and present circumstances, especially regarding their own actions and opinions. This is especially true if the respondent is asked questions about both current and past matters. When analysing data based on retrospective questions, there is a risk that changes in patterns of behaviour and opinions will be under-reported or underestimated. Recall problems and recall errors can be reduced by linking the retrospective questions to specific events or events that were important in the respondent's own life, such as when the respondent got married, had a child, moved to a new home, completed their education or started their first job.

In addition to questions about current and past matters, we can also ask questions about anticipated future matters. Such expectation questions are used, for example, in studies of consumers' expectations of future economic developments, partly regarding the country's economy as a whole, partly regarding the economic situation of the consumer's own household (Katona, 1964). Expectation questions can be compared with the hypothetical questions mentioned above. They can be just as difficult and demanding, and it is useful if they are linked to specific and concrete circumstances with which the respondents are familiar. In this way,

it is easier for respondents to have certain expectations about their own financial situation than about the country's economy. In both cases, it will also be easier to answer if the question specifies the time horizon for the expectations, for example regarding 'economic development in the next six months' or 'economic development next year'.

General requirements for the formulation of the questions

In addition to the assessments of the formulation of questions that relate especially to specific types of questions, there are some general considerations that apply to all question types. Firstly, it is important to make sure that the questions are neutral. We must avoid questions that are *leading*: the respondent must not be led or invited to choose a particular response option. A question is leading if, for example, it refers to just one of several contradictory positions in a debate, or if it discusses one of the positions in a more positive or attractive way than the other positions. Furthermore, a question is leading if it gives the impression that one of the positions is more acceptable than the others, or if it indicates that one of the positions has greater support than the others.

Figure 13.5 presents five examples of questions about the respondent's opinion on British membership of the EU. The first two of these questions are neutral, while the other three questions are leading in different ways. Questions 3 and 5 favour the position of EU supporters, while question 4 is slanted in favour of the position of the EU opponents.

Secondly, the questions should be *one-dimensional*. Each question formulation must contain only one question, so that neither the respondent nor the researcher is in doubt about what the answer refers to. The following wording is an example of a multidimensional question:

---

1   Are you for or against British membership of the EU?

  ☐ For

  ☐ Against

  ☐ Unsure, have no opinion

2   Some are supporters of British EU membership, while others are opposed to this. What do you think? Are you for or against British membership of the EU?

  ☐ For

  ☐ Against

  ☐ Unsure, have no opinion

3   Are you in favour of British membership of the EU?

  ☐ Yes

  ☐ No

  ☐ Unsure, have no opinion

4   At the last referendum on British membership of the EU, there was a majority against membership (Brexit). Are you for or against British membership of the EU?

  ☐ For

  ☐ Against

  ☐ Unsure, have no opinion

5   Opinion polls in recent times have shown increasing support for British membership of the EU. Are you for or against British membership of the EU?

  ☐ For

  ☐ Against

  ☐ Unsure, have no opinion

Figure 13.5   Examples of neutral (1–2) and leading (3–5) questions about British membership of the EU

Are you a supporter of continued Norwegian membership of NATO, or do you think that Norway should rely on military cooperation through the EU?

This formulation includes two different questions. It is possible to be in favour of Norwegian military cooperation through both NATO and the EU, and it is possible to be against both. Such multidimensional questions are also called *double-barrelled questions*. The formulation should be divided into two separate questions, while making the questions more neutral, such as:

1   Do you support or oppose Norwegian membership of NATO?
2   Are you for or against Norwegian participation in EU military cooperation?

Thirdly, the question formulations should be *clear, unambiguous* and *precise*. Here is a common example of a question formulation that does not take this into account:

What is your income?

This example contains a number of problems. It is unclear what period the income should refer to: Does it refer to monthly income or annual income? The concept of income is not clear: does it refer to gross income before pension contributions and tax allowance, income used as a basis for tax on gross earnings, income calculated for net taxes or income after tax? The sources of revenue to be included are not specified: does the question only cover salary income, or should dividends, income from interest and other capital income also be included? The question can be clarified in different ways, depending on what information the researcher wants. These questions are examples of more unambiguous and more accurate questions about income:

1　What was your total gross annual income last year, before tax allowances and deduction of tax? Include both salary and capital income.
2　How much did you receive in salary last month after pension contributions and deduction of tax?

Fourthly, the linguistic formulation of the questions should be adapted to the respondents selected, and the language used must be *understandable* for all the respondents. A good rule is to avoid foreign words or phrases that many people may find difficult to understand. On the other hand, it is also important that the questions are not perceived as being banal. If the respondents are experts on the topics raised in the questioning, it may be a good idea to use the professional terminology with which these respondents are familiar.

General requirements for response options

When formulating the questionnaire, the wording of the question itself must be seen in conjunction with the formulation of the response options. In conjunction with the step-by-step procedure for selecting information outlined in Chapter 7 (Table 7.3), each question corresponds to one dimension or variable, while each response option corresponds to a category or value. The construction of the response options is based on the operational definitions of the variables and their values, and we follow the categorization procedure described in Chapter 7.

In line with this description, we emphasize that the response options should be mutually exclusive and generally exhaustive for all possible answers to the question. In other words, the response options

should not overlap, and it should be possible for all respondents to find an appropriate response option. The formulation of the response options therefore requires thorough planning and understanding of which answers may be relevant. However, it is not always possible to predict all the answers. The response options can nevertheless be made exhaustive by including a residual category that can be used for all respondents who cannot place their response under one of the specified response options.

When categorizing, we also emphasize that the different categories should be *equivalent* so that there is a balanced relationship between them. Equivalence and balance between the response options in a questionnaire helps to avoid leading questions. For example, if we ask about respondents' attitude to banks' customer care, there should be as many response options for positive attitudes as for negative attitudes, and the positive response options should be designed in the same way as the negative response options. In such cases it is also common to have a middle category that can be used for respondents who do not have a clear positive or negative attitude. The response options could look like this:

- Very satisfied
- Satisfied
- Undecided, neither satisfied nor dissatisfied
- Dissatisfied
- Very dissatisfied

For example, if we removed the 'very dissatisfied' category, the set of response options would be unbalanced, and the question would be leading because positive response options would be marked more strongly than negative options. On the other hand, we could remove the *middle category* without the question becoming unbalanced. The disadvantage of that would be that respondents without a particular opinion could be 'forced' to express either satisfaction or dissatisfaction. On the other hand, an explicit middle category can cause many respondents to place themselves there for convenience, even though they actually have an opinion. Whether we should include a middle category should be determined specifically for each question based on an assessment of the different considerations.

With the same number of response options on both sides of a middle category, the number of response options for this type of attitude question becomes an odd number (3, 5, 7, etc.). For other question types, the number of response options may be an even number (2, 4, 6, etc.). The number of response options we should have for a question may depend on the question as well as what answers we can expect. We should not have so many response options that it will be difficult for the respondent to maintain an overview of the options or distinguish between them.

When designing response options, we need to make a separate assessment of questions that basically refer to variables at the interval or relationship level, such as age or income. Such questions may be open-ended, so that the age is stated in years and the income in pounds, dollars or euros. However, the questions can also be given a closed-ended form by grouping the values into a number of fixed response options. For example, the response options for the question of income could be:

- Less than €10,000
- €10,000–19,999
- €20,000–29,999
- €30,000–39,999
- €40,000–49,999
- €50,000–59,999
- €60,000 or more

The advantage of grouping the values in fixed response options for such questions is that respondents may find it easier to respond. There is no problem entering an exact figure for age in years, so there is no need to group the values of the age variable. However, it may be more difficult to enter an exact figure for income in euros than to place the income in one of the groups specified above.

The disadvantage of such a grouping of values is that we obtain less accurate information and that we reduce the measurement level of the variable from the ratio level to the ordinal level. This limits the analytical options because we cannot utilize analysis methods that assume continuous variables at the interval or ratio level.

Response options in the form of scales

A set of response options that are arranged in relation to each other in such a way that they form a variable at the ordinal, interval or ratio level is called a *scale*. The term 'scale' is used especially in relation to attitude questions. If we number the response options for the question about attitude towards the banks' customer service that we discussed above, the response options would be an example of a simple attitude scale at the ordinal level:

1 Very satisfied
2 Satisfied
3 Undecided, neither satisfied nor dissatisfied
4 Dissatisfied
5 Very dissatisfied

Increasing numerical values on this scale represent increasing negative or decreasing positive attitude towards banks' customer service.

A scale with only five values is a rather simple scale. However, if each value is to be specified with a particular wording, it will be difficult to have a finely divided scale with many values because the respondents may lose their overview. We could use a *graphical scale* instead, where the scale is visually illustrated for the respondent. Graphical *rating scales* are especially common. Such scales can be illustrated by a straight line that is divided into numerical values, for example from 0 to 10 or from 0 to 100. For some of the numerical values, especially the extremes and perhaps also the midpoint, there is a description of what attitude or

Based on a referendum, UK has decided to leave EU (Brexit). There is a lot of debate about this decision.

What is your opinion about Brexit?

On this scale, the value 0 corresponds to the strongest opposition to Brexit, while the value 10 corresponds to the strongest support for Brexit. Place a circle around the number that most closely describes your opinion.

Strongly against					Uncertain				Strongly in favour	
0	1	2	3	4	5	6	7	8	9	10

Figure 13.6 Example of graphical rating scale

attitude intensity the value represents. The answer can then be specified by the number on this scale that best fits the respondent's own attitude. Figure 13.6 is an example of a rating scale.

A graphical rating scale can be illustrated in other ways than by a simple line. For example, the scale can be expressed in the form of a thermometer, where 0 degrees and 100 degrees symbolize the extremes on the attitude scale. In newspapers and other media, it has become common to use dice to indicate ratings for films, concerts or books, for example. This appears as a simple scale with values from 1 to 6, where 1 indicates the most negative assessment and 6 indicates the most positive assessment. However, dice are not a very well-chosen illustration of such a rating scale. Dice are mostly used in games and are one of our most common symbols for chance. Dice throws are therefore associated with random numbers, not numbers that are deliberately chosen to match a systematic assessment.

The graphical rating scale in Figure 13.6 represents the response options for a single question. Other scales can be based on an index that combines or weights the answers to several questions. Such scales are called *composite scales*. There are many different types of composite scales for studying attitudes. One of the most common attitude scales is the *Likert scale*, which was developed in the 1930s by the American social psychologist Rensis Likert (1903–1981). This scale is based on a number of statements that express positive or negative attitudes to a particular phenomenon. For each statement, a question is asked about whether the respondent agrees or disagrees. The number of statements may vary, depending on how many aspects of the phenomenon we want to include in the scale. The number of response categories may also vary, depending on how closely we wish to measure the strength of the attitude. It is most common to have five categories: 'strongly agree', 'agree', 'neither agree nor disagree', 'disagree' and 'strongly disagree'. Such a five-point Likert scale was used in several questions in the study of workaholism mentioned above (Andreassen et al., 2014). If you want to 'force' the respondent to express a certain opinion, the middle category can be omitted. This was done in a study of attitudes among American and Chinese students towards the police response to domestic violence, where four-point Likert scale was used (Sun et al., 2011: 3300). Figure 13.7 shows an example of statements and response categories in a five-point Likert scale for examining attitudes to shopping malls.

Experience shows that some respondents will agree or disagree with all statements, without this reflecting their true attitude to the phenomenon covered by the statements. Such patterns in the answers are called *response sets*. Response sets can be detected and may be

For each of the five statements below, indicate whether you strongly agree, agree, disagree or strongly disagree with the statement. Circle the answer that best describes your opinion about each of the statements.

			Neither agree nor disagree		
1 Shopping malls draw too many customers away from the smaller shops	Strongly agree	Agree	Neither agree nor disagree	Disagree	Strongly disagree
	1	2	3	4	5
2 It is good to have the large product range in the shopping malls	Strongly agree	Agree	Neither agree nor disagree	Disagree	Strongly disagree
	5	4	3	2	1
3 Shopping malls are attractive due to the excellent parking facilities	Strongly agree	Agree	Neither agree nor disagree	Disagree	Strongly disagree
	5	4	3	2	1
4 Shopping malls provide too few opportunities for social contact during shopping	Strongly agree	Agree	Neither agree nor disagree	Disagree	Strongly disagree
	1	2	3	4	5
5 It is too stressful to shop at shopping malls	Strongly agree	Agree	Neither agree nor disagree	Disagree	Strongly disagree
	1	2	3	4	5

Figure 13.7 Example of statements and response categories in a Likert scale for measuring attitudes to shopping malls

excluded from the data analysis if the battery of questions includes both positive and negative statements, as illustrated in the figure.

In the example in the figure, each response option is assigned a number that indicates how strongly a positive attitude to shopping malls is expressed. The higher the number, the stronger the positive (or weaker the negative) attitude the answer expresses. For each respondent we find the value on the total Likert scale by adding up the numbers for each of the five answers. Thus, the scale consists of values from 5 to 25, where 5 corresponds to the least positive (or most negative) attitude, and 25 correspond to the most positive attitude towards shopping malls. Since the scale values are based on addition of the values for the answers to the individual question elements or indicators, the Likert scale constitutes an additive index.

There are also scales and indexes that are based on procedures other than addition for comparing the values for the individual indicators. Indexes and scales can also be constructed during the data analysis. This will be discussed in more detail in Chapter 17.

The order of the questions and the layout of the questionnaire

The design of the questionnaire also involves determining the order of the questions. Regarding the order of the topics raised, the same considerations apply as for unstructured interviewing. We should start with simple and interesting questions and follow up with more demanding topics. Controversial or sensitive questions should be asked at the end of the questionnaire, but the questionnaire should be rounded off with simple and uncontroversial topics. A good rule is to place questions about the same theme one after another, so that all the questions about a single theme are asked before the next theme is introduced. It is often a good idea to describe the background for the topic before the individual questions are asked. In that way, good transitions can also be achieved between the different topics and questions.

It is important, both within each topic and in the questionnaire generally, to avoid what are known as *sequence effects*, or *context effects*, whereby the answer to a particular question is influenced by the answers to previous questions. The risk of such effects is minimized if we follow a funnel principle and proceed from the general to the specific, so that the most general questions about a topic are asked first, before we follow up with increasingly specific questions about the topic.

When assessing the sequence of the questions, we should take into account that some of the questions will only be asked of some of the respondents. If a questionnaire contains questions about the respondent's children, there is no reason to ask these questions to respondents who do not have children. Therefore, we ask a *filter question* first: whether the respondent has children. If the answer is no, the respondent or interviewer is instructed to skip all the questions about children. The filter question filters out the respondents who should skip certain questions. In order to achieve good progression in the questionnaire, it is important that all the questions that should be skipped are placed directly after the filter question and before the next question that is common to all respondents.

Once the questions and the answers have been formulated and the sequence has been determined, the final task is to ensure that the questionnaire as a whole is given a satisfactory design, especially in terms of its size and layout. As already mentioned, the scope or length of the questionnaire will depend on the method of questioning, but also on the respondents and their relationship to the topic of the study. Questioning of particularly articulate respondents who are familiar with questionnaires about topics that they find highly interesting may be more comprehensive than questioning of other respondents. Personal interviews should preferably last no more than 1 hour, or perhaps up to 1½ hours, while telephone interviews should usually last less than 20 minutes, or possibly up to half an hour. Questionnaires that are completed by the respondents themselves should be shorter than questionnaires used in interviewing.

However, the scope or length of the questionnaire should be seen in conjunction with the layout, especially when the questionnaire is handled by the respondents themselves. If the layout is good, so that the questionnaire is transparent and appealing, even relatively long questionnaires can work reasonably well.

Survey experiments and vignette questions

Surveys based on structured questionnaires may be used in experimental studies. The basic principle in such survey experiments is to use different versions of the questionnaire in different subgroups of the sample of the study, and to compare the responses from the subgroups. Although most questions in the questionnaire are the same for all respondents, one or more of the questions are systematically posed in different ways to the different subgroups. Apart from receiving different questions, the subgroups should be as equal as possible in all other respects. This can be ensured, for example, by *randomization*, which means that each respondent in the original sample is randomly selected for one of the subgroups. This means that any difference between the groups in the responses to different formulations of a question in the questionnaire may be regarded as an effect of the particular formulation of the question. The main purpose of survey experiments, as well as for experiments in general, is to conduct causal analyses, examining empirical effects of selected specific factors. A more detailed and thorough discussion of experimental research will be presented in Chapter 21.

An example of a survey experiment is a study in Catalonia and Scotland, focused on how support for establishing these regions as new independent states is influenced by the prospects for the new states to become EU members (Muro and Vlaskamp, 2016). The sample of 1200 respondents in each region was divided into three representative subgroups with 400 respondents in each group. Different scenarios were presented to the three subgroups. The scenario for the first group was that the new state would be accepted as an EU member. The second group got the scenario that the new state would not be accepted as an EU member. The third group was used as a reference or control group and did not get a special scenario regarding EU membership. All respondents were asked about whether or not they supported secession. Differences between the subgroups in their responses to the question of support were interpreted as effects of the prospects for EU membership.

In this study, the scenarios regarding EU membership were presented to the respondents as vignettes. A *vignette* has been defined as 'a short, carefully constructed description of a person, object, or situation, representing a systematic combination of characteristics' (Atzmüller and Steiner, 2010: 128). Vignettes may be used in all surveys, in particular for specifying and clarifying questions about hypothetical conditions or situations. In survey experiments, vignettes are used as the most typical way of formulating different versions of questions to different subgroups of respondents. In the study in Catalonia and Scotland, the vignettes described particular circumstances under which

the respondents would support or oppose the creation of a new independent state. For example, in one of the subgroups, the respondents were asked how they would vote in a referendum under the following circumstances (Muro and Vlaskamp, 2016: 1122):

Before the referendum on the independence of Catalonia/Scotland, the EU authorities and the Member States issue a statement saying that if the majority of Catalans/Scots vote in favour, the new Catalan/Scottish state can be a member of the EU from its first day of independence.

In Catalonia, respondents in the second subgroup were asked how they would vote in a referendum under these circumstances (Muro and Vlaskamp, 2016: 1123):

Before the referendum on the independence of Catalonia, the EU authorities and the Member States issue a statement saying that, regardless of the result, Catalonia has no prospect of joining the EU.

In the construction of vignette questions, it is a challenge to formulate scenarios, conditions, or situations that are realistic and credible, even though they might be hypothetical. The respondent should consider it possible that the hypothetical phenomena or circumstances described in a vignette could be real, or that they could actually occur. If the description in the vignette is perceived to be unbelievable or unrealistic, the respondents may find it difficult to answer the question, or they may give unreliable responses.

Pretesting and instruction

Since the questionnaire is crucial for successful questioning, and since it cannot be altered after data collection has commenced, the questionnaire must be pretested before the actual questioning begins. The questionnaire is then tested by questioning a few selected persons. These could be people similar to the respondents in the study, but they could also be professionals with knowledge and experience of structured questioning. The pretesting shows how the various questions work and provides a basis for improving the questionnaire before it is used for data collection. Pretests are described, for example, in the study of attitudes towards the police response to domestic violence mentioned above (Sun et al., 2011: 3298), as well as in a study of attitudes to conflicts of interest among French medical students (Etain et al., 2014).

If the data collection is conducted as an interview, the interviewers must be instructed. Some instructions can be contained in the questionnaire itself. Written interviewing instructions should also be prepared. It is also an advantage if the interviewers obtain an oral briefing or training. The purpose of this is to ensure that the interviewers understand how the interview should be conducted and that the questionnaire is used in the same way by all the interviewers.

Transparency and information

As pointed out in Chapter 3, surveys cannot be conducted without informed consent from the respondents. It is required that respondents should receive certain types of information, about the purpose of the questioning, about confidentiality and anonymity, and about the right to refuse to participate in the study or withdraw during the questioning process.

The researcher must decide how much transparency there should be about the purpose of the study, and how the respondents should be informed. The information may be provided in writing, in the form of a letter or an e-mail, or on a website before the data collection is conducted. In telephone interviewing, however, the information may be given on the phone, as an introduction, before the questioning starts.

Respondents' consent to participate may be formalized as a signed declaration in a particular document, or it may be clarified that answering the questions is regarded as a consent to participate in the survey.

Implementing the data collection

How the data collection is carried out will depend on the method of questioning. When the respondents complete the questionnaire themselves, the data collection starts with the respondent receiving the questionnaire by regular mail, e-mail, online or by personal delivery. The respondent then completes the questionnaire and sends it back. This can also be done by regular post, e-mail or online. The questionnaire can also be collected personally from the respondent.

Special approaches and systems have been developed for using the Internet in surveys and structured questioning (Tourangeau et al., 2013). This procedure is usually referred to as a *web survey*. The selected respondents receive an e-mail with an invitation to participate in the survey. The e-mail contains a link to the web page for the survey. In the study of attitudes among French medical students mentioned above, the students received an e-mail from their dean with the link to the online questionnaire. Alternatively, the invitation can be sent to the respondents in a letter by regular mail, providing information about logging in to the relevant web page. In the study of workaholism in Norway, which was referred to above, the respondents received a letter in which they were asked either to return a completed paper version of the questionnaire or to use a link to find, complete and submit an online questionnaire version (Andreassen et al., 2014).

The website has detailed information about the survey and how to complete the questionnaire. The questionnaire is completed on the website. Filter questions can be entered here, and each respondent will then only see questions on the screen that are relevant based on the answer to the filter question. After all the questions have been answered, the respondent can click on a box to automatically submit the questionnaire.

In some web surveys respondents may find the questionnaire, along with an invitation to complete and submit it, more or less accidentally while surfing or searching for information on the Internet. However, such studies may create special challenges regarding assessments of how representative the respondents are. It is difficult to know the number and characteristics of all those Internet users who saw the information about the study but decided not to participate.

If the respondents complete the questionnaire themselves, the delivery, completion and collection of the questionnaire may sometimes take place at the same time in a whole group of respondents, for example in a school class, where all the students are respondents. The actual completion, however, is carried out individually by each respondent. The advantage of this is that the researchers themselves or their assistants can be present and encourage or provide information to the respondents. This procedure for data collection in groups was used in the survey on attitudes among American and Chinese students, which was mentioned above. The questionnaire was distributed, completed and collected in the students' classrooms (Sun et al., 2011: 3298–3299).

When the questioning is in the form of interviewing, the respondent is called on the telephone or receives a visit and answers the questions asked by the interviewer. The interviewer records the respondent's answers and takes back the questionnaire. The interview can be based on a questionnaire in printed form, but it is becoming increasingly common to conduct the interview with the help of a computer. In a personal interview, the interviewer relies on a laptop computer, tablet, or smart phone. The terms for these forms of interviewing are *computer-assisted telephone interviewing (CATI)* and *computer-assisted personal interviewing (CAPI)*.

In personal interviewing, it is particularly important to ensure that the interview can be conducted without interruptions. The respondent's response may be affected by the presence or interference of other people.

Typical problems during the data collection

One of the biggest challenges when conducting surveys is to ensure that as many as possible of the people in the sample are included in the questioning. Structured questioning is usually linked to relatively large probability samples and statistical generalization. *Drop-out* from the original sample may cause the final selection of respondents to be systematically biased, so that the generalization possibilities are weakened. Dropping out may be due to several factors. Some people may have died or moved after the sampling was made. These people are removed from the sample, which is thus adjusted. While the original sample is called the *gross sample*, the adjusted sample is a *net sample*. Drop-outs from the net sample may include people who cannot be found or contacted, people who are too ill to participate in the survey, and people who refuse to participate. It is the extent of this drop-out from the net sample that is interesting. The drop-out rate shows the percentage of people in the net sample that did not participate in the survey. We do not usually announce the drop-out rate, but specify the *response rate* instead, as this shows the percentage of the net sample that became actual respondents (100% minus the drop-out rate).

When the respondents complete the questionnaire themselves, it is usually necessary to send out one or more reminders to avoid an excessive drop-out rate. For example, one reminder was used in the Norwegian study of workaholism (Andreassen et al., 2014), and two reminders were sent out in the French study of attitudes towards conflict of interest (Etain et al., 2014). In order to avoid excessive drop-out during interviews, it may be necessary to visit or telephone a person a second time if they cannot be contacted at the first attempt. Nevertheless, there will always be some level of drop-out in structured questioning. For personal interviewing, a response rate of 80% or higher is considered to be a reasonably good result. The response rate will usually be somewhat lower in the case of telephone interviewing, and for questioning where the respondents themselves complete the questionnaire, it is not uncommon to have response rates as low as 50–60%. For example, in the study of workaholism in Norway, a response rate of 54 percent was obtained (Andreassen et al., 2014). The way in which this drop-out could affect the data must be assessed specifically for each study.

In addition to drop-out, data based on structured interviewing can be affected by unreliable answers. This form of impact on the data are mainly related to three typical problems that may occur during data collection. These problems may occur in different ways depending on the different methods of questioning.

One of the typical problems relates to the *respondents' willingness to answer*. Respondents who do not want to answer leads primarily to drop-out, but it can also be expressed in the form of inappropriate or deliberately incorrect answers. The latter problem is greatest when the respondents themselves complete the questionnaire. A lack of willingness to answer may be due to the respondent being provoked by the interviewer or reacting negatively to sensitive questions. It may also be due to animosity towards the particular study, or to

questionnaires or research in general. Recently, there has been a sharp increase in the number of inquiries and requests for participation in questionnaires, especially by e-mail and telephone. Most of these inquiries relate to various types of somewhat frivolous marketing surveys, which are often combined with ongoing sales activities. This development tends to increase people's general dislike of survey studies and makes it difficult to obtain high response rates in social science studies based on structured questioning.

The researcher can reduce this problem by focusing on adapting the questionnaires to the relevant sample, providing information about the study and its purpose, motivating the respondents, and instructing any interviewers.

Another typical problem during data collection is related to the *respondent's ability to answer*. Respondents' inability to answer will lead to drop-out, but it can also result in unreliable answers because some respondents will answer even if they do not really have the prerequisites to provide an answer. Not having the prerequisites to give an answer may be due to the respondents having general problems articulating clear opinions or difficulty completing the questionnaire. Problems with answering may also be due to the questions raising issues with which the respondent is unfamiliar, such as questions about other people's actions or opinions, or because the questions are about issues that the respondent does not remember, such as retrospective questions about events and actions too far back in time. Inability to answer could also be due to the questions being about circumstances that the respondent has not thought through, such as general attitude questions that are not related to the respondents' practical experiences.

In order to reduce this problem, we should focus on choosing questioning methods and question formulations that are well-adapted to the respondents who are included in the study. As far as possible, the questions should be linked to topics with which the respondents have a close or practical relationship. The use of retrospective questions and opinion questions should be assessed with particular care.

The third typical problem is related to the *respondents' understanding of the questions*. Questions not being understood or being misunderstood will first and foremost lead to unreliable answers, but it could also result in drop-out because incomprehensible questions can affect both the ability and the willingness to answer. Failure to understand the questions may be due to the questions dealing with circumstances about which the respondents have no knowledge, or because the wording of the questions is leading, ambiguous, unclear or linguistically difficult. Comprehension of the questions can also be impacted by context effects caused by the order of the questions. Furthermore, the background, status and experiences of the respondents can be decisive for how the questions are understood. Identical question formulations may be understood in different ways by different respondents.

The problems can be reduced if we focus on assessing the wording and positioning of the various questions, and whether the questionnaire is adapted well to the linguistic modes of expression and forms of communication used by the respondents in the particular study.

If the sample includes respondents from different countries or cultures, the questionnaire may need to be formulated in different languages, tailored to the different native languages of the respondents. It then becomes a particular challenge to ensure that the questions and answers are presented in the same way in the various linguistic versions of the questionnaire. Typically, this is based on *double translation*, including a first translation from the original language to the other language, and then a second translation from the other language back to the original language again. Based on differences between the original questionnaire and the double translated questionnaire, the first translation can be improved. A double translation was used in the survey among American and Chinese students, which was mentioned above (Sun et al., 2011: 3298), as well as in the European survey of quality of life (Eurofound, 2016).

During the data analysis, the researcher must consider how these problems may affect the data and the results of the analysis. Such assessments should be made for each question and for the questionnaire as a whole. The impact on the data may vary between different questions. Even if a respondent participates in the survey, some of the questions may be left unanswered or may result in particularly unreliable answers. Even if the overall response rate for the study is satisfactory, the response rate for some of the questions may be very low. Such questions should not be included in the analysis. Questions that are believed to have resulted in many unreliable answers should also be excluded from the analysis.

CHAPTER HIGHLIGHTS

- Structured questioning is based on a questionnaire with fixed questions in a particular order and with predefined response options for most questions. The questionnaire can be used by

  1 the respondents themselves, who receive and return the questionnaire as normal post, as an e-mail, via the Internet or by personal delivery

  2 an interviewer, through telephone interviews or personal interviews.

- Before conducting data collection through structured questioning, the researcher must choose the questioning method and must construct and pre-test the questionnaire, instruct any interviewers and provide information to the respondents.

- The design of the questionnaire is about formulating the questions and responses options, as well as clarifying the sequence of the questions and the layout of the questionnaire.
- We distinguish between different types of questions. The questions must be neutral, one-dimensional, clear and understandable.
- The response options must be mutually exclusive, exhaustive and of equal importance. They can be constructed as scales.

- The implementation of data collection depends on the questioning method. Response rates are maximized through motivation, reminders or re-visiting.
- Typical problems with structured questioning are drop-out, or unreliable answers associated with

  o the respondents' willingness to answer
  o the respondents' ability to respond
  o the respondents' understanding of the questions.

RESEARCH EXAMPLES

I recommend that you read the publications used as research examples in this chapter. One of these examples is the questionnaire used in the fourth survey about quality of life in most European countries, conducted by Eurofound:

Eurofound (2016) *Fourth European Quality of Life Survey: Source Questionnaire.* Luxembourg: Publications Office of the European Union.

Four other examples are articles presenting survey studies on different topics and in different countries:

Andreassen, Cecilie Schou, Mark D. Griffiths, Jørn Hetland, Luca Kravina, Fredrik Jensen, and Ståle Pallesen (2014) 'The prevalence of workaholism: A survey study in a nationally representative sample of Norwegian employees', *PLoS One* 9(8), e102446.

The article presents a survey study of workaholism, based on a national, representative sample of employees in Norway. By regular mail the employees in the sample received a letter with information on the study, a four-page questionnaire and a prepaid return envelope. Respondents could return the completed questionnaire by mail or use a link to a website for completing and submitting the questionnaire. After one reminder letter, a response rate of 54 percent was obtained. The questionnaire included several questions intended to identify workaholism. The findings indicate that the prevalence of workaholism was about 8 percent.

Etain, Bruno, Lydia Guittet, Nicolas Weiss, Vincent Gajdos, and Sandrine Katsahian (2014) 'Attitudes of medical students towards conflict of interest: A national survey in France', *PLoS One* 9(3), e92858.

This article discusses attitudes towards conflict of interest among medical students, based on a national survey in France. After several pretests of the questionnaire, an e-mail was sent to the dean of each medical school in France. The dean was asked to send an e-mail with information about the study and a web link to the questionnaire to all their students, who could complete and submit the questionnaire online. Participation was voluntary and anonymous. The study suggests that there is a need for improved education about conflict of interests among the medical students.

Muro, Diego, and Martijn C. Vlaskamp (2016) 'How do prospects of EU membership influence support for secession? A survey experiment in Catalonia and Scotland', *West European Politics* 39(6), 1115–1138.

The article is an example of an online survey experiment in Catalonia and Scotland. The research question is whether support for secession (from Spain and UK, respectively) and the formation of independent states in the two regions is influenced by different scenarios regarding EU membership for the new states. The sample of 1200 respondents in each region was divided in three representative subgroups with 400 respondents in each group. Different vignettes were presented for the three subgroups. For the first group, the vignette stated that the new state would be accepted as an EU member. The second group got a vignette stating that the new state would not be accepted as an EU member. The third group was used as a reference or control group and did not get a special vignette regarding EU membership. All respondents were asked about whether or not they supported secession. Comparing the three subgroups within each region, the researchers found that 'the prospects of EU membership had only limited effect on support for the creation of a sovereign state' (Muro and Vlaskamp, 2016: 1115).

Sun, Ivan Y., Mingyue Su, and Yuning Wu (2011) 'Attitudes toward police response to domestic violence: A comparison of Chinese and American college students', *Journal of Interpersonal Violence* 26(16), 3289–3315.

The study presented in this article examines attitudes among American and Chinese students toward proactive and traditional police response to domestic violence. A questionnaire with 100 items was prepared in both a Chinese and an American version, based on double translation between the two languages. After a pretest, the questionnaire was used in samples of students at one Chinese and one American university. The questionnaires were distributed, completed and collected mainly in the students' classrooms. The findings indicate that Chinese students are more positive to traditional police response and less positive to proactive police response than American students are.

STUDENT EXERCISES AND QUESTIONS

1 What is the difference between open-ended and closed-ended questions?
2 What is the purpose of using composite questions?
3 What is a leading question?
4 Why is it difficult to use retrospective questions in surveys?
5 What are the main questioning methods in surveys?

6 Discuss how attitudes towards climate change and global warming could be studied by means of a structured questionnaire. What types of questions could be used, and which problems might arise in the data collection?
7 Construct a questionnaire for examining the study conditions for various groups of students at a university. Conduct a pretest of the questionnaire among 3–5 selected students at your school.

RECOMMENDED LITERATURE

Sapsford, Roger (2014): *Survey Research* (2nd edn). London: Sage.

This book presents the main theoretical and practical aspects of survey research, including construction of scales and use of the Internet in surveys. The discussion is illustrated by means of examples. The book is useful for social science students who are conducting small research projects.

Fowler, Floyd J., Jr. (2013) *Survey Research Methods* (5th edn). London: Sage.

The book is a step-by-step guide to the survey research process. It discusses the growth of online survey usage, the drop in response rates, the improvement in pretest techniques, and the growing role of individual cell phones in surveys.

Punch, Keith F. (2014) *Survey Research: The Basics* (1st edn). London: Sage.

This book is a short, practical `how-to' book for beginning researchers, focusing on small-scale surveys. It describes the elements of the survey, providing a set of steps and guidelines for implementing each element.

QUANTITATIVE CONTENT ANALYSIS

This chapter provides the knowledge that is necessary for understanding and assessing how quantitative content analysis is used in social science. The chapter will enable you to carry out studies based on this type of data collection.

The chapter will teach you how to

- use quantitative content analysis to examine various types of texts and visual materials
- construct a coding schedule
- use the schedule in coding of selected texts or visual materials

- handle different problems that might arise in quantitative content analysis
- use computer programs in automated content analysis.

Quantitative data collection from different types of documents

The theme of this chapter is the collection of quantitative data based on documents as the source. This design is called *quantitative content analysis*.

Like qualitative content analysis, which was described in Chapter 11, quantitative content analysis is based on systematic review of the content of documents. The purpose is to find relevant information about the phenomena to be studied, as they are specified in the research questions. The relevant parts of the content are processed, systematized and recorded in such a way that they can be used as data in the particular study.

Quantitative content analysis can be used for all types of documents, such as texts, numbers and images, as well as audio, audio-visual and digital materials. However, this design is most common in connection with verbal presentations in the form of various texts. The texts may be written or oral. Traditionally, there are written texts on paper and oral texts on audio or video tapes, but it is becoming increasingly common that both written and oral texts are available on the Internet or on special data files. Oral texts are usually transcribed before their content is analysed.

Quantitative content analysis differs from qualitative content analysis in various ways. The selection or sampling of the documents is fully completed before the data collection starts. The review of these texts is not intended to generate or develop categories. The text content, on the other hand, is evaluated based on a structured schedule with variables and categories that are developed and specified before the data collection starts. This schedule is called a *coding schedule*. The registration of data involves ticking off on the coding schedule, which variables and categories are relevant for each text unit. This registration is referred to as *coding* the text. The data analysis can thus be based on the number of text units placed in each of the categories. However, the analysis of these quantitative data does not start until the data collection is completed.

This means that the review of the texts and the data registration are more structured in quantitative content analysis than in qualitative content analysis. The data collection can therefore be performed by persons other than the researcher. These are called *coders*. It may also be necessary for the researcher to receive assistance from other coders to review the texts because quantitative content analyses usually include larger volumes of text than qualitative content analyses. On the other hand, the use of coders imposes great demands on the construction of the coding schedule. In addition, the researcher must formulate coding instructions, which are detailed descriptions of how the coding schedule should be used and how the coding should be performed. Quantitative content analysis therefore requires more comprehensive and more detailed preparations for the data collection than qualitative content analysis does.

Instead of using coders for manual coding of readable texts, it is also possible to use computer programs for automated coding in quantitative content analysis. Various types of software have been developed for extracting the relevant content from the selected texts and for generating quantitative data based on these extracts. Such programs require that the texts are available in digital form, such as texts on the web, which can be used in web content analysis (Ackland, 2013: 35–40). However, texts on paper or in audio recordings may also be digitized, so that they may be processed by computer for content analysis.

This chapter will describe and discuss the data collection in quantitative content analysis. First, based on Table 14.1, and with reference to manual coding of readable texts, it is shown how the data collection is prepared and implemented, as well as what problems may arise during the data collection. Then, content analysis of visual materials is presented, and the use of computer programs for automated content analysis is examined.

Quantitative content analysis of texts

Preparing the data collection

The construction of the coding schedule and the formulation of the coding instructions are the main tasks in preparing for data collection.

Table 14.1 Overview of data collection in quantitative content analysis

Aspect of data collection	Characteristics of quantitative content analysis

Preparations for data collection	• Find the sampled texts
	• If necessary, arrange to obtain access to the texts and evaluate the degree of transparency
	• Construct the coding schedule:
	   ○ Specify variables
	   ○ Consider the variables in light of the selected texts
	   ○ Consider the relationship between manifest and latent content in the selected texts
	   ○ Specify the unit of measurement and categories for the different variables
	   ○ Specify the recording unit and the context unit
	• Formulate the coding instructions and instruct the coders
	• Pretest and possibly improve the coding schedule and coding instructions

Implementation of data collection	• Systematically review the selected texts and fill out a coding schedule for each unit of analysis:
	   ○ Identify specified variables
	   ○ Register a category for each of the identified variables
	• Compare different coders' registrations for the same texts

Typical problems during data collection	• The coders' backgrounds and perceptions may affect the assessment and registration of the content of the texts • Limited contextual understanding may affect the assessment of words and expressions in the text • Focusing on quantitative aspects of the text can affect the interpretation of the content

However, these tasks cannot be performed in isolation from the specific texts to be analysed. The variables and categories in the analysis must be defined and specified in such a way that they can be applied to the selected texts.

The selected texts

The first task during the preparations is therefore to find the texts that are sampled. The degree of difficulty of this task will depend on a variety of characteristics of the texts to be studied, such as whether the texts are public or private, new or old, open or confidential, and whether they are available in many or few copies. As a rule, the texts can be obtained from archives, libraries or the Internet. In the case of contemporary texts from the mass media, for example, the researcher can obtain the texts gradually as they become available, by purchasing newspapers or making recordings of radio and television programmes.

Generally, quantitative content analysis is based on texts that are widely available and are published openly, especially texts from mass media and increasingly from online social media. However, in some cases there may be restrictions on the use of the texts. They may be difficult to access or confidential. In such cases, the researcher must arrange for permission to use the texts. Such agreements must be made with those who administer the rights to the texts. The question then arises as to how much openness is required in relation to these rights holders concerning the purpose of analysing the texts and the study more generally. The same methodological, research ethical and practical considerations apply here as for qualitative content analysis and other research designs. In principle, there should be as much transparency as possible.

Variables

The design of the coding schedule is an extensive process. The specification of variables is an important part of this process. In this work, the researcher starts with the research questions and follows the procedure described in Chapter 7 (Table 7.3). The Twitter study referred to in Chapter 6 can be used as an example of this process (Humphreys et al., 2013). Table 14.2 provides an overview of the variables in the coding schedule in this study. The table presents the variables in the study, organized into three groups of variables: subject, topic and style of the tweet. For each variable, the table shows an example of how the variable is found in a tweet. Furthermore, the table includes a column showing the reliability coefficient (alpha) for each variable. This coefficient is a measure of the degree of similarity between different coders' assessments of the same texts, which is explained later in this chapter.

The research question was to compare the content of the tweets with the content of diaries from the eighteenth and nineteenth centuries. Historical literature about the content of such diaries was therefore used as a basis for the development of the coding schedule in the content analysis of the tweets. Based on the literature review, it was considered particularly relevant to focus on three main groups of variables: the tweets' references to actors or subjects, as well as the topic and style of the messages. A set of more specific variables was selected for each of these groups. For example, the style of the messages was defined as the purpose or form of the messages and specified using the variables accounting, commentary, information seeking, content sharing, and response.

The variables specified with reference to the research question of the study must be assessed in light of the selected texts. We must ensure that we have included all the variables necessary for the most exhaustive registration possible of the relevant content in the texts. In the Twitter study, the variables would provide opportunities to record all the content in the selected messages that were relevant to the research question.

Table 14.2 Coding schedule and reliability for quantitative content analysis of tweets, based on Humphreys et al. (2013: 420)

Variables		Examples	Reliability coefficients (alpha)
Tweet subject	First person singular	I love twitter	0.91
	Third person singular	Gloria loves twitter	0.85
	Third person plural	Teachers love twitter	0.74
	Audience	Do you guys love twitter?	0.74
	None	Twitter is so slow	0.86
Tweet topic	Weather	It's snowing in April	0.74
	Family	My dad loves baseball	0.72
	Media	Just watched American Idol	0.81
	Food/beverage	Enjoying a beer on the porch	0.91
	Religion	I'll keep you in my prayers	0.72
	Health	I have a splitting headache	0.78
	Sleep	It's 4am and I should be sleeping	0.81
	Activities	Just updated my blog	0.79
	Home activities	Making lasagna for dinner	0.73
	Work activities	Finished the report for my boss	0.78
	Outside of home & work activities	Running errands at the mall	0.80
Tweet style	Accounting	Drivin' to work	0.71
	Commentary	I hate "family" dinners	0.78
	Information seeking	What's the best pizza in NYC?	0.73
	Content sharing	http://tinyurl.com/34abql	0.80
	Response	@cutegirl sure thing!	0.71

On the other hand, there is no reason to include variables that are not found in the texts.

In practice, the assessment of the variables in light of the texts can be done by reading through a smaller sample of the texts to identify whether different variables exist and how the variables are expressed. The texts chosen for this purpose would usually be determined based on the researcher's discretion. It is important to capture as much of the variation width in the text as possible.

The Twitter study included a total of 21 variables, as illustrated in Table 14.2. These variables were both specified with reference to the research question and evaluated in light of the texts in the messages to be analysed.

Manifest and latent content

The reading of a discretionary selection of the texts also provides a basis for assessing the relationship between manifest and latent content. *Manifest content* refers to particular words, phrases or formulations that are recorded in the same way each time they appear in the text. Sometimes the coding can be based on such manifest content. The coding then becomes a routine and can be accomplished using computer programs that identify and register instances of particular letter combinations. The problem with coding of manifest content is that identical words or phrases can have many different meanings, depending on the context in which they appear.

Latent content refers to the specific meaning of particular words, expressions or formulations, as they are included in the specific context of the text. In order to reveal the latent content in a particular part of the text, this part of the text must be seen in conjunction with a larger part of the text. It may also be appropriate to see the text itself in a larger social context, such as the background, origin and purpose of the text, or the authors' background and characteristics. This applies particularly to analyses of very short texts, such as tweets. In Twitter, each message is such a short text that its latent content may be understood from larger sequences of multiple messages or in light of other contextual circumstances. Quantitative content analysis is very often based on coding of latent content. This can be demanding and requires that we specify the clearest possible criteria for how relevant statements should be understood in different contexts.

Categories and units of measurement

The assessment of manifest or latent content is intended to ensure that for each variable, we should be able to select a particular category to match the text. In other words, we must define and specify a set of categories or values for each variable (see Table 7.3). In quantitative content analysis, the specification of categories is associated with the choice of the unit of measurement.

The simplest unit of measurement is *occurrence*. This means that for each variable, we choose between two categories. We record whether the variable is mentioned in the text (value 1 in the coding schedule) or not mentioned (value 0 in the coding schedule). This unit of measurement was used in the Twitter study.

Another type of unit of measurement is *direction*, which is common when registering attitudes to different phenomena, such as organizations or institutions. Each organization or institution then represents a variable, and, for each variable, categories are used for positive or negative attitudes. For each variable, we can distinguish, for example, between the following categories:

0. No mention
1. Positive mention
2. Neutral mention
3. Negative mention

A third type of measurement unit is *intensity*, which is used to assess the strength of attitudes. For example, it would be possible to combine direction and intensity by using categories such as 'strong positive mention' and 'strong negative mention' in addition to the categories listed above.

A fourth type of measurement unit is *frequency*, which entails that you register the number of times a variable is referred to in the same unit of analysis. In analyses of editorials in newspapers, for example, this would mean counting how many times each variable is mentioned in each of the editorials.

A fifth type of measurement unit is *text volume*. This measure shows how much text is used to refer to each variable. For example, it can be measured in the number of column inches in a newspaper or the number of seconds in a radio programme.

Recording unit and context unit

Simply put, the coding schedule includes the variables and the categories that are specified.

For each unit of analysis, the coding schedule is used to specify which category on each of the variables is most appropriate for the content of this text. If we analyse the content of a large sample of editorials in one or more newspapers, each article will be the unit of analysis. One coding schedule is used for each unit of analysis (article).

In order to use the coding schedule in this way, we must specify two more units within this text. These units are called the recording unit and the context unit.

The *recording unit* is the part of the text that forms the basis for assessing whether or not a variable is mentioned. In analyses of newspaper articles, the recording unit may be a sentence or statement in the article. For each statement or each individual sentence, we assess which variables are mentioned and what category is relevant for this mention.

The *context unit* is the part of the text to be read through to assess which category should be selected when a particular variable is mentioned. This unit refers to the evaluation of latent content and is not relevant when the coding is restricted to the manifest content. The context unit is larger than the recording unit. In analyses of newspaper articles, the context unit could be a paragraph in the article. If a mention of a particular variable is identified in a statement, the coder must then read through the entire paragraph or section containing the statement in order to assess which category is appropriate for the mention, for example if the mention is positive, neutral or negative.

When the unit of analysis is a text that consists of many sentences and several paragraphs, such as editorials in newspapers, both the recording unit (a statement) and the context unit (a paragraph) may be less than the unit of analysis (the entire article). In other studies, these units may be identical. This is especially true when each unit of analysis consists of a very short text, such as in the Twitter study (Humphreys et al., 2013). Each message was

both the unit of analysis and the recording unit. Each message was also the context unit, although it could be relevant to assess the content of each message in light of several messages and other contextual circumstances.

Coding schedule and coding instructions

The coding schedule is given a final design based on all these assessments and specifications, either on paper or in a computer version.

Before the coding schedule can be used, the researcher must formulate coding instructions and instruct the coders. The coding instructions provide a detailed guide on how to perform the coding. In addition to a general overview of the procedure during coding, the instructions usually contain a description of each variable and each category. The description includes definitions of the individual variables and categories, criteria for the coders' assessment of the text in relation to the coding schedule, as well as examples of text elements that are included in the various variables and categories. Table 14.2 shows which examples of text elements were used for each of the variables in the Twitter study.

Usually, the coders also receive oral guidance from the researcher. This can happen, for example, in connection with general training or exercises before the coding commences. The purpose is to ensure that all the coders have a common understanding of the coding schedule and that they understand and interpret the text in the same way, so that the coding is not affected by varying interpretations among the coders.

The training of the coders is usually conducted in the form of practical training in the use of the coding schedule on selected parts of the text material to be encoded. This also functions as pretesting of the coding schedule. The pretesting is intended to reveal problems or weaknesses in the coding schedule, especially in relation to how it works for the specific texts to be coded. Based on the pretesting, both the coding schedule and the coding instructions can be changed and improved.

In the Twitter study, the coders were trained for four hours per week for a period of 2½–5 months before the data collection began. This training period helped improve both the coding schedule and the qualifications of the coders. However, in many studies based on quantitative content analysis, the training period for the coders is much shorter.

Implementing the data collection

The implementation of the data collection consists of coding the selected texts. The texts are thoroughly reviewed and evaluated systematically with reference to the coding schedule. The variables and categories contained in the text are recorded in the coding schedule. The coder uses one schedule for each unit of analysis. For each recording unit in the text, the coder assesses whether it is relevant to any of the variables in the form. If the recording unit corresponds to a variable, it is evaluated in conjunction with the context unit and possibly in the light of other contextual factors in order to determine which category should be registered for this variable in the schedule.

The schedule can be on paper, but it can also be designed in a digital version, so that the coder performs the registrations using a computer. If the coding is concentrated on the manifest content of the texts, both the identification of the variables and the registration of the categories can be performed using a computer and special computer programs. If the text is not already in a digital form, it can be digitized, for example by scanning, and organized as a computer file, so that the coding can be performed automatically.

Coding of latent content assumes that the individual recording units are interpreted and assessed in relation to the contextual unit or in a larger contextual setting. This cannot be done automatically. These assessments must be carried out by coders. In this context, it is important that the different coders understand the categories in the same way and interpret the texts as similarly as possible. The more the coding varies between different coders, the less reliable the data will be. One of the advantages of quantitative content analysis is that we can estimate the size of the differences between the assessments of the different coders. We can ask all the coders to code the same texts independently of each other and then compare their evaluations. The degree of similarity between the coders can then be calculated, both for each variable, and for the entire coding schedule. This comparison of the coders is usually an integral part of the data collection process and is usually based on coding a sample of all the texts to be coded.

In the tweet study, 24% of all messages in the analysis were coded by two or three coders, and the similarity between different coders' coding of the same messages was calculated using a procedure developed by the German researcher Klaus Krippendorff (1970, 2018). The degree of similarity is expressed using a reliability coefficient called Krippendorff's alpha, which varies between 0 (no similarity) and 1 (full similarity). Table 14.2 gives these reliability coefficients for each of the variables in the tweet study. As we can see, the coefficients vary between 0.71 and 0.91 (Humphreys et al., 2013). This is a relatively good match.

The coefficients are called reliability coefficients, because the degree of similarity between different coders' assessments of the same texts is a measure of the *reliability* of the data. Reliability is an aspect of data quality, which will be further discussed in Chapter 15.

Typical problems during the data collection

Coders perceiving the categories differently and evaluating the texts in different ways is one of the common problems during the data collection in quantitative content analysis. How the text is understood and interpreted may depend on the background and perspective of the coder, and the data may be affected by differences between the coders in their interpretations and perspectives.

In principle, the researcher has three options to prevent or reduce this problem. Two of the options concern reducing the differences between the researchers' assessments. This must be done before the data collection starts. One of these options is to improve the coding schedule and the coding instructions, preferably based on extensive pretesting and systematic comparison of the coders' assessments before the final coding takes place. A more precise design of the measuring instrument can lead to a clearer understanding of the assessment criteria, greater similarity between the coders and more reliable coding.

The second option to reduce the differences between the coders is to improve their training. Systematic guidance of the individual coders, and possibly of all the coders jointly, can contribute to a common understanding of the coding schedule and greater similarity in the assessments of the texts.

The third option to reduce the problem of differences between the coders' assessments concerns reducing the consequences of these differences during the data analysis. For example, the researcher can restrict the analysis to the variables where the similarity between the coders is greatest and disregard variables with major discrepancies between different coders. However, if this applies to many variables or particularly important variables, the analysis may become too limited in relation to the research question of the study.

A high degree of similarity between the coders is no guarantee that the coding reflects a correct understanding of the content of the text. The interpretation of the text may be influenced by the researcher's special perspective, which forms the basis for the formulation of the coding instructions and the training of the coders. All the coders are instructed to comprehend the text in a particular way. A typical problem in this regard is that limited contextual understanding may affect the assessment of words and expressions in the text. The researcher may not have an adequate overview of the background to the text or the social function the text had when it was disseminated. Comprehension may also be inadequate in terms of the authors' wording or writing style. This is especially true of old texts and texts from distant cultures. The problem can also be significant in connection with special types of texts, such as ironic statements.

Researchers can reduce the extent of these types of problems by familiarizing themselves with the contextual circumstances related to the formulation, dissemination and use of the texts to be content-analysed. The content of the texts can thus be understood in the light of their representativeness and meaning. Insights into what or whom the texts represent, and the meaning that the texts have for different actors, are often a prerequisite for interpreting the content in a meaningful manner. In this connection, however, it is important to be aware that the same text may have different meanings for the author and the readers, and that the meaning of the text may vary between different groups of reader. Appreciation of such contextual circumstances is important for the construction of the coding schedule and the formulation of coding instructions, but it is also important for the data analysis and the interpretation of the results of the analysis. The researcher should constantly consider whether the content should be understood on the basis of the text's internal structure, as an expression of the authors' intentions, in light of the readers' perceptions or in conjunction with other contextual conditions.

A third typical problem during the data collection is that the focus on quantitative aspects of the text can affect the interpretation of the content. This problem can occur, for example, when quantitative content analysis is used to study interests or attitudes among different actors. In such studies, it is often assumed that interest in a phenomenon is reflected in how much this phenomenon is mentioned in the analysed texts, and that the attitude of a phenomenon can be understood based on how much positive or negative mention of this phenomenon is found in the texts. Such assumptions about the relationship between the amount of text and interests or attitudes can often be valid, but not always. More qualitative assessments of the text could result in other interpretations or in a more sophisticated understanding. How different quantitative aspects of the text can be understood will vary between different texts. For example, there may be significant differences between party programmes, newspaper commentaries, social media messages, and personal diary notes.

In order to avoid misinterpretations of the meaning of texts, the researchers should familiarize themselves with the specific texts to be analysed, as well as the contextual circumstances of these texts. This insight is important for the construction of the coding schedule and the formulation of the coding instructions, as well as for the interpretation of the findings and results of the analysis.

Content analysis of visual materials

In addition to examining texts, quantitative content analysis may be used to study visual materials, such as drawings, paintings, photographs, or videos. Like texts, images may be systematically reviewed with reference to specified variables and categories, in order to record data on those content elements of the pictures that are relevant to the research question of the study.

The main challenge for studies of images is to develop variables and categories that are adapted to the special nature of visual materials, taking into account that the elements of pictures are very different from the elements of texts. However, in spite of this difference, the principles and procedures for content analysis of visual materials are the same as those for content analysis of texts. A coding schedule is constructed, with the specified variables and categories, coding instructions are formulated, and the schedule is used by coders to record data from the materials to be content-analysed.

An example of a quantitative content analysis of visual materials is a study of Facebook profile photographs which was carried out by Hum et al. (2011). They examined gender differences in the content and amount of such profile photographs among college students. They constructed a coding schedule consisting of variables and categories that were adapted to the relevant content elements of the pictures to be examined. The coding schedule is presented in Table 14.3.

Some of the variables and categories are quite easy to identify and record, such as number of photos in profile picture album, and number of subjects in the photograph. Other variables and categories are more demanding to code, requiring more thorough assessments and interpretations, for example physical activity and appropriateness.

The photographs were coded by the six collaborating researchers. They participated in 3 hours of training in order to reach a common understanding of the picture elements in relation to the specific variables and categories, and thus to achieve sufficient reliability of the data.

Table 14.3 Coding schedule for quantitative content analysis of Facebook profile photographs, based on Hum et al. (2011: 1831)

Variables	Categories
Sex	Male
	Female
Number of photos in profile picture album	1–10
	11–20
	21+
	Other (not able to view profile album)
Physical activity	Completely physically active
	Moderately active
	Inactive
	Other (Facebook account holder is not in the profile photograph)
Candidness	Candid
	Between candid and posed
	Posed
	Other
Appropriateness	Inappropriate
	Moderate
	Appropriate
	Other
Number of subjects	Alone
	Couple (two individuals, but does not have to be just romantic in nature)
	Group (three or more individuals)
	Other

Compared to texts, visual materials may be more difficult to assess and interpret. This means that data based on pictures may be even more affected by the coders' background and perspectives than data based on texts. Furthermore, this difference between texts and visual materials means that using computer programs for automated coding is usually more difficult for visual materials than it is for texts. However, this depends on the type of visual materials that are analysed, as well as the kind of content elements that are specified in the coding schedule.

In terms of the typical problems related to limited contextual understanding and the focus on quantitative aspects of the content, there are, in general, few differences between studies of texts and studies of visual materials.

Automated content analysis

The coding process in quantitative content analysis can be performed manually, by coders, or automatically, by means of computer programs. Automated content analysis requires that the documents to be analysed are available in a digital, machine-readable form. Studies based on computer programs for the coding are called *automated content analyses*.

An example of an automated content analysis is a study of North Korean nuclear rhetoric in news from the Korean Central News Agency (KCNA), which was carried out in 2010 by Rich (2012). The research question is specified in the form of three hypotheses. The hypotheses state that references to nuclear issues are positively correlated with references to the USA (H1), negatively correlated with references to China and Russia (H2), and negatively correlated with references to contemporary Korean events. These events include the sinking of the South Korean ship *Cheonan*, the North Korean shelling of sites on the South Korean island of Yeonpyeong, and the announcement of Kim Jong Un as the next North Korean leader (H3).

Daily news sources from KCNA in 2010 were collected, and a computer program was used to identify the occurrence and frequency of specified variables in these news sources for each day. The variables are listed in a content dictionary, which also specifies the exact words that are included in the computer search for each variable. The content dictionary in an automated content analysis is equivalent to the coding schedule in a content analysis based on manual coding. The content dictionary of the KCNA study is shown in Table 14.4.

Table 14.4 Content dictionary (coding schedule) for automated content analysis of KCNA News in North Korea, based on Rich (2012: 79)

Variables	Inclusion
Nuclear Issues	Denuclearization, Denuclearize, NPT, Nuclear, Nuclearization, Nuclear War, Nuke
Cheonan	Cheonan
Yeonpyeong	Yonphyong
Kim Jong Un	Kim Jong Un
War	War, Warfare, Warhawks, Warlike, Warman, Warmaniac, Warmonger, Wartime
Peace	Peace, Peaceful, Peacefully, Peacekeeping
Friendship	Friend, Friendly, Friendship
Against the DPRK	Against the DPRK
Sovereignty	Sovereign, Sovereignty
North Korea	North Korea, DPRK
South Korea	South Korea, South Koreans
Japan	Japan, Japanese
China	China, Chinese
Russia	Russia, Russians, Soviet Union
USA	America, Americans, The United States, The US, USA

This content dictionary was constructed before the data collection started, based on the hypotheses, as well as '..the literature on automated content

analysis and historical knowledge of North Korea' (Rich, 2012: 78). Although automated content analysis typically relies on a content dictionary that is constructed before the computer-based extraction of data from the texts, an alternative approach is to use the computer program and various types of algorithms for a more open clustering and categorization of the selected texts. Such open approaches are usually referred to as *text mining*. Text mining is a special form of data mining and related to data scraping, which was described in Chapter 7.

In the study of North Korean news, the computer program WordStat was used for the automatic coding of the texts. This software package, developed by the company Provalis Research, is one of several computer programs that are available for automated quantitative content analysis. Other software packages include Textpack, Textstat, TACT, SAS Text Miner, and General Inquirer, which was the first computer program for content analysis.

By means of such computer programs, it is possible to use content analysis to examine large amounts of text. Thus, automated content analysis can be an appropriate design for big data research, such as studies of the content of social media. Furthermore, in automated content analysis, one of the typical problems related to manual coding is avoided. When all data recording is conducted by a computer, the data are not affected by the backgrounds and perspectives of different coders.

However, in automatic coding by computers, a word or a phrase is usually registered in exactly the same way every time it occurs in the text. In the study of North Korean news, only explicit text references to the specific words in the content dictionary were identified and registered by the computer program (Rich, 2012: 78). This is a typical limitation of automated content analysis. Computers are usually not able to discover more implicit references to variables or topics, or to understand different meanings of particular words within larger contexts. For example, it is difficult for computers to distinguish between an ironic and a more serious usage of a word or a phrase. Thus, whereas automated content analysis may be very useful for finding and recording manifest content of texts, it is less

appropriate for examining the latent text content. In automated content analysis, it is easy to obtain consistency in terms of wording, but not necessarily in terms of meaning. For this reason, automated content analysis is also less appropriate for examining visual materials than it is for analysing texts.

CHAPTER HIGHLIGHTS

- In quantitative content analysis of texts, the content of selected texts is evaluated and recorded using a structured coding schedule developed prior to data collection.
- Before conducting the data collection in quantitative content analysis, the researcher must find the sampled texts, construct the coding schedule and formulate the coding instructions, instruct the coders and pretest the schedule. The construction of the coding schedule includes specification of variables, categories, units of measurement, recording units and context units.
- During the data collection, the coders assess the selected texts. One coding schedule is used for each unit of analysis, and a particular category is recorded for each variable in this schedule.
- The following problems are typical for data collection based on quantitative content analysis:
  1 The coders' backgrounds and perceptions may affect the assessment and registration of the content of the texts.

  2 Limited contextual understanding may affect the assessment of words and expressions in the text.
  3 Focusing on quantitative aspects of the text can affect the interpretation of the content.
- Content analysis may be used to examine visual materials, in addition to texts.
- Visual materials may be difficult to interpret and may be especially affected by the coders' background and perspectives.
- Quantitative content analysis may be based on automatic coding by computers, instead of manual coding by coders.
- Such automated content analysis can be used in big data studies with large amounts of texts, and problems related to coders' background and perspectives are avoided. However, automated content analysis is typically limited to the manifest content of texts and less appropriate for examining meanings of words and phrases within larger contexts. It is also less useful for examining visual materials than for analysing texts.

RESEARCH EXAMPLES

I recommend that you read the publications used as research examples in this chapter.

One of these articles was also referred to in Chapter 6. The study presented in this article is an example of a quantitative content analysis of texts from Twitter, based on manual coding:

Humphreys, Lee, Phillipa Gill, Balachander Krishnamurthy & Elizabeth Newbury (2013) 'Historicizing new media: A content analysis of Twitter', *Journal of Communication* 63(3), 413–431.

Two other articles are referred to as research examples in this chapter:

Hum, Noelle J., Perrin E. Chamberlin, Brittany L. Hambright, Anne C. Portwood, Amanda C. Schat, and Jennifer L. Bevan (2011) 'A picture is worth a thousand words: A content analysis of Facebook profile photographs', *Computers in Human Behavior* 27:1828–1833.

This article presents a study that exemplifies quantitative content analysis of visual materials. The study examines gender differences in the content and amount of Facebook profile photographs. The data collection was based on a coding schedule consisting of variables and categories that were adapted to the relevant content elements of the pictures to be examined. The photographs were coded by the six collaborating researchers. They participated in 3 hours of training in order to reach a common understanding of the picture elements in relation to the specific variables and categories, and thus to achieve sufficient reliability of the data. The findings show that profile pictures for both men and women are inactive, posed and appropriate, including only the subject.

Rich, Timothy S. (2012) 'Deciphering North Korea's nuclear rhetoric: An automated content analysis of KCNA News', *Asian Affairs: An American Review* 39(2), 73–89.

This article presents a study that is an example of automated content analysis. It is an analysis of North Korean nuclear rhetoric in news from the Korean Central News Agency (KCNA). The purpose is to examine how references to nuclear issues are correlated with references to the USA, China, Russia, and some contemporary Korean events. Daily news sources from KCNA in 2010 were collected, and a computer program was used to identify the occurrence and frequency of specified variables in these news sources for each day. The variables are listed in a content dictionary, which also specifies the exact words that are included in the computer search for each variable. The findings indicate that nuclear issues are mainly associated with the USA and rarely referred to in connection with Korean events.

STUDENT EXERCISES AND QUESTIONS

1 What is the difference between a recording unit and a context unit?
2 How do we construct a coding schedule in a quantitative content analysis?
3 Why is it important to distinguish between manifest and latent content in quantitative content analysis?
4 Why are coding instructions and training of coders important in quantitative content analysis?
5 What are the main advantages and limitations of automated content analysis?
6 Discuss how TV commercials could be examined by means of a quantitative content analysis.
7 Select a particular debate in a newspaper, construct a coding schedule, and conduct a quantitative content analysis of the debate.

RECOMMENDED LITERATURE

Krippendorff, Klaus (2018) *Content Analysis: An Introduction to its Methodology* (4th edn). London: Sage.

This book presents a general and comprehensive introduction to content analysis. The book is divided into three parts, covering conceptual aspects, important components and perspectives of content analysis.

The fourth edition includes discussion of new developments in content analysis, such as studies of social media.

Neuendorf, Kimberly A. (2017) *The Content Analysis Guidebook* (2nd edn). London: Sage.

This comprehensive guidebook explains core concepts and techniques in content analysis. It presents step-by-step instructions and practical advice for conducting content analyses. The presentation is an accessible core text for students in different social science disciplines.

Weber, Robert Philip (1990) *Basic Content Analysis* (2nd edn). London: Sage.

This book is a concise introduction to content analysis from a social science perspective. In addition to describing approaches and procedures for doing content analysis, it discusses problems and issues that can arise when carrying out content analysis.

DATA QUALITY, RELIABILITY
AND VALIDITY

This chapter provides the knowledge that is necessary for understanding how the quality of data is assessed in different types of social science studies.

The chapter will teach you about

- criteria for data quality
- different types of reliability and validity
- tests and calculations of reliability in quantitative studies

- assessments of reliability in qualitative studies
- assessments of validity
- strategies for improving reliability and validity.

What is data quality?

Chapters 9–14 showed how data collection is done in various social science studies. This chapter deals with the quality of the data collected.

Data collection is a process. We can consider this process as a production process, where we produce the data that we require in order to shed light on specific research questions. We could also say that we construct data on the basis of the relevant information that we can obtain from various sources. In this sense, it could be argued that the data are generated through a form of social construction.

This means that the data can be perceived as a product, and just like other types of products, social science data can be of varying quality. We are concerned with ensuring that our data is of the best quality possible. Good quality data are necessary to ensure that the results of the analysis are valid and useful.

This chapter will first discuss what is meant by quality of social science data, and what criteria are used to assess the quality. Then the two most important quality criteria, reliability and validity, are examined. Different types of reliability and validity are described, and it is discussed how reliability and validity can be assessed. Finally, it is shown how data quality can be improved.

The quality of social science data cannot be assessed in an entirely general manner. The quality must be seen in connection with the intended use

of the data. The purpose of a set of data is that it should be used to shed light on specific research questions. The quality of the data is higher if it is more suitable for shedding light on these problems. The quality of the same data set can therefore vary depending on the research questions to be examined. Data that could be considered to be of high quality for one type of research question could be of low quality for other types of research question. For example, we can collect data that are very suitable for describing the living conditions of different groups in the population, but these data are not necessarily good enough to explain the differences in living conditions between the different groups.

The extent to which data are suitable for answering the research questions to be examined in a particular study will depend on a variety of conditions. The most important prerequisites for satisfactory examination of the particular research questions can be summarized as follows:

1 The data must be based on the principles of the researcher's *commitment to truth*, as discussed in Chapter 1. The data collected should, as far as possible, represent actual conditions and reflect true information related to the specific research questions. The theoretical, methodological and contextual anchoring of this relationship between data and truth should be clarified as much as possible by explicit description and documentation of both the data collection and the data collected. The clarification of how the

data reflect true information should be based on rational and logical criteria.

2   Data collection must be based on *scientific principles for logic and language use*, so that the data form the basis for systematic theoretical discussion and argumentation. This was described in Chapter 2. The collection of data should be based on the most precise terms and linguistic formulations possible, and the use of terms should be linked to the usual social science terminology in the research area to which the research questions to be studied belong. The data collection should be based, as far as possible, on valid assumptions, anchored in previous research in this area.
The data should also be as complete as possible, in the sense that they should shed light on all the relevant aspects of the issues in question.

3   The *selection of units* must be carried out in an appropriate manner. The selection or sampling must be based on the assumptions and procedures described in Chapter 8. Both the type of units and the level of the units must be in accordance with the research questions to be examined. The sample size and sampling method must be adapted as well as possible to the types of generalizations required by the research questions.

4   *The selection of information types* must be performed in a systematic manner. As pointed out in Chapter 7, the information selection must be based on the concepts that arise from the research questions to be examined, and dimensions and categories must be specified that are most relevant and fruitful for these concepts. The operational definitions of the dimensions and the categories must be in agreement with the theoretical concepts, while also being well adapted to the types of sources and data to be used.

5   The *implementation of data collection* must be carried out in a proper manner, based on the assumptions and procedures that apply for the various research designs, as described in Chapters 9–14. We must avoid or reduce the typical problems that may occur during data collection. The data should be affected as little as possible by the study being conducted or by the design of the data collection.

The quality of the data can be regarded as an overall expression of how well these assumptions are fulfilled. The data quality is good if the data are based on scientific principles of truth and logical discussion, and if both the selection of units and types of information, as well as the collection of data, have been carried out in a systematic and responsible manner, in accordance with the prerequisites and procedures of the research designs used. The better these prerequisites are fulfilled, the higher the quality of the data.

Quality assessment criteria

This clarification of what is meant by data quality implies that we can assess the quality of data by conducting a systematic and critical discussion of the data production and the data with reference to each of the five assumptions highlighted here. The overall data quality can be examined if we assess the extent to which each of the five assumptions are fulfilled. We can identify and review possible problems associated with the various assumptions, and we can discuss the consequences that these problems will have for the data and their quality. For each of the problems, we should then consider *how* the data may be affected by the problem, the *extent* to which the data may be affected, and the likely *direction* of the impact.

In structured questioning based on telephone interviews, for example, problems may arise in connection with both the sampling of units and the implementation of the data collection. Such studies have traditionally been based on random sampling of landline numbers throughout a country or within a more limited geographical area. There are several problems linked to this sampling if the objective is to achieve a probability sample of the population at the individual level. People who have secret phone numbers, and people who do not have their own phone, for example because they live in an institution, cannot be included in the sample. People with multiple phone numbers will be more likely than others to be included in the sample. When several people have the same phone number, each of these persons will have a smaller probability than others of being included in the sample. People in families or in large households will therefore be less likely to be included in the sample than individuals who live alone. Biases in the sample may also arise because it may be easier within families to make contact with certain family members than with others. These are all issues related to the selection of units. Problems may also arise in connection with the data collection. Some of these problems concern drop-out, partly because the interviewers do not receive an answer when they call the selected phone numbers, and partly because the people who are called are not willing to be interviewed. This can lead to further biases in the final data. People who do not spend much time at home will have a smaller probability of being interviewed than others. People who are extrovert and like to engage in long phone calls would usually be more likely than others to be interviewed. The topic of the interview may also systematically determine who is willing to be interviewed.

The extent of such problems will vary between different studies and must therefore be assessed specifically for each study. The consequences that the various problems may have for the quality of the data must also be assessed specifically for each study because the consequences will depend on the research questions to be studied. For example, if the telephone interview is intended to study people's leisure activities, the data quality may be relatively strongly affected by the problems highlighted here. In research on leisure activities, it is common to distinguish between home-oriented and outdoor-oriented activities. The distribution of time between the two activity categories varies with age and family situation. Young people are usually more outdoor-oriented in their leisure time than older people, and single people also have more outdoor-oriented leisure activities than people in relationships. As mentioned above, telephone interviewing may reduce the probability of young people, who are living with their parents, being included in the sample. This may lead to an underestimation of the scope of outdoor-oriented leisure activities in the study. On the other hand, single people are more likely than others to be included. This may result in outdoor-oriented leisure activities appearing more popular than they really are. In other words, these two opposing problems in connection with the sampling of units can offset each other. The problems associated with drop-out during data collection are probably more important in this context. The fact that people who do not spend much time at home have a smaller probability of being interviewed than others could have particularly large consequences in terms of underestimating the extent of outdoor-oriented leisure activities. Since people with home-oriented leisure activities are over-represented in the data, not only the extent of different leisure activities but also the attitudes to different types of activity may be misjudged in the study. For example, people's positive attitudes toward home-oriented leisure may be overestimated, while the positive attitudes towards outdoor-oriented leisure may be underestimated.

In studies with other research questions, data quality may be less affected by such issues in connection with telephone interviewing, or the impact may be different.

Choosing mobile phone numbers instead of landline numbers will reduce some of the issues identified here. Mobile phones are primarily owned by individuals and are rarely shared by more than one person. This reduces the difference between single people and people in larger households with regard to the likelihood of being included in the sample. Mobile phones are also taken outside the home, so the likelihood of being included in the sample is less dependent on whether or not the person is often at home. On the other hand, not everyone has a mobile phone, and some people have a mobile phone with a secret number, while others have multiple mobile phones. Therefore, some of the issues associated with telephone interviews will apply to both landlines and mobile phones.

Specific consideration must be given to how data quality is affected by various problems during data production, depending on the research questions to be studied. However, the discussion of which problems may be associated with data production can be systematized based on the five *general* requirements for good data quality described in the previous section.

In this sense, the five preconditions can be considered criteria for assessing the data quality. However, there is an even more systematic approach to assessing the quality of data in social science studies. This procedure is based on two overall criteria for quality assessments. These criteria summarize the most important aspects of the five prerequisites for good data quality mentioned above. The criteria are called reliability and validity.

Reliability refers to the accuracy or trustworthiness of the data. Reliability is high if the research design and data collection provide accurate data. Reliability manifests itself in the fact that we get identical data if we use the same design and methods for different collections of data about the same phenomena. Reliability is an expression of the degree of consistency between the data sets from such repeated data collections. The greater the degree of consistency, the greater the reliability. In practice, it is not always possible to carry out such repeated collections of data on the same phenomena. One reason for this is that many societal phenomena are constantly changing. Another reason is that some research designs are too complex or too flexible for the data collection to be repeated in exactly the same way. This applies particularly when collecting qualitative data. In some cases, for example when questioning respondents, it may also occur that data from a repeated data collection are affected by the fact that a similar data collection has been carried out earlier. This fundamental clarification of what is meant by reliability is nevertheless a useful starting point for discussing and assessing the reliability of all types of studies.

The reliability shows the extent to which variations in the data are due to particular features of the research design or the data collection. Reliability is low if a large part of the variation in the data is due to the design of the study or the implementation of the data collection. High reliability means that the data differ to a small extent due to such methodological circumstances, and that the variations in the data mainly reflect real differences between the units of the analysis. This is important with regard to the level of trust in the data and the interpretation of the results of the analysis.

The reliability depends on how the research design is constructed and how the data collection is conducted. High reliability requires a clear and adequate design as well as careful and systematic data collection. In view of the five preconditions for good data quality that were highlighted in the previous section, this entails that reliability is primarily linked to the selection of information types and the execution of the data collection. A good foundation in the principles of truth can also help the research design to work well for the information to be collected, and a good utilization of the principles of logical discussion may be important for the research design to be understood in an unambiguous way.

Validity concerns the adequacy or relevance of the data for the research questions and the phenomena to be examined. Validity is high if the research design and data collection result in data that are relevant to the research questions. Validity is an expression of how well the actual data correspond to the researcher's intentions with the research design and data collection. The better the actual data correspond to the researcher's intentions, the higher the level of validity. It can be difficult in practice to determine how well this correspondence is achieved, but this basic definition of validity is nevertheless a good basis for discussing and assessing validity, no matter how the study is conducted, and irrespective of what data are used.

The validity shows the extent to which the research design is suitable for collecting data that are relevant to the research questions in a particular study. The level of validity is low if the research design is not very appropriate for the research questions, so that we actually study something other than what is required for the research questions. A high level of validity requires that both the universe of units and the various concepts in the study are defined in a systematic manner, both theoretically and operationally, that there is good consistency between the theoretical and operational definitions, and that the choice of methods for selecting units and collecting data is well adapted to these definitions.

Thus, the validity depends primarily on how the research design is constructed. Seen in connection with the five preconditions for good data quality that we have highlighted, validity is primarily related to the selection of units and information types. The more specific preparations for data collection are also important for validity. This applies especially to the choice of focus or themes, as well as to the construction of procedures or instruments for data collection. In addition, the principles of truth are important for assessing what type of information about actual circumstances is most relevant to the research questions, and the principles for logical discussion are useful for assessing the relationship between theoretical and operational definitions.

As overall criteria for assessing data quality, reliability and validity complement each other, since they refer to different preconditions for good data quality. At the same time, the two criteria are also partly overlapping, first and foremost because high reliability is a prerequisite for high validity. Data cannot be valid for or relevant to the research questions if the data are not reliable. On the other hand, reliability is independent of validity, and high reliability is no guarantee that the level of validity is high. Data may be reliable, even if they are not relevant to the research questions in the particular study. The reliable information provided by the data is in this case different from what is addressed by the research questions. Thus, reliability is a necessary but not a sufficient prerequisite for validity.

The next two sections will discuss reliability and validity in more detail. First, different types of reliability will be described, and it will be shown how we can assess the reliability of different types of data. Then validity and validity assessments for different types of data will be examined.

Reliability

As mentioned, reliability shows how accurate or trustworthy the data are. Generally, reliability is defined as the level of consistency between different collections of data about the same phenomenon based on the same research design.

Types of reliability

Based on various specifications of this definition, we can distinguish between different types of reliability. Usually, it is focused on two main types, stability and equivalence.

Stability

Stability refers to the level of consistency between data about the same phenomenon collected using the same research designs at different times. Assuming that the phenomenon being investigated is stable, so that it does not change between the times it is investigated, the level of reliability is high if there is a high degree of consistency between the data collected at different times. The study is stable over time, in the sense that it works in the same way at different times.

This type of reliability is particularly important when we study real development trends or change processes in society. The fact that the research design is stable means that there is a high degree of consistency between data from different times when we study stable conditions in society. If we study societal conditions that change over time, a stable research design will result in differences between the data gathered at different times. Since the research design is stable, the differences between the data gathered at the two different times will be an accurate reflection of the changes in the social conditions we are studying. If the research design is not stable, some of the differences in the data will be due to the research design itself, so that the differences between the data at the two different times will not be an accurate reflection of the changes in social conditions. In other words, if reliability in terms of stability is high, we can be confident that the differences between data about the same social conditions at different times are not due to particular features of the research design, but instead reflect real changes in these social conditions over time. If this type of reliability is low, we cannot know if certain differences between different data collections reflect real changes in the social conditions we are studying, or whether these changes in the data are a result of the research design working differently at different times. The interpretations of the results of the analysis may then be very uncertain.

However, a high level of reliability in terms of stability is also important when we study social conditions at a single point in time. Confidence in the results of the analysis will depend on the fact that the data are not affected by an unstable research design. If the research design works differently at different times, the results of the analysis will have little general or lasting scientific value.

Equivalence

The other main type of reliability is *equivalence*. While stability concerns consistency between data collected at different times, equivalence is based on consistency between mutually independent data collections executed at the same time. For example, the different data collections may be mutually independent because they are performed by different persons. Equivalence is based on comparison of data gathered using the same research design, but by different observers, different interviewers, different coders or different researchers. Reliability in the form of equivalence is high if there is a high degree of consistency between data about the same phenomenon, collected by different persons using the same research design. This form of reliability is an indication that the data are not affected by who uses the research design. The research design functions in the same way, regardless of who executes the data collection.

Equivalence is used not only with reference to comparison between different people's use of the same research design. Particularly in connection with quantitative studies, this type of reliability can also be based on a comparison of different indicators that are included in the same index or the same scale. Reliability in the form of equivalence is then high if there is a high degree of consistency between data based on different indicators, so that the data are consistent across the various indicators. In a questionnaire, for example, we can study people's attitude to the EU using a composite scale. As pointed out in Chapter 13, we ask several different questions about the respondent's attitude towards the EU, so that each question corresponds to an indicator. If the different indicators indicate approximately the same degree of positive or negative attitude towards the EU, the scale has a high level of reliability in terms of equivalence. If there are large differences between the indicators with regard to what attitude they indicate, the scale has a low level of reliability. The greater the differences between the indicators, the lower the reliability of the scale.

Reliability in the form of equivalence is particularly important when data are collected by several different persons, and when the research design contains many indexes or composite scales. If reliability is high, we can be confident that variations in the data are not due to differences between different people's use of the research design or differences between different indicators. The variations found in the data can be interpreted unambiguously as the result of real differences between the units of analysis. If reliability in the form of equivalence is low, we cannot know if certain variations in the data are due to substantive or methodological conditions, and the interpretation of the results of the analysis becomes uncertain.

However, satisfactory reliability in terms of equivalence is of major importance even if the data collection is carried out by a single person, for example by one researcher. In terms of the overall validity and long-term scientific value of the study, it is important to have confidence that the research design in question would have led to the same data being collected, regardless of who conducted the study.

Assessments of reliability in quantitative studies

In principle, reliability is an important criterion for assessing data quality in all types of social science studies, and regardless of the type of data used, reliability should be assessed in a critical and thorough manner. However, in practice there are significant differences between qualitative and quantitative studies with regard to how reliability can be assessed. In many quantitative studies, reliability can be tested and calculated in a relatively precise manner. This will rarely be possible in qualitative studies. Reliability assessments of qualitative data must be based on systematic discussions of the various elements of the research design and the data collection, with reference to the relevant types of reliability. The most important types of reliability tests and calculations used in quantitative studies will now be presented, before reliability assessments in qualitative studies are discussed.

Table 15.1 Overview of reliability tests in quantitative studies

Reliability type	Definition	Reliability test
Stability	Consistency between independent data collections with regard to the same phenomenon at different times	The test–retest method
Equivalence between different data collections	Consistency between independent data collections with regard to the same phenomenon at the same time	The inter-subjectivity method
Equivalence between different indicators	Consistency between data based on different indicators in the same index	The split-half method

The kind of test used in quantitative studies depends on the type of reliability to be examined. Table 15.1 presents an overview of this relationship between reliability types and reliability tests.

The test–retest method

The stability of the research design is tested by using the design on the same sources at different times, so that the data sets from different times can be compared. This procedure is called the *test–retest method*. The repeated collection of data is usually limited to a small sample of the units in the study. As a rule, this is a random sample of all the units in the study, so that the results of the reliability test can be considered representative of the entire study.

In quantitative content analyses, the test–retest method involves the same texts being coded on two or more occasions by the same coder and based on the same coding schedule and the same coding instructions. In structured questioning, the same questionnaire is used at different times with the same respondents, and possibly by the same interviewer. In structured observation studies, the same actors are observed in almost identical situations by the same observer and with the same observation form, but at different times.

In practice, the test–retest method is easiest to use in quantitative content analysis. The text to be studied is itself stable and is not affected by repeated coding. We can be certain that a deviation between data based on repeated coding of the same text is not due to changes in the phenomenon being studied, but rather to lack of stability in the research design. The entire deviation can be considered a reliability problem.

The test–retest method is more problematic when it comes to questioning and observation. It may be more difficult here to interpret deviations between data at the different times. In addition to the lack of stability in the research design, such deviations may be due to changes in the actual conditions being investigated. Between the dates of the study, the observed actors may have changed their behaviour, and the respondents in the questionnaire study may have changed their opinions. Data from repeated data collections may be affected by the fact that such data collection has been conducted earlier. These problems can be reduced if the reliability test emphasizes comparisons of the test and retest data about circumstances that are very likely or certain to be stable.

The test–retest method was used by Rath et al. (2013) in a study of the reliability and validity of a questionnaire about personality styles in depression. It was also used by Spanemberg et al. (2014), in a study of the reliability and validity of a questionnaire about personality styles in depression.

The inter-subjectivity method

Reliability in the form of equivalence between individuals is tested by comparing data based on different people's use of the same research design with the same sources. This procedure is referred to as the *inter-subjectivity method*. In the same way as the test–retest method, this procedure is generally limited to a random sample of the units in the current study. The comparisons of the mutually independent data collections from this sample are regarded as representative of the entire study. The equivalence is assessed on the basis of comparisons between different coders in quantitative content analysis, between different observers in structured observation, or between different interviewers in structured questioning. The inter-subjectivity method is not relevant to surveys where the questionnaire is completed by the respondents themselves.

This procedure is usually easy to use in both content analysis and observation. In content analysis, different coders can code the same text independently of each other, but based on the same coding schedule and the same coding instructions. Regardless of whether the coding takes place simultaneously or at different times, the text will be the same, so that the entire deviation between the coders can be regarded as a lack of inter-subjectivity and thus as a reliability problem. In observation studies, the same actors and the same situations can be observed by different observers simultaneously and based on the same observation schedule. Since the mutually independent observations are conducted simultaneously, the observed phenomena are exactly the same, and the deviations between the observers can be entirely interpreted as inter-subjectivity or reliability problems.

For interviewing, however, the inter-subjectivity method may be just as problematic as the test–retest method. The same questions cannot be asked of the same respondents at the same time by different interviewers. In practice, there must always be a certain amount of time between the different interviewers questioning the same respondents. Thus, there are several possible explanations for deviations between data from the different interviewers. In addition to the lack of inter-subjectivity, the deviation may be due to a lack of stability in the research design, effects caused by the first data collection on data from the new collection, as well as real changes among the respondents between the times of the interviews. The problem can be reduced by testing the reliability using both the inter-subjectivity method and the test–retest method, so that it is possible to compare data, both from different interviewers and from the same interviewer at different times. If both tests concentrate on comparisons of data about conditions among the respondents that can be expected to be relatively stable, we can distinguish between stability problems and inter-subjectivity problems by seeing the results of the two tests in relation to each other. This can be difficult to do in practice, not least because there are limits to how many times the same respondents would be willing to answer the same questions. In all cases, the two reliability tests should be based on different samples of the units in the study.

The split-half method

Reliability in the form of equivalence between indicators in a composite scale can be tested by randomly dividing the indicators into two groups of equal size. Data based on one half of the indicators is then compared to data based on the other half of the indicators. The comparison applies to data from the same units. Reliability is high if both groups of indicators show the same scale value for the same units. This procedure is referred to as the *split-half method*. For example, if we have eight different indicators in a scale for attitude to the EU, these indicators are randomly distributed into two groups. Each group is comprised of four indicators. For each unit, the attitude to the EU displayed by one group of indicators is compared with the attitude to the EU displayed by the second group of indicators.

Here, it is not data from different data collections that are compared, but rather data based on different parts of the research design. Unlike the other two reliability tests, the split-half method can therefore be used on the basis of a single data collection. Split-half tests can usually be performed after the data collection has been completed and are often based on data for all the units in the study. The procedure is also independent of the types of sources used in the study. The split-half method can be used in the same way in quantitative content analysis, structured observation and structured questioning.

Tests of the equivalence between different indicators in a scale are also referred to as *internal consistency tests*. Rath et al. (2013) and Spanemberg et al. (2014) used internal consistency tests, in addition to the test–retest method, in their studies of the reliability of questionnaires. Bergland et al. (2015) also used internal inconsistency tests in their study of the reliability of a scale for measuring the thriving of older people.

Reliability calculations

The comparisons based on the various test methods provide a basis for calculations of the level of reliability. Such reliability calculations can be carried out in different ways. The simplest method of calculation is to express the level of consistency as a proportion of the entire data being tested. Thus, the reliability can be calculated, for example, when we compare two different coders in quantitative content analysis. If the two coders have coded the same 100 texts based on a coding scheme with 20 variables, each coder has made 20 × 100 = 2000 evaluations and registrations in total. If we find that there is agreement between the coders on 1800 of these registrations, and that there are deviations between the coders on 200 of the registrations, the level of agreement can be calculated by determining what fraction of 2000 is represented by the figure 1800. The fraction can be expressed as a proportion and can then be calculated as follows: 1800/2000 = 0.9. Reliability is measured on a scale from 0 (no consistency) to 1 (full consistency). A consistency of 0.9 is an expression of high reliability. The same proportion can also be expressed as a percentage and is then calculated as follows: (1800/2000) × 100% = 90%.

A weakness of this simple method of calculation is that it does not take into account the level of consistency that could be expected solely on the basis of chance. If we imagine, in the example above, that the codes for each of the 20 variables and each of the 100 units were recorded on the basis of random draws instead of the coders' evaluations, there would still be a certain level of consistency. The level of random consistency we can expect between two such (imagined) random draws for the same variables and units can also be calculated and expressed as a proportion or percentage. How this could be done will not be discussed here. The point is that no matter how unreliable the coding schedule and the coding instructions, and no matter how unreliable the coders' use of the schedule and the instructions, there will still be a certain (random) consistency between the two coders' recordings. If the consistency between the coders is not significantly *greater* than the random consistency, the reliability is too low.

When the expected random consistency is calculated, the reliability can be expressed as a measure of the difference between the actual consistency and the random consistency. This reliability measure is called *Scott's pi* and is calculated as follows:

$$pi = \frac{\% \text{ actual consistency} - \% \text{ random consistency}}{100\% - \% \text{ random consistency}}.$$

Based on this calculation, pi will vary between 0 (if the actual consistency is equal to the random consistency) and 1 (if the actual consistency is 100%). If we imagine in the example above that the random consistency between the registrations for the 20 variables and the 100 units is calculated to be 25%, the reliability could be expressed as follows:

$$pi = \frac{90 - 25}{100 - 25} = 0.87.$$

This is also an expression of high reliability.

There are also other measurements for consistency that can be used for reliability calculations. As shown in Chapter 14, reliability in the Twitter study was expressed in the form of *Krippendorff's alpha* (see Table 14.2). This measurement, which varies between 0 and 1, has been developed specifically with the aim of testing the level of consistency between different coders in quantitative content analyses.

When testing reliability in the form of equivalence between indicators, based on the split-half method, it is normal to use a measurement called *Cronbach's alpha*. This measure of reliability also varies between 0 and 1. However, such calculation methods will not be discussed in more detail here.

Regardless of the kind of reliability measurement used, reliability can be calculated for the entire body of data, as in the example above, or separately for different parts of the data. For example, reliability can be calculated separately for each variable. In the example above, then, we would get 20 different reliability calculations. In the tweet study, the reliability for the individual variables varied between 0.71 and 0.91 (Chapter 14, Table 14.2). Such a differentiation of the reliability calculations is useful when we interpret results of analyses based on different combinations of variables. Some of the results may be more reliable than others, depending on which variables are included in the analyses.

In the example above, the reliability calculation refers to the consistency between the coders' evaluations for each unit and each variable. A cruder reliability calculation is based on the consistency between the coders regarding how the units are distributed across different values for each variable. Calculations of the consistency for the units' distribution often show higher reliability than calculations of the consistency for each unit, because deviations in different directions can cancel each other out when they are aggregated for all the units. The different coders in a content analysis may have recorded a certain value for a given variable for the *same number* of units, even though they have not necessarily registered this value for the *same* units. Such reliability calculations based on the units' distributions are sufficient if only these simple distributions are included in the data analyses. As a rule, however, the analyses are based on the individual units' values on the various variables. The reliability calculations should then be based on the consistency for each unit.

Assessments of reliability in qualitative studies

In qualitative studies, it is usually not possible to test and calculate reliability using such standardized methods. This is due to several factors,

including the fact that the research design and data are less structured than in quantitative studies, and that the data collection is closely related to data analysis and interpretation and cannot be separated as a distinct phase in the research process. Above all, the assessment of reliability in qualitative studies is characterized by the fact that the importance of the researcher is greater in collecting qualitative data than it is in quantitative data collection. In quantitative studies, the assessment of reliability will mainly focus on how the measuring instrument works. The standardized and structured instrument for data collection, in the form of an observation schedule, questionnaire or coding schedule with coding instructions, is expected to work in the same way regardless of who uses it. In qualitative studies, the procedures for data collection are typically developed during the data collection process itself, in part depending on the researcher's analyses and interpretations of data, at the same time as new data are collected. The researcher's interpretations are linked to the particular context in which the data collection process takes place, and the approaches and procedures are adapted to this particular context. In practice, therefore, it becomes impossible to make mutually independent data collections based on exactly the same procedures. This applies to both stability and equivalence: the data collection process will depend on *when* the study is conducted, and *who* conducts the study.

Due to these differences between qualitative and quantitative studies, it has been argued that the concept of reliability is not relevant to or useful for quality assessments of qualitative data. Some literature on qualitative research uses the term *credibility* instead of reliability (Marshall and Rossman, 2015; Morse, 1994). Although different terms are used, importance is attached to the same type of assessments of the qualitative data. In qualitative studies, both reliability and credibility mean that the findings are based on data about actual conditions. The data are not credible if they are based on the researcher's purely subjective assessment or on random circumstances that occur during the research process. Credibility requires that the data collection is conducted systematically and in agreement with established assumptions and procedures that apply in the research design used. The assessments of reliability (or credibility) will thus enhance trust in the results of the empirical analysis and in the qualitative data that are analysed. Table 15.2 presents an overview of types of reliability and reliability assessments in qualitative studies.

Table 15.2 Overview of reliability (credibility) assessments in qualitative studies

Reliability type	Reliability assessment
Stability	Consistency between descriptions of the same conditions at different times
Equivalence	Consistency between descriptions of the same conditions produced by different researchers
Internal consistency	Consistency between different elements of the data within the study
External consistency	Consistency between the data in the study and other available information about the conditions studied

Assessments of stability

Although the reliability assessments in qualitative studies cannot be based on standardized tests, it is often possible to establish a certain empirical basis for assessing reliability in terms of both stability and equivalence. In terms of stability, the researcher can carry out repeated data collections concerning conditions that are assumed to be relatively stable. This is usually concentrated on a strategic sample of the data, with particular emphasis on data that are particularly suitable for such repeated collections, or data that are particularly important in the

study. In qualitative content analysis, the same texts can be reviewed at different times. In participant observation, the same actors can be observed several times in almost the same situations. In informal interviews, the researcher can have several different conversations with the same respondents about the same themes.

A simpler empirical approach to reliability assessments is that the researcher does not carry out repeated data collections, but instead conducts a critical review of the same data at different times. In qualitative content analyses, the archived text sections with markings and comments can be reviewed and reassessed again. In observation studies the field notes can be read again, and in interview studies the audio recordings or the transcripts of the conversations can be critically reviewed repeatedly.

The purpose of such repeated data collections or repeated reviews of the data is to clarify the stability of the researcher's descriptions of the conditions being studied. The stability can be assessed based on the degree of consistency between the descriptions of the same conditions based on the data collection or data review at different times. Although the researcher's analyses and interpretations during the first data collections may affect the descriptions at a later date, the comparison of such repeated descriptions of the same conditions is often a useful basis for systematic discussions about the stability of the descriptions.

Assessments of equivalence

Reliability in the form of equivalence can be assessed by comparing different researchers' descriptions of the same conditions. These descriptions can be based on separate data collections from each of the researchers. The various researchers can conduct content analyses of the same texts, simultaneous observations of the same actors, or conversations with the same respondents about the same topics. Especially when several researchers collaborate on the execution of the same study, it may be appropriate to make such comparisons of different researchers' descriptions of the same conditions.

Comparisons of different descriptions may also be based on different researchers' reviews and assessments of the same data independently of each other. Each of the researchers can conduct a critical review of the archived text sections in a content analysis, field notes in an observation study or audio recordings in an interview study.

The equivalence can then be assessed based on the consistency between the descriptions produced by the different researchers. Such comparisons of descriptions from different researchers may be problematic, because different researchers can perceive and understand the same conditions from different perspectives. Nevertheless, these comparisons are also a useful empirical basis for discussions and assessments of possible sources of error during the collection of qualitative data.

However, it is quite common that reliability assessments of qualitative data are not based on such empirical studies of stability or equivalence. The reliability is assessed on the basis of a systematic and critical discussion of the data. The data are evaluated in relation to various aspects of the particular study, such as the choice of research design, the implementation of the data collection, the credibility of the sources, the role of the researcher and the context of the study. The discussion of how the data are affected by the particular context of the study is particularly important in assessing the reliability of qualitative data.

Assessments of internal and external consistency

When reliability assessments are based on comparisons between mutually independent data collections carried out at different times or by different researchers, it is the consistency between the different data collections that is evaluated.

Assessments of consistency are also central to reliability discussions that are not based on direct empirical studies of stability or equivalence. It is common to emphasize two types of consistency in critical discussions of the reliability of qualitative studies.

One type is *internal consistency*. This is about the relationship between different parts of the data collected. Internal consistency is high if the different data elements are plausible or reasonable, viewed in relation to each other and in light of the data as a whole. This means that the different parts of the data fit well together and are consistent with an overall picture of what is being studied.

External consistency is the other type of consistency that is important in discussions about reliability. This concerns the relationship between the data collected and other relevant information. External consistency is high if there is consistency between the data in the study and other available information about the conditions studied. This means that the data fit well into the context of the study and appear reasonable in this larger context. The prerequisite for using consistency with other available information as the basis for assessing reliability is that this external information is also evaluated and discussed in a critical manner and, on this basis, can be regarded as credible and well-founded knowledge. On the other hand, social science studies will often aim to verify and possibly revise different types of available information about conditions in society. Thus, lack of compliance with such information will not necessarily be a sign of low reliability. Instead, it can be considered an interesting empirical finding.

Regardless of whether the reliability assessments are based on empirical studies of stability or equivalence, or if they are associated with systematic discussions of the data, it is important that the data collection is described and documented as explicitly and thoroughly as possible. For example, good field notes will be crucial for assessing the reliability of participant observation. Not only the observation notes but also the analytical and methodological notes must be written in such an explicit way that both the researcher and others can use them to recapitulate and discuss the data collection after the study has been completed.

Validity

Even if the reliability is high, it is not certain that these reliable data are relevant to what we intend to study. The data may have low validity even if the reliability is high. As mentioned, validity refers to the adequacy of the data regarding the research questions to be investigated. We can distinguish between different types of validity based on this definition.

Compared with the concept of reliability, the concept of validity is less precise and more comprehensive, because validity refers to more aspects of the data collection and the data than reliability does. The scope and complexity of the validity concept become clear when we distinguish between different types of validity. The distinction between different types of validity refers primarily to what criteria are emphasized when assessing validity. It is possible to specify a number of different criteria for validity, so it is also common to distinguish between many different types of validity. Which of these are the most useful for the assessment of data quality may vary between different research designs. Some of the main types of validity, partly in quantitative studies and partly in qualitative studies, will be considered here. In other words, different criteria for validity will be reviewed for each of the two data types.

One form of validity that is relevant to both qualitative and quantitative studies is *face validity*. This form of validity refers to very simple criteria, and the validity assessment is not based on

in-depth studies or thorough discussions, but on characteristics of the data collection and the data that are evident to both the researcher and others. In other words, the perception of face validity is uncontroversial and is considered unproblematic. Face validity is considered satisfactory if it is obvious that the data collected are good and appropriate given the intentions of the study. It may also occur that the data are obviously not very relevant to the current research questions to be studied. In that case, the face validity is low.

In addition to face validity, there are several other types of validity, based on more systematic assessments. An overview of different types of validity in quantitative and qualitative studies is presented in Table 15.3.

Table 15.3 Types of validity in quantitative and qualitative studies

Type of study	Type of validity

Quantitative studies	Definitional validity
	• Content validity
	• Criterion validity
	   ○ Concurrent validity
	   ○ Predictive validity
	• Construct validity

	Internal validity (experiments)
	External validity (experiments)
Qualitative studies	Competence validity
	Communicative validity • Actor validation • Collegial validation
	Pragmatic validity

Validity in quantitative studies

Generally, the concept of validity refers to more specific criteria and more systematic assessments than those used for face validity. As mentioned above, the criteria and assessment methods may vary between different research designs.

First, some common forms of validity in quantitative studies will be presented.

Definitional validity

In its most specific sense, validity refers to the relationship between theoretical and operational definitions of concepts. While the *theoretical definition* clarifies what the researcher intends to study, the *operational definition* will determine what is actually being studied. High validity therefore assumes that there is consistency between the theoretical and operational definition of each concept.

Definitional validity can be specified in three different ways. The first of these specifications emphasizes that validity is an expression of how adequate the operational definition is for the theoretical content of the concept. Validity is low if, for example, the operational definition is narrower than the theoretical definition. This form of definitional validity is often referred to as *content validity*. Content validity is particularly relevant when the operational definition includes several indicators for the same concept. For example, in a study of people's quality of life, the concept of quality of life may be theoretically defined as 'satisfaction with your own situation regarding financial resources, health, social relationships and opportunities for activities'. In this case, high content validity assumes that the operational definition includes one or more indicators for each of the four areas of satisfaction that are specified in the theoretical definition. For example, if the study is limited to indicators of satisfaction with financial resources, the content validity will be low.

The second specification of definitional validity refers to the degree of consistency between data based on different operational definitions of the same concept. One of these operational definitions is generally known as a valid and good expression of the term in question and is therefore used as a criterion for the validity of data based on the other operational definitions. The definitional validity is considered to be high if there is good consistency between these data and data based on the criterion definition. This form of definitional validity is usually referred to as *criterion validity*.

For example, if we study intelligence based on various operational definitions, we can use a well-known and established intelligence test as a criterion for validity. The criterion validity will then be high if there is good consistency between data based on the operational definitions in the study and data based on the established intelligence test. The validity is low if the established intelligence test and the other operational definitions result in different intelligence for the same persons. When we thus compare data from the same time for both the criterion definition and the other operational definitions, the validity is usually referred to as *concurrent validity*.

Criterion validity can also be based on comparisons where data for the criterion definition is from a later point in time than data for the other operational definitions. For example, we can compare data on child intelligence based on specific operational definitions, with data about the same persons' school performance. School performance is then used as a criterion for the validity of the intelligence study, because we can assume that school performance is linked to intelligence. The criterion validity is high if there is a high consistency between intelligence and school performance. If those who have high intelligence according to the study later perform poorly at school, the study has low validity. The validity is an expression of how well the study of intelligence can anticipate or predict school performance. As such it is therefore often referred to as *predictive validity*. Concurrent validity and predictive validity are two different types of criterion validity.

While criterion validity is based on comparison between different operational definitions of the same concept, the third specification of definitional validity is based on the relationship between operational definitions of different concepts. This form of definitional validity is usually referred to as *construct validity*. The starting point is a known link between two different concepts, such as between the concepts of political interest and political activity. We know from previous research that there is a positive relationship between the two concepts, so that the more interested people are in politics, the more politically active they are. In an empirical study of political interest and political activity, the two concepts must be operationally defined. In a structured questionnaire, for example, we can use a graphical rating scale for political interest and a composite scale for political activity. If the study finds a positive relationship between the two scales that corresponds to the known relationship between the two concepts, we can consider the scales as valid expressions of the concepts. Construct validity is then high. If the relationship between the scales is different from the known relationship between political interest and political activity, the construct validity is low for one or both of the scales. In general, therefore, construct validity shows the extent to which the relationship between indicators for different concepts corresponds to the known relationship between these concepts.

Rath et al. (2013) refer to convergent and discriminant validity in their assessment of validity of a questionnaire-based scale about smoking behaviour. These validity types are subcategories of construct validity. *Convergent validity* is used for tests of validity based on an expected relationship between concepts, and *discriminant validity* is used for validity based on tests of an expected lack of relationship between concepts.

Assessments of construct validity are also presented by Spanemberg et al. (2014) in their study of the validity of a questionnaire about personality styles in depression, and by Bergland et al. (2015) in a study of the validity of a scale for measuring the thriving of older people.

Internal and external validity

In connection with experimental studies, reference is often made to two other types of validity – internal and external validity. Experimental studies, which will be discussed in more detail in Chapter 21, are structured studies of causal relationships. Such studies are based on quantitative data and are conducted under highly controlled conditions, often as laboratory studies. *Internal validity* concerns whether the experiment itself is conducted satisfactorily, so that the conclusion concerning causality is valid under the controlled study conditions. *External validity* is an expression of whether the results of the experiment are realistic and can be generalized to apply to common situations in society, so that the conclusion regarding causality is valid not only under artificial study conditions, but also for real social conditions.

In most experimental research designs, there will be some contradiction between internal and external validity. Prioritizing of internal validity usually occurs by tightening control of the study conditions, and this can easily occur at the expense of realism and external validity. In such studies, therefore, it is a challenge to find a good balance between the two types of validity.

Validity in qualitative studies

The types of validity mentioned so far are particularly common in quantitative research designs. While internal and external validity refer specifically to experimental testing of causal hypotheses, content validity, criterion validity and construct validity are often associated with the use of precise measurements for certain concepts. In principle, these types of validity can also be a good starting point for discussing the quality of data in qualitative studies. Reasoning about content validity, criterion validity and construct validity may be useful when qualitative data are used for concept development and clarification of the content of concepts and categories. The distinction between internal and external validity may be important when the objective of qualitative studies is to clarify causal relationships and develop causal hypotheses. The assessments of these types of validity will be less precise in qualitative studies than they are in quantitative studies.

However, there are some special types of validity that are particularly common in assessing qualitative data because they are especially appropriate for the characteristic features of qualitative research designs. Three types of validity for quality assessments of qualitative data will be highlighted here: competence validity, communicative validity and pragmatic validity.

Competence validity

Competence validity refers to the researcher's competence for collecting qualitative data in the relevant research field. Competence is an expression of the researcher's experience, background and qualifications related to this type of data collection. The more competent the researcher is in this field, the greater the chances of obtaining high-quality data. The researcher's competence improves confidence that the collected data is of good quality and is suitable for investigating the research questions to be addressed. In this way, the validity of the data is linked to the researcher's competence. The fact that the data collection has been carried out in a competent manner forms the basis for assuming that the validity is satisfactory.

This emphasis on the researcher's competence is related to the particularly important role of the researcher during data collection in qualitative studies. While the collection of quantitative data is based on structured research designs in the form of specific measuring instruments, the researcher is the most important component in the collection of qualitative data. This will be discussed in Chapter 20.

The emphasis on the researcher's competence is also linked to the fact that the collection of qualitative data is performed in a flexible manner and partly on the basis of analyses and interpretations during the data collection process. Thus, the validity is evaluated and possibly improved during the data collection process itself. The data collection procedures are adjusted or revised if it proves necessary in order to enhance the validity. All in all, this is a challenging and demanding process in which the researcher's competence is of great importance for the validity of the data.

Competence validity refers to knowledge about the sources and the empirical field, as well as theoretical understanding of what is being studied. The validity depends on the researcher being able to develop a close relationship with the sources, so that it becomes possible to find and collect the data that are most relevant to the research questions. At the same time, the validity depends on the researcher being able to develop a theoretical interpretation of these data, so that it becomes possible to assess how relevant and appropriate they are for the concepts or hypotheses that are central to the study.

However, it must be emphasized that the researcher's competence is not a guarantee that the validity will be high. Even if the researcher is very competent, problems may arise during the data collection that adversely affect the validity. In other words, the researcher's competence is a necessary, but not a sufficient prerequisite for high validity.

Communicative validity

Communicative validity is another type of validity that can be emphasized in qualitative studies. This type of validity is based on dialogue and discussion between the researcher and others about whether the data are good and appropriate for the research questions to be addressed in the study. Such discussions can be effective for uncovering potential problems and weaknesses in the data. The validity can be considered satisfactory if the discussions result in agreement or consensus that there are no particular problems or weaknesses in relation to the intentions of the study.

In this context, the researcher can enter into a dialogue with various discussion partners. Firstly, it is quite common that the data are discussed with the sources themselves, for example the actors who are observed or the respondents who are interviewed. If they recognize themselves in the researcher's descriptions and 'approve' the presentation, the validity can be considered satisfactory. The dialogue with the sources regarding the data can also reveal problems and weaknesses, which the researcher then has an opportunity to correct, so that the validity is improved. This process is usually called *actor validation*.

A possible problem with actor validation is that the actors and the researcher can have different perspectives as a basis for assessing the quality or validity of the data. Therefore, the researcher cannot rely solely on the actors' own descriptions of reality, but must consider these descriptions in conjunction with the analytical concepts and theoretical perspectives that are important in the study. The sources' assessments of data may also be affected by their own particular interests, especially in descriptions of conflicting or controversial conditions. Sometimes the sources will attempt to take control of the researcher's descriptions by setting conditions for how certain circumstances are to be described and discussed. This can be particularly problematic if the sources are powerful or have high status.

Other researchers can also be discussion partners for assessing communicative validity. The researchers can discuss the validity of the data with their academic partners and colleagues. This critical discussion of the data can also reveal problems and weaknesses. Colleagues' appraisals are usually not based on first-hand knowledge of the particular empirical conditions described in the study in question. On the other hand, colleagues can assess the data on the basis of more general theoretical insights within the area of the study and their methodological experience with this type of study. If the discussion with colleagues leads to consensus that the data have no particular weaknesses or limitations relative to the issues to be studied, the validity may be considered satisfactory. If, on the other hand, the discussion shows that there are certain weaknesses, the researcher has the option to correct these and thereby enhance the validity. This process is commonly referred to as *collegial validation*.

A potential problem associated with collegial validation is that different researchers may assess the data from different academic perspectives. They may represent different schools of thought within a subject field, reflecting different theoretical traditions or different methodological approaches. Occasionally, the relationship between such schools may be conflictual and characterized by rivalry or power struggle. This may also result in conflicts and disputes regarding the perception of reality. At worst, researchers within the most powerful or most established traditions may try to verify that the descriptions of reality are in line with their own academic perspectives, so that the opportunities for new discoveries and academic innovation are weakened. It will then be a challenge for the researcher to ensure that collegial validations are not characterized by such rivalries, but that the validity of the data is discussed on the basis of the issues being investigated in the current study and on the study's own approaches and perspectives.

Pragmatic validity

A third type of validity that can be utilized in qualitative studies is *pragmatic validity*. This type of validity shows the extent to which the data and the results of a study form the basis for particular actions. The level of validity is high if the study constitutes a good basis for action. Validity is thus an expression of the consistency between the empirical study and the actions that are highlighted for development. For example, a study of the working environment in a company can be said to have high pragmatic validity if the study provides the basis for improvement of the environmental conditions in the company.

Pragmatic validity can be compared with predictive validity, which was discussed above. Both validity types concern the degree of consistency between the results of a study and subsequent actions or events. However, there is an important difference: predictive validity shows the extent to which certain events or actions can be *predicted* by the study, while pragmatic validity expresses the extent to which particular events or actions can be *prescribed* or suggested by the study. Pragmatic validity therefore refers specifically to research that is used to develop a particular practice. The concept is therefore primarily relevant for action research, where the researcher interacts with different actors to utilize their research results in practical action, or applied research, where the research results are used by other actors for practical purposes.

A possible problem with pragmatic validity is that the validity assessments can be influenced by conflicting interests with regard to what actions should be developed or supported. Such problems can be particularly serious in commissioned or contract research. Resourceful or powerful clients may commission research projects in order to promote certain actions in line with their own special interests. If these interests conflict with the interests of the actors who are studied, the study may not be particularly suitable for promoting the clients' interests, even though the data are both relevant and appropriate to the research questions studied. In this case, the clients may assess the pragmatic validity differently than those involved in the

study. It is then a challenge for the researcher to clarify the basis for the validity assessment and to clarify the action preferences that underpin the pragmatic validity.

Assessment of validity

Since the concept of validity is less precise and more complex than the concept of reliability, validity assessments are usually more complicated than reliability assessments. In practice, it is not possible to achieve perfect validity in social science studies, and there are no simple criteria for what can be considered as satisfactory validity. There are also no precise measurements of validity, and it is not possible to test or calculate the validity in an exact way.

The most important procedure for assessing validity is to conduct systematic and critical discussions of the research design, data collection and data, emphasizing the validity types that are most relevant to the current study, and referring to the various aspects of each of these types of validity.

For example, in some studies, it may be particularly important to assess content validity. This validity type is particularly relevant in studies aimed at developing or utilizing complex concepts. It is then necessary to conduct a systematic review of all the components in the different concepts and to assess whether they are adequately covered by the collected data. In other studies, it may be particularly important to consider, for example, the question of external validity. This applies above all to experimental studies conducted under laboratory-like conditions, but which are intended to highlight real causal relationships between phenomena or conditions in society. The validity assessments then require thorough discussions of all the elements of the research design, with emphasis on how the artificial study conditions differ from the so-called natural conditions in society, and how these differences affect the possibilities of considering causal relationships identified in the experiment as valid expressions of real causal relationships in society.

Although validity cannot be tested or calculated in an exact manner, validity assessments can often be substantiated by special empirical investigations or analyses. The possibilities for empirical substantiation of validity assessments are particularly important for criterion validity and construct validity in quantitative studies. As mentioned above, these types of validity refer to the relationship between different operational definitions, either the consistency between different indicators for the same concept (criterion validity) or the relationship between indicators for different concepts (construct validity). In quantitative studies, the relationship between different indicators can be analysed empirically and expressed in terms of coefficients of agreement, correlation coefficients or other statistical measures. Such analyses of relationships will be discussed in Chapter 18.

More generally, assessments of validity can be substantiated empirically through comparisons of different types of data about the same phenomena. Such comparisons can be carried out internally in the data for the study in question. This not only applies to the relationship between different indicators in quantitative studies, but also may involve similarities or differences between different perspectives or approaches in qualitative studies. The comparisons may also be external, in the sense that data from a given study are compared with similar data from other sources or from previous research. In essence, the validity can be assumed to be high if there is high consistency between different data about the same phenomena. When such comparisons show low consistency, the empirical basis for detecting and clarifying validity problems is strengthened.

In qualitative studies particularly, it is important to discuss such comparisons in light of the context of the data collection. A main purpose of qualitative studies is to interpret and understand certain phenomena in light of the specific context in which these phenomena occur. This entails that the validity of the data must also be discussed and assessed specifically in light of the particular context in which data collection has been performed. In other words, differences between data about the same phenomena may be due to the fact that the data collection has been performed under different contextual conditions, and therefore do not necessarily reflect validity problems.

Qualitative studies also have other procedures for empirical substantiation of validity assessments. Competence validity can be assessed by systematically discussing the methodological experiences from the relevant study in the context of the researcher's previous experience and general qualifications for this type of study. Communicative validity can be assessed from the perspective of actor validation, based on conversations about the data with the sources in the current study, or collegial validation, based on comments on the data from other researchers.

Improving data quality

Data quality assessments are necessary in order to properly interpret the results of the analysis in a responsible manner. This is especially true for the quality assessments that are carried out after the data collection has been completed. The interpretations can then take account of problems with reliability or validity. Another, and perhaps more important, purpose of assessing reliability and validity is to improve data quality. During the planning and implementation of empirical investigations, therefore, reliability and validity should be assessed on a continuous basis, and part of the quality assessments should be undertaken early enough in the research process that they could provide a basis for quality improvements before the data collection is completed.

Quantitative studies

The opportunities for quality improvement in quantitative studies are primarily related to the quality assessments that are made during the preparation of research designs and measuring instruments, as well as in connection with the pretesting of designs and instruments. Both reliability and validity can then be enhanced through changes in the research design and measuring instruments before the actual data collection begins. For example, it may be relevant to clarify and specify theoretical and operational definitions of concepts, change the measurement level of variables, or use multiple indicators for complex concepts.

During data collection, the quality of the data can be ensured by following the selected research design in a responsible manner, and by using the observation schedule, questionnaire or coding schedule in accordance with the researcher's instructions.

After the data collection, the researcher can take account of quality assessments of the data through the data processing and analyses. For example, the analyses may pay particular attention to those parts of the data that are believed to have the highest reliability and validity, and variables with low reliability or validity can be excluded from the analyses. It may also be appropriate to improve the quality by merging variables and constructing indexes or by merging the values for some variables. Indexes usually have higher reliability than single variables, and index construction can also be effective in improving the content validity. Merging values on a variable can improve reliability, especially if the variable is initially divided into many values and if it has proved difficult during data collection to distinguish clearly between values that are close to each other.

Qualitative studies

In qualitative studies, there are great opportunities to improve both reliability and validity throughout the data collection process. The design is flexible, so that it can be adapted and changed based on the researcher's experiences and assessments as the study progresses. Data quality assessments should be central in this connection.

We can highlight two main strategies to improve data quality when implementing qualitative studies. These strategies complement each other. One strategy entails strengthening the work with field notes. These notes and their preparation form the basis for assessments of data quality, for example. Methodological notes are particularly important in connection with these assessments. These notes deal with experiences and problems during the data collection, as well as reflections on these experiences and problems. Methodological notes are essential in studies based on participant observation, but it is also recommended to use them during informal interviewing and qualitative content analysis. The better the methodological notes are designed, the better the researcher's basis for assessing the quality of the data, and the better the preconditions will be for revising the research design and adjusting the data collection in order to improve the data quality.

The second strategy for improving data quality in qualitative studies involves systematic adaptation of the data collection. The purpose is partly to arrange the data collection in order to obtain the best possible basis for assessing the data quality, and partly to adjust the data collection process based on the assessments of data quality that the researcher performs during the process. It is particularly important during the first part of the data collection process to establish a good foundation for the quality assessments. During the research process, it becomes increasingly important to adjust the data collection process based on these assessments.

Systematic adaptation of data collection in order to establish a good basis for data quality assessments can be achieved in two ways. Firstly, researchers can utilize methodological experiences and discussions from previous research. By making use of designs and procedures that have been used in other similar studies, researchers can discuss their own data in relation to other comparable research. As a rule, a good match with previous studies can be considered an indication that the data quality is high. In this way, the quality of the data can be discussed with reference to *external consistency*.

Secondly, the researcher can provide systematic variation in the data collection so that data about the same phenomena are collected in different ways. This involves, for example, choosing different positions and perspectives in participant observation, using different question formulations in informal interviewing, or performing different categorizations of the texts in qualitative content

analysis. The researcher can then compare the data based on the different collection methods. Generally, the quality of the data can be assumed to be high if there is high consistency between the data based on different perspectives, question formulations or categorizations. This type of data quality is referred to as *internal consistency*.

Systematic adaptations of data collection based on previous research and with a view to variations in perspectives, questions or categories not only help improve the basis for *assessing* the quality of the data. Such adjustments can also be an important strategy for *improving* data quality. When data collection is based on approaches and experiences from previous research, the level of trust and credibility in the data is improved. In the same way as indexes tend to have higher validity and reliability than individual variables in quantitative studies, qualitative data will usually have higher quality if multiple approaches are used to investigate the same phenomena.

CHAPTER HIGHLIGHTS

- Data quality must be evaluated in connection with the research questions to be investigated, and based on five key prerequisites for data quality:
  1 The data must be based on the principles of the researchers' commitment to truth.
  2 The data collection must be based on the scientific principles for logic and language use.
  3 The selection of units must be conducted in an appropriate manner.
  4 The selection of information types must be performed in a systematic manner.
  5 The implementation of data collection must be performed in a proper manner.
- The five assumptions are summarized in two overall criteria for data quality: reliability and validity.

- Reliability refers to the data's accuracy or trustworthiness. We distinguish between two main types of reliability: stability and equivalence.
- In quantitative studies, reliability is assessed using the test–retest method, the inter-subjectivity method or the split-half method. Reliability can be calculated in different ways.
- In qualitative studies, there are no standardized methods to assess reliability. The assessments are based on empirical studies of stability and equivalence, as well as critical discussions of internal and external consistency.
- Validity concerns the adequacy or relevance of the data for the research questions and phenomena to be examined. We distinguish between different types of validity: definitional

validity, internal validity and external validity in quantitative studies; and competence validity, communicative validity and pragmatic validity in qualitative studies.

- Validity assessments are based on systematic and critical discussions of the research design, data collection and data, with particular emphasis on relevant validity types. Such assessments of validity can be substantiated empirically through comparisons of different types of data about the same phenomena.

- The purpose of reliability and validity assessments is to improve data quality. In quantitative studies, this must be done especially during preparation for the data collection process. In qualitative studies, data quality can also be improved throughout the data collection process.

RESEARCH EXAMPLES

I recommend that you read the publications used as research examples in this chapter.

Bergland, Adel, Marit Kirkevold, Per-Olof Sandman, Dag Hofoss, and David Edvardsson (2015) 'The thriving of older people assessment scale: Validity and reliability assessments', *Journal of Advanced Nursing* 71(4), 942–951.

This article presents reliability and validity assessments of a scale for measuring the thriving of older people. Data based on the scale were analysed in order to identify different dimensions of thriving. Construct validity was assessed by examining the correspondence of these dimensions with thriving theory. Reliability was assessed by examining the internal consistency and homogeneity of the scale. The article concludes that the Thriving of Older People Assessment Scale has satisfactory reliability and construct validity.

Rath, Jessica M., Eva Sharma, and Kenneth H. Beck (2013) 'Reliability and validity of the Glover-Nilsson smoking behavioral questionnaire', *American Journal of Health Behavior* 37(3), 310–317.

The purpose of this article is to assess the reliability and validity of a questionnaire-based scale for smoking behaviour. Reliability was examined in terms of both stability (test–retest) and internal consistency. In order to assess the validity, the relationship between the smoking behaviour scale and a test for nicotine dependence was examined. It was concluded that the questionnaire-based scale has high reliability, in terms of both temporal stability and internal consistency, and satisfactory validity, in terms of both discriminant and convergent validity. These validity types are subcategories of construct validity.

Spanemberg, Lucas, Giovanni Abrahão Salum, Marco Antonio Caldieraro, Edgar Arrua Vares, Ricardo Dahmer Tiecher, Neusa Sica Da Rocha, Gordon Parker, and Marcelo P. Fleck (2014) 'Personality styles in depression: Testing reliability and validity of hierarchically organized constructs', *Personality and Individual Differences* 70, 72–79.

This article presents assessments of reliability and validity of a questionnaire on personality styles in depression. Data based on the questionnaire were analysed to identify different dimensions of personality. Construct validity was assessed by examining relationships between these dimensions, and relationships between data based on the personality questionnaire and data based on quality of life measurements. Reliability was assessed in terms of both stability (replication of questioning) and internal consistency.

STUDENT EXERCISES AND QUESTIONS

1   What is the difference between reliability and validity?
2   What is the difference between stability and equivalence as expressions of reliability?
3   How is reliability assessed
    a   in quantitative studies?
    b   in qualitative studies?
4   What is meant by definitional validity?
5   Why is it more challenging to assess reliability and validity in qualitative studies than in quantitative studies?
6   Why are reliability and validity important in social research?
7   Discuss strategies for improving data quality in quantitative and qualitative studies.

RECOMMENDED LITERATURE

Carmines, Edward G., and Richard A. Zeller (1979) *Reliability and Validity Assessment*. London: Sage.

This book explains how the reliability and validity of empirical measurements in social science can be evaluated. Different types of validity are discussed, and different types of reliability tests are examined.

Drost, Ellen A. (2011) 'Validity and reliability in social science research', *Education Research and Perspectives* 38(1), 105–123.

This article provides insight into the concepts of validity and reliability and describes the main methods for assessing reliability and validity in behavioural research. Different types of reliability and validity are discussed, and different strategies for improving reliability and validity are suggested.

Kirk, Jerome, and Marc L. Miller (1986): *Reliability and Validity in Qualitative Research*. Beverly Hills, CA: Sage.

In this book, the role of reliability and validity in qualitative research is discussed, and the importance of reliability and validity is emphasized. The book presents a paradigm for the qualitative research process that makes it possible to pursue validity without neglecting reliability.

PART IV

DATA ANALYSIS

The online resources are here to help with analysing data!

Visit https://study.sagepub.com/gronmo to access real-world practice datasets, videos, case studies, key term definitions, and critical thinking exercises that will help you learn more about data analysis.

ANALYSIS OF QUALITATIVE DATA

This chapter provides the knowledge that is necessary for understanding and conducting analysis of qualitative data.

The chapter will teach you how to

- distinguish between different purposes of the analysis
- select appropriate methods for the data analysis
- use coding and categorization in qualitative analyses
- use matrices and figures in the analysis
- use qualitative data for developing concepts, typologies, hypotheses and theories

- apply the constant comparative method
- make use of analytical induction
- develop grounded theory
- conduct theoretical generalizations
- use computer software in qualitative data analysis.

Processing and analysing texts

The purpose of qualitative data analyses is to obtain a comprehensive understanding of specific circumstances or to develop theories and hypotheses about specific social contexts. If the conditions or relationships specified in the research questions are more comprehensive than those included in the empirical study, the analysis should provide a basis for theoretical generalization. As pointed out in Chapter 8, this requires a strategic sampling of the phenomena that are included in the empirical study.

In qualitative studies, data are usually analysed while they are being collected. Analyses occur continuously in parallel with the data collection, but, as the study progresses, the analysis work becomes an increasingly dominant part of the project. The analyses will then be continued and completed after the data collection has been terminated. In qualitative research designs, therefore, we cannot isolate the data analysis process as a distinct phase in the study. The methods for qualitative analysis that will be discussed in this chapter can be used at different stages of the project, both during and after the data collection process.

The specific selection of methods for the analysis in a particular study must be made primarily on the basis of the particular research questions to be addressed, the specific research design and the particular context of the study. However, the majority of qualitative studies share an important common feature: regardless of how the data are collected, the data will usually be in the form of texts, which are available in written, printed or digital form. Occasionally, qualitative data may also be available in other forms, such as audio recordings, visual materials or audio-visual presentations, and some computer programs can be used for analysing these types of materials. However, this is less common, mainly because such materials are typically regarded as documentary sources, which are transcribed or described and transformed into textual data before they are analysed. Content analysis of such documentary sources was discussed in Chapters 11 and 14. In this chapter, the discussion of procedures for qualitative data analysis will concentrate on data in the form of text.

The ways in which these procedures are used in practice can vary widely from study to study. There are no standardized analytical techniques that can be used for analysis of qualitative data. While quantitative data can be analysed using more or less advanced statistical techniques, analysis of qualitative data is characterized by greater flexibility and is based on more general strategies.

In this chapter some of the most common approaches for qualitative analyses in social science are reviewed. First, coding of qualitative data is described. This is the most usual procedure for processing and sorting text data in order to obtain a better overview of the data set. There is then a section on how the coding forms the basis for categorization and concept development. Next, a more specific method for generating categories and concepts based on qualitative data is reviewed. This method involves systematic and repeated comparisons of different elements in the qualitative data. It is also discussed how qualitative data can be used to develop distinctions between different types of phenomena and how such types can be related to each other in typologies. Then, it is described how matrices and figures can be important analytical tools for arranging different text elements in relation to each other, and to illustrate the relationships between these elements. Next, two common purposes of qualitative analyses are discussed, namely a general understanding of specific conditions and the development of hypotheses and theories. Then, it is discussed how qualitative data can be used for theoretical generalization. Finally, the use of computers and various types of software in qualitative data analysis is explained.

through the texts to be analysed and forms an impression of what is important or typical. Through such inspection of the data, surprising or special trends and patterns are also discovered. This is combined with the researcher's experience and impressions from the data collection, and all of this will be processed in the researcher's consciousness. Based on further reflection and repeated readings of the text data, often combined with the writing of *analytical memos*, the researcher gradually develops deeper insights and increased understanding of important empirical patterns. Data elements, empirical findings and more theoretical interpretations are thus assembled, compiled and summarized at an ever higher level and in an increasingly general form. Although this process is scientific, it can also have much in common with artistic activities. There is an art to carrying out qualitative analyses in this creative fashion. The impressionist approach is extremely demanding. It requires a great deal of experience, adequate theoretical insight and considerable ability to form an overview of complex empirical patterns.

As a rule, data in qualitative studies are both comprehensive and complex. In order to identify general and typical patterns, it is necessary to simplify and summarize the content of the texts so that it is easier to obtain an overview of the central and important trends in the data.

Coding of qualitative data

The textual data in qualitative data analysis could be field notes from participant observation, transcripts of unstructured interviews, or texts that have been selected and registered for qualitative content analysis.

The data analysis involves identifying general or typical patterns in these texts. Occasionally, this can be done in ways that have a certain impressionistic character. The researcher then reads

Codes

Coding the data is an important procedure for creating an overview by simplifying and summarizing the content of the text. This involves finding one or a few keywords that can describe or characterize a larger section of the text, such as multiple sentences or entire paragraphs. The keywords are called codes.

This meaning of 'coding' is different from the meaning commonly used in quantitative studies. In quantitative studies, coding involves marking a respondent's response, a text unit or another data element with a specific value or number, corresponding to the category on a specific variable in which the individual data element will be placed. Such coding of quantitative data is part of the data collection or data processing that occurs prior to the analysis of the data. A code is the numerical value of a particular category for a variable, and these codes are determined and defined before the data analysis commences. In qualitative studies, on the other hand, coding may be part of the analysis. The codes are developed during the analysis and are not expressed in numbers, but as text.

In qualitative data analysis, a code is an abbreviation or a symbol that is used for a segment of words (a sentence or paragraph) to classify the words (Miles et al., 2019). For example, a code for a particular section could specify a topic that the section is about, or something that is mentioned in the section, such as an actor, an action, an event or a relationship.

Codes can be descriptive, interpretive or explanatory. *Descriptive codes* are purely descriptive characteristics of the actual and explicit content of the text. *Interpretive codes* express the researcher's interpretation or understanding of the content of the text. For example, it may be the researcher's interpretation of the meaning of an action for a particular actor. *Explanatory codes* express the researcher's explanation of the circumstances that are explicitly mentioned in the text. Such codes may indicate, for example, a possible reason or cause for what is described in the text.

Descriptive codes are directly generated from the empirical data, as these are expressed through the explicit presentation in the text that is being analysed. Interpretive and explanatory codes will be based on an understanding of the text in light of a larger contextual or theoretical context.

A contextual understanding of the text can be developed from the researcher's knowledge of the context of the study, based on their experience and observations made while collecting the data, but the text element that is coded can also be understood contextually by viewing it in conjunction with larger parts of the text in which the particular element is included. A particular section can become more understandable and more meaningful when we read it in conjunction with what has been written immediately before and immediately after that particular section.

A theoretical understanding of the content in the text is developed by assessing and discussing the text in relation to theoretical concepts or categories.

The research questions of the studies represent an important basis for the researcher's assessments of which contextual or theoretical interpretations are most relevant for the particular text to be coded. In this way, codes will be developed both *inductively*, based on empirical data, and *deductively*, based on the concepts and theories of previous research.

Open coding

Coding can be done in several steps. The first step is usually called *open coding*. In open coding, the codes appear as an initial characterization and classification of the key content elements in the data. The fact that the coding is open means that the researcher's choice of codes is primarily determined by the empirical data. At the same time, the research question of the study will be a guideline for the researcher's assessment of how the content of the data should be divided and characterized. In the first coding, however, openness to empirical evidence is more important than the guidelines from the research question. In this connection, descriptive codes are more common than interpretive and explanatory codes. The intention is that the researcher should be open-minded enough to discover unforeseen and surprising empirical phenomena, patterns and contexts.

How coding is done is exemplified in an article by Fung and Adams (2017) on motivations for environmental activism among college students. The study is based on unstructured interviews with students and observations from a meeting of a student activist group. After reviewing the data and memos from the data collection, the researchers 'developed a list of themes and concepts that occurred repeatedly in the data. Based on these themes, we created a set of codes, a definition for each code, rules for applying the code, and examples of how to use and *not* use each code' (Fung and Adams, 2017). The codes were developed by identifying themes that were both relevant to the research questions and frequently found in the data. These codes are shown in Table 16.1.

Categorization and concept development

The first step of the coding process is based on the raw data, that is, the text that constitutes the study's data. The next steps can be based on both the text itself and on the codes developed during the open coding. Through this process, the coding is developed further in order to form the basis for categories and concepts.

Table 16.1 Example of coding in qualitative data analysis. Reproduced here from Fung and Adams (2017: 6)

Research question	Code	Code definition
Main RQ: What reasons do self-identified environmentalists or activists give for taking action against environmental problems that concern them? That is, what is their motivation?	EXPERIENCE	One's previous experiences and education (can be formal education, learning on one's own, learning from others, indirect education) that influence one's desire (or lack thereof) to participate in activism
	AWARENESS	Being made or making others aware of an issue, idea, concept, problem, etc., by any method (talking to someone, reading, education, etc.)
	SELF-IMPROVEMENT	Doing something because of a desire to improve one's own life/character or to further one's self-interest
	PASSION	Doing something because of a connection with that subject and/or because of one's passion for that subject
	INCENTIVES	Having an external (that is, outwardly-motivated) reason to do something. Usually this involves getting something in return, but that is not a necessary condition to be met
	PWYP (Practice What You Preach)	The desire to take action against a concern to 'be the change you want to see'
	COMMUNITY	The desire to do something in order to improve or become engaged with a community, or to get the community involved in one's cause
Sub RQs: What prevents or discourages self-identified environmentalists (SIEs) from taking action on their concerns (environmental or otherwise)? That is, what thresholds or barriers, if any, exist for taking action? Why?	INVOLVEMENT	The perception of being easily able to become involved with a group, project, campaign, etc.
	TIME	Having or not having enough time to become involved in something, or to do something, related to one's activistic concerns

Categories

A *category* is a collection or class of phenomena with specific common characteristics. The category is defined by these common attributes of the phenomena, in contrast to attributes of phenomena that are not included in the category. For example, in a content analysis of newspaper articles, we can place all statements containing positive or negative mention of the EU into the same category, where the statements share in common that they express an attitude towards the EU. Similarly, we can place all statements with positive or negative mention of NATO into another category, where expressing an opinion about NATO will be the common feature of the statements.

Coding that aims to develop categories is not completely open. It must be more *systematic* than the first coding of the qualitative data. The coding must now be based on certain common attributes of the various phenomena described in the data. These common features must first be identified and defined. This is done by reviewing the codes or keywords produced by the open coding, and possibly by reassessing parts of the data with a view to finding common features of several of the codes and several of the coded text elements. As such common features are identified and defined, they will form the basis for the gradual development of an increasing number of increasingly well-defined categories. This is how the coding is developed towards a categorization of the qualitative data. At the same time, the research question of the study will form the basis for ongoing assessments of which categories are most relevant and most useful. Generally, the categorization will be based mainly on the empirical data, so that the researcher can still be as open-minded as possible with regard to discovering new and unforeseen trends and relationships. Eventually, however, the research question will be given greater and greater emphasis, so that the empirical patterns can be interpreted and understood in light of more theoretical perspectives, for example in order to arrive at a theoretical generalization of the empirical results.

In this categorization process, it may be appropriate to adjust the generality level or abstraction level of the categories. A category can be divided into several new and more specific categories. For example, a general category for attitude towards the EU can be divided into one category for support of the EU and another category for opposition to the EU. Multiple categories can be merged into a more general category. An example of this would be to merge the categories for attitude towards the EU and attitude towards NATO (and possibly other similar categories) into an overall category for attitudes towards international organizations. The level of generality or specificity that the categories should have in a particular study will depend partly on the categories that are appropriate for the data, and partly on which categories are most meaningful with regard to the research question.

Thus, the categories will be gradually generated and continually revised as different parts of the data are reviewed. The coding helps to develop categories, and when new categories are developed, revised and specified, each category will be designated with its own code. As the different categories become increasingly well-defined, they will be used as a basis for a systematic coding of the entire data set. This allows the researcher to determine whether the categories work well for the entire data set, or whether they require further adaptation and improvement. When the entire body of data is evaluated in relation to each of the new categories, the researcher also obtains a better basis for clarifying the content of each category and the boundaries between the different categories. Systematic coding that uses a well-thought-out set of meaningful categories will also allow even more simplification of the complex data and provide an even better overview of relevant and useful empirical patterns.

Concepts

Typically, this categorization is important for the next step in the coding, which is about developing concepts. A *concept* is a theoretical construct, a designation or a general notion for a particular type of phenomena. In conjunction with categories, a concept may be the general notion for the phenomena included in the category. The concept can thus be a name for the category. Any name for a category, however, will not necessarily be a social science concept. Such concepts constitute basic elements in social science theories. A theory consists of a set of relations between concepts, where the relations are in a certain systematic relationship with each other. *Street corner society* is a well-known social science concept based on analysis of qualitative data. The concept was developed by the sociologist William Foot Whyte (1943), based on participant observation among young boys and street gangs in an Italian-American slum area in Boston in the late 1930s. Street corner society is a general term for the typical patterns, relationships and structures that Whyte observed in this environment. The concept constitutes unifying or integrating characteristics of relatively complex phenomena. Social science concepts may vary with regard to complexity, generality and level of abstraction.

When the coding is further developed from categorization to concept development, the challenge is to find notions for the categories that are theoretically useful, so that they can be related to established concepts or form the basis for new concepts. In this way, the concepts can make links between the empirically generated categories and more general social science perspectives. At the same time, the confrontation between established concepts and the empirical clarification and delimitation of the content of the various categories can help to clarify, differentiate or revise the concepts. The result may also be the development of completely new concepts. This is all of major importance for the development of theories and for theoretical generalization.

This third step in the coding process is based on both the categories that have been developed and the text that is associated with the different categories. When we search for conceptually useful designations for the categories, and when the categories are confronted with different concepts, it may prove necessary or appropriate to revise the categories once more. It is particularly important in connection with the development of concepts to carefully consider the boundaries between the categories and the relationship between different categories. A concept does not necessarily refer to a single category, but may also be a collective term for a set of categories or for a particular relationship between different categories.

The development of concepts is usually based on *selective* coding. The coding goes into depth for each concept and concentrates on the categories and text elements that are particularly relevant for the individual concept. It may be useful to use analytical memos or memos for this purpose. The researcher often writes such a memo for each of the concepts that may be useful for the data being analysed. The memo discusses the meaning and dimensions of the concept in depth, with special emphasis on theoretical and operational definitions, how it has been developed and utilized in previous research, how it is included in various theoretical perspectives and, not least, how the concept may be related to the data in the current study. Here, various alternative classifications, codes and categorizations of the data are also discussed, with particular emphasis on how to establish the best possible connection between the concept and the data.

As the qualitative analysis gradually develops from open coding via categorization to concept development, we place ever more emphasis on guidelines from the research question and theoretical perspectives, increasing emphasis on deductive approaches and increasing emphasis on interpretive and explanatory codes. However, we are constantly concerned with maintaining a close relationship with the data. Codes, categories or concepts are rarely used in isolation from the data from which they are generated. Quotes from the data are presented as illustrations, elaborations and documentation of the content in the categories and the concepts. This applies especially to the final research reports from qualitative studies.

Constant comparative method

The American social researchers Barney Glaser and Anselm Strauss have developed a special method for coding and categorizing qualitative data (Glaser and Strauss, 1967). This method, which is referred to as the *constant comparative method*, involves making repeated systematic comparisons of the various elements in the data.

A data element is a delimited part of the text to be analysed. The amount of text that is demarcated in each element will depend on both the content of the data and the purpose of the analysis. A data element may be an entire passage or a single sentence. In certain cases, a single word may also constitute a separate data element. Often, the delimitation of data elements will place greater emphasis on the meaning of the text, rather than on the form of presentation and the formal division of sentences and paragraphs. For example, if we have observed relations between participants at an international congress, we may be concerned with identifying different attributes of the relationships recorded in the text from the field notes.

Such attributes could be, for example, the types of relationships observed (social gatherings, conversations or various types of more active interaction) or the number of actors involved in the relationships (dyads or groups of different sizes). Relevant attributes could also be which actors are involved (gender, age, nationality, status and position), where the relationships are manifested (during meetings, coffee breaks or completely outside the congress programme), or what the relationships are about (matters relating to the congress, other professional matters or personal relationships). Each section or part of the text that provides information about such characteristics of the observed relationships will be considered a data element.

Although the researcher starts with certain assumptions about which type of characteristics of the relationships are relevant to identify, it is important to remain completely open to the data, so that the analysis itself provides good opportunities to detect unforeseen aspects of the relationships. In the same way, the researcher starts with a completely open attitude to how different aspects and characteristics of the relationships should be classified into types and categories. In other words, the actual analysis of the data may result in categories other than those indicated in the example above. The categories develop gradually through the specific analysis of the particular data.

The constant comparative method developed by Glaser and Strauss is a systematic procedure for generating such empirically based categories. In turn, all relevant data elements are systematically compared and arranged in relation to each other. In practice, this occurs by the researcher reading through the text and identifying the first text section that refers to the phenomenon to be analysed and categorized (e.g. the relationships mentioned above). Then the researcher continues reading the text until the next mention of the phenomenon is identified in a new section of the text. These first two text sections are then compared in order to determine what they show about the phenomenon in question. In the example with relationships among congress participants, the comparison will clarify whether the two sections of text deal with the same or similar characteristics in the relationships. If so, they can be placed together in a common category. If the text sections describe different characteristics of the relationships, they are each placed in different categories. The researcher then continues reading the text until the third relevant section of text is identified. This section is then compared with the first two sections. If this third data element closely resembles one of the first two elements, they are placed in a common category. If the third data element resembles both of the first two elements, all three will be placed in the same category, and if the third element is different from both of the first two elements, it is placed in a separate category. The first three data elements will thus form the basis for one, two or three categories. The fourth data element identified during the further reading is then placed together with one or more of the first three elements, or forms the basis for another new category. The reading and the systematic comparison continue in this way. All relevant data elements will gradually be compared to each other, and the numerous data elements will be reduced to a smaller number of categories.

This repeated, systematic comparison means that an increasing number of the different data elements are placed into different categories. The content of the categories can also be revised, the boundaries between the categories may be shifted or changed, some categories may be subdivided into new ones, and some established categories may be merged into a single new category. Throughout this process, the researcher maintains a close relationship with the data. The categories are *generated* by the text being analysed. The content and demarcation of each category are also *defined* and *illustrated* by the parts of the text that are placed in the category. This provides a good basis for finding suitable and accurate designations for the categories, so that the categorization can lead to conceptualization and concept development. Through this systematic work, the researcher clarifies the differences between different categories, detects certain relations between the categories and identifies possible relationships between different parts of the data. This provides opportunities to develop hypotheses and theories, especially when the relationships are discussed with reference to the concepts that are gradually linked to the various categories. Glaser and Strauss (1967) stressed that their constant comparative method is useful for theory development. They discussed how the method can be incorporated into a more general strategy of analysis, where qualitative data form the basis for what they called *grounded theory* or empirically based theory. This strategy will be further discussed later in this chapter, in a separate section on the development of hypotheses and theories.

The constant comparative method was used in a study of teacher feedback in the classroom in Swedish primary schools (Eriksson et al., 2017). The study was based on observations in classrooms in four primary schools with 7–9-year-old students. The data consisted of field notes and transcriptions of some audio recordings from dialogues, conversations and unstructured interviews. Using the constant comparative method, the researchers coded these data and identified recurring patterns, and the codes were gradually grouped into more and more comprehensive codes. Thus, the analysis resulted in five main categories of teacher feedback to students in the classroom (Eriksson et al., 2017: 320).

Types and typologies

A category is comprised of phenomena with one or more specific characteristics in common.

This means that a category contains a certain type of phenomenon. A category can therefore be understood as a *type*. When multiple categories are arranged in relation to each other in a particular system, these categories form a *typology*. A typology thus consists of a set of types that are arranged in a logical relationship to each other. Developing typologies can be a useful analytical method in qualitative studies. It helps to clarify and specify both the differences and the relationships between different categories. This can be of great importance when developing both concepts and hypotheses.

In typology development in qualitative studies, the researcher starts with a relatively general category that is relevant to the particular study. For example, in a study based on unstructured interviews on consumption patterns, a typology of attitudes towards shopping was developed (Lavik, 1979). Reviewing the transcripts of the interviews, the researcher identified all statements from respondents that expressed attitudes to shopping. Coding and categorization of these statements made it possible to distinguish between four main types of attitudes towards shopping: economic, ideological, social and practical attitudes.

This classification is related to two dimensions that represent the most important divisions between the different types. One of these concerns the importance of the purchases for the consumer. Some consumers emphasize the supply importance of shopping: that the importance of shopping is limited to obtaining various products. These consumers have a purely instrumental attitude to their purchases. Other consumers have a more expressive attitude to their shopping. They are concerned with the psychosocial and social significance of the shopping process: that the act of shopping is significant as a break and as an opportunity to engage in social contact, either with the employees in the shop or with other customers. The second dimension that distinguishes between different attitudes to shopping refers to the distinction between the results of the shopping and the act of shopping as a process. While some consumers pay particular attention to the outcome of the shopping process, others are more concerned with what happens during the actual shopping process.

When the four attitude types are arranged along these two dimensions, the logical relationship between the types can be visualized, as shown in Table 16.2. The economic attitude and the practical attitude entail that the consumer emphasizes the significance of the supply aspect of shopping. While the first of these types of attitude emphasizes the results of shopping in terms of obtaining good and reasonable products, the other attitude emphasizes that shopping as a process can be carried out in a quick and efficient manner. Ideological and social attitudes emphasize the psychosocial and social importance of shopping. The former attitude is result-oriented and concerns, for example, shopping in particular types of shops, such as local shops or consumer cooperatives, because this means that the social or societal importance of these types of shops can be maintained. The latter attitude is process-oriented

Table 16.2 Example of a typology: attitudes towards shopping

| | Dimension no. 1 | |
Dimension no. 2	Emphasis on the significance of the supply aspect of the purchases	Emphasis on the purchases' psychosocial and social significance
Emphasis on the results of the shopping	Economic attitude	Ideological attitude
Emphasis on shopping as a process	Practical attitude	Social attitude

and emphasizes the psychosocial and social importance that the shopping activity itself has for the specific consumer.

Table 16.2 shows how the four types of attitude constitute a typology of attitudes towards shopping. The four types are related to the two dimensions and are thus also arranged in relation to each other. The dimensions form a logical basis for the relationship between the types, and together the four attitude types form a system for classifying the statements. The designations of the different attitudes also constitute concepts, so that the typology clarifies some conceptual relationships. This example shows how the actual development of the typology contributes to the formation of concepts. The clarification of the distinctions and the relationships between the types increase the ability to find appropriate concepts for the different categories.

In a study of Dutch mothers and their life histories, based on semi-structured interviews, Ruitenberg (2014) developed a typology of the mothers. The typology distinguished between different 'narratives of choice and considerations regarding the ideal gender division of labour, work and motherhood' (Ruitenberg, 2014: 58). Four types of mothers were included in the typology: drifters, privilegeds, balancers, and ambitious (Ruitenberg, 2014: 76).

Another example of a social science typology is Durkheim's classification of suicide. In his famous study of suicide, Durkheim (1897) emphasizes that suicide can be understood in light of two different social conditions. One of these concerns individuals' integration into society. The second relationship concerns society's regulation of individuals and their actions. According to Durkheim, both excessively strong and excessively weak social regulation of individuals can lead to suicide, and suicide can also be due to both overly strong and overly weak integration of individuals in society. Regulation and integration thus constitute dimensions for a typology of suicide. The dimensions form a basis

for distinguishing between four different types of suicide, as illustrated in Table 16.3.

Table 16.3 Durkheim's suicide typology

	Society's regulation of the individual	The individual's integration into society
Weak	Anomic	Egoistic
Strong	Fatalistic	Altruistic

The development of *ideal types* is a special form of identification and delimitation of types in qualitative analyses. An ideal type is a representation of a particular phenomenon, where the most important and most typical features of the phenomenon are isolated, highlighted and described in an idealized or pure form. An ideal type therefore functions roughly like a model.

The development of ideal types as a social science method is particularly associated with Max Weber. Best known is his depiction of bureaucracy as an ideal type (Weber, 2013). The features of bureaucracy emphasized in Weber's ideal-type depiction include a fixed division of labour, recruitment based on technical qualifications, permanent employment, fixed salary, hierarchical relationships, distinction between position and person, clear rules, and the right to appeal against decisions.

Ideal types do not refer to 'ideal' in the normative sense. The features of a phenomenon included in an ideal type are not especially desirable features. Ideal-type traits are based on actual conditions that are investigated empirically. The method is therefore well suited to qualitative analyses, because it can clarify the most distinctive features of certain conditions in society. It is the data that determine which features should be isolated and highlighted. It is also the data that form the basis for assessing how the features should be isolated and idealized.

On the other hand, ideal-type depictions are not quite as empirically based representations as other categorizations and typologies. The isolation and idealization of selected characteristics will often combine purely empirical analysis with more conceptual and theoretical interpretation. Some of the characteristics observed may be magnified or exaggerated in the depiction of the ideal type, while other observed characteristics may be toned down or minimalized. What is crucial is what appears to be most significant and most typical from a particular theoretical perspective.

Matrices and figures

Matrices and figures can be very useful analytical tools in qualitative studies. The way in which such tools can be used in analyses of qualitative data is described in detail by Miles et al. (2019).

Use of matrices

A *matrix* in this context is a chart for systematizing and arranging quotes from qualitative data. The matrix is arranged in the same way as a table. The examples of the typologies presented in Tables 16.2 and 16.3 are arranged as matrices. Here, the designations of the different types make up the content of the individual cells or boxes in the matrices. Such matrices are often used to summarize the results of comprehensive and in-depth qualitative analyses.

Matrices are also used during the analysis process. Different matrices can be used at different stages in the analysis of qualitative data. Especially during the initial stages, it is the text sections from the data that are rendered inside the matrices. As the analysis evolves more and more towards categorization and concept development, the content of the matrices can gradually change from quotes to codes, type descriptions, category designations, or concepts.

Table 16.4 shows an example of a matrix that can be used to systematize and arrange quotes from informal interviews about attitudes to shopping. One line is set aside in the matrix for each person interviewed, and one column for each type of attitude referred to by the respondents. The starting point for the division into attitude types is the typology that was presented in Table 16.2. The typology may be based on previous research or previous stages in the analysis of the data from the same study. Quotes from the transcripts of the interviews are placed in the individual cells or boxes. If Ann states that her emphasis is on finding the best and cheapest goods when she shops, this is a statement concerning economic attitude, which is placed in the box at the top in the left-hand column of the matrix. When such matrices are filled with content in the form of quotes in the different boxes, they will be far larger than the matrix in Table 16.4. Each box must be large enough to accommodate the relevant quotes from the data.

Table 16.4 Matrix for arranging quotes from informal interviews about attitudes to shopping

| Respondent | Attitude to shopping | | | | |
	Economic attitude	Social attitude	Ideological attitude	Practical attitude	Other attitudes
Ann					
Bill					
Jane					
Ruth					

When the relevant quotes are placed in the appropriate boxes in the matrix, we obtain a better overview of the structure of the data. If we look at all the quotes in the column for economic attitude in Table 16.4, we obtain a better understanding of the content in this category and the significance of this attitude type. Similarly, we can clarify the content of the social attitude category. If we compare the quotes in the column for economic attitude with the quotes in the column for social attitude, we obtain a more specific and more empirically based insight into the boundaries between the two categories and the distinction between the two attitude types. We can thus develop an increasingly in-depth understanding of the relationship between all of the attitude categories. Since we include a separate column for the residual category of 'other attitudes', we can also determine whether there are attitudes that do not fit into the four defined categories, and how comprehensive the four attitude types really are for people's attitudes to shopping. The boundaries and usefulness of the typology can thus be challenged, explored and clarified.

Analyses of data using matrices like that in Table 16.4 can be carried out in two different ways. Referring to the matrix, the analyses can be conducted horizontally or vertically. Horizontal analyses consider each row in the matrix and identify empirical patterns based on all the boxes in that row. The patterns in the different rows can then be compared to each other in order to reveal more general traits. The special matrix in Table 16.4 is arranged in such a way that a horizontal analysis in this case would be *person-centred*. This implies that we take each individual person involved in the study and identify typical features of this person with regard to all the themes that are included in the matrix. Based on these themes, we can then obtain a comprehensive understanding of the individual people. We can then compare the different people with each other. On the basis of similarities and differences between the people in

the data, we can develop, for example, new categories or types. Depending on the attitudes most stressed by the individual consumers, we can distinguish between different types of consumers, such as economic, social, ideological and practical consumers.

Vertical analyses consider each column in the matrix and identify empirical patterns based on all the boxes in this column. The patterns in the different columns can then be compared to each other, in order to identify more general features. A vertical analysis based on the matrix in Table 16.4 would be *theme-centred*. This means that each theme that is included in the matrix is reviewed in its entirety and on the basis of quotes from all the people included in the matrix. The purpose is to obtain an overall understanding of what characterizes this theme across different people. Then the different topics may be compared or viewed in relation to each other. In this example, it is a matter of clarifying how each of the different types of attitude manifests itself in the different consumers. This enables us to gain an insight into how different aspects of each type of attitude are emphasized and expressed in different contexts. This provides a basis for a comprehensive understanding of what characterizes the different attitudes to shopping.

In her study of Dutch mothers mentioned above, Ruitenberg (2014: 66) used four large matrices to arrange the data from the interviews, and these matrices were thematically analysed.

Matrices can also provide a basis for identifying relationships or links between different categories or phenomena. The matrix in Table 16.4 could, for example, be expanded with more columns, so that in addition to the different attitude categories, we also had columns for respondents' gender, age, education, employment and family circumstances. In that case, we could discover certain covariations between, say, employment situation and attitudes. For example, economic and practical attitudes could be relatively more widespread among consumers with long working hours than among other consumers. Such patterns may be easier to detect if we sort the rows in the matrix to some extent, so that people with the same background traits are grouped in series. Any similarities in attitudes will also appear in series in the matrix.

Use of figures

When matrices are filled with text instead of numbers, they appear as a special type of *figure*. Many other types of figures are also used in qualitative data analysis, especially when it comes to illustrating possible relationships or links between different categories and different units. The kind of figures used can vary from analysis to analysis and will depend on both the type of patterns and correlations to be illustrated, as well as the researcher's creative abilities. A few examples of figures used in qualitative analyses will be given here.

A typical purpose for using figures in such analyses is to illustrate *structural patterns*. *Structure* refers to a set of relations that are in a certain relationship with each other. Usually, we also emphasize that only relations with a certain duration or stability can be regarded as parts of a structure.

Social networks constitute a type of structural pattern that is often analysed in qualitative studies. A network is a pattern of relations or connections between people or other actors, such as organizations. The network may include different types of relations between the actors, such as friendships, family relations or collegial relations between individuals. Typically, qualitative network studies are based on data about such relations. The German-American social-psychologist Jakob Moreno (1934) developed a particular type of figure to illustrate network patterns. In such figures, which are called *sociograms*, the actors are presented as points, while the relations between the actors are illustrated by lines or arrows between the points.

Figure 16.1 is an example of a sociogram. It shows a network of friendship relations between boys and girls based on data from informal interviews. The four boys and the three girls have answered questions about whom they regard as their closest friends. An arrow pointing in both directions illustrates a mutual relation. John has named Jill as a friend, and Jill has named John as a friend. An arrow in one direction illustrates a one-sided relation. John has named Jack as a friend, while Jack has not mentioned John among his closest friends.

Such sociograms can be made more advanced, especially regarding the relations presented. We can have different types of arrows for strong and weak relations or for relations with different content. The arrows can also be marked with a number to indicate how many different connections exist between two actors (such as both spouses and colleagues), and plus or minus next to the arrow can be used to symbolize positive relations (friends) or negative relations (enemies). The sociograms can also be far more extensive than those shown in Figure 16.1.

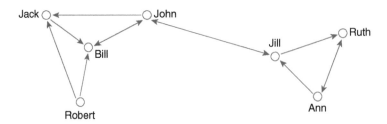

Figure 16.1 Example of a sociogram

The problem is that the sociograms quickly become incomprehensible or unreadable when we increase the number of actors and relations. There are many computer programs for analysing social networks. Using such programs, sociograms can be produced automatically, by means of special software packages. In Chapter 23 analyses of social networks will be discussed in greater detail.

Another type of structural pattern is *hierarchies*. These concern hierarchical structures, where the relationships represent relations between superior and subordinate categories or units. Such structures are typical of the relations between the employees in a bureaucracy or a business company. This can be presented, for example, as illustrated in Figure 16.2. This shows an example of a formal structure in an organization, focusing on formal relations between people in leading positions in the organization. Such a figure is called an *organization chart*. Such figures can also be used to illustrate more informal structures. Informal structures do not necessarily coincide with formal organizational structures. For example, if we conduct a study based on participant observation of the organization presented in Figure 16.2, we may discover that section manager Andrews has a powerful position in the organization because she has developed a particularly close and friendly relationship with CEO Johnson. In a similar figure presenting the informal organizational structure, therefore, Andrews would be placed higher up in the hierarchy. It is a fairly common result of qualitative studies of hierarchical organizations that the

researcher identifies and interprets structures that deviate from the formal organization chart.

The hierarchical structure illustrated in Figure 16.2 covers relations between actors. Such figures can also be used to illustrate hierarchical patterns of relations between categories and concepts. As we have pointed out above, categories can be divided into more specific subcategories or merged together into more general overall categories. This is an expression of a hierarchical arrangement of the relations between different categories. Similarly, a set of specific concepts may refer to different dimensions of a more general and overall concept.

In addition to presenting structural patterns, an important purpose of figures in qualitative analyses may be to illustrate possible causal relationships. As pointed out above, analyses using matrices may allow us to discover patterns in the form of covariation between different categories or phenomena. For example, if we discover that it is typical for people with long working hours to have economic and practical attitudes to shopping, this can form the basis for a hypothesis about a causal relationship between their work situation and their attitude to shopping. We could also discover that it is typical for people with small children to have a more social attitude to shopping, so that we can develop a hypothesis about a causal relationship between family situation and attitude to shopping. A very simple figure that summarizes and illustrates these two possible causal

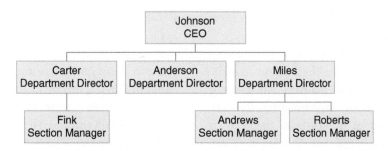

Figure 16.2 Example of a hierarchical structure: organization chart of the management in a bureaucracy

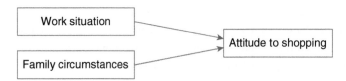

Figure 16.3 Example of possible causal relationships between work situation, family circumstances and attitude to shopping

relationships could look like Figure 16.3. As discussed in Chapter 2, this causal model is a conceptual model. Each of the phenomena that are possible causal factors, and each of the phenomena that the causal factors could affect (i.e. the effects) are placed in a separate box in the figure. The possible causal relationships between these phenomena are illustrated in the form of arrows from the causal factors to the effects.

Such causal models can be specified in different ways. For example, Figure 16.3 can be made more detailed in order to highlight the type of work situation (long working hours) that is assumed to affect attitudes to shopping, and what kind of attitude this particular work situation is expected to lead to (economic or practical attitude). Similarly, we can specify the possible causal relationship between family situation (small children) and attitude to shopping (social attitude). The empirical data may also show a particular relationship between family situation and work situation, for example that it is typical for people with young children to have short working hours. Thus, the model can be expanded so that we also specify a possible causal relationship between family situation and work situation. Different types of causal models will be discussed in more detail in Chapter 21.

The examples of figures that have been shown here are very simple. During the analysis of qualitative data, not only the matrices but also the figures will contain many elements from the data. Typical and important quotes from the text are inserted into the figures so that the researcher constantly maintains close proximity to the empirical data. This provides the basis for identifying and discovering new patterns, and this is how the various empirical patterns can be interpreted and understood. Like the matrices, the figures will still be revised, refined and specified in new ways in order to examine different combinations of data elements and thus discover new trends in the data. As the analysis gradually develops and as the researcher's overall understanding is strengthened, both the matrices and the figures will increasingly be based on summaries and interpretations of the empirical data, in the form of codes, categories and concepts.

In the study of feedback from teachers in Swedish primary schools, which was mentioned above, Eriksson et al. (2017) used figures for visualizing the content of the different categories of teacher feedback. A figure is also presented in the article on motivations for environmental activism among college students, which was described above (Fung and Adams, 2017). This figure shows the effects of different motivations on activism.

Holistic understanding of specific contexts

The purpose of qualitative analyses is usually either to arrive at a holistic, comprehensive understanding of specific conditions or to develop hypotheses and theories. First, let us see how the analyses can form the basis for a comprehensive understanding of specific contexts. Such specific contexts could be companies, organizations or institutions, small groups or communities, relations or limited structures, actions or interaction processes, incidents or events, opinion statements or debates.

The prerequisite for achieving a comprehensive understanding of such conditions is that the conditions are sufficiently delimited. An overall understanding requires both overview and insight. It will be difficult to develop such an understanding if the conditions being analysed are very extensive or very complex. In principle, we can limit both the scope and the complexity of the conditions being studied. Limitation of complexity can be achieved by focusing the study or analysis on certain aspects of the conditions. However, this is not very relevant when the purpose is to develop a comprehensive understanding. In such analyses, the delimitation must primarily apply to the extent of the conditions to be analysed. In other words, if we want to develop a comprehensive understanding of a particular type of enterprise, it is more useful to conduct in-depth analyses of *one* typical enterprise than to concentrate the analysis on certain features of the business in several such enterprises. The more complex the conditions we intend to analyse, the more the scope of the conditions should be delimited if the analysis aims to obtain an overall understanding. Usually, this delimitation is performed before data collection commences. During the data analysis process, it is important to be aware of what this delimitation entails, and it is important to clarify exactly what should be understood in a comprehensive way. It is essential to clarify the boundaries of the *entirety* to be understood, because any entirety is merely a part of an even greater entirety.

Coding and categorization of qualitative data actually involve a breakdown of the data into different elements and a division of these data elements into different types or groups. If the purpose is to use this as a basis for developing a comprehensive understanding of what is being studied, it becomes particularly important that the data elements be combined again, and that the different parts of the data are viewed in context. In such analyses, it is especially necessary to maintain a close connection between the codes and the text sections that are characterized by the codes. At the same time, the individual text sections should also be considered and evaluated in light of larger parts of the data and in a more general contextual perspective. Interpretive codes are therefore of major importance. A combined interpretation of the entire data set forms the basis for a comprehensive understanding of the conditions being analysed. Compared with a pure reading of the data, however, systematic coding and categorization can provide a different and perhaps more insightful understanding of the entire data set.

In order to strengthen the overall understanding and the overall perspective, coding and categorization can be combined with the writing of analytical memos. Such memos could deal with a single concept, as is the case when analytical memos are used in connection with concept development. When we wish to develop a holistic understanding, the purpose of analytical memos is precisely to tie together the various threads, create an overview and provide as complete a presentation as possible of the data being analysed. As the analysis progresses, new analytical memos are written and the overall understanding is brought to an ever higher level.

When the purpose of the analysis is to obtain a comprehensive understanding, it may be relevant to use methods other than coding and categorization. One alternative method is *condensation*. This means that the content of the data is presented in an abbreviated or condensed form. The main content of one or more paragraphs in the text is reproduced in a shorter text, preferably a simple formulation or a few sentences. The challenge is to concentrate the new presentation on the essential meaning of the original data. The difference from coding is that this approach does not simply use short keywords to characterize the individual data elements, but creates shorter summaries of the data instead. Such a summary provides a better overview of the whole of the data set, which then provides a basis for an overall understanding of the conditions being analysed. The difference from categorization is that the various data elements are not divided into types or groups, but the short versions of the different text sections are seen in relation to each other, as important parts of a larger whole.

Another method for developing an overall understanding is *narrative analysis*. This approach is particularly suitable for establishing a comprehensive understanding of specific sequences or processes. A narrative analysis entails that the text being analysed is organized or systematized with reference to typical elements in a story or narrative. Such elements could be typical phases in a sequence of events or in the life story of an actor. Other typical elements of the narrative could be which actors, actions and relations are part of specific events or processes. During the analysis, information about these typical elements is identified and this information is presented in the form of a narrative. In some cases, such narratives may be explicitly provided by the data. This can occur, for example, in data from informal interviews, especially if the elements of the narrative are included as the organizing principle for the interview guide, so that the respondents are invited to share their life story or tell about specific events. The analysis then consists of identifying, interpreting and clarifying the narratives. In other cases, the data contain information about the different elements, but this information is not organized in the form of narratives or stories. The analysis then involves identifying this information and reorganizing it so that it can form the basis for constructing empirically based narratives. Such narratives can be identified or constructed for each unit of analysis or aggregated for groups of units. These narratives

form an overall description and interpretation of the events or processes being analysed. Thus, a comprehensive understanding of specific events or processes can be developed on the basis of such narratives.

A third approach in analyses intended to obtain a comprehensive understanding is *discourse analysis*. This is an approach that is used to establish a comprehensive understanding of expressions of opinion and communication processes. The purpose of the analysis is to identify and interpret different forms of expression and opinion in the texts that form the qualitative data set. The purpose is to understand the discourses expressed in the texts. *Discourse* refers to a system of ideas, perceptions and concepts about conditions in society. Discourse analyses help us to understand what types of discourses are expressed in different texts and how the different discourses are expressed. Discourse analysis was described in Chapter 11, as a special form of qualitative content analysis.

Development of hypotheses and theories

The other common purpose of qualitative analyses is to develop hypotheses and theories. As pointed out above, systematic use of matrices in analyses of qualitative data can enable us to discover relationships between different categories, and these relationships can form the basis for assumptions about possible causal relations between the phenomena contained in the different categories. An assumption concerning such causal relations is a good example of a hypothesis. When we use figures for an overall presentation of several such hypotheses in the form of a model, we are well on the way to developing a theory.

However, the development of theories in qualitative analyses is not always linked to the production of models, and the theories that are developed in this way are also not always focused on causal relationships. Moreover, it is not always the case that theory development in qualitative studies takes place through the compilation and combination of several individual hypotheses. The empirical analysis can also form the basis for a more general theoretical understanding and formulation of more complex theories, which can then be specified and possibly subdivided in the form of different hypotheses.

Both hypothesis formulation and theory development are usually empirically based. The hypotheses and theories are generated or evolve on the basis of the empirical data. This procedure is discussed in detail by Glaser and Strauss (1967). They describe this kind of empirically based theory as *grounded theory*. This approach was used by Eriksson et al. (2017), in their study of teacher feedback at Swedish primary schools, which was described above. The approach is also called *analytical induction*, and such studies are commonly referred to as theory-generating studies.

Analytical induction differs somewhat from the constant comparative method, which was discussed earlier in this chapter. In analytical induction, the empirical patterns are not only described but also interpreted. Interpretation occurs partly contextually, by the results of the analysis being understood in light of a larger social context, and partly theoretically, by the empirical tendencies being discussed on the basis of previous research and established theories. The theoretical interpretation is of particular interest in this context, because it constitutes an important part of the interaction and the exchange between theory and empirical evidence in such analyses. Hypotheses and theories are generated on the basis of the empirical data, but other studies and existing theories are also an important starting point for understanding how the data form a basis for new hypotheses and further development of theories.

Qualitative analyses are not usually intended to be used for comprehensive testing of hypotheses or theories. Such testing is more common in quantitative analyses. However, hypothesis formulation and theory development in qualitative analyses are based on the empirical data and are focused on hypotheses and theories that are as consistent with the data as possible. A common approach for achieving the best possible empirical foundation of hypothesis and theory development is commonly referred to as the *search for deviating cases*. This approach requires the researcher to systematically search for elements in the data that do *not* conform to the hypotheses or theories that are generated. First, the researcher formulates a hypothesis or theory based on a relationship or other empirical pattern identified during the analysis. The data are then reviewed systematically in order to find any data that deviate from the hypothesis or the theory. As soon as such a deviating data element is identified, the hypothesis or theory formulation is reassessed and reformulated so that the new formulation is in accordance with both this new data element and the data that formed the basis for the original formulation. The systematic review of the data then continues with the goal of detecting data elements that deviate from the new hypothesis or theory formulation. When such a new deviation is detected, the hypothesis or theory is once again reformulated, so that the new formulation accommodates both the new data element and all the parts of the data that formed the basis for the previous formulation. In this way, the systematic review of the data and the repeated reformulations of the hypothesis or theory continue until a formulation has been achieved that is compatible with all of the data, so that the researcher is no longer able to detect more deviating cases.

The search for deviating cases in qualitative analyses is a parallel to hypothesis testing in quantitative analyses, which will be discussed in

Chapter 19. The two approaches are based on the same strategy. The strategy involves finding empirical evidence that does not support a given hypothesis. The purpose of the analysis is to detect deviations between the hypothesis and the empirical evidence. However, the consequence of finding such deviations is different in the two types of analyses. In quantitative analyses, the hypothesis is rejected, but in qualitative analyses, deviations lead to the hypothesis being reformulated. In both cases, however, the more a hypothesis is assessed on the basis of empirical data without having to be rejected or reformulated, the greater the confidence we can have that the hypothesis is supported by empirical evidence.

When researchers consider their own analyses in conjunction with relevant theories from previous research, they can assess how the hypothesis formulation and theory development will contribute to new understandings and insights into the relevant research field. This reduces the risk of generating hypotheses and theories that are pure repetitions or replications of previous contributions from other researchers.

However, this does not mean that the hypothesis formulation and theory development necessarily lead to completely new theories. Much of the theoretical work associated with qualitative analyses involves further development of theories that are already established. Thus, new empirical analyses can help to nuance, clarify or specify existing theories.

Theoretical generalization

Assessing the results of the empirical analysis in connection with previous research and established theories is not only important with regard to hypothesis formulation and theory development. Such a theoretical foundation of qualitative analyses is also important in theoretical generalization of results of the analysis. By discussing the empirical patterns in light of the strategic selection of units and types of information, and by looking at these patterns in conjunction with relevant theories, the researcher can evaluate whether the results of the particular study can be assumed to also apply in more general contexts.

Theoretical generalization can be conducted in connection with several of the approaches for qualitative data analyses described here. The special feature of theoretical generalization is the systematic assessments of the area in which the empirical findings may be valid. Can the results of the analysis be generalized? Do the results only apply to the units and contexts that are included in the specific empirical study, or do they have more general validity?

As pointed out in Chapter 8, theoretical generalization may be intended both for the establishment of a comprehensive understanding and for the development of concepts, hypotheses and theories. Qualitative studies of selected units within a limited context can result in a comprehensive understanding of this specific context, but this understanding may also apply to other similar contexts, or to a larger context of which the analysed context is a part. Analyses of qualitative data based on a limited number of units can also form a basis for new concepts or theoretical reasoning. Such concepts and theoretical perspectives are assumed to be valid for the units and the conditions contained in the particular empirical study, and sometimes it is also assumed that they can be generalized, as valid for a larger number of units and more general or extensive conditions.

Theoretical generalization requires systematic discussions of the empirical findings in conjunction with results from other research. Theoretical insight, empirical knowledge and methodological experience from previous research provide a basis for assessing whether the analytical results from a particular qualitative study can be generalized from this empirical study to more units, other contexts or larger contexts. Systematic comparison of the findings with findings from studies of other units and contexts allows us to clarify the types of units and contexts for which the results of the study may apply. More generally, the purpose is to investigate the following questions. Under which conditions do the empirical results of the analysis apply, and under what conditions are they not valid? Comparisons with results from studies of both similar and different units and contexts increase the possibilities for such clarification of the scope and limitations of the study. This also strengthens the basis for theoretical generalization. We will have opportunities to assess whether the empirical results of the study can be generalized, as well as the types of units and contexts to which they can be generalized.

Such systematic discussions of a particular qualitative study in conjunction with results from previous research may take place after the data collection and most of the data analysis has been completed. The basis for theoretical generalization is then considered on the basis of the units and the contexts that have already been selected for the current study. A new qualitative study can also be discussed in conjunction with the results of previous research, even before the new empirical survey starts, or while data collection is ongoing.

As pointed out in Chapter 8, a strategic selection of units may be conducted in order to provide the best possible basis for theoretical generalization. The possibilities for theoretical generalization will then become an important criterion for the selection of units. Based on the results and experiences from previous studies, we can also assess the contexts and types of information that could be strategically important to prioritize in the new study, in order to strengthen the possibilities for theoretical generalization. In some cases, it may be appropriate to choose the same type of units and information as in previous studies. In other cases, it may be appropriate to include other types of units and information than those that were studied

previously. In some studies, it may be particularly interesting to find units and information that appear from previous research to be typical. In other studies, it may be important to use knowledge from previous research to obtain a wide variety of units and information in the new study. What is most appropriate with regard to theoretical generalization must be assessed specifically and strategically in each study.

When the selection of contexts, units and information types is based on such strategic assessments and in light of previous research, it strengthens not only the foundation for assessing whether theoretical generalization is possible, but also the likelihood that the results of the study can actually be generalized.

Computer-assisted qualitative data analysis

In recent years, it has become more and more common to use computers in qualitative data analysis, and an increasing number of software packages have been developed for this purpose (Kelle, 1995). These packages are referred to as *computer-assisted qualitative analysis software* (CAQDAS).

Obviously, using computers in data analysis requires that the data or texts to be analysed are available in digital form. Increasingly, such textual data are available in digital form anyway. Computers are used for producing and processing field notes and transcripts from unstructured interviews, and various types of documentary sources for content analysis are found on the web. Textual data that are printed or handwritten have to be scanned or digitized in other ways before they can be analysed by means of computers.

If the textual data are available in digital form, computers can be very useful in the process of analysing qualitative data. Some software packages even make it possible to analyse images, audio recordings or videos without transforming them into texts before the analysis. The only requirement is again that these materials are available in digital form. Typically, however, in the analysis, audio recordings or visual materials are coded, and these codes are handled and processed in the same way as codes based on textual data.

By using computers in qualitative data analysis, many of the tasks in the analysis can be performed more easily and faster. Computers make it possible to process and analyse larger data sets, or larger amounts of texts. Complex data can be simplified in different ways, and data displays can be easily created, changed and adjusted as the analysis develops. This may provide a better overview of the whole data set. Switching back and forth between different parts of the data can be done more efficiently. Thus, different data elements can be compared and related to each other, and empirical relationships can be detected and pursued in the further analysis.

One of the most common functions of software for qualitative data analysis refers to the coding of the data. Manual coding is based on printed text and a paper format with wide margins, so that the key words can be written in the margin, next to the sentences or sections that the keywords refer to. When computers are used in the coding process, it is easy to search in the digital text for particular data elements, based on various specifications. It is easy to view these text elements, to determine a special keyword or code for each element, and to mark it with the selected code.

Furthermore, data elements that have been marked with particular codes can easily be retrieved by the computer and shown on the computer screen. Several data elements with the same code, or elements with different codes, can be displayed simultaneously and compared. Based on this, computer programs can be used very efficiently for recoding parts of the data, and for reorganizing the recoded data.

Based on this coding and recoding process, computer software can be used to facilitate the categorization of the qualitative data. Using the computer makes it easier to identify common features between various data elements, to group them together, and to distinguish them from other data elements. This process of identifying similarities and differences is useful for developing categories, defining the content of each category and determining the boundaries between different categories.

CAQDAS usually has functions for creating matrices and figures, and for arranging and rearranging both coded and uncoded data in these displays. Repeated experiments with different groupings of both rows and columns in matrices can be conducted, in order to identify patterns and relationships between different themes. It is easy to see that these functions are useful for developing categories as well as typologies.

The code and retrieve functions of CAQDAS are also very efficient and flexible for using the constant comparative method. By means of these software functions, different text elements can be identified, displayed and compared with previously coded texts.

Another typical software function is to link or relate particular data elements to other parts of the data. This linking, based on selected criteria, is useful for identifying possible empirical relationships between data elements or between categories. Thus, computer-aided analysis can facilitate the development of hypotheses and theories.

Sometimes, computer programs may also be useful tools in analyses aiming for holistic understanding of specific contexts. By means of such software, larger parts of the textual data can be retrieved, displayed and moved around in various ways. This can make it easier to discover general patterns in the data and to develop an overall understanding of the data set as a whole.

In general, however, computer programs seem to be less useful for developing a holistic understanding of the whole data set than they are for constructing categories and typologies, or for discovering relationships and formulating hypotheses. There are two main reasons for this. First, the major functions of CAQDAS are focused on characteristics of different parts of the data sets, rather than overall patterns of the entire data set. Thus, the risk of using computer software for the analysis is a fragmentation of the data, which may be useful for categorization, but not for condensation and holistic understanding.

Second, it is a general limitation of computers that they cannot be used for interpretations of data and findings, which are necessary for developing a general understanding of the data set as a whole. Interpretations are also necessary for conceptualizations, explanations and theoretical generalizations. Thus, computer software is also less useful for these parts of qualitative data analysis than it is for the more descriptive parts of the analysis.

There are a large number and a wide variety of software packages available for qualitative data analysis. Four of the most common packages are briefly described here, mainly with reference to their most important functions. One of these packages, NVivo, is presented, described and discussed in detail by Jackson and Bazeley (2019). Their book is included in the list of recommended literature at the end of this chapter.

NVivo is used for analysis of qualitative data based on different designs for data collection and different methods of analysis. The software supports data in many different formats, not only various types of texts, but also audio files, videos and other types of digital images. NVivo can be used for coding, classifying, sorting and arranging data, for examining relationships in the data, for constructing models based on the data, and for creating a variety of diagrams. Furthermore, the software has efficient search and query functions, including matrix searching, which enables search based on combinations of search criteria.

ATLAS.ti also can be used for analysing digital data in the form of audio files, videos and images, in addition to textual data. Atlas.ti makes it possible to locate and code data, to annotate findings in the data, to weight and evaluate the importance of the findings, and to visualize complex relations between them. The software can handle large volumes of coded and uncoded data, and it can keep track of codes, notes, annotations and memos that are produced during the analysis. Atlas.ti has a network function, which supports theory building, analysis of relations between data elements or categories, as well as creating diagrams for visualization of networks.

N6 is used for analysing data in the form of plain text. The software can handle large volumes of data and is useful for providing a basis for a general overview of the data set. The functions include coding of each paragraph in the text, matrix searching based on combinations of search criteria, text editing, flexible display of categories and coding information, and construction of matrices for coded data and categories. Furthermore, N6 has a command language, which can be used for programming special tasks for the processing and analysis of the data. Thus, the software can be used for different needs in a particular project, such as for repetitive or massive data handling.

MaxQDA can be used for analysing different types of digital data, including audio files, videos and images, in addition to texts. Data can be coded, and the codes can be given a weighting depending on how certain the code is, or how important it is. Data can be annotated with memos. Links between data elements can be used, and tools for summarizing text content are available. Coded and uncoded data can be searched and retrieved based on combinations of criteria, including the weightings of the codes.

The data can be effectively displayed on the computer screen in up to four different panes in the working window, and the displays ensure a close integration of data, codes, memos and other documents. This provides a good overview and possibilities for comparing data elements as well as keeping the analysis well grounded in the data.

CHAPTER HIGHLIGHTS

- Typically, qualitative data analyses are based on textual data. Audio recordings, videos or images may also be analysed, but these are usually transformed into text, by transcription, descriptions, or coding.
- The analysis takes place partly in parallel with the data collection.
- Coding the data creates an overview through simplification and summarizing of the content of the texts.
- A code in qualitative analyses generally refers to an abbreviation or a symbol that is used for a segment of words (a sentence or paragraph) in order to classify the word segment. For example, a code for a particular paragraph could specify a topic that the paragraph is about, or something that is mentioned in the paragraph.
- Codes can be descriptive, interpretive or explanatory.
- Coding can be performed in several steps:
  1 open coding, for an initial characterization and classification of the important data elements
  2 systematic coding, with focus on category development
  3 selective coding, with emphasis on concept development.
- The constant comparative method is a special procedure for coding and categorization, often with the aim of developing empirically grounded theory.
- Qualitative analyses are often intended to identify types and developing typologies. A typology is a set of types that are arranged in a logical relationship to each other, and in relation to one or more general dimensions.
- Matrices and figures are important aids to help identify and highlight patterns and relationships in qualitative data. Matrices provide an overview of the structure in the data and can form a basis for theme-centred or person-centred analyses. Figures can illustrate relationships between units or categories.
- We highlight two important purposes of qualitative analyses:
  1 Holistic understanding of specific conditions. In addition to coding and categorization, this can be based on, for example, condensation, narrative analysis or discourse analysis.
  2 Hypothesis formulation and theory development. This can be based on analytical induction, and search for deviating cases.
- Theoretical generalization can take place in connection with different approaches to qualitative data analysis. It requires systematic discussions of the results of the empirical analysis in conjunction with results from other research. When such discussions are conducted before the data collection process has been completed, they provide a basis for strategic selection of contexts, units and information types that improve the basis for theoretical generalization.
- Many different types of software are available for qualitative data analysis.
- Computers are useful tools in data analysis, especially for coding, creating displays, constructing categories and typologies, and for discovering relationships and formulating hypotheses.
- Computers are less useful for developing a holistic understanding of the whole data set, and for interpretation, conceptualization, explanation and theoretical generalization.

RESEARCH EXAMPLES

I recommend that you read the publications used as research examples in this chapter.

Eriksson, Elisabeth, Lisa Björklund Boistrup, and Robert Thornberg (2017) 'A categorisation of teacher feedback in the classroom: A field study on feedback based on routine classroom assessment in primary school', *Research Papers in Education* 32(3), 316–332.

This article presents a study of teacher feedback in the classroom in Swedish primary schools. The study is based on observations in classrooms in four primary schools with 7–9-year-old students. The data consist of field notes, combined with transcriptions of audio recordings from dialogues, conversations and unstructured interviews. The analysis of these data is based on grounded theory. Using the constant comparative method, the researchers coded the data and identified recurring patterns, and the codes were gradually grouped into more comprehensive codes. Thus, the analysis resulted in five main categories of teacher feedback to students in the classroom. In the article, the content of the different categories is visualized by means of figures.

Fung, Cadi Y., and Ellis Adjei Adams (2017) 'What motivates student environmental activists on college campuses? An in-depth qualitative study', *Social Sciences* 6(4), art. 134.

This article presents a study of motivations for environmental activism among college students. The study is based on unstructured interviews with two students and observations from a meeting of a student activist group. The article shows how coding is done in qualitative data analysis. After reviewing the data and memos from the data collection, the researchers listed themes and concepts that occurred repeatedly in the data. Based on these themes, a set of codes was developed, with definitions of the codes, rules for applying the codes, and examples of how to use and *not* use each code. The codes were developed by identifying themes that were both relevant to the research questions and frequently found in the data. A figure is presented showing the relationships between different motivations and their effects on activism.

Ruitenberg, Justine (2014) 'A typology of Dutch mothers' employment narratives: Drifters, privilegeds, balancers, ambitious', *Gender Issues* 31(1), 58–82.

This article is based on semi-structured interviews with 39 mothers living in Amsterdam. The interview data are focused on the life histories of the mothers. The article shows how large matrices were used in the data analysis, and how a thematic analysis of these matrices provided a basis for developing a typology of the mothers. The typology is based on varieties in the mothers' narratives of choice and considerations regarding the ideal gender division of labour, work and motherhood. The typology consisted of four types of mothers: drifters, privilegeds, balancers, and ambitious.

STUDENT EXERCISES AND QUESTIONS

1 What are the main purposes of qualitative data analyses?

2 What is the relationship between coding, categorization and concept development in the analysis of qualitative data?

3 Why is construction of typologies useful in qualitative data analysis?

4 Why is it important to search for deviant cases?

5 What is meant by theoretical generalization?
6 How can computers be used in qualitative data analysis?
7 Select a current debate in a newspaper for a qualitative content analysis. Show how the content of the debate can be analysed by using

a Categorization
b Condensation.

RECOMMENDED LITERATURE

Jackson, Kristi, and Patricia Bazeley (2019) *Qualitative Data Analysis with NVivo* (3rd edn). London: Sage.

This book provides an introduction and a step-by-step guide to planning and conducting qualitative data analysis with NVivo. It presents methodological discussion, practical instruction and research examples. The book shows how NVivo software can assist analysis across a wide range of research questions, data types, perspectives and methodologies. It demonstrates the power and flexibility of the NVivo software, and explains how NVivo can be used at each stage in a research project.

Harding, Jamie (2018) *Qualitative Data Analysis: From Start to Finish* (2nd edn). London: Sage.

This book introduces the basics of qualitative data analysis. It presents the different steps of a qualitative analysis and describes the practical tools and techniques that can be used for analysing the data. Examples from multidisciplinary use of data from interviews and focus groups are provided. The book offers advice and guidance on key activities in qualitative data analysis, such as making summaries, identifying similarities, drawing comparisons and using codes.

Miles, Matthew B., A. Michael Huberman, and Johnny Saldaña (2019) *Qualitative Data Analysis – International Student Edition: A Methods Sourcebook* (4th edn). London: Sage.

This book is focused on how qualitative data and findings can be displayed. It shows how different displays, such as matrices and figures, can be used to arrange and systematize data and findings, not only for presenting the results of the analysis, but also for facilitating the process of analysis. The book distinguishes between five different methods of analysis: exploring, describing, ordering, explaining, and predicting. A number of examples from recent research are presented.

INDEXES AND DISTRIBUTIONS

This chapter provides the knowledge that is necessary for understanding how quantitative data can be organized for analysis, and how univariate analysis is conducted.

The chapter will teach you how to

- use computer software for quantitative data analysis
- create a data matrix
- recode variables and construct various types of indexes

- distinguish between central tendency and dispersion
- perform analysis of univariate distributions in terms of frequency tables, graphical presentations and various types of statistical measures.

Processing and analysing quantitative data

Chapter 16 dealt with qualitative data analysis. The theme for this and the next two chapters is analyses of quantitative data.

The objective of quantitative analyses is usually to establish a representative overview of general conditions or to test theories and hypotheses about specific relationships in society. If the conditions or relationships emphasized in the research question of the study involve more units than those included in the empirical study, the purpose of the analysis will be to arrive at a statistical generalization. As pointed out in Chapter 8, this requires that the selection of units for the empirical study is based on a probability sample of the universe referred to in the research question.

In quantitative studies, data analysis is a separate phase in the research process. The analysis does not commence until the data collection process is completed. The types of analyses to be performed should therefore be planned before the data collection commences. The collection of data must be arranged in such a way that it will be possible to carry out the necessary analyses to investigate the research question.

Unlike qualitative analyses, analyses of quantitative data can be based on statistical methods and standardized techniques. Analyses based on such methods and techniques are performed using computers and special software packages. Thanks to these analytical methods and computer programs, it is possible to process and analyse large amounts of data. In qualitative studies, computer software may be a useful but not a necessary tool for processing and analysing the data. Qualitative analyses may be conducted without using computers, especially if the data set is not too large. However, in quantitative data analysis, computer software is a necessity, partly because the data sets usually are large, and partly because the data analysis typically is based on advanced statistical methods.

A number of statistical methods of analysis have been developed for quantitative studies. The methods that can and should be used in a particular study will depend on the research question as well as the nature of the data. Both the selection of units and the construction of variables are of major importance for which analyses can be conducted. However, all quantitative studies share an important common feature: the data will be in the form of numbers, regardless of how they have been gathered. In structured observation, structured questionnaires and quantitative content analysis, it is always numerical data that will be analysed. Generally, therefore, it is not necessary to develop separate analysis methods for each of the three research designs. In principle, the data analysis can be based on the same approaches, no matter what types of sources the data collection is based upon.

Some of the methods for quantitative analysis are used to identify, describe and characterize actual patterns in the data being analysed. These methods are based on *descriptive statistics*. In reviewing such methods, we will pay particular attention to how we can combine multiple variables into *indexes*, how we can illustrate the *distribution* of units on individual variables, and how we can identify *relationships* between two or more variables. Indexes and distributions will be reviewed in this chapter, while relationships are the theme of Chapter 18.

In addition to descriptive statistics, certain methods have been developed for statistical generalization. We can use these methods to assess whether it is advisable to make generalizations from the sample in the study to the universe from which the sample has been drawn. As mentioned in Chapter 8, such methods can be used to determine precision and certainty when drawing conclusions about particular conditions in the universe, based on analyses of the corresponding conditions in the sample. The statistical basis for these methods is called *inductive statistics*. Methods for statistical generalization will be discussed in Chapter 19.

This chapter starts with a review of some common software packages for quantitative analysis, with particular emphasis on SPSS, which is widely used in social science. This software review is relevant for the methods that will be presented in this chapter as well as in the next two chapters. Furthermore, in this chapter it is shown how a set of quantitative data can be organized in a data matrix for statistical analyses, and the most important methods for index construction and analysis of distributions are described, with a focus on different types of frequencies, graphical presentations and statistical measurements.

Software packages for quantitative data analysis

There are several software packages available for quantitative data analysis. The most common

software tools for social science data include Stata, SAS, and SPSS.

Stata is developed by StataCorp. The software can be used for data management and editing, simple and complex statistical analysis, and graphical visualizations. Stata can import data in different formats, including various Excel formats. Selection of analyses or other tasks to be performed can be made in menus and dialog boxes, but a command syntax can also be used for this purpose. Commands are entered into the Command window and recorded in the Review window. The available list of variables and their values are displayed in the Variables window, and the results of analyses are shown in the Results window.

SAS (Statistical Analysis System) is developed by SAS Institute. This is a powerful program, which is used in research as well as for business purposes. The software can retrieve data from many different sources. It can be used for large data sets and can handle complex and advanced analyses. SAS has a number of functions in addition to statistical analysis, such as graphics production, report writing, business planning, project management, quality improvement, and forecasting. The software provides a graphical point-and-click user interface, but more advanced options are based on a programming syntax, which requires some knowledge of the SAS programming language.

SPSS (Statistical Package for the Social Sciences) is an IBM product, officially named *IBM SPSS Statistics*. It is a comprehensive and flexible program. It can be used for different types of data and can handle large data sets. It is easy to enter data into SPSS, and it is easy to edit existing data files in the program. The software can be used for generating statistical measures and graphical presentations, as well as for performing advanced and complex statistical analyses. Selection of analyses, editing activities or other tasks to be performed is made by means of dialog boxes with standardized options. Tasks that are more specialized can be defined by using a command syntax language.

Since SPSS is the most widely used software for data analysis in social science, it is reasonable to explain briefly how it is used. When the SPSS program is started, a dialog box in the program invites the user to open a file. The program operates with three main windows, and dialog boxes or menus with options for what to do. One of the windows is the *Data Editor*, with a *Data Viewer* and a *Variable Viewer*. This window is used for entering new data or editing existing data files. New data may be entered by typing the data into the Data Viewer or by opening another file, for example importing a data file from Excel. In the Data Viewer the whole data set is displayed and organized as a data matrix, which will be explained in the next section of this chapter. In the Variable Viewer, each variable is displayed in more detail for viewing and editing. For example, names of the variables and labels for the values of the variable can be defined.

Another window is the *Output Viewer*. The results of any analysis are shown in this window. Which analysis to perform is usually selected in dialog boxes. The results of the analysis shown in the Output Viewer can be edited, saved, printed, or exported to another program, for example to Microsoft Word.

The third window is the *Syntax Editor*. This window is used for entering commands that are more specific than those found as standard options in the dialog boxes. For example, a command can be formulated for conducting a special type of analysis. Such commands have to be formulated in a certain way, so that they can be interpreted and executed by the program.

A simple guide to using SPSS is presented by te Grotenhuis and Matthijssen (2016). Their book is included in the list of recommended literature at the end of this chapter.

SPSS or other software packages for quantitative analysis can be used for all the methods that will be described in this chapter and the next two chapters. However, in order to apply the software in a meaningful way, it is necessary to understand when the methods can be used, how they work, and how the findings based on different methods can be interpreted. Therefore, the most common methods will be described and explained in detail. However, the descriptions will be as straightforward and intuitive as possible, with only the most necessary references to statistical theory, and simple examples will be used to demonstrate how each method is used.

From registration schedule to data matrix

Before the actual analysis work can start, the data must be organized and arranged for the statistical methods that will be used. The data are usually arranged in a large table, where there is one row for each unit and one or more columns for each variable. In the boxes or cells in the table, we enter the numbers for the value that each unit has on each of the variables. These numbers are called *codes*. The table has one column for each digit in the codes on the different variables. This table, which includes all of the data, including all units and all variables, is called a *data matrix*.

Quantitative studies usually involve very many units and quite a few variables, so that the data matrix becomes rather extensive. Table 17.1 shows an example of a small section of a typical data matrix. This section of the data matrix comprises ten units (U1, ..., U10) and nine variables (V1, ..., V9). Three of the variables (age, income and the number of visits to the cinema last month) have multi-digit codes and thus more columns, while each of the other variables can fit in one column because they have codes with only one digit.

The data matrix is filled out on the basis of the registration schedule from the data collection. This could be an observation schedule from

Table 17.1 Example of a section of a data matrix

Units	Variables											
	V1 Gender	V2 Age		V3 Type of residence	V4 Educational level	V5 Annual income (in EUR '000)				V6 Number of visits to the cinema last month	V7 Number of newspapers read regularly	V8 Political interest	V9 Attitude to the European Union (EU)
U1	1	2	3	2	3	0	0	2	9	0	4	1	4	1
U2	1	6	0	4	3	0	0	5	2	0	0	3	1	2
U3	2	4	4	3	5	0	0	3	5	0	1	2	2	1
U4	1	1	9	5	2	0	0	0	4	1	0	0	5	5
U5	2	6	6	1	2	0	1	2	4	0	0	2	3	3
U6	2	3	7	1	3	0	0	3	6	0	6	1	3	3
U7	1	3	8	4	1	0	0	2	9	0	1	3	5	4
U8	2	6	4	5	3	0	0	2	8	0	0	4	4	3
U9	2	2	1	3	2	0	0	1	0	0	8	1	1	2
U10	1	5	8	2	3	0	0	3	4	0	0	2	3	3

structured observation, a questionnaire from structured questioning or a coding schedule from quantitative content analysis. For each unit, we have a registration schedule, but only one row in the data matrix. In other words, the data matrix is a simplified and clearly set out presentation of the quantitative data.

The better structured the registration schedule is, the easier it is to fill out the data matrix. The registration schedule could be a questionnaire, for example. In that case, the schedule would usually contain fixed response options for most of the questions. Generally, the questionnaire also indicates which number code corresponds to each of the response options. These codes can then be transferred directly to the data matrix. However, some of the questions may be open. Then the answers must be divided into categories, so that each category represents a value for the relevant variable, and we have to decide which numerical code should be used for the different values.

In such cases, the transfer of data from the registration schedule to the data matrix must be based on a *codebook*. The codebook is an overview of the criteria and rules for completing the data matrix. It shows which numbers should be entered into the data matrix for different values of the different variables. The codebook also constitutes our most important basis for understanding and keeping account of the significance of the different numbers in the data matrix. It therefore contains a complete overview of all the variables and values in the data, regardless of whether the codes for the values are explicitly stated in the registration schedule. Table 17.2 shows the codebook for the nine variables in Table 17.1.

Based on the codebook in Table 17.2, we can see what characterizes the different units in the data matrix in Table 17.1. For example, unit no. 1 (U1) is a 23-year-old man, living in a rural municipality with more than 5000 inhabitants, and with upper

Table 17.2   Codebook for the variables in Table 17.1

Variable no.	Variable name	Code	Value name
1	Gender	1	Man
		2	Woman
2	Age	[number of years]	[Age at the time of the interview]
3	Type of residence	1	Rural municipality with up to 5000 inhabitants
		2	Rural municipality with more than 5000 inhabitants
		3	Town with less than 50,000 inhabitants
		4	City with 50,000–200,000 inhabitants
		5	City with more than 200,000 inhabitants
4	Educational level (highest completed education)	1	Primary school
		2	Short vocational education
		3	Upper secondary school
		4	Up to 4 years of higher education
		5	More than 4 years of higher education
5	Annual income	[amount in EUR '000]	[Gross income (before tax deductions) in last full calendar year]
6	Number of visits to the cinema last month	[number of times]	[Number of visits to the cinema in the 30 days before the interview date]
7	Number of newspapers read regularly	[number of newspapers]	[Number of different newspapers read at least once a week]
8	Political interest	1	Very little interest
		2	Little interest
		3	Medium interest
		4	Significant interest
		5	Very significant interest
9	Attitude to the European Union (EU)	1	Strongly negative
		2	Negative
		3	Uncertain, neutral
		4	Positive
		5	Strongly positive

secondary school as his highest level of education. He has an annual income of €29,000, he has visited the cinema four times during the last month, and he reads one newspaper regularly. He also has a high level of political interest, and he is strongly negative towards the EU.

Such a review of the overall data pattern for each unit can provide a basis for controlling the data quality. In this way, we can reveal any logical inconsistencies or contradictions in the data. For example, if the data matrix showed that a person who is only 19 years of age has completed a university education, it would probably be due to an error in the data. Such errors can then be corrected before the analysis itself takes place.

In practice, the researcher will usually not have data for all units on all variables. In structured observation, not all the actors perform the actions we want to observe. In a structured questionnaire, there will be a number of respondents who do not answer all the questions, and in quantitative content analysis, there may be a number of text units that do not contain a reference to all of the theme categories that are included in the coding schedule. In addition to the codes shown in the codebook in Table 17.2, therefore, there may be separate codes to specify that data are missing for a particular unit on a given variable.

In large quantitative studies, both the data matrix and the codebook may be very extensive. As pointed out above, this is handled using computers and special software packages. As a rule, the recorded data are scanned or typed directly into a separate data file that is adapted to the software to be used during the analysis. Both the data matrix and the codebook are thus stored and processed in electronic form.

Recoding, index construction and levels of measurement

Basically, the data matrix is the most accurate presentation possible of the information recorded during the data collection process, and the codebook is designed in order to render this information in as detailed a fashion as possible. However, the variables can be processed further. They can be restructured and simplified in two different ways. We can reduce the number of values by recoding each variable, and we can reduce the number of variables by constructing indexes based on multiple variables.

Recoding of variables

Recoding means that multiple values for a single variable are combined or grouped. For example, the 'political interest' variable in Table 17.2 can be recoded in order to reduce the number of values from five to three. This can be done by combining values 1 and 2 and values 4 and 5, so that we get the following three values:

1   Little interest (original values 1 and 2)
2   Medium interest (original value 3)
3   Significant interest (original values 4 and 5).

For another example, the variable 'annual income' could be recoded from absolute amounts in euros to a smaller number of income levels or income categories, such as:

1   Very low income (less than €20,000)
2   Low income (€20,000–44,999)
3   Average income (€45,000–54,999)
4   High income (€55,000–79,999)
5   Very high income (€80,000 or more).

The assessment of how the original values should be grouped together in new values can be based on two different criteria. One is a *logical* criterion, which emphasizes that both the delimitation of each value and the relationship between the values must be logically, theoretically or conceptually meaningful. The recoding of the variable 'political interest' is in line with such a criterion. When the values of small and very little interest are merged into one value, it is logical that the values of significant and very significant interest should also be merged, not least in order to maintain the overall balance between the values for the variable. Logically, it would be more problematic, for example, to merge the values very little interest and little interest, as well as the values of medium interest and great interest, and to retain the value for very great interest as the new third value.

The assessment of how the values should be grouped together in a recoding process can also be based on an *empirical* criterion. The emphasis is then placed on ensuring that the units are distributed roughly evenly on the new values after the recoding of the variable. This could be a useful criterion for recoding the variable 'annual income'. There are no precise logical limits between, for example, low and medium income. It may therefore be reasonable to start with the actual income distribution in the empirical data and then define the income categories in such a way that about 20% of the units are included in each of the five categories.

The advantage of implementing such recoding in order to combine values is that we achieve some simplification of the information and a better overview of the data. The disadvantage is that the recoded variables provide less detailed information than the original ones. In many cases, the recoding will also cause the variable's level of measurement to change. This happens, for example, in the case of the recoding of the income variable as described here. While the original variable is at the ratio level, the recoded income variable will be at the ordinal level. This has consequences for which methods or techniques we can use in the analysis. Generally, the higher the measurement level of the variables, the more advanced the methods we can use. The original income variable can therefore be analysed using more advanced methods than the recoded variable.

Construction of indexes

While recoding individual variables involves combining values on each variable, *index construction* involves combining multiple variables into a new index. The variables included in the index are called *indicators*. The value that a unit in the data is assigned on the new index is determined on the basis of the combination of values that the unit has on the different indicators. There are various procedures for combining the values of the indicators to values on the new index. The procedures for the construction of two different types of indexes are presented here. The two types are typology-based indexes and additive indexes.

Typology-based indexes

As mentioned in Chapter 16, a typology constitutes a set of types that are in a mutually logical relationship to each other. Development of typologies in qualitative analyses is usually done in two stages. First, we identify the most important dimensions in the differences between different types. Then, each type is placed into the appropriate combination of positions on the dimensions identified. The construction of *typology-based indexes* in quantitative analyses is based on a similar two-step approach. We first choose the variables that correspond to important dimensions in the differences between different types. We then determine which value combinations of the selected variables correspond to the different types in the typology. Table 17.3 shows an example of an index that is constructed as a typology.

The variable 'attitude to the EU' is seen here in conjunction with the variable 'activity in the EU debate'. As regards people's relationship to the debate on the EU, these two variables can be considered as important dimensions in the differences between different types of people. One dimension refers to the position or attitude in the debate, while the other dimension concerns how actively this position is argued in the debate.

Based on these dimensions, the population can be divided into different types, and this typology forms the basis for an index. The two dimensions

Table 17.3   Index construction based on a typology

Activity in the EU debate	Attitude to the EU				
	1 Strongly negative towards EU	2 Negative towards EU	3 Uncertain, neutral	4 Positive towards EU	5 Strongly positive towards EU
1 Very little activity	2 Passive EU opponents		3 Not engaged	5 Passive EU supporters	
2 Little activity					
3 Medium activity	1 Active EU opponents		4 Neutral debaters	6 Active EU supporters	
4 Great activity					
5 Very great activity					

or variables constitute indicators in the index, and each type in the typology represents a value on the index.

Since each of the two indicators has five values, there are a total of 25 possible value combinations when the indicators are viewed in context. In principle, it is possible to operate with an index value for each of the 25 possible value combinations. However, the purpose of index construction is to simplify and make it easier to get an overview and understanding. Therefore, it is common to merge value combinations that are close together, so that each index value includes multiple combinations of values for the indicators. In other words, index construction involves both the merging of variables and the merging of values. The number of index values established and which value combinations are merged will vary, depending on the purpose of the index in the further data analysis. In Table 17.3 we distinguish between six values.

The measurement level may be changed when different variables are combined in an index. In Table 17.3, each of the indicators is at the ordinal level (degree of positive attitude to the EU and degree of activity in the EU debate). However, the index is at the nominal level because there is no common ranking for all the six values, especially for the values 3 and 4 (not engaged and neutral debaters). However, through further recoding, these two values could be merged, which would

change the index's measurement level from the nominal to the ordinal level. The index would then have five values instead of six, and it would be a measure of the level of active support for EU membership.

In this example of a typology-based index, we combine two variables. However, the number of variables merged in such indexes can vary. When we include more variables, the complexity of the value combinations increases, and it becomes more difficult to keep track of both the dimensions and the division into types in the typology.

In typology-based indexes, logical and theoretical assessments determine which variables should be included in the index, and which value combinations should form the basis for the different types in the typology and the values of the index.

Additive indexes

Additive indexes are constructed by adding up the values of all variables included in the index, so that a unit's value on the index equals the sum of the values of the indicators. Table 17.4 gives an overview of five possible indicators in an additive index for quality of life. The indicators show the degree of satisfaction with different aspects of life. The index thus constitutes a subjective

Table 17.4 Overview of possible indicators in an index for quality of life

Variable (indicator)	Value				
	Very little satisfaction	Little satisfaction	Reasonable satisfaction	Great satisfaction	Very great satisfaction
Satisfaction with financial situation	1	2	3	4	5
Satisfaction with employment situation	1	2	3	4	5
Satisfaction with family circumstances	1	2	3	4	5
Satisfaction with health condition	1	2	3	4	5
Satisfaction with leisure activities	1	2	3	4	5

measurement of quality of life. When we add up the values for the different indicators, we get index values that vary between 5 and 25. The lowest value (5) means that all the indicators show very little satisfaction, while the highest value (25) indicates very great satisfaction on all the indicators.

One of the problems with additive indexes is that the same index value can be based on quite different combinations of values for the individual indicators. For example, a value of 15 on the quality of life index may indicate reasonable satisfaction on all the indicators or the combination of very little satisfaction on one of the indicators, little satisfaction on two other indicators and very great satisfaction on the last two indicators, as well as a range of other combinations of values. The index value, then, does not show which indicators have high values and which ones have low or medium values. In other words, the simplification from five variables to a single index leads to a reduction in the information content.

The construction of additive indexes reduces the number of variables but, at the same time, the number of values on the index becomes greater than the number of values on each of the original variables. It may therefore be appropriate to combine index construction and recoding. By aggregating the values on the new index, we can reduce the number of index values. In this way, the

21 values on the quality of life index, for example, can be reduced to the following three values:

1 Low quality of life (values 5–11 on the additive index)
2 Medium quality of life (values 12–18 on the additive index)
3 High quality of life (values 19–25 on the additive index).

In the index in Table 17.4, all the indicators are assigned the same weight. The five indicators make the same contribution to the summation to a total index value. However, some indicators could be considered as more important quality of life components than other indicators, so that the indicators should be assigned different weightings in the index. This can be achieved by changing the numbers for the individual indicator values. For example, if we double the figures for the values on the health indicator (2, 4, 6, 8 and 10 instead of 1, 2, 3, 4 and 5), this indicator would be assigned twice as much importance in the index as each of the other four indicators. The additive index's minimum value would then increase from 5 to 6, and the maximum value would increase from 25 to 30.

The quality of life index in Table 17.4 is comprised of five variables, each of which represents a particular component of people's quality of life. The index could have been limited to fewer quality of life components, or it could have been expanded with more components. How many and which variables to include in the index is not only based on conceptual, logical and theoretical assessments. The choice of indicators in additive indexes is also based on empirical analyses. Such analyses can clarify whether the different variables can be regarded as valid measurements for the same phenomenon, so that the index generally has a satisfactory level of validity for what is being studied. Based on Table 17.4, the question will be whether all five variables constitute a valid expression of quality of life. As a rule, this is clarified by examining the relationship between the variables. This can be done using correlation analysis and factor analysis. Factor analysis will not be discussed in more detail in this book, but correlation analysis will be presented in Chapter 18.

Two different variables are considered to be measurements for the same phenomenon if there is a positive correlation between the variables, so that units with a high value on one of the variables consistently also have a high value for the other variable. If there is such a correlation between the indicators in an additive index, all the indicators will make a meaningful contribution to the overall measurement that the index represents, and the values of the various indicators will produce a result in the same direction in this overall measurement.

The assessments of which variables should be included in an additive index can be linked to the discussion of different types of validity, which was presented in Chapter 15. While the theoretical assessments mainly concern the content validity of the index, the empirical analyses of the relationships between the indicators will refer to the construct validity of the index.

Univariate distributions

The simplest form of quantitative analysis is to describe how the units in the study are distributed across the different values of each variable. Based on the data matrix, we take the relevant variable and count how many of the units are registered for each of the values.

Frequency tables

The number of units registered with a particular value is called the *frequency* for that value. The distribution of the units on this particular variable is thus an overview of the frequencies of all the values of the variable. A distribution on a single variable or in a single index is often referred to as a *univariate distribution*. The example in Table 17.5

Table 17.5 Example of absolute, relative and cumulative frequency distribution: attitude to the EU

Attitude to the EU	Absolute frequencies	Relative frequencies (%)	Cumulative frequencies (%)
1 Strongly negative	345	23	23
2 Negative	330	22	45
3 Uncertain, neutral	300	20	65
4 Positive	285	19	84
5 Strongly positive	240	16	100
Total	1500	100	100

shows the distribution of 1500 units across the five values of the variable 'attitude to the EU'. This could be, for example, 1500 respondents in a structured questionnaire or 1500 newspaper articles about the EU in a quantitative content analysis.

The variable in Table 17.5 is at the ordinal level. The values express the degree of positive attitude to the EU. The table displays the distribution in three ways.

The *absolute frequencies* are based on the actual counts of the units for the different values. The *relative frequencies* show what percentage of units fall within each of the five values. The relative frequencies will then always add up to 100%. The percentages are often presented as decimals. As a rule, it is advisable to stick to whole numbers that are rounded off and adjusted so that the sum is exactly 100%. Due to the rounding up or down of each percentage, the sum of all percentages may sometimes be a little more or a little less than 100%. Then the largest percentages may be adjusted down or up, until the sum is exactly 100 %. Whole numbers provide the best overview. Numbers with decimals also give the impression of greater accuracy than the data can usually provide, especially when they are based on probability sampling. When the distribution is based on relative frequencies, it is referred to as a *relative distribution* or *percentage distribution*. Such a distribution is very useful and very common. Compared to absolute frequencies, relative frequencies provide a better overview and a better basis for comparisons of distributions with varying numbers of units.

Relative frequencies and relative distributions may be used to describe the characteristics of the sample of a study, as well as to examine various aspects of the research question. For example, relative distributions are presented by Pflug and Schneider (2016) in an analysis of school absenteeism, based on a survey among high school students in Germany. Relative frequencies are also used by Gardner et al. (2016) in an analysis of advanced practice in the nursing workforce, based on a national survey in Australia.

The *cumulative frequencies* in the table show the percentage share of a particular value, plus the percentages of all lower values. For the highest value, the cumulative frequency is always 100%, because it includes the percentage for both this value and the percentages for all lower values, that is, the percentages for all the values. Cumulative frequencies can also be based on absolute frequencies rather than relative frequencies. We can also calculate reverse or inverse cumulative frequencies, where we start with the frequency of the highest value and end up with the sum of the frequencies for the lowest value and all higher values. Since cumulativity refers to a particular order between the values, cumulative frequencies do not make sense for variables at the nominal level.

Otherwise, overviews of univariate distributions in table form can be used regardless of the measurement level of the variable. However, variables at interval or ratio level may have so many values that such tables become very large and difficult to understand. In such cases, it may be useful to recode the variable so that several of the original values are grouped together into larger and fewer categories.

Graphical presentations

Univariate distributions can also be described and visualized by means of graphical presentations. The distribution is then not presented as a table, but in the form of a graph or chart. The graph is usually based on the relative frequencies, but it is also possible to use the absolute frequencies as a basis for the graphical presentation. There are many types of graphical presentations, and a more general discussion of such visualizations is presented in Chapter 25. Three types of graphs or charts which are particularly useful in univariate analysis are described here. One of these is called

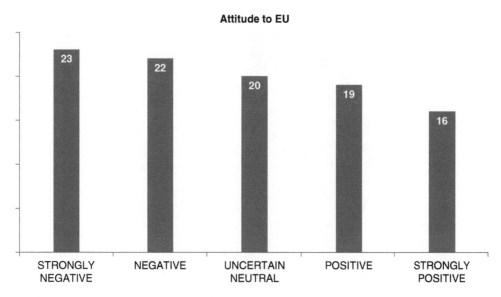

Figure 17.1   Example of a bar chart: attitude to the EU (created by means of Chart in Microsoft Word)

a *bar chart*, because the frequencies are illustrated as bars. The chart consists of a bar for each value of the variable, and the length of the bars illustrates the proportion of the units that are included in each value. Figure 17.1 shows the distribution from Table 17.5 in the form of a bar chart.

A *pie chart* is another type of graphical presentation. The graph resembles a pie. It consists of a circle that is divided into segments. Each segment corresponds to a value of the variable, and the colour of the segment shows which value it represents. The size of the segments illustrates how large a share of the units is registered on the various values. The entire circle symbolizes all the units (100%). A segment's share of the total circle corresponds to the proportion of all the units that have the value represented by the segment. Figure 17.2 shows how the distribution above can be presented in the form of a pie chart. A limitation of pie charts is that it may be difficult to compare the sectors of a given pie chart, and that it may be even more difficult to compare sectors across different pie charts. When using or considering the use of pie charts, this limitation should be taken into consideration.

In principle, both a bar graph and a pie chart could be used regardless of the measurement level of the variable. If the variable has many values, however, the number of bars or segments may be so large that the figure becomes difficult to understand. This is often the case for variables at the interval or ratio level, and especially for continuous variables such as age or income. In such cases, the variable can be recoded so that the number of values is reduced before we present the distribution in the form of a bar chart or pie chart.

However, there are also special types of graphical presentations that are specifically adapted to variables at the interval or ratio level, and particularly suitable for continuous variables. A *line chart* is such a presentation. Basically, the line chart is constructed in the same manner as a bar chart. The values are presented in ascending order along a horizontal axis in the figure, and frequencies (usually in percentages from 0 to 100) are indicated along a vertical axis. Instead of placing a bar for each value, we mark the top of each such bar in the form of a point. In other words, the point is the intersection of an

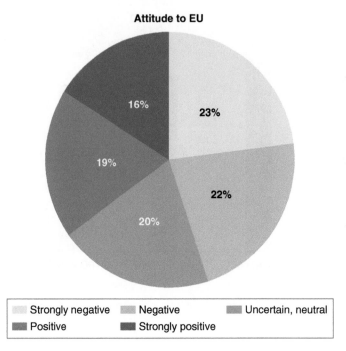

Figure 17.2 Example of a pie chart: Attitude to the EU (created by means of Chart in Microsoft Word)

(imagined) straight vertical line from the value the point represents, and an (imagined) straight horizontal line from the frequency corresponding to this value. We then draw a straight line between all these points. This line is a representation of the univariate distribution. Figure 17.3 shows an example of the distribution of income, based on the income variable in Table 17.1.

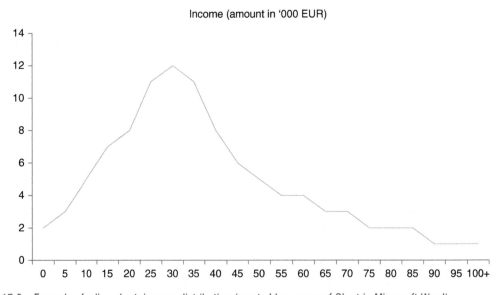

Figure 17.3 Example of a line chart: income distribution (created by means of Chart in Microsoft Word)

Line charts are especially useful if we wish to analyse the same type of distribution at different times or in different societies. For example, we may have separate lines within the same axis system for income distribution in 1960, 1980 and 2000, or separate lines for income distribution in the UK, Germany and France.

Bar charts and line charts are presented in the article on advanced practice among Australian nurses that was mentioned above (Gardner et al., 2016). Such graphical presentations are also used by Noh et al. (2015) in an analysis of gender differences in the relationship between work status and quality of life, based on national survey data in the Republic of Korea.

The line in a line diagram is usually referred to as a *curve*. The curve becomes smoother or more even when more values and points are marked on the chart before the line is drawn between the points. The shape of the curve will vary, depending on how the units are distributed over the different values. If the highest values are most common among the units, the curve will be lowest to the left of the chart and then rise towards the right. We say then that the curve is *negatively skewed*. If the lowest values have the highest frequencies, the curve will be highest to the left of the chart and then decline towards the right. In this case, the curve is *positively skewed*. The income distribution in Figure 17.3

is an example of a positively skewed curve. A third possibility is that we find most of the units on the middle values, and that the frequencies gradually reduce with both increasing and decreasing values from the average value of the variable. The curve is then symmetrical and is called a *bell curve*. Such a symmetrical distribution, with the highest frequency at the average value and with an even distribution of units on both sides of the average value, is called a *normal distribution*. Figure 17.4 shows the shape of the curve for a typical normal distribution.

The normal distribution is important in quantitative analysis. One reason is that many empirical distributions have this form. For example, the distribution of intelligence, measured as values on an IQ scale, is shaped like a bell curve. However, the most important reason why the normal distribution is important in quantitative analysis is that this form of distribution is central in probability theory and statistics. The normal distribution plays an important part in connection with probability sampling of units as well as statistical generalizations of empirical findings. The normal distribution and its importance in inductive statistics will be further discussed in Chapter 19.

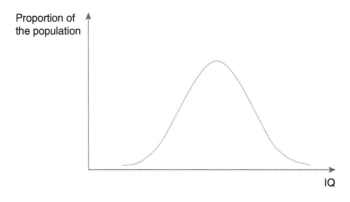

Figure 17.4 The shape of the curve for a typical normal distribution (e.g. the distribution of IQ in the population)

Statistical measures

Univariate distributions can also be described by means of statistical measures. Characteristic features of the distribution are then calculated and presented using one or a few numbers. There are two particular characteristics of distributions that can be characterized by statistical measures. One set of measures specifies which value of the variable is most central in the distribution of the units. We call this the *central tendency*. The second set of measures shows what characterizes the *dispersion* of the units across the different values.

Central tendency: Mode, median and mean

There are various statistical measures for both central tendency and dispersion. The measure used will depend on the variables' measurement level. Let us first look at different measures for central tendency.

For nominal-level variables, we can use a measure called the *mode*. This is simply the value of the variable having the highest frequency. In other words, this value is the most common of all the values for the variable. The mode for the variable 'attitude to the EU' in Table 17.5 is the value '1. Strongly negative', because the frequency of this attitude is greater than the frequency of any of the other attitudes. As we can see particularly well in this case, the mode is a very rough measure of the central tendency. There is very little difference between the frequencies of the different values, and the mode value covers less than a quarter of the units. Since this is a variable at the ordinal level, it is also particularly striking that it is one of the extreme values of the variable that constitutes the mode. This would be no problem if the variable was at the nominal level, because the order of the values would then be unimportant.

For ordinal-level variables, it is better to use a measurement for the central tendency that takes account of the order of the values. The *median* is

such a measure. When the values are arranged in ascending order, the median is the value that divides the units into two equal parts. Half of the units have values at or below the median, and half of the units have values at or above the median. The median for the variable 'attitude to the EU' in Table 17.5 is then the value '3. Uncertain, neutral'. Units with the values 1 and 2, as well as part of the units having the value 3, make up half of all the units, while the other half consists of the remainder of those having the value 3, as well as the units with the values 4 and 5. As we can see, the cumulative frequency distribution is particularly useful for finding the median. We can see that the two lowest values only comprise 45% of the units, while the three lowest values include 65% of all the units. Consequently, it is on the third value that the units are divided into two equal parts.

Both the mode and the median can also be used for variables at the interval or ratio level. For such variables, however, it would be more appropriate to indicate the central tendency in the form of an arithmetic mean. This measure, which is usually referred to simply as the *mean*, is affected by distances between the values of the variable, and therefore it is not meaningful at the nominal or ordinal level. The mean is calculated by adding together the values for all the units and dividing this sum by the total number of units. This can be done based on the data matrix. We can also start with the absolute frequency distribution for the variable, multiplying each value by the frequency of this value. Then all these products are added together, and this sum is divided by the total number of units. The formula for mean is as follows:

$$M = \frac{\sum x}{N},$$

where M is the mean, $\sum x$ is the sum of the values for all units ($\sum$ is the Greek letter *sigma*, which means sum in mathematical and statistical equations), and N is the total number of units.

Table 17.6 Number of visits to the cinema last month: absolute, relative and cumulative frequency distribution

Number of visits to the cinema	Absolute frequencies	Relative frequencies	Cumulative frequencies
0	525	35	35
1	255	17	52
2	195	13	65
3	180	12	77
4	120	8	85
5	75	5	90
6	60	4	94
7	30	2	96
8	30	2	98
9	15	1	99
10	15	1	100
Total	1500	100 %	100 %

As a simple example of calculating the mean, we can look at the variable 'number of visits to the cinema last month' in Table 17.1. The distribution of this variable is shown in Table 17.6.

The starting point for calculating the mean is the absolute frequency distribution. We can first calculate the sum of the values (number of visits to the cinema) for all of the 1500 units:

$$\Sigma x = (525 \cdot 0) + (255 \cdot 1) + (195 \cdot 2) + (180 \cdot 3) + (120 \cdot 4)$$
$$+ (75 \cdot 5) + (60 \cdot 6) + (30 \cdot 7) + (30 \cdot 8) + (15 \cdot 9) + (15 \cdot 10)$$
$$= 0 + 255 + 390 + 540 + 480 + 375 + 360 + 210 + 40$$
$$+ 135 + 150$$
$$= 3135.$$

Then we can calculate the mean using the formula above:

$$M = \frac{\Sigma x}{N} = \frac{3135}{1500} = 2.09.$$

The mean for the 1500 persons in the table is 2.09. In other words, these people have visited the cinema 2.09 times on average during the last month before the study was conducted.

Means are used as a measure in the data analysis in all the articles mentioned above, on school absenteeism in Germany (Pflug and Schneider, 2016), on nursing practice in Australia (Gardner et al., 2016), and on gender differences in work status and quality of life in the Republic of Korea (Noh et al., 2015).

Comparing the three measures of central tendency, we can see from Table 17.6 that the mode for the variable is 0 visits, and that the median is 1 visit, whereas the mean was calculated as 2.09 visits. Such differences between the three measures for the central tendency are characteristic of skewed distributions. This distribution of visits to the cinema is positively skewed. The mean is therefore higher than the median, which in turn is higher than the mode. In negative skewed distributions, the relationship between the measures is reversed: the mode is higher than the median, and the median is higher than the mean. In normal distributions, the three measures are identical.

Dispersion: Standardized modal percentage, quartile deviation, variance and standard deviation

Statistical measures of dispersion in a univariate distribution show the extent to which the units are dispersed across different values, or the extent to which they are clustered around the mode, the median or the mean. We will now look at four different measures of dispersion. One of these is the *standardized modal percentage*, which can be used for variables at all measurement levels, and which is based on the mode. The modal percentage is the percentage of all units that have the mode value for the variable. If all units have this value, the modal percentage is 100. This will always be the maximum number for the modal percentage. There is then no dispersion. All the units are concentrated on the same value. The minimum number for the modal percentage, which expresses the widest possible dispersion, varies with the number of values for the variable. If there are two values for the variable, the minimum number for the modal percentage will be 50. If there are four values, the minimum number will be 25. To make the measure of the dispersion independent of the number of values for the variable, therefore, the modal percentage is standardized. The standardized modal percentage is calculated as follows:

$$\text{Standardized modal percentage} = \frac{\text{Modal percentage} - \dfrac{100}{\text{Number of values}}}{100 - \dfrac{100}{\text{Number of values}}} \cdot 100$$

The standardized modal percentage will vary between 0 (when there is maximum dispersion) and 100 (when there is no dispersion).

For the variable 'attitude to the EU' in Table 17.5, the standardized modal percentage can be calculated from the formula above:

$$\text{Standardized modal percentage} = \frac{23 - \dfrac{100}{5}}{100 - \dfrac{100}{5}} \cdot 100 = 3.75.$$

The standardized modal percentage is very low, and the dispersion is therefore high.

Similarly, we can find the standardized modal percentage for the variable 'number of visits to the cinema last month' in Table 17.6:

$$\text{Standardized modal percentage} = \frac{35 - \dfrac{100}{11}}{100 - \dfrac{100}{11}} \cdot 100 = 28.5.$$

Here, the standardized modal percentage is higher, and the variable 'number of visits to the cinema last month' therefore has less dispersion than the variable 'attitude to the EU'. The higher the standardized modal percentage, the *lower* the dispersion. Therefore, this measure is actually an expression of concentration, which is the opposite of dispersion. The three other measures to be discussed here are more direct measures for dispersion.

Quartile deviation refers to the dispersion on both sides of the median. When the values are arranged in ascending order, the quartile deviation is calculated on the basis of the values that divide the units into four equal parts. These values are called *quartiles*. The first quartile, Q_1, is the value that separates the 25% of units that have the lowest values and the 75% of units that have higher values. The second quartile, Q_2, is identical to the median. The third quartile, Q_3, is the value that separates the 75% of the units with the lowest values and the 25% of the units that have higher values. The difference between the third and first quartiles is called the *quartile difference*. The quartile deviation is defined as half of the quartile difference and is calculated from the following formula:

$$Q = \frac{Q_3 - Q_1}{2}.$$

The quartile deviation is an expression of distance between the first and third quartiles, which thereby emphasizes the dispersion of the middle 50% of the units.

Like the median, the quartiles can be identified on the basis of the cumulative distribution. If we look at the distribution of the variable 'attitude to the EU' in Table 17.5, we find that the first quartile is the value 2 and that the third quartile is the value 4. If we insert this into the formula above, we can calculate the quartile deviation for the variable:

$$Q = \frac{4-2}{2} = 1.$$

Similarly, we can find the quartiles and calculate the quartile deviation for the variable 'Number of visits to the cinema last month' in Table 17.6:

$$Q = \frac{3-0}{2} = 1.5.$$

Unlike the standardized modal percentage, quartile deviation does not provide a basis for comparing the dispersion for the two variables. The quartile deviation can be used, however, to compare different samples or groups of units with respect to the dispersion on the same variable. For example, we can compare the quartile deviations for women and men in terms of the distribution of the number of visits to the cinema.

Since the calculation of the quartile deviation assumes that the values are arranged in a particular order, this measure cannot be used at the nominal level, but it can be used at the other measurement levels.

However, when the variables are at the interval or ratio level, it is common to express the dispersion in the form of *variance* or *standard deviation*. These dispersion measures are closely linked to each other, as the standard deviation is the square root of the variance. The variance and standard deviation are calculated on the basis of each unit's distance from the mean for the entire distribution. Since the measures are based on distances between values, they cannot be used at the nominal or ordinal level.

Table 17.7 Example of calculation of squared deviations from the mean: number of visits to the cinema last month for ten units

Unit	Value (x)	x – M	(x – M)²
U1	4	1	1
U2	0	–3	9
U3	1	–2	4
U4	10	7	49
U5	0	–3	9
U6	6	3	9
U7	1	–2	4
U8	0	–3	9
U9	8	5	25
U10	0	–3	9
Total	30	0	128
Mean (M)	3		

The variance and standard deviation can be regarded as measures of the unit's average distance from the mean value of all the units. Since we must then find each unit's distance from the mean value, we start with the data matrix. Let us look at the variable 'number of visits to the cinema last month' as an example of this. Table 17.7 shows the values for this variable (x) for the ten units (U1, ..., U10) that are included in the data matrix in Table 17.1.

We can see that the number of visits to the cinema varies between 0 and 10. The sum of the values for all ten units is 30 visits to the cinema, and the mean (M) is then 3 visits to the cinema. We will now find each unit's distance from this mean ($x - M$). For the first unit (U1), which has 4 visits to the cinema, the distance is $4 - 3 = 1$. For the second unit (U2), the distance is $0 - 3 = -3$. Some of the distances have a positive sign, and others have a negative sign. The sum of the absolute values of the distances will therefore be 0. In order to remove the signs so that we can find the sum of the actual distances, regardless of whether they are above or below the mean value, we square the distances, $(x - M)^2$. The squared distances are calculated in the rightmost column of Table 17.7. As we can see, the sum of these is 128. This sum is an expression of all the units' *total* (squared) distances from the mean. The greater the sum, the greater the dispersion of the distribution. We will now find the *mean* (squared) distance from the distribution's mean value. We therefore divide the sum of the (squared) distances for all the units by the number of units (N). The result is the variance (V), which is calculated from the following formula:

$$V = \frac{\sum (x - M)^2}{N}.$$

If we insert the numbers from Table 17.7 into this formula, we find the variance for the variable:

$$V = \frac{128}{10} = 12.8.$$

As mentioned, the variance is the mean of the *squared* distances. The square root of the variance will then be a measure that is closer to the mean of the actual distances. This is the standard deviation, which has the following formula:

$$s = \sqrt{\frac{\sum (x - M)^2}{N}}.$$

The standard deviation for the variable 'number of visits to the cinema last month' in Table 17.7 will then be

$$s = \sqrt{\frac{\sum (x - M)^2}{N}} = \sqrt{12.8} = 3.58.$$

When the variance and the standard deviation are calculated for probability sampling, it is common to divide the squared distances by $N - 1$ instead of N. This is due to the uncertainty associated with random differences between the sample and the universe. When the sample (N) is large, however, both the variance and the standard deviation will be approximately equal in size, whether we divide by N or by $N - 1$.

In quantitative studies, the standard deviation of a variable is usually presented together with the mean, in order to show both the central tendency and the dispersion of the distribution. This combination of the two measures is used in all the articles mentioned above (Gardner et al., 2016; Noh et al., 2015; Pflug and Schneider, 2016).

The variance and standard deviation are important statistical measures in several of the methods of analysis that will be discussed in Chapter 18, and these measures will also be further discussed in Chapter 19, in connection with hypothesis testing and statistical generalization.

- Quantitative data appear in the form of numbers.
- The analysis of quantitative data is conducted after the data collection process and is based on statistical methods and standardized techniques.
- The analyses are performed by means of computer programs. Several software packages are available for this purpose.
- The data are organized in a data matrix based on a codebook.
- Recoding means that multiple values for a single variable are combined on the basis of logical or empirical criteria. The measurement level of the variable may be changed in connection with recoding.
- Index construction entails combining several variables (indicators) into an index. We distinguish between different types of indexes, such as typology-based and additive indexes.
- The distribution of the units on a variable is called univariate distribution. Such distributions can be analysed using different types of frequencies, graphical presentations and statistical measures.
- We distinguish between absolute, relative and cumulative frequencies.
- We distinguish between different types of graphical presentations, such as bar charts, pie charts and line charts.

- There are different types of statistical measures for univariate distributions, such as:
  - Measures for central tendency
    - The mode is used especially for nominal-level variables
    - The median is used especially for ordinal-level variables (cannot be used at the nominal level)
    - The mean requires interval- or ratio-level variables.
  - Measures for dispersion
    - The standardized modal percentage is used especially for nominal level variables
    - The quartile deviation is used especially for ordinal-level variables (cannot be used at the nominal level)
    - The variance requires interval- or ratio-level variables
    - The standard deviation requires interval- or ratio-level variables.
- Distributions may be positively skewed, negatively skewed or symmetrical. A symmetrical distribution is referred to as a normal distribution. Normal distributions play an important role in probability sampling of units and statistical generalization of empirical findings.

I recommend that you read the publications used as research examples in this chapter.

Gardner, Glenn, Christine Duffield, Anna Doubrovsky, and Margaret Adams (2016) 'Identifying advanced practice: A national survey of a nursing workforce', *International Journal of Nursing Studies* 55, 60–70.

This article presents a study of advanced nursing practice, based on a national sample of nurses in Australia. The purpose is to identify and delineate advanced practice from other levels of nursing practice. The analysis includes examinations of relative frequency distributions, medians, means and standard deviations, as well as bar charts and line charts. The study provides new knowledge about the structure of nursing practice and provides a foundation for a standardized national career structure for nurses.

Noh, Jin-Won, Jinseok Kim, Jumin Park, Hyun-jung Kim, and Young Dae Kwon (2015) 'Gender difference in relationship between health-related quality of life and work Status', *PLoS One* 10(12), e0143579.

The study presented in this article examines how health-related quality of life is associated with employment status, focusing on gender differences in this relationship. The study is based on national survey data in the Republic of Korea. Statistical measures, including the mean and standard deviation, are used in the analysis, and graphical presentations, both bar charts and line charts, are presented. The analysis shows that quality of life is positively affected by employment, and that this effect is more important for men than for women.

Pflug, Verena, and Silvia Schneider (2016) 'School absenteeism: An online survey via social networks', *Child Psychiatry & Human Development* 47(3), 417–429.

This article deals with school absenteeism, which is investigated by means of data from a survey among high school students in Germany. The purpose is to examine the extent of absence from school, as well as relationships between absence and potential risk factors. The analysis includes frequency tables, as well as means and standard deviations. The study shows that 9% of the students reported absenteeism during a 7-day period, and that these students have lower socioeconomic status, more emotional and behavioural problems, and less prosocial behaviour than students with no absence.

STUDENT EXERCISES AND QUESTIONS

1 What is a data matrix?
2 Why are computers important in analysis of quantitative data?
3 What is the difference between recoding of variables and construction of indexes?
4 Why do we need different measures of central tendency and dispersion in quantitative analysis?
5 What is a normal distribution?
6 What measurement level of the variable is required for the use of

  a the mode?
  b the mean?
  c the quartile deviation?
  d the standard deviation?

7 Discuss which statistical measures of central tendency and dispersion could be used for the following variables:

  a age (in number of years)
  b education (with the values low, medium, high)
  c education (in years)
  d attitude to feminism (with the values very negative, negative, neutral, positive, very positive).

RECOMMENDED LITERATURE

Blaikie, Norman (2003) *Analysing Quantitative Data: From Description to Explanation*. London: Sage.

This book is an introduction to the theory and practice of quantitative analysis, which does not require an in-depth understanding of statistical theory. Presenting a scheme of classification of methods of analysis, the book explains what procedures to use under what circumstances. Real research examples are used as illustrations of methodological issues. The book is written for students doing research in different social science disciplines.

Rose, David, and Oriel Sullivan (1996) *Introducing Data Analysis for Social Scientists* (2nd edn). Buckingham: Open University Press.

This book explains the principles of analysing data in different stages, and it provides an introduction to using computers and SPSS. Underlying principles are illustrated with examples focusing on the role of theory and the logic of data analysis. Requiring only elementary mathematics and no previous knowledge of statistics, the book is intended for social science students taking their first course in quantitative data analysis.

te Grotenhuis, Manfred, and Anneke Matthijssen (2016) *Basic SPSS Tutorial*. London: Sage.

This book presents the basic knowledge for using SPSS. Readers are guided through point-and-click sequences, illustrated with examples from research. Based on the use of SPSS, the book provides a basic knowledge of the most commonly used procedures in statistics.

RELATIONSHIPS BETWEEN VARIABLES

This chapter provides the necessary knowledge for understanding quantitative analyses of relationships between variables, and for conducting such analyses.

The chapter will teach you how to

- select appropriate methods for analysis
- distinguish between bivariate and multivariate analysis
- conduct table analysis, correlation analysis and regression analysis
- distinguish between effect and interaction in multivariate analysis

- distinguish between gamma and Pearson's *r* in correlation analysis
- interpret regressions coefficients and explained variance in regression analysis.

Selection of methods for analysis

While Chapter 17 dealt with indexes and univariate distributions, this chapter will look at the relationships between different variables. Many research questions in quantitative studies relate to relationships between variables. A statistical relationship between two variables implies a probability that units with specific values for one of the variables will also have certain values for the other variable. For example, there may be a probability that those with a high level of education also have a high income, or that those who have little interest in politics also participate little in political activities. The greater this probability, the stronger the relationship between the variables. If there is no such systematic pattern in the unit's values for the two variables, there is no statistical relationship between the variables.

Quantitative analyses are often about identifying statistical relationships between variables, as well as clarifying how strong these relationships are, what direction the relationship has and the form it takes. There are a large number of methods and techniques for such analyses. This chapter is focused on three of the most important and common methods, namely table analysis, correlation analysis and regression analysis. These methods of analysis will be discussed in turn. First, however, an overview of some important differences between the three methods is presented, with emphasis on the types and constellations of variables that each of the methods is particularly suitable for analysing.

The methods of analysis that can and should be used in a particular analysis will depend on the research question of the study, in addition to the characteristics of the variables that are included in the analysis. The research question determines the relationships to be investigated, and thus which variables should be analysed. Both the properties of each of these variables and the constellation of all the variables in the analysis are critical for the choice of analysis method. Table 18.1 provides an overview of four key features of the variables and the relationship between them for each of the three methods of analysis to be discussed here. Let us take a closer look at each of these key features.

Bivariate or multivariate analyses

Firstly, the choice of analysis method depends on the number of variables in the analysis. Analyses that are limited to the relationship between two variables are called bivariate analyses. Multivariate analyses are intended to clarify the relationships between three or more variables.

Table 18.1 Typical features of the variables in table analysis, correlation analysis and regression analysis

Characteristics of the variables in the analysis	Method of analysis		
	Table analysis	Correlation analysis	Regression analysis
Number of variables	Two or three	Two	Two or more
Measurement level of the variables	Nominal or ordinal level	All levels, but especially ordinal, interval or ratio level	Interval or ratio level
Number of values for each variable	Few	Many	Many
Relationship between variables	One dependent and one or two independent variables	Symmetrical relations between the two variables	One dependent and one or more independent variables

Table analysis may include both bivariate and multivariate analyses. In principle, there is no fixed limit on the number of variables that can be included in a table analysis, but in practice, such analyses will concentrate on two or three variables. If more than three variables are included in the same table, both the table and the analysis can become quite complex.

Correlation analyses are carried out primarily as bivariate analyses. Admittedly, there are also more complicated methods for multivariate or multiple correlation analyses, but they will not be discussed here. Typically, correlation analyses often include many variables, but the relationships between them are clarified between each pair of variables. These relationships are expressed in the form of correlation coefficients that are presented in a correlation matrix, where all the variables are included. The matrix thus builds on separate bivariate analyses for each pair of these variables, and it is the results of these different bivariate analyses that are shown in the correlation matrix.

Regression analysis may include two or more variables. This analysis method is particularly suitable for analysing relationships between many variables.

Measurement level of the variables

The measurement level of the variables will also determine which methods can and should be used.

Table analysis is used primarily when the variables are at the nominal or ordinal level. Variables at the interval or ratio level can be included in table analyses, but this assumes that we can distinguish clearly between different values for the variables, and that the number of values is relatively limited. Table analysis is not suitable for continuous variables with very many values, because the tables would then become very extensive and complex. If such variables are to be included in a table analysis, they are often recoded so that both the number of values and the measurement level are reduced.

In the case of correlation analysis, this book concentrates on methods that can be used at the ordinal level, and methods for variables at the interval and ratio levels. However, there are also simple methods for correlation analysis at the nominal level.

Regression analysis requires the variables to be at the interval and ratio level. Such analyses can also include variables at the nominal level, if these are dichotomies with the values 0 and 1. In regression analyses, such nominal-level variables are referred to as *dummy variables*. It is also relatively common for regression analyses to include variables at the ordinal level, provided that these variables have a large number of values.

Number of values

Not only the number of variables, but also the number of values for each variable affects the analysis methods that can be selected. Table analysis requires variables with few values. Otherwise, both the tables and the analyses will be complex and difficult to understand. The analysis will be simplest if each variable has only two values. On the other hand, the analysis will often be more balanced and more meaningful if the variables have three or more values.

Both correlation analysis and regression analysis are better suited when there are many values for each variable. Especially in regression analyses, it is an advantage to have variables with many values. However, dummy variables are an exception to this general rule, because each of these variables only has the two values 0 and 1.

The relation between the variables

In addition to the characteristics of each variable, the relation between the variables is important for the selection of analysis methods. Here a distinction is made between dependency relations and symmetrical relations between the variables.

Dependency or symmetry

A dependency relation between two variables entails that one variable is expected to affect the other. A unit having a specific value for the second variable is considered to be an effect of this unit having a certain value for the first variable. Thus, income can be perceived as an effect of education, and political interest can be said to affect political activity. The variable that exerts an effect is called the *independent variable*, and the one that is affected is referred to as the *dependent variable*.

If we do not distinguish between independent and dependent variables in the analysis, the relation

between the variables is symmetrical. A symmetrical relation between two variables implies that the variables are treated as equivalent in the analysis. Even if we find a statistical relationship between the variables, we do not assume that one variable affects the other. The relationship may mean instead that both variables are affected by a common underlying cause, or that they are part of a common underlying dimension. In this way, we will assume for example that there is a symmetrical relationship between the indicators in the additive index for quality of life described in Chapter 17 (Table 17.4).

Even if we find a relationship between the quality of life components 'satisfaction with employment situation' and 'satisfaction with leisure activities', there is not necessarily a dependency relation between the two variables.

Table analysis is usually based on assumptions about dependency between the variables, although the relation between the variables in the table can also be considered as symmetrical. It is most common that table analysis involves one dependent and one or two independent variables. Correlation analysis usually assumes a symmetrical relation between the two variables that are analysed. Regression analysis, on the other hand, requires a clear distinction between dependent and independent variables. Such analyses always involve one dependent variable and one or more independent variables.

Independent and dependent variables

How can we determine in practice whether there is a dependency or a symmetrical relation between the variables in an analysis, and how can we distinguish between independent and dependent variables? The most important criterion for such assessments is the chronology between the variables. When we examine the relation between two variables, the key question is whether we can assume that each unit's value for one variable is determined *before* they got their value for the other variable. This applies, for example, to the relation between the variables gender and income. Whether a person is a woman or a man is determined before this person achieves a certain income level. If it is possible to assume such a chronology between the variables, the analysis can be based on a dependency relation between the variables. This chronology is then also critical for the distinction between dependent and independent variables. In a dependency relation between two variables, the variable that is determined first will be the independent variable, and the variable that is determined last will be the dependent variable. In the relation between gender and income, gender must be the independent variable, and income will be the dependent variable. Income can be affected by gender, but gender cannot be affected by income.

In studies of individuals, variables associated with the individuals' social background or personality will usually be considered as independent variables, while variables associated with the individuals' actions or opinions will often appear as dependent variables. In content analyses of texts, aspects of the text's context or author will often be analysed as independent variables, while aspects of the text's content will usually be presented in the form of dependent variables. However, it is not always easy to determine which variables should be independent and which ones should be dependent. The assessment of this can also vary from study to study. The relation between the variables 'political interest' and 'political activity' is an example of this. On the one hand, political activity could be motivated by an interest in politics, so that the interest variable is independent, while the activity variable is dependent. On the other hand, an interest in politics can also be inspired by political activity. In that case, the activity variable becomes independent, while the interest variable is dependent. In such cases, the choice of dependent and independent variable is determined by the research question to be examined and the perspective from which the relation between the variables is understood.

In many cases, it is not possible to assume a specific chronology between the variables. It may then be more useful or appropriate for the analysis to be based on a symmetrical relation between the variables, as in connection with the additive index for quality of life mentioned above. Generally, it may be difficult to assume a particular chronology between general attitude variables or between general behaviour variables.

Causal relations

A causal relation is a particular type of dependency between variables. The independent variable is then considered to be the cause and the dependent variable is the effect. A causal relation between two variables assumes that there is a statistical relationship between the two variables, and that this relationship is not *spurious*. A bivariate relationship between two variables is spurious if the bivariate relationship is actually due to a statistical relationship between each of the two variables and a third variable. In that case, the statistical relationship between the two original variables will disappear when we analyse the relationship between all three variables together. The original relationship is spurious because it disappears when we *control* for the third variable.

For example, a bivariate relationship between income and home size could actually be due to the fact that both income and home size are related to age. People achieve a higher income when they grow older and become more senior. Most people also acquire a larger home as they grow older and have bigger families. The bivariate relationship between income and home size is then spurious and will disappear when we conduct a multivariate analysis of the relationships between all three variables. Then income cannot be considered as a cause of home size.

In other words, clarification of causation through control for spuriosity requires multivariate analyses. Such clarifications can be included in both table analyses and regression analyses. This will be shown in the presentation of these two analysis methods in this chapter. Furthermore, analyses of causal relations will be discussed in more detail in Chapter 21.

Table analysis

As noted above, table analyses are used to investigate both bivariate and multivariate relationships, but cannot include more than a few variables. Such analyses are usually limited to two or three variables. Since the variables must be divided into distinct values, table analyses are especially suitable for variables at a nominal or ordinal level, and these variables should have few values. The analysis becomes clearest if each of the variables has only two values, but on the other hand, it may be more interesting if the variables have three or more values. Table analysis is usually based on a dependency relation between the variables, with one dependent and one or more independent variables.

Contingency tables

Table 18.2 shows the relationship between the two variables 'income' and 'home size'. As the variables are presented in this table, they are at the ordinal level and have three values each. Such tables of relationships between variables are often called *contingency tables* or *cross tables*. They show the intersections between the distributions for the different variables. Separate distributions are shown for each of the variables, based on each of the values for the other variables in the table. The columns in Table 18.2 show separate distributions of home size for each of the values on the income variable. The rows of the table show separate income distributions for each of the values for the home size variable. These separate distributions are called *conditional distributions* because they show how, for example, the distribution of home size is conditional upon different values for the income variable. In the rightmost column, the table shows the sum of the frequencies for the other columns, which is the distribution of home size for all of the 1500 units in the table, regardless of income level. Similarly, the row at the bottom shows the corresponding sum of the frequencies of the other rows, which represents the income distribution for all the 1500 units, regardless of the size of their home. The distributions in the rightmost column and the bottom row are thus unconditional distributions, but are referred to as *marginal distributions*. The marginal distribution for a variable in a cross table is identical to the univariate distribution for this variable.

Table 18.2   Bivariate relationship between income and home size: absolute frequencies

Home size	Income			Total
	Low	Medium	High	
Small	250	100	50	400
Medium	150	400	50	600
Large	100	200	200	500
Total	500	700	300	1500

If there is a relationship between the variables in the table, the conditional distributions of each of the variables will be mutually different and different from the marginal distribution of the variable. If all the conditional distributions are equal and identical to the marginal distribution, there is no relationship between the variables.

This comparison of the conditional distributions becomes easier if we look at relative frequencies instead of the absolute frequencies in Table 18.2. In such a cross table, relative frequencies in the form of percentages can be calculated in three different ways. All three methods of calculation are illustrated in Table 18.3.

Table 18.3 Bivariate relationship between income and home size: relative frequencies (percentages) calculated vertically, horizontally, and based on the grand total

(a) Vertical percentages

Home size	Income			Total
	Low	Medium	High	
Small	50	14	17	27
Medium	30	57	17	40
Large	20	29	66	33
Total	100%	100%	100%	100%
N	500	700	300	1500

(b) Horizontal percentages

Home size	Income			Total	N
	Low	Medium	High		
Small	62	25	13	100%	400
Medium	25	67	8	100%	600
Large	20	40	40	100%	500
Total	33	47	20	100%	1500

(c) Percentages based on the grand total

Home size	Income			Total
	Low	Medium	High	
Small	16	7	4	27
Medium	10	27	3	40
Large	7	13	13	33
Total	33	47	20	100% (N = 1500)

The percentage sums (100%) in the table indicate the direction of calculating the percentages, and the number of units (*N*) below or to the right of the percentage sums shows the absolute frequencies that form the basis for the percentage calculation.

It is the vertical and horizontal percentages that provide the basis for comparing the conditional distributions and for assessing whether there is a relationship between the variables. The vertical percentages (Table 18.3a) focus on the distributions of home size, conditional upon income levels. Here we compare the four different columns with vertical distributions in the table. For example, the marginal distribution in the rightmost column shows that 33% of all the units, regardless of income, have a large home. The conditional distributions in the table show that only 20% of units with low income have a large home, while over 66% of high-income units have a large home. Thus, there are large differences between the conditional distributions mutually, and between the conditional distributions and the marginal distribution. This means that there is a relationship between the variables. There is a clear tendency for people to have a larger home if they have a higher income.

The horizontal percentages (Table 18.3b) highlight the income distributions for units with different home sizes. Here we compare the four rows with horizontal distributions in the table. The marginal distribution in the bottom row, for example, shows that 20% of all the units, regardless of the size of their home, have a high income. According to the conditional distributions in the table, only 13% of the units with a small home and only 8% of the units with a medium-sized home have a high income. On the other hand, the income level is high among 40% of those who have large homes. We can again see the clear relationship between the variables, since the conditional distributions are both mutually different and different from the marginal distribution.

The percentages based on the grand total (the total sum of all units) show the proportion of all the 1500 units in the analysis that have different combinations of values for the two variables. Table 18.3c shows, for example, that 16% of the units have both a low income and a small home, and that 13% have both a high income and a large home. On the other hand, according to the table, only 7% of all the units have large homes and low incomes, and only 4% have small homes and high incomes. These percentages can be useful, for example, in assessing the extent of expected or surprising value combinations, and as a basis for index construction based on the two variables.

The method for calculating the percentages that should be used in a given analysis is usually assessed on the basis of the distinction between dependent and independent variables. In the example here, it would be reasonable to regard income as an independent variable and home size as a dependent variable. For the individual units, income is usually established prior to the purchase of a particular home. Generally, people acquire a home based on what they can afford. It is common to draw up cross tables as we have done here, with the values of the independent variable at the top and the values of the dependent variable at the far left of the table. The analysis of the table is primarily about how the distributions of the dependent variable are conditional on different values for the independent variable. We must therefore compare the conditional distributions of the dependent variable. When we set up the table as we have done here, the distributions of the dependent variable will appear vertically. Therefore, it is the vertical percentages values (Table 18.3a) that should be used. These percentages provide the basis for comparing the vertical distributions in the table. On the other hand, the comparison must be done horizontally, across the direction of the percentage calculations. It is the percentages in the different vertical distributions that should be compared. The procedure can be summarized in three points:

1 Prepare the table with the values of the dependent variable to the left, and the values of the independent variable at the top.
2 Calculate percentages vertically.
3 Compare percentages horizontally.

Percentage differences

It is the difference between the conditional distributions that shows that there is a relationship between the variables. The greater the difference, the stronger the relationship. The table expresses the difference between the distributions through the horizontal difference between the percentages for the vertical distributions. This *percentage difference* can therefore be used as a measure of the strength of the relationship. This measure is easiest to use if each of the variables in the table has only two values. Let us look at an example of this based on the same variables as above. The variables are recoded, so that we only distinguish between low and high income and small and large homes. The vertical percentages in the conditional distributions are shown in Table 18.4.

Table 18.4 Home size conditional on income. Relative frequencies

Home size	Income		Total
	Low	High	
Small	56	33	47
Large	44	67	53
Total	100%	100%	100%
N	900	600	1500

Here, the percentage difference will be calculated horizontally for one of the values of the dependent variable. For the value 'small home size', the percentage difference (d) will be

$$d = 56 - 33 = 23.$$

The percentage difference could also be calculated on the basis of the value 'large home size':

$$d = 44 - 67 = -23.$$

The absolute values of the two differences are identical, but the differences have different signs. This will always be the case in such *fourfold tables*, where each of the two variables has only two values. The sign must always be interpreted in light of the order between the values of the two variables, as they are set up in the table. In this case, the signs reflect that high income increases the likelihood of a large home. Since these are variables at the ordinal level, we can say that the relationship between the variables is positive: home size increases with increasing income. If home size decreased when income increased, the relationship would be negative.

It is the absolute value of the percentage difference that indicates the strength of the relationship. In this case, the percentage difference is large and is therefore an expression of a strong relationship between the two variables. If we interpret this as a causality, income can be regarded as a cause of home size, and home size appears as an effect of income. This can be illustrated in the form of a simple causal model, as shown in Figure 18.1.

Income ⟶ Home size

Figure 18.1 Causal relationship between income and home size

Percentage difference can also be used as a measure of relationship when the variables have more than two values. However, we will get multiple percentage differences for the same table, and we must either calculate the average of the different percentage differences or make a combined interpretation of all percentage differences. This will not be discussed in further detail here.

Multivariate table analysis

On the other hand, we will discuss how percentage difference can be used as a measure of relationships between three or more variables in multivariate table analysis. Let us look at an example with three variables. In addition to the two variables in Table 18.4, we include age as a third variable. As with income, age will be an independent variable, and home size will continue to be a dependent variable. For simplicity, we will stick with the two values 'younger' and 'older' for the age variable, which is thus at the ordinal level. The table with the three variables is drawn up as shown in Table 18.5.

We still place the values of the dependent variable to the left of the table, but now we set up the combinations of values for both of the two independent variables at the top of the table. With this layout of the table, we also need to express the values as percentages vertically in order to compare the distributions of the dependent variable. These distributions are now conditional on both of the independent variables at the same time. Instead of two conditional distributions, we now get four, since there is one conditional distribution for each combination of values for the two independent variables.

Effects

The multivariate analysis involves both clarifying how strong an *effect* each independent variable has on the dependent variable, and clarifying whether there is *interaction* between the independent variables. We will first look at how to calculate the effects. The purpose is to find the effect of each of the independent variables, *controlled for* the other independent variable. This means that we calculate the effect of one of the variables, while keeping the value of the other variable constant. In the example here, we find the separate effect of income on home size, both among only the younger and among only the older homeowners. The overall effect of income controlled for age is then the average of the two *partial effects*. Similarly, we find the partial effect of age separately for those with low income, and the partial effect of age separately for those with a high income. The average of these two partial effects will be the combined effect of age controlled for income. The partial effects are expressed in terms of percentage differences, and when there are only two values for the dependent variable, we can rely on one of these values. As pointed out in connection with Table 18.4, the absolute value of the percentage differences will be the same, regardless of which of the values we rely on.

When the variables are at the ordinal level, it is best to rely on the highest value of the dependent variable and calculate the percentage difference between the high and low value for each of the independent variables. Positive percentage

Table 18.5 Home size conditional on age and income: relative frequencies

Home size	Younger		Older		Total
	Low income	High income	Low income	High income	Total
Small	60	60	31	32	47
Large	40	40	69	68	53
Total	100%	100%	100%	100%	100%
N	600	200	300	400	1500

differences will then correspond to positive relationships, while negative percentage differences will correspond to negative relationships. We therefore focus on the percentages in the row for large home in Table 18.5. In order to keep an overview of the partial effects of the two variables, we can transfer these four numbers to a new table, where the values of one independent variable (older and younger) are placed at the top, and the values for the other independent variable (high and low income) are placed on the far left of the table. This has been done in Table 18.6.

Table 18.6 Percentage with a large home conditional on age and income

	Older	Younger	Partial effects of age
High income	68	40	28
Low income	69	40	29
Partial effects of income	−1	0	

The partial effects of age are calculated horizontally in the table, both for units with high income (68 − 40 = 28) and for units with low income (69 − 40 = 29). The total effect of age controlled for income is equal to the average of the two partial effects: $\frac{1}{2}(29 + 28) = 28.5$.

The partial effects of income are calculated vertically, both for the older (68 − 69 = −1) and for the younger homeowners (40 − 40 = 0). The total effect of income controlled for age is equal to the average of the two partial effects: $\frac{1}{2}(−1 + 0) = −0.5$.

Thus, we find that age has a strong effect on home size. The relationship is positive: home size increases with increasing age. On the other hand, the effect of income is approximately equal to zero. When we control for age, income has no effect on home size.

If we see this in relation to the relationship in Table 18.4, we have an example where the bivariate

relationship between two variables (income and home size) disappears when we control for a third variable (age). The bivariate relationship between income and home size turns out to be spurious. This is because the third variable, age, is associated with both of the two original variables. The fact that age has an effect on home size is shown above. The fact that age also has an effect on income is illustrated in Table 18.7. Thus, both home size and income increase with increasing age. Presented in the form of a causal model, this result of the analysis appears as shown in Figure 18.2.

Table 18.7 Income conditional on age: relative frequencies

Income	Age		Total
	Younger	Older	
Low	75	43	60
High	25	57	40
Total	100%	100%	100%
N	800	700	1500

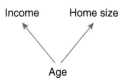

Figure 18.2 Causal relationships between age and income, and between age and home size

Interaction

Finally, another possible result of the multivariate analysis of the relationships between these three variables will be discussed. The purpose is now to show how we analyse both effects and *interaction*. Table 18.8 is set up in the same way and includes the same variables as Table 18.5, but the two tables contain different numbers, so that the analyses show different results. We transfer the percentages in the row for large home to Table 18.9, so that the partial effects and the total effects can be calculated in the same way as above.

Table 18.8 Home size conditional on age and income: relative frequencies

| Home size | Younger | | Older | | |
	Low income	High income	Low income	High income	Total
Small	75	25	75	10	47
Large	25	75	25	90	53
Total	100%	100%	100%	100%	100%
N	600	200	300	400	1500

Table 18.9 Percentage with a large home conditional on age and income

	Older	Younger	Partial effects of age
High income	90	75	15
Low income	25	25	0
Partial effects of income	65	50	

Based on Table 18.9, we can calculate the total effects (E):

$$E_{income} = \frac{1}{2}(65 + 50) = 57.5,$$

$$E_{age} = \frac{1}{2}(15 + 0) = 7.5.$$

This shows that both income and age have positive effects on home size, and that the effect of income is much stronger than the effect of age.

In addition, Table 18.9 shows that there is an interaction between age and income with regard to their effects on home size. Such an interaction entails that the effect of one independent variable varies between the values of the other independent variable. In our example, this is reflected in the fact that the income effect is stronger among the older than among the younger homeowners, and that

the age effect is stronger among people with high incomes than among those with low incomes. More precisely, age has no effect on home size for the low-income group, but it does for the units with high income. The interaction between the two variables can also be expressed as follows: the income effect is strengthened with increasing age, and the age effect is strengthened with increasing income.

While the total effect of each independent variable is calculated as the average of the partial effects, the interaction between the variables is expressed as the difference between the partial effects. The greater the difference between the partial effects, the stronger the interaction. If there is no difference between the partial effects, as in Table 18.6, there is no interaction between the variables.

In other words, it is the difference between the percentage differences that must be calculated in order to find the interaction. The difference between the partial effects is the same for both of the variables. The interaction can therefore be calculated on the basis of one of the variables, such as age:

$$15 - 0 = 15.$$

The usual *formula* for interaction is based on a formal definition of interaction as half of the difference between the partial effects. The interaction I will then be

$$I = \frac{1}{2}(15 - 0) = 7.5.$$

This is a clear interaction.

If we interpret the relationships in Table 18.8 as causal relationships, the results of the analyses can be presented in the form of a causal model, as shown in Figure 18.3. Both income and age have an effect on home size (arrows 1 and 2). In addition, there is an interaction between age and income, so that the age effect varies with the income (arrow 3) and the income effect is affected by age (arrow 4).

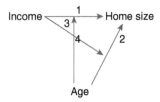

Figure 18.3 Effects of income (1) and age (2) on home size, and interaction between income and age (3 and 4) with regard to their effects on home size

Multivariate analyses of effects and interaction can also be performed for tables with more than three variables, but the calculations become more complex and difficult to understand when the number of variables increases. In such cases, it may be useful to use *correspondence analysis*, which is a more advanced method for summarizing information in cross tables in order to produce graphical presentations of this information (Hjellbrekke, 2019). However, this method will not be discussed here.

Correlation analysis

Correlation analysis aims to find a single statistical measure that can characterize the relationship between two variables. This measure, which is called the *correlation coefficient*, is a figure that usually ranges between –1 and +1. The absolute value of the correlation coefficient is an expression of the *strength* of the correlation. If the coefficient is 0, there is no correlation between the two variables. The stronger the correlation, the more the coefficient will approach –1 or +1. The sign shows the *direction* of the correlation, whether it is negative or positive.

Correlation analysis is carried out primarily as bivariate analysis and it is based on a symmetrical relationship between the two variables that are analysed. Each variable can have many values.

Correlation analysis can be performed with variables at all measurement levels, and there are several different methods for correlation analysis. With variables at the nominal level, we can express the correlation by means of the correlation coefficient known as *Cramér's V*, developed by the Swedish mathematician and statistician Harald Cramér (1893–1985). This coefficient, which varies between 0 and 1, shows how strong the correlation is between the variables. Since the variables are at the nominal level, it makes no sense to distinguish between positive and negative correlation or positive and negative sign for the coefficient. If the variables at the nominal level are dichotomies, with the values 0 and 1, we can also use the correlation coefficient *phi*, after the Greek letter ϕ.

When the variables are at the ordinal level, we can also use different methods and coefficients for correlation analysis. One of these is *Spearman's rho*, developed by the British psychologist Charles Spearman (1863–1945) and usually denoted by the Greek letter ρ. In an article by Franzen (2003), this coefficient is used to examine the correlations between various environmental attitudes and gross domestic product (GDP) per capita in different countries. Another correlation coefficient is *Kendall's tau*, which was developed by the British statistician Maurice Kendall (1907–1983), and is denoted by the Greek letter τ. A third correlation coefficient for ordinal-level variables is *gamma*, launched by the American statisticians Leo Goodman (born 1928) and William Kruskal (1919–2005). The coefficient is denoted by the Greek letter γ. All of these coefficients are also called *rank correlation coefficients*, since they show the degree to which the units are ranked in the same way along both variables.

For variables at the interval and ratio level, the correlation coefficient *Pearson's r* is usually used. It was developed by the British statistician Karl Pearson (1857–1936). This coefficient is also called the *product-moment correlation coefficient*.

Two of the methods for correlation analysis, gamma and Pearson's r, will be described here.

The purpose is to show how these correlation coefficients are calculated and how they are interpreted.

Gamma

The gamma correlation coefficient shows the extent to which the units in a study are arranged or ranked equally or differently for the two variables analysed. For example, we can look again at the variables income and home size, and compare two different units with regard to their positions on these two variables. If one unit has both a higher income and a larger home than the other unit, the two units are ranked equally on the two variables. However, if one has a higher income but a smaller home than the other, the units are ranked differently on the two variables. We can thus make a paired comparison of all the units in the study.

The fact that the units are arranged or ranked equally for the two variables is an expression of a positive correlation between the variables. Different ranking of the units, however, signifies a negative correlation between the variables. The calculation of gamma is therefore based on the number of pairs of units that are ranked equally or similarly (N_s), relative to the number of pairs ranked differently (N_d). The calculation is made based on the formula

$$\gamma = \frac{N_s - N_d}{N_s + N_d}.$$

This formula is constructed so that gamma will vary between –1 and +1. If absolutely all the pairs of units are ranked differently on the two variables, we will have the strongest possible negative correlation between the variables. N_s is then equal to 0 (there are no pairs of units that are arranged equally), and gamma = $-N_d/N_d = -1$. We have the strongest possible positive correlation if absolutely all of the pairs of units are ranked equally on both variables. Then N_d equals 0, and gamma = $N_s/N_s = +1$.

If the number of pairs with the same ranking on both variables is as large as the number of pairs of different rankings on the two variables, there is no correlation between the variables. Then N_s is equal to N_d and we get gamma = $(N_d - N_d)/2N_d = 0$.

Calculation of gamma

How can we count the number of pairs that are ranked equally and the number of pairs that are ranked differently so that we can find N_s and N_d? We can show this based on the bivariate relationship between income and home size shown in Table 18.2. We do not use percentages when calculating gamma. We use absolute frequencies instead. The calculation is illustrated in Table 18.10.

We disregard the marginal distributions and concentrate on the frequencies for the combinations of values on the two variables. It is an advantage to arrange the values in the same order on both variables. In Table 18.10, both of the variables are set with the values in ascending order. We can find the number of pairs of units in the study by multiplying the frequency in each cell by the frequencies in all the other cells. To find the number of pairs of units *that are equally ranked for both variables* (N_s), we must multiply the frequency in each cell by all the frequencies below and to the right of the cell that we use as a basis. For example, we can look at the cell second from the top in the far left of the table, and compare it with the other cells. The 150 units in this cell have a low income and a medium-sized home. All of the units in the row above this cell have a smaller home, but they have an income that is equal to or higher than the 150 we are comparing with. This means a different ranking of the units for the two variables. The units in the two cells to the right of the 150 have the same size home, but higher income. This also implies a different ranking of the units. The units in the cell immediately below the 150 have larger

Table 18.10 Example of calculation of gamma: correlation between income and home size

	Income			
Home size	Low	Medium	High	Total
Small	250	100	50	400
Medium	150	400	50	600
Large	100	200	200	500
Total	500	700	300	1500

Calculation of the number of pairs ranked equally for both variables (N_s):

250	100	50	+	250	100	50	+	250	100	50	+	250	100	50
150	400	50		150	400	50		150	400	50		150	400	50
100	200	200		100	200	200		100	200	200		100	200	200

250(400+50+200+200) +   100(50+200) +   150(200+200)   +   400(200)

N_s = 250(850) + 100(250) +150(400) + 400(200) = 212,500 + 25,000 + 60,000+80,000 = 377,500

Calculation of the number of pairs that are ranked differently for the two variables (N_d):

250	100	50	+	250	100	50	+	250	100	50	+	250	100	50
150	400	50		150	400	50		150	400	50		150	400	50
100	200	200		100	200	200		100	200	200		100	200	200

50(150+400+100+200) +   100(150+100)   +   50(100+200)   +   400(100)

N_d = 50(850) + 100(250) + 50(300) + 400(100) = 42,500 + 25,000 + 15,000 + 40,000 = 122,500

$$\gamma = \frac{N_s - N_d}{N_s + N_d} = \frac{377,500 - 122,500}{377,500 + 122,500} = \frac{255,000}{500,000} = 0.51$$

homes, but equal income. Again, the ranking of the units is different for the two variables. The units in the two cells below and to the right of the 150, however, have both higher incomes and larger homes than the 150. This implies an equal ranking of the units for both variables. It is therefore the sum of the frequencies in *these* two cells that should be multiplied by the frequency 150. This cell combination is marked with blue numbers in the calculation of N_s in Table 18.10. The three other combinations of frequencies to be multiplied in order to calculate N_s are also marked with blue numbers.

Similarly, we can find the number of pairs of units *that are ranked differently for the two variables* (N_d). Then we need to multiply the frequency in each cell by all the frequencies below and to the left of the cell we are using as a basis. For example, we can look at the cell at the top right of the table. The 50 units in this cell that have a high income but a small home can be compared with the units in the other cells in the table. All of the units immediately below these 50 have a larger home, but not lower income, and all of the units to the left of the 50 have lower income, but not a larger home. Consequently, the units are not ranked differently for the two variables. Only the units in the four cells below and to the left of the 50 have both a lower value for one variable and a higher value for the other variable, that is, both a lower income and a larger home. Therefore, it is the frequencies in *these* four cells that should be multiplied by the 50 units. The sum of this multiplication and the other three multiplications required to calculate N_d, are marked with blue numbers in the cells for calculation of N_d in Table 18.10. Once we have calculated both N_s and N_d, we can put the numbers into the formula and calculate gamma, as shown at the bottom of Table 18.10. The calculation shows a gamma of 0.51. This is an expression of a fairly strong positive correlation between income and home size. Home size increases with increasing income.

Linear and nonlinear relationships

Gamma shows the strength and direction of the correlation, but not what *form* the correlation has. The form of the correlation can be illustrated by means of a *scattergram*. Such a diagram resembles

line charts for frequency distributions, as described in Chapter 17 (Figure 17.3). In both cases, the diagram consists of a horizontal and a vertical axis. In the scattergram, the values of one of the two variables are placed along the horizontal axis. The vertical axis does not have the frequencies for this variable, as is the case for a line diagram, but the values for the other variable instead. Each unit in the study is then marked with a point in the diagram. The point is the intersection of the vertical line from the unit's value on the horizontal axis, and the horizontal line from the unit's value on the vertical axis. Figure 18.4 shows how a unit with a medium income and a large home would be placed in such a scattergram.

Thus, each of the 1500 units in Table 18.10 can be marked with a point in the scattergram. Of these units, 200 have the mean income and a large home and would therefore be placed at the intersection marked in Figure 18.4. If we draw a line through the value combinations or points of intersection, where most of the units are located, this line would form a curve showing the form of the correlation between the variables. Table 18.10 shows that most of the units are in the intersection points that mark equal values for both variables: low income and small home size, medium income and medium home size, and high income and large home size. A total of 850 of the 1500 units have these value combinations. The line through these points constitutes the curve for the correlation between the two variables. This is illustrated in Figure 18.5.

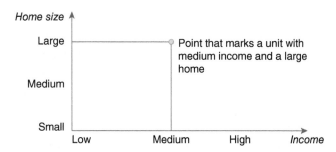

Figure 18.4 Example of the construction of a scattergram: correlation between income and home size

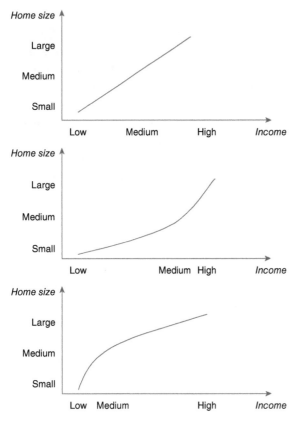

Figure 18.5 Graphical presentation of the correlation between income and home size: three different curve shapes

As Figure 18.5 shows, the shape of the curve, and hence the form of the correlation, can be presented in different ways. For positive correlations between variables at the ordinal level, there are essentially three different curve shapes. The shape of the curve will depend on how large is the distance between the variable values on the two axes in the diagram. The top curve is a straight line because there is an equal distance between the variable values on both axes. The curve rises continuously, and the increase is constant for the entire curve. When the curve appears as a straight line, the correlation is called *linear*. The other two curve shapes in Figure 18.5 are not linear. The entire curve rises, but the increase varies for different parts of the curve. Such correlations are called *monotonic*. Both linear and monotonic correlations can also be negative, so that the entire curve falls instead of rising. For linear negative correlations, all parts of the curve will fall equally.

For variables at the ordinal level, only the order between the values is fixed. The distances between the values can vary. Therefore, all three curve shapes in Figure 18.5 can be equally accurate representations of the correlation between income and home size. In other words, the correlation coefficient gamma is a measure of monotonic, but not linear, correlations. Linear correlations are meaningful only when the distances between the values for the variables are defined in a clear and unambiguous manner, as they are for variables at the interval or ratio level.

Pearson's *r*

Unlike gamma, Pearson's *r* is a correlation coefficient that takes account of distances between the values of the variables, and therefore requires that the variables are at interval or ratio level. Pearson's *r* is a measure of linear correlations between such variables. More precisely, this correlation coefficient expresses the extent to which there is a linear correlation between two variables.

What Pearson's *r* shows

In simple terms, we could say that Pearson's *r* is based on the dispersion around the mean for each of the variables and appears as a measure of how much of this dispersion is *common* to the two variables. The fact that the dispersion or the variance is common means that there is systematic covariation between the two variables. In other words, there is a systematic relationship between the units' values on one variable and their values on the other variable. The more of the dispersion that is common, the stronger the correlation between the variables.

As we have demonstrated earlier, the dispersion around the mean for each of the variables (x and y) is expressed as the standard deviation (s_x and s_y). The product of the two standard deviations ($s_x \cdot s_y$) expresses the combined dispersion for both the variables. The dispersion that is common to the two variables is expressed in a measure called the *covariance* (s_{xy}).

Pearson's r shows how large a proportion the common dispersion (covariance) represents of the combined dispersion (the product of the standard deviations). The calculation is based on the formula

$$r = \frac{s_{xy}}{s_x \cdot s_y}.$$

To calculate Pearson's r, we must find the standard deviation for each of the variables and the covariance between the variables. The standard deviation was described in Chapter 17. Let us now take a closer look at covariance. While the standard deviation for *one* variable is based on the individual units' distance from the mean, $(x - M_x)^2$ and $(y - M_y)^2$, the covariance between *two* variables is calculated based on each unit's distance to the mean for both variables, $(x - M_x)(y - M_y)$. The covariance is the average of this product of the deviations for all the units. The formula for the covariance (s_{xy}) is therefore

$$s_{xy} = \frac{1}{N} \cdot \sum (x - M_x)(y - M_y)$$

Figure 18.6 illustrates how the direction of the correlation is reflected in the sign of the covariance. The two axes represent the variables x and y. We have marked the means for the variables (M_x and M_y) on each of the axes. If we now mark each unit's position for the two variables with a point, this will be the scattergram for the variables x and y. As we can see, the lines based on the two averages will divide the scattergram into four fields. The sign of the covariance will depend on how the units are distributed on these fields. Units that have higher values than the means for both variables are located in the field to

the top right of the diagram. Both deviations from the averages will be positive, and the product of the two deviations will also be positive. If both the units have a lower value than the mean value for both variables (the field at the bottom left), both the deviations are negative and the product will be positive. If the units have a lower value than the mean for one of the variables and a higher value than the mean for the other variable (the top left and bottom right fields), one deviation will be positive and the other will be negative, so that their product will be negative.

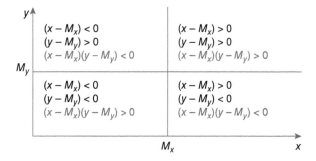

Figure 18.6 Overview of how the sign of the covariance depends on the location of the units relative to the means of the two variables

If there is a positive linear correlation between the variables, the curve in the scattergram will be rising. This means that there will be more units in the fields at the bottom left and top right than in the other two fields. Products with a positive sign will dominate compared to products with a negative sign. Thus, the covariance will be positive, as the correlation between the variables is positive. Similarly, a negative linear correlation between the variables will mean that the curve is evenly falling. The points of the units will then be located in the fields at the top left and bottom right. Negative products will dominate compared to positive products, and the covariance will be negative, as an expression of the negative correlation.

The formula for Pearson's r means that the coefficient will vary between −1 and +1. The strongest possible correlation between the variables entails that the entire dispersion is common for the two variables. The absolute value of the covariance will then be equal to the product of the standard deviations, so r = −1 or +1. If the correlation is negative, the covariance will have a negative sign, so that r = −1. If the correlation is positive, the covariance will have a positive sign, so r = +1. If there is no correlation between the two variables, the variables will not have any common dispersion. The covariance will be equal to 0 and we will have r = 0. The greater the proportion of the dispersion that is common, the greater the absolute value of the covariance, and the higher the absolute value of Pearson's r.

Calculation of Pearson's r

Let us look at how Pearson's r is calculated using a simple example. The example is based on the ten units in the data matrix presented in Chapter 17 (Table 17.1), and focuses on the two continuous variables 'number of visits to the cinema last month' and 'age'. Table 18.11 contains the key figures needed to calculate the standard deviation for each of the variables and the covariance between the two variables. For each variable, the table shows the units' values, deviation from the mean and the square of this deviation. In the rightmost column we have calculated the product of the deviations from the mean of both variables.

Table 18.11 Example of calculation of Pearson's r: correlation between age and number of visits to the cinema last month

Unit	Age (x)	(x − M_x)	(x − M_x)²	Number of visits to the cinema (y)	y − M_y	(y − M_y)²	(x − M_x) (y − M_y)
U1	23	−17	289	4	1	1	−17
U2	60	20	400	0	−3	9	−60
U3	44	4	16	1	−2	4	−8
U4	19	−21	441	10	7	49	−147
U5	66	26	676	0	−3	9	−78
U6	37	−3	9	6	3	9	−9
U7	38	−2	4	1	−2	4	4
U8	64	24	576	0	−3	9	−72
U9	21	−19	361	8	5	25	−95
U10	28	−12	144	0	−3	9	36
Total	400	0	2916	30	0	128	−446
Mean (M)	40			3			

Calculation of the standard deviation for age:

$$s_x = \sqrt{\frac{\sum (x - M_x)^2}{N}} = \sqrt{\frac{2916}{10}} = 17.08$$

Calculation of the standard deviation for the number of visits to the cinema:

$$s_y = \sqrt{\frac{\sum (y - M_y)^2}{N}} = \sqrt{\frac{128}{10}} = 3.58$$

Calculation of the covariance between age and number of visits to the cinema:

$$S_{xy} = \frac{1}{N} \times \sum (x - M_x)(y - M_y) = \frac{1}{10} \times (-446) = -44.6$$

Calculation of Pearson's r:

$$r_{xy} = \frac{S_{xy}}{S_x \times S_y} = \frac{-44.6}{17.08 \times 3.58} = -0.73$$

These key figures can be inserted into the formulas for standard deviation and covariance, and Pearson's *r* can then be calculated as shown in Table 18.11. It turns out that Pearson's *r* is –0.73. This is an expression of a negative correlation. The number of visits to the cinema decreases with increasing age.

We can see from the rightmost column of the table that negative products are dominant compared to positive products. This is also apparent from the scattergram in Figure 18.7. In the figure, the means (3 visits to the cinema and 40 years of age) are marked with lines, so that the scattergram is divided into four fields, similar to the scattergram in Figure 18.6. We can see that all the units, except two, are located in the top left and bottom right fields. If we drew in the straight line that lies as close as possible to the ten points in the scattergram, we would get a curve that started high up in the top left field and then descended down through the field at the bottom right of the scattergram.

Pearson's *r* is used by Franzen (2003) in an article on environmental attitudes in different countries. The coefficient is used to examine the correlation between an index for environmental concern and GDP per capita, as well as relative growth in GDP per capita. Using the countries as units of analysis, Pearson's *r* is 0.79 for GDP per capita and 0.60 for growth in GDP per capita, which indicate rather strong positive correlations. Furthermore, by using scattergrams, Franzen (2003: 302–305) shows that the correlations reflect basically linear relationships.

Regression analysis

While Pearson's correlation coefficient *r* shows the extent to which the correlation between two variables can be presented in the form of a straight line in the scattergram, a regression analysis will clarify where this line can be placed in the diagram.

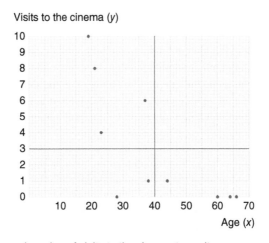

Figure 18.7   Scattergram for age and number of visits to the cinema: ten units

In contrast to correlation analysis, regression analysis assumes a dependency relation between variables. The analysis includes a dependent variable (the *y*-variable) and one or more independent variables (*x*-variables).

Regression analysis generally requires variables at the interval or ratio level, but may also include dummy variables and, occasionally, variables at the ordinal level, especially if these variables have many values and if we can assume even distances between the values. Generally, it is an advantage if each variable has a large number of values, except that dummy variables always have only two values (0 and 1). If the dependent variable is a dummy variable, we can also use a special form of regression analysis called *logistic regression*. This analysis method could be an alternative to table analysis. However, logistic regression will not be discussed here.

Regression analysis is used for both bivariate and multivariate relationships and is a suitable method for analysing relationships between many variables. For the sake of the simplest possible presentation, the most important methodological principles for regression analysis will be reviewed with reference to bivariate analyses. Then the features of multivariate regression analysis will be described. Multivariate regression analysis is usually called *multiple regression*.

The regression line

A bivariate regression analysis is based on the scattergram for the two variables. The dependent variable (*y*) is placed along the vertical axis of the graph, while the independent variable (*x*) is placed along the horizontal axis. Figure 18.7 is an example of this. The number of visits to the cinema is the dependent variable, and age is the independent variable.

Simply put, the main purpose of regression is to find the location of the straight line in the scattergram that best fits all the units in the data set. This line is called the *regression line*. No matter how the line is drawn, there will be a certain distance between this line and the actual location of the individual units. The challenge is to draw the best-fitting line, so that the sum of these distances for all units is minimized.

The distance between a unit's actual location and the regression line is assessed in relation to the dependent variable, and it will appear in the diagram as a vertical distance from the unit to the regression line. The distances can be calculated or estimated as a difference between the unit's value on the dependent variable and the value of the dependent variable that the regression line directly above or below the unit corresponds to. For those units that are located above the regression line, this difference will be positive. For the units below the line, the difference is negative. By a simple addition of the distances themselves, the positive and negative differences will offset each other. The differences are therefore squared, so that the negative signs are removed before performing the addition. It is therefore the squared deviations between the units and the regression line that are summed up, and this sum should be as small as possible. This regression method is therefore referred to as the *least-squares method*.

The regression equation

The location of the regression line is determined by a particular formula, called the *regression equation*:

$$y = a + bx + e,$$

where *y* is the dependent variable, *x* is the independent variable, *a* is the *constant*, *b* is the *slope*, also called the *regression coefficient*, and *e* is a *residual*.

The residual shows the size of the deviation between the regression equation and the actual location of the units in the diagram. If all the units were located on the regression line, *e* would be equal to 0, and the empirical relationship would be a perfectly linear correlation. Usually, empirical relationships are not completely linear. The units' location will appear as a larger or smaller dispersion around the regression line. The purpose of the least-squares method is to calculate where the regression line must be placed if the combined deviation between the regression line and the actual positions of the units is to be minimized. This involves finding the lowest possible value for e.

Based on the regression equation, the residual can be expressed as

$$e = y - (a + bx) = y - a - bx.$$

The main point in the regression analysis is not to identify the actual value of e, but rather to find the values of a and b that result in the lowest possible value of e. It is the values of a and b that show the location of the regression line. We find the best fit of the regression line to the units' actual positions when the values of a and b are calculated so that the value of e is minimized.

The constant (a) corresponds to the intersection of the regression line and the vertical axis (y-axis). Since the residual (e) expresses the deviation between the regression line and the actual positions of the units, the value of e is 0 for positions on the regression line itself. Thus, if $x = 0$ in the regression equation, then $y = a$. In other words, the constant is the probable value of the dependent variable for units with the value 0 for the independent variable.

The regression coefficient shows how steeply the regression line rises or falls in the scattergram. When b is positive, the line rises and the correlation is positive. When b is negative, the line falls, as the correlation is negative. In other words, the regression coefficient shows how much the value of the dependent variable increases or decreases when the value of the independent variable increases by one measurement unit. With reference to Figure 18.7, the regression coefficient shows how much the number of visits to the cinema decreases as age increases by one year.

To calculate the constant (a) and the regression coefficient (b) in order to obtain lowest possible

value for the residual (e), we can use a formula that is based on the means of the two variables (M_x and M_y), the covariance between the two variables (s_{xy}) and the standard deviation of the independent variable (s_x). The formula is

$$y - M_y = \frac{s_{xy}}{s_x^2}(x - M_x).$$

How this equation was developed will not be discussed here, but, by inserting the relevant numbers from Table 18.11, we can find the regression equation for the relationship between age and the number of visits to the cinema:

$$y - 3 = \frac{-44.6}{291.6}(x - 40)$$
$$y = -0.15x + 0.15 \cdot 40 + 3$$
$$= 9 - 0.15x.$$

In this example, $a = 9$ and $b = -0.15$. With this information, we can draw the regression line on the scattergram, as shown in Figure 18.8. The line intersects the y-axis at the value 9 visits to the cinema, and for each year the age increases, the number of visits to the cinema decreases by 0.15. As we can see, the line passes through the intersection of the mean values of the two variables. That will always be the case. We can see this if we put $x = M_x$ in the formula above. Then we will get $y = M_y$. As the figure shows, the vast majority of the units in the diagram are located at a certain distance from the regression line. Using the least-squares method based on the formula above, however, we have found the location for the regression line in the diagram which overall minimizes the distances between the line and the points for all units.

Since the regression line is a straight line, we only need two points on the line (the intersection of the regression line and the y-axis, and the intersection of the mean values for the two variables) in order to draw the entire line. In this example, the calculation of the constant ($a = 9$) has only theoretical interest to determine the intersection of the regression line and the y-axis. In practice, of course, the number of visits to the

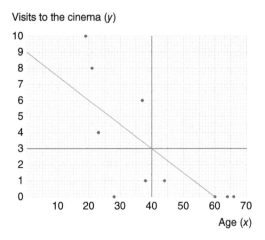

Visits to the cinema (y)

Age (x)

Figure 18.8 Scattergram and regression line (highlighted line) for age and number of visits to the cinema: ten units

cinema is not 9 for persons who are 0 years of age. The substantive significance of the regression line applies for the age groups from 19 years (which is the age of the youngest unit in the material) and older.

The fact that the regression coefficient (*b*) has a negative sign is consistent with the fact that the correlation between these two variables is negative. The regression line is falling from left to right in the scattergram. If the correlation between the variables were positive, the regression coefficient would be positive. The regression line would be rising from left to right in the scattergram.

The stronger the correlation between the two variables, the greater the absolute value of the regression coefficient (*b*). However, this absolute value depends not only on the strength of the correlation, but also on the measurement units of the two variables. In principle, this absolute value also has no upper limit. This regression coefficient is therefore referred to as an *unstandardized regression coefficient*. Such unstandardized coefficients cannot be regarded directly as an expression of the strength of the effect that the independent variable has on the dependent variable. They also cannot be used to compare the effects of different independent variables, especially because different variables may have different measurement units. For example, the variable 'age' is measured in years, while the variable income is measured in euros.

However, the regression coefficients can be standardized so that they become independent of varying units of measurement for the different variables. The basis for this standardization is the standard deviations for the two variables. The *standardized regression coefficient*, called *beta* (and denoted by the Greek letter β), is calculated by multiplying the unstandardized regression coefficient (*b*) by the ratio between the standard deviations for the independent and the dependent variable:

$$\beta = b \frac{s_x}{s_y}.$$

We can insert the figures for the regression coefficient (*b*) from the regression analysis above, and for the standard deviations (s_x and s_y) from Table 18.11, and thus find the value for beta in our example:

$$\beta = -0.15 \cdot \frac{17.08}{3.58} = -0.72.$$

This is an expression for the negative effect of age (*x*) on the number of visits to the cinema (*y*). Beta has fixed limits and varies between –1 and +1, regardless of the variables' units of measurement. The stronger the effect that the independent variable (*x*) has on the dependent variable (*y*), the higher the absolute value of beta. The sign of beta shows whether the effect is positive or negative.

When there is no correlation between the two variables, beta will be equal to 0.

Beta, however, is not only affected by the correlation between the two variables (x and y), but also by the units' dispersion on the two variables. The larger this dispersion is, the greater the standard deviations (s_x and s_y) will be. As we can see from the formula for beta, the larger s_x is, the larger beta will be, and the larger s_y is, the smaller beta will be.

This means that it is not entirely unproblematic to interpret standardized regression coefficients as an expression of the strength of an effect, even if the standardized coefficients are more suitable for such interpretations than unstandardized regression coefficients.

Explained variance

In bivariate regression analysis with only one independent variable in addition to the dependent variable, the standardized regression coefficient (beta) is equal to the correlation coefficient (Pearson's r). In this example, there is a small difference between Pearson's r in Table 18.11 (–0.73) and beta above (–0.72). This is due to inaccuracies related to the rounding of the figures in the calculations.

In the review of correlation analysis, it was mentioned that Pearson's r can be regarded as an expression of how much of the total dispersion in the two variables is common to both the variables. In regression analysis, where we distinguish between dependent and independent variables, the question will be how much of the total dispersion on the dependent variable is explained by the independent variable. In this connection, the dispersion is not expressed in the form of standard deviations, but as variance, and the stronger the correlation between the two variables, the greater the proportion of the total variance in the dependent variable that can be explained by the independent variable. The proportion of variance explained (R^2) is not expressed directly by Pearson's r, but rather by the square of Pearson's r:

$$R^2 = r_{xy}^2.$$

Since Pearson's r varies between –1 and 1, R^2 will vary between 0 and 1. R^2 is thus a more direct measure of the *proportion* of the total dispersion that is common to the two variables. If we insert Pearson's r for the relationship between age and education (from Table 18.11), we find how large a proportion of the total variance in the variable 'number of visits to the cinema' is explained by age:

$$R^2 = (-0.73)^2 = 0.53.$$

This means that 53% of the total variance in the number of visits to the cinema is explained by age.

The proportion of variance explained is thus a measure of how strong an effect the independent variable (x) has on the dependent variable (y). As a measure of the strength of the effect, the proportion of variance explained (R^2) can be used instead of or in addition to the standardized regression coefficient (beta).

Multiple regression analysis

Regression analyses will often involve more than two variables. Such analyses are useful for investigating the effects of many different independent variables on a single dependent variable. The regression equation for the correlations between a dependent variable (y) and four independent variables (x_1, x_2, x_3, x_4) would look like this:

$$y = a + b_1 x_1 + b_2 x_2 + b_3 x_3 + b_4 x_4 + e.$$

As in bivariate regression analysis, we have a constant (a) and a residual (e), but a separate regression coefficient is calculated for each independent variable (b_1, b_2, b_3, b_4). The regression coefficient for each variable is an expression of the correlation between this independent variable and the dependent variable, controlled for the other independent variables.

In multiple regression, the least-squares method is used to find the values of the constant (*a*) and all the regression coefficients (*b*) for all the independent variables that give the least possible value for the residual (*e*). Since the analysis includes several independent variables, the regression equation will not represent a single line in a two-dimensional diagram. The equation involves different dimensions in a multidimensional 'space'. It is not easy to illustrate this by means of diagrams, and it is also not easy to imagine how the adaptation of the regression equation appears in relation to the actual pattern of units in this 'space'.

In the regression equation, the constant (*a*) shows what value the dependent variable (*y*) has when all the independent variables (*x*) have the value 0. The regression coefficient for a particular independent variable shows how much the value of the dependent variable changes when the value of this particular independent variable changes with a measurement unit, while the values of all the other independent variables remain unchanged. For example, b_2 will show how much the value of *y* changes when x_2 changes by one measurement unit and all the other *x*s are held constant.

In multiple regression, we find the effects of various independent variables as they are expressed through the regression coefficients. The effect of each independent variable is then controlled for the effects of all the other independent variables, so that the analysis also takes account of any spurious correlations. Multiple regression allows us to compare the effects of the various independent variables. The unstandardized regression coefficients (*b*) are not directly comparable because the independent variables may have different units of measurement (e.g. age in years and income in euros). Therefore, we usually use the standardized regression coefficients (beta) to compare the effects of the independent variables (*x*) on the dependent variable (*y*). The standardized coefficients are

calculated or estimated in the same way in multiple regression as in bivariate regression.

When comparing the beta values for the various independent variables, we must remember that these values are not only expressions of the effects of the variables, but also affected by the dispersion on the variables, expressed as the variables' standard deviation. When we compare the effects of different independent variables on the same dependent variable based on the same regression equation, the standard deviation for the dependent variable will be common to the calculation of all the beta values. It is therefore the standard deviation of the independent variables that can affect the beta values differently for the different independent variables.

These properties of the beta values must also be taken into account if we compare beta values from regression analyses based on different samples of units. In regression analyses of samples from two different countries with income as a dependent variable and education as one of the independent variables, for example, we can find different beta values for education in the two countries. This may be interpreted as a stronger effect of education on income in one country than in the other, but the beta value may also be affected by differences between the two countries as to the distributions of income and education. By comparing the standard deviations for each of these variables in the two countries, we can assess whether it is reasonable to interpret the beta coefficients as expressions of the strength of the effects.

The proportion of variance explained (R^2) can also be calculated in multiple regression. Here, R^2 will show how much of the variance in the dependent variable (*y*) is explained by all the independent variables (*x*) combined. While the regression coefficients (*b* or beta) show how strong an effect each of the independent variables has on the dependent variable, controlled for the other independent variables, the proportion of variance explained (R^2) is an expression of the overall explanatory power of all the independent variables combined.

Multiple regression can be carried out in several steps. We can add a new independent variable at each step. The change in the proportion of variance explained from one step to the next will then be an expression of how strong an effect the new independent variable has on the dependent variable, controlled for the effects of the other independent variables that are included in the analysis. By varying which independent variables are included in the multiple regression, we can use the proportion of variance explained as a basis for comparing the effects of the independent variables. Like the standardized regression coefficients, the proportion of variance explained can be an expression of the strength of the effects.

In multiple regression, we can also analyse the interaction between different independent variables. As pointed out in the discussion of table analysis (see Table 18.9), interaction between two independent variables entails that the effect of one independent variable on the dependent variable differs for different values on the other independent variable. For example, the effect of income on home size may be stronger among older people than among younger people. There is then an interaction between the income variable and the age variable with respect to the effect of these two variables on the home size variable.

In regression analysis, we can identify interaction between two independent variables by calculating a separate coefficient for the product of the two independent variables. In the following regression equation, b_5 will be an expression of the interaction between the variables x_1 and x_2:

$$y = a + b_1x_1 + b_2x_2 + b_3x_3 + b_4x_4 + b_5x_1 \cdot x_2 + e.$$

Referring to our example, the dependent variable (y) could be home size, while x_1 could be income and x_2 could be age (x_3 and x_4 would be two other independent variables). The regression coefficient b_5 would then be larger, the stronger the interaction between income (x_1) and age (x_2). If there is no interaction, b_5 will be equal to 0.

Multiple regression analysis was used in a study by Johnson and Ali (2004) to examine how different countries' participation and medal-winning success at the Olympic Games can be explained by economic and political factors. Different analyses were performed with participation and medal-winning as the dependent variables (y). In each of these analyses, 13 independent variables ($x_1, ..., x_{13}$) were included as specifications of economic and political factors. By comparing the beta coefficients, the researchers concluded that 'socioeconomic variables explain Olympic participation and success remarkably well' (Johnson and Ali, 2004: 974).

Furthermore, Halikoupoulou and Vlandas (2016) used multiple regression in a study of how the success of far right parties in elections to the European Parliament can be explained. Analysing different European countries, with country as the unit of analysis, the researchers defined the support for far right parties as the dependent variable (y) in several regression analyses, which included a number of independent variables (x), mainly related to economy, unemployment and labour market institutions. Comparison of the beta coefficients showed an effect of unemployment on the support for far right parties, but only in countries without well-developed labour market institutions, including unemployment regulations and dismissal regulations. The multiple regression analyses were conducted in several steps, gradually increasing the number of independent variables. The proportion of variance explained (R^2) by all the independent variables was 0.44.

- Table analysis can be both bivariate and multivariate. The analysis involves a small number of variables with a small number of values for each variable. Usually, one of the variables is considered dependent and the others as independent. The analysis can be used at all measurement levels, but is most common at the nominal and ordinal level.
- Table analysis involves comparing conditional distributions. Percentage difference (absolute value) is a measure of the strength of the relationship.
- Multivariate table analysis controls for spuriosity and clarifies:
  1. How strong an effect each of the independent variables has on the dependent variable
  2. Whether there is interaction between the independent variables.
- Correlation analysis is bivariate. The variables are considered to be symmetrical and may have many values. There are different correlation coefficients for different measurement levels:
  1. Gamma is used at the ordinal level. The coefficient shows the extent to which the units are ranked equally or unequally on the two variables. Gamma varies between –1 and +1 and explains the strength and direction of monotonic correlations.

2. Pearson's r is used at interval or ratio levels. The coefficient is an expression of what proportion of the dispersion around the mean for each of the two variables is common for both variables. Pearson's r varies between –1 and +1 and explains the strength and direction of linear correlations.

- Regression analysis can be either bivariate or multivariate. The analysis is suitable for analysing correlations between a dependent and one or more independent variables. As a rule, the interval or ratio level is required. The variables usually have many values.
- Regression analysis involves finding the straight line (regression line) in the scattergram that has the best fit to all units. This is achieved by calculating an equation (the regression equation).
- Multiple regression controls for spuriosity and explains:
  1. How strong an effect each of the independent variables has on the dependent variable (expressed through standardized regression coefficients)
  2. How large a proportion of the variance in the dependent variable is explained using all the independent variables (expressed by R^2).

I recommend that you read the publications used as research examples in this chapter.

Franzen, Axel (2003) 'Environmental attitudes in international comparison: An analysis of the ISSP Surveys 1993 and 2000', *Social Science Quarterly* 84(2), 297–308.

This article examines relationships between economy and environmental attitudes in different countries. Both Spearman's rho and Pearson's r are used as correlation coefficients. Using country as the unit of analysis, an index of environmental concerns is found to be strongly correlated with GDP per capita as well as with relative growth in GDP per capita: Pearson's r is found to be 0.79 and 0.60 for the two correlations. Scattergrams are presented to show that these correlations reflect basically linear relationships.

Johnson, Daniel K. N., and Ayfer Ali (2004) 'A tale of two seasons: Participation and medal counts at the Summer and Winter Olympic Games', *Social Science Quarterly* 85(4), 974–993.

The purpose of this article is to examine how different countries' participation and medal-winning success at the Olympic Games can be explained by economic and political factors. Referring to country as the unit of analysis, the authors present different multiple regression analyses with participation and medal-winning at the Olympic Games as the dependent variables. In each of these analyses, 13 independent variables are included as specifications of economic and political factors. By comparing the beta coefficients, the researchers conclude that 'socioeconomic variables explain Olympic participation and success remarkably well' (Johnson and Ali, 2004: 974).

Halikoupoulou, Daphne, and Tim Vlandas (2016) 'Risks, costs and labour markets: Explaining cross-national patterns of far right party success in European Parliament elections', *Journal of Common Market Studies* 54, 636–655.

This article presents a study of how the success of far right parties in elections to the European Parliament can be explained. With country as the unit of analysis, the researchers define support for far right parties as the dependent variable in several regression analyses, which include a number of independent variables, mainly related to economy, unemployment and labour market institutions. Comparison of the beta coefficients show an effect of unemployment on the support for far right parties, but only in countries without well-developed labour market institutions, including unemployment regulations and dismissal regulations. The multiple regression analyses are conducted in several steps, gradually increasing the number of independent variables. The proportion of variance explained (R^2) by all the independent variables is 0.44.

STUDENT EXERCISES AND QUESTIONS

1 What is the difference between bivariate and multivariate analyses?
2 What is the difference between a conditional distribution and a marginal distribution in a contingency table?
3 Why do we control for spurious relationships between variables?
4 What are the differences between the correlation coefficients gamma and Pearson's r?
5 Why do we need variables at the interval or ratio level of measurement to do a regression analysis?
6 What relationship between education and income is expressed by the regression equation $y = 20 + 5x$ (where x is education measured in years, and y is income measured in thousands of euros per year)? The residual, e, can be disregarded in this discussion.
7 Consider the hypothetical data in Table 18.12 and discuss the following questions:
   a What are the variables in the table?
   b What are the values and measurement level of each variable?
   c Which of the variables is dependent, and which variables are independent?
   d What are the relationships between the variables, in terms of effects and interaction?

Table 18.12 Attitude to the EU conditional on gender and age

| | Women | | Men | | |
Attitude to EU	20-50 years of age	51-80 years of age	20-50 years of age	51-80 years of age	Total
Positive	40	30	65	30	41
Negative	60	70	35	70	59
Total	100%	100%	100%	100%	100%

RECOMMENDED LITERATURE

Foster, Liam, Ian Diamond, and Julie Banton (2014) *Beginning Statistics: An Introduction for Social Scientists* (2nd edn). London: Sage.

This book presents basic principles in statistics for students with no prior knowledge or experience. It is a step-by-step guide to using statistics. The book describes concepts and explains statistical analysis, referring to tables and graphs, correlation and regression. Graphs and displays are used as illustrations of main points, and examples from real research are provided.

Schroeder, Larry D., David L. Sjoquist, and Paula E. Stephan (2017) *Understanding Regression Analysis: An Introductory Guide* (2nd edn). London: Sage.

This book presents the fundamentals of regression analysis, including what it means and how it is used. The presentation is concise and non-technical. The estimation, interpretation and use of regression coefficients in different disciplines are explained in intuitive ways. The book includes few equations, but many examples.

Treiman, Donald J. (2009) *Quantitative Data Analysis: Doing Social Research to Test Ideas*. San Francisco: Jossey-Bass.

This book is an introduction to quantitative data analysis, including how to decide which statistical procedure is suitable, and how to interpret the subsequent results. Table analysis as well as correlation analysis and regression analysis are described and explained. A number of examples are used as illustrations of how various methods of analysis are used in research.

STATISTICAL GENERALIZATION

This chapter provides the necessary knowledge for understanding how empirical findings can be generalized from a probability sample of units to the larger universe of the units.

The chapter will teach you about

- the difference between random and systematic errors
- the basic characteristics of sampling distributions
- the difference between estimation and hypothesis testing

- the distinction between Type I error and Type II error
- the essentials of different types of hypothesis testing.

Inductive statistics

In Chapters 17 and 18, methods of analysis were discussed with reference to *descriptive statistics*, the purpose of which is to describe patterns or trends in the data being analysed. This chapter is focused on *inductive statistics*, whose purpose is to clarify how findings based on a sample of units can be generalized to a larger universe of the units. Inductive statistics may also be call *inferential statistics*.

The prerequisite for this form of statistical generalization is that the study is based on a probability sample of the units in the universe. In the review of probability sampling in Chapter 8, it was pointed out that there are always certain statistical margins of error associated with such samples. These margins of error are due to random differences between the sample and the universe. The size of these differences will vary from sample to sample. For specific findings in a particular study, we need to calculate how large the margins of error can be assumed to be for the specific sample on which these findings are based. Such calculations form an important part of the statistical generalization.

However, differences between actual conditions in the universe, and the knowledge about these conditions that is obtained from a sample study, are not only due to the margins of error in the sampling of the units. As pointed out in Part III of this book, on the collection and quality of data,

different types of systematic errors can occur during data collection. Such errors occur in addition to the random errors associated with the sampling. In statistical generalization, only the random errors are taken into account.

Before the review of different methods of statistical generalization, therefore, the relationship between random and systematic errors will be discussed. Then, the calculation of margins of error in probability samples will be described. Next, two main types of statistical generalization are examined. One of these is called estimation. The second type of generalization is called hypothesis testing. Three different methods of hypothesis testing will be considered. One of these is a chi-square test, which is used in connection with table analysis. Another method is the *t*-test, which is used for correlation analysis and for each regression coefficient in regression analysis. A third method is the *F*-test, or analysis of variance, which is used for regression analysis, either for several of the coefficients together, or for the entire regression equation.

Random and systematic errors

The purpose of statistical generalization is to clarify whether empirical findings based on data from a probability sample are valid for the larger universe from which the sample is drawn. We must always expect certain deviations between the findings and the corresponding conditions in the universe as a whole. The challenge for statistical generalization is to calculate how large these deviations can be assumed to be.

There are several different reasons for the deviations between the findings in a study and the conditions in the universe. One of these causes is deviations arising from the actual sampling. The advantage of probability sampling is that the deviations from the universe will then be *random* and that they can be calculated using statistical methods. It was pointed out in Chapter 8 that such margins of error will be reduced if we increase the size of the sample, and that the margins of error will be greater if we want to increase the certainty of the generalization.

The other causes of deviations between the empirical findings and the corresponding conditions in the universe are linked to various types of problems during data collection. Two main types of problems are important in this context. One of these problem types is the *drop-out* of units from the original sample. The final data set does not necessarily include all of the units that were included in the original sample. Some of the sampled units may be difficult to find, and some of the units in the sample may not be available for data collection. In a content analysis, selected texts may no longer exist or the researcher may no longer have access to them. In an observation study, some of the selected actors may not be present when the observation is conducted or they may not be willing to be observed. In a survey based on a questionnaire, drop-out can occur because some of the selected respondents cannot be traced and because some respondents cannot or will not participate in the study.

The consequence of drop-out during data collection is that the final data set and the empirical findings are not based on all of the original sample,

but on a smaller sample. As pointed out earlier, drop-out can lead to *systematic* deviations from the original sample. In that case, there will also be systematic differences between the results of the analysis and the conditions in the universe. This will occur, for example, if we wish to compare different age groups in a study where there has been a particularly high drop-out rate among the oldest people in the sample.

The second main type of problems during data collection is related to the quality of the data recorded. Even though we obtain data about most of the units in the original probability sample, the quality of the data may still not be satisfactory. As described in Chapter 15, both *reliability* and *validity* must be assessed before we can have confidence in a particular set of data and the findings based on these data.

Like drop-out problems, low reliability or low validity will usually lead to *systematic* discrepancies between the results of the analysis and the corresponding conditions in the universe. The data can provide a systematically biased impression of the conditions among the units included in the study. In other words, low reliability or validity can lead to significant differences between the empirical findings and the corresponding conditions in the universe, because the findings do not even match the actual conditions in the sample itself.

For statistical generalization, only the random margins of error associated with the sampling are considered. Systematic errors due to drop-out, low reliability or low validity are not taken into account by the statistical methods for generalizing from the sample to the universe. It is therefore important to perform separate assessments of such systematic errors. We must assess how extensive the systematic errors can be, as well as the extent to which they can be expected to lead to particular bias in the data, compared to the corresponding conditions in the universe. If the data are systematically biased, the statistical generalization will be of little value. In other words, the prerequisite for a meaningful statistical generalization is that we start with a probability sample and that neither drop-out problems, reliability problems nor validity problems lead to significant bias of the data. The possibilities for such bias should therefore be considered before we perform statistical generalization of the analysis results.

Sampling distribution and margin of error

Before different methods of statistical generalization are described, the statistical and probability theory basis for such generalization will be reviewed.

Table 17.5 in Chapter 17 shows the distribution of attitudes to the European Union in a probability sample of 1500 units. The table shows that 45% of the units in the sample are opposed to the EU (negative or strongly negative). Let us assume that this sample is a simple random sample of the British population and that 46% of the population are opposed to the EU. If the study is otherwise conducted 'flawlessly', this difference between 46% in the universe and 45% in the sample will be due to chance.

If we draw many random samples with 1500 people from the population, opposition to the EU in these samples will vary. Some samples will have more than 46% opposed, and other samples will have less. In the vast majority of the samples, the proportion of those opposed will be close to 46%, and in a few samples the proportion will be significantly smaller or significantly greater. We can consider the distribution of all these samples as a univariate frequency distribution, where each *sample* is a unit and the percentage of EU opponents in the sample is the variable. Figure 19.1 is a graphical presentation of this in the form of a line chart.

The frequency distribution presented in Figure 19.1 is a probability distribution, which is called the *sampling distribution*. It has been demonstrated statistically that such sampling distributions will appear as normal distributions. The formulation of this statistical insight is referred to as the *central limit theorem*. According to this theorem, the mean of the percentages of EU opponents in all the samples will be equal to the actual percentage of EU opponents in the universe. For the majority of the samples, the percentage will be equal to or close to this mean. There will be an equal number of samples with a higher and a lower percentage, and the farther away from the mean we move on the horizontal axis, the fewer samples there will

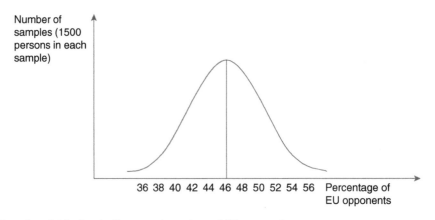

Figure 19.1 Sampling distribution for the percentage share of EU opponents

be for each value. The curve has the same shape on both sides of the average.

The knowledge that the sampling distribution has this shape is of major importance in inductive statistics. The fact that the distribution has the characteristics of a normal distribution is an important basis for statistical generalization. One of the characteristics of normal distributions is that there is a clear relationship between the distance from the mean value, measured in the number of standard deviations, and the proportion of the samples that are located within this distance from the mean. This can be clarified if the normal distribution is standardized, so that the mean is given the value 0 and the standard deviation is given the value 1. These values, which express the number of standard deviations on each side of the average, are called z-values, or z-scores. This standard deviation for a sampling distribution is called the *standard error*.

It has been demonstrated statistically that, for example, 95% of the samples in a sampling distribution are within 1.96 standard errors of either side of the mean (z = ±1.96). This is illustrated in Figure 19.2. Similarly, 99% of the samples have been shown to be within 2.58 standard errors of either side of the mean (z = ±2.58).

We can calculate (see below) that the distance of 1.96 standard errors in this case corresponds to 2.5 percentage points, so that in 95% of a large number of random samples with 1500 people from the same population, the percentage of EU opponents will be between 43.5 and 48.5. In other words, in any random sample of this size, there is a 95% probability that the percentage of EU opponents will be within this range. When we find 45% EU opponents in our one sample, then this is a very likely result.

In this simplified presentation of the probability theory basis for statistical generalization, the starting point has been the actual percentage in the universe, and it has been shown what percentages are likely to be found in different random samples from this universe. In the actual generalization, the reasoning is in the opposite direction. The reason for the generalization is precisely that we *do not* have knowledge of the conditions in the universe. On the contrary, based on knowledge of specific characteristics of the sample, we want to show what probably characterizes the universe. Simply put, we employ the same reasoning about the relationship between the number of standard errors and the proportion of samples in the sampling

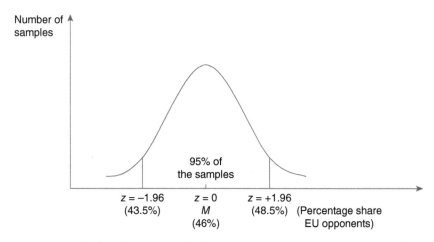

Figure 19.2 Sampling distribution for the percentage of EU opponents: the relationship between the number of standard errors (z) and the proportion of samples

distribution, but we start with the empirical findings and the standard deviation in the sample instead of the real attributes of the universe. Since we do not know the standard error of the sampling distribution, we use instead the standard deviation for the percentage of EU opponents in the sample, which can be calculated.

Methods of generalization

We distinguish between two main types of statistical generalization. One key type is called *estimation*. The starting point for estimation is a particular finding regarding a characteristic of the sample, such as the percentage of EU opponents or the mean income in the sample. The estimation is based on calculating a probable minimum value and a probable maximum value for the corresponding feature in the universe.

The second main type of generalization method is called *hypothesis testing*. Simply put, hypothesis testing is about clarifying whether a relationship between different features of the sample is strong enough to assume that the relationship also applies to the corresponding relationship in the universe.

Estimation and hypothesis testing are based on the same probability theory foundation, but the two types of generalization are somewhat different in terms of purpose and procedure. Let us now take a closer look at estimation and hypothesis testing.

Estimation and confidence intervals

The probability that a particular finding in the sample can also be assumed to apply in the universe is assessed on the basis of the number of standard deviations from the measure that is calculated for the sample. Once again, we can use the example of the proportion of EU opponents.

The starting point is that the percentage of EU opponents in the probability sample of 1500 persons turns out to be 45%. There is then a 95% probability that the percentage of EU opponents in the population will be within a range of 1.96 standard deviations from 45%.

The procedure for calculating the standard deviation varies between different measures. For the measure 'percentage', or 'proportion', the calculation is based on the formula

$$s = \sqrt{\frac{p(1-p)}{N}},$$

where p is the proportion (45% corresponds to the proportion 0.45), N is the number of units, and s is the standard deviation for the proportion.

If we enter the relevant figures, we get

$$s = \sqrt{\frac{0.45(1-0.45)}{1500}} = 0.0128.$$

The distance of 1.96 standard deviations will thus be

$$1.96\,s = 1.96 \cdot 0.0128 = 0.025.$$

This corresponds to 2.5 percentage points, so that there is a 95% probability that the percentage of EU opponents in the population is between 45% − 2.5% and 45% + 2.5%, that is, between 42.5% and 47.5%. This range is an expression of the statistical margin of error associated with the sample. This is called the *confidence interval* for the percentage of EU opponents and can also be expressed as 45% ± 2.5%. In other words, the confidence interval is the distance between the probable minimum value and the probable maximum value for the relevant feature of the universe – in this case the percentage of EU opponents in the population.

The confidence interval always refers to a certain *level of confidence*. The level of confidence is the probability that we are correct when we claim that the real percentage in the universe lies within the confidence interval. In this case, the level of confidence is 95%.

We *choose* a certain level of confidence and *calculate* the confidence interval based on the selected level of confidence. It is common to choose a level of confidence of at least 95%. We can choose a higher level in order to be even more certain that the generalization is valid. The consequence will be that the generalization becomes less *precise*, because the confidence interval is larger. As mentioned above, for 99% confidence we must multiply the standard deviation by 2.58 instead of 1.96:

$$2.58s = 2.58 \cdot 0.0128 = 0.033.$$

Expressed in percentage points, the confidence interval at this level of confidence is thus 45% ±3,3%, that is, between 41.7% and 48.3%.

Hypothesis testing

The purpose of hypothesis testing is to clarify whether a particular relationship that has been demonstrated in the sample can be assumed with a certain level of probability to apply in the universe. The starting point is a hypothesis (H_1) about a particular relationship, such as

H_1: There is a relationship between income and home size.

This hypothesis can be investigated on the basis of Table 18.4, which was used as an example in the review of table analysis in Chapter 18.

The table shows that there is a clear relationship between income and home size, with a percentage difference of 23%. The question now is whether this relationship is strong enough for us to say, with a high level of probability, that it is not due to random differences between the sample and the universe. To clarify this, we formulate a hypothesis that there is *no* relationship between the two variables. This hypothesis is called the *null hypothesis* (H_0):

H_0: There is no relationship between income and home size.

The hypothesis test does not focus on the actual hypothesis, but on the null hypothesis.

The reason is that it is statistically easier to *reject* a hypothesis than to prove that a hypothesis is correct. If the null hypothesis cannot be rejected, we still cannot assume that the actual hypothesis is correct, or proved. If the null hypothesis can be rejected, the actual hypothesis will be strengthened and we can assume that the relationship in the sample also applies to the universe. This thinking corresponds to the reasoning that underlies the search for deviating cases in qualitative analyses, as discussed in Chapter 16.

Thus, the purpose of hypothesis testing is to clarify whether or not the null hypothesis should be rejected. In the same way as in estimation, we must decide how certain we wish to be when we reject the null hypothesis. We risk committing one of two types of errors. On the one hand, we may risk rejecting a null hypothesis that is correct. This is called a *Type I error*. On the other hand, we may risk that an incorrect null hypothesis is not rejected. This would be a *Type II error*.

Compared to the actual hypothesis in the study (H_1), the consequence of a Type I error is that we mistakenly consider the hypothesis as strengthened, while the consequence of a Type II error is that the hypothesis is mistakenly rejected. In a scientific context, the first type of error is usually regarded as more serious or more worrying than the second. Making an error when we reject the actual hypothesis is therefore more acceptable than making an error when we accept the hypothesis. Basically, scepticism is considered to be the most important factor. The correct strategy is to be especially certain before accepting a statement as truth. Thus, we can have great confidence in those hypotheses that pass this stringent test.

For hypothesis testing, therefore, we place the greatest emphasis on avoiding Type I errors. The consequence of rejecting a null hypothesis that is correct would be that we incorrectly accept the actual hypothesis concerning a particular relationship. We want to minimize this risk. Generally, we will reject the null hypothesis only if it is at least 95% likely that it is incorrect. This means that there is less than a 5% probability that we will be wrong when the null hypothesis is rejected. This risk probability (p) is usually expressed in terms of a proportion instead of a percentage ($p < 0.05$) and is called the *significance level*. This corresponds to a 95% level of confidence in estimation. Compared to the probability distribution in Figure 19.2, a significance level of $p < 0.05$ has the following meaning: if the null hypothesis is to be rejected, the H_1 relationship must be so strong in our sample that there is at least a 95% probability that it will exist in any corresponding sample from the same universe. In that case, the relationship is *significant* at this level of significance.

That the relationship is significant is a prerequisite for it to be generalized from the sample to the universe. Therefore, hypothesis testing is also referred to as *significance testing*.

We can choose a higher level of significance if we wish to be even more certain. We usually distinguish between two significance levels in addition to $p < 0.05$. We can require that the probability of making an error when the null hypothesis is rejected should be less than 1% ($p < 0.01$) or less than 0.1% ($p < 0.001$). The higher the significance level we choose, the stronger the relationship must be in the sample (H_1) for the null hypothesis (H_0) to be rejected. The relationship must be stronger in order to be considered significant.

There are various methods to clarify whether or not the null hypothesis should be rejected. All of these methods are based on the characteristics of the sampling distribution as a normal distribution, as described above. The method that is best suited to a specific hypothesis test will depend on the type of relationship to be investigated. Examples of three different methods will be demonstrated here: the chi-square test, the *t*-test and the *F*-test.

These methods involve calculating the chi-square value, the *t*-value or the *F*-value for the relationship between the variables specified in H_1. These values are called *test estimators*. The stronger the relationship between the variables in H_1, the higher the chi-square-value, *t*-value or *F*-value for the relationship will be. It is the size of these values that forms the basis for the assessment of the null hypothesis: at a certain level of significance, the chi-square value, *t*-value or *F*-value must be greater than a certain *critical value,* if the null hypothesis is to be rejected. In other words, the value of the selected test estimator must be greater than the critical value if the empirical relationship is to be considered significant and generalized from the sample to the universe.

The critical values for the chi-square distribution, *t*-distribution and *F*-distribution at different levels of significance are presented in statistical critical value tables.

Chi-square test

Chi-square tests are usually used for table analysis. Let us look at how we can calculate the *chi-square value* for a particular relationship. We start with H_1, that there is a relationship between income and home size, and we look at the table analysis of this relationship in Table 18.4 in Chapter 18. H_0 would then be that there is no relationship between income and home size.

Chi-square takes its name from the Greek letter χ and is written χ^2. The formula for the calculation is as follows:

$$\chi^2 = \sum \frac{\left(f_o - f_e\right)^2}{f_e}.$$

Here, f_o is the observed (actual) frequencies in our table analysis, and f_e is the expected frequencies if there is no relationship between the variables, that is, the frequencies as they would be if H_0 is correct. The stronger the relationship is, the greater the difference between the observed and the expected frequencies ($f_o - f_e$). When this difference is squared, $(f_o - f_e)^2$, the problem that some of these differences may have a negative sign is eliminated. By dividing the squared difference by the expected frequency, $(f_o - f_e)^2 / f_e$, a certain adjustment is made for differences between the frequencies in the different cells in the table. This calculation is performed for each cell in the table, and the results of the calculations for all the cells are added together in order to find the chi-square value.

Table 19.1 shows the calculation of the chi-square value for the relationship between income and home size. As mentioned, the basis for this calculation is Table 18.4 in Chapter 18. That table showed the relative frequencies. The chi-square value, however, is calculated on the basis of the absolute frequencies. In Table 19.1a, it is the absolute frequencies that make up f_o. In Table 19.1b,

we have calculated the expected frequencies (f_e). These frequencies are based on the marginal distributions in the table, which are fixed. The expected frequencies in each of the four cells in the table can then be calculated as shown in the cell at the top left. For a particular cell, we find the expected frequency by multiplying the sum of the row in which the cell is located, by the sum of the column in which the cell is located, and then dividing this product by the total sum in the table. In this way, we calculate how the conditional distributions would be if they were identical to the marginal distribution. The calculation thus shows how the frequencies would be if there were no relationships between the two variables.

Table 19.1 Calculation of the chi-square for the relationship between income and home size

a) Observed frequencies (f_o):

Home size	Income Low	High	N
Small	500	200	700
Large	400	400	800
N	900	600	1500

b) Expected frequencies, given that H_0 is correct (f_e):

Home size	Income Low	High	N
Small	(700•900) / 1500 = 420	280	700
Large	480	320	800
N	900	600	1500

c) The difference between observed and expected frequencies $(f_o - f_e)$:

Home size	Income Low	High	N
Small	80	−80	700
Large	−80	80	800
N	900	600	1500

d) The squared differences $(f_o - f_e)^2$:

Home size	Income Low	High	N
Small	6400	6400	700
Large	6400	6400	800
N	900	600	1500

e) The squared differences divided by the expected frequencies $\dfrac{(f_o - f_e)^2}{f_e}$:

Home size	Income Low	High	N
Small	6400/420 = 15.24.	6400/280 = 22.86.	700
Large	6400/480 = 13.33.	6400/320 = 20.00.	800
N	900	600	1500

f) Calculation of the chi-square (χ^2):

$$\chi^2 = \sum \frac{(f_o - f_e)^2}{f_e} = 15.24 + 22.86 + 13.33 + 20.00 = 71.43$$

We can do this for all the cells, but in a fourfold table like this, the frequencies in the three other cells will be determined by the frequency in the first cell, because the numbers in both the rows and both the columns must match the sums in the marginal distributions. No matter how large the table is, the frequency for the last value of each variable will be given as soon as the frequencies of the other values are determined. We then no longer have any *degrees of freedom* regarding which frequencies can be included in the table. The number of degrees of freedom for a table is then defined on the basis of how many cells can be filled with numbers until the content of all the cells is given. The number of degrees of freedom (df) can be calculated using the formula $df = (k_1 - 1)(k_2 - 1)$, where k_1 is the number of values of one variable and k_2 is the number of values of the second variable. The number of degrees of freedom is important in connection with the assessment of the chi-square value. The more degrees of freedom we have in the table, the higher the critical value of the chi-square.

In Table 19.1c, we have calculated the differences between observed frequencies and expected frequencies. These differences are squared in Table 19.1d, and in Table 19.1e the squared difference in each cell is divided by the expected frequency in the same cell. As we can see in Table 19.1f, chi-square can then be calculated by adding up the numbers in the four cells in Table 19.1e. The chi-square value is 71.43.

By looking it up in a statistical table of the probability distribution of chi-square values, we can find the critical value of chi-square for different levels of significance and for different degrees of freedom. In our case, the number of degrees of freedom is equal to 1. The critical value of chi-square is then 3.84 for the significance level $p < 0.05$, 6.64 for significance level $p < 0.01$, and 10.83 for the significance level $p < 0.001$.

The chi-square value is so high in this case that it will be higher than the critical value, regardless of which of the three significance levels we choose. It is therefore extremely unlikely that we will be wrong if the null hypothesis is rejected. The probability of making such an error would be less than 0.1%. We can conclude that the relationship between income and home size is highly significant ($p < 0.001$) and that it can therefore be assumed that it is highly probable that the relationship applies for the entire universe.

Chi-square tests were used by Armsworth (1989) in a study of therapy for incest survivors in the USA in the 1980s. The study focused on female clients with incest experiences who had sought help from various kinds of professional therapists. In a questionnaire study, the clients rated their therapists' degree of helpfulness. The rating was summarized on a six-point scale, ranging from 'more harm than good' to 'very helpful'. Contingency tables indicated that the rating of male therapists was lower than the rating of female therapists, and chi-square tests showed that this relationship between the clients' rating and the gender of the helping professionals was statistically significant.

t-test

t-tests are often used to determine whether correlation coefficients or regression coefficients are statistically significant. As an example, we can consider the correlation analysis of the relationship between age and the number of visits to the cinema, which was discussed in Chapter 18. Hypothesis H_1 is that there is a correlation between these two variables, and the null hypothesis assumes that there is no such correlation.

In Table 18.11, Pearson's r for this correlation was calculated to be –0.73. The question is whether this correlation coefficient is high enough for us to reject H_0 and accept H_1.

There are different procedures for calculating *t*-values. For correlation coefficients, we can find the *t*-value for the correlation using the simple formula

$$t = r \sqrt{\frac{N-2}{1-r^2}},$$

where r is the correlation coefficient and N is the number of units. If we enter the relevant figures, we obtain

$$t = -0.73 \sqrt{\frac{10-2}{1-(-0.73)^2}} = -0.73 \sqrt{\frac{8}{1-0.53}} = -3.01.$$

Here, the number of degrees of freedom is calculated in a slightly different way than for table analysis. The degrees of freedom are determined based on the number of units $(N-2)$. The correlation analysis in Table 18.11 is based on ten units. The number of degrees of freedom is therefore $10 - 2 = 8$.

We can look up a statistical table of the probability distribution of t-values to find the critical value of t for different levels of significance and for different degrees of freedom. When the number of degrees of freedom is equal to 8, t has a critical value of 2.31 for the significance level $p < 0.05$, 3.36 for the significance level $p < 0.01$ and 5.04 for the significance level $p < 0.001$.

When we compare the actual t-value (-3.01) with the critical values of t, we can disregard the sign and concentrate on the absolute value. In this case, the absolute value of t is higher than the critical value for the significance level $p < 0.05$, but lower than the critical value for the significance levels $p < 0.01$ and $p < 0.001$. When the null hypothesis is rejected, the probability of making an error is less than 5%, but greater than 1%. Whether or not the null hypothesis is to be rejected will then depend on the level of significance we choose. The conclusion here will be that the relationship between age and the number of visits to the cinema is statistically significant at the level $p < 0.05$, but not at the level $p < 0.01$.

In this example, the sample consists of only 10 units. This is a very small sample. If the sample had been larger, say 1000 or 1500 units, which is normal in survey studies, a correlation coefficient of -0.73 would be statistically significant, also at the level of $p < 0.001$. There are two reasons for this. Firstly, a larger number of units (N) in the formula for calculating the t-value would result in a significantly higher t-value. Secondly, the greater the number of degrees of freedom ($N - 2$), the lower the critical values will be for t.

Similarly, the t-test can also be used in regression analysis. The purpose is then to clarify whether the regression coefficients are statistically significant. In multiple regression, the t-test is used for each of the coefficients in the regression equation. Further details about this calculation will not be presented here.

t-tests are presented in an article by Persson (2014) on relationships between children's personality and their psychosocial family and school environment. The study was based on questionnaire data from a sample of 10–19-year-old Swedish boys and girls, and the relationships were examined by means of correlation analyses and multiple regression analyses. t-tests were conducted to test the statistical significance of the correlation coefficients and the regression coefficients. A number of significant relationships between psychosocial factors and personality variables were identified.

F-test and ANOVA

In multiple regression, the F-test is used for several of the regression coefficients together, or for the entire regression equation. The test shows whether the entire group of the selected coefficients or the entire equation is statistically significant.

The null hypothesis (H_0) here would be that none of the independent variables (x_1, x_2, x_3, ...) have any effect on the dependent variable (y). This means that all the regression coefficients (b_1, b_2, b_3, ...) are equal to 0. The alternative hypothesis (H_1) assumes that at least one of the independent variables has an effect on the dependent variable, so that at least one of the regression coefficients is not equal to 0.

The F-test is based on the comparison of variance and is therefore called an analysis of variance; the abbreviation ANOVA is frequently used.

When using the *F*-test in multiple regression, we start with the total variance (*V*) of the dependent variable (*y*). As shown in Chapter 17, the variance is calculated using the equation

$$V = \frac{\sum (y - M)^2}{N - 1},$$

where $\sum (y - M)^2$ is the sum of the squared distances from each unit's actual *y*-value (*y*) to the average value of *y* (*M*), and *N* is the total number of units. The purpose of the regression analysis is to explain as much as possible of this variance in the dependent variable (*y*) using the independent variables ($x_1, x_2, x_3, \ldots$). As mentioned in Chapter 18, R^2 is a measure of the proportion of the total variance in the *y*-variable that is explained by all the *x*-variables. This can be expressed as

$$R^2 = \frac{V_{explained}}{V_{total}}.$$

As a rule, the proportion of variance explained (R^2) is less than 1, because the residual (*e*) in the regression equation is usually greater than 0. The residual expresses the proportion of the total variance in the *y*-variable that is not explained by the *x*-variables. The total variance in the *y*-variable (V_{total}) then consists of two components, one component that is explained by the *x*-variables ($V_{explained}$) and one component that is not explained by the *x*-variables, namely, the residual of the variance ($V_{residual}$). This can be expressed as

$$V_{total} = V_{explained} + V_{residual}.$$

The part of the variance in *y* that is explained by the *x*-variables can be calculated based on the value that each unit would have if the unit were located on the regression line. This is the *y*-value that is predicted by the regression equation, as a result of the values this unit has on the *x*-variables. This predicted *y*-value can be called $\hat{y}$. The main element in the calculation of the variance explained is the sum of the squared distances from each unit's predicted *y*-value ($\hat{y}$) to the average value for *y* (*M*): $\sum (\hat{y} - M)^2$. The variance explained is calculated by

dividing this sum by the number of degrees of freedom (*k*), which here is the number of independent variables (*x*) in the regression equation. The variance explained is therefore calculated

$$V_{explained} = \frac{\sum (\hat{y} - M)^2}{k}.$$

The variance not explained expresses the dispersion around the regression line. It is calculated from the sum of the squared distances from each unit's actual *y*-value (*y*) to the unit's predicted *y*-value ($\hat{y}$): $\sum (y - \hat{y})^2$. The residual variance is calculated by dividing this sum by the number of degrees of freedom, which in this case is the number of units minus the number of independent variables in the regression equation minus 1. This gives the formula

$$V_{residual} = \frac{\sum (y - \hat{y})^2}{N - k - 1}.$$

When we use the *F*-value as a test estimator, the variance explained is not compared with the total variance, as in the calculation of R^2. In the *F*-test, the variance explained is compared instead with the variance not explained, so that the *F*-value is calculated from the formula

$$F = \frac{V_{explained}}{V_{residual}} = \frac{\sum (\hat{y} - M)^2 / k}{\sum (y - \hat{y})^2 / (N - k - 1)}.$$

As the equation shows, the *F*-value will be 0 if the variance explained is equal to 0. None of the independent variables have any effect on the dependent variable. All the regression coefficients are equal to 0. When variance explained increases, the numerator in this fraction will increase, while the denominator in the fraction will decrease. The *F*-value will thus increase. How big the *F*-value needs to be in order for the null hypothesis to be rejected (the critical value) will depend on the number of degrees of freedom in both the numerator and the denominator of the fraction.

In a regression analysis with, for example, 6 independent variables (k) and 1500 units (N), the number of degrees of freedom in the numerator will be 6, and the number of degrees of freedom in the denominator will be 1493.

In a table of the F-distribution, we can find the critical F-values for these degrees of freedom (k, $N - k - 1$) and for different levels of significance ($p < 0.05$, $p < 0.01$ or $p < 0.001$). If the calculated F-value is higher than the critical F-value, H_0 can be rejected. In that case, the group of regression coefficients included in the F-test can be considered statistically significant, in accordance with H_1.

F-tests and ANOVA were used by Elliott et al. (2005), in a study of factors that can explain drivers' intentions to comply with speed limits in the UK. Questionnaire data were collected from a random sample of drivers. Multiple regression analyses were conducted in order to examine relationships between the drivers' intentions to comply with speed limits and a number of factors, including beliefs, attitudes, norms, and perceived control. The regression analyses were carried out stepwise, including additional independent variables for each step. In addition to the regression coefficients of each independent variable, the increase in the proportion of variance explained for each step was identified in order to find the effects of different independent variables. In this analysis of variance, F-tests were used to examine the statistical significance of the increase in the variance explained. The study showed several significant effects of various belief factors on drivers' attitudes and intentions.

CHAPTER HIGHLIGHTS

- The purpose of statistical generalization is to clarify whether empirical findings based on data from a probability sample are valid for the larger universe from which the sample is drawn.
- For statistical generalization, only the random margins of error associated with the sample selection are considered. Systematic errors due to drop-out, low reliability or low validity are not taken into account.
- Statistical generalization is based on the central limit theorem. The sampling distribution is a normal distribution, and there is therefore a clear relationship between the distance from the mean value, measured in the number of standard deviations, and the proportion of the samples located within this distance from the mean. The standard deviation of a sampling distribution is called standard error.
- We distinguish between two main types of statistical generalization: estimation and hypothesis testing.

- Estimation is based on a particular finding of a property of the sample and involves calculating a probable minimum value and a probable maximum value for the corresponding property in the universe. The distance between the two values is called the confidence interval.
  1 We choose a level of confidence (e.g. 95%).
  2 We calculate the confidence interval based on the level of confidence selected.
- Hypothesis testing involves clarifying whether a relationship between different features of the sample is strong enough to assume that the relationship also applies to the corresponding features of the universe.
  1 We formulate a hypothesis and a null hypothesis.
  2 We select a significance level ($p < 0.05$, $p < 0.01$ or $p < 0.001$).
  3 We choose a test estimator and a test method: a chi-square test (for table analysis), t-test (for correlation coefficients and regression coefficients) or F-test (for

combinations of regression coefficients or entire regression equations).

4   We calculate the chi-square value, *t*-value or *F*-value.

5   We compare the calculated value with the critical value for the selected test estimator, the selected significance level and the number of degrees of freedom.

6   The null hypothesis is rejected and the actual hypothesis is strengthened if the calculated value is greater than the critical value. If the calculated value is less than the critical value, the null hypothesis cannot be rejected and we cannot assume that the actual hypothesis is correct.

RESEARCH EXAMPLES

I recommend that you read the publications used as research examples in this chapter.

Armsworth, Mary Witham (1989) 'Therapy of incest survivors: Abuse or support?', *Child Abuse & Neglect* 13, 549–562.

This article provides an example of the use of chi-square tests. It presents a study of therapy for incest survivors in the USA in the 1980s. The study focused on female clients with incest experiences who had sought help from various kinds of professional therapists. In a questionnaire study, the clients rated their therapists' degree of helpfulness. The rating was summarized on a six-point scale, ranging from 'more harm than good' to 'very helpful'. Contingency tables indicated that the rating of male therapists was lower than the rating of female therapists, and chi-square tests showed that this relationship between the clients' rating and the gender of the helping professionals was statistically significant. It is pointed out that the most frequently cited reason for low rating was sexual intimacy or harassment from the therapist.

Elliott, Mark A., Christopher J. Armitage, and Christopher J. Baughan (2005) 'Exploring the beliefs underpinning drivers' intentions to comply with speed limits', *Transportation Research Part F: Psychology and Behaviour* 8(6), 459–479.

This article contains examples of the use of *F*-tests and ANOVA. Questionnaire data collected from a random sample of drivers in the UK were used to study factors that can explain drivers' intentions to comply with speed limits. Multiple regression analyses were conducted in order to examine relationships between the drivers' intentions to comply with speed limits and a number of factors, including beliefs, attitudes, norms, and perceived control. The regression analyses were carried out stepwise, including additional independent variables for each step. In addition to the regression coefficients of each independent variable, the increase in the proportion of variance explained for each step was identified in order to find the effects of different independent variables. In this analysis of variance, *F*-tests were used to examine the statistical significance of the increase in the variance explained. The study showed several significant effects of various belief factors on drivers' attitudes and intentions.

Persson, Nils Bertil Gerhard (2014) 'A study of personality and family- and school environment and possible interactional effects in 244 Swedish children – A multiple regression analysis', *Psychology* 5, 886–895.

This article includes examples of the use of *t*-tests. The study presented in the article was focused on relationships between children's personality and their psychosocial family and school environment. The analysis was based on questionnaire data from a sample of 10–19-year-old Swedish boys and girls, and the relationships were examined by means of correlation analyses and multiple regression analyses. *t*-tests were conducted to test the statistical significance of the correlation coefficients and the regression coefficients. A number of significant relationships between psychosocial factors and personality variables were identified.

STUDENT EXERCISES AND QUESTIONS

1 What is the difference between descriptive and inductive statistics?
2 What is the purpose of statistical generalization?
3 What kind of error margins are calculated in statistical generalization?
4 Why is the normal distribution important in statistical generalization?
5 Why is the Type I error regarded as more important than the Type II error in hypothesis testing?
6 Discuss what is meant by the following statements:

   a The relationship between education and income is highly significant ($p < 0.001$)
   b The relationship between gender and environmental activism is not significant ($p > 0.05$).

7 Calculate the chi-square value for the data in Table 19.2, determine the degrees of freedom, find a table of critical values for chi-square on the web, and discuss whether there is a statistically significant relationship between the variables in the table.

Table 19.2 Attitude to the EU in different age groups

Attitude to EU	20-50 years of age	51-80 years of age	Total
Positive	180	250	430
Negative	270	300	570
Total	450	550	1000

RECOMMENDED LITERATURE

Bowen, Chieh-Chen (2016) *Straightforward Statistics*. London: Sage.

This book provides a general understanding of foundational statistics. It is written for students in different social science disciplines. Using plain language, the book presents a cumulative approach to statistics and a gradual development of statistical insight, from simple to more complex concepts.

Roberts, Maxwell J., and Riccardo Russo (1999) *A Student's Guide to Analysis of Variance*. London and New York: Routledge.

This book covers a number of statistical concepts and topics, with a particular focus on variance. Among the topics included are random error, Type I and Type II errors, null hypotheses, *t*-tests, significance levels, and degrees of freedom. The book provides an intuitive discussion of various sources of variance in a data set, as well as practical advice for using ANOVA in research.

Shafer, Douglas, and Zhiyi Zhang (2012) *Introductory Statistics*. Saylor Academy (https://open.umn.edu/opentextbooks/textbooks/135).

This is an introductory book that concentrates on core concepts, which are well described and explained. The book covers central statistical topics, such as probability, sampling distributions, estimation, hypothesis testing, chi-square tests and *F*-tests. Furthermore, the book contains a number of exercises and references to larger data sets that can be used for statistical analysis.

MIXED METHODS AND COMBINING DATA

This chapter provides the knowledge that is necessary for understanding the differences between qualitative and quantitative data and how the two data types can be combined in mixed methods research.

The chapter will teach you about

- how qualitative data collection differs from quantitative data collection
- how qualitative data analysis differs from quantitative data analysis

- how to select a strategy for combining qualitative and quantitative data
- important relationships that should be considered in analysis of such data combinations.

Data differences and data combinations

In Chapter 6, differences between qualitative and quantitative research designs were described, and mixed methods designs for combining different sources and data were discussed. In this chapter, differences between the two data types and strategies for combining them will be further discussed.

Previously, data collection and data analysis have been discussed separately, in two different parts of the book, data collection in Part III and data analysis in this part of the book. Furthermore, qualitative and quantitative studies have been discussed in separate chapters. This chapter points out major differences between qualitative and quantitative data and examines mixed methods strategies for data collection as well as for data analysis.

The first section of the chapter deals with differences between the two data types. Qualitative and quantitative data are compared with regard to four key aspects of data collection and four key aspects of data analysis. The second section of the chapter is focused on combinations of qualitative and quantitative data. First, four strategies for combining the two types of data are suggested. Then, some challenges in the analysis of such data combinations are discussed, with reference to five important relationships.

Differences between qualitative and quantitative data

Chapter 6 discussed the differences between qualitative and quantitative data with reference to four *general* aspects of social science studies (cf. Table 6.3). The two data types will now be compared with reference to particular aspects of the *data collection* and the *data analysis* in various studies. This discussion will refer to examples from the studies that were described in the presentation of the six different research designs in Chapter 6.

Aspects of data collection

The differences between qualitative and quantitative data collection will be examined in relation to each of the three types of data sources (actors, respondents and documents). The discussion is based on Table 20.1, which provides an overview of important features in the collection of qualitative and quantitative data in various research designs. The table also gives an overview of the studies used as examples in this discussion.

The relation to the sources

Table 20.1 distinguishes between four important aspects of data collection. The first of these is about

Table 20.1   Main features of the collection of qualitative and quantitative data

Source type	Data type	Example of study (described in Chapter 6)	Relation to sources	Principle for the treatment of the sources	Principle for data recording	Key part of data collection
			Aspect of data collection			
Actor	Qualitative data	Ethnography and participant observation: election campaign study	Natural interaction	Accessibility of relevant events and actions	Completeness	Observer
	Quantitative data	Structured observation: passenger study	Focus on selected events and actions	Comparability between selected events and actions	Precision	Instrument
Respondent	Qualitative data	Unstructured interviews and focus groups: nursing study	Open interaction	Accessibility of the individual respondent	Completeness	Interviewer
	Quantitative data	Questionnaires and surveys: quality of life study	Programmed interaction	Comparability between all respondents	Precision	Instrument
Document	Qualitative data	Qualitative content analysis: newspaper study	The data are supplemented along the way	Accessibility of relevant information	Completeness	Researcher
	Quantitative data	Quantitative content analysis: tweet study	Text units selected in advance	Comparability between selected text units	Precision	Instrument

the relation to the data sources. This relation was also described in Chapter 6, but in a more general way. Here, the focus is specifically on the process of data collection.

In observation, the relation to the actors observed can vary greatly. In qualitative studies based on participant observation, the relation is characterized by natural interaction between the researcher and the actor. Ensuring that the interaction is as natural as possible is an important challenge in such studies. In this regard, it may be a problem that the researcher must write notes about what is observed. In the election campaign study (Nielsen, 2012), which was about political communication in a US congressional election, this problem was

reduced by most of the notes being written when the researcher was alone.

In structured observation designs intended to collect quantitative data, the observer's relation to the observed actor may vary. In the passenger study (Russell et al., 2011), where bus and train passengers and their activities were observed in their natural surroundings, there was no contact between the observers and the actors. Other structured observation studies may include some form of interaction. This is especially true when the observation is carried out in more experimental contexts, such as in Bales's small-group studies (Bales, 1952). The main point is that the observer focuses on selected events and actions.

The collection of respondent data involves a certain interaction between the respondent and the interviewer. In qualitative studies, this interaction is open. Each new question is to a large extent dependent on the preceding answer. The interview usually develops as an ordinary conversation, such as in the nursing study (Gould and Fontenla, 2006), where 27 nurses spoke in detail about various aspects of their work at the hospital. Although the conversation was guided by the interviewer, this steering was adapted to the respondent's individual nature, and its purpose was only to ensure that all the selected conversation topics were covered satisfactorily. This data collection assumes that the interviewer is able to interpret the respondent's answers and statements and is able to improvise questions while the interview is ongoing. The answers may be misinterpreted and the questions may be leading. In such cases there is a risk that the information we receive is not of the kind we need, nor has the content we want.

The relation to the respondent is different in quantitative studies based on structured questioning. If the questionnaire is completed by the respondents themselves, the researcher's contact with the respondents is very limited. If the structured questioning is conducted in the form of an interview, there is more extensive interaction between the interviewers and the respondents, but this interaction is tightly structured. The collaborative process is based on the established structure in the questionnaire, such as the quality of life study (Eurofound, 2012), where nationwide population samples in 27 European countries answered questions about different aspects of their quality of life. A prerequisite for this process to work is that the questionnaire is well prepared and tested through a pretesting process before the actual data collection commences. If it turns out that some questions do not work well, there are few adaptation options available while the interview is in progress. For many respondents, however, this form of structured interaction will in any case be a relatively

unusual situation. It can often be problematic to structure life in such a way, not least for women, and especially mothers with small children. A life situation that is complex and unpredictable may not be investigated very well using highly structured research designs. The information provided by the respondents in structured interviews can thus be both different and more limited than what they could contribute in more natural situations.

In connection with document data, the relation to the source is also more open in qualitative than in quantitative studies. In qualitative content analysis, the data may be supplemented along the way during the data collection process. A specific document may contain information about both the research question in the study and other relevant sources. Examining a selected source may thus lead to the selection of new sources. More generally, the choice of sources in qualitative content analyses may depend on the content of the sources. The purpose of the newspaper study (Oosthuizen, 2012) was to study how nurses are referred to in South African newspapers. The content analysis took a pragmatic sample of all the newspaper articles over a 5-year period that contained the word 'nurse' or 'nursing'. This sample included articles that, in combination, were well suited to shedding light on the research question to be studied. One of the problems of such a pragmatic approach is that the selection of sources may be influenced by the researcher's preference for specific conclusions.

This problem is less pronounced in quantitative content analysis. In such studies, the text units are selected in advance, before the actual data recording commences. The selection of sources is assumed to be independent of the specific content of the sources. The selection is often based on different types of considerations regarding representativeness, for example that the selected texts should be representative of a larger volume of texts or that they should be representative of the communication with a particular population of individuals, groups, organizations or other actors. Such considerations were the basis for the selection of text units in the tweet study (Humphreys et al., 2013), where the intention was to compare the content of the tweets with the content of personal diaries from the eighteenth and nineteenth centuries. In line with this research question, it was desirable to obtain the most representative overview possible of the content of today's tweets. Therefore, a probability sample of people who had published tweets during a particular 3-week period was used, and a random sample of these people's tweets was included in the analysis. These tweets were considered representative of today's tweets, so that they could be compared to diaries from earlier times. In general, such representativeness assessments may be problematic, and it may also be a problem that it is not possible to take account of information about relevant additional sources that may appear during the data recording.

The treatment of the sources

The relation to the sources that develops during data collection is based on more general methodological principles for the treatment of the sources. These principles can be considered as a separate aspect of the data collection. This is not about processing the collected data, but about the treatment of data sources during the data collection process.

In qualitative observation studies, it is a key principle that the researcher should gain access to relevant events and actions. The purpose of the participation in the processes observed, such as in the election campaign study, is precisely that the researcher should have direct access to all the circumstances that may be relevant to the research question of the study.

In quantitative observation studies, however, the aim is to achieve the greatest possible comparability between the selected events and actions. The circumstances that are assumed to be relevant to the research question are selected before the observation starts, as in the passenger study. The purpose of the structuring of the observation is to be able to compare the observed conditions systematically.

A key principle in connection with qualitative interview studies is to ensure the researcher's access to the individual respondent. Each respondent is treated according to his or her nature, as in the nursing study. The stimuli (or questions) presented by the interviewer are adapted to each respondent's own background and conditions. This provides great opportunities to obtain answers to the questions asked, but it can also make it difficult to compare the answers from different respondents.

When collecting quantitative respondent data, however, it is an important principle that the data set is based on comparability between all respondents. All respondents are given identical stimuli, as in the quality of life study. The idea is that this will produce equivalent answers. Such reasoning is unproblematic if the respondents are similar to each other, so that they constitute a homogeneous sample. The more heterogeneous the sample is, the more problematic is the assumption that identical stimuli lead to equivalent answers. Respondents with different characteristics can react differently to the same stimulus. The same question can be perceived in different ways. This may affect both the respondents' willingness to answer and the content of the responses. In such cases, the answers may not be equivalent and comparable without the use of different stimuli.

This distinction between accessibility and comparability is also found in relation to document data. Qualitative content analyses are based on the principle of access to relevant information. Such analyses may include many different types of texts and may combine a variety of different aspects of these texts. Quotations of different types and of varying lengths and content can be included and combined in the ways that eventually appear to be most fruitful based on the research question of the study. In the newspaper study, the various articles were treated in this way. The purpose was to show how the nurses were mentioned in South African newspapers, and the analysis resulted in a set of categories that showed the types of statements the newspapers contained. The analysis also provided the basis for concluding that there were plenty of positive statements on the nurses in the newspapers, but that the positive statements were overshadowed by more negative statements. However, this analysis could not show how much space each of the categories received in the newspapers, or how much weight was attributed to each category. Analyses of such questions would assume equivalence and comparability between the individual articles and the quotes in the content analysis.

This kind of issue, however, was central to the tweet study. The quantitative content analysis of the tweets was about clarifying how large a percentage of the messages mentioned different types of actors, and how the messages were distributed across different types of themes and styles. The counting of messages that was thus required assumed a high degree of comparability between the selected texts. The analysis had to be limited to the same type of messages and the same aspects of these messages. One problem with this procedure is that it could be difficult to capture special features of the messages that are specific to certain groups, cultures or contexts. The tweets analysed came from many different countries, and it may be that the tweets' statements about actors, as well as their themes and styles, vary between countries in such a way that it is problematic to assume that the tweets from all the countries are fully equivalent and comparable.

The data recording

Qualitative and quantitative research designs are not only based on different principles for the treatment of the sources. The two types of data are also different with regard to the principles for data

recording. In this respect, however, the differences between the different source types are not very large. In observation studies, interview studies and content analysis, completeness is a key principle for recording qualitative data. The most important task during data recording is to include all available information that is relevant to the research question. This principle of complete data recording is more important for qualitative studies than for quantitative studies, because the latter type of study is usually based on clearer assumptions about which selected aspects of the sources should be covered by the data collection.

In connection with quantitative designs, the question of relevance and completeness is expected to be largely clarified before the data collection process. During the actual recording of data, therefore, accuracy or precision is the key principle. Especially for reasons of comparability, it is important to ensure that the information collected is recorded as accurately as possible, and that it is placed into the correct categories on the observation schedule, questionnaire or coding schedule.

This distinction between complete and precise data recording is parallel to the distinction between relevant and precise interpretations, as discussed in Chapter 6 (cf. Table 6.3). There will often be a risk that the emphasis on precision and accuracy in quantitative designs may occur at the expense of the fruitfulness of the study. On the other hand, due to the emphasis on relevance and completeness in qualitative designs, it may be difficult to carry out a critical assessment of the reliability of the data and the validity of the conclusions. This is especially true for unstructured interview studies, where it may be unclear which stimuli or questions form the basis for the qualitative data recorded.

The key part of the data collection

A fourth difference between qualitative and quantitative data collection concerns what is the most important part of the data collection.

When collecting quantitative data, the measuring instrument is the most important part of the design. This instrument will have been thoroughly prepared, properly structured, and is often tested before the data collection begins. The instrument is available as an observation schedule for structured observation, as a questionnaire for structured questioning or as a coding schedule for quantitative content analysis. It may be a problem that it is usually difficult to change the instrument after the data collection has commenced. It is important that the entire data collection process is based on the same instrument, not least for the sake of comparability between the actors, respondents or text units. Therefore, it is usually not possible to correct any defects in the instrument that are only discovered during data collection. This applies especially to structured interviews. Once a respondent has answered the questions in a particular questionnaire, it is problematic to return to the same respondent with a revised questionnaire. The answers obtained in the new interview could then be affected by the participation in the previous interview. This problem can also occur during structured observation, but it is less serious in quantitative content analyses, since documents are more stable and permanent sources than actors and respondents. The tight structuring of the instrument in the collection of quantitative data means that data collection is relatively easy to carry out. However, the less the researcher participates in the data collection, the greater the problems associated with the interpretation of the results of the analysis.

The implementation of the data collection is far more difficult in qualitative studies. The instrument is less thoroughly prepared and less determined in advance. The most important part of the collection process, therefore, is not the procedures or instruments used for the collection of data, but the persons who conduct the data collection.

In participant observation, the observer is the most important part of the design. More than in any other research design, the participating observers use themselves as a means of obtaining relevant data, and more than in any other design, the observers make use of their own participation as a means of understanding the data collected. The election campaign study is a good example of this. Therefore, it is almost unthinkable that the participant observation can be performed by anyone other than the researchers themselves.

Similarly, when collecting qualitative respondent data, the interviewer constitutes the most important part of the design. Usually, the researcher will be the interviewer in such designs. This is not only because data collection is difficult to implement, but also because the interpretation of the data is largely based on the impressions and experience gained through the fieldwork itself.

Not least because of such interpretative possibilities, it is also the researcher who constitutes the most important part of the collection of qualitative document data. In order for the selection and compilation of quotes from a text to be complete and relevant, the researcher must have an overview of the entire body of text from which the quotes are taken.

The collection of qualitative data is thus highly dependent on the person who carries out the collection. The main problem is that this person's characteristics and sociocultural background can affect which data are collected. Such circumstances can affect the interaction that develops between observed actors or the answers given by a respondent, and they could also influence the interpretation of the interaction between actors, the respondents' answers or the content of documents. These problems can have consequences for both the continuing data collection process and the final interpretation of the data.

In general, therefore, the significance of the researcher is greater during the collection of qualitative data than it is during the collection of quantitative data. This is partly due to the fact that the distinction between data collection and data analysis is less marked in qualitative designs than in quantitative designs. In qualitative studies, it is common for the data analysis to start before the data collection has been completed.

Aspects of the data analysis

In a comparison of qualitative and quantitative analyses, it is not necessary to distinguish between the different designs for data collection. The important distinction refers to the types of data to be analysed, typically numbers in quantitative studies and texts in qualitative studies. Table 20.2 shows an overview of some important features of analyses of the two data types. The differences between qualitative and quantitative analyses will be discussed in connection with four different aspects of the analysis.

Purpose of the analysis

The first difference between qualitative and quantitative analyses highlighted in Table 20.2 refers to the purpose of the analysis. Analyses of qualitative data are often intended to achieve a more or less comprehensive understanding of specific conditions. Such studies are usually intensive, in the

sense that they go into depth in relatively limited areas. They are usually concentrated on relatively few units, but they investigate a large number of properties of these units. This is particularly true for the election campaign study, which emphasized obtaining an overall understanding of personal communication and its importance in two constituencies in the US Congressional elections. The purpose of the nursing study was to develop a comprehensive understanding of the work situation of only 27 nurses from two selected hospitals in England. The newspaper study involved detailed analyses of 161 pragmatically selected newspaper articles from South Africa in order to obtain an overall understanding of how the nursing profession is discussed in the media.

Qualitative data analyses attach great importance to empathy and insight. The analyses are therefore suitable for developing hypotheses and theories. Qualitative analyses, however, have clear limitations when it comes to assessing whether the hypotheses and theories developed are valid in wider-ranging contexts. These limitations are related to the lack of association of the data with larger groups or larger areas. In other words, a significant problem with qualitative data is its limited range and validity, not primarily in terms of time, but especially in space.

Table 20.2 Key features of the analysis of qualitative and quantitative data

Aspect of the analysis	Qualitative data	Quantitative data
Purpose of the analysis	Overall understanding of specific conditions Depth Development of hypotheses and theories	Representative overview of general conditions Breadth Testing of hypotheses and theories
Key elements of the analysis	Concepts, categories and typologies	Frequencies, distributions and correlations
Organization of the analysis	Analysis and interpretation in parallel with data collection No standardized analysis techniques The data set may become overly complex	Large volumes of data can be processed and analysed using statistical techniques and computer programs
Presentation of the results of the analysis	Illustration using quotes	Documentation using tables

However, it is especially on this point that the quantitative analyses are strongest. The purpose of these analyses is usually to achieve the most representative overview possible of general conditions. The analyses are based on more extensive strategies, by providing broad presentations of some limited phenomena. They often include a relatively large number of units, but then they concentrate on a limited number of characteristics of these units. The passenger study provides a representative overview of the activity patterns among bus and train passengers, based on observation of 812 passengers in Wellington in 2008. The quality of life study provides an overview of selected aspects of the quality of life among more than 35,500 people who are assumed to be representative of the entire population of 27 European countries in 2011. The tweet study provides an overview of subjects, theme and style in 2100 randomly selected English-language tweets in 2008. In other words, overview is prioritized over insight in such analyses. Quantitative data analyses are often used in the testing of hypotheses and theories. Quantitative analyses, however, are not as suitable for the further development of theoretical reasoning. While the results of the analysis are set out clearly, they may also be superficial. Quantitative data do not provide a very good basis for understanding dynamic relationships, processes and patterns of interaction. This limitation of quantitative analyses, therefore, is not about space, but about time: this approach can form the basis for time series data, but it is not good at capturing the time dimension and the dynamics of social processes. Using time series data based on records from many different times with short intervals can reduce, but not eliminate, this problem.

Key elements of the analysis

Another difference between qualitative and quantitative data analyses concerns what are important elements of the analysis. The key elements in qualitative analyses are usually concepts, categories and typologies. Such analyses may entail arranging and systematizing the qualitative data into appropriate categories. These can form the basis for developing and clarifying concepts. Various categories and concepts can then be seen in context, so that it becomes possible to construct more comprehensive typologies. These elements of the data analysis help to ensure that descriptions based on qualitative data are analytical. The development of categories and concepts was a key analysis strategy in the newspaper study. The statements about nurses were first divided into many different categories. Many of the original categories were then merged into more general categories. The analysis resulted in 18 such general categories, which were then discussed in light of the concepts about the nursing profession's work situation and its relationship with the health-care sector. Thus, the analysis helped to clarify the meaning of the various categories and to specify the content of the concepts used. The content of the individual categories thus becomes a core theme in qualitative analyses. In the election campaign study, great importance was attached to the meaning associated with the different types of personal contact and communication. An objection could be made that the content and meaning of a category are of little interest if we do not know anything about who or how many it applies to.

However, the scope of different categories constitutes a main theme in quantitative data analysis. The key elements of such analyses are frequencies, distributions and correlations. The data provide the basis for explaining how many of the units in a study have a given attribute. Thus, it can also be determined how the units are distributed in terms of various characteristics and how different characteristics are related to each other. The quality of life study therefore focuses on how the population is distributed on various quality of life components and what aspects of quality of life are correlated. This means that quantitative analysis clarifies the number of units that are included in the different categories. The actual development and clarification of the different categories is rarely a part of the analysis. The discussion of the content and meaning of the categories is usually completed before the data collection begins. The categories are determined during the construction of the questionnaire or the schedules for the data collection. These categories are to a large extent considered unproblematic, or at least as given, during the analysis of the data. In any case, the possibilities for changing the content of the categories are relatively small once the data have been collected. This can be a significant weakness in quantitative analyses. The set of categories may be rigid, and the content and meaning of the categories may be unclear. It can thus be argued that it is not very interesting to know the number of units in a category if we do not have a proper understanding of what the category means. This problem can be reduced if the quantitative study is based on thorough preparations.

Organization of the analysis

As pointed out above, the distinction between data collection and data analysis is less marked in qualitative studies than in quantitative studies. Thus, the two approaches differ in terms of how the analysis is organized. In qualitative approaches the analysis and the interpretation are partly conducted in parallel with the data collection. The fact that the researchers themselves actively participate in the collection of qualitative data is not only because this data collection is more demanding than the collection of quantitative data. The experience gained from the fieldwork also constitutes an important context for the interpretation of the data. The interpretation conducted during the recording of the data is not only about steering the continuing data collection process in the most relevant direction. It is also focused on obtaining a

more general insight into and understanding of the phenomena to be analysed. Such a form of empathy is central to qualitative analyses, such as in the election campaign study and the nursing study. This becomes all the more important because such analyses cannot be based on statistical techniques. The data set must be limited, because overly extensive data can easily become too complex to follow. In particular, the number of research units is usually limited in qualitative studies. This was the case in the election campaign study, which focused on delimited environments of electoral campaigners in two local constituencies. It was also the case in the nursing study which involved 27 nurses, and in the newspaper study, which included 161 newspaper articles. Gradually, however, new and improved software is being developed for qualitative data analysis, especially for identifying patterns in large volumes of text. Nevertheless, the analysis and interpretation of qualitative data can sometimes have a certain impressionistic quality. It is possible to delve deeply into the specific circumstances that the analysis is focused on. In return, the limited scope of the data may restrict the perspective. The analysis may lead to in-depth knowledge of the phenomena being studied, but less knowledge about how these phenomena are related to more extensive conditions in society.

In quantitative studies, the analysis and interpretation are usually conducted after the data collection is completed. The collection of quantitative data is not only highly structured. It is also carried out in a routine manner. The researcher usually only participates to a very small extent in the data collection process. In the quality of life study, the researchers did not participate in any part of the interviewing. Although it can also be an advantage in quantitative studies for the researcher to have as good a knowledge as possible of the primary sources, such studies are often so extensive that it is impossible for the researcher to obtain an overview of more than a limited portion of the primary data. This is especially true of the quality of life study, which includes interviews with more than 35,000 people in 27 different countries. However, since the data recording is structured and the data are quantified, it is possible to process and analyse these large data sets using statistical techniques. Structuring, quantification and statistical calculations help to reach precise conclusions, as well as to keep track of large amounts of data. In other words, precision and overview are prominent features of quantitative analyses. Being able to process large amounts of data can also provide a basis for examining and evaluating relationships that apply to relatively wide-ranging social conditions. On the other hand, there is a risk that the analysis results in limited insight into the conditions studied. It is possible that not only the data collection, but also the analyses and the interpretations may become too routine. The utilization of the data can become a matter of purely technical skills. This could cause the entire study to be characterized by a lack of imagination, creativity and originality.

Presentation of the results of the analysis

A fourth difference between qualitative and quantitative analyses relates to the presentation of the results. The different characteristics of the two types of data affect not only the processing of the data, but also the presentation of the findings resulting from the analysis. The most common form of presentation of qualitative data involves using quotations from observation notes, interview transcripts or documents for illustrative purposes. This is how the results of the election campaign study, the nursing study and the newspaper study were presented. General points, arguments, concepts or categories are exemplified, elaborated and explained by selecting relevant quotes from the data, putting them together and presenting them

in the most appropriate manner. In combination, the quotes presented help to describe the phenomena being analysed. With this selection and compilation of quotes, the researcher usually strives to achieve as comprehensive a description as possible. Since the quotes largely reproduce the primary source's own expressions and formulations, the description can be both detailed and nuanced at the same time. Thus, it can also be quite complex. There is a danger that the presentation will not only become unclear, but also too detailed. It can also be characterized by a lack of perspective, in that it may be difficult to distinguish between significant and insignificant aspects of the descriptions. On the other hand, a strict prioritization and selectiveness regarding the presentation of quotes may be problematic because the selection may be too strongly influenced by the researcher's personal opinions and sociocultural background. Generally, the less analytical the description is, the greater these problems will be.

The results of quantitative analyses are usually documented using tables. This is the most important form of presentation in the passenger study, the quality of life study and the tweet study. The frequencies, distributions or correlations that form the basis for the different interpretations and conclusions are compiled and presented in tables of varying complexity. These are designed and assembled in the most appropriate manner in order to comment on and highlight the general trends, patterns and contexts that are most relevant to the research question of the study. In this way, the tables can summarize and simplify large amounts of information. Such presentation of the results may be suitable for providing a clear overview of the most central and general features of the data. It provides a good starting point for distinguishing between significant and less significant aspects of the phenomena being studied. On the other hand, the information presented in this way may become too crude. The information may be not just simplified, but oversimplified. Thus, it may be argued that presentations of results from quantitative studies are focused on overviews, whereas presentations of results from qualitative studies emphasize insights.

Combinations of qualitative and quantitative data

Having reviewed the differences between qualitative and quantitative data, the rest of this chapter is focused on how the two types of data can be combined in order to conduct mixed methods research.

As shown above, qualitative and quantitative data have different strengths and limitations. Thus, the main reason for combining the two types of data in mixed methods research is that they will be complementary. The limitations of qualitative data may be balanced by the strengths of quantitative data, and vice versa. Being combined in the same study, the two data types may provide more comprehensive knowledge on the research question of the study than each data type could do separately. Qualitative and quantitative data may shed light on different aspects of the phenomena being examined. By combining the two types of data, we may be able to examine more aspects of the phenomena, and we may be able to use more perspectives for understanding the phenomena.

However, it has been pointed out that combinations of qualitative and quantitative data in a particular study should be based on thorough considerations of the possibility that the two data types may be too different to be combined in the same study. Using mixed methods approaches, we should take into account possible problems related to ontological or epistemological incoherence between qualitative and quantitative data.

Such philosophical or theory of science perspectives on differences between qualitative and quantitative data have been discussed by Onwuegbusie et al. (2009). Discussing philosophical frameworks for mixed methods research, they emphasize a pragmatist paradigm in social science as an appropriate epistemological justification and logic for combining different data and methods. Furthermore, they point out that both qualitative and quantitative data are also used within other research paradigms, including post-positivism, constructivism, the critical theory paradigm, and the participatory paradigm.

Mixed methods research, which is also called methodological triangulation, was described in Chapter 2, and in Chapter 6 it was discussed how mixed methods research can be implemented by combining elements from different research designs. In this connection, field research was highlighted as a typical design for mixed methods research based on combinations of different sources and data, and the bureaucracy study carried out by Blau (1963) was referred to as a good example of this.

In this chapter, mixed methods research is discussed in more detail. First, four strategies for combining qualitative and quantitative data are outlined. Then, some challenges in the analysis of such data combinations are discussed.

Strategies for combining data

Qualitative and quantitative data can be combined in different ways and with different aims and purposes. Mason (2006) distinguishes between different logics for such data combinations. In some studies, one of the data types is used as the main basis for the study, while the other type is used as supplementary or additional data. In other studies, the two data types are equally important and are either used in parallel, but separated from each other, or more integrated. Furthermore, the two data types may be used in a complementary way, to examine distinctive but intersecting questions, or each of the data types may be used to corroborate findings based on the other type of data. In addition, Mason (2006) points out that mixed methods may be used for opportunistic reasons, for example because such designs have a high academic prestige or are favoured by research funding sources.

In this subsection, four different strategies for combining qualitative and quantitative data are outlined. Two of these strategies entail that the use of the different data types constitutes different phases in the research on social conditions. The two data types are used sequentially. The other two strategies relate to different forms of parallel or simultaneous utilization of the different data types. Qualitative and quantitative data are used concurrently.

Qualitative studies preparing for quantitative studies

One of the strategies for sequential use of qualitative and quantitative data is to conduct qualitative studies in preparation for quantitative studies. Then the qualitative study is an exploratory phase of a research project. Typically, the purpose is to obtain a certain empirical basis for constructing the best possible measuring instrument for the collection and recording of the quantitative data in the next phase of the research project. Traditionally, this is probably the most common combination of the two data types.

In connection with large surveys based on structured questionnaires, such qualitative exploratory studies are conducted in the form of preliminary studies or pretesting. These preliminary studies can be carried out both before and during the construction of the questionnaire. The qualitative studies can also contribute to revision or clarification of the research questions before the collection of the quantitative data is commenced.

It may be important to carry out certain types of qualitative preliminary investigations, not only in the case of structured interviewing, but also in connection with quantitative content analyses. These preliminary studies usually entail reading through and systematizing different parts of the documentary sources. This first qualitative approach provides the basis for selecting the most relevant texts and developing the most useful categories. This phase of a study can be important for constructing a coding schedule that not only is appropriate for the research question, but also works well on the texts to be analysed.

In practice, such qualitative studies in preparation for quantitative studies are more widespread than we would think based on the social science literature. This is because the qualitative preliminary studies are not always adequately reported. The reports are often limited to accounts of the more comprehensive quantitative studies. In many cases it would be of great interest to obtain more explicit presentations of which considerations led to the quantitative research design and how different types of qualitative data were used in connection with these considerations. What alternative designs were evaluated or tested and to what extent did the qualitative preliminary studies contribute to such alternative procedures being rejected?

Thus, qualitative data could be utilized better during discussions of approaches and methods. It can also be argued that such qualitative data are often utilized too little during the interpretation of the results of the quantitative analysis. The experiences gained from fieldwork or text studies during qualitative preparations for quantitative studies usually provide an important basis for understanding what the quantitative data mean. Together with the recorded qualitative data, such experiences can be used to explain, clarify and communicate the content of the concepts and categories that are included in the quantitative analysis.

In other words, the problem with this first strategy for combining qualitative and quantitative data is not that more quantitative studies should be prepared using qualitative studies. On the contrary, the challenge consists of achieving a better *utilization* of the qualitative data that *are* collected during the preparations for quantitative studies. This involves the *integration* of the qualitative and quantitative data during analysis and interpretation, and it involves the *presentation* of experiences from the qualitative preliminary study in addition to results from the quantitative analyses.

Lawson et al. (2018) present a mixed methods study of female students at an American university, where qualitative focus group data were collected and analysed before the collection and analysis of quantitative survey data. The purpose of this research was to examine the importance of professors' behaviour and attributes for the success of female students in university studies dominated by male students. The qualitative focus group data were used to identify common themes in the professors' behaviour and attributes that were useful for female students. Based on the results from this study, the survey study was carried out to extend the research. Using the quantitative survey data, the researchers examined hypotheses on relationships between the academic achievements of female students and various factors, including their professors' behaviour and attributes. Although the two types of data were analysed separately, the results of the analyses were presented together and integrated in an overall discussion of the findings. The researchers concluded that 'our results indicated that proximal environments are important and that professors' behaviors that support women without singling them out were most helpful' (Lawson et al., 2018: 542).

Qualitative studies following up quantitative studies

Another strategy for combining qualitative and quantitative data entails that the sequence for using the two data types is different than for the first strategy: the qualitative study does not constitute a preparation for, but a follow-up to the quantitative study. This strategy is based on the following fundamental considerations. On the one hand, it may be necessary to supplement quantitative studies with more qualitative studies in order to understand the general results of the quantitative analyses. On the other hand, the general overview obtained through quantitative analyses may provide an important basis for strategic assessments of which phenomena or issues are particularly important to study in more depth using more intensive, qualitative follow-up studies.

This reasoning is particularly relevant for larger, representative survey studies based on structured questionnaire and quantitative data. Such studies primarily help to reveal general trends and patterns. In many cases, it would be interesting to delve deeper into some of these trends and patterns. By conducting a qualitative and intensive study as a follow-up to quantitative survey studies, we can combine general overviews with specific insights into strategically important areas.

However, this second strategy for combining qualitative and quantitative data is not as prevalent as the first. It is more common that quantitative studies are prepared using qualitative studies, rather than being followed up by such studies.

In a mixed methods study of Asian-Canadian children and families involved in the child welfare system in Canada, Lee et al. (2017) collected and analysed qualitative data to follow up their quantitative data analyses. Secondary analyses of nationwide quantitative data on child-maltreatment-related investigations were conducted to compare Asian-Canadian and White Canadian children and families involved in the child welfare system. Results of these analyses were presented and discussed in focus groups with child-welfare workers as participants. Qualitative data from the focus groups and from semi-structured interviews were used to examine the child-welfare workers' experiences and perceptions of working with Asian-Canadian children and families involved in the child welfare system. Thus, the qualitative analyses were conducted to explain results from the quantitative analyses in more depth. The results of the two analyses were presented together and combined in an overall discussion. The study showed that Asian-Canadian children are substantially different from White Canadian children, and that they represent a diversity of cultural values and family norms, with important implications for social work practice and policies.

Parallel use of qualitative and quantitative data

The third strategy for combining qualitative and quantitative data is perhaps the most interesting of the four combination strategies. It is based on collecting both types of data in parallel. The data analyses are also conducted in parallel. The qualitative study is conducted neither before nor after the quantitative study. Both types of data are used concurrently.

Apart from this parallelism and the simultaneous utilization of the two types of data, there are no decisive or major differences between this strategy and the two previous ones. The two types of data can complement each other. The quantitative data provide the basis for a clear presentation of general patterns linked to the phenomena being investigated. This presentation can be elaborated and clarified using the qualitative data. These data can also be used to offset the limitations of the measuring instruments and analysis techniques that underlie the quantitative results. The collection of qualitative data can also provide experiences that are important for the interpretation of the various results of the analysis.

It can be very valuable that this combination of overview and insight takes place through a parallel and simultaneous utilization of the two types of data. In principle, this strategy means that both qualitative and quantitative approaches are applied to the same units of analysis at the same time, and thus under the same circumstances and research conditions. In the first two strategies, both data types can also be collected from the same units of analysis, but then the qualitative and quantitative data collection takes place at different times. Thus, the two data types can refer to different research conditions. Both the units themselves and their surroundings may have undergone major or minor changes between the two times. The greater the gap between the two times, the more difficult it may be to find all the original units in the subsequent study. This applies especially in studies based on questioning of respondents.

As pointed out in Chapter 6, field research is a typical design for parallel utilization of qualitative and quantitative data. The bureaucracy study carried out by Blau (1963), which was presented in Chapter 1 and further discussed in Chapter 6, was based on this type of field research. Blau studied the dynamics of bureaucratic activity in two public offices. He conducted 3 months of fieldwork at each of the two offices. During this period, he collected both qualitative and quantitative data based on observation and questioning of his colleagues, as well as reviews of various types of documents in the archives and in the ongoing case processing (see Table 6.4). He also carried out structured interviewing of the employees at the offices. Although this quantitative data collection was launched after the field visit, both qualitative and quantitative data were collected and utilized completely in parallel during the field visit.

Quantification of qualitative data

The fourth combination strategy is also a form of parallel utilization of the two data types. However, this strategy is simpler than the previous one. In this strategy, the data collection is mainly based on a qualitative approach, whereas the data analysis is largely based on a quantitative approach. Both approaches, however, refer to the same data. These data are collected as qualitative data, but they are transformed to and analysed as quantitative data. In other words, the collected qualitative data are quantified during the analysis.

In this context, the parallel and simultaneous utilization of qualitative and quantitative approaches entails that the two approaches are included in the same study and that they are linked to the same units of analysis and the same research conditions. On the other hand, the two approaches are related to different phases in the research process, one for data collection and the other for data analysis. Thus, the parallelism and simultaneity is somewhat less obvious and less genuine in this fourth strategy than in the third strategy.

This form of quantification of qualitative data is probably the most problematic of the four strategies. The problematic aspect is especially that the two approaches refer to both the same data and separate phases of the research process, that the data are treated qualitatively during the collection, but quantitatively during the analysis. This could mean that there is a risk of falling between two stools. Usually the collection of qualitative data is not based on the requirements for structure and precision that are essential for conducting quantitative analyses of the data. When qualitative data are used in quantitative analyses, phenomena that are grouped together and counted during the analysis may not be comparable. Thus, this strategy can be characterized as a form of *quasi-statistics*.

Despite these problems, however, this strategy for combining qualitative and quantitative approaches can also be carried out in a reasonable manner and can work both efficiently and fruitfully. The prerequisite is that the limitations of such quantification of qualitative data are taken into account during the interpretation and presentation of the analysis results.

In an article on nurses' perceptions of teamwork, staffing and workload, Yanchus et al. (2017) present a secondary analysis of qualitative data based on unstructured interviews with 271 nurses. These nurses were selected from different clinical units at seven Veterans Health Administration hospitals in the USA. In a previous study, the qualitative data had been collected and coded into a number of thematic categories. In their secondary analysis of these data, Yanchus et al. quantified the coded data set, focusing on the themes of teamwork, staffing and workload. They examined the frequencies of the themes and the relationships between the themes, using Pearson's correlation analysis. The authors 'found that the quantification of qualitative data was possible, and useful, when the characteristics of the qualitative data lend themselves to this process, and when a quantitative analysis of text data provides greater insight into the overall findings of a study' (Yanchus et al. 2017: 318).

Analysing data combinations

In the following discussion of how to analyse data combinations, the strategy for parallel use of qualitative and quantitative data is of most interest. This strategy represents the most genuine combination of the two types of data. The qualitative and quantitative data are utilized concurrently in both data collection and data analysis. As pointed out above, field research is usually based on such data combinations.

Based on general experience from field research, and with particular reference to examples from the study conducted by Blau (1963), some challenges associated with the analysis of data combinations are now discussed. The discussion is focused on five relationships that are important in such analyses.

The relationship between analysis and collection of data

The first issue to be discussed concerns the role of the analysis in the overall research process. As pointed out above (Table 20.2), there are clear differences between qualitative and quantitative approaches. In quantitative studies, the data analysis is a separate phase in the research process: the analysis only begins after the entire data collection process has been completed. In qualitative studies, we cannot distinguish between the analysis and collection of data as completely different phases in the research process: the analysis takes place partly in parallel with the gathering of the data.

In field research designs, where qualitative and quantitative data are combined, we must rely on the latter process. Even in this type of mixed methods research, the data analysis cannot be separated as a distinct phase in the research process. Instead, it must be carried out in parallel with other operations throughout the entire research process. Field research is characterized by a constant alternation back and forth between data collection and data analysis. Generally, this also involves constantly switching back and forth between theory and empirical data. The data collection is usually organized on the basis of theoretical ideas and can be regarded as a connecting line from theory to the empirical data. The data analysis is usually intended to achieve a theoretical understanding of the empirical data and can be said to establish the link from the empirical data to the theory. Field research strives to ensure a continuous development of such connecting lines back and forth between theory and empirical data.

As suggested above, the relationship between analysis and data collection is about the same in purely qualitative studies as in field research based on a combination of qualitative and quantitative data. Thus, field research is strongly influenced by the fact that qualitative data are included in the data combination that is used. However, this does not mean that the constant switching between analysis and data collection is limited to only the qualitative part of the field research.

In principle, the same analysis strategy also applies to the quantitative part of the design. Blau (1963) emphasized such an approach in his bureaucracy studies. From the very start of his field stay, he performed analysis work in parallel with his data collection. During each 3-month fieldwork period, the weekends were largely used to analyse the data that he had collected during the preceding week. These preliminary analyses included both qualitative and quantitative data.

Blau's bureaucracy studies also illustrate another point in the relationship between analysis and data collection. Although these two operations are conducted in parallel in the combination designs that we are discussing here, there is nevertheless a certain change in the relationship between analysis and data collection during the research process. At the beginning of the process, data collection is completely dominant, while the analysis forms a much smaller part of the project work that is carried out. Eventually, this relationship changes, and towards the end of the research process, data collection becomes less and less central, while the emphasis is increasingly placed on the analysis work. In Blau's studies, the analysis activities were restricted to the weekends for as long as the fieldwork was ongoing. During this period, data collection was the most important activity. However, after about 3 months, Blau took a break from the data collection process and focused the work more intensely on analysing the collected data. Although the data collection process was not yet completed, the analysis work gradually consumed an increasingly large part of the researcher's time and attention.

The researcher faces two important challenges in this constant shifting between analysis and data collection. One challenge is to continually review and improve the research design and the data. This is one of the main reasons why the design is initially flexible. As the time spent in the field and the data collection lead to better insight into the problems and processes being studied, the researcher will discover both new data requirements and new data possibilities. A prerequisite for this, however, is that the data collected and the experience gained from the fieldwork are systematized and analysed as they become available. It is primarily such analyses that give the researcher an insight into the issues that are being investigated. Without this improved insight based on the systematization of relevant experiences and data, it is difficult to determine which data, methods and procedures will be most useful for the further fieldwork. In order to be able to develop the fieldwork in a useful manner, the researcher must constantly assess which sources of data are available and which of these are most relevant. It is the interaction between data collection and data analysis during the time spent in the field that can form the basis for these assessments.

The second challenge associated with switching between analysis and data collection is to carry out a continuous reassessment and improvement of the results and interpretations of the analyses. Thus, it is not only the research design that can be revised during the research process. The results of the analyses may also be subject to revision. Analyses based on the first data and field experiences will be provisional. The results of these preliminary analyses can gradually be reassessed in light of new data and new insights. They can be interpreted in the context of an increasing number of ever larger contexts. Thus, the results can be nuanced and modified to provide a basis for other interpretations. The analyses start at an early stage, they proceed continuously and they are raised to an increasingly higher level, viewed in light of the research question. It is an important point in this connection that the earlier the analysis work begins, the better the final results of the analysis

will be. This is not only because the ongoing analyses can lead to a continual improvement of the data set, but also because this continuous analysis process can result in better clarification of concepts, hypotheses and theories. Through this process, the researcher's ideas and interpretations can be explicitly formulated, systematized and confronted with empirical data at an early stage. In his bureaucracy studies, Blau (1963) emphasized that the first interpretations were only provisional, but that it is nevertheless important to begin such interpretations at an early stage. Through confrontation with the increasingly comprehensive empirical evidence, these preliminary interpretations can be refined or replaced by other possible interpretations. It is therefore important to begin an ongoing analysis process at an early stage, even if the first results of the analysis may not be correct. In the initial phases, incorrect results may be better than no results.

It should be pointed out that there is a clear connection between the two challenges discussed here in connection with the process of switching back and forth between analysis and data collection. The first challenge is methodological, while the second is substantive. The relationship between the two challenges can be perceived as a kind of means–ends relationship. Improving the design of the study and the data is a means of achieving better results and interpretations, which can be regarded as an overall objective. On the other hand, the ongoing development of empirical findings and interpretations is an important means of improving the research design and the data. In other words, there is a mutual, dialectical connection between the two challenges.

The relationship between generating and generalizing analyses

The next issue to be discussed refers to the relationship between different types of analyses.

More precisely, this concerns the relationship between analyses with different purposes. As pointed out in connection with Table 20.2, there are clear differences between qualitative and quantitative analyses in this regard.

Qualitative analyses are particularly suitable for analytical descriptions and the development of hypotheses and theories. They emphasize concept formation, typology construction and clarification of the content and meaning of different categories. Such analyses have a *generating* purpose. Quantitative analyses are usually intended to test hypotheses and theories based on statistical overviews and calculations. The units of analysis are classified into different categories, and based on this classification, the study focuses on frequencies, distributions and correlations. These analyses have a *generalizing* purpose.

When we combine qualitative and quantitative data, it is important to take account of this difference between the two types of data. The difference means that combinations of qualitative and quantitative data provide good opportunities to combine generating and generalizing analyses. When this data combination is part of a field research design, the two forms of analysis can be integrated within the framework of an overall analysis strategy. Such a strategy is based on continuously alternating between generating and generalizing analyses. A typical analysis process can thus be initiated with qualitative, generating analyses that prioritize concept development or hypothesis formulation. The concepts or hypotheses that are generated can then form the basis for quantitative, generalizing analyses intended to test whether the concepts are adequate or whether the hypotheses are empirically supported. The generalizations established in this way can then provide the basis for generating new concepts and hypotheses, which must in turn be tested through new generalizing analyses, and so forth. By alternating in this way between the two forms of analysis, both concept formation and hypothesis

testing can be raised to an increasingly higher theoretical level.

This analysis strategy was central to the bureaucracy study carried out by Blau (1963). He formulated a twofold objective for his analyses. He wished to develop theoretical insights that could explain the activities at the public offices, and he also wished to examine which explanatory principles were correct and which were incorrect. In order to achieve this, Blau continuously alternated between generating and generalizing analyses. In this regard, however, he emphasized that generating analyses need not necessarily be based on qualitative data. In many cases, quantitative data can also provide a good basis for developing concepts or hypotheses. This is especially true when quantitative analyses result in unexpected findings or exhibit surprising patterns. Such findings can provide important impulses and ideas for concept development. Blau emphasized that continuously refining different concepts became an important part of his analyses, and he stressed that this clarification of concepts not only took place in connection with the purely generating analyses, but also was a key aspect of the alternation and interaction between the generating and the generalizing analyses.

Although it is *usually* the case that generating analyses are based on qualitative data and generalizing analyses are based on quantitative data, we can see here that this is not *always* the case. Blau used quantitative data in a generating manner. Others have argued that qualitative data not only are suitable for hypothesis development, but also can form the basis for hypothesis testing. This can be seen in connection with the use of qualitative data for theoretical generalization, as discussed in Chapter 16. Glaser and Strauss (1967) argued that qualitative as well as quantitative data can be used to both develop and test hypotheses. In this regard, they highlight *analytical induction* as a systematic approach to combine hypothesis development and hypothesis testing based on the same qualitative data. This approach is used particularly to develop and test relatively limited and integrated theories of causal relationships.

Each hypothesis is developed through constant confrontations with different individual phenomena that deviate from or contradict the hypothesis. This inspection of each part of the data set forms the basis for ongoing reformulations of the various hypotheses. The testing associated with analytical induction entails that the hypotheses are assessed more systematically on the basis of the total data set in the study. As part of this procedure, however, the qualitative data are coded and quantified.

The relationship between formal and informal data processing

The discussion about generating and generalizing analyses is concerned with how we relate to hypotheses and theories. Partly related to this discussion is the question of how to process the data upon which the analyses are based.

We can distinguish between formal and informal processing of data. *Formal* data processing is based on standardized rules, procedures and techniques. This is the most common approach employed for theory testing and generalizing analyses. Many of the generalizing analyses require formal data processing. Such formal procedures can also be the basis for developing concepts, hypotheses and theories. In connection with theory development and generating analyses, however, data processing is often more informal. This means that the procedure is more pragmatic and flexible. *Informal* data processing is not based on standardized rules or techniques. Instead, the data are systematically utilized in all the ways that gradually prove appropriate in order to investigate the research question in the study. In generating analyses, such informal approaches can often be used in conjunction with more formal data processing.

Thus, field research based on a combination of qualitative and quantitative data not only involves alternating between analysis and data collection and between generating and generalizing analyses. Field research designs also entail alternating between formal and informal data processing. The purpose is to achieve the most comprehensive utilization of the data in relation to the specific research question. This requires, on the one hand, using methods that are possible and useful with regard to creative concept development and relevant insights. On the other hand, this should be combined with procedures that are reliable and reasonable with regard to accurate hypothesis testing and general overview.

The distinction between formal and informal data processing differs from the distinction between quantitative and qualitative analyses. Certainly, qualitative analyses are typically based on informal data processing and quantitative data are usually formally processed. However, this does not have to be the case. Firstly, qualitative data can be processed in a formal manner. We could say that this is what happens when qualitative data are quantified during the analysis. This was the approach recommended by Glaser and Strauss (1967) when they argued for combining theory development and theory testing through analytical induction. As noted above, this formal processing of qualitative data may be problematic, because it is not certain that the qualitative data have been gathered in accordance with the structure and precision required for quantitative analyses. However, this problem is greatest when such quantification of qualitative data is used for the purpose of testing hypotheses or as the basis for a clear description of more general conditions. The problem becomes far less serious if the formal processing of qualitative data is included as part of concept development or hypothesis formulation. In such generating analyses, numerical or other formal expressions for different characteristics of the qualitative data can serve as a simple and clear presentation of key features of data that are otherwise very complex. A formalized presentation of the qualitative data can also provide opportunities for experimenting with varied combinations of different features of the data. In this way, formal processing of qualitative data can be an effective means of identifying categories or relationships that would otherwise be difficult to detect. Although this formalization of the data is imprecise, it may generate ideas. Although the concepts and hypotheses that are developed have an uncertain empirical basis, they may be relevant and useful, and their scope and validity can be clarified later using more accurate data.

Another approach involves taking an informal approach to quantitative data. This approach is more unusual than the formal processing of qualitative data. However, it may also be appropriate to process quantitative data in informal ways in connection with the development of concepts and hypotheses. If quantitative data are used in such informal analyses, we can ignore many of the requirements for structure and precision that must otherwise be fulfilled when we apply more standardized analytical techniques. Thus, the number of units that are included in different groups, the measurement level of the variables, or the statistical significance of correlations will not be important in informal processing of quantitative data. The purpose of this data processing is not to establish a general overview, but to clarify special concepts or detect interesting relationships. It may be useful for these purposes to work intensively and flexibly with selectively chosen and highly delimited parts of the quantitative data. One of the methods recommended for such quantitative analyses is index construction. Glaser and Strauss (1967) emphasize that systematic development of both formal and informal indexes can be a very useful strategy for generating and refining concepts regarding the social conditions being studied. The results obtained through informal processing

of quantitative data can then be used as the basis for generalizing analyses, where the quantitative data are processed more formally. Thus, field research not only involves a combination of qualitative and quantitative data, but may also involve alternating between formal and informal processing of both types of data.

The relationship between approaches and research questions

So far, three relationships involved in analyses of data combinations have been discussed. A key point in the discussion of all three relationships has been that such data analyses should be as flexible as possible. Above all, this concerns *methodological* flexibility. The analysis strategies are designed to exploit the methods and method combinations that gradually prove to be appropriate or useful for examining the specific research questions. The analysis should also be characterized by *empirical* flexibility. During the analysis, we may discover new and relevant aspects of the social conditions to be studied. It must then be possible for the analysis to be expanded to include these newly identified empirical phenomena. Finally, there is a need for *theoretical* flexibility. The results of the analysis during the research process can provide a basis for incorporating more theoretical perspectives. New theories may be generated, or established theories may be tested, revised and further developed.

The combination of qualitative and quantitative data, as well as the switching between analysis and data collection, between generating and generalizing analyses and between formal and informal data processing must therefore be a flexible approach. As Blau (1963) pointed out, the main purpose of such flexible approaches is that during the analysis, we should be able to detect and understand unforeseen aspects of the matters being studied.

However, the fact that the approach is flexible does not mean that such research designs are characterized by a complete lack of planning and systematics. One of the most important fixed points is the research question of the study. In principle, it could be argued that a certain rigidity with regard to the research question is just as important as the flexibility in the approach. Even when we approach the empirical data with openness, this approach is nevertheless not free of preconceptions. It is not only in connection with more structured research designs that the research question should be discussed thoroughly before the empirical investigations begin. For flexible field research designs, it is equally important to carry out such systematic preparations based on both thorough literature studies and more general insights into social conditions. In this way, the empirical studies can be developed on the basis of a general, overall research question.

As Glaser and Strauss (1967) emphasized, it is important that such theoretical preparations do not develop into a straitjacket, so that they later become a barrier to discovering new aspects of the empirical data. On the contrary, the flexible approach should ensure an openness towards unexpected findings. Such unforeseen results and new interpretations can also entail that the general, overall research question will be specified, clarified, expanded and perhaps partly revised. Nevertheless, it is important that we essentially adhere to the original overall and general research question to be examined. This is one of the prerequisites for using flexible approaches. The basis for the flexible approach to theory, empirical evidence and method is not relativism, but relevance. During the research process, we constantly emphasize the theories, data and methods that are most relevant. Both in principle and in practice, the research question is the most important point of reference for assessing what is relevant. Theories, methods and empirical findings are only relevant to the extent that they can help to investigate the research question. If we also adopt a flexible approach to the research question, the basis for such assessments of relevance will be eliminated and the entire study can easily become dominated by relativism and a lack of planning. This is the point of view that justifies our insistence that the choice of approaches must be governed by the research question.

In some studies, the original research question may turn out to be completely unfruitful and uninteresting. Such an outcome may be due to the fact that the empirical investigations were too poorly prepared and that the research question was not thoroughly discussed in advance. In each case, the consequence of abandoning the original research question will in reality be that the planned project will be terminated or completely changed. Seen from this perspective, there are good reasons to stick to what will be studied, even though we are open to how this is to be analysed.

In other words, it is generally important to combine flexible approaches with a certain rigidity towards the research question to be studied. This research question provides a basis for strategic choices of relevant theories, data, methods and mixed methods designs.

The relationship between triangulating strategies and integrating perspectives

When qualitative and quantitative data are combined in field research, the approach is not only characterized by flexibility. It is also designed for mixed methods and triangulation. Such approaches are intended to achieve openness, diversity and versatility. It is not simply a matter of being able to incorporate the data, methods and theories that gradually seem to be the most useful. It is also important to connect together so many different types of data, methods and theories that the research question is investigated as comprehensively as possible.

As already mentioned, the research question represents a fixed point in this connection. It provides a basis for assessing which data, methods and theories are relevant. The last relationship to be discussed here concerns another systematizing principle. This is a principle about linking together the various results of the analysis with the aid of integrating perspectives. On the one hand, the various data and theories used during the analysis should be relevant to the problem being studied. On the other hand, the various findings and interpretations produced by the analysis should be related to each other and integrated on the basis of more general and unifying perspectives.

Particularly in triangulating research that focuses on combining many different types of data, methods and theories, the analysis can result in very different findings and interpretations. It is important that these results are coordinated and related to one another. Otherwise, the analysis can easily end up with a set of separate and isolated individual results. The insight achieved on the basis of such results can be quite fragmentary. A more comprehensive understanding of the conditions studied will often require that we emphasize the interaction and relationship between the different empirical findings and theoretical reasoning. In some studies, such a discussion of the total pattern of empirical findings can provide a basis for accentuating common features and formulating syntheses. In other studies, the results of the analysis may be more contradictory, so that they point in the direction of alternative hypotheses and competing theories. In all cases, it is important that the different results are discussed in relation to each other and interpreted in light of more general perspectives.

Blau (1963) attached great importance to integrating the various results from his analyses of the activities in bureaucracies in the USA. Blau's point of departure was previous research on bureaucracy, especially Weber's analyses of bureaucratic structures and their ideal typical features (cf. Weber, 2013).

Blau was more concerned with dynamic aspects of the bureaucracy. His research question focused on processes and development trends related to daily activities and interpersonal relationships among employees in public offices. From an early stage in his study, he related different data and methods to different aspects of the research question. During the research process, he developed a central *thesis* about bureaucracy. The thesis suggested that bureaucratic structures continually create conditions that modify these structures. Eventually, the different approaches, results and interpretations were increasingly discussed, organized and integrated with reference to this thesis.

Strongly inspired by Robert Merton, with whom he worked, Blau developed a functionalist understanding of bureaucracy (cf. Merton, 1957). With his emphasis on interaction and dynamism, Blau studied different aspects of the bureaucracy than Weber, who had been more concerned with structures and ideal types. Blau further developed Merton's functionalist paradigm as an integrating perspective on his analyses of processes and relationships in the bureaucracy.

Blau's bureaucracy studies also demonstrated the form that interaction between research questions and integrating perspectives can take in connection with such data combinations and triangulation strategies. Blau's interest in the dynamic character of the bureaucracy seems to be a general guideline throughout his study. Already in his formulation of the research question he directed his attention to these aspects of the bureaucracy. On the one hand, this acted as a guide for the data collection and analysis, as the relevance of different data, methods and theories was considered on the basis of the research question's emphasis on processes and development trends. On the other hand, the flexible and triangulating approach contributed to the research question being empirically examined in a comprehensive manner and partly by means of unforeseen data. Thus, the understanding of the dynamic aspects of the bureaucracy could be clarified by a central thesis and related to a more general, functionalist frame of reference. This frame of reference was gradually developed into an integrating perspective that made it possible to coordinate all the different results of the analysis.

To summarize, a typical approach in the mixed methods research discussed here can be described in the following, highly simplified manner. Initially, an overall research question is formulated as clearly as possible. The research question is investigated through a combination of qualitative and quantitative data, as well as by alternating between data collection and analysis, between generating and generalizing analyses and between formal and informal data processing. The approach is characterized by openness towards unforeseen data and empirical findings, and emphasis is placed on capturing diversity in the social conditions studied. In this process, the research question is a criterion of relevance, while it can also be clarified, expanded and partly revised. Eventually, increasing emphasis is placed on a more comprehensive understanding and coordination of the different results of the analysis, with reference to integrating perspectives.

CHAPTER HIGHLIGHTS

- There are clear differences between qualitative studies and quantitative studies with regard to key aspects of the data collection:
  1 The relation to the data sources is different. In qualitative studies, the relationship is open and flexible. In quantitative studies, the relationship is programmed and structured.
  2 The principles for the treatment of the sources are different. Qualitative studies focus on the accessibility of all relevant information, while quantitative studies emphasize comparability between the units selected.
  3 The principles for data recording are different. Qualitative studies prioritize completeness, while quantitative studies emphasize precision.
  4 The key part of the data collection is different. In qualitative studies the researcher is the most important part, while the instrument is the most important part in quantitative studies.
- There are clear differences between qualitative and quantitative studies with regard to key aspects of the data analysis:

1 The purpose of the analyses is different. Qualitative analyses emphasize depth and aim to achieve a comprehensive understanding of specific conditions, as well as developing hypotheses and theories. Quantitative analyses emphasize breadth and aim to achieve a representative overview of general conditions, as well as testing hypotheses and theories.
2 The key elements of the analyses are different. Qualitative analyses emphasize concepts, categories and typologies, while quantitative analyses emphasize frequencies, distributions and correlations.
3 The organization of the analyses is different. In qualitative studies, analysis and interpretation take place in parallel with the data collection. Such analyses are not based on standardized techniques, and the data set may become overly complex. In quantitative studies, the analysis takes place after the data collection, and large volumes of data can be processed and analysed using statistical techniques and computer programs.
4 The presentation of the results of the analysis is different. Qualitative analyses emphasize illustration using quotes,

while quantitative analyses emphasize documentation using tables.

- Qualitative and quantitative data can be combined in mixed methods research, which is also called methodological triangulation.
- Four different strategies for combining qualitative and quantitative data have been suggested:

  1 The most common strategy is to perform certain qualitative studies in preparation for quantitative studies.
  2 A less traditional strategy is based on the opposite sequence between the two approaches: conducting qualitative studies to follow up quantitative studies.
  3 Probably the most interesting strategy entails parallel and concurrent utilization of qualitative and quantitative data.
  4 A simpler and more problematic form of parallel utilization of the two types of data involves collecting qualitative data that are quantified during the analysis.

- In analysing combinations of qualitative and quantitative data, we have to consider five important relationships:

  1 The relationship between analysis and collection of data
  2 The relationship between generating and generalizing analyses
  3 The relationship between formal and informal data processing
  4 The relationship between approaches and research questions
  5 The relationship between triangulating strategies and integrating perspectives.

RESEARCH EXAMPLES

It is recommended that you read the articles that are referred to as research examples in this chapter.

Several publications are referred to as research examples in this chapter. Six of these publications were also presented and described as research examples in Chapter 6:

Eurofound (2012) *Third European Quality of Life Survey – Quality of Life in Europe: Impacts of the Crisis*. Luxembourg: Publications Office of the European Union.

Gould, Dinah, and Marina Fontenla (2006) 'Commitment to nursing: Results of a qualitative interview study', *Journal of Nursing Management* 14, 213–221.

Humphreys, Lee, Phillippa Gill, Balachander Krishnamurthy, and Elisabeth Newbury (2013) 'Historicizing new media: A content analysis of Twitter', *Journal of Communication* 63(3), 413–431.

Nielsen, Rasmus Kleis (2012) *Ground Wars: Personalized Communication in Political Campaigns*. Princeton, NJ: Princeton University Press.

Oosthuizen, Martha J. (2012) 'The portrayal of nursing in South-African newspapers: A qualitative content analysis', *Africa Journal of Nursing and Midwifery* 14(1), 49–62.

Russell, Marie, Rachel Price, Louise Signal, James Stanley, Zachery Gerring, and Jacqueline Cumming (2011) 'What do passengers do during travel time? Structured observations on buses and trains', *Journal of Public Transportation* 14(3), 123–146.

Furthermore, the bureaucracy study which was presented in Chapter 1 and further discussed in Chapter 6, is also used as a research example in this chapter:

Blau, Peter M. (1963) *The Dynamics of Bureaucracy: A Study of Interpersonal Relationships in Two Government Agencies* (rev. edn). Chicago: University of Chicago Press.

In addition, three other research examples are referred to in this chapter:

Lawson, Katie M., Laura Y. Kooiman, and Olyvia Kuchta (2018) 'Professors' behaviors and attributes that promote U.S. women's success in male-dominated academic majors: Results from a mixed methods study', *Sex Roles* 78(7–8), 542–560.

The mixed methods study presented in this article is an example of how qualitative studies can be used to prepare quantitative studies. The purpose was to examine the importance of professors' behaviour and attributes for the success of female students in university studies dominated by male students. Based on results of a qualitative focus group study, a survey study was carried out to extend the research. Although the two types of data were analysed separately, the results of the analyses were presented together and integrated in an overall discussion of the findings. The results indicated that professors' behaviour as well as environmental factors were important for the academic achievements of the female students.

Lee, Barbara, Esme Fuller-Thomson, Barbara Fallon, Nico Trocmé, and Tara Black (2017) 'Asian-Canadian children and families involved in the child welfare system in Canada: A mixed methods study', *Child Abuse & Neglect* 70, 342–355.

This article presents a mixed methods study that exemplifies how qualitative studies can be used to follow up quantitative studies. Secondary analyses of nationwide quantitative data on child-maltreatment-related investigations were conducted to compare Asian-Canadian and White Canadian children and families involved in the child welfare system. Results of these analyses were presented and discussed in focus groups with child-welfare workers as participants. Qualitative data from the focus groups and from semi-structured interviews were used to examine the child-welfare workers' experiences and perceptions of working with Asian-Canadian children and families involved in the child welfare system. Thus, the qualitative analyses were conducted to explain results from the quantitative analyses in more depth. The results of the two analyses were presented together and combined in an overall discussion. The study showed that Asian-Canadian children are substantially different from White Canadian children, and that they represent a diversity of cultural values and family norms, with important implications for social work practice and policies.

Yanchus, Nancy J., Lindsey Ohler, Emily Crowe, Robert Teclaw, and Katerine Osatuke (2017) '"You just can't do it all": a secondary analysis of nurses' perceptions of teamwork, staffing and workload', *Journal of Research in Nursing* 22(4), 313—325.

This article is an example of how qualitative data may be quantified. The article presents a secondary analysis of qualitative data on nurses' perceptions of teamwork, staffing and workload, based on unstructured interviews with 271 nurses. These nurses were selected from different clinical units at seven Veterans Health Administration hospitals in the USA. In a previous study, the qualitative data had been collected and coded into a number of thematic categories. In their secondary analysis of these data, Yanchus et al. (2017) quantified the coded data set, focusing on the themes of teamwork, staffing and workload. They examined the frequencies of the themes and the relationships between the themes, using Pearson's correlation analysis.

1 What are the most important differences between qualitative and quantitative studies in the treatment of data sources?

2 What are the typical differences between qualitative and quantitative studies in the purpose of the analysis?

3 What are the most important differences between qualitative and quantitative studies in the key elements of the analysis?

4 Why should ontological and epistemological issues be considered when qualitative and quantitative data are combined in mixed methods research?

5 Discuss how the quality of life study, described in Chapter 6 and in this chapter, could be followed up by a qualitative study.

6 Discuss how the nursing study, described in Chapter 6 and in this chapter, could be followed up by a quantitative study.

7 Discuss how unemployment could be examined in a mixed methods study. Formulate one or more research questions and suggest a strategy for combining qualitative and quantitative data in the study.

RECOMMENDED LITERATURE

Brannen, Julia (ed.) (1995) *Mixing Methods: Qualitative and Quantitative Research*. Aldershot: Avebury.

This book provides a comprehensive discussion of the theoretical, methodological and practical issues of mixing different methods and combining qualitative and quantitative data in social research. The use of data combinations is illustrated by means of examples from a number of studies that have successfully combined qualitative and quantitative approaches.

Creswell, John W. (2014) *A Concise Introduction to Mixed Methods Research*. London: Sage.

This book presents an introduction to mixed methods research, and provides a foundation for understanding the methodology of such research. It is written for students in different social science disciplines and is recommended as a text for workshops or seminars, or as supplementary reading in undergraduate and graduate classes.

Teddlie, Charles, and Abbas Tashakkori (2009) *Foundations of Mixed Methods Research: Integrating Quantitative and Qualitative Approaches in the Social and Behavioral Sciences*. Los Angeles: Sage.

Starting with a historical overview of the development of mixed methods research, this book describes how such research can be carried out. Mixed methods approaches are discussed with reference to all stages in the research process, including formulating research questions, constructing research designs, sampling units, collecting and analysing data, as well as interpreting findings.

PART V

ASKING AND ANSWERING QUESTIONS IN SOCIAL SCIENCE

The online resources are here to help with asking and answering questions!

Visit https://study.sagepub.com/gronmo to access real-world practice datasets, videos, case studies, key term definitions, and critical thinking exercises that will help you learn more about answering social science questions.

DESCRIPTION, EXPLANATION
AND UNDERSTANDING

This chapter provides the necessary knowledge for understanding the differences between descriptive, explanatory and interpretive studies, as well as how qualitative and quantitative data can be used in such studies.

The chapter will teach you about

- how social conditions can be described in qualitative and quantitative studies
- the meaning of causal relations in social science
- strategies for developing causal hypotheses in qualitative studies
- the differences between multivariate analysis and experimental studies

- the essential features of phenomenological and hermeneutical studies
- how to develop holistic understanding in qualitative studies.

Typical social science questions

Part IV of this book (Chapters 16–20) examined various approaches, methods and techniques for analysing qualitative and quantitative data, as well as strategies and challenges for analyses based on combinations of the two types of data. Methodological discussions of social science analyses, however, are about more than how different analyses are carried out. It is also important to understand how the analyses form the basis for developing new social science knowledge and insights. This requires not only knowledge of different methods of analysis, but also an understanding of how different analyses are related to more general social science perspectives. In addition to specific methods, we need to discuss more general approaches and perspectives for asking and answering typical questions in social science. This is the topic of this part of the book, which consists of this chapter and the next three chapters.

In Chapter 4, it was pointed out that the content of research questions can be used as a basis for distinguishing between different types of questions. In terms of substantial content, research questions may focus on different kinds of knowledge, or they may deal with different kinds of social phenomena.

Whereas these types of questions were briefly described in Chapter 4, they will be discussed more thoroughly in this and the following two chapters. In addition, Chapter 24 is devoted to big data and computational social science, which provide new possibilities as well as new challenges for asking and answering questions in social science.

Questions referring to different *types of social conditions* will be examined in Chapters 22 and 23. Chapter 22 is focused on questions that refer to time, space or different levels in society, whereas Chapter 23 deals with questions referring to social relations, networks or structures. This chapter concentrates on questions related to different *kinds of knowledge*. As pointed out in Chapter 4, such questions may be focused on description, explanation or understanding of the social conditions to be studied.

The next section will review descriptive studies. Such studies are intended to map and discuss different characteristics or features of the social conditions being studied. The primary purpose is to clarify the facts about these social conditions, how they vary, or how they change. Such descriptions of actual circumstances include ethnographic descriptions based on qualitative analyses, as well as descriptive quantitative analyses.

The presentation of descriptions is followed by a section on explanatory studies. The purpose of such studies is to explain the social conditions that are of interest. The questions are focused on how certain phenomena in society can be explained by other phenomena. After a general discussion of the distinction between causal relationships and statistical correlations, the development of causal hypotheses based on qualitative analyses and the testing of causal hypotheses based on quantitative analyses will be discussed. In connection with quantitative causal analyses, two different analytic strategies are explored: multivariate causal analysis and experimental studies.

Finally in this chapter, interpretive studies are examined. Such studies are based on understanding or interpreting the meaning of the social conditions that are of interest. Interpretive studies are mainly based on qualitative data, although some quantitative studies may also provide a basis for interpreting the meaning aspects of different phenomena. The section on interpretive studies deals with phenomenological and hermeneutical studies, which are focused on understanding based on the participants' own intentions, opinions and perspectives. Finally, it is shown how the researcher can develop a comprehensive or holistic understanding through contextual interpretation.

In practice, there are no sharp boundaries between description, explanation and understanding, and elements of all types of knowledge may be combined in the same research project. Nevertheless, it is important and useful to be aware of the most important differences between these three typical social science questions.

Descriptive studies

The purpose of descriptive studies is to identify and investigate actual conditions or phenomena in society. The kinds of relationships or phenomena that are described may vary. Descriptive studies may include units at different levels and different types of information about these units. The descriptions can focus attention on, for example, action and interaction patterns, expressions of opinion, group differences, distribution patterns, structural conditions, change processes and development trends.

The manner in which the descriptions are formed may also vary. However, descriptive social science studies differ from other types of descriptions of social conditions, such as journalistic presentations and reports. The most important feature of social science descriptions is that they are analytical. The analytical nature of the descriptions can be expressed in different ways. An important analytical characteristic is that the descriptions are related to previous research and are based on social science concepts. Another way of making descriptions analytical is that the conditions studied are discussed with reference to certain norms or standards for how the circumstances should be expected to be. For example, descriptions of income level and income distribution can be described with reference to poverty line standards and norms for economic equality in society. A third way of ensuring the analytical nature of descriptions is that the descriptions are comparative. Studies of income conditions could, for example, focus on inequalities between men and women, social class or different countries with regard to both income level and income variations. A fourth analytical feature of social science descriptions could be that they are dynamic. Dynamic descriptions of income conditions highlight how the income level and income distribution develop or change over time.

Such descriptions may have both scientific and social significance. They may be important for discovering new and unknown aspects of society and for developing new knowledge about social conditions. Descriptive studies can help to demonstrate and document that certain social conditions are as we have assumed, or that they are not as expected. Systematic descriptions of different conditions in society can form the basis for criticism of these social conditions, and they can be a starting point for changing those circumstances. Systematic descriptions of income conditions and their development can, for example, contribute to criticism of income policy and may result in this policy being changed.

Descriptive studies in social science can be based on both qualitative and quantitative analyses. The main features of the two types of descriptive studies will be discussed.

Ethnographic description

Descriptions based on qualitative analyses are usually called *ethnographic* descriptions. It is common to distinguish between thin and thick ethnographic descriptions. The term *thick description* is particularly associated with the American anthropologist Clifford Geertz (1926–2006). Such descriptions emphasize not only the actual conditions, but are also intended to identify the meaning of the observed conditions for the actors involved, in light of the context in which they occur (Geertz, 2000). In this sense, a thick description entails not only a purely descriptive presentation, but also interpretation and understanding, which will be reviewed at the end of this chapter, in the section on contextual interpretation and holistic understanding. Ethnographic descriptions that concentrate on only presentations of actual conditions as they are observed by the researcher are called *thin descriptions*. These descriptions will be discussed in this section.

Ethnographic descriptions can illustrate different conditions in bounded environments, such as particular organizations, institutions or communities. The descriptions can highlight selected actors and their actions or opinions, or they can highlight specific events. Such studies may also be suitable for revealing patterns of relationships or interaction,

and they can shed light on events and processes within limited time-frames.

As pointed out in Chapter 16, analysis of qualitative data is often based on coding the data with a view to categorization and concept development. This procedure can be used to develop an ethnographic description. The systematic sorting and processing of the material that the coding entails helps the ethnographic description to be analytical. The analytical character of the description will also be enhanced if the presentation is arranged and organized with reference to the concepts and categories that are developed, or based on the types and typologies into which the material can be divided. Ethnographic descriptions can also be linked to categories, concepts or typologies that have been developed and discussed in previous research.

However, the use of social science concepts and categories in ethnographic descriptions may be more or less systematic and more or less explicit. Ethnographic descriptions can be very detailed. The presentation usually places great emphasis on accurate reproduction of actual observations and empirical conditions. In many cases, ethnographic descriptions are presented in the form of *narratives*. Such a narrative is a consistent and comprehensive report on the conditions the researcher has studied. The qualitative analysis, in the form of coding and categorization, entails that the qualitative data are divided into different text elements, and that these are grouped and arranged in relation to each other and with reference to more general concepts. When this analysis is used as the basis for an ethnographic description in the form of a narrative, the different text elements are combined together in a new way so that together they constitute the comprehensive and coherent narrative or story that the scientist wishes to tell.

In ethnographic descriptions, the content of such narratives is based on the researcher's observations of actual conditions but, at the same time, the narrative is designed in such a way that the researcher produces an analytical presentation of these conditions. In other words, the narrative is both based on empirical facts and designed by the researcher.

In designing the narrative, the researcher usually uses certain analytical or systematizing steps so that the presentation clarifies the key features of the conditions being studied. The narrative is often developed on the basis of some basic dimensions.

The most common dimension in narratives is the *chronology*, or the sequence between the elements that are included in the narrative. This time dimension is particularly useful in studies of events and processes, but it can also work well in studies of action and interaction patterns. In the study itself, and especially in the analysis of the qualitative data, the actual chronology of events or actions can be pushed to the background or toned down in favour of other analytical principles. Particularly in connection with coding and categorization, there will be features of the text elements other than their position in the time that become central. When the researcher designs a narrative that emphasizes chronology as the systematizing dimension, the actual, natural or typical chronology of the events and the actions in the data is reconstructed.

When narratives are included in ethnographic descriptions, the researcher usually uses other organizing dimensions in addition to chronology. The purpose of such dimensions is to pay special attention to particular circumstances. These may be circumstances that are particularly emphasized in the research question, or circumstances that have become particularly prominent during the data collection process. In studies of interaction patterns, such a narrative may emphasize, for example, which actors interact at different times, what they interact about, and what characterizes the relationship between the interaction partners. In studies of negotiation processes, for example,

the narrative can be organized on the basis of different phases, different turning points, different driving forces and different actor constellations in the negotiations. Such organizing dimensions in narratives are commonly referred to as *configurational* dimensions. We can also say that the narrative is constructed around a particular *plot*.

Ethnographic descriptions can also be based on other types of linguistic or rhetorical devices in order to highlight particular features of the conditions being studied. The use of *metaphors* is important in this context. For example, the Canadian sociologist Erving Goffman (1922–1982) used dramaturgical metaphors in his studies of people's daily lives. Everyday life was described as if it was a theatre performance, with emphasis on concepts such as *actor*, *role* and *stage* (Goffman, 1959).

An article by Maddox (2015) includes an ethnographic description that is related to a framework developed by Goffman (1964). The article is focused on standardized assessments of adult literacy among nomadic herders in the Gobi desert in Mongolia. Based on participant observation, the researcher presents an ethnographic description of *the situation and the context* in which the assessment tests took place. Within this situation and context, the interaction between the testing team, as representatives of the state, the selected herder, as respondent, and other herders, as bystanders, is described and related to some of Goffman's concepts. The purpose of this ethnographic description was to analyse how the assessment performance was influenced by the particular linguistic interaction, considering 'larger cultural and institutional dimensions of the test as a social occasion' (Maddox, 2015: 440).

The researcher's choice of configurational dimensions, metaphors and other devices in the presentation requires a certain amount of interpretation of the qualitative data and their significance, as well as the actual description of the specific circumstances. The use of such pres- entation devices is therefore even more important in interpretive studies than in purely descriptive studies.

Descriptive quantitative analyses

The simplest form of descriptive quantitative analy- sis is univariate analysis, where we describe how the units are distributed on the different values of each variable. Overviews of the age distribution in the population, the income distribution in the working population, and the distribution of votes for different political parties among voters are examples of such analyses. Descriptive quantitative analyses can also be bivariate or multivariate. Such analyses reveal relationships or covariations between two or more variables, but without the relationships being linked to causal hypotheses or explanatory models. This means that we do not distinguish between dependent and independent variables, but assume instead that there is a sym- metrical relationship between the variables in the analysis. Correlation analyses can thus be descrip- tive analyses. Such analyses can describe, for example, covariations or correlations between age, income and home size.

Descriptive quantitative analyses can also reveal more complex structural patterns. Such patterns can be described, for example, on the basis of net- work analyses and can be presented using sociograms or measures of centrality, centraliza- tion, density, and other features of the network. In this way, we can analyse phenomena such as social networks between residents in a neighbourhood or network connections between large companies in a country. Studies of relations, networks and struc- tures will be further discussed in Chapter 23.

Some descriptive quantitative analyses concen- trate on distributions, relationships or structural patterns for a particular group of units or for a particular society at a single point in time. Such

studies can, for example, provide an overview of special conditions or circumstances in Australian society in 2004, among young people in Europe in the mid-1990s, or in the fishing industry in Iceland at the end of the 1980s.

Descriptive quantitative analyses can also compare different groups of units or different societies at a single point in time. We can then identify differences in distributions, relationships or structural patterns. These include salary differences between women and men in Canada today, differences in the state of health of different age groups, productivity differences between different enterprises, differences between Texas and California regarding income distribution in the two states, and differences between Norway and Sweden with regard to the degree of concentration and centralization of grocery stores. In other words, such analyses can include both correlations between different variables, such as gender and salary, and larger comparative analyses of different organizations, communities or countries.

A third design for descriptive quantitative analyses examines how distributions, contexts or structural patterns change over time for a particular group of units or for a particular society. By comparing the same conditions at different times, we can identify stability or changes in these conditions for the group or society being analysed. Both short-term and long-term changes can be described. For example, we can examine changes in support for various political parties during the 1990s, or analyse the structural changes in the German banking system from 1945 to 2000.

A fourth type of descriptive quantitative analysis involves combinations of differences and changes. By comparing different groups at different times, we can describe how the differences between groups change over time. We can clarify whether wage differences between women and men have increased or decreased from 1980 to the present day, or whether differences in the provision of child day-care between different municipalities have changed over the last ten years.

Studies of changes and studies focusing on comparisons will be discussed in more detail in Chapter 22.

Explanatory studies

In the presentation of the results from a descriptive analysis, the researchers will usually append various types of comments to the analysis. In such comments, the researchers can discuss the results of their own study in light of concepts, perspectives and results from previous research. They can also comment on the results of the analysis in light of the research question, views expressed in public debate, or decisions, plans and measures in politics, public administration or business. Such comments may include reflections and speculations about possible explanations of the empirical findings produced in the study. In descriptive studies, however, such explanatory possibilities are not followed up in further empirical analyses.

The most important feature of explanatory studies is that the empirical data are analysed systematically in order to develop or test different possibilities for explaining the social conditions studied. The analysis includes both data on social conditions to be explained, and data on other social conditions that can explain why the first-mentioned conditions are as they are. If the researcher wishes to investigate whether pay differences between women and men can be explained by discrimination against women in working life, a preliminary study would include analyses of data about both pay gaps and discrimination, in order to clarify the relationship between these conditions. Ideally, the analysis should also include data about other possible explanations for differences in pay between women and men, so that the importance of gender discrimination as an explanation

can be compared with the importance of other possible explanations.

Explanatory studies in social science are often concerned with clarifying causal relationships between two or more social phenomena. Such analyses, which are also known as *causal analyses*, are about developing and testing hypotheses about specific causal relationships.

Some key features of various types of causal analyses will now be considered. First, it is explained how the concept of causality is understood in social science studies, with particular emphasis on the distinction between causal relationships and statistical correlations. Then, it is shown how qualitative analyses can be used to develop causal hypotheses, and how causal hypotheses can be tested using different types of quantitative analyses.

Causal relationships and statistical correlations

Hypotheses about causal relationships are usually linked to more general theories of social mechanisms or social processes that can explain why specific social patterns are formed, maintained, changed, developed or dismantled.

A strict and precise understanding of the concept of causality entails that a particular phenomenon (B) always has the same cause (A), and that a particular cause (A) always has the same effect (B). Such a causal relationship is called *deterministic*. Deterministic causal relationships exist between phenomena in nature, but we cannot expect to find such relationships between societal phenomena.

While deterministic causal relationships are important in natural science, social science usually focuses on another understanding of the concept of causality. Based on such an understanding of the concept, a phenomenon (A) will be regarded as the cause of another phenomenon (B) if there is a certain probability that A leads to B, or that A increases the probability of B. Such a causal relationship is called *stochastic*. The relationship could also be called *tendential* because there is a tendency for A to cause B. The connection between education and income can be regarded as a stochastic causal relationship. There is a certain likelihood that a higher level of education will lead to higher income, but not everyone with high education has a high income and not everyone with a low level of education has a low income.

Stochastic or tendential causal relationships between two phenomena require that there is a certain covariation between the two phenomena that can be demonstrated empirically. In qualitative studies, such covariations can be detected through description and interpretation of different patterns in the data being analysed. In quantitative studies, stochastic causal relationships can be expressed in the form of statistical correlations. For example, the relationship between education and income can be expressed as a relatively high correlation between the two variables.

However, not all covariations or statistical correlations are expressions of causality. Simply put, a statistical correlation between two phenomena is a necessary but not a sufficient condition for a causal relationship between the two phenomena. Another necessary condition for causality is that the statistical correlation is not spurious. As pointed out in Chapter 18, a statistical correlation between two phenomena is spurious if the relationship is due to the fact that both phenomena are the effects of a third phenomenon. The spurious correlation will then disappear when we control for the effect of the third phenomenon. A statistical correlation between income and visits to the opera, for example, may prove to be spurious because both income and visits to the opera are linked to education. In such a case, there is a tendency for people with a high level of education to have high income and a relatively high level of interest in opera, and the correlation between income and visits to the opera will disappear when we control for education. In this case, education constitutes a common underlying cause of both income and visits to the opera. The bivariate statistical correlation between income and visits to the opera is then spurious and cannot therefore be an expression of causality.

A third necessary condition for a causal relationship between two phenomena is that there is a certain *chronology* between the two phenomena, so that the phenomenon that is assumed to be the cause occurs *before* the phenomenon that is believed to be the effect. In the relationship between education and income, education usually comes before income. We get an education before we enter the labour market and receive an income. Admittedly, we can also take further education and continuing education after we have been working for many years, but this can in turn affect the income we receive, so that the income level increases after we have obtained supplementary education. In many cases, the chronology of different phenomena can be explained purely logically or intuitively. In other cases, this may be more unclear or complicated. It may then be necessary to carry out an empirical study of the chronology between the phenomena that are part of a causal hypothesis.

A fourth condition for a causal relationship between two phenomena is that there is a certain *proximity in time (and space)* between the two phenomena. If high education is a cause of high income, we must assume that this effect will materialize quite quickly. If highly educated people only achieve a high income after they have been working for many years, the high income could be explained by a number of other factors, such as age, seniority, experience or networking. Such explanatory factors may act in addition to education, in combination with education or instead of education. In any event, a causal relationship between education and income is less likely the longer people with high education must be employed before they earn a high income.

To clarify whether there is a causal relationship between different social phenomena, we therefore need to do the following:

1 Examine whether there is an empirical *covariation* between the phenomena.
2 Check whether this empirical relationship is *spurious*.
3 Identify the *chronology* between the phenomena in order to clarify whether the phenomenon that is assumed to be the cause, exists or occurs prior to the phenomenon that is assumed to be the effect.
4 Determine whether there is sufficient *proximity in time* between the assumed cause and the assumed effect.

These four assumptions for determining causality form the basis for both the development of causal hypotheses in qualitative analyses, and testing of such hypotheses in quantitative analyses.

Qualitative causal analyses

Chapter 16 explained in general how qualitative analyses can be used for developing hypotheses and theories. Let us now consider in particular the development of causal hypotheses in qualitative analyses, with particular focus on how this hypothesis development relates to the four prerequisites for determining causality.

In view of the first prerequisite for empirical covariation, qualitative analyses are particularly well suited to *discovering* such covariations. Such analyses can go into detail and thus find patterns or connections that are difficult to detect through more general quantitative analyses. Qualitative analyses are also flexible, so that any patterns and connections discovered during the analysis can be followed up and investigated further as the data collection and data analysis progress. Thus, the analysis can provide both better evidence *that* there

is a systematic relationship between certain phenomena, and better insight into *how* these phenomena are interrelated. Since qualitative analyses focus on observing different phenomena in light of the specific context in which these phenomena occur, they can also provide good opportunities to understand *why* particular phenomena are linked together in a particular way.

The researcher will endeavour to investigate whether such relationships can be assumed to be typical and general, or whether they only apply to a few special actors or in a few specific situations. Two of the approaches discussed in Chapter 16 are particularly important when it comes to clarifying whether observed relationships can be assumed to apply across different actors and situations. One of these is the search for deviating cases, which is a method for assessing the empirical basis of causal hypotheses. Using this approach, the hypothesis can be formulated so that we are sure that the relationship applies for all the cases in the data. The more types of actors, events, actions and situations included in the analysis, the more empirically founded the hypothesis will be.

The other important approach for assessing the basis of the causal hypothesis is theoretical generalization. The researchers discuss their own empirical analyses of the assumed causal relationship in light of relevant empirical results and theoretical insights from previous research. This forms the basis for assessing whether the hypothesis can be assumed to also apply beyond the context, situations and units examined by the researcher.

Both the search for deviating cases and theoretical generalization contribute to the causal hypothesis being specified and clarified in such a way that the assumed empirical basis and theoretical foundation for the hypothesis become as general and solid as possible. For a more comprehensive empirical examination of the general foundation of the hypothesis, however, we must analyse data from larger areas and from across different contexts, as we can do in quantitative studies, with emphasis on probability sampling and statistical generalization.

The second prerequisite for clarifying causal relationships, that the empirical relationship is not spurious, must be considered already in the formulation of a causal hypothesis. In qualitative analyses, the researcher will try to find indications of alternative possible explanations, both different effects of the same phenomenon and different causes for the same phenomenon. In this connection, various possibilities are also evaluated regarding whether there is a common underlying cause of two different phenomena that seem to covary, so that the correlation is spurious. Since qualitative studies are both intensive and flexible, they can provide good opportunities to investigate such opportunities as the analyses gradually reveal new patterns.

Through such investigations and considerations the probability of spuriosity can be reduced. This reinforces the researcher's basis for formulating a causal hypothesis based on the original empirical connection. On the other hand, the investigations and considerations of the possibilities of a common underlying cause may increase the likelihood of spuriosity. This weakens the basis for formulating a causal hypothesis based on the covariation that was initially identified. Instead, it may be appropriate to develop two other hypotheses that specify causal relationships between the underlying cause and each of the two phenomena that were included in the original empirical connection. A third outcome of the researcher's investigations and evaluations of possible common underlying causes could be that it is difficult to determine whether or not the empirical connection is spurious, and that both possibilities are considered to be equally probable. In that case, three different and partly competing hypotheses can be formulated, one based on the original empirical connection, and two that clarify the causal relationship between

the possible underlying cause and each of the two phenomena in the original connection.

Qualitative analyses can rarely progress further than this in clarifying questions about spuriosity. Further and more comprehensive analyses of possible underlying causes are usually based on quantitative data.

Qualitative analyses can often provide a good basis for assessing the last two preconditions for clarifying causal relationships, about the chronology and proximity in time between the assumed cause and the assumed effect. This is not only because qualitative analyses are intensive and flexible enough to closely examine the relationship between different phenomena as such relationships gradually prove to be interesting. Such analyses are usually also suitable for providing detailed insights into the development of social processes and courses of events over time. This applies in particular to studies where the research question itself is concerned with such processes and courses of events. The manner in which different phenomena are related to each other in terms of chronology and proximity in time is usually a key part of such research questions. Formulations of causal hypotheses can then be based on first-hand empirical knowledge of these two prerequisites for clarifying the causal relationship between phenomena that are included in the hypotheses.

A limitation of qualitative studies, however, is that the investigation period is usually relatively short. Processes and events can be studied in great detail, but rarely over long periods of time. The empirical explanation of the chronology and proximity in time between different phenomena is therefore limited to actions, events, opinions or situations that are within the defined period of time for the current study. More specifically, this means that such analyses do not have particularly good potential for direct empirical investigation of possible causes that occur prior to the investigation period, or possible effects that may occur after the investigation period has passed. Such direct empirical clarification is mainly limited to phenomena that occur closely to each other in time. On the other hand, it is precisely such phenomena that are of most interest in relation to causality, since proximity in time is one of the four prerequisites for such conditions.

Quantitative causal analyses

While qualitative analyses can be suitable for the development and formulation of causal hypotheses, quantitative analyses are more suitable for examining or testing such hypotheses. Hypothesis testing is based on both descriptive and inductive statistics and emphasizes the analysis of correlations between variables based on the four preconditions for clarification of causal relationships.

With regard to the assumption of empirical covariation, quantitative analyses can provide good insights into the characteristics of empirical relationships between different variables. As we have seen, there are a number of methods and techniques to identify the strength, direction and form of the relationships, and to assess whether the relationships are statistically significant. Such analyses can be based on wide-ranging probability samples, and thus they can show whether the relationships apply to large populations and across many different contexts.

Quantitative analyses also provide good opportunities for checking whether empirical correlations are spurious. In principle, there are two different strategies for such checks. One strategy is *multivariate causal analysis*, which entails investigating whether the bivariate correlation between two variables in a causal hypothesis (assumed cause and assumed effect) changes when we control for the effect of one or more other *specified* variables (possible underlying causes). The effects of selected potential underlying causes are controlled in turn.

The second strategy is *experimental studies*, where the relationship between the two variables in a causal hypothesis is examined under conditions that allow us to ignore the systematic effects of *all* variables other than the causal variable. The effects of all potential underlying variables are controlled by a particular form of probability sampling called *randomization*. In the further review of quantitative explanatory studies, multivariate causal analysis as well as experimental studies will be discussed.

Experimental studies are conducted in such a way that both the precondition of the chronology between the cause variables and the effect variable, and the precondition of the proximity in time between the two variables, are under full control.

A *dynamic analysis* is another design for quantitative analysis of causal relationships that also provides a good overview of the chronology and temporal proximity between the variables. This is a special design for analysing different types of series of events, such as people's career development. While experiments involve the researcher controlling the chronology and the proximity between the two variables, a dynamic analysis entails that the chronology and the temporal proximity can be identified empirically in the analysis itself. However, dynamic analysis will not be discussed further here.

In multivariate causal analysis, the temporal relationship between the variables may be rather unclear. In many such analyses, the preconditions regarding chronology and temporal proximity are neither controlled by the researcher nor clarified empirically in the data to be analysed. The researcher must then consider these questions based on current theories, previous empirical research and general social science insights. When it is particularly difficult to determine the chronology of two variables, it may also be appropriate to perform two alternative versions of the causal analysis, one version for each of the two possible chronologies between the variables.

Multivariate causal analysis

A general discussion of multivariate analysis was presented in Chapter 18. Let us now focus on how such analyses are used to test causal hypotheses. That is what we call *multivariate causal analysis*.

Hypotheses about causal relationships are called *causal hypotheses*. Independent variables are called *causal variables* or *causes*, while dependent variables are called *effect variables* or *effects*. Multivariate causal analysis can be used to test one or more causal hypotheses, and each of the hypotheses tested can specify causal relationships between two or more variables. In other words, such an analysis can be applied to relationships between one or more causal variables and one or more effect variables.

The first step in a multivariate causal analysis is to clarify the relationship between the variables that will be included in the analysis. We do this by specifying a *causal model*. A very simple causal model consists of just one causal hypothesis with one causal variable and one effect variable. If the hypothesis assumes that there is a causal relationship between education and income, the model can be presented as shown in Figure 21.1. The specification of the causal model is based on the wording of the causal hypothesis. Both the hypothesis formulation and the model specification are based on the preconditions of chronology and temporal proximity of the variables.

Education ⟶ Income

Figure 21.1 Causal relationship between education and income

The next step in the causal analysis is to identify and describe the empirical relationship between the variables. In connection with the simple model in Figure 21.1, this concerns the bivariate relationship between education and income. For example, the analysis could be based on personal data from a probability sample of the population in the 30–65-year age group. The empirical relationship can be analysed using, for example, table analysis or regression analysis. Based on a chi-square test or a *t*-test, we can determine whether the relationship is statistically significant, so that it is not due to random errors in the sampling, but can be assumed instead to apply to the entire population.

If we find a significant bivariate relationship between the two variables, the third step in the causal analysis will consist of checking whether this relationship is spurious. We control for certain potential underlying variables, such as gender, age, class background and place of residence. In principle, the choice of such control variables is based on theoretical reasoning about which factors can be assumed to affect the two variables in the causal hypothesis. In practice, we usually need to concentrate on only some of the theoretically interesting control variables, partly because we cannot select variables other than those available in the current data, and partly because there are limits to how many variables can be included in a single analysis.

This entails that we expand the analysis from bivariate to multivariate relationships. We also conduct significance testing of the individual relationships in this multivariate analysis. If both education and income are effects of one or more of the other variables, the control for the other variables will cause the relationship between education and income to disappear. In that case, the original relationship is spurious, and the causal hypothesis can be rejected.

If the correlation between the two variables in the hypothesis survives the control for the other variables, the likelihood of spuriosity has been weakened and the causal hypothesis has correspondingly been strengthened. It must be emphasized, however, that this conclusion regarding spuriosity applies solely to the control variables included in the multivariate analysis.

It will always be possible that controls for *other* potential underlying variables could detect spuriosity. We must always allow for this uncertainty in multivariate causal analysis, because it will never be possible to control for all potential underlying causes.

One or more of the control variables can also be included in the causal model itself. The model will then become more complex, as in the trivariate model shown in Figure 21.2, where place of residence is assumed to be an underlying causal variable for education and income. This model entails that the original causal hypothesis is replaced by two new hypotheses, one about education as an effect of place of residence, and one about income as an effect of place of residence. In this case, it is assumed that there is no bivariate relationship between education and income, or that such a relationship is spurious. Each of the two new relationships can then be controlled for other underlying variables. For example, it can be envisaged that class background affects all three variables in the new causal model. This can also form the basis for a further expansion of the model, as shown in Figure 21.3.

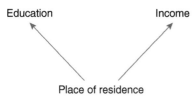

Figure 21.2   Education and income as effects of place of residence

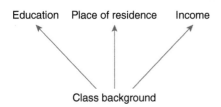

Figure 21.3   Education, place of residence and income as effects of class background

A causal model can also include *indirect causality*. For example, income could be an effect of education, which in turn is an effect of place of residence. The model can then be presented as shown in Figure 21.4.

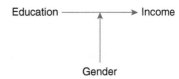

Figure 21.4   Indirect causal relationship from place of residence through education to income

Furthermore, multivariate causal analysis may include interaction between variables, as discussed in Chapter 18. For example, it could be envisaged that education would have a stronger impact on income among men than among women. The causal relationship between education and income would then be conditional on gender. Figure 21.5 shows how this would be presented in a causal model.

Education ————————→ Income

Gender

Figure 21.5   Causal relationship between education and income, conditional on gender

When the causal model is complex and includes both direct and indirect causal relationships, as well as possible interaction effects, the multivariate causal analysis is often called a *path analysis,* because the causalities in the model appear in the form of paths between the variables. The multivariate analysis will then clarify not only whether each of the relationships is significant and not spurious, but also how strong each of the relationships is. We can determine which causal variables have the greatest effect on a particular effect variable, and we can calculate the overall effect of all the causal variables on a given effect variable.

Experimental studies

Experimental studies constitute another design for testing causal hypotheses. As already mentioned, such studies are based on a different strategy than multivariate causal analysis with regard to control of spuriosity. Special characteristics of experiments are also that they are carried out under strictly controlled conditions, often in laboratories, and that the assumed causal variable is controlled and manipulated by the researcher. This means that the researcher decides who should be exposed to the causal variable, and when they should be exposed to it.

In its simplest form, an experiment involves testing a single hypothesis about a causal relationship between two variables. For example, the hypothesis could be that a particular television marketing campaign against smoking reduces the prevalence of smoking in the population. The test is based on a comparison of two equal groups of units. The units are usually individuals. The units are selected as a probability sample from the population on which the causal hypothesis is to be tested. For example, the population may be 15–25-year-olds in the United States, and the sample could be 2000 randomly selected persons from among this age group. The selected units are then randomly assigned to the two groups in the experiment so that each group consists of 1000 persons. One of the two groups is called the *experimental group* or the *treatment group*. The other is called the *control group*. The procedure for compiling the groups is called *randomization*. This is based on both probability sampling from a population and random distribution of the units in the two groups.

The 1000 people in the experimental group are then invited to a closed viewing of the television campaign programme against smoking, while the 1000 in the control group do not see this campaign programme. Generally, we say that the experimental group is *exposed to* the assumed causal variable, while the control group is not exposed to this variable.

Some time after the closed viewing of the television advertisements, the researcher conducts an empirical study of the smoking habits among the young people in both the experimental group and the control group. The two groups are compared with regard to the prevalence of smoking. If there is no significant difference between the groups, the hypothesis must be rejected. The television campaign has had no noticeable effect on smoking. However, the hypothesis is strengthened if smoking appears to be less prevalent in the experimental group than in the control group and if this difference is statistically significant. The campaign has then had the expected and intended effect. It could also be envisaged that the study showed a significant difference in the opposite direction: that smoking is more prevalent in the experimental group than in the control group. In this case, the campaign has functioned contrary to its intended purpose and the causal hypothesis must be rejected or reformulated.

An overview of an experimental study, in its simplest form, is presented in Figure 21.6.

Experimental studies may also be more complex. By using more than two groups, we can include several causal variables in the study. For example, we can study the effects of different types of anti-smoking campaigns. In that case, we usually have one experimental group for each causal variable. We can also compare the groups with regard to the effect variable at more than one point in time. In the study of smoking, for example, we could investigate the smoking habits of the two groups both before and after the experimental group watches the television campaign programme. The effect of the campaign would then be expressed by the *change* in the prevalence of smoking being greater in the treatment group than in the control group. We could also investigate the smoking habits of both groups at several different times after showing the

Steps	Action	Illustration
1 Causal hypothesis	Formulate a causal hypothesis	
2 Sampling	Draw a probability sample from the universe of units	
3 Randomization	Randomly divide the sampled units equally into an experimental group and a control group	
4 Exposure to X	Expose the experimental group to the causal variable X	
5 Examine Y	Examine the two groups as to the effect variables Y_e and Y_c	
6 Conclusion	Test whether the two groups are significantly different as to the effect variable	

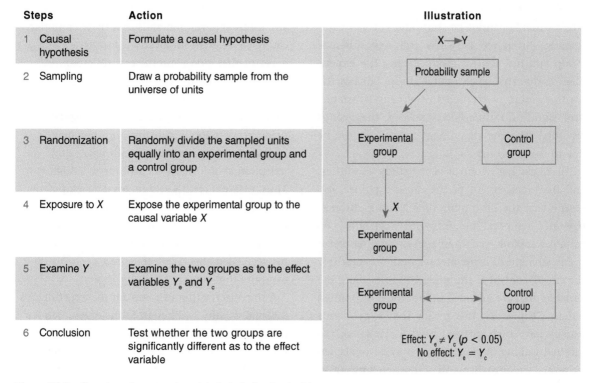

Figure 21.6 Overview of an experimental study in its simplest form

television programme, so that we could identify both the immediate, short-term and long-term effects of the anti-smoking campaign.

An article by D'On Jones (2015) presents an experimental study of writing achievements among kindergarten students in the US. In total, 112 kindergarten students were randomly divided into three groups. Two of the groups were experimental groups with new and special teaching methods for learning to write: one group was involved in writing workshops, and one group was involved in interactive writing. The third group was a control group with traditional teaching methods. The experiment with the different teaching methods lasted for one school year, and the students' writing skills were tested before and after the experiment. The effects of the causal variables were identified by comparing the writing achievements during the year in the three groups. The achievements were higher in the experimental groups than

in the control group, showing that new teaching methods had substantial effects on the writing skills of the students.

Both simple and complex experiments are in accordance with the four preconditions for clarifying causal relationships. The empirical relationship between the causal variable and the effect variable is systematically investigated and probability sampling combined with significance testing ensures that the correlation can be generalized to the larger population.

The randomization of the composition of the two groups means that in principle there are only random differences between the groups in terms of smoking behaviour. Randomization also means that there are only random differences between the groups with regard to effects from all factors other than the causal variable. As mentioned above, this is in principle a control for all possible underlying variables, so that the correlation between the causal variable and the effect variable cannot be spurious. The only systematic difference between the experimental group and the control group during the experiment is that the experimental group, but not the control group, is exposed to the causal variable. Any significant difference between the groups recorded after the experiment must therefore be due to this exposure.

The researcher's control of the study conditions and the management of the cause exposure also ensure that the preconditions regarding chronology and temporal proximity between the two variables are followed up in a reassuring manner.

The strength of experimental studies is precisely the strong control of the study conditions and the variables that are included in the study. As pointed out in Chapter 15, this means that experiments usually have high internal validity. However, the internal validity of experiments may be weakened by several circumstances. All of these circumstances are related to the fact that the similarity or equivalence between the groups, which was ensured through randomization, strictly applies only at the start of the study when the sampling and grouping of the units is performed. During the study, the people in both groups may undergo changes other than those controlled by the researcher. Some changes are due to other forms of *external factors* than the cause exposure included in the experiment. In the study of the relationship between anti-smoking campaigns and smoking behaviour, all of the units in the experiment may be affected by, for example, general information about and discussion of smoking in different types of media while the experiment is being conducted. Other changes are due to *internal development* or *maturation* of the persons participating in the experiment. Young people's attitude to smoking can change as they grow older and gain more experience. The likelihood of effects of external factors and internal development will be particularly large if the experiment is conducted over a relatively long period.

The main problem with both external factors and internal development is that these conditions can have different implications for the experimental group and the control group. Precisely because the experimental group is exposed to television programmes about smoking, they may also become more aware of regular media reports about smoking, and they may become more aware and have stronger self-reflection about their own attitude to smoking. Thus, external factors and internal development may have a greater effect on smoking habits in the experimental group than in the control group. It is difficult for the researcher to distinguish between such effects and the effect of the cause exposure that is part of the experiment.

A third factor that can weaken the experiment's internal validity is different forms of *reactivity*, or *control effects*. Control effects entail that the actual participation in a study has an impact on those who are being studied and that this in itself can lead to changes in their behaviour. The young people participating in an experiment concerning the effects of an anti-smoking campaign may change their smoking habits as a result of participation in the experiment, more or less irrespective of the content of the campaign being studied. Usually, the control effect is also stronger in the experimental group than in the control group, because participation is most extensive and most intense for the units in the experimental group.

Although such circumstances could weaken the experiment's internal validity, it is in connection with external validity that we find the greatest limitations of experimental studies. The highly controlled study conditions can easily become artificial and unrealistic compared to the conditions that really exist in society. The participation of a large number of young people in well-planned and well-organized viewings of a particular television programme, with subsequent follow-up surveys, creates a special and artificial setting for the participants. In this artificial setting, the impact may be different than it would be if the same young people watched the television programme in a natural setting, in their own home and as part of the regular broadcasting schedule, with the possibility of choosing whether to watch the programme or not. In many cases, experimental studies are conducted under even stricter conditions. It is particularly important in these cases to assess whether the causal relationships that are documented in the experiment have satisfactory external validity, so that they can also be assumed to apply under normal conditions in society.

Due to the strict requirements for control of the study conditions and the management of cause exposure, it may be difficult in many cases to conduct an experiment in its purest or most classical form, as described here. Such designs can give rise to both practical problems and research ethical concerns. However, there are many research designs based on some of the elements and logical principles of the classical experiment, but which are nevertheless better adapted to the common conditions in society. Such modified experiments are called *quasi-experimental research designs*.

As pointed out in Chapter 13, experimental or quasi-experimental designs can be used in connection with survey studies. These are usually called *population-based survey experiments* (Mutz, 2011). Such surveys include structured questioning of respondents, but the form of the design is based on the principles from experimental studies. As usual in survey studies, a probability sample is selected from the population in the area where the study is conducted, for example a probability sample of the Spanish population. However, the people in the sample are randomly assigned to two or more groups. In connection with the questioning, the groups are exposed to different information or different attempts at persuasion. As explained in Chapter 13, such information is typically presented in various types of vignette questions. In its simplest form, the design comprises two groups: an experimental group that is exposed to the information, and a control group that is not exposed to it. By comparing the groups' answers to the same questions, we can identify possible effects of the particular information given to the experimental group. Due to the randomized distribution of the respondents in the different groups, we can assume that initially there are only random differences between the different respondent groups. We can therefore assume that all statistically significant differences between the groups with regard to the respondents' answers to the same questions are due to the information or the effects during the questioning.

Interpretive studies

While explanatory studies aim to clarify the causes and effects of different social phenomena, the purpose of interpretive studies is to develop a more comprehensive understanding of the conditions studied and to identify the meaning or significance associated with actions and events in society. With reference to the classic works of social sciences, explanatory studies can be linked to Emile Durkheim, while interpretive studies are primarily associated with Max Weber.

Interpretation in order to achieve a comprehensive understanding and identify aspects of meaning requires the researcher to develop a familiarity, sensitivity and closeness to the actors studied, and thus a deep insight into the actions, events or statements of opinion being analysed. Holistic understanding and interpretation of intentions also assumes that the actors or conditions that are explored are studied as parts of a larger historical, cultural and social context, and that they are analysed in light of this specific context. It is precisely within a certain context that actions or events appear as whole phenomena and become meaningful, both for the involved actors themselves and for outside observers.

For example, interpretive studies can be intended to develop a holistic understanding of social life in a limited community, either in the researcher's own country or in more exotic parts of the world. In the 1950s, the British social anthropologist John Barnes conducted a study over several years of a fishing community in western Norway. His interpretation of the social relations and their significance in this rural community formed the basis for, among other things, the launch of the *social network* concept in social science literature (Barnes, 1954). Interpretive studies can also establish a holistic understanding of a particular organization or institution, such as a hospital or a business, or they can identify the meaning attached to important processes or activities within the organization. Many interpretive studies focus on individual actors and their everyday lives and daily activities, partly in order to understand the meaning that different activities, routines or rituals have for the actors themselves, and partly in order to interpret how these circumstances can be understood in light of the actors' context. Such studies can also develop a holistic understanding of the overall life situation of particular actors. In the late 1960s, the Norwegian social anthropologist Cato Wadel conducted in-depth and long-term studies of one particular unemployed person in Canada. The holistic understanding of this person's overall situation and the interpretation of the meaning attached to various aspects of this situation also helped to shed light on conditions for unemployed people more generally (Wadel, 1973).

With their emphasis on proximity, empathy and insight into specific contexts, interpretive studies are mainly based on qualitative data. Two main types of interpretive studies will be presented here. The first type of study includes phenomenological and hermeneutical studies, which emphasize the interpretation of the meaning aspects of different actions, primarily based on the actors' own intentions with the actions. The second type of interpretive study is focused on holistic understanding, mainly based on contextual interpretation. However, this is not a sharp distinction. All interpretive studies include both interpretation of meaning and holistic understanding.

Intention and meaning

Both phenomenological and hermeneutical studies emphasize the interpretation and understanding of the meaning attached to different actions. Both approaches start with the actors' own understanding of their actions and emphasize that the meaning of the actions must be interpreted in light of the actors' intentions with the actions.

Phenomenological studies

Phenomenological studies are largely based on the philosophical works of Edmund Husserl (1859–1938). In social science, it was first and foremost Alfred Schütz (1967) who developed the methodological basis for phenomenological studies. Phenomenological analyses are particularly concerned with analyses of actions and experiences in people's everyday life.

The basic starting point for phenomenological analyses is that reality is the way the actors themselves perceive it. It is the actors' own experience of the phenomena, or the actors' lifeworld, that is the basis for the analyses. Such analyses therefore attach great importance to understanding actions from the actors' own perspective. The purpose is to find the actors' own perception of their actions and the meaning the actors themselves attach to their actions. The researcher's understanding of the actions and their meaning is based on the actor's own understanding of this.

In order to interpret the actions and their meaning, the researcher must obtain an insight into the intentions or objectives of the actors' actions. The researcher will also be interested in gaining an insight into the actors' experiences, knowledge and perceptions in a more general sense, so that the intention of the individual action can be put into a broader context. In this way, phenomenological analyses can exceed the actors' own immediate formulations of what various actions mean. The analyses can reveal the essential features of the actions and obtain a deeper understanding of the meaning that different actions actually have for the actors.

It is primarily the actor's own general world of ideas that constitutes the larger context and background for understanding the actions and their significance. In phenomenological analyses, less emphasis is placed on the researcher's observations of the external context for the actors and their actions. The actors' own experience and understanding of the context is more important.

In this connection, it may also be useful for researchers to start from the perspective of their own everyday experiences, using this primarily as background to reflect on the actors' experiences and knowledge. In phenomenological analyses it is important to avoid the researcher's own personal experiences or knowledge becoming too prominent or too dominant. The researcher is on guard against possible prejudices and attaches importance to downplaying preconceived perceptions of the actors or their actions.

An interpretive study based on phenomenology is presented by Perrin-Wallquist and Lindblom (2015), in an article on gay and lesbian adolescents disclosing their homosexuality to their parents. Based on unstructured interviews with three men and three women, the article describes how gays and lesbians make sense of their experiences of telling their parents about their sexual orientation. The analysis focused on the meaning of these experiences for the adolescents themselves.

The phenomenological analysis was carried out in different steps, ending up with a narrative of the results of the analysis. Different emotional themes were identified as involved in the respondents' disclosure of their homosexuality, and liberation was summarized as the overall meaning of this disclosure for the respondents themselves.

Hermeneutical studies

The philosophical basis for *hermeneutical studies* was developed by the German philosophers Wilhelm Dilthey (1833–1911) and Hans-Georg Gadamer (2008). As in phenomenological analyses, hermeneutical analyses aim to understand the meaning of actions in the context of, among other things, the intentions of the actors, but the latter approach is not as closely linked to studies of people's everyday lives as the former approach. Hermeneutical studies are conducted across a broad range of social science themes and fields of research.

Hermeneutics is the theory and methodology of interpretation. Although hermeneutical analyses are based on the participants' own understanding and views when they interpret actions and their significance, hermeneutical interpretation is conducted on a broader basis and in light of a broader context than the phenomenological interpretation. Hermeneutical analyses are not as strongly focused on the participants' own understanding as phenomenological analyses. In hermeneutical studies the researcher places more emphasis on interpretation of the actors and their views. Insight into the intentions of the actors is an important basis for understanding the meaning of the actions, but insight into the intentions is also developed in an interaction between the participants' self-perception and the researcher's interpretation of this self-perception.

In other words, the researcher performs a further and more comprehensive interpretation in hermeneutical analyses than in phenomenological analyses. More specifically, this is expressed in the form of two important differences between the two approaches. Firstly, hermeneutics attaches greater importance to the researcher's *preconceptions* than phenomenology does. In hermeneutical analyses, the researcher's interpretation will not only be based on the specific understanding established during the study itself. The interpretation is also based on the more general understanding that the researcher has before the study begins. This preconception can include the researcher's own experiences and attitudes, results from previous research, academic concepts and theoretical frames of reference. The researchers utilize this as an important basis for their understanding of the actors and their actions, and for their interpretation of the significance of the actions. Hermeneutical analyses assume that all understanding is based on various types of preconception.

Secondly, hermeneutics differs from phenomenology in placing greater emphasis on the *holistic understanding* of the researcher. Hermeneutical analyses regard the actors and their actions as part of a more comprehensive whole. The intentions and actions of the actors are not only seen in connection with the actors' more general world of ideas. The actions are also interpreted in light of the researcher's understanding of the context in which a particular actor operates, and based on the researcher's view of the situation or process in which the action occurs. Hermeneutical analyses assume that no phenomenon can be understood independently of the greater whole of which it is a part.

Hermeneutical analyses are conducted in this way as alternating between understanding and preconception and between partial understanding and holistic understanding. This alternation between different bases for interpretation and modes of understanding constitutes a kind of circular movement and is often referred to as the *hermeneutical circle*.

This means that hermeneutical interpretation takes place at several levels. At one level, the researcher emphasizes the actors' own interpretations. At another level, the emphasis is on the researcher's interpretation of the actors' interpretations, partly on the basis of both preconception and holistic understanding. This interpretation of the actors' interpretation is often called *double hermeneutic* (Giddens, 2013).

Contextual interpretation and holistic understanding

With its emphasis on understanding the actors and their actions as part of a larger whole and in light of the context in which they occur, hermeneutical analysis includes both contextual interpretation and holistic understanding. In other words, hermeneutical analysis constitutes a particular form of development of holistic understanding through the interpretation of certain phenomena in light of the specific context of these phenomena.

However, there are also other forms of contextual interpretation intended to obtain a holistic understanding of conditions in society. Hermeneutical studies are primarily focused on understanding certain actions and their significance, based on the interpretation of the relevant actors and their intentions. In other interpretive studies, contextual interpretation can provide a basis for a holistic understanding of other phenomena or social conditions, such as local communities, institutions, organizations, groups, processes, events or debates.

Chapter 16 showed how qualitative analyses can generally provide a basis for a holistic understanding of such specific circumstances. In this connection, it was emphasized that it is important to delimit the conditions or units to be studied, partly with regard to the scope of the conditions, partly with regard to the complexity of the conditions. It was also pointed out that there are special analytical strategies to develop a holistic understanding based on qualitative data, such as condensing, narrative analysis and discourse analysis.

Based on this review of interpretive studies as a particular analytical perspective, it can be added here that *contextual interpretation* can be regarded as a fundamental prerequisite for developing a holistic understanding. Regardless of how we delimit the phenomenon being studied, this phenomenon as a whole must be understood in light of a larger contextual whole, beyond the boundaries of the phenomenon. Whichever analytic strategy is used to investigate the whole phenomenon, the phenomenon cannot be understood as a whole without considering it in light of the more extensive context in which it occurs. A holistic understanding involves not only describing all aspects of the phenomenon, but also understanding the significance of the different aspects for the phenomenon as a whole, and how the phenomenon as a whole makes sense in an even wider social context.

This perspective on holistic understanding forms the basis for the kind of analyses developed by Geertz (2000) under the term *thick description*. As pointed out earlier in this chapter, such analyses are not limited to descriptive presentations of actual conditions. What makes the description thick is that the presentation of actual conditions is combined with an interpretation of how the various conditions are meaningful in a wider context. Geertz himself was particularly interested in studying different types of rituals, for example in Indonesia. Through interpretation of the specific rituals in light of the local cultural context, Geertz was able to develop a holistic understanding of the rituals and their symbolic significance. Such a holistic understanding would have been impossible without the contextual interpretation of the rituals as part of a larger cultural context.

CHAPTER HIGHLIGHTS

- Descriptive studies detect and shed light on actual conditions in society.
  - Ethnographic descriptions based on qualitative studies are often designed as narratives and are usually organized based on different configurative dimensions, metaphors or other analytical devices.
  - Descriptive quantitative studies provide analytical overviews of distributions, correlations or structural patterns. Such overviews may also include comparisons and changes.
- Explanatory studies include systematic analyses intended to develop or test different possibilities for explaining the social conditions being studied. We distinguish between different types of social science explanations. Explanatory studies are often about developing and testing hypotheses about causal relationships.

  - Causalities require stochastic relationships that are not spurious, as well as a particular chronology and temporal proximity.
  - Qualitative analyses are suitable for developing causal hypotheses. Through the search for deviating cases and theoretical generalization, the hypothesis is increasingly specified.
  - Quantitative analyses are suitable for testing causal hypotheses. The tests can be based on multivariate causal analysis or experimental designs.
- Interpretive studies are based mainly on qualitative data. Such studies develop a holistic understanding of the conditions being studied, and they highlight the meaning or significance attached to actions and events in society.

○ Phenomenological and hermeneutical studies develop an understanding of the meaning attached to different actions, based on the intentions of the actor and the actor's own understanding of their actions. Compared with phenomenological studies, hermeneutic studies are concerned with a wider range of topics, and they place greater emphasis on the researcher's preconceptions and the researcher's holistic understanding.

○ Contextual interpretation is intended to achieve a holistic understanding of different conditions in society. Such interpretation may include, for example, thick descriptions.

RESEARCH EXAMPLES

I recommend that you read the publications used as research examples in this chapter.

Jones, Cindy D'On (2015) 'Effects of writing instruction on kindergarten students' writing achievement: An experimental study', *Journal of Educational Research* 108(1), 35–44.

This article presents an experimental study of writing achievements among kindergarten students in the USA. In total, 112 kindergarten students were randomly divided into three groups. Two of the groups were experimental groups with new and special teaching methods for learning to write: one group was involved in writing workshops, and one group was involved in interactive writing. The third group was a control group with traditional teaching methods. The experiment with the different teaching methods lasted for one school year, and the students' writing skills were tested before and after the experiment. The effects of the causal variables were identified by comparing the writing achievements during the year in the three groups. The achievements were higher in the experimental groups than in the control group, showing that new teaching methods had substantial effects on the writing skills of the students.

Maddox, Bryan (2015) 'The neglected situation: Assessment performance and interaction in context', *Assessment in Education: Principles, Policy & Practice* 22(4), 427–443.

This article presents an ethnographic description. It is focused on standardized assessments of adult literacy among nomadic herders in the Gobi desert in Mongolia. Based on participant observation, the researcher presents an ethnographic description of the situation and the context in which the assessment tests took place. Within this situation and context, the interaction between the testing team, as representatives of the state, the selected herder, as respondent, and other herders, as bystanders, is described and related to a framework developed by Goffman (1964). The purpose of this ethnographic description was to analyse how the assessment performance was influenced by the particular linguistic interaction, considering 'larger cultural and institutional dimensions of the test as a social occasion' (Maddox, 2015: 440).

Perrin-Wallqvist, Renée, and Josephine Lindblom (2015) 'Coming out as gay: A phenomenological study about adolescents disclosing their homosexuality to their parents', *Social Behavior and Personality* 43(3), 467–480.

The article presents an interpretive study based on phenomenology. Based on unstructured interviews with three men and three women in Sweden, the article describes how gays and lesbians make sense of their experiences of telling their parents about their sexual orientation. The analysis focused on the meaning of these experiences for the adolescents themselves. The phenomenological analysis was carried out in different steps, ending up with a narrative of the results of the analysis. Different emotional themes were identified as involved in the respondents' disclosure of their homosexuality, and liberation was summarized as the overall meaning of this disclosure for the respondents themselves.

1 What is the difference between thick and thin descriptions?

2 How are narratives used in ethnographic descriptions?

3 Why are causal relationships in society stochastic rather than deterministic?

4 How can we determine whether there is a causal relationship between two social phenomena?

5 Why are interpretive studies typically based on qualitative studies?

6 What is the difference between phenomenological and hermeneutical studies?

7 Formulate a hypothesis about a causal relationship between knowledge of climate change and involvement in environmental activities, and discuss how this hypothesis could be tested in different ways.

RECOMMENDED LITERATURE

Atkinson, Paul (1992) *Understanding Ethnographic Texts*. London: Sage.

This book provides advice on reading as well as writing ethnography. The author explains how field notes and interview transcriptions are used for developing ethnographic descriptions. Literary conventions used in ethnographic descriptions are explained, and different styles of ethnographic writing are discussed.

Bevir, Mark, and Jason Blakely (2018) *Interpretive Social Science: An Anti-naturalist Approach*. Oxford: Oxford University Press.

This book deals with interpretive approaches in social science, with particular emphasis on hermeneutics. It presents critical views on various kinds of naturalist research and provides philosophical foundations of interpretive approaches. Furthermore, implications of interpretive approaches for methods and empirical research are discussed.

Shadish, William R., Thomas D. Cook, and Donald T. Campbell (2002) *Experimental and Quasi-experimental Designs for Generalized Causal Inference* (2nd edn). Boston: Houghton Mifflin.

This is a book about field experiments, discussing how different elements of the classical and pure experimental design can be included in various types of quasi-experiments. The book includes such topics as causation, validity, randomized experiments, and causal inference.

TIME, SPACE AND LEVEL

This chapter provides the necessary knowledge for understanding the differences between longitudinal, comparative and multi-level studies, as well as how qualitative and quantitative data can be used in such studies.

The chapter will teach you about

- how short-term processes and long-term trends can be examined
- the differences between recall data, time series data and panel data
- the differences between cohort effects and life-phase effects
- the differences between most similar and most different strategies in comparative studies

- the differences between global, aggregated and contextual variables
- the significance of temporal fallacies, equivalence problems and cross-level fallacies
- the combination of temporal, spatial and multi-level perspectives in historical-comparative studies.

Temporal, spatial and multi-level questions

Chapter 21 discussed typical social science questions with reference to different kinds of knowledge about social conditions. This chapter focuses on common social science questions about different kinds of social conditions. One type of such questions is temporal questions, which deal with processes, stability and changes in society. Another question type is spatial questions, which refer to similarities and differences between different contexts or societies. A third type of questions is multi-level questions, which are focused on the relationship between different levels in society.

Challenges and problems associated with analyses of these three types of social science questions will now be discussed. For each type of question, both qualitative analyses and quantitative analyses will be examined, and some important issues associated with these analyses will be pointed out. Finally, the chapter will discuss historical-comparative studies, which combine all three question types, often based on mixed methods approaches.

Longitudinal studies

Analyses focusing on *temporal* research questions are very common in both qualitative and quantitative studies. Such analyses can concern how large or small social processes progress, how the lives of individuals or families develop, how patterns of behaviour or opinions change, or how the historical development of society proceeds.

Analyses of processes and modes of development are called *longitudinal studies*. Such studies can vary with regard to the length of the time-frame that is being examined. Some analyses may be limited to short-term processes or short-term changes, while others may examine long-term trends or development tendencies. The analyses may also differ with regard to the length of the intervals between the different data recordings within the time-frame being analysed. In some studies, data recording continues throughout the entire process. The progression of the process is monitored continuously from one moment to the next. Other studies examine stability and change by comparing data on the same phenomena at different times. Both the number of times compared and the length of the interval between these times may vary. In practice, the more long-term the processes are, the more difficult it will be to follow the processes continuously, and in long-term analyses, there can often be relatively large intervals between the moments being compared.

Qualitative analyses

Qualitative studies are usually more suitable than quantitative studies for capturing the continuous development of a particular process. The most important method for such studies is participant observation. The researcher participates in the process that is observed and analysed. Since such research designs are very intensive and demanding, there is a limit to how long the study can last. As a rule, it is relatively short and clearly defined processes that can be analysed in this way. For example, the study may concern specific negotiation processes in business or specific decision-making processes in political or administrative bodies. The challenge for the analysis is to bring out the dynamics of the interaction between different actors and how the process as a whole develops through this dynamic interaction.

Qualitative analyses can also be used in studies over longer periods of time. An example of this is biographical studies. These studies analyse the life histories of different individuals. They address the entire lives of individuals or essential parts of their lives. Data can be based on unstructured interviews, written accounts that individuals are asked to provide, or various documents in the form of, for example, letters and images that provide information about their lives. These retrospective data are then used to reconstruct the life stories, often with particular emphasis on important or critical events in the life. Each individual's life story may be of interest in itself. However, the life cycles of different types of individuals are often analysed. By comparing these analyses and interpreting the

individual life courses in a historical context, the researcher can also understand key features of social development during the period of time that the individuals have experienced. The challenge for the analysis is precisely to develop such a historical-contextual understanding of individual life courses.

Another example of qualitative studies over extended time periods is qualitative content analyses of documents about comparable circumstances at different times far back in the past. For example, we could study whether significant changes have occurred in the arguments for and against Norwegian membership in the EU (formerly the EEC and EC). This debate has been ongoing ever since the early 1960s, and it was particularly intense in the early 1960s, the early 1970s and the early 1990s. In two national referendums (1972 and 1994), a majority voted against membership. Qualitative content analyses of parliamentary debates, newspaper articles, or radio and television programmes at different times can show what types of arguments have been central among the supporters and opponents of membership, and how the arguments have changed from the 1960s until today. The challenge for such analyses is to ensure that the documents from the different times are comparable and to understand the more general development of society during the time period being analysed.

Kallio et al. (2015) present an in-depth, longitudinal case study of a newspaper organization in Finland. Data were collected before and after the organization moved to a new location and changed the physical design of the facilities, from a rather hierarchical to a more open space design of the workplace. The empirical study was based on qualitative observation and interview data, in addition to some survey data and photographs of the facilities. The purpose of the study was to examine the organizational culture before and after the change in the physical space, with particular emphasis on cultural conditions for creativity. The study indicates that the move from a hierarchical to an open design of the workplace had an impact on the organizational culture. In particular, the cultural change was characterized by more equality, openness and collectivity, which seemed to strengthen the creativity in the newspaper organization.

Quantitative analyses

Quantitative analyses are not particularly suitable for observing processes continuously over a certain period of time. Structured observation can certainly be used to record selected features in strictly defined processes, but this only provides a limited understanding compared with participant observation. On the other hand, quantitative analyses are very suitable for detecting changes through comparisons of data about particular phenomena on many occasions over long periods. For example, structured observation of comparable conditions at different times can show whether and how these conditions change over time.

Quantitative content analysis of comparable documents can also be repeated on many different occasions over extended periods. Such analyses could be conducted concerning the debate on Norwegian EU membership since the 1960s. While a qualitative content analysis could show what kinds of arguments were central at different times, a quantitative study of the same documents could show how much weight different arguments were given and how the weight of the different arguments has changed up to the present.

Quantitative analyses of stability and change can also be based on data that are available in different types of registers, and which are available in comparable forms for different times. Quantitative data based on structured questioning of respondents can provide the basis for analyses of development processes and change processes in three different

ways. Firstly, the respondents can be asked about conditions at earlier times, yielding *recall data*. For example, like qualitative biographical studies, structured questioning can be used to analyse the respondents' own life course. Secondly, different probability samples of respondents from the same universe can be asked the same question at different times. If the questioning occurs at regular intervals, we obtain data for a whole series of times. Such data are called *time series data*. Thirdly, the same sample of respondents can answer the same question at different times. Such a sample is called a *panel*, and the data is referred to as *panel data*.

Compared with time series data, both recall data and panel data are more limited with respect to the period of time that can be analysed. The respondents' memories are limited to their own lifetime, and questions about circumstances far back in time can provide unreliable answers because the respondent may not remember well enough. Experience shows that such recall errors often entail that the respondent exaggerates the conformity between past and present situations, so that changes are underestimated in the analysis. This applies especially to questions about the respondent's own actions or opinions. It is a challenge in the analysis to reduce such effects caused by recall errors.

Neither time series data nor panel data are affected by recall errors. Panel data, however, can be even more limited than recall data with regard to how long a period of time can be analysed. There are limits to how often and how many times the same respondent panel can be asked the same questions. The greatest problem with panel studies over long periods of time is drop-out from the sample. Drop-outs due to death and relocation become increasingly common as time passes. Problems due to denial can also increase over time. Since drop-out applies to different respondents at different times, the problems will be amplified during the investigation period. The number of respondents included in the panel at any given time will be smaller and smaller, and thus the full panel will become less and less representative of the universe.

Another problem with panel studies is that the respondent's answer at one time can affect the answer to the same question provided the next time. There may also be a risk here that the respondent attaches too much importance to conformity, especially regarding questions about their own actions and opinions, so that changes can be underestimated in the data and in the analysis. The shorter the interval between the rounds of questioning, the greater this problem will be.

Compared to time series data, however, panel data has the advantage that it provides information about changes for each respondent. These changes are called *gross changes*. Time series data only show the aggregated changes for the entire sample combined. These are called *net changes*. Net changes are usually less than gross changes because changes in one direction among some individuals can be counterbalanced by changes in the opposite direction among other individuals. For example, if we are interested in changes in people's attitudes to Norwegian membership of the EU over a 20-year period, we can use time series data to find that the proportion of opponents has increased from 45% to 55%, while the proportion of supporters has decreased from 55% to 45%. We disregard the respondents who have not made a decision on the issue. This 10% change is the net change, because it is based on a comparison of the entire sample questioned the first time with the entire new sample questioned 20 years later. However, there were far more extensive changes at the individual level during this period. Panel data might show that 25% of the population have changed from being supporters to being opponents, while 15% of the population have changed their position in the opposite direction. The gross change reflects the sum of the two figures (40% of the population),

while the net change is the difference between the figures (10%). In this case, the gross changes will be even more extensive because many individuals may have changed their position back and forth several times during the period. The complexity and scale of the gross changes will also increase further if we consider those individuals who have not adopted a position, and how this varies between the times when they were questioned.

While time series data can be used for analysis of longer periods than panel data, panel data will provide more detailed information about the changes that occur during the period analysed. However, analyses of time series data are not limited to comparisons of the *entire sample* at the different times. Time series data over extended periods can also be analysed on the basis of the respondents' age at the different times. Such an analysis is called a *cohort analysis*. A *cohort* is a number of people in a population who share in common that they have experienced a significant event in their lifetime at the same time. A birth cohort consists of people born at the same time. A cohort analysis is usually based on different birth cohorts. If we have time series data for every 10 years in a 40-year period, the sample at each time can be divided into age groups with an age span of 10 years in each age group, distinguishing, for example, between people in their twenties, people in their thirties, people in their forties, and so on. Thus, each age group can be monitored over time. Those who are in the forties the first time they are questioned can be compared to those who are in their fifties 10 years later, and with those who are in their sixties 20 years later, and so on. In this way, we can identify changes in each birth cohort between the different times.

Tables 22.1 and 22.2 show examples of cohort analysis of changes in attitudes to Norwegian membership of the EU in the period 1960–2000. The tables contain constructed numbers and show two different outcomes of the cohort analysis, so that we can illustrate the design of the analysis as well as possible. We can analyse the trends in each cohort by comparing the numbers diagonally in the table. The blue numbers in the tables, for example, show the proportion of EU supporters in the cohort that are in their twenties in 1960, in their thirties in 1970, in their forties in 1980, and so on. These people were born in the period 1931–1940.

Table 22.1 Example of cohort analysis of changes in the proportion of supporters of Norwegian membership of the EU: constructed numbers for illustration of the generation effect (cohort effect)

Respondent's age	Time of questioning				
	1960	1970	1980	1990	2000
20–29	60	55	50	45	40
30–39	60	60	55	50	45
40–49	60	60	60	55	50
50–59	60	60	60	60	55
60–69	60	60	60	60	60
Entire sample	60	59	56	53	50

Table 22.2 Example of cohort analysis of changes in the proportion of supporters of Norwegian membership of the EU: constructed numbers for illustration of the life phase effect

Respondent's age	Time of questioning				
	1960	1970	1980	1990	2000
20–29	70	69	66	63	60
30–39	65	64	61	58	55
40–49	60	59	56	53	50
50–59	55	54	51	48	45
60–69	50	49	46	43	40
Entire sample	60	59	56	53	50

According to Table 22.1, 60% of the members of this cohort were supporters throughout the period. The table shows that the proportion of EU supporters is stable, as it is also within each of the other cohorts. The attitudes established at an early age follow the cohort throughout their lives. There are no differences between the life stages. If we compare the different cohorts in Table 22.1, we find no differences between the oldest cohorts, those born in 1940 or earlier (the cohorts below the blue numbers in the table). However, we find differences between the youngest cohorts, those born after 1940 (the cohorts above the blue numbers in the table). For each 10-year period that passes, the proportion of supporters among the youngest respondents is reduced. Within each cohort, the proportion remains stable at this lower level throughout the remainder of the study period. The younger the cohort, the lower is the proportion of EU supporters. The differences between the cohorts can be termed a *cohort effect*. Since the different cohorts can be said to represent different generations, the difference between the cohorts is also referred to as a *generation effect*.

Table 22.2 shows a different outcome of the cohort analysis than Table 22.1. There are significant changes here in the proportion of EU supporters in each cohort. Within all the cohorts, the proportion of supporters decreases as time passes, and as the cohorts grow older. In other words, there are clear differences between the age groups or the life stages within the different cohorts. These differences within the cohorts are referred to as an *age effect* or a *life-phase effect*. Table 22.2 also shows a certain generation effect in addition to the life-phase effect, as the proportion of supporters is generally lower for the youngest cohorts than for the oldest. However, this generation effect is weaker than the life-phase effect.

Time series and cohort analyses can also provide a basis for identifying a third type of change effect known as the *period effect*. Changes due to more intense campaign activity prior to the referendums in 1972 and 1994 would be examples of period effects. Tables 22.1 and 22.2 both show that the proportion of EU supporters overall decreases throughout the study period. This is reflected in the bottom row of each table, which shows that the proportion of supporters fell from 60% to 50% over the 40 years. This long-term trend can be regarded as a period effect. In Table 22.1 this period effect is primarily found among the youngest age groups, but in Table 22.2 it is evenly distributed among all age groups.

The challenge in the analysis is to distinguish as well as possible between the three effects. In practice, this can be quite difficult.

Quantitative time series analyses can be based on simple comparisons of the figures for the different times that are included in the study period. The change trends or development lines can be illustrated using time series diagrams, or line charts, which are similar to the line charts for univariate distributions. The different times in the study period are placed along the horizontal axis (time axis). The sizes or measurements to be compared are placed along the vertical axis. Figure 22.1 shows an example of such a diagram for the development of the proportion of EU supporters as expressed in Table 22.1.

Special methods have been developed for more advanced *time series analyses*. Such methods involve conducting a more combined analysis of data for all the times together, and the purpose can be, for example, to express the change trend mathematically, such as in the form of an equation or function. Such time series analyses will not be further described here.

Another special method for conducting quantitative analyses of developments over time is *event history analysis*. This type of analysis emphasizes changes in the form of specific events. The analysis is based on how long it takes before such events occur for different units, and special regression techniques are used to clarify the various courses of events. For example, event history analysis is used to analyse people's career paths, where starting or leaving a job is the type of event that forms the basis for the analysis. Such analyses will not be reviewed in this book.

Fallacies related to time

As noted above, there are various limitations and problems associated with the different approaches to analysing processes or changes over time. The most general problem with the time perspective in social science analyses is that conclusions are

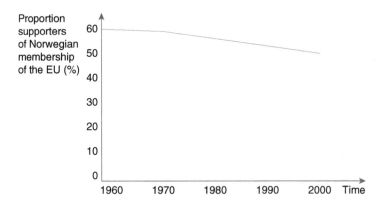

Figure 22.1 Example of a time series diagram for the development of the proportion of EU supporters, 1960–2000: constructed data

sometimes drawn about developments over time, even though the data upon which the conclusion is based refer to only one point in time. Such conclusions are called *temporal fallacies*.

Data about conditions at a single point in time are referred to as *synchronous* data, whereas data about conditions at multiple times are referred to as *diachronic* data. Longitudinal studies, in other words, are based on diachronic data. We need diachronic data in order to analyse processes and changes and in order to be able to draw reliable conclusions about developments over time.

Sometimes it may be tempting to use synchronous data as the basis for conclusions about development processes. This applies especially when we analyse actions or attitudes among people from different age groups. Attitudes towards Norwegian membership of the EU can again serve as an example. Table 22.2 shows a negative relationship between age and support for membership of the EU. The proportion of EU supporters is greatest among the youngest respondents. If we had demonstrated this correlation at a single point in time, say in 1980, we might be tempted to assume that support for EU membership would generally be more common in the period after 1980. We could assume that young people would retain their opinion as they grew older, and that cohorts with many supporters would thus replace cohorts with fewer supporters. This would be a correct assumption if the generation effect was stronger than the life-phase effect. According to Table 22.2, however, the opposite is the case.

Regardless of whether the assumption is correct or not, the actual conclusion about change over time will be a fallacy. The basis for the conclusion is insufficient. Only diachronic data can form the basis for conclusions about change or development.

Comparative studies

While temporal questions concern stability and change over a period of time, *spatial* questions refer to similarities and differences between different places. Both types of questions emphasize the comparison of social conditions. A temporal question requires comparing conditions at different times, while a spatial question involves comparison of conditions in different places in space. The term *space* is used here in a social geography sense with reference to the geographical location of society, and conditions in different places are clarified as conditions in different contexts or different societies.

Spatial questions are central in *comparative studies*. Such studies involve comparing different societies or conditions in different societies. This may concern different local communities or society generally in different countries or nations. Comparative studies may, however, also include social conditions that are more institutionally or organizationally demarcated, so that the studies entail comparing different institutions or organizations.

Comparative studies have in common that they usually only involve a small number of units, but each unit is usually extensive and complex. Each unit corresponds practically to a case in case studies. The difference between case studies and comparative studies is that case studies can comprise only a single unit, while comparative studies require analyses of at least two units that are systematically compared.

As a rule, the number of units in comparative studies is too small to allow probability sampling of these units. In some such studies, the universe also involves so few units that probability sampling is not relevant. This is the case, for example, in comparative studies that are based on national societies as units. Comparative studies are therefore usually based on a strategic selection of units.

This selection is usually based on one of two alternative *strategies* for comparing the units. While one of these comparative strategies involves comparing units that are as *similar as possible*, the second strategy involves comparing units that are as *different as possible*. Which of these strategies is chosen will depend on the characteristics of the units that the comparative study is intended to explain, and whether the units are similar or different in terms of these particular conditions.

For example, if we wish to compare countries to find possible causes of criminality among the population, we can either compare countries that are similar in terms of the extent and types of criminality in the population, or countries with different patterns of criminality. If we wish to compare countries that are *different* with respect to criminality, we would preferably choose countries that are otherwise as *similar as* possible. The thinking is that none of the conditions that are similar in the countries studied can explain that the criminality is different. Different conditions in the countries can only be explained by other factors that are also different. All the conditions that are similar can thus be eliminated as potential causes of crime. The analysis can concentrate on identifying potential causal factors among the few conditions that are different in the countries included in the study. In other words, to explain differences between the units, units are chosen that are as similar as possible with respect to all conditions other than those to be explained. This is the *most similar strategy*.

If we wish to compare countries that are *similar* in terms of criminality, we should choose countries that are as *different* as possible with respect to all conditions other than criminality. The point here is that none of the conditions that are different in the countries studied can explain the similar patterns of criminality. All the different conditions can be eliminated as potential causal factors. Such factors can only be identified among the few conditions that are not different in the countries studied. To explain similarities between the units, the general strategy is to choose units that are as different as possible with respect to all conditions other than those to be explained. This is *the most different strategy*.

In such studies, the basis for rejecting potential causal factors will be more reliable than the basis for accepting such factors. The challenge is therefore to make such a strategic selection of units that as many potential causal factors as possible can be rejected. The greater the number of potential factors rejected, the greater the probability that the factors *not* rejected will be the correct causal explanation. Since comparative studies always involve relatively few units, such explanations can nevertheless be quite unreliable because there can be many alternative explanatory possibilities that are not investigated.

Comparative studies may be important in order to develop general knowledge in social science. Analyses of the same phenomena in different societies can provide a basis for determining whether these phenomena are general or context-specific, and how they manifest themselves under different contextual conditions.

Comparative studies can be based on both qualitative and quantitative analyses.

Qualitative analyses

Qualitative comparative studies usually emphasize a holistic understanding of each unit in the study. This requires that each unit is clearly defined and relatively easy to understand, and that the number of units is very limited. Such units could be small local communities, institutions or organizations. Participant observation will often be an important method in this type of comparative study, but both informal interviewing and qualitative content analysis can also be appropriate designs, possibly in combination with participant observation.

The various units are mainly studied individually, and the emphasis is primarily placed on analysing the distinctive features of each unit and understanding the individual entity as a whole within a unique context. Both the data collection and the analysis, however, are intended to identify comparable features of the various units and highlight similarities and differences between the units.

Like qualitative analyses in general, such comparative analyses may be based on more or less systematic approaches. Based on so-called Boolean algebra, a systematic procedure has been developed specifically for qualitative analyses in comparative studies (Ragin, 1987). This procedure entails that comparable features of the various units in the analysis are identified, and that a clear distinction between two different categories is defined for each of these features. One category is given the value 0 and the other category is given the value 1. In a comparison of different local communities, for example, we could distinguish between a high level of crime (1) and low level of crime (0), between high unemployment (1) and low unemployment (0) and between many immigrants (1) and few immigrants (0). In this way, the data set is simplified and an easy-to-follow overview is established of similarities and differences with respect to different features of the units. A more comprehensive comparison of the units can then be made based on the configurations or patterns generated by the numbers for all the features of each unit.

This procedure has much in common with the use of variables and values in quantitative analyses, but in the qualitative analyses referred to here, the numbers are not analysed in a quantitative manner. These analyses focus on qualitative differences between the combined patterns that are formed by different number combinations.

The challenge is to analyse and interpret these patterns in light of the contextual understanding of each individual unit as a unique whole, so that the emphasis on different features of the units and the division into simple categories do not result in an unfortunate fragmentation of the analysis.

Quantitative analyses

While comparative studies based on qualitative analyses emphasize a holistic understanding of each individual unit in the study, quantitative comparative studies refer to specific variables to characterize the units that are included in the analysis. The number of variables can be quite large. The more extensive and complex the units studied, the more variables it may be relevant to use in order to characterize and compare the units. Thus, it is possible to handle more comprehensive and complex units in quantitative studies than in qualitative studies. The number of units can also be larger in quantitative analyses than in qualitative analyses. Comparative studies based on quantitative analyses can include comparisons between social conditions in relatively many countries. For example, comparative studies have been carried out on people's use of time in 12 different countries in the 1960s (Szalai, 1972), and on networks in business in 10 Western industrialized countries in the 1970s (Stokman et al., 1985).

Variables can be used in several ways in the analysis. Firstly, the same variables can be used for the different units separately, so that the units are compared with respect to their distribution on these variables. The variables are then used for specific types of sub-units within each main unit in the analysis. A sub-unit is a unit on a lower level than the main unit. If the comparative analysis includes countries as units, we could use regions, counties, municipalities or individual residents in the country as sub-units. For example, we can compare average incomes in EU countries or income distributions in Germany and France.

This type of comparison is used by Hansen et al. (2006), in a study of poverty among households with children in Norway and Germany. The study is based on survey data from the two countries, and separate analyses were carried out for each country, based on the same variables. The purpose was to examine poverty among single-parent and two-parent households, with reference to different measures of poverty. As to income poverty and material deprivation, the analysis indicates that there is more poverty in Germany than there is in Norway, and that, in both countries, there is more poverty among single-parent households than there is among two-parent households. Furthermore, in both countries, single-parent households receive more social assistance than two-parent households.

Secondly, we can use a set of variables for all the units in the comparative study, so that each unit has a value on each of the variables. For example, in a comparative study of different countries, such variables could be gross national product per capita or research expenditure as a percentage of gross national product. The comparison between the countries would then be shown by the distribution on the variables in the analysis. The latter procedure is particularly relevant in comparative analyses involving relatively many units. When there are a small number of units, it becomes less meaningful to conduct analyses of how the units are distributed across the different variables.

There is also a third way of using variables in studies of different societies. Again, this concerns studies of sub-units within the societies to be compared. The sub-units from all the societies are then analysed together, and the sub-units' societal affiliation is defined as a separate variable. For example, if we have data from structured questioning based on probability samples from the populations in the UK, USA, Canada and Australia, where the same questionnaire is used in every country, the respondents from all four national samples can be combined into a single data set. The variables are common to all the respondents, and the respondent's nationality is specified as a separate variable. The comparison between the countries can then be based on analyses of correlations between the nationality variable and the other variables in the analysis.

The latter procedure can be more problematic than the first two. When social affiliation or nationality is only treated as one variable in line with other variables, the contextual and holistic understanding of the peculiarities of each society can be very limited, and the interpretation of the differences between countries may therefore be inadequate. Due to the contextual features of the societies being compared, it can also be problematic to treat the sub-units from all the societies as fully equivalent in a common data set. The greater the cultural differences between the different societies, the more problematic this will be. Since the analysis concentrates much more on the sub-units than on the main units to be compared, there may also be doubt about whether it is justified to characterize this analytic design as a comparative study.

It is generally a challenge to interpret results of a variable-oriented analysis in light of a contextual understanding of the characteristics of each unit in the analysis. It is also important to consider whether the conditions being compared are really comparable. Problems related to comparability are among the most fundamental and common problems in comparative studies. Such problems are called equivalence problems. This is the theme of the next subsection.

Problems related to equivalence

Equivalence is the most important prerequisite for comparability. In order to compare particular phenomena, we must have equivalent data about these phenomena. Since different types of comparisons are central to most social science studies, the question of equivalence is of general importance in social science. In comparative studies, however, this question becomes particularly important. The comparison between different societies is then the main purpose of the analysis. Different societies are often characterized by different cultures, and it is particularly challenging to obtain equivalent data from across such cultural differences.

Problems with producing equivalent data can occur in different ways and in connection with various aspects of the study. In comparative studies, we can distinguish between four types of equivalence. One of these is *linguistic equivalence*. This is about equivalence between words, expressions and formulations in the societies that are being compared. The question is whether the same words and expressions have the same meaning across the societies in the analysis. Linguistic equivalence assumes that the researcher has a correct understanding of linguistic formulations in the different societies studied, and that the researcher's words and expressions are correctly understood by the actors or respondents studied in these societies.

Linguistic equivalence becomes a particularly difficult challenge in comparative studies of societies with different languages, as is usual in comparisons between different countries. It is then important to assess whether the translations are good enough in terms of what specific formulations mean in the different languages. A common procedure for controlling this is to translate the same text both ways. For example, the questions in a French-language questionnaire can be translated into English, and the English-language version can then be translated back into French again by another translator. Deviations between the original and the translated French-language versions can be considered as a lack of linguistic equivalence. The linguistic equivalence is assumed to be satisfactory if there is a high level of compliance between the original and the back-translated version.

Another type of equivalence is *contextual equivalence*. This refers to equivalence with regard to the contextual meaning of particular phenomena or conditions in different societies. The question is whether a given phenomenon, seen in relation to the larger context in which it occurs, has the same meaning in each of the societies that are being compared.

For example, certain occupational groups or positions may have different meanings in different countries because they are part of different systems or different institutional contexts. Priests exist in many religions, but there can be major variations between the religions regarding the priests' background, status and functions. In other words, the title of 'priest' can have very different meanings in different religious contexts. In comparative studies, therefore, it can be problematic to compare priests in different religions. In such studies, it would be a challenge to assess whether the contextual equivalence is satisfactory.

A third prerequisite for comparability in comparative studies is *conceptual equivalence*. This refers to the meaning of social science concepts in different societies. Not all concepts can be used in the same way and with the same meaning in different cultures, contexts or types of society. Some concepts are context-specific, so that the same term has different meanings in different societies. Some concepts will even be meaningless in some societies.

For example, if we compare economic conditions and income differences in the Netherlands and Haiti, one of the world's poorest countries, the term 'poverty' will have very different meanings in the two countries. Similarly, the term 'social class' may have a different meaning in developing countries than in industrialized countries.

Generally, it is a problem that concepts developed on the basis of studies in specific types of society are not equally suitable for understanding the conditions in other types of society. In comparative studies, the researcher must consider this possible problem particularly carefully. The concepts used in comparisons across cultures and societies will be absolutely crucial to the conceptual equivalence of such studies.

The fourth type of equivalence can be called *methodological equivalence*. The question here is whether certain methods work the same way in different types of society. Even if we use the exact same methodological design in different societies, this may not result in equivalent data from the different societies.

For example, the use of structured questioning may function very differently depending on the level of education in the societies that are being compared. In countries with low levels of education and extensive illiteracy, the use of questionnaires will work far worse than in countries with high levels of education. Cultural differences will also affect what questions can be asked, how the questions should be formulated and how the questions are answered. Identical questions do not necessarily elicit equivalent answers. In order to obtain equivalent data based on questioning, it may be necessary sometimes to use different formulations of the questions.

In comparative studies, such problems related to methodological equivalence may pose major challenges with regard to both the construction of the research design and the interpretation of the data obtained from the societies that are being compared.

Multi-level studies

Multi-level studies include units at two or more levels in society. The division into different levels refers primarily to actors as the units of analysis. We usually distinguish between three different levels of analysis in social science studies, namely *micro*, *meso* and *macro*. Multi-level questions and multi-level studies focus on the relationship between different levels.

When data about units at different levels are combined in a single study, the phenomena being studied will be investigated in a more comprehensive manner than if the study included only one level. Multi-level data provide more balanced insights and a more in-depth understanding of the phenomena than data from just one level. The purpose of multi-level studies is often to explain or understand conditions at one level in light of the conditions at other levels. The most common approach is to analyse how micro-level conditions are contingent on meso-level or macro-level conditions, or how conditions at the meso level are contingent on conditions at the macro level. The conditions at the lower levels are examined in light of conditions at higher levels. The latter conditions then constitute contexts or contextual conditions for the former conditions. Such designs, known as *contextual analyses*, are a special type of multi-level study.

One of the best-known contextual analyses in social science is Durkheim's study of suicide (Durkheim, 1897). He studied, among other things, the frequency of suicide among Catholics and Protestants in Germany and France, and found that variations in the inclination to commit suicide are largely due to differences between the social contexts of individuals in different countries and within different religions. As pointed out in Chapter 16, suicide can be understood in light of two different social conditions, partly how well integrated the individuals are in society, and partly how strongly society regulates individuals and their actions. These conditions constitute contextual conditions for suicide.

Multi-level studies may include both qualitative and quantitative analyses.

Qualitative analyses

Qualitative analyses are often intended to develop a holistic understanding of the phenomena being studied. The actors, actions, events or opinions being analysed must then be understood in light of the wider contexts in which they occur.

This requires that we have information about both the units themselves and the contexts in which the units are situated. Since the units' context usually refers to a higher level than the units themselves, this means that qualitative analyses are often multi-level studies, especially in the form of contextual analyses.

More specific designs for qualitative multi-level analyses may concern, for example, studies of organizations and their members or companies and their employees. On the one hand, the analyses can focus their attention on individual members or individual employees and their characteristics, actions or opinions. This all concerns actors at the micro level. On the other hand, the analyses can focus on each organization or company as a whole, with emphasis on typical characteristics, actions or opinions for these actors also. These are actors at the meso level.

Another example of a qualitative multi-level analysis could be a study that focuses on conditions in voluntary organizations in a local community, as well as on the entire local community. Each organization and the local community itself are considered as entities. Although it is common to assume that both organizations and local communities are at the meso level, the local community in this case will be at a higher level than the individual organizations.

Qualitative multi-level analyses may also involve more than two levels, but there is a limit to how many levels it is possible to keep track of in such intensive studies. The analyses may be based on data from participant observation, informal interviewing as well as qualitative content analysis. The analytical challenge is to investigate the relationship between the different levels, so that each level is not described separately, isolated from the other levels. It is common for conditions at higher levels to be regarded as contextual prerequisites for conditions at lower levels, and that the latter conditions are understood in light of the context created by the former conditions.

Quantitative analyses

The relationship between individuals, organizations and local communities can also be analysed using quantitative data. Quantitative analyses generally provide opportunities for studying units at many levels and many units at each level. Quantitative analyses can also be used if the multi-level analysis includes selected features of extensive and complex units, especially at the macro level.

In the case of a parliamentary election, for example, we can study variations in election participation and party preferences on the basis of respondent data from a nationwide probability sample of the population. Data from such questioning can be combined with data from public election statistics about election participation and vote distribution in the different municipalities and in the different counties. This provides a basis for a multi-level analysis, where data at the individual level are seen in connection with data at the municipal and county level. The dependent variables, election participation and party preference, can be analysed in relation to various independent variables on each of the three levels, so that we can determine how election behaviour is conditional on both individual circumstances and the features of the municipalities and the counties.

In contrast to qualitative analyses of relationships between different levels, quantitative multi-level analyses generally attach great importance to correlations between selected specific variables. In multi-level analyses, variables are combined with reference to the different levels of the analysis. For each level, a set of variables is specified that expresses different relevant properties of the units at this level.

Depending on how the variables are specified and how they are used in the analysis, we can distinguish between three types of variables in multi-level analyses. One such type is *global variables*. These variables refer only to one of the levels in the analysis. They are unique to this level. The variables are constructed on the basis of distinctive features of the units on this level and are used in the analysis to express characteristics of the *same* units. In the example above, the variables from the structured questioning are global variables when they are used as expressions of characteristics of the individual respondents. They are both constructed and used at the individual level. Similarly, the business structure in the municipality will be a global variable when it is used to express a characteristic of the municipality. The variable is designed and used with reference to the same level, namely the municipal level.

Another type of variable is *aggregated variables*. These are variables that are designed based on units at one level and are used in the analysis as expressions of properties of units at a *higher* level. Election participation in a county is an aggregated variable because it is designed on the basis of election participation in the individual municipalities in the county, but is used in the analysis as a property of the county. Each unit at the higher level (county) consists of a number of units at a lower level (the municipalities in the county). The value of the units on the aggregated variable (election participation in the county) appears as a result or aggregate of the values for the units at the lower level (election participation in county municipalities).

The third type of variable is *contextual variables*. These variables are designed based on units at one level and are used in the analysis as expressions of properties of units at a *lower* level. The business structure variable in the municipality is a contextual variable when it is used in the analysis as a characteristic of the individual respondents' context or as a contextual condition for the individual's election participation and party preference. Belonging to such a context is then regarded as a characteristic of the units at the individual level. In this sense, the variable is used as an expression of

the units' situation at the individual level, while the variable is constructed based on characteristics of the units at the municipal level.

In quantitative multi-level analyses, therefore, there are many possibilities for combining data and variables at different levels. Special analytic techniques have also been developed for such multi-level analyses. However, these techniques will not be discussed here.

A quantitative multi-level analysis is presented by Brady et al. (2009), who conducted a study of how the poverty of individuals in 18 affluent countries is influenced by the political context in these countries. The study focuses on individuals as the unit of analysis and combines global and contextual variables. The global variables refer to micro-level characteristics of each individual, including poverty (poor or not poor) as the dependent variable, in addition to several independent variables, such as gender, age, education, family situation and unemployment. The contextual variables refer to macro-level features of the country in which the individuals live, including welfare generosity, unemployment rate, economic growth, and the strength of labour unions and leftist political parties. The data from all countries were organized as one data set, which means that all individuals within each country have the same values on the contextual variables. The analysis shows that poverty is explained by both individual characteristics and contextual features of the countries. Welfare generosity reduces poverty, and it reduces the effects of individual characteristics on poverty. The strength of unions and leftist parties also reduces poverty, mainly by strengthening welfare state generosity.

Fallacies related to levels

As mentioned above, the purpose of multi-level analyses is to investigate the relationship between the different levels included in the analysis, and this requires data about units at all these levels. If we have no data about conditions at a particular level, we cannot include this level in the analysis or draw conclusions about units at this level. If we draw a conclusion about conditions at a level without having data referring to this level, we run the risk of a *cross-level fallacy*.

Like temporal fallacies, cross-level fallacies are conclusions reached on an erroneous basis. It is the data that are erroneous in connection with the conclusions. While temporal fallacies are conclusions about trends over time based on data from just one point in time, cross-level fallacies are conclusions about conditions at one level based on data from another level. The crucial thing is not whether or not the conclusions prove to be empirically correct. It is the way the conclusions are reached, and especially the lack of a basis for the conclusions in the data, which makes them fallacies.

We distinguish between two types of cross-level fallacy. The most common of these is called *ecological fallacy* or *aggregative fallacy*. This entails that we reach conclusions about conditions at a particular level based on data about conditions at a *higher* level. In this case, we make statements about individual units solely on the basis of *aggregated* data about these units – without having data at the individual level.

If we have data about how voters' votes are distributed across parties in different municipalities, it would be an ecological fallacy to use these data to state how the individual voters in the different municipalities cast their votes. Even if it appeared that a party had strong support in municipalities with a large share of industrial workers, this would not automatically mean that the party had its greatest support among industrial workers. It is not certain that it is the industrial workers in these municipalities who are voting for the party. Another possibility is that the political differences are particularly strong in industrial municipalities, and that such differences increase the level of

support for the particular party among those who are *not* industrial workers. It is possible to empirically investigate which of these options are correct, but this requires data about the voters at the individual level.

The second type of cross-level fallacy is called *atomistic fallacy*. In this case, the conclusion goes in the opposite direction: conclusions are drawn about conditions at a certain level, based on data about conditions at a *lower* level. In this case, we make statements about features of larger units based only on data about each of the smaller units included in the larger unit. However, it is a basic principle in social science that the whole is often more or different than the sum of its parts. The characteristics of institutions, organizations and societies cannot simply be ascertained by aggregating the characteristics of the individuals that make up these larger units. The interaction between the individuals in institutional and societal contexts, and the dynamics of this interaction, create conditions and processes that cannot possibly be determined based solely on data about each individual that forms a part of the institution or society.

Historical-comparative studies

So far, we have considered social science questions that focus on each of the three perspectives of time, space and level. A summary of typical qualitative and quantitative analyses as well as typical problems related to these perspectives is presented in Table 22.3.

There are also more complex studies in which all three perspectives are combined into a single analytic design. Such analyses of stability and change at different levels in different societies are called *historical-comparative studies* or *comparative-historical studies*.

Table 22.3 Typical qualitative and quantitative analyses of longitudinal, spatial and multi-level questions, and typical problems related to such analyses

Type of questions	Typical qualitative analyses	Typical quantitative analyses	Typical problem
Longitudinal questions	• Analyses of short-term processes, based on participant observation • Analyses of longer periods, based on biographical or documentary data	• Analyses of trends and developments, based on documentary or respondent data, including recall data, panel data or time series data. • Cohort analyses based on time series data	Temporal fallacies (based on synchronous data)
Spatial questions	• Comparative analyses of organizations or communities, based on holistic understanding of each unit	• Comparative analyses of organizations, communities, or countries, based on selected variables that characterize the units	Equivalence problems • Linguistic • Contextual • Conceptual • Methodological
Multi-level questions	• Analysis of relationships between micro, meso and macro levels, based on holistic understanding of various types of units as well as their contexts	• Analysis of relationships between micro, meso and macro levels, based on global, aggregated or contextual variables	Cross-level fallacies • Ecological • Atomistic

These types of studies are usually concerned with large and comprehensive issues such as similarities and differences between important, long-term development processes in different countries, or conditions for major societal changes in different types of society or in different epochs. For example, historical-comparative studies have been conducted on the causes of the major revolutions in France, Russia and China (Skocpol, 1979), and why there are major differences between the USA and South Africa in relation to the historical development of the relationship between different races (Fredrickson, 1981).

Historical-comparative studies can be compared to field research. Like field research, historical-comparative studies are based on flexible designs. The collection and analysis of data take place largely in parallel. As more and more data are collected and analysed, and as the researcher's insight deepens, the research question can be revised and clarified. At the same time, the researcher's deepening insight may lead to a modification of the design for collecting and analysing the data during the study.

The types of sources, data and methods to be used are not finally settled until the data collection begins, and they are assessed continuously as the study progresses. The researcher wishes to find as fruitful a formulation of the research question as possible, and to use all available sources, data and methods that are appropriate in order to investigate the research question of the study.

This means that, like field research, historical-comparative studies are often based on combinations of qualitative and quantitative data. Chapter 20 discussed some problems, challenges and strategies associated with analyses of such data combinations. These problems, challenges and strategies are relevant in both field research and historical-comparative studies. Historical-comparative studies must also consider the distinctive possibilities and limitations we have discussed earlier in this chapter in connection with analyses of developments over time, differences between types of society and the relationship between levels. For example, historical-comparative studies must focus on avoiding both temporal and cross-level fallacies, as well as assessing different types of equivalence problems.

Since historical-comparative research combines not only different types of sources, data and methods, but also the three perspectives of time, space and level, such research designs will usually be even more complex than field research designs. The data can be extensive and the analysis can be very demanding. The studies are usually intended to develop a holistic understanding of conditions in different societies and at different times. Establishing a holistic understanding of the conditions in each society and at each time requires a complex design in itself. Comparing these conditions over time and between societies increases the complexity even further.

The main difference between historical-comparative studies and field research is about the distance between the actors, the actions, the opinions and the events being studied. Field research is usually based on participant observation as a central method. The researcher is present in the field during the data collection. The actors are observed while performing the actions that are being studied, and the researcher participates in these actions. The researcher is very close to the conditions being studied. Such designs are most suitable for studying micro-level conditions within relatively short periods of time and in closely demarcated communities. However, historical-comparative studies include conditions at both micro and macro level, in relatively long periods of time and in several different societies. The researcher's distance from these conditions must necessarily be quite large.

The distance is especially great for conditions far back in time. The most important source will then be documents of various kinds, such as newspapers, books, reports, letters, statistical overviews, and public or private records. Both qualitative and quantitative content analyses may be relevant. As pointed out in Chapter 11, it is also important to make source-critical and contextual assessments of the documents, with particular emphasis on discussing the authenticity, credibility, representativeness and bias of the sources. The older the documents are, the more challenging and demanding these assessments will be.

CHAPTER HIGHLIGHTS

- Longitudinal studies examine processes and developments over time.
  - Qualitative longitudinal analyses are suitable for continuous studies of processes, especially through participant observation. Based on, for example, biographical studies or document studies, qualitative analyses can also cover longer periods of time.
  - Quantitative longitudinal analyses are suitable for comparing many moments of time within extended time periods. Questioning of respondents can form the basis for three types of diachronic data: recall data, time series data and panel data. Time series data over extended periods provide opportunities for cohort analyses.

  - Temporal fallacies are conclusions about developments over time based on data about a single moment.

- Comparative studies involve comparing different societies, either societies that are as similar as possible, or societies that are as different as possible.
  - Qualitative comparative analyses focus on obtaining a holistic understanding of each unit.
  - Quantitative comparative analyses are based on specific variables to characterize the units. The variables can be used for the units individually, for all the units together, or such that each unit represents its own value for a particular variable.

- ○ Equivalence problems may weaken the prerequisites for comparability. We distinguish between linguistic, contextual, conceptual and methodological equivalence.

- • Multi-level studies include units at two or more levels in society. In contextual analyses, conditions at a given level are considered in light of conditions at higher levels.

  - ○ Qualitative multi-level analyses provide a comprehensive understanding of the phenomena that are being studied.

- ○ Quantitative multi-level analyses focus on relationships between selected variables and combine variables with reference to the different levels. We distinguish between global, aggregated and contextual variables.

- ○ Cross-level fallacies are conclusions about conditions at a particular level based on data about a different level. We distinguish between ecological and atomistic fallacies.

- • Historical-comparative studies address comprehensive issues and combine the time, spatial and level perspectives in the same analysis.

RESEARCH EXAMPLES

I recommend that you read the publications used as research examples in this chapter.

Brady, David, Andrew S. Fullerton, and Jennifer Moren Cross (2009) 'Putting poverty in political context: A multi-level analysis of adult poverty across 18 affluent democracies', *Social Forces* 88(1), 271–299.

This article presents a multi-level analysis of how the poverty of individuals in 18 affluent countries is influenced by the political context in these countries. The study focuses on individuals as the unit of analysis and combines global and contextual variables. The global variables refer to micro-level characteristics of each individual, including poverty (poor or not poor) as the dependent variable, in addition to several independent variables, such as gender, age, education, family situation and unemployment. The contextual variables refer to macro-level features of the country in which the individuals live, including welfare generosity, unemployment rate, economic growth, and the strength of labour unions and leftist political parties. The analysis shows that poverty is explained by both individual characteristics and contextual features of the countries. Welfare generosity reduces poverty, and it reduces the effects of individual characteristics on poverty. The strength of unions and leftist parties also reduces poverty, mainly by strengthening welfare state generosity.

Hansen, Hans-Tore, Olaf Jürgens, Anne Hege H. Strand, and Wolfgang Voges (2006) 'Poverty among households with children: A comparative study of Norway and Germany', *International Journal of Social Welfare* 15(4), 269–279.

This article presents a study of poverty among households with children in Norway and Germany. The study is based on survey data from the two countries, and separate analyses were carried out for each country, based on the same variables in both countries. The purpose was to examine poverty among single-parent and two-parent households, with reference to different measures of poverty. As to income poverty and material deprivation, the analysis indicates that there is more poverty in Germany than there is in Norway, and that, in both countries, there is more poverty among single-parent households than there is among two-parent households. Furthermore, in both countries, single-parent households receive more social assistance than two-parent households.

Kallio, Tomi J., Kirsi-Mari Kallio, and Annika Johanna Blomberg (2015) 'Physical space, culture and organisational creativity: A longitudinal study', *Facilities* 33(5–6), 389–411.

This article presents an in-depth, longitudinal case study of a newspaper organization in Finland. Data were collected before and after the organization moved to a new location, with a substantial change in the physical design of the facilities, from a rather hierarchical to a more open space design of the workplace. The empirical study was based on qualitative observation and interview data, in addition to some survey data and photographs of the facilities. The purpose of the study was to examine the organizational culture before and after the change in the physical space, with particular emphasis on cultural conditions for creativity. The findings indicate that the move from a hierarchical to an open design of the workplace had an impact on the organizational culture. In particular, the cultural change was characterized by more equality, openness and collectivity, which seemed to strengthen the creativity in the newspaper organization.

STUDENT EXERCISES AND QUESTIONS

1 Why are qualitative studies more suitable than quantitative studies for examining social processes?

2 What are the most important differences between qualitative and quantitative comparative studies?

3 Discuss the most important differences between recall data, time series data and panel data in longitudinal studies.

4 Describe the typical equivalence problems in comparative studies.

5 What is a contextual analysis?

6 Describe different types of cross-level fallacies.

7 Formulate a research question about changes in people's attitudes to gender equality, and discuss how the research question could be examined by means of different types of empirical studies.

RECOMMENDED LITERATURE

Lange, Matthew (2013) *Comparative-Historical Methods*. London: Sage.

This book presents an overview of different methods and techniques in comparative-historical or historical-comparative research. It is a comprehensive introduction to such research, offering examples from classic and recent studies. The book describes the development of historical-comparative analysis and refers to methodological debates within this area.

Snijders, Tom A. B., and Roel J. Bosker (2012) *Multilevel Analysis: An Introduction to Basic and Advanced Multilevel Modeling* (2nd edn). London: Sage.

This book is an introduction to methods, techniques and issues in multi-level research. It presents conceptual explanations and practical guidance for designing and conducting multi-level studies in social science. The book provides step-by-step coverage of a number of relevant topics, such as multi-level theories, ecological fallacies, model specification, and multivariate multi-level models.

Taris, Toon W. (2000) *A Primer in Longitudinal Data Analysis*. London: Sage.

This book provides an introduction to the theory and practice of longitudinal research. Both the strengths and weaknesses of such research are discussed. The book presents a broad overview of longitudinal research as well as practical advice for designing and implementing these types of studies, including how to use statistical techniques and how to interpret findings.

RELATIONS, NETWORKS AND STRUCTURES

This chapter provides the necessary knowledge for understanding how typical relational questions can be analysed in social science.

The chapter will teach you about

- how different relations form social networks
- the relationship between sociomatrices and sociograms
- how to measure the density and centralization of networks

- how to measure the centrality of an actor in a network
- the relationship between networks and structures
- how different types of data can be used in network studies.

Relational questions

Temporal, spatial and multi-level questions, which were discussed in Chapter 22, refer to different kinds of social conditions. *Relational questions*, which will be explored in this chapter, are also typical social science questions with reference to special kinds of social conditions. Such questions are not limited to characteristics of individual units, but deal with relations between units.

A *relation* constitutes a connection between two units. When the relations between many pairs of units are considered together, they make up a *social network*. Such networks can also be regarded as social structures.

Studies of social networks can be focused on, for example, interaction between friends or colleagues, contact between companies or organizations, or communication and collaboration between politicians from different countries. In research on welfare and health, social networks are often regarded as important resources for both individuals and families. In such studies, network connections can also be analysed as a basis for individuals' identity and belonging to the society. In studies of organizations and companies, networks can be understood from strategic perspectives, where deliberate and planned network building provides the basis for promoting particular interests or strengthening the power and influence of

different actors. In analyses of society as a whole, network patterns can be regarded as expressions of integration or cohesion between different individuals or groups. Network analyses can show how different relations rise and develop, what form the network patterns have, and how important the networks are for different actors or for society as a whole.

There are specific concepts in social science for characterizing different types of relations and different patterns in social networks and structures. Special methods have also been developed for analysing and answering questions about relations, networks and structures. Such concepts and methods will be presented in this chapter. First, it is shown how we can distinguish between different types of relations, focusing on both substantive and formal characteristics of the relations. Then, it is demonstrated how networks of such relations can be analysed using sociograms and graph theory. In the following section, it is demonstrated how such analyses can be used to reveal different features of the network as a whole. Then, methods for examining the positions of different actors in the network are reviewed. Furthermore, it is discussed how network analysis can provide a basis for understanding larger structures in society. Finally, the chapter describes how network analyses can be based on both quantitative and qualitative data, as well as mixed methods approaches.

Types of relations

Social science studies can address relations between all the types of units discussed in Chapter 7, including actors, actions, opinions and events. This chapter, however, is focused on relations between actors. These are social relations, and the networks formed by such relations are called social networks.

Social relations exist between all types of actors and between actors at all levels in society, but the types of relations that exist can vary between different actors and different levels.

The so-called *pattern variables* developed by the American sociologist Talcott Parsons (1951) are based on a main distinction between primary and secondary relations. As Table 23.1 illustrates, this distinction is specified using five different pattern variables. Overall, these variables can be regarded as a general typology for social relations. The typology conceptualizes and arranges different characteristic features of the relations, emphasizing how an actor can relate to other actors. Each of the five pattern variables forms a dimension in the typology. Each dimension is defined through a concept pair, where one concept denotes traits of near or primary social relations, while the other concept denotes features of more distant or secondary relations.

Social relations can otherwise be classified or categorized in many different ways. As pointed out in Chapter 7, such distinctions between different types of relations can be based on the content of the relations or on their more formal characteristics.

As to the content of the relations, we think about what the relations are about and what the relations between the actors consist of. It could be friendship, acquaintance, neighbourly or collegial relations between people. There may be customer relations or cooperative relations of various kinds between companies, and relations in the form of interlocking directorates can be established by a single person being a board member in several different companies. Municipalities can develop cooperative relations in order to promote common interests in larger regional contexts. Relations between states can be developed through international negotiations, agreements, organizations and alliances. Generally, relations can include different activities, such as social gatherings, conversation or other communication, coordination or interaction, negotiation or exchange of goods and services; a number of other examples could be mentioned. The point is that the content of social relations can vary, and that the study of relations with varying content is a core feature of social science.

We can also distinguish between different formal characteristics of social relations. A relation can be *symmetrical* or *asymmetrical*. A relation between two actors is symmetrical, or mutual, if it has the same meaning for both actors, or if it reflects equality between the two actors. A friendship relation is symmetrical if both actors consider the other actor as their friend. A cooperative relation is symmetrical if the two cooperating actors are equally strong. A relation is asymmetrical if it has a different significance for the two actors, or if the two actors have different value or strength in the relation. An asymmetrical

Table 23.1 A typology of social relations: the pattern variables described by Parsons

Primary relations	Secondary relations
Affectivity	Affective neutrality
Diffusiveness	Specificity
Particularism	Universalism
Ascription	Achievement
Self-orientation	Collectivity-orientation

friendship relation means that only one of the two actors regards the other as a friend. A relation is also asymmetrical if it entails that one actor has power or influence over the other actor. An asymmetrical relation has a specific *direction*, from one actor to the other actor, for example from the actor who exercises power to the actor exposed to power.

A relation can be *positive*, *neutral* or *negative*. While friendship is a positive relation, animosity is a negative relation. While cooperative relations are positive, conflictual relations are negative. Relations that involve communication or information exchange may also be positive or negative, but will often be neutral.

Relations can also have different *weight* or *value*. In other words, different importance can be attached to relations, or they may be more or less valuable to those actors who are involved in the relations. Such a rating of the relations can be based on different criteria. For example, the distance between the actors can be such a criterion. In a friendship relation, the distance between the two friends may vary. A relation between two close friends can be considered more important than a relation between two friends who are not so close.

A relation can be *uniplex* or *multiplex*. A uniplex relation between two persons means that the relation has only one type of content. For example, the two actors are just friends or just neighbours or just colleagues. Relations that include multiple types of content are called multiplex relations. Two persons who are not only friends, but also neighbours and colleagues, have a multiplex relation to each other. Multiplexity can be used as a criterion for rating relations, so that the more types of content a relation involves, the higher the rating it is assigned.

A formal characteristic of relations that has been very important in recent theories on social networks is the *strength* of the relations. A relation between two actors can be strong or weak.

The strength of a relation depends on a combination of several factors, including how much time the actors spend on the relation, how emotionally intense the relation is for the actors, how intimate the relation is, and how many reciprocal services are associated with the relation. The more the relation is characterized by these factors, the stronger the relation. Relations between close friends who meet often are strong relations, while relations between acquaintances who meet less often are weak. The American sociologist Mark Granovetter (1973) has demonstrated that the distinction between strong and weak relations, or ties, is very useful for understanding social networks as important structures in society. He emphasizes that weak ties have a special strength in this context. This paradoxical insight will be further discussed below, in the section on social networks and structures in society.

Sociograms and graph theory

When a set of actors have relations with each other, they constitute a social network. As pointed out in Chapter 16, social networks can be illustrated by means of a certain type of figure or diagram. In such figures, which are called *sociograms*, the actors are presented as points, and the relations between the actors are presented as lines between the points. Figure 23.1 is an example of a simple sociogram. It illustrates a

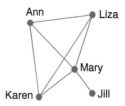

Figure 23.1 Example of a sociogram: network between five women

network between five women. It could be a network of friends, for example. Mary has relations with all the others in the network. She is a friend of all the other women in the network. Karen, Ann and Liza have relations with everyone except Jill, and Jill has only one relation, to Mary. In other words, Jill has a friendship with only Mary, while Karen, Ann and Liza are friends with each other and with Mary.

This sociogram is called a *simple graph* because it only shows whether or not there is a relation between each pair of actors. All the relations in the sociogram appear to be symmetrical. If any of the relations were asymmetrical, they could be marked in the sociogram with arrows instead of just lines. If Jill considered Mary to be her friend, but without this being reciprocated by Mary, we would draw an arrow from Jill to Mary. A sociogram with arrows instead of lines is called a *digraph* (abbreviated from directed graph).

None of the relations in Figure 23.1 are weighted. None of the relations have greater weight than the others. For example, if Mary has a closer friendship with Karen than with the other three women, this difference could be marked with different numbers on the lines, so that the line between Mary and Karen had a higher number than the other lines from Mary. However, numbers associated with the lines can also be used to indicate that the relations are multiplex. If Mary and Ann are not just friends but also colleagues, this could be expressed by marking the line between them with the number 2.

In this sociogram, we do not distinguish between positive, negative and neutral relations. This could be marked by providing the lines with symbols (+, – or 0). If the relation between Mary and Jill were characterized by conflict or animosity, this could be expressed by adding a minus sign to the line between the two. If the relations between the four other women were friendly, the other lines in the sociogram would get a plus.

Positive and negative relations can also be marked by different types of line. Normal practice in this case is that solid lines (———) indicate positive relations, while dashed lines (----------) indicate negative relations. However, different types of line can also be used to mark the difference between strong and weak relations. Solid lines then represent strong relations, while dashed lines represent weak relations.

In addition to graphic representation, we can also use matrix algebra to illustrate social networks. The network is then expressed in the form of a *sociomatrix* instead of a sociogram. Table 23.2 shows the sociomatrix corresponding to the sociogram in Figure 23.1. We refer to a particular cell in the matrix by the name of the person represented by the row in which the cell is located, followed by the name of person represented by the column where the cell is located. Thus, the cell in the top row and the rightmost column of Table 23.2 is referred to as the (Karen, Jill) cell. In the matrix, a 0 indicates that there is no relation, while a 1 means that there is a relation. For example, the number 1 in the (Ann, Karen cell) means that there is a relation between Ann and Karen, while the 0 in the (Karen, Jill) cell means that there is no relation between Karen and Jill. Since none of the women has such a relation to themselves, there are no numbers in the diagonal in the matrix.

Table 23.2 Example of a sociomatrix: network between five women

	Karen	Ann	Liza	Mary	Jill
Karen		1	1	1	0
Ann	1		1	1	0
Liza	1	1		1	0
Mary	1	1	1		1
Jill	0	0	0	1	

The matrix is symmetrical because this is about symmetrical relations. The triangle above the diagonal is a mirror image of the triangle below the diagonal. Often, therefore, only the lower triangle is rendered in such symmetrical matrices. If the matrix contained asymmetrical relations, however, it would be asymmetrical. If Jill considered Mary to be a friend, without the friendship being reciprocated, there could be a 1 in the (Jill, Mary) cell, but a 0 in the (Mary, Jill) cell.

If the relations were weighted or multiplex, the weight or multiplexity could be expressed by numbers other than 0 and 1 in the matrix, so that a higher number would indicate a relation of greater weight, or of more types of content. Strong and weak relations could also be marked with different numbers in the matrix, with higher numbers for strong than for weak relations.

Finally, the numbers in the matrix could be given different algebraic signs if we wished to distinguish between positive and negative relations. Positive relations would then be marked with positive numbers and negative relations with negative numbers.

As already mentioned, social networks can be analysed using both sociograms and sociomatrices. The advantage of sociograms is that they provide a visual overview of the network as a whole and the positions of the various actors within the network. The limitation of sociograms, however, is that they are primarily suitable for analysing relatively small and limited networks. As the numbers of actors and relations increase, sociograms become increasingly complex and increasingly difficult to understand. Admittedly, computer programs to draw sociograms based on information about network connections are continuously being improved. There are limits, however, to how many points and lines can be included in a single figure before it becomes difficult or impossible to distinguish the different points and lines from each other.

In large-network analyses, it is more appropriate to rely on various statistical measures to characterize different features of the network patterns and network positions. The advantage of sociomatrices is that they can be used as a basis for calculating such measures. We can use computer programs to handle very large matrices that allow us to analyse patterns and positions in extensive networks and large social structures.

Features of networks

Network analyses are intended to highlight patterns or features in the network as a whole, as well as aspects of different actors' positions in the network. Let us first take a look at some important features of the overall network.

The five women in the sociogram in Figure 23.1 constitute a *network component*. In a component, all of the actors are directly or indirectly connected to each other, and there are no relations between the actors in the component and other actors.

There is no *direct relation* between Jill and Liza, but since Jill may have contact with Liza through Mary, there is an *indirect relation* between Jill and Liza. Indirect relations can go through several actors. The number of direct relations that are part of an indirect relation between two actors constitutes the *distance* between the actors in the network. A direct relation then corresponds to a distance of 1. Jill is located at a distance of 2 from Karen, Ann and Liza, but at a distance of 1 from Mary.

In addition to the five friends in Figure 23.1, a network analysis could include a corresponding group of five men with friendship relations between them, but without relations with any of the five women. The five male friends would then constitute another network component.

The patterns of direct and indirect relations, distances and components are important features of social networks. Such features can be summarized in various statistical measures that are used to characterize different network patterns. One of these measures is *density*. This measure shows how many relations exist in the network, expressed as a proportion of the number of theoretically possible relations between all the actors. The density (*d*) is calculated using the following formula, where *l* is the number of relations in the network and *n* is the number of actors:

$$d = \frac{l}{n(n-1)/2}.$$

The network in Figure 23.1 has seven relations (*l*). The number of theoretically possible relations between the five women, [*n*(*n* − 1)/2], is 10. The density of this network is then 7/10 = 0.7. If all the theoretically possible relations actually existed in the network, the density would be equal to 1. Such a network with maximum density is called a *clique*. The network in Figure 23.1 would be a clique if we disregarded Jill. The network between the four other women in the figure is a clique because each of the four has direct relations with all the other three.

Centralization is another feature of a network that is often expressed in the form of a statistical measure. Simply put, centralization is an expression of differences between the actors with regard to how centrally they are positioned in the network. If one or a few actors are much more centrally positioned than the other actors, the network has a high degree of centralization. If there are only small differences between the actors' centrality, the network has a low level of centralization. Figure 23.2 shows sociograms for two small networks with very different levels of centralization. The network in Figure 23.2a has a high degree of centralization because the actor in the centre is far more centrally positioned than the five other actors. The network in Figure 23.2b has a low degree of centralization, because none of the six actors is more centrally positioned than the others.

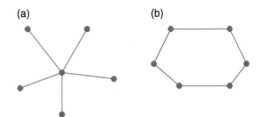

Figure 23.2 Examples of networks with (a) a high degree of centralization and (b) a low degree of centralization

There are different measures of centralization. One of these measures is called the *heterogeneity index* because it shows how heterogeneous the network is with regard to the actors' centrality. The calculations of the different measures of centralization can be rather complicated and will not be discussed in more detail here.

The network's centralization is based on the distribution of the individual actors' centrality. Thus, centralization is an example of how the properties of the network as a whole are closely linked with the positions of the various actors in the network. The theme of the next section is how we can analyse different features of the actors' positions in the network.

Features of the actors' positions in the network

The network's characteristics, especially its density and centralization, can be important for interaction processes within the network. The denser the network is, and the more centralized it is, the greater the opportunities for information exchange, interaction and coordination between the actors. The role of different actors in these processes will depend on their positions in the network. The actors' *centrality* is most crucial in this regard. The more centrally placed the actors are, the greater their opportunities for influencing or controlling the communication, interaction or coordination that takes place in the network.

Centrality can be defined and measured in different ways. The simplest measure is called *degree*. An actor's degree is defined as the number of direct relations between this actor and other actors in the network. This measure of centrality is also referred to as the number of *neighbours* to the relevant actor. The more direct relations or neighbours an actor has, the more central the actor is in the network. The position is central because the actor has direct connection to many other actors. In Figure 23.2a, the actor in the centre has a degree of 5, while each of the other actors has a degree of 1. In Figure 23.2b, all the actors have a degree of 2.

This measure of centrality may vary with network size because the likelihood of having many direct relations increases as the number of actors in the network increases. However, we can standardize, or normalize, the measure by controlling for the network's size. The degree is then divided by the maximum number of direct relations that the actor could have ($n - 1$). This *normalized degree centrality* is then calculated as

$$C = \frac{\text{degree}}{n-1}.$$

Looking at Figure 23.2 again, we find for Figure 23.2a that the normalized degree centrality of the actor in the centre is $C = 5/5 = 1.0$. The normalized degree centrality for each of the other actors is $C = 1/5 = 0.2$. In Figure 23.2b, all actors have the same normalized degree centrality ($C = 2/5 = 0.4$).

This degree-based centrality measure can be expanded to include indirect relations at a certain distance in addition to direct relations. For example, centrality can be calculated as the number of neighbours at distance 1 and 2. The standardized version of this expanded measure of centrality

shows the proportion of the total number of actors in the network that can be reached in one or two steps. Therefore, the measure is called *2-step reach*. However, such expanded centrality measures based on degree are not very useful in small networks, where there are relatively few indirect relations.

Another measure of centrality is called *closeness*. While centrality in the form of degree refers to the actor's nearest neighbours, closeness is defined on the basis of the actor's distances to all the other actors in the network. The idea is that the actor has a central position if the average distance to the other actors in the network is small. Centrality in the form of closeness is therefore calculated by summing up the distances to all other actors. The smaller this sum is, the more central is the actor. In Figure 23.2a, the sum of the distances from the actor in the centre to all of the five other actors is equal to 5, while each of the other actors has a distance sum of 9.

Based on this summation of distances, there are various indexes for closeness. Some of these involve a standardization of the closeness measure, so that it is made independent of the size of the network. The calculations can be relatively complicated and will not be described here.

Centrality may also be measured in terms of *betweenness*. This entails that an actor is central if the actor's position is between many other actors. This is illustrated in Figure 23.3, where the two networks in Figure 23.2 are linked by an indirect relation between one of the actors in network (a) and one of the actors in network (b). This indirect relation goes through actor A. Thus, in the new and larger network, actor A has a very central position between the two original networks. All the actors in each of the original networks must go through A to get in contact with the actors in the other original network. A's position is central because it provides great opportunities for information access, information dissemination and coordination.

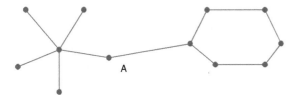

Figure 23.3 Example of centrality in the form of betweenness (A)

Using sociograms and statistical measures, such as density and degree, the authors show how the networks in the class changed during the role-playing period. The number of both friendship and acquaintance ties increased dramatically, which means that the density of both networks increased in the role-playing period.

If we follow the lines from one point in the sociogram to another point, possibly through intermediate points, these lines constitute a *path* between the starting point and the end point. In Figure 23.3, point A lies on the shortest path between all the points in one original network (a) and all the points in the other original network (b). The betweenness for a point is calculated on the basis of how many of the shortest paths between the other points in the network pass through the point in question. The greater the number of such paths that pass through the point, the more central the point is. In other words: the greater the number of other actors a particular actor is between, the more central this particular actor is in the network. The calculation of betweenness centrality can be rather complicated and will not be described here.

Betweenness is very important in terms of establishing links between small networks so that they can be integrated into larger structures. Actors in intermediate positions establish bridges between smaller networks. These bridges are often weak relations. Thus, weak relations are strategically important for the development of social structures, which will be discussed in more detail in the next section.

An example of a network study is presented by Webb and Engar (2016). They examined how relations between students evolved while using a particular role-playing game. Students in a class at a US university were interviewed before, during and after a 3-month period of playing a game called 'Reacting to the Past'. In each of four interviews, the students were asked to name their friends and acquaintances among their classmates.

Social networks and structures in society

Research on social networks is an important area of social science, not least because such networks have a high degree of social significance. For individual actors, networks may have significance as a resource. Good network connections can provide help and support or access to affordable goods and services. Networks provide social contact, integration into the community, a sense of belonging and identity. They can also provide access to information and be a basis for influence. Various actors can also develop or utilize networks strategically, in order to enhance their position or promote their interests. For companies, organizations and political actors, network building is an increasingly common strategy. The way in which a network works as a resource and how it can be developed and utilized strategically will depend on both the network's properties and the positions of the actors in the network. Thus, it is important to analyse both network patterns and network positions.

Such analyses are not only important for understanding the significance of networks for different actors. Analyses of social networks are also important for understanding larger social structures. A social structure can be defined as a relatively stable pattern of relations between social positions. In this sense, a social network can be regarded as a social structure. Such networks appear as concrete, observable expressions of structural conditions in society. Structural patterns in a particular area of society are expressed through network connections between actors in this area.

Therefore, network analyses can reveal the form of a given structure and how different structures develop and function. For example, analyses of networks in business and industry can provide a basis for an increased insight into economic power structures in society. On the one hand, the network as a whole may be a basis for communication and coordination among companies, which strengthens the general power of business and industry in society, especially if the network is dense and centralized. On the other hand, a central position in the network provides a basis for influencing or controlling the communication and coordination, which strengthens the power of the most central companies within business and industry.

One type of such intercorporate networks is based on interlocking directorates among companies. An interlocking directorate between two

companies means that one person is a member of the board of both companies. Networks of interlocking directorates have been studied in many countries. For example, an analysis of interlocking directorates between all the banks and the 200 largest companies in Norway in 1985 showed that the most central company (Elkem) had 64 neighbours at distances 1 and 2 (Grønmo and Løyning, 2003). This means that through its board relations, this company had regular contact with 64 other companies. The sociogram in Figure 23.4 illustrates this network around Elkem.

As the most important company, Elkem is positioned at the centre of the sociogram. The inner circle contains the companies with which Elkem had *direct* relations. This means that each of these companies shared one or more board members with Elkem. The outer circle consists of the companies with which Elkem had *indirect* relations. This means that one or more board

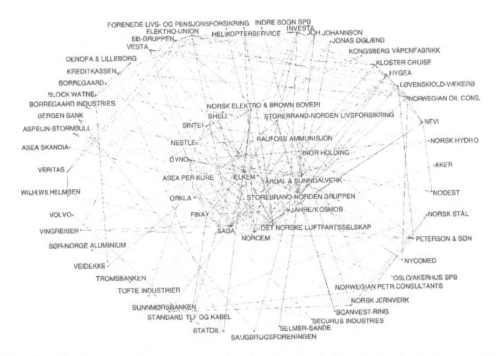

Figure 23.4 Example of an economic power structure, based on the network of interlocking directorates around the most central company in Norway in 1985. Reproduced from Grønmo and Løyning, 2003: 153)

members from each of these companies met with board members from Elkem at board meetings of companies in the inner circle. These direct and indirect links to Elkem constitute a large and almost nationwide network of companies.. This network can be understood as a power structure in which the relations between the companies formed the basis for communication and coordination, and where Elkem, through its central position, could be a dominant actor in the communication and coordination processes.

A relation based on interlocking directorates between two companies is regarded as strong if it is the managing director, or CEO, of one company that is a board member of the other company. Otherwise, such relations are regarded as weak. On this basis, the majority of the network connections in Figure 23.4 are weak relations.

The sociogram in Figure 23.4 shows only the network connections of the most central company. If the sociogram included the relations between all the companies in the network, the figure would become extremely complex and difficult to read. In connection with such extensive structures, the network patterns and the actors' positions must be described using different statistical measures, such as density, centralization and centrality.

A similar study was carried out by Heemskerk (2011). He examined the network of interlocking directorates among the 300 largest European companies in 2005. Using sociograms, he visualized the transnational network among the companies. Referring to the home country of each company, he also identified the corporate network relations among the European countries. Furthermore, based on the interpersonal relations between directors meeting as members of the same board, he revealed the European interpersonal network of directors. Analysing the characteristic features of these intercorporate and interpersonal networks, and focusing on the most central companies and the directors with most relations, Heemskerk

(2011) identified a European corporate elite. He concluded that the European corporate network is based on only a small number of European directors, and that the European interpersonal network is sparse compared with many national corporate elite networks.

Since the 1970s, social science network research has undergone extensive theoretical and methodological renewal. This renewal has had particular importance for the understanding of networks as structures and for network analyses in larger structural contexts. An important part of this renewal is the theory of the *strength of weak ties*, developed by the American sociologist Mark Granovetter (1973). A key point in this theory is that strong relations, or strong ties, are mainly found in small cliques, and that it is mainly weak relations, or weak ties, that make up the connections between different cliques. This insight has helped to expand the perspective of network research in social science. Previous network research was largely focused on strong relations within limited networks in small groups or local communities. Recent research in the field has increasingly focused attention on weak relations and their importance, and in this way it has also become possible to study more extensive network patterns in larger social contexts.

This expanded perspective is further enhanced by the methodological development of network research. It has become possible to conduct empirical network studies that incorporate large numbers of actors and relations, and the analyses can reveal patterns and positions in complex and comprehensive social networks. Various types of big data as well as new computer software and analytical methods, based primarily on graph theory and matrix algebra, have allowed us to deal with large networks. Analysis as well as visualizations of social networks can be based on a number of special software packages, such as UCINet and Pajek.

Qualitative and quantitative network analyses

Social networks can be analysed using both qualitative and quantitative data as well as mixed methods. The two types of data form the basis for conducting different kinds of analyses, and for understanding different aspects of the networks.

Quantitative analyses

In quantitative network analyses, we start with a particular type of actor and particular types of relations between these actors, such as large companies and their interlocking directorates. We can study the entire universe of these actors, that is, all the companies above a certain size. We can also study a sample of actors. As a rule, we rely on a probability sample, such as a simple random sample of all the companies above a certain size. There are many different types of relations between the selected actors. Quantitative analyses concentrate on one or more of these types of relations. Between companies there are ownership relations, board relations, negotiation relations, transactional relations, and more informal relations between the leaders of the companies. By analysing board relations in the form of interlocking directorates, we concentrate on one type of relation.

There is also an alternative procedure for sampling in network studies. Instead of starting with a sample of actors and then identifying relations between the selected actors, we can start with a sample of a particular type of relations and then identify the actors involved in the selected relations. This assumes that we can obtain an overview of the universe of such relations or that we can rely on a sampling method that can be assumed in principle to result in a probability sample of the universe. In studies of interlocking directorates, for example, we can select a probability sample of all the people who are board members of two or more

companies, and thus for each of the selected persons we can identify which companies are connected to each other by interlocking directorates.

Quantitative data about such selected network connections consist of specific measures for the relations between each pair of the selected actors. The relational measures may be limited to showing whether or not a relation exists between the actors, but they may also be more nuanced and reflect, for example, the number of relations, the strengths of the relations or their direction.

The analyses of such quantitative network data provide an overview of general patterns and characteristic features of the network as a whole, or different actors' positions in the network. In such analyses, we can use sociograms to visualize or illustrate patterns and positions, but we can also use statistical measures of different characteristics of the network patterns and network positions. The larger and more complex the networks analysed, the more difficult it will be to use sociograms. However, statistical measures can be used in connection with both small and large networks.

One of the major advantages of quantitative network analyses is that such analyses allow us to study comprehensive and complex network patterns. Such analyses may include large amounts of data in the form of information about a large number of actors and relations.

A limitation of quantitative network analyses is that they primarily focus on the *form* of the network patterns, and that they are not specifically concerned with the *content* of the network connections or the *importance* of the relations that are part of the network. Admittedly, the overview of the form of the network patterns can provide a good basis for discussing which processes are related to the network and the importance of the network connections, both for the network as a whole and for the individual actors. Such discussions, however, are not based on direct empirical observations, but are developed on the basis of interpretations of the empirical findings and theoretical reflections about the patterns revealed by the analyses.

Another limitation of quantitative network analyses is that they do not take account of the context in which the network connections exist. The more extensive the networks that are analysed, the greater this limitation will be. When analysing small networks, contextual conditions can be considered while interpreting the results of the analysis, while this will be difficult in large networks. Partly it will be difficult to obtain an overview of such larger contexts, and partly the contextual conditions will be different for different parts of the network.

Here, as elsewhere, there is a connection between context and significance or meaning. The meaning that different network connections have for the actors themselves will depend largely on the context in which these connections occur. Viewing the network connections in their context is thus a prerequisite for understanding the significance or meaning that the connections have for the actors themselves. This also entails that the same type of relation may have different meanings for the actors, because the relation type and the actors are parts of different contexts. In quantitative analyses of large and complex networks, it can thus be difficult to assess whether the relations that are part of the network are equivalent and comparable.

Qualitative analyses

Both the content and significance of the relations, as well as the context of the network, can be empirically investigated using qualitative network analyses. Qualitative analyses are particularly well suited to investigating precisely such conditions.

Qualitative network analyses are usually based on strategically selected actors or strategically selected relations. Studies based on selected actors are often intended to investigate what type of relations exists between these actors internally or between the selected actors and other actors. Studies based on selection of relations focus on investigating which actors are linked through these relations.

The strategic sampling is based on the actors or relations being either unique and of great interest in themselves, or typical and interesting in a larger and more general context. As pointed out in Chapter 8, snowball sampling is a form of strategic sampling that is particularly well suited for qualitative network studies. Regardless of whether the qualitative data are based on the sampling of actors or relations, an important part of the analysis will consist of obtaining an overview of the network patterns that are formed by the relations between the various actors. In qualitative analyses of such network patterns, it is not adequate to use statistical measures of features of the network or of the actors' positions. However, as pointed out in Chapter 16, both figures and matrices can be important analytical tools in qualitative analyses generally. In line with this, qualitative network analyses will use sociograms and simple sociomatrices to present and illustrate the network patterns that are revealed.

In addition to revealing the patterns of the networks, qualitative network analyses are also intended to establish knowledge, insights and understanding regarding the content of the different relations and the importance of the relations for the various actors. The processes associated with the network connections are investigated and analysed in light of both the features of the network and the context around the network. Generally, this is the most important objective of qualitative network analyses, and this type of analysis constitutes the primary strength of qualitative network studies. Special software has been developed for this kind of qualitative network analysis (Lonkila and Harmo, 1999).

The largest limitation of qualitative network analyses is that they can only be conducted for small, clearly delimited networks. Intensive studies of the content, meaning and context of the relations are very demanding and will be insurmountable if the study involves very many relations, if the network is very large and complex, or if the network's context is diverse and diffuse.

Mixed methods in network studies

As we can see, the weaknesses and limitations of quantitative network analyses can be offset by the strengths of qualitative network analyses, and vice versa. In other words, here as elsewhere, it may be appropriate and useful to combine qualitative and quantitative approaches. Quantitative analyses can provide an overview of patterns and positions in large networks and social structures, while qualitative analyses can provide an insight into the processes associated with these structures, as well as an understanding of the content, meaning and significance of the various network connections for different actors and under different contextual conditions.

Such a combination of qualitative and quantitative network analyses was used in the study of interlocking directorates between banks and large companies mentioned above (Grønmo and Løyning, 2003). In addition to the quantitative analyses of patterns in the nationwide corporate networks and power structures, qualitative analyses were conducted based on informal interviews of 11 centrally placed board members in key companies. The interviews provided important knowledge about, for example, the importance of interlocking directorates, not least in a power perspective. This knowledge is not only of interest in itself. It also provided a valuable basis for interpreting the network patterns that were identified in the quantitative analyses.

Another example of a mixed methods network study is presented by Bernardi (2011). The purpose of her study was to examine the influence of social networks on family formation and fertility decision-making among young adults in transnational families. The data collection was based on interviews with 28–32-year-old men and women in Germany in 2004 and 2005. The interviews provided quantitative data on network relations among the respondent and the 10 most important members of the respondent's network, and qualitative data on emotional and material exchanges among these network members, as well as the meaning of the relations of exchanges in the network. The network analysis focused on the strength or importance of the relations as well as structural features of the network, including density and closeness. Sociograms were used to visualize the network patterns. The article concludes that 'describing and understanding the structure and composition of children's social environments and identifying strong and weak ties in their networks are powerful tools for identifying the vulnerabilities and strengths of transnational families in the context of childrearing' (Bernardi, 2011: 801).

CHAPTER HIGHLIGHTS

- A social relation is a connection between two actors. We distinguish between different types of social relations, partly based on the content of the relations, partly based on their formal features.
- Relations can be primary or secondary, symmetrical or asymmetrical, positive, neutral or negative, uniplex or multiplex, and they can have different directions, weight and strength.
- A set of actors who have relations with each other constitute a social network. We distinguish between direct and indirect relations in the network.

- In a network component, all of the actors have direct or indirect relations to each other, and there are no relations between the actors in the component and other actors. In a clique, all the actors have direct relations to each other.
- Social networks can be presented in the form of sociograms and sociomatrices.
- Network analyses are intended to investigate patterns or features of the network as a whole, such as density and centralization, as well as aspects of different actors' position in the network, such as centrality (in terms of degree, closeness or betweenness).
- Social networks can be regarded as social structures. The strength of weak ties is that they often constitute bridges between small groups and thus are important for the development of larger structures.

- Quantitative network analyses can provide an overview of general patterns and characteristic features of the network as a whole or different actors' position in the network. Such analyses are based on specific types of actors and relations. The analyses are often based on probability samples of actors or relations and may include large networks.
- Qualitative network analyses can provide contextual understanding of the network and insights into the content and meaning of network relations. Such analyses are based on strategically selected actors or relations within limited contexts.
- It can be useful to combine qualitative and quantitative network analyses.

RESEARCH EXAMPLES

I recommend that you read the publications used as research examples in this chapter.

Bernardi, Laura (2011) 'A mixed-methods social networks study design for research on transnational families', *Journal of Marriage and Family* 73, 788–803.

The study presented in this article is an example of a mixed methods network study. The study examined the influence of social networks on family formation and fertility decision-making among young adults in transnational families. The data collection was based on interviews with 28–32-year-old men and women in Germany in 2004 and 2005. The interviews provided quantitative data on network relations among the respondent and the 10 most important members of the respondent's network, and qualitative data on emotional and material exchanges among these network members, as well as the meaning of the relations of exchanges in the network. The network analysis focused on the strength or importance of the relations as well as structural features of the network, including density and closeness. Sociograms were used to visualize the network patterns. The article argues that the mixed methods approach is very useful in this type of research.

Heemskerk, Eelke M. (2011) 'The social field of the European corporate elite: A network analysis of interlocking directorates among Europe's largest corporate boards', *Global Networks* 11(4), 440–460.

This article presents a network analysis of interlocking directorates among the 300 largest European companies in 2005. Using sociograms, the article visualizes the transnational network among the companies, the interpersonal network among the companies' directors, and the corporate network relations among the European countries. Analysing the characteristic features of the intercorporate and interpersonal networks, and focusing on the most central companies and the directors with most relations, the article identifies a European corporate elite. The conclusion is that the European corporate network is based on only a small number of European directors, and that the European interpersonal network is sparse compared with many national corporate elite networks.

Webb, Jeff, and Ann Engar (2016) 'Exploring classroom community: A social network study of Reacting to the Past', *Teaching & Learning Inquiry* 4(1).

This article presents a network study of how relations between students evolved while using a particular role-playing game. Students in a class at a US university were interviewed before, during and after a 3-month period of playing a game called 'Reacting to the Past'. In each of four interviews the students were asked to name their friends and acquaintances among their classmates. Using sociograms and statistical measures, such as density and degree, the authors show how the networks in the class changed during the role-playing period. The number of both friendship and acquaintance ties increased dramatically, which means that the density of both networks increased in the role-playing period.

STUDENT EXERCISES AND QUESTIONS

1 What is the difference between symmetrical and asymmetrical relations?

2 What is a network component?

3 What is the difference between density and centralization in a network?

4 What is the difference between degree and betweenness as measures of an actor's centrality in a network?

5 Why are weak ties important in social networks?

6 Why are social networks regarded as social structures?

7 Consider the sociogram in Figure 16.1 in this book and discuss the following questions (you may disregard the directions of the relations):

   a How can this network be presented in a sociomatrix?

   b What is the density of the network?

   c Which actors are most central in the network, based on degree as the measure of centrality?

   d Which actors are most central in the network, based on betweenness as the measure of centrality?

RECOMMENDED LITERATURE

Prell, Christina (2011) *Social Network Analysis: History, Theory and Methodology.* London: Sage.

The book provides an overview of social network analysis, including the field's historical development, theoretical perspectives and frameworks, and analytical procedures. The presentation helps students learn how to study, think about and analyse social networks.

Scott, John (2017) *Social Network Analysis* (4th edn). London: Sage.

This book is a comprehensive guide to social network analysis. It presents an introduction to social network analysis and an overview of the field. The book includes discussions of the most important developments in research on social networks, the key theories and techniques in this research, as well as practical exercises and real-world examples of social networks.

Yang, Song, Franziska B. Keller, and Lu Zheng (2017) *Social Network Analysis: Methods and Examples.* London: Sage.

This book presents basic methodological tools for social network analysis. It is based on a conceptual rather than a mathematical approach, and methods for network studies are discussed in relation to research designs, as well as collection and analysis of data. The discussion of methods is illustrated by means of examples from various fields, including politics, work and organizations, mental and physical health, and crime and terrorism studies.

BIG DATA AND COMPUTATIONAL SOCIAL SCIENCE

This chapter provides the necessary knowledge for understanding how big data and computational social science can be used to ask new questions and provide new answers in social research.

The chapter will teach you about

- characteristic features of big data and computational social science
- different types of big data
- typical questions that can be examined by means of big data and computational social science
- some major challenges related to big data in social science.

Opportunities for new questions and answers

In the previous chapters, typical social science questions have been discussed, partly with reference to different kinds of knowledge (Chapter 21), and partly with reference to different kinds of social phenomena (Chapters 22 and 23). This chapter is focused on new possibilities for asking and answering social science questions, based on new data sources and new tools for collecting, storing and processing data. Big data and computational social science provide opportunities for asking new questions as well as answering old questions in new ways.

In several chapters of this book it has been described how big data can be collected and analysed, and how computer programs can be used for collecting and analysing data. The use of big data and software packages has been described in relation to different methods for data collection and analysis. The purpose of this chapter is to summarize the main aspects of big data and computational social science, and to discuss what types of questions can be answered by means of these new sources and tools. First, the main features and types of big data are emphasized, and the major characteristics of computational social science are explained. Then, the special opportunities provided by big data and computational social science for examining important social science questions

are discussed. Finally, some major challenges related to big data and computational social sciences are pointed out.

Features and types of big data

As pointed out in Chapter 7, it is common to emphasize three typical features of big data. The first and most obvious feature is that such data are very voluminous. A set of big data, such as a national tax register, consists of very large amounts of data. The second feature of big data is variety. Typically, a big data set is quite complex and characterized by much diversity. A wide variety of information is included in big data, such as the mixture of texts, pictures and videos in social media. The third feature is velocity, which means that big data are frequently updated and changed. For example, in registers on people's income, new information on a person's income regularly replaces or is added to older information on the income. Thus, the register will always include the most recent income information, and perhaps information on income changes as well. Other big data sets, such as data on people's use of smart phones, will show more or less continuous processes of movements or changing behaviour. Thus, big data are usually characterized by the three Vs: volume, variety and velocity.

There are many different sources for big data and many different types of such data. Big data can be obtained, for example, from public registers, registered business transactions, recordings from surveillance cameras or sensors, or various types of social media. Such data may be available as numbers, texts, pictures, or videos, and they may be qualitative or quantitative.

Sources of big data can be categorized in more systematic ways. As referred to in Chapter 7, Kitchin (2014: 85–97) distinguishes between three categories of big data sources, based on how the data are provided or produced. These categories are:

- *volunteered information*, which is traded or gifted by people to a system;
- *automated information*, which is generated as an inherent automatic function of a device or a system; and
- *directed information*, which is based on traditional forms of surveillance, focused on a person or a place by a human operator.

Another categorization of big data sources is presented by Lazer and Radford (2017: 21–23). Based on the 'loci of data collection', or type of information provided by the data, they distinguish between information about:

- *digital life*, which includes information about behaviour that is digital, such as social media activities;
- *digital traces,* which refers to information about records of actions, but not the actions themselves – for example, such information includes call detail records from phone calls, or information in national tax registers;
- *digitalized life*, which includes digitalized information about activities that are not digital, such as video recordings of city life.

What is computational social science?

In previous chapters of this book, it has been pointed out how computers and computer software can be used in data collection and analysis. All types of collection and analysis of qualitative as well as quantitative data can be more or less computer-based or computer-assisted, and special software packages have been developed for different research designs and different data types. Computers may be very useful tools in all kinds of social research, but in typical quantitative analyses the use of computer programs is essential, especially if the data set is relatively large, and if the analysis is based on advanced statistical methods.

In big data studies, the use of computers and computer programs is absolutely necessary. Due to the volume, variety and velocity of big data, such data cannot be handled without computers. Computers with large capacity and high speed are required for registering, processing and storing various kinds of big data. Computer networks are needed for transferring, linking and integrating big data from different sources. Adequate and specialized computer software is important for collecting and analysing big data for different purposes, including social science studies.

Although computational social science could refer to all kinds of computer-based social research, this term is typically used in a more limited and narrow sense. Usually, computational social science is defined as a subfield of social research based on big data, which is particularly focused on using computers and big data for analysing social networks, social geographic systems, and content of social media as well as traditional media (cf. Shah et al., 2015). In such big data studies, computer programs are used for examining social and behavioural relationships and interactions through simulation, modelling, network analysis and media analysis.

For example, Kogut et al. (2014) used simulation and network analysis in a computational social science study of quotas for women directors on corporate boards in the USA. Actual data from the implementation of such quotas in Norway were used as a basis for simulating the minimal quota in the USA for obtaining structural gender equality on American corporate boards.

In a study of the roots and spreading of fake news, Jang et al. (2018) used evolution tree analysis, which is a recent development in computational social science focusing on networks. In the context of the 2016 US presidential election, more than 300,000 tweets about 30 fake and 30 real news stories were examined in terms of the root content, original source, and evolution pattern.

In a computational criminology study of cyberhate in social media, Williams and Burnap (2016) focused on the Twitter network, analysing approximately half a million tweets during the two weeks following a terrorist attack in London in 2013.

Based on these tweets, the escalation, duration, diffusion and de-escalation of cyberhate after the terrorist event were examined.

Big data and computational social science: Typical questions

Big data and computational social science provide a basis for asking and answering new social questions, and for developing new answers to old social science questions (Lazer and Radford, 2017). The most typical of these questions will be discussed here. An overview of these questions is presented in Table 24.1. For each of the questions, the table summarizes the limitations of traditional

Table 24.1 Overview of typical questions for big data research and computational social science

Questions related to	Limitations of traditional research	Strengths of big data research and computational social science
Actual behaviour	Only self-reports, reports or traces of behaviour, or actual behaviour observed in only small contexts	Ongoing behaviour in large populations recorded as it occurs
Dynamic processes	Only time series data, with intervals between time points, or continuous processes observed in only small contexts	Continuous development of processes recorded in real time, for large populations and at different levels of society
Social systems	Either static features of networks with low complexity, or dynamic features of more complex but small networks	Ongoing processes of contact and interaction recorded for large and complex networks, and analysed empirically or through modelling and simulation
Field experiments and causal relationships	Difficult to separate experimental and control groups, to manipulate the causal factor, and to avoid control effects. Usually only small contexts and few participants	Especially social media useful for large-scale experiments, with manipulation of exposure in different experimental and control groups, and without control effects
Weak but meaningful relationships	Weak relationships are not statistically significant	In studies based on large samples or whole populations, even very weak relationships can be analysed with emphasis on substantial meaning, rather than statistical significance
Few or dispersed units	Too few units included in general samples and multivariate analysis, and limited accessibility for data collection	Sufficient numbers of all categories can be included in large samples or population studies, or extracted for special studies, with a variety of big data available for analysis

research and the strengths of research based on big data and computational social science.

Actual behaviour

Based on big data and computational science, questions about people's actual behaviour can be examined in more detail and in more reliable ways than before.

In traditional social research, based on ordinary data, neither respondents nor documents can be used as sources for examining what people actually do. Respondents are asked to report about what they or other people usually do, or what they or other people did at some time in the past. Documents are analysed as traces or reports of what people have done in the past. Only observation of actors can provide data on what people actually do at the time of the study. However, both participant observation and structured observation must be limited to relatively few actors, small contexts, and short time periods.

In contrast, big data and computational social science provide opportunities to collect and analyse data on present and concurrent activities and interactions in large populations. People's actual behaviour is registered or recorded as it occurs. These data show the behaviour itself, rather than self-reports, reports or traces of the behaviour.

For example, Jungherr et al. (2016) examined the content of tweets during the 2013 election campaign in Germany. Almost 1.4 million tweets from almost 100,000 persons were analysed, in order to identify people's images of political reality. Thus, the analysis was based on actual individual behaviour, in the form of writing a tweet and expressing an immediate and current view or image of political reality. This form of actual behaviour of individuals was the basis also for the Twitter studies mentioned above, on fake news (Jang et al., 2018) and on cyberhate (Williams and Burnap, 2016).

Dynamic processes

Questions on dynamic processes may also be examined in new ways, based on big data and computational social science.

In traditional social research, longitudinal studies are often based on various kinds of time series data, especially if long time periods are examined. Such studies are typically based on quantitative data and compare the same social phenomena at different time points within the whole time period. Since there will always be a shorter or longer time interval between these time points, the studies can provide information on stability and change over time, but not about the dynamic or continuous processes during the time period. In quantitative studies, the dynamics of such processes can be examined in indirect ways, based on recall questions to respondents or descriptions in documents. More direct studies of dynamic and continuous processes can be conducted in qualitative research, mainly in research based on participant observation. In such studies, actors and their activities and interactions can be observed more or less continuously over some time. However, as pointed out above, observation studies are limited to relatively short time periods, which means that they are not appropriate for examining longer-term processes. Furthermore, the limitation of participant observation studies to few actors and small contexts, which was emphasized above, in connection with actual behaviour, is also relevant for questions about dynamic process.

Big data and computational social science provide possibilities to overcome these limitations of studies of processes in traditional social research. Not only actual behaviour and events are registered and stored. Changes in the behaviour and events are also recorded as they occur. Thus, in addition to current events, activities and interactions, previous events, activities and interactions are recorded and available for analysis. Thus, big data contain information about the continuous development of various types of processes in real time, in large populations and at different levels of society. The utilization of big data for monitoring processes has been called *nowcasting* (Lazer and Radford, 2017: 24). Computers, computer programs and computational social science make it possible to collect or retrieve this information, as well as to process and analyse it.

For example, in a study of the Arab Spring, Levin et al. (2018) used big data to quantify conflict intensity. The Arab Spring was a protest movement that started in Tunisia in 2010 and spread to several other Arab countries. In this study, different Arab countries in the Middle East were compared as to conflict intensity several years before, during and after the Arab Spring. Conflict intensity was analysed by means of remote sensing data showing the amount of night lights, social media data (Flickr photos), and data on conflict-related events mentioned in different types of media.

In their Twitter study of the German election campaign, Jungherr et al. (2016) organized the tweets along the time dimension and examined the development of topics in the tweets as a process. The dominant topics in the tweets at different time points were analysed and discussed in relation to key political events in the ongoing election campaign.

Furthermore, the dynamic process perspective is very important in the evolution tree analysis of the roots and spreading patterns of fake news (Jang et al., 2018), as well as in the study of the escalation, duration, diffusion and de-escalation of cyberhate in social media (William and Burnap, 2016).

Social systems

Big data and computational social science provide new opportunities for examining questions about social systems.

A social system may be defined as a network of relations between individuals, groups, organizations or institutions, which constitutes a coherent whole. As pointed out in Chapter 23, various types of data about relations may be used to examine network patterns. Traditional network studies may be based on many different types of data on relations. For example, data on relations between individuals may be based on questions to respondents about their contacts, friends or colleagues. Documentary sources may contain information about relations between organizations or institutions, such as collaboration, negotiations or alliances. Observation of actors may provide data on various types of relations between individuals or groups.

Traditional network studies based on participant observation or other qualitative approaches are usually focused on a limited number of actors within small contexts but may examine several types of relations between the actors, including both formal and informal ties, as well as various forms of interaction. On the other hand, traditional quantitative studies of networks typically comprise a relatively large number of actors, but they are limited to relatively few types of relations between these actors. Furthermore, quantitative data are less appropriate than qualitative data for examining dynamic interaction processes in social networks. The network patterns that are identified in such studies may be rather static and more relevant for detecting stable structures than for revealing dynamic systems. Thus, if traditional network studies are used for analysing social systems, qualitative studies are limited in terms of size of the systems that can be analysed, whereas quantitative studies are limited in the complexity and the dynamics of the systems that can be examined.

These limitations can be overcome in studies of social systems based on big data and computational social science. Social media, e-mails, mobile phone calls and several other kinds of big data provide information about different types of relations, contacts and interactions in large populations of individuals, organizations or institutions. Contacts are recorded as they occur, in real time, and interaction processes are registered as they develop. Thus, very large and complex networks can be examined, and the dynamic, ongoing processes of contact and interaction within these networks can be analysed in detail. Thus, the usefulness of big data for examining both actual behaviour and dynamic processes makes such data useful also for studying social systems.

In computational social science, big data can be used as a basis for modelling or simulating interactions within social systems as well as responses of a social system as a whole to various events and changes in the system's environment. For example, in the study of quotas for women directors on corporate boards, which was mentioned above, Kogut et al. (2014) used simulation to examine how different quotas would affect the intercorporate system, especially in terms of gender equality in network centrality and influence. The simulation showed that even low numerical quotas could create conditions for well-connected networks of women directors with increased structural equality.

Field experiments and causal relationships

Big data provide new opportunities for answering questions about causal relationships, based on large-scale field experiments.

In traditional social research, it may be difficult or challenging to conduct field experiments under natural conditions, and such studies may have several limitations. It may be difficult to separate experimental groups from control groups, to manipulate or control the causal factor, and to avoid control effects. Furthermore, in traditional

field experiments, the data collection may be very resource-intensive, which creates limitations as to the size of the contexts and the number of actors that can be involved in the experiments.

Such difficulties and limitations are reduced in field experiments based on big data. Especially social media are adequate for big data field experiments. Social media are used naturally by large numbers of people, who can be involved in large-scale experiments. To some extent, it is possible to manipulate such media as to what different groups of media users are exposed to. Thus, it is possible to control the causal factor and to separate experimental groups from control groups. What is written by users of the media, before and after their exposure to the manipulated content, is accessible and can be analysed by researchers. Typically, the media users are not aware of the researchers' manipulation of the media content or their analysis of the messages, which means that traditional control effects in field experiments are avoided.

For example, Kramer et al. (2014) present an experimental study of emotional contagion on Facebook. A total of 689,003 Facebook users reading messages in English during one week in January 2012 were selected for the study. These users were randomly divided into two experimental groups and two control groups. Facebook's news feed was manipulated for the users. In one of the experimental groups, the exposure to positive emotional content in messages from their friends was reduced. In the other experimental group, the exposure to negative emotional content in their friends' messages was reduced. Each experimental group was compared to one of the control groups. The focus of the comparison was the positive and negative emotions expressed in the users' own messages after the exposure to the manipulated messages in the experimental groups. The study showed that the experimental group with reduced exposure to positive emotional content produced fewer positive messages, whereas the experimental group with reduced exposure to negative emotional content produced fewer negative messages. Thus, the field experiment indicated a causal relationship between the emotional content of messages that are read by the media users, and the emotional content of the messages that are written by the users. This is described as an 'emotional contagion through social networks' (Kramer et al., 2014: 8788).

Weak but meaningful relationships

Although the effects of the causal factor in the experiment mentioned above were as expected and theoretically meaningful, these effects were rather small (Kramer et al., 2014). However, due to the large number of units involved in the study, the effects were statistically significant. This illustrates another advantage of using big data. Such data make it possible to examine questions about relationships that are weak but meaningful.

In traditional social research, based on quantitative data and probability samples, it is difficult to examine weak relationships, since such relationships may not be statistically significant. The smaller the sample is, the stronger a relationship has to be in order to be statistically significant. In studies based on small samples, relationships may be theoretically meaningful without being statistically significant. However, the lack of statistical significance means that the relationship may be due to random errors, and it does not make sense to analyse or interpret such relationships as if they were real.

In studies based on larger samples, weaker relationships may be statistically significant, and in population studies the issue of random errors due to sampling is not relevant. If the whole population of units is examined, it is not necessary or relevant to test the statistical significance of relationships. Any empirical relationship identified in a population study can be regarded as real.

In big data studies, very large samples and whole populations can be examined. In such studies, even very weak empirical relationships can be analysed and interpreted as real relationships in society. Weak relationships can be analysed in more detail, with less emphasis on statistical significance and more focus on substantial meaning and theoretical implications of the relationships.

Few or dispersed units

Not only weak relationships between variables, but also categories of few or dispersed units can be examined more effectively in big data studies than in traditional social research.

In most societies, there are minorities of people that are so small that they will not be sufficiently represented in traditional studies based on probability samples. Such minorities could be groups of indigenous peoples or immigrants from particular parts of the world. Also other categories or groups of people consist of so few individuals that they will be almost invisible in traditional probability samples. Examples of such categories are very rich people, and various social elites. Although each of these categories with few units could be examined in special studies focusing only on the category itself, such categories cannot be adequately analysed as parts of general samples of the whole population. This problem could be reduced by constructing weighted samples where minorities or small groups are over-represented. However, in addition to being few in number, members of minority groups are often geographically dispersed. Thus, in traditional social research, especially in surveys based on personal interviews, it may be difficult or very resource-intensive to conduct the collection of data from all units in such samples. Sometimes, minorities or elites are also less accessible than other groups, because they are more reluctant to participate in research.

The problem of having too few units from various categories or groups included in traditional studies is not only related to the sampling of units and the collection of data. This problem may be strengthened in the analysis of the data. Especially in multivariate analyses including many variables and many values on each variable, the number of units may be too small for certain combinations of values on the different variables. If several value combinations are affected by this problem of small numbers of units, it is difficult to carry out the analysis in a meaningful way. The problem can be reduced by reducing the number of variables included in the analysis, or by merging values on each variable in the analysis. However, this will also reduce the nuances and detail in the analysis.

Using big data and computational social science, we can include sufficient numbers of small categories of units in social research. Such studies can be based on whole populations, including all units in different categories, or very large samples, with sufficient numbers of units in all relevant categories. More and more types of big data on all the selected units can be gathered from private or public registers, social media or other sources, regarding a wide variety of actual behaviour or ongoing interactions. Thus, the collection of data can be conducted without the traditional problems related to dispersion and limited accessibility of units in some small categories of people. Furthermore, due to the large number of units as well as the powerful computers and the advanced software, very complex multivariate analysis can be carried out, including very small categories of units and combinations of very specific values on many different variables. Thus, it is possible to identify patterns within very small or dispersed categories of units,

and to relate or compare these patterns to more general patterns within larger groups or the whole population.

In addition to examining small groups or categories as parts of larger general samples or whole populations, big data can also be used for more focused studies of one or more selected categories of units, for example units with a special and unusual type of health problem. The units with the selected characteristics can be identified within the whole population of units, and data on these particular units can be extracted from the relevant set of big data. Thus, further analysis can focus on these extracted data on the selected category of units. The analysis can include all units with the relevant characteristics or a large enough sample of units within this category. This procedure has been described as a way of making big data small (Welles, 2014; Lazer and Radford, 2017).

New challenges

In addition to providing new opportunities, big data and computational social science also create a number of new challenges in social research. Some of these challenges have been described in previous chapters of this book. Two of the most important challenges will be emphasized and summarized here.

One challenge is to develop a contextual understanding of the big data that are used in social research. This may be difficult, since a lot of big data are recorded, stored and used with very limited reference to the temporal or spatial context in which they were collected. This is a typical limitation of quantitative data sets in general, and it is usually more difficult to develop a contextual understanding the larger the data sets are. Thus, the contextual interpretations of empirical findings are particularly challenging in big data research. To some extent, such problems may be reduced in the data analysis, for example by using variables related to time and place as independent variables, and by discussing temporal and spatial differences in relation to historical and geographical contexts. Furthermore, some kinds of big data provide more opportunities for contextual understanding than others. For example, data based on social media may be more context-specific than data based on national registers. Thus, the possibilities for contextual understanding may be increased by combining different types of big data in the same study. Nevertheless, in big data studies it is always important to be aware of possible contextual limitations and to discuss potential implications of such limitations for the interpretation of the empirical findings.

Another important challenge related to the use of big data in social research is to make sure that the research is based on the relevant ethical norms and standards. As pointed out in Chapter 3, regarding some types of big data, for example registers for surveillance, the establishment of the data may in itself be ethically problematic. The individuals do not know that these data exist or how they are used.

For researchers using such data in particular and big data in general, the main ethical challenge is to ensure that the rights of participants or sources in the research are protected. In big data studies, it is especially important to consider very carefully how the ethical norm of informed consent should be handled.

For some big data sources this is not necessarily a problem. For example, big data based on social media usually consist of messages that are published by individuals themselves. They know that the social media are open and public, and that their messages can be read by everyone. In this sense, social media messages are similar to newspaper articles. They can be read and analysed by researchers. Informed consent from each author is usually not needed, although there are still several other ethical norms that have to be considered in such studies.

In many other big data sources, such as private or public registers, data about individuals are included without any information to these individuals and without any consent from them. Even if the individuals have given their informed consent to be included in the data set, this consent does not refer to specific studies based on these data. Sometimes, the individuals' consent to be included in a big data set is based on general information about the possibility that these data may be used for various types of research. However, it is important to consider whether this type of general informed consent is sufficient as an ethical foundation for a particular study based on the big data set.

In traditional social research, informed consent from individuals included as participants in a study is usually obtained after contact and dialogue with each individual participant. Typically, in big data studies, it is very difficult to use this procedure. Such studies involve so many individuals that it would be extremely resource-intensive to locate and get in contact with each and all of them. Often, this would not even be possible, since the individuals in registers or other big data sources may have been anonymized.

However, as pointed out in Chapter 3, when big register data on individuals are used in research, it is advisable to consider if some kind of informed consent is necessary and possible. It is important to be aware of any guidelines, rules or conditions that regulate the use of the specific registers for social research. It may also be necessary to contact relevant ethics committees or agencies for advice, ethical clearance or permission to use data from these registers.

- Big data are characterized by the three Vs:
  - Volume
  - Variety
  - Velocity.
- Based on how the data are produced, we can distinguish between three categories of big data sources:
  - Volunteered information
  - Automated information
  - Directed information.
- Based on the type of information provided by the data, we can distinguish between three categories of big data sources:
  - Digital life
  - Digital traces
  - Digitalized life.
- Computational social science is a subfield of social research based on big data, which is focused on using computers and big data for analysing social networks, social geographic systems, and content of social media and traditional media.
- Big data provide a basis for asking new questions and for answering old questions in new ways. The most typical of these questions refer to:
  - Actual behaviour
  - Dynamic processes
  - Social systems
  - Field experiments and causal relations
  - Weak but meaningful relationships
  - Few or dispersed units.
- Big data create a number of new challenges in social research, mainly related to
  - the possibilities of developing a contextual understanding of the empirical findings
  - the possibilities of protecting the rights of participants and sources in the research.

RESEARCH EXAMPLES

I recommend that you read the publications used as research examples in this chapter.

Jungherr, Andreas, Harald Schoen, and Pascal Jürgens (2016) 'The mediation of politics through Twitter: An analysis of messages posted during the campaign for the German federal election 2013', *Journal of Computer-Mediated Communication* 21(1), 50–68.

This article presents a study of tweets during the 2013 election campaign in Germany. Almost 1.4 million tweets from almost 100,000 persons were analysed, in order to identify people's images of political reality. Thus, the analysis was based on actual individual behaviour, in the form of writing a tweet and expressing an immediate and current view or image of political reality.

Kramer, Adam D. I., Jamie E. Guillory, and Jeffrey T. Hancock (2014) 'Experimental evidence of massive-scale emotional contagion through social networks', *Proceedings of the National Academy of Sciences of the USA* 111(24), 8788–8790.

This article presents an experimental study of emotional contagion on Facebook. Nearly 690,000 Facebook users reading messages in English during one week in January 2012 were selected for the study. These users were randomly divided into two experimental groups and two control groups. Facebook's news feed was used to manipulate the emotional content of the messages read by the users. The field experiment indicated a causal relationship between the emotional content of messages that are read by the media users, and the emotional content of the messages that are written by the users. This is described as an 'emotional contagion through social networks' (Kramer et al., 2014: 8788).

Levin, Noam, Ali Saleem, and David Crandall (2018) 'Utilizing remote sensing and big data to quantify conflict intensity: The Arab Spring as a case study', *Applied Geography* 94, 1–17.

In the study presented in this article big data were used to quantify conflict intensity in the Arab Spring, which was a protest movement that started in Tunisia in 2010 and spread to several other Arab countries. In the study, different Arab countries in the Middle East were compared as to conflict intensity during several years before and after the Arab Spring. Conflict intensity was analysed by means of remote sensing data showing the amount of night lights, social media data (Flickr photos), and data on conflict related events mentioned in different types of media.

Whereas all studies used as examples in this chapter are based on big data, the following three articles also exemplify the use of computational social science:

Jang, S. Mo, Tieming Geng, Jo-Yun Queenie Li, Ruofan Xia, Chin-Ter Huang, Hwalbin Kim, and Jijun Tang (2018) 'A computational approach for examining the roots and spreading patterns of fake news: Evolution tree analysis', *Computers in Human Behavior* 84, 103–113.

This article presents a study of the roots and spreading of fake news. The study was based on evolution tree analysis, which is a recent development in computational social science focusing on networks. In the context of the 2016 US presidential election, more than 300,000 tweets about 30 fake and 30 real news stories were examined in terms of the root content, original source, and evolution pattern. Thus, the analysis was based on actual individual behaviour, in the form of writing a tweet and expressing an immediate and current view or image of political reality.

Kogut, Bruce, Jordi Colomer, and Mariano Belinky (2014) 'Structural equality at the top of the corporation: Mandated quotas for women directors', *Strategic Management Journal* 35(6), 891–902.

This article presents a computational social science study of quotas for women directors on corporate boards in the USA, using simulation and network analysis. Actual data from the implementation of such quotas in Norway were used as a basis for simulating the minimal quota in the USA for obtaining structural gender equality on American corporate boards.

Williams, Matthew L., and Pete Burnap (2016) 'Cyberhate on social media in the aftermath of Woolwich: A case study in computational criminology and big data', *British Journal of Criminology* 56(2), 211–238.

This article presents a computational criminology study of cyberhate in social media. The study focused on the Twitter network, analysing approximately half a million tweets during the two weeks following a terrorist attack in London in 2013. Based on these tweets, the escalation, duration, diffusion and de-escalation of cyberhate after the terrorist event were examined.

STUDENT EXERCISES AND QUESTIONS

1 What are the characteristic features of big data?
2 Describe different types of big data.
3 How is computational social science defined?

4 Why do big data provide possibilities for asking new questions in social science?
5 Why are big data useful for examining

a weak relationships between variables?

b small categories of units?

6 What are the main challenges related to the use of big data in social science?

7 Formulate a research question on the development of an election campaign before a national election, and discuss how various types of big data could be used for examining the research question.

RECOMMENDED LITERATURE

Cioffi-Revilla, Claudio (2017) *Introduction to Computational Social Science* (2nd edn). London: Springer.

This is a comprehensive introduction to computational social science. It introduces the key concepts and definitions in the field, and it contains a list of acronyms as well as a glossary. The book covers the methodological approaches of automated social information extraction, social network analysis, social complexity theory, and social simulation modelling. Numerous review questions, exercises and problems with solutions are included in the book.

Kitchin, Rob (2014) *The Data Revolution: Big Data, Open Data, Data Infrastructures and Their Consequences.* London: Sage.

This book provides an overview and a critical analysis of the new landscape of big data, open data and data infrastructures. It introduces ways of thinking conceptually about this new data landscape, and it emphasizes critical discussions of the technical shortcomings and the social, political and ethical consequences of the data revolution. Issues on surveillance, privacy, security, profiling, social sorting, and intellectual property rights are covered in the book.

Welker, Martin, Cathleen M Stützer; and Marc Egger (2018): *Computational Social Science in the Age of Big Data: Concepts, Methodologies, Tools, and Applications.* Cologne: Herbert von Halem Verlag.

This book is focused on the establishment of computational social science as an emerging field of research and application. Emphasizing a multidisciplinary presentation, the book describes concepts, methodologies, tools, and applications within this field. Different topics that are relevant for research and practice in the field are covered.

PART VI

WRITING AND PRESENTING RESEARCH

The online resources are here to help with writing and presenting research!

Visit https://study.sagepub.com/gronmo to access real-world practice datasets, videos, case studies, key term definitions, and critical thinking exercises that will help you learn more about writing, visualizing, and presenting research.

WORKING WITH DATA VISUALIZATION

This chapter provides the necessary knowledge for understanding how different types of data visualizations may be used in theses or other research reports, as well as in presentations of research results.

The chapter will teach you how to

- use visualizations as accurate representations of data
- use visualizations for effective presentations of selected data
- choose appropriate visualizations for different types of data

- use visualizations based on big data
- avoid visualizations that are deceptive or misleading.

What is data visualization?

Visualizations have been used frequently in this book. Several of these are visualizations of data or findings. In Part IV of the book (Chapters 16–20), on data analysis, it was shown how various types of visualizations, or figures, may be used to document and illustrate findings in analyses of qualitative and quantitative data. The most common forms of data visualizations are various types of charts, such as the bar, pie and line charts, which were described in Chapter 17. In addition to these 'classic three', there are many other types of visualizations that can be used for presenting data and findings.

This chapter presents a more systematic and more thorough discussion of different types of visualizations, showing how to work with data visualization for different purposes, and how to choose the most appropriate visualizations for different types of data. Furthermore, the impact of big data and new technology on data visualization is discussed, and the importance of avoiding deceptive or misleading visualization is emphasized.

First, however, it should be clarified, more precisely, what data visualization means. Visualizing data refers to the illustration of selected data or empirical findings by using images, or figures, in order to create accurate, clear and effective presentations or overviews for an audience of readers or viewers. The idea is that an image may work better as a presentation of the data than a textual description does. An image or figure may also be a more effective presentation than a table with numbers. Although tables might be regarded as a form of visualization (Sue and Griffin, 2016: xii), tables are not included in the discussion of data visualization in this chapter.

There are many different types of visualizations that can be used for presenting data. The choice of one particular type of visualization depends on the type of data we want to present, and the type of audience we want to address. We should choose the type of visualization that is most accurate and appropriate for the specific data to be presented, and that is most effective for the particular audience of the presentation.

As pointed out by Kirk (2016: 19), data visualization is a 'representation and presentation of data to facilitate understanding'. This is illustrated in Figure 25.1. Visualization is a way of presenting data to an audience. The first step in the process of working with the visualization is to find the type of visualization that is the best representation of the data. This activity is called *encoding*, since the visualization may be regarded as a code for the data. Accuracy is the main criterion for finding the best, or most appropriate, visualization for the specific data. The visualization should represent the data as accurately as possible.

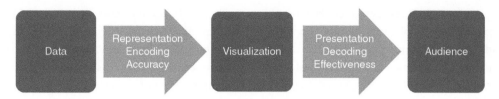

Figure 25.1 Data visualization: presenting data to an audience

The second step in working with data visualization is to present the visualization to the audience. Seeing the visualization, the audience will understand the data. This is called *decoding*: the readers or viewers decode the visualization. Effectiveness is the most important criterion for doing a good presentation. The visualization should facilitate the understanding of the data (Kirk, 2016: 21–28).

This means that effectiveness, in addition to accuracy, should be taken into consideration in the choice of visualization. Among the different types of visualizations that would represent the data accurately, we should choose the visualization that is expected to be most effective for the audience.

Purposes of data visualization

Data visualizations are important in different types of research reports as well as in presentations of research for various types of audiences (Sue and Griffin, 2016). In a thesis or an article, visualizations of data are included as documentation or illustration of empirical findings and results of the research. Different kinds of visualizations may be used, depending on the type of report, and the background of the expected readers.

Data visualizations may be even more important in presentations of research than they are in research reports. In presentations, there are more possibilities for using data visualizations, but this may also be more challenging. In research reports, we may use only static visualizations, such as

pictures, diagrams, charts or other figures, whereas presentations may include interactive, online and live visualizations, such as videos and films, in addition to static visualizations. The choice of visualizations is adapted to the type of presentation, and the background of the expected audience. Working with data visualizations for presentations involves the creation as well as the delivery of the presentation.

In reports as well as presentations, data visualizations are used for several purposes. The most important purpose is to make it as easy as possible for readers or viewers to understand the information that is visualized. As pointed out by Sue and Griffin (2016: xii), a visualization makes it possible to present complex information quickly and effectively. The visualization may simplify and summarize the information, and it may focus on key aspects of a complex pattern. By means of data visualization, empirical findings become more accessible for readers and viewers (Kirk, 2016: 32–37). It becomes easier to see what the analysis shows, and to understand what this means.

Another purpose of data visualization is to emphasize a main result or a key finding in the data analysis. The visualization is used to make a point (Evergreen, 2017: 1). By visualizing particular data, or by visualizing data in a particular way, it is possible to focus on a special message, which can be clarified and made visible.

Furthermore, visualizations may be used to add legitimacy and credibility to the presentation of data and empirical findings (Evergreen, 2017: 4–5). Diagrams, charts or graphs may be more convincing than textual or numerical presentations of data. Since visualizations are based on accurate and reliable representation of the data, visual presentations may be perceived as trustworthy (Kirk, 2016: 32–37).

Visualizations are also used to present data in a more elegant way than textual or numerical presentations do. By designing elegant visualizations, it is possible to stimulate the interest among potential readers or viewers. A wider audience may be interested in the information presented, and the motivation for reading a report or following a presentation may be increased when it includes data visualizations. Elegant visualizations make the data presentations attractive for readers and viewers (Kirk, 2016: 42–46). Elegant visual presentations may be enjoyable and entertaining.

In addition to making presentations accessible, clear, trustworthy, and attractive for the readers, data visualizations are also useful for researchers. Working with visualizations may reveal and clarify empirical patterns and relationships, which might be difficult to discover with only textual or numerical presentations of the data. Similarly, special deviations from general patterns may be easier to identify and interpret by visualizing the data (Sue and Griffin, 2016: xii). In general, visualizations may be used to simplify complex data, to create overviews of large amounts of data, or to focus on particular aspects of the data. Thus, data visualizations are developed and applied for the purpose of data analysis, in addition to data presentation. As will be pointed out later in the chapter, using visualization in the data analysis is particularly useful in big data research.

Types of visualizations

A typical form of data visualization is a chart, which is a combination of two elements. These are called *marks* and *attributes* (Kirk, 2016: 151–157). Typical marks are *points*, *lines* and *areas*, as shown in Figure 25.2. The marks are symbols of units or categories that are represented in the charts. For example, different age groups in a society may be represented by one line each in a bar chart, or each person in a network may be represented by a point.

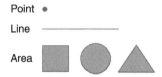

Figure 25.2 Marks used in charts

Attributes in a chart represent variations or differences in the data about the units or categories. Kirk (2016: 153–154) distinguishes between *quantitative, categorical* and *relational* attributes. Quantitative attributes include, for example

- *position* on a scale, shown by points that are placed along the scale;
- *size*, indicated by different lengths of lines or different sizes of circles;
- *angle*, indicated by smaller or larger sectors of a circle; and
- *quantity*, shown by number of points or triangles.

Categorical, or qualitative, attributes symbolize

- *distinctions* between categories of units, for example a triangle for men and a circle for women.

Relational attributes show

- *connections* or relations between units, such as ties between personal friends, indicated by a line for the tie and points for the persons.

In addition to these examples, there are a number of other types of quantitative, qualitative and relational attributes that may be used in charts.

Thus, there are very many ways of combining marks and attributes to design charts. The aim is to find the combination of marks and attributes that is the most accurate representation of the specific data and the most effective presentation for the particular audience. Working with data visualizations means combining analytical skills and creativeness.

Although there is a large number of charts and other visualizations that may be used for reports and presentation, it is important to keep in mind that most of these visualizations can be used for only certain types of data. As pointed out above, accurate representation of the specific data is the most important criterion for selecting the best visualization. Thus, the process of choosing a particular visualization should start by clarifying what type of data are to be represented by the visualization, and then consider those visualizations that are possible and appropriate for this data type.

Categorical charts

Systematic discussions of the most appropriate visualizations for different types of data are presented by Evergreen (2017) and Kirk (2016). Kirk (2016: 161–209) presents an overview of 49 different charts. These are classified into five main types, based on their usability for different types of data

and findings. One of the five chart types is *categorical* charts, which compare categories of units as to selected attributes. An example of this is the *clustered bar chart*; an example is shown in Figure 25.3, which is based on constructed data. The colours of the lines, or bars, represent different levels of education (low, medium and high), and the lengths of the lines indicate the level of income. The scale along the horizontal axis shows income in 10,000 euros, so that, for example the value 4 represents the income of 40,000 euros. Thus, Figure 25.3 shows how income increases with increasing education, in four different years, from 2000 to 2015. Furthermore, the figure shows how the income at all levels of education increases over time, within this period.

In this chart, the lines are horizontal, but they may also be designed as vertical columns. The bar chart is *clustered*, because it shows separate lines for the different educational categories within each year. If we had only one line for each year, for example income regardless of education, the chart would still be a *bar chart*, but not a clustered bar chart.

In Figure 25.3 the income for each year is indicated by the length of the lines or bars. If we wanted to show the income for a time period, for example 2005–2010, rather than separate years,

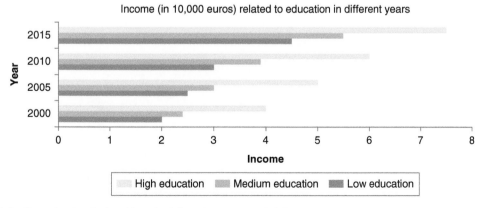

Figure 25.3 Example of a clustered bar chart, based on constructed data

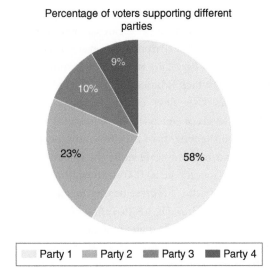

Percentage of voters supporting different parties

Figure 25.4 Example of a pie chart, based on constructed data

Hierarchical charts

Another type of charts is *hierarchical* charts. They show how a whole set of units are divided into parts, or how different parts are related to each other in hierarchies. The *pie chart*, as presented in Figure 25.4, is an example of a part-to-whole chart, illustrating the division of all units into different parts. In this example, which is based on constructed data, the whole circle, or pie, represents the total number of votes in a general election, the colours show different political parties, and the sizes of the different sectors indicate each party's share of all votes. Pie charts have been criticized, based on arguments that it may be difficult to compare the sectors of a given pie chart, and especially that it may be difficult to compare sectors across different pie charts. This should be taken into consideration when pie charts are used.

Figure 25.5 presents a *stacked bar chart*. This is another hierarchical, part-to-whole chart, which may be used as an alternative to the pie chart. The chart, which is based on constructed data, shows how the voters in each of four regions are distributed on four political parties. Each line, or bar, represents all voters in one region. The coloured parts of the lines represent different parties, and the length of a coloured part of a line

the breadth of each bar could show the length of each period, and then the income would be indicated by the area of the bar, rather than its length. This categorical chart is called a *histogram* (Kirk, 2016: 173). In a study of the effect of election promises on electoral behaviour, Born et al. (2018) used a histogram to visualize the distribution of kept and broken election promises.

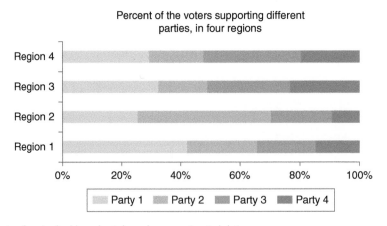

Percent of the voters supporting different parties, in four regions

Figure 25.5 Example of a stacked bar chart, based on constructed data

indicates a party's share of all votes in the region. Thus, the figure visualizes the relative strength of the parties within each region, as well as the strength of each party in different regions.

In an article on publication patterns in developmental psychology, Doberman and Hamilton (2017) present a stacked bar chart to visualize the distribution of different types of cross-country collaboration on publication in different years.

Relational charts

A third type of charts is *relational* charts. These are used to present connections between units or correlations between variables. Figure 25.6 shows a *sociogram*, which is an example of a network of connections between friends. For example, each point could represent a person, and the lines between points could indicate friendship between the two persons.

Figure 25.6 Example of a sociogram

In their article on publication patterns in developmental psychology, Doberman and Hamilton (2017) use sociograms to visualize social networks among authors. Separate networks are used to distinguish between male and female authors, authors from different countries, and authors of articles in different journals. Sociograms are also presented to identify the most influential authors in the networks.

Whereas the sociogram illustrates connections between units, the *scattergram* or *scatter plot* is an example of a chart for visualizing relationships between variables. In Figure 25.7, which is based on constructed data, the values of one variable (education) are plotted along the horizontal axis, and the values of the other variable (income) are plotted along the vertical axis. The points represent units (individuals), which are placed in the chart according to their exact values on the two variables. The scattergram is a common data visualization in correlation and regression analyses (Jacoby, 1998). This was shown in Chapter 18 (cf. Figures 18.4 and 18.5).

If we drew a line between the points in the scattergram in Figure 25.7, the relationship between education and income would be visualized as a line chart. In their article on the effect of election promises, Born et al. (2018) present line charts as visualizations of both predicted and empirical relationships between promises and voting.

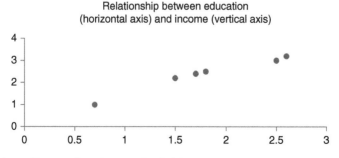

Figure 25.7 Example of a scattergram, based on constructed data

Temporal charts

A fourth type of charts is *temporal* charts, which show trends and changes over time. The most common example of this chart type is the *line chart*. This is illustrated in Figure 25.8, which is based on constructed data. When the line chart is used to present trends or time series, different time points, for example years, are placed along the horizontal axis. In this figure, the years 2000, 2005, 2010 and 2015 are included. In the example, the coloured lines indicate the number of PhD graduates at different universities. Thus, the lines show the changes in the number of graduates at each university over time, as well as the differences in number of graduates between the universities in each year.

In their article on publication patterns in developmental psychology, Doberman and Hamilton (2017) present a line chart to visualize trends of collaboration among authors between 2005 and 2014.

If the area between the horizontal axis and each of the lines in the line chart (for example in Figure 25.8), were filled with colour, the trends would be visualized as an *area chart* (Kirk, 2016: 195). In a study of the relations between new suburban areas and other parts of the Prague metropolitan area in 2004, Novák and Sýkora (2007) used area charts to visualize activity distribution and spatial mobility for different groups during a weekday.

Spatial charts

The fifth type of charts is *spatial* charts, which illustrate spatial patterns by means of maps. The maps are used to relate patterns of different types of data to geographical areas. One example of a spatial chart is the area *cartogram*. Compared to the geographical map, the cartogram may look different or distorted. Figure 25.9 presents a cartogram showing the population of different countries in the world. This cartogram looks different from a traditional geographical map, since the size of each country depends on the number of inhabitants instead of the area.

Another example of a spatial chart is the *choropleth map*, as shown in Figure 25.10. In this chart, the form of the geographical map is kept, and data on average household expenditures on housing, water electricity, gas and other fuels in different European countries are indicated by special colours of the countries. As shown in the figure, each colour indicates a certain range of expenditures.

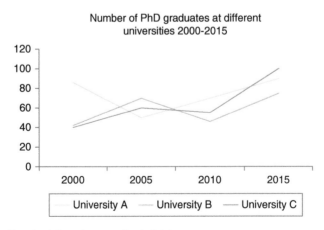

Figure 25.8 Example of a line chart, based on constructed data

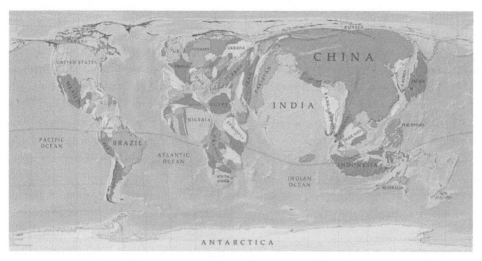

Figure 25.9 Cartogram showing the human population of the countries of the world. Created by Mark Newman and reproduced here from his web page (http://www-personal.umich.edu/~mejn/cartograms/)

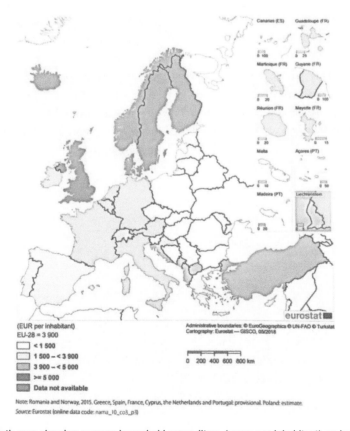

Figure 25.10 Choropleth map showing average household expenditure (euros per inhabitant) on housing, water electricity, gas and other fuels in European countries in 2016. Reproduced from Eurostat, 2018: 76)

Instead of using different colours for the areas on the map, we could use symbols, such as dots or circles on each area to show the characteristics of the areas. For example, the average expenditure in a country could be indicated by a certain number of dots or a circle with a certain size. Such charts are called *proportional symbol maps* (Kirk, 2016: 203). In their article on the relations between new suburban areas and other parts of the Prague metropolitan area, Novák and Sýkora (2007) used symbol maps as visualizations of people's locations in the city at different times of the day.

Other types of visualizations

All the charts shown above, except the sociogram, are designed to visualize quantitative data. There are fewer charts available for visualizing qualitative data (Evergreen, 2017: 175). One visualization that has been used in qualitative analyses of texts is the *word cloud*. An example of a word cloud is presented in Figure 25.11. This pattern is based on an article in the American business magazine *Forbes* (Friedman, 2016). This article discusses why a majority of the British people voted for the UK to leave the European Union (Brexit) in 2016.

The word cloud reflects the frequencies of different words in the article. The more frequently a word is used in the text, the larger is the image of the word in the visualization. Although the frequency of the words is a quantitative feature of the text, it is the pattern of the cloud that is used for interpretations in a qualitative analysis. Furthermore, word clouds may be combined with categorizations of words into more general topics, as well as identification of phrases in which the words are used.

In addition to the few examples presented here, there are a large number of other possible charts within each of the five chart types. Furthermore, visualizations of data or empirical findings may also include other forms of illustrations or documentation than these types of charts. Data visualizations in theses, articles or other research reports normally have to be charts or other still pictures. Sometimes, paintings, drawings or photographs may be used as illustrations of key features or typical situations uncovered by empirical studies. For example, in qualitative studies based on participant observation, photographs of events, meetings, encounters or interaction during the fieldwork may be included in the final report as visualizations of important findings in the study.

Figure 25.11 Word cloud (created in WordArt.com) of a magazine article on Brexit (Friedman, 2016)

In conference presentations it is possible to use charts as well as all kinds of pictures. In addition, presentations may use interactive visualizations, links to online visualizations, and different types of live visualizations, such as animations, videos, and films. Links to online visualizations usually add flexibility to presentations and increase the possibility of showing the most updated versions of the visualizations. Typically, online visualizations also provide increased possibilities for interactive use of visualizations.

Interactivity means that a visualization may be changed during a presentation by altering the specified types of data included in the visualization. For example, in a chart it is possible to add or remove categories, to add or remove attributes, or to change between different types of charts. This may be planned before the presentation, or it may be decided during the presentation, for example because of questions from the audience.

Live visualizations include animations, such as animated cartograms, which may show, for example, how the population of the countries of the world has changed since 1950. Furthermore, presentations may use videos or films to visualize processes and interactions that were discovered during a fieldwork, or to illustrate typical or important information revealed during interviews. Especially in anthropology there is a rich tradition of using both films and pictures to visualize data and findings.

Big data, new technology, and data visualization

The increasing use of big data and the development of new information technology represent new challenges for data visualization. Some of these challenges will be pointed out here. Miller (2017) presents a more thorough discussion of big data visualization.

Big data includes data based on a number of different sources, such as *public registers* on people's education, income, taxes, travel activities, health, or other information, *business transactions* in shopping or banking, *recordings* from surveillance cameras or sensors, and *social media*, such as Facebook, Twitter, Instagram, and YouTube. Such data may be available as numbers, texts, pictures, or videos, and they may be qualitative or quantitative.

In general, big data are characterized by the three Vs: volume, variety and velocity. Big data are available in large amounts. Typically, the diversity and complexity of such data are high. Moreover, big data are frequently updated and changed.

On the one hand, this means that visualization of big data is even more important than visualization of traditional data. Due to their size, complexity and speed, big data are more difficult to read, interpret and understand. Visualization may be necessary, not only to present key findings to different audiences, but sometimes also to find or identify the most central patterns or trends. Visualization may be an important tool in the analysis as well as in the reports and presentations.

On the other hand, visualization of big data is more difficult than visualization of traditional data. Traditional data may be visualized by means of rather small computers and existing program packages, such as Microsoft Office, including Excel, and the Chart function in Word and PowerPoint (Sue and Griffin, 2016). Handling the volume, variety and velocity of big data is much more demanding. However, the recent development of new information technology has made it possible to store, process, analyse and visualize big data. The opportunities to utilize big data depend on the development of both hardware and software. New and more powerful computers, with larger memory capacity and faster processing capability, have facilitated the handling of big data in general. New program packages have made it possible to create big data visualizations in particular.

A number of new program packages have been developed for analysing and visualizing big data, such as SAS Visual Analytics, Tableau, Gephi, Visual.ly, TIBCO Spotfire, and Google Chart API.

Some of these software tools have been constructed mainly for marketing and business purposes, as parts of the more general management information system called Dashboard, and integrated into the strategy that is called Business Intelligence. However, most of the program packages are also useful for more general visualization purposes in social science.

Although new visualization programs and techniques are necessary for handling the volume, variety and velocity of big data, most of the chart types used in traditional data visualization may also be used in the visualization of big data. For example, the 'classic three', the bar, pie and line charts, are used for both traditional visualizations and big data visualizations.

Some types of visualizations seem to be particularly useful for big data. For example, it would be reasonable to use word clouds to detect and present patterns in large amounts of texts from social media, especially if this is combined with categorization of topics and identification of phrases in which key words are used. Furthermore, it would be interesting to identify trends or contextual variations, by comparing word clouds from different points in time and from different places.

The sociogram is another type of visualization that may be especially useful for organizing and presenting large amounts of data on connections among persons or organizations. A semantic network is a similar type of diagram, which presents connections among concepts, words or phrases instead of relations among actors or social units.

Word clouds and network diagrams are used in qualitative studies of big data. In quantitative studies it is quite common to use line charts to visualize big data, especially to show trends. Large amounts of data based on public registers or business transactions may be used for line charts of both long-term trends and short-term changes. Since many sources of big data are frequently updated, big data visualization may capture such frequent changes by means of interactive functions and online links to the data sources.

A similar chart, which is called *parallel coordinates* (Kirk, 2016: 185), is also common in visualization of big quantitative data. However, this chart does not show variations between different points in time, but between different variables. A line in the parallel coordinates chart may run from the variable age through the variables education, income, and family situation, to health. The chart may include several such lines, for example one for each region of a country. Thus, each line indicates the average values of the different variables within the region. Typically, the parallel coordinates chart is used for visualizations in multivariate analyses of big data based on public registers or business transactions.

As mentioned above, data visualization is not only used to present results of the data analysis. Visualization may also be used as a part of the data analysis, to discover and understand patterns or trends in the data. In Chapter 16, it was pointed out how figures and matrices may be useful in qualitative data analysis. In big data research, visualizations are useful in both qualitative and quantitative data analysis.

When visualizations are used to analyse big data, there are four issues that should be taken into consideration (cf. Tay et al., 2018):

- *Identification*. Due to the large volume of data, it is necessary to identify the most relevant units and the most interesting parts of the data for the visualization. This identification is based on the research questions and analytical perspectives in the particular study. The data may be reduced or aggregated, and different subsets of the data may be selected for simplified visualizations.

- *Integration*. Due to the variety of big data, it is useful and interesting to integrate different types of data in the visualizations. This can lead to more creative visualizations as well as new discoveries of empirical patterns and trends.

- *Immediacy*. The velocity of big data makes it possible to visualize the most recent and updated patterns as well as the changes and trends in real time. This is very useful for revealing and understanding dynamic processes as well as continuous streams of activities and interactions.

- *Interactivity*. Due to the variety as well as the velocity of big data, it is interesting and useful to develop interactive visualizations, which may be particularly useful in inductive analyses. Thus, it is possible to detect variations in patterns depending on interactive changes of the visualizations. Such changes may include filtering of data elements of the visualization, zooming in and out within the visualization, or focusing on selected details of the visualization.

Avoiding deceptive visualizations

Although the purpose of visualization is to make it easy for readers or viewers to understand the information that is visualized, some visualizations may be deceptive or misleading. A chart or a diagram may be designed in such a way that it does not give a correct image of the data or finding that it represents. This may be done on purpose, as a conscious and deliberate manipulation of the visualization,

in order to hide some information, or to give a biased or incorrect picture of the information. Deceptive or misleading visualizations may also be made unintentionally, due to mistakes or lack of competence. In any event, it is important to make sure that visualizations do not 'lie' about the data.

There are several ways of designing deceptive or misleading data visualizations. One well-known way is to manipulate the horizontal axis in a bar chart.

This is demonstrated by the difference between the bar charts in Figure 25.12 and Figure 25.13. The two figures are based on the same constructed data, but the presentations of the data are different. Figure 25.12 shows substantial differences between the three categories, whereas Figure 25.13 shows no differences between the categories. In Figure 25.12, the horizontal axis shows values to one decimal place, so that the differences between the values may appear as more substantial than they really are. As the figure shows, the difference in value between category 1 and category 3 is only 0.4. In addition, the visual image of big differences between the three categories is strengthened by the fact that the horizontal axis does not start at 0, but at the value 2.8. In Figure 25.13, the values at the horizontal axis have been rounded off to whole numbers, and the horizontal axis starts at the value 0. Due to the rounding of the values, the similarity between the three categories in Figure 25.13 may appear as greater than it really is.

Thus, both figures may be misleading. Whereas the differences between the three categories may be overestimated in Figure 25.12, the differences may be underestimated in Figure 25.13. However, sometimes only differences between whole numbers are considered to be significant or interesting. Then, Figure 25.12 would be regarded as more misleading than Figure 25.13. Furthermore, starting the horizontal axis at a value different from 0 is typically regarded as potentially misleading.

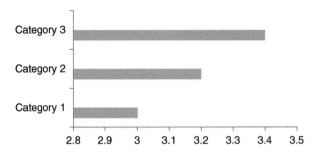

Figure 25.12 Example of a bar chart, indicating substantial differences between the three categories. The horizontal axis does not start at 0, and it shows values to one decimal place

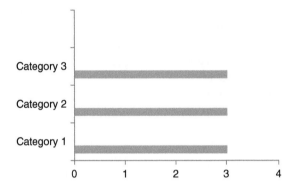

Figure 25.13 Example of a different bar chart, based on the same data as Figure 25.12, indicating no differences between the three categories: The horizontal axis starts at 0, and it shows values rounded off to whole numbers

Another way of creating deceptive or misleading visualizations is to present only selected parts of the data, leaving out other parts. An example of this is presented in Figure 25.14, where a line chart shows a linear increase in the time period between 1980 and 2010. However, this is a misleading chart, because the chart includes data for only four time points, one point for every tenth year. Thus, the chart does not present changes within each of the three decades.

The correct line chart for the changes between 1980 and 2010 is presented in Figure 25.15. The same data are used for the charts in both figures, but Figure 25.15 includes information for more time points within the period, showing data for every fifth year. Thus, the more detailed information

in Figure 25.15 reveals that there is no linear increase between 1980 and 2010. Within this period, there are both increases and decreases, although there is a long-term increasing trend.

In addition to the examples presented here, there are a number of other possibilities for creating deceptive or misleading data visualizations. It is important to be aware of such problems, so that they can be revealed when visualizations are viewed and interpreted, and prevented when visualizations are created and presented. Misleading visualizations are problematic in terms of both research quality and research ethics, not only if they are due to intended manipulations, but also if they are caused by mistakes or incompetence.

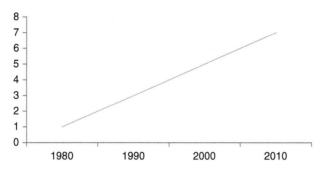

Figure 25.14   Example of a misleading line chart, indicating a linear increase between 1980 and 2010: data are presented only for every tenth year, omitting data for 1985, 1995 and 2005

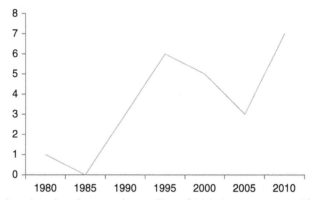

Figure 25.15   Correct line chart, based on the same data as Figure 25.14: data are presented for every fifth year

···

CHAPTER HIGHLIGHTS

- Data visualizations are illustrations of selected data or empirical findings by means of images or figures, in order to create accurate, clear and effective presentations for an audience of readers or viewers.
- When the visualization is created, the data are encoded by the researcher, so that the visualization represents the data as accurately as possible.
- When the visualization is presented, it is decoded by the audience. The presentation should facilitate the understanding of the data as effectively as possible.

- Purposes of data visualizations include:
  - Documenting or illustrating empirical findings in a research report, such as a thesis or an article
  - Showing research results in presentations, for example at conferences
  - Facilitating the understanding of data or findings by readers or viewers
  - Emphasizing key results of a research project
  - Adding credibility to data and findings
  - Stimulating interest in the research among potential readers and viewers

- o Simplifying and clarifying complex data for the researcher.
- A data visualization is a combination of marks, such as points, lines or areas, and attributes, including
  - o Quantitative attributes (positions, sizes, angles, quantities)
  - o Qualitative attributes (distinctions)
  - o Relational attributes (connections).
- A typical form of data visualization is a chart. Charts are classified into five main types, based on their usability for different types of data:
  - o Categorical charts, which compare categories or units as to selected attributes, for example the bar chart
  - o Hierarchical charts, which show how a whole set of units is divided into different parts, such as the pie chart or the stacked bar chart
  - o Relational charts, which show connections between units, such as the sociogram, or correlations between variables, such as the scattergram
  - o Temporal charts, which show trends or changes, such as the line chart
  - o Spatial charts, which show spatial patterns of different types of data related to maps of geographical areas, such as the area cartogram and the proportional symbol map.
- These five types of charts (except the sociogram) are used mainly for quantitative data. In addition, there are some visualizations that are designed for qualitative data, such as the word cloud.

- In addition to charts, data may be visualized by means of different kinds of pictures, animations, videos or films. Visualizations may also be interactive and include online links.
- Visualization of big data requires powerful computers and special software.
- Most of the chart types that are used in traditional data visualization may also be used in big data visualization.
- Some types of visualizations seem to be particularly useful for big data, for example
  - o Word clouds, which are used for visualizing data from social media
  - o Sociograms, which visualize big data on connections among persons or organizations
  - o Semantic networks, which present connections among concepts, words or phrases
  - o Line charts, which visualize big data on trends and changes
  - o Parallel coordinates, used for visualization in multivariate analyses of big data.
- Data visualization is not only used for presenting results of the data analysis. Visualization may also be used as a part of the data analysis, to discover and understand patterns or trends in the data. Using visualization in the data analysis is particularly important in big data research.
- It is important to avoid deceptive or misleading visualizations. Such visualizations may be intended or due to incompetence or mistakes, but they are always problematic for the quality and ethics of the research.

RESEARCH EXAMPLES

It is recommended that you look at articles in social science journals to see whether, and how, data visualizations are used. Three articles are described here:

Born, Andreas, Pieter van Eck, and Magnus Johannesson (2018) 'An experimental investigation of election promises', *Political Psychology* 39(3), 685–705.

This article analyses the effect of election promises on electoral behaviour. The analysis is based on quantitative data, which were collected by means of an experiment in Germany. The participants in the study were students at the University of Erfurt. The experiments focused on how voter behaviour is affected by politicians' promises for the next election period as well as their fulfilment or breaking of promises for the previous election period. The analysis shows that voters reward politicians with high promises, but only up to a certain point, since the highest promises have low credibility. Furthermore, in addition to rewarding politicians for promising contributions, voters seem to punish politicians for breaking promises. The article presents line charts to visualize both predicted and empirical relationships between promises and voting. A histogram (cf. Kirk, 2016: 173) is used as a visualization of the distribution of kept promises versus broken promises. Clustered bar charts (cf. Kirk, 2016: 162) are presented to visualize politicians' promise keeping and contributions over time.

Dobermann, Darja, and Ian S. Hamilton (2017) 'Publication patterns in developmental psychology: Trends and social networks', *International Journal of Psychology* 52(4), 336–347.

This article is focused on patterns of publication in development psychology. The analysis deals with publication differences between countries, collaboration on publishing between universities and between countries, relationships between authors and editorial boards, and patterns of influence on the publishing within different journals. The study is based on quantitative and relational data. Two journals were selected for the study. All empirical articles in the two journals between 2005 and 2014 were examined. The analysis demonstrates a North American dominance in publication, and social networks among authors are identified. Furthermore, it is shown that there are 15 'chief influentialists binding groups of authors together' (Dobermann and Hamilton, 2017: 336). The article presents a number of data visualizations. Line charts are presented to show trends of collaboration between authors. Stacked bar charts (Kirk, 2016: 177) are used to demonstrate the different types of cross-country collaboration for each year of the study period. Sociograms are presented to illustrate social networks among authors. Separate sociograms are used to distinguish between male and female authors, and between authors from different countries, as well as to identify the most influential authors in the network. Moreover, separate sociograms are used to show the author network for each of the two journals.

Novák, Jakub, and Luděk Sýkora (2007) 'A city in motion: Time-space activity and mobility patterns of suburban inhabitants and the structuration of the spatial organization of the Prague metropolitan area', *Geografiska Annaler: Series B, Human Geography* 89(2), 147–168.

This article presents a study of the relations between new suburban areas and other parts of the Prague metropolitan area in 2004. It is focused on the time-space activity and mobility patterns of the inhabitants of the new suburban areas. Using a time geography approach, and referring to structuration theory, the purpose is to understand the structuration of metropolitan spatial organization. The analysis is based on quantitative data, collected from a sample of respondents by means of time use diaries combined with questionnaires and interviews. The diaries were used to record what the respondents did, where and with whom they were, as well as how and where they were moving, during a period of three full days. In the questionnaires and interviews, the respondents were asked about background information and attitudes. The analysis shows that people in the new suburbs are dependent on the core of the metropolitan area, where they have to go for work and services, although some new suburban shopping centres make it possible to keep some activities within the suburbs. In addition to geographical maps showing the location of the selected suburbs and the core of the city, several visualizations are presented to illustrate data and empirical findings. Area charts (Kirk, 2016: 195) are used to illustrate activity distribution and spatial mobility for different categories of respondents, and for weekdays compared to weekend days. Symbol maps are presented to show the location of the respondents at different time points during the day.

1 What is data visualization?
2 Why are data visualizations valuable for presenting social research?
3 What are the characteristics of the bar, pie and line charts, and how are they used?
4 What are the differences between a sociogram and a scattergram?
5 Why are visualizations useful in the analysis of big data?
6 Find a data visualization in a newspaper or magazine article, for example on an opinion poll.

    a What type of visualization is this?

    b Discuss whether (or how) the visualization may be deceptive or misleading.

    c Discuss how you could manipulate the visualization to make it (more) deceptive or misleading.

7 Select an article in a social science journal that includes one or more data visualizations.

    a What types of visualizations are used in the article?

    b Discuss whether other data visualizations could have been used in the article, and specify the types of such additional visualizations.

Evergreen, Stephanie D. H. (2017) *Effective Data Visualization: The Right Chart for the Right Data*. London: Sage.

This book describes types of visualizations that can be used for different types of data. The description of each type of visualization includes detailed guidelines for creating the visualization, mainly by means of Excel.

Kirk, Andy (2019) *Data Visualisation: A Handbook for Data Driven Design* (2nd edn). London: Sage.

This book provides a thorough discussion of how to create data visualizations, and it includes an overview of a large number of charts, classified into five different categories.

Sue, Valerie M., and Matthew T. Griffin (2016): *Data Visualization & Presentation with Microsoft Office*. London: Sage.

This book describes how to use Microsoft Office (Excel, PowerPoint, and Word) to create data visualizations, such as bar, line and pie charts. The book shows how to prepare data for making charts, and how charts are used in writing reports, as well as creating and delivering presentations.

WRITING ABOUT RESEARCH

This chapter provides the necessary knowledge for understanding how research reports are written and organized, and for writing a research essay or a report on your own research, for example a master's thesis or a PhD dissertation.

The chapter will teach you how to

- write a research essay
- organize the process of writing a thesis, an article or another report
- use the appropriate style of writing for an academic text
- organize a thesis or an article according to the typical structure of academic texts
- include references to literature and avoid plagiarism in academic texts
- publish a book based on a whole thesis or another major report
- publish articles based on parts of a thesis or report.

Writing about research: Purposes and formats

Chapter 5 dealt with literature reviews, discussing how to do and write a literature review. It was pointed out that the review of the literature may be a part of a larger research project or a separate, stand-alone study. In its most comprehensive form, as a separate study, the final written literature review is a complete research report. Thus, most of the description and discussion of how to write a literature review that was presented in Chapter 5 is relevant and applicable also for writing about research in general, which is the topic of this chapter.

This chapter presents a more extensive and thorough discussion of how to write about research, which is also called *academic writing*. This first section presents an overview of different purposes of and formats for writing about research. In the following section it is described how to write research essays or exam essays. Next, some general features of academic writing are presented, before two specific forms of reporting about your own research are described and discussed in more detail. These are writing a thesis for a degree, and writing an article for a journal. The last part of the chapter deals with different ways of publishing research, focusing on different types of publications.

The main reason researchers write about research is to present and discuss their own research or research done by other researchers. The general purpose is to make this research available and known to the research community and to a wider audience. Presenting new theoretical insights, empirical evidence and methodological experiences, and discussing these in relation to previous research, is necessary for the long-term development of specific research fields as well as social science in general. Furthermore, reporting about new knowledge and new perspectives generated by research on particular social phenomena is important for people's understanding of these phenomena, and for practical application of the research.

In addition to these scientific and societal purposes of academic writing, researchers have personal reasons to write about their research. Writing and publishing their research reports is the most important way of demonstrating and documenting their merits, qualifications and competence as researchers.

Students also have personal reasons to write about research, as a part of their education. They have to write term papers, essays, or course-work exams about research in a selected field or on a particular topic, mainly for learning and grading purposes. Furthermore, students have to write a thesis, for training and graduation purposes, for a master's degree or PhD. Students' academic writing, especially a master's or PhD thesis, may also be important for scientific and societal purposes, in addition to the student's personal purposes.

In addition to shorter essays, there are two basic formats for writing about research. One of these is the major report format, and the other is the article format.

A *major report* is a comprehensive and large report from a research project. A master's or PhD thesis, which will be discussed in more detail in this chapter, is a typical example of a major report. A major report is the main outcome of a research project. It is typically a complete description and discussion of the background, research process and results of the project. This report may be the final presentation of the outcome of the project, but parts of a major report may also be selected for further and more in-depth elaboration in shorter papers or articles.

Typically, major research reports are made publicly available and distributed more or less widely by the centre or institution where the research has been done. In particular, the major report is sent to those institutions and persons who have been involved in the project or contributed to the research, such as funding agencies, sponsors, contract partners, collaboration partners, and advisers. Furthermore, it is good practice to send the major report to those who have contributed with data in the research, for example, persons who have been observed or interviewed, or institutions that have provided access to archives or other data sources. Theses are made available by the universities where they are submitted for a master's degree or a PhD.

Recognized publishers may also publish theses as well as other major research reports as books, which are called *monographs*. Publishing a major report as a monograph widens the distribution of the report, and it increases the researcher's prestige.

Compared to the major report format, the *article* format is shorter. Typically, an article is published in a recognized academic journal. Journal articles will be discussed more extensively later in this chapter. However, an article may also be published as a book chapter, in an anthology, which is an edited book consisting of a collection of articles. Typically, such anthologies are published by recognized publishers. Furthermore, the article format is also used for papers that are written and presented at academic conferences. Conference papers are often revised and improved, and later published as journal articles or book chapters. Papers presented at a conference may be included in conference proceedings, which are an edited collection of papers from the conference. Some conference proceedings are published as anthologies by recognized publishers.

In addition to the two basic formats of academic writing, which will be emphasized in this chapter, there are some other forms of writing about research. Among these additional forms are students' term papers, essays, or course-work exams, which were mentioned above. Writing research essays or exam essays will be described before the presentation of how to write theses and articles.

Academic writing also includes online writing, focusing on research in blog comments or Wikipedia contributions, and book reviews, presenting summaries and critical evaluations of research monographs or anthologies.

A special form of academic writing is the research proposal, which deals with research intentions rather than research results. The research proposal presents an initiative for a new research project, and a plan for the new project. The proposal describes the background of the project, its relation to previous research, and its scientific and societal significance. Furthermore, the research proposal presents the research question, the research design, the methodological approach, the ethical issues, and the estimated time-frame for the project. Students may have to write a research proposal for their thesis, as a basis for being accepted for a master's degree or PhD programme. A research proposal is also a necessary part of an application for funding for a new research project.

Writing a research essay or exam essay

Students on social science courses may have to write various kinds of essays, as a basis for their learning, and as a part of their exams. Often, these essays are focused on social research and are therefore called *research essays*. How to write such research essays will be discussed here, with emphasis on the most important aspects of the writing process and the essay text. However, although the advice and recommendations presented here may be useful for writing a typical research essay, it is important to emphasize that research essays and exam essays can be written in different ways, depending on the particular type of essay and the specific topic of the essay.

Students may write research essays under different *conditions*. Essays may be written as a test or exam under controlled conditions in the classroom, with only a few hours available to complete the assignment. They may or may not have access to various types of sources, such as books or online connection. Typically, there are strict rules as to what kinds of sources students can, and cannot, use. Alternatively, students may write essays at home, over a period of a few days or weeks, with full access to all kinds of sources. Usually, there are certain rules as to the minimum and maximum length of the essay, especially if the essay is written at home. For example, it may be decided that such an essay should be between 1200 and 1500 words in length.

It is important to consider these conditions carefully. The ambitions for the essay should be adapted to the time available for writing it. It is recommended to plan how the essay should be organized and to decide approximately how many words can be used for each part of the essay. It is advisable to plan the work systematically, to determine how much of the available time should be used for the different parts of the essay and the different parts of the writing process. The selection and specification of the topic of the essay, the number and kinds of sources used, and the breadth and depth of the discussion should be considered thoroughly, to ensure that the writing of the essay will be manageable within the limited length of the essay and the limited time available for the writing process.

The *topic* of the essay may be given, without any choice on the students' part. Alternatively, students will be free to choose one topic from a list of a few different topics, or they may be free to select any topic within certain limits, usually related to the general theme of the course.

When students have a choice regarding topics, it is a good idea to select a topic that they find most interesting or engaging, or a topic that they are most familiar with and have most knowledge about. Choosing such topics ensures that the writing is based on the student's best possible motivations and qualifications, which are important for the quality of the essay.

When the topic has been given or selected, it should be carefully read and interpreted, to make sure that it is understood in a reasonable way. The student's interpretation and understanding of the topic should be briefly explained in the introduction of the essay. By explaining how the topic is understood, the student describes the topic as precisely as possible.

Furthermore, a given or selected topic also has to be specified or narrowed. The purpose is to make the discussion as focused as possible within the limited length of the essay, and to make the writing process manageable within the limited time available. Specifying the topic can be related to principles and procedures for specification of research questions, which was explained in Chapter 4 of this book. The specification must be reasonable and closely related to the original formulation of the topic, although the original formulation is wider and more general. The specification should be explained and justified in the introduction to the essay.

The main content of the research essay is a presentation and discussion of research on the topic that has been specified. If the student is allowed to use *sources* from the research literature, these sources should be selected carefully. Due to the limited length of the essay and the limited time available for the writing, it is not possible to find and use all sources. It is necessary to concentrate on a few books or articles from the relevant research area. This will also give a more focused discussion of the topic. There are several criteria for selecting the most appropriate sources. For example, the selection could give priority to sources that

- are most relevant to the topic of the essay
- are representative of the most recent research in the area
- present the most general summaries of the relevant research area
- present the best overview of different approaches and perspectives within the research area.

The selection of the sources should be briefly justified in the essay, for example with explicit reference to the criteria that are used for this selection.

Furthermore, it is necessary to be selective in the use of each source. The presentation and discussion should focus on some major parts of each book or article that are used as sources. For example, introductions and literature reviews may provide good overviews of the whole research area, while discussions of findings and conclusions may summarize the main approach and contribution provided by the research in the book or the article. In addition, it may be necessary to use other parts of the content of the source to understand and explain important aspects of the research.

The selection of sources as well as the focus on selected parts of each source are guided by the specified topic of the essay. Moreover, based on the topic specification and the reading of relevant sources, *the text of the main parts* of the essay is often organized and written according to the student's own *message* regarding what the social research shows about the topic of the essay. This message may be formulated as one overall statement about the research contributions on the essay topic, or as a summary of two or more contradicting research perspectives on the topic. The message can also consist of a few main *ideas* regarding important aspects of the topic. It is often wise to present the message and ideas early in the essay, so that they can be a frame of reference for the presentation and discussion of the research. The research can then be presented in relation to *arguments* for and against these ideas. Different research contributions may be referred to in this argumentation. The student's ideas may be supported or strengthened by some contributions and weakened by other contributions. The presentation of arguments should be balanced, and the reference to research contributions should be representative for the development of the relevant research area.

The last part of the essay consists of a very brief summary of the presentation and discussion, and a main conclusion on what the relevant research shows about the topic of the essay. This conclusion should be related to the student's message and ideas and to the research-based discussion of the arguments for and against these ideas.

The essay should include proper and correct references to the literature used as sources in the text, and the student is responsible for avoiding plagiarism. How to reference sources and avoid plagiarism is discussed in Chapter 5 of this book. The problem of plagiarism is also explained in Chapter 3.

General features of academic writing

As parts of social science courses, research essays or exam essays written by students are rather short texts, which are focused on specific topics and produced within a very limited time period. Although some of these essays may be based on new small empirical studies, most student essays use literature from previous research as sources for the presentation and discussion.

The rest of this chapter refers to the writing of theses and articles, which are two major types of reports based on new research in social science. Some aspects of this academic writing, for example the style of academic texts, are also relevant to students' research essays.

The writing process

A thesis or article is a report on a study that has been carried out. The report cannot be completed before the results of the study are clear. Thus, the main writing process takes place towards the end of the research project, usually as the last stage of the project. However, the planning of the research report and the preparations for the writing process should start at the beginning of the research project (Becker, 2007).

The research report deals with the background, development and results of the study. For the writing of the report it is very useful to have good notes and documentation from the whole research process. Thus, it is important to write notes when the study is planned, when the research question is identified and developed, when the literature review is done, when the methods are considered and selected, and when the data are collected, analysed and interpreted. Such notes should consist of information about what was done in the research process, how it was done, and why it was done. Considerations regarding alternative approaches or methods should also be included in the notes. Keeping accurate records of the relevant literature and systematic documentation of the findings are also necessary for the writing process. Such notes, records and documentation should be made during the research project, with the final writing process in mind. Some of the notes may even be written as preliminary drafts of chapters or sections for the final report.

Preliminary drafts of chapters on the research question, the literature review, and the methodological approach may be written before starting the data collection. Sometimes, especially in quantitative research, it is also possible to write about the data collection before starting the data analysis. In qualitative studies and mixed methods research, it is usually more difficult to start the report writing during the research process, since the research question and the methodological approach may be modified during the project, and since data collection and data analysis are carried out simultaneously. Thus, especially in such studies, notes and memos written during the whole research process are very useful in the process of writing the research report.

In any event, drafts that have been written during the research project have to be reconsidered and most likely revised or rewritten when the data analysis has been completed. The reason is that the report as a whole should be consistent, and each part should be related to the other parts and well integrated within the whole report. The report should be organized and written with a clear message or story in mind, focusing on the relationship to previous research, the major findings and conclusions, and the importance of this new contribution. All chapters or parts should be adapted to this overall story, convincing the readers of the credibility of the conclusions and the importance of the research. Since this story may not be fully clarified before the data analysis, it is necessary to have a concentrated writing process at the end of the research project, in order to write through and edit the whole report, regardless of how much writing the researcher has done during the project.

Before the concentrated writing process it is essential to establish good conditions for thinking and writing. It is useful to have access to a quiet office space without noise or other disturbances, and to have a desk where the computer as well as the notes and literature can be kept during the writing process. The computer should be equipped with a good word processing program, such as Word, and preferably software for checking spelling, grammar and style.

Usually the writing process is most efficient if it can be carried out with full concentration and attention, using the whole day for the writing during a period of time. It is a good idea to make a writing schedule for this time period, estimating how much you will be able to write per day and per week, and planning when each chapter or section of the report can be drafted and revised (cf. Zerubavel, 1999). Furthermore, the planning of the writing process should include arrangements for receiving comments on drafts from supervisors, fellow students, or colleagues. During the writing process it is also very valuable to participate in research seminars or writing seminars, where drafts can be presented, commented on and discussed.

The writing schedule should be based on time estimates that are as realistic as possible. However, it is a common experience that the time required is underestimated. Thus, it may be necessary to adjust the schedule during the process. Nevertheless, a schedule that has to be adjusted is better than no schedule. Moreover, good writing habits often include the aim of writing a certain amount of text every day, even though the quality of the text, and the need for revision and improvement, may differ from day to day.

Since the writing is based on notes, references and documentation from the research process, the concentrated writing process may start with this material. It is recommended to organize and systematize the notes, references and documentation. Considering this material as a whole is useful for developing and clarifying the main story or message that should be presented in the report. An example of a research report presenting such an overall story is the book *Street Corner Society,* which is based on a qualitative study of the social life among Italian immigrants in a slum area in Boston in the 1930s (Whyte, 1943). Observing the social structure of this environment, Whyte became particularly interested in how local groups of young boys were developed and organized. He observed relations and activities among these groups, which were meeting on street corners and in nearby shops. The main story of the book is that these groups of boys seemed to form their own society, described as the street corner society. This story is reflected in the line of argumentation in each chapter and in the book as a whole, including the book title.

Whereas each chapter or section of the research report should be adapted to the main overall story of the report, the different chapters or sections also have their own specific content. This specific content may be identified and developed by sorting and categorizing the notes, references and documentation in relation to the different parts of the research report. Thus, this sorted material is valuable for outlining and writing each chapter of a major report or each section of an article. As pointed out by Joyner et al. (2013: 174), the planning of each chapter may follow a bottom-up or a top-down approach. A bottom-up approach starts with the notes from the research process, using them to generate the outline of the chapter. The notes are systematized as a basis for organizing the chapter. A top-down approach, on the other hand, starts with a more analytical and logical consideration of how the chapter should be organized and outlined, and then the notes are related to the different parts of the chapter, according to this analytical outline.

Regardless of how the outline of a chapter is developed, the next step is to start writing the full text of the chapter. The text is divided into paragraphs. Each paragraph should be coherent, dealing with one idea, one topic, or one argument, and it typically starts with general statements, which gradually are more specified. The text should flow and proceed logically from one paragraph to the next. Headings, and perhaps subheadings, are used to show how the chapter is organized and divided into different parts. References are inserted in the text where the literature is used, and documentation of findings, such as tables, figures, or quotes, are placed where the findings are described or commented on.

It is a good idea to revise while writing (Joyner et al., 2013: 175). This process is illustrated in Figure 26.1. First, a paragraph, or a small and limited part of the chapter, is written. Then, this text is read and assessed. If necessary, the text is revised and improved. After this revision of what has just been written, the writing continues with the next paragraph, or the next part of the chapter.

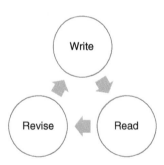

Figure 26.1 Revising while writing

When a larger part of the text, such as a whole chapter, has been written, it is reasonable to ask for comments from supervisors, fellow students, or colleagues, or to present the text for comments and discussion at a seminar. Such comments are valuable for improving and ensuring the necessary quality of the text. However, it is important to consider each comment carefully, keeping in mind

that some comments may not be reasonable or meaningful. Based on the comments, the text is revised, and the writing continues with another chapter, or another part of the text, as shown in Figure 26.2.

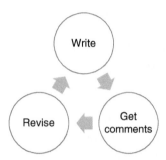

Figure 26.2 Revising based on comments from others

When all parts of the text have been written, it is necessary to read through the whole report, not only reconsidering and revising each part, but also examining how the various parts are related to one another and integrated within the whole report. This revising implies re-editing in addition to rewriting. After re-editing based on your own reading, it is useful to get comments from others on the complete draft of the thesis or article. These comments should be considered very carefully and utilized thoroughly, since they provide a basis for the final revision and improvement of the report, including rewriting and re-editing.

An overview of a typical writing process is presented in Table 26.1. This description of a typical writing process is focused on academic writing as such, referring to different kinds of research reports, including theses and articles. What is said about chapters of theses, is also relevant for sections of articles.

However, it must be emphasized that the description of the writing process presented here is quite general and based on common experiences. There are wide varieties among individuals in working habits and ways of

Table 26.1 Overview of a typical writing process

Stages in the writing process	Activities involved in the process
Planning and preparing the writing during the research process	• Writing notes • Keeping records of references • Securing documentation of findings • Writing preliminary and limited drafts, if possible
Organizing good working conditions for a concentrated writing process	• Securing good conditions for thinking and writing, including an undisturbed space and a well-equipped computer • Drawing up a writing schedule • Making arrangements for comments
Writing with full concentration and attention after the data analysis	• Organizing and systematizing notes, references and documentation • Developing and clarifying the main story or message of the report • Writing an outline of the report • Outlining each chapter or section, based on a bottom-up or a top-down approach • Writing and organizing paragraphs and headings within each chapter or section • Inserting references to literature and documentation of findings (tables, figures, quotes) • Revising while writing: Write – read – revise – continue writing • Getting comments to drafts and revising the text

organizing their writing. What is important is that each individual develops and follows those approaches and procedures that work best for himself or herself.

Style and structure of academic texts

There are some variations between different disciplines in the *style* of academic texts. Typically, a thesis or an article is written within the tradition of one discipline and will be evaluated and eventually approved or accepted by experts in this discipline. These disciplinary experts are very important readers of the academic text, even though they will evaluate the readability of the text for a wider audience. Thus, before starting their writing, the researchers should be aware of any specific requirements or expectations regarding the style of their own discipline. What will be emphasized and described here are some style features that are common to most academic texts. For a better understanding of what these features mean, it is advisable to look at a few journal articles, such as those articles that are referred to and listed as examples later in this chapter.

Academic texts are characterized by a clear, precise, formal and consistent style. These aspects of the style are focused on the importance of finding the right words and formulations, and using these words and formulations consistently through the whole text. Using the correct disciplinary terminology is one way of ensuring the clarity, precision, formality and consistency of the text. Using words from everyday language that are precise and unambiguous is another way of writing in this academic style. A third way is to write concisely, not using more words than necessary to express an idea, explanation or argument in a paragraph.

The challenge is to obtain clarity and precision without making the text too rigid and too difficult to read, and to keep the text formal without making it boring for the readers. Furthermore, consistency should be combined with creativity and variety in the language, using synonyms and different formulations to express the same meaning.

Academic texts should follow the formal rules and common conventions in terms of language, including grammar, spelling, and punctuation. Such rules and conventions should be applied consistently throughout the report. In particular, it is important to use non-discriminatory language, including gender-neutral formulations. Referring in general to a teacher, for example, the correct wording is not 'he', but 'he or she'. Alternatively, it is possible to use the plural form, 'they'.

Another aspect of formality is that academic texts traditionally have been written in the third person, such as 'the researcher collected the data', or in the passive voice, for example 'the data were collected by the researcher'. However, this tradition is no longer followed as strictly as it used to be, and the formal style of writing in the third person or in the passive voice has even become somewhat controversial. It has been argued that this style is too formal, and that it is more reasonable for the researcher to write in the first person, such as 'I collected the data'. Writing academic texts in the first person has become more common than before, especially in qualitative research, where the researcher is personally involved in the data collection, and where this personal involvement may be important for understanding and interpreting the findings. Summarizing this debate and development, Oliver (2014: 80) concludes:

A position has now been reached in writing about research, where although the third person is generally favoured in most cases, it is acknowledged that the first person is appropriate in a number of different contexts, and is favoured by some.

As pointed out by Joyner et al. (2013: 179–180), it is important to find the right balance between confidence and tentativeness in academic texts. On the one hand, the text should demonstrate or signal the researcher's confidence about the importance of the study and the credibility of the findings. On the other hand, such certainty or confidence should not be exaggerated. It may be necessary to use more tentative formulations. Formulations such as 'this study proves' are usually too confident. More tentative, and better, formulations might be 'this study suggests', or 'according to this study, it is likely that'. However, too much tentativeness should also be avoided, for example formulations like 'this study seems to suggest'.

Balancing confidence and tentativeness is one way of ensuring that the text is written with caution. Being careful in the writing also means that assertions should be documented, and that assumptions and arguments should be justified. Typically, references to literature from previous research are used for such documentation and justification. How to use and reference literature correctly, and how to avoid intentional or accidental plagiarism, were described in Chapter 5. This description, which referred to the writing of literature reviews, is relevant and applicable for the writing of all kinds of research reports.

Findings should also be documented. In quantitative research, this is done mainly by means of tables, presenting numbers based on the analysis of the quantitative data. In qualitative research, findings are documented mainly by means of quotations from field notes, interviews, or texts from a qualitative content analysis. In both types of research, figures may be used, in addition to tables or quotations, to present conceptual or verbal summaries and overviews of main patterns from the analysis. However, the text should not be overloaded with these types of documentation. The challenge is to design, select and present tables and figures that are easy to read and focused on the most important findings, and to identify, select and present those quotations that are typical examples of more general findings. In mixed methods research, the documentation of findings are adapted to the different types of data that are analysed. The challenge is to integrate findings from both qualitative and quantitative data. How to visualize data and findings was described in Chapter 25. This description may be useful for creating good documentation of findings in research reports.

Although tables, figures or quotations are important as documentation of findings, they do not speak for themselves. In the text, the main patterns within tables and figures are described and commented, and the quotes from qualitative studies are justified and commented in relation to more general patterns in the data.

Table 26.2 presents a summary of style features that should be given particular attention when writing academic texts.

Table 26.2 Style features to be emphasized in writing academic texts

Strive for

- clarity
- precision
- formality
- consistency

Follow formal rules and common conventions in

- language
- grammar
- spelling
- punctuation

Write with caution,

- using gender-neutral and non-discriminatory language
- choosing the first person, third person or passive voice
- balancing confidence and tentativeness
- documenting assertions
- justifying assumptions and arguments
- using correct references
- avoiding intentional or accidental plagiarism
- documenting and commenting findings

When it comes to the *structure* of research reports, there are some differences between different types of texts. However, some aspects of structure are common to most academic texts. Such aspects will be emphasized here, whereas the structure of theses and articles will be described more specifically later in the chapter.

A typical research report consists of four major parts: introduction, methodology, results, and conclusion. An overview of these parts and the typical elements in each part are presented in Table 26.3. The figure also shows some elements of the report that may be placed before the introduction, and some elements that may be included after the conclusion. A few comments regarding this typical structure will be presented here.

Table 26.3 Typical structure of research reports

Parts of the report	Elements of each part
Before the introduction	Different types of reports may include different types of elements, including table of contents, abstract, acknowledgements, preface, list of tables, and list of figures
Introduction	Background Research questions Literature review
Methodology	Research design Data Methods of data collection Methods of data analysis
Results	Data analysis Findings of the study
Conclusion	Discussion of findings Major conclusions Limitations of the study Recommendations for further research
After the Conclusion	Different types of reports may include different types of elements, including list of references, abbreviations, glossary, index, and appendices

The introduction may start with a presentation of the background to the report, such as a description of the topic of the report, and the context in which the research has been done. Furthermore, the introduction includes the description and discussion of the research question, and the literature review. The research question is justified. The presentation of the background may be used to point out the importance of the research question for society. Its importance for science and relation to previous research are clarified by means of the literature review, which is also used to show how the research question is developed and specified.

The methodology part presents the research design, the data, and the methods for the collection and analysis of the data. In general, this part of the report contains a systematic description of how the research was carried out, and usually also a discussion of why it was done in this way. The discussion includes reflections on strengths and limitations of the methods that have been used, compared with alternative methods that could have been used.

The third main part of the report is focused on the results. This part includes a presentation of the data analysis and a description of the relevant and important findings based on the analysis. The findings are documented by means of tables, figures or quotations, and they are described and summarized in the text.

In the conclusion of the report the findings are systematically discussed with reference to the research question and in relation to previous research. Based on this discussion, the major conclusions of the study are presented. Furthermore, this concluding part of the report presents reflections on the limitations of the study that has been carried out, and recommendations for further research.

Most research reports also contain some elements before the introduction and after the conclusion. However, there are variations between different types of reports as to such elements. Typically, an abstract of the report, and some expressions of acknowledgements to institutions and persons for support of the research are presented before the introduction of both major reports and articles. In addition, major reports may include a preface, as well as lists of tables and figures at the beginning of the report.

At the end of the report, a list of references is included in both major reports and articles, whereas major reports also may present a list of abbreviations used in the report, a glossary of the important terms and concepts, an index of different subjects dealt with, and an index of the main names referred to, as well as one or more appendices, presenting for example questionnaires or schedules for data collection, or detailed results of data analyses.

Basically, this typical report structure is common for both qualitative and quantitative research. However, in qualitative research, the development of the research question may be discussed throughout the report, for example in the discussion of methods and in the discussion of findings. Formulating a more precise research question may also be a major conclusion of the study. Furthermore, as pointed out by Golden-Biddle and Locke (2007), qualitative research reports are often characterized by narrative perspectives, based on a 'theorized storyline' and telling a story, with the author as an explicit and visual storyteller.

Reports based on mixed methods research may also follow the basic structure outlined in Table 26.3. In such reports, a special challenge for the methodology part is to describe and discuss the methods related to both the qualitative and qualitative data, and in addition to explain how and why the combination of data and methods is particularly useful and valuable for the study and its research question. For the results part, and especially for the conclusion part, it is important that the findings based on the different data and methods are not presented and discussed as separate studies, isolated from one another. They should be integrated and discussed together. It should be emphasized how the qualitative and quantitative parts of the research complement each other, providing different kinds of knowledge and insights, and thus contributing to a broader and more comprehensive analysis of the research question.

The report structure presented here is focused on empirical studies. However, with some adjustments, it is relevant also for more theoretical or conceptual reports. In such reports, the methodology part does not refer to collection and analysis of empirical data, but describes and discusses, for example, the approach to the selection of literature and theoretical contributions, and strategies for analysing the literature and developing the theoretical argumentation. Moreover, the results part of the report may present a theoretical argumentation or a construction of a model, instead of an analysis of empirical data.

In an article, each of the main parts may be divided into different sections, covering one or more elements of the report. Similarly, a major report is divided into different chapters, which may be further divided into different sections. The structure of the report, as well as the content of each part of the report, is clarified and visualized by using headings and subheadings. A heading or a subheading should be concise, but also informative, regarding the content of the text it covers.

Signposting is another way of visualizing the structure of the report. Signposting provides explicit information on the development of the text, either a summary of the presentation so far, or a plan for the further presentation, or both. This type of information to the reader may be placed at the beginning or at the end of a chapter or section, or when the text changes from one topic to another or moves from one line of argumentation to another. Typical formulations would be for example 'in the previous chapter it was shown that…', 'this chapter will present the main theoretical contributions in this area…', or 'having described the main findings, I now turn to a discussion of the implications of these findings…'.

Furthermore, as pointed out above, it is important to work with the coherence of each paragraph and the logical linkage between paragraphs. This is a third way of developing and improving the structure of a report.

Writing a thesis

A thesis is a type of major report, which is similar to a book. It is written as a part of a graduate or postgraduate course of study, for the purpose of research training, and in order to obtain an academic degree. A master's thesis is required for a master's degree, and a doctoral thesis is necessary for the award of a PhD. A thesis may also be called a 'dissertation', and sometimes a distinction is made between master's theses and PhD dissertations. In this chapter the words 'thesis' and 'dissertation' are regarded as synonyms, and the word 'thesis' will be used with reference to both the master's degree and the PhD.

Furthermore, in this presentation, the thesis is described as a coherent report, like a monograph, written as one original piece of work. Another type of thesis is a collection of articles, published or submitted for publication in one or more academic journals. This type of thesis consists of three to five articles which are more or less related to one another. In addition to the set of articles, the thesis includes an introduction where the relationships between the articles are described and explained, clarifying the major research question, methodology, results, and conclusion of the thesis as a whole. Writing an article is the topic of the next section of this chapter.

A thesis is a research report based on a study. Typically, this is an empirical study, but some theses present a theoretical or conceptual study, focused on argumentation or model building rather than the collection and analysis of empirical data. In any event, a thesis should provide an original contribution to knowledge. It should be based on a study that is new and different from previous studies, and it should present new findings, interpretations, or perspectives.

Master's theses and doctoral theses are similar in terms of style, structure, and types of content, but a doctoral thesis is more advanced and more sophisticated than a master's thesis. Compared to a master's thesis, a PhD thesis is longer, and it presents a more extensive literature review, a more thorough methodological discussion, a larger empirical or conceptual study, and a more elaborated discussion and reflection on findings and theoretical perspectives. Typically, the expectations of original contributions to knowledge are higher for PhD theses than they are for master's theses.

In terms of length, there are considerable variations among different types of theses. As pointed out by Oliver (2014: 6), a master's thesis may be up to about 40,000 words in length, whereas a PhD thesis may be 80,000 words or more. However, some degree studies, such as various types of 'professional' degrees, are based on shorter theses: about 15,000 words for a master's thesis, and about 50,000 words for a PhD thesis.

Usually the study programme for a master's degree or a PhD specifies not only an expected length of the thesis, but also an estimated amount of time that could or should be used for the research and writing involved in the thesis work. The aims for the thesis and the planning of the writing process should be based on the expected length of the text as well as the time available for the thesis work. It is important to limit the work to what is realistic and possible to do within the length and time restrictions. Furthermore, it is important to start writing early in the research process, and to develop and follow a systematic plan for the whole writing process.

Different universities, and different degree programmes within a university, may have their own specific requirements, rules, expectations and recommendations regarding length, format, content, structure, and style of theses. Students should find as much information as possible about this before starting work on their thesis. It is also a very good idea to look at a variety of previous theses within your degree programme and your own research area, in order to understand how they are written and structured. Previous theses may be found online or at the university library. References to a few theses are included in the research examples section at the end of this chapter.

With the necessary adaptations to university-specific or disciplinary-specific rules and recommendations for theses, the general description of academic writing that was presented above is relevant for the process of writing a thesis, as well as for the style and structure of the thesis. Typically, the thesis is organized according to the structure shown in Table 26.3.

Writing an article

As pointed out above, a thesis may consist of a number of articles, in addition to an introduction that describes and explains how the articles are related to each other, and clarifies the research question, methodology, findings and conclusion of the thesis as a whole. When a thesis is written as a coherent major report, parts of the thesis may be selected as a basis for writing one or more articles in addition to the thesis. Usually, this is done after the thesis has been completed and submitted. An article by Beckfield (2006) on European integration and income inequality was based on his PhD thesis on the same topic, which was submitted the year before (Beckfield, 2005). Articles may also be written during the thesis work, but that is more demanding and challenging. Since the two writing tasks are different, it might be difficult to combine them, and to divide the attention between the thesis and the article.

Although there are different types of articles, the articles described here are academic or scholarly pieces of work that are based on research and written within a shorter format than major research reports. Articles may be empirical, presenting analyses of qualitative or quantitative data, or they may be theoretical or conceptual, discussing theoretical perspectives or developing models.

Typically, an article is published in an academic journal, but it may also be included as a chapter in a book, or it may be presented as a scholarly paper at an academic conference. As to style and structure, the general features of academic writing presented above are relevant to writing articles, but it may be necessary to adapt to specific requirements of the particular journal, book or conference where the article is presented. Thus, where the article is supposed to be presented or published may be important for determining how it should be written. Therefore, some aspects of publishing will be presented in the next section of this chapter.

The typical length of an article is about 8000 to 10,000 words. Since the article is shorter than a major report, it has to be more focused and more concise. A thesis or a larger research project may be a basis for several articles. Each article may be limited to certain aspects of the general research question, certain parts of the empirical data, or certain selected types of analyses. In his article cited above, Beckfield (2006) deals with a more specific research question than he did in his PhD thesis (Beckfield, 2005). In an article on gender inequalities among staff in British and German universities, Pritchard (2010b) refers to two other articles, where she had written about the same research question, based on different types of data (Pritchard, 2007, 2010a).

Although there are some variations among articles as to how they are written and structured, most articles are organized according to the overall structure shown in Table 26.3. This is exemplified by three different articles, which are compared in Table 26.4. All three articles present empirical analyses of various aspects of inequality, but they are based on different types of data. The first article is based on a quantitative study, the second presents a qualitative study, and the third article refers to a mixed methods study, using both quantitative and qualitative data. The table shows how the headings and subheadings of the elements in each article are related to the main parts within a typical article structure.

The article by Beckfield (2006), based on a quantitative study of European integration and income inequality, starts with an abstract, and some acknowledgements of support from persons and institutions. In the introduction part of the article, the author describes the European context, and the background to the study. The research question, which is focused on impacts of economic and political integration on income equality, is discussed in relation to relevant literature from previous research. In the next part of the article, the data and methods are described. In the results part, the analyses are presented, and the findings are described and documented by means of tables and figures. The conclusion part of the article starts with a brief summary of the research question, the methodology, and the main results of the analysis. Then the implications of the results are discussed in relation to previous research, recommendations for further research are suggested, and limitations of the study are discussed. Finally the overall conclusion is presented, maintaining that 'the recent rise in income inequality within Western European societies is partly explained by regional integration' (Beckfield, 2006: 981). After the conclusion part only the list of references is included.

The article on gender inequalities among staff in British and German universities (Pritchard, 2010b) is based on a qualitative study. An abstract is placed at the beginning of the article. The introduction describes the gender status quo in academia in the two countries. It reviews relevant literature and describes the research question, which is about 'perceptions of gender equality among female academics in British and German higher education' (Pritchard, 2010b: 517). The methodology part describes the study design,

Table 26.4 Elements and structure of three different articles

Typical structure of articles	Selected examples of articles		
	Beckfield, Jason (2006) 'European integration and income inequality', *American Sociological Review* 71, 964–985.	Pritchard, Rosalind (2010b) 'Gender inequalities among staff in British and German universities: A qualitative study', *Compare* 40(4), 515–532.	Crosnoe, Robert, and Chandra Muller (2014) 'Family socioeconomic status, peers, and the path to college', *Social Problems* 61(4), 602–604.
	Quantitative study	**Qualitative study**	**Mixed methods study**
Before the introduction	Abstract Acknowledgements	Abstract	Abstract Acknowledgements
Introduction	Background • Economic integration, labour, and income inequality • Political integration, the welfare state, and income inequality	The gender status quo in British and German academia	• Secondary socioeconomic status effects on high school course work • Mechanisms of secondary effects
Methodology	Data and method	Methodology	Methods • Data • Quantitative measurement • Quantitative analyses • Qualitative analyses
Results	Results • Additional controls	Presentation of the results • Factors impeding the professional progress of female academics in British and German universities • Gender-related career behaviour and academic disciplines • Differences in networking and sponsorship	Results • Course work trajectories • Parents, course mates, and course work • Instrumental support from parents • Instrumental support from peers
Conclusion	Discussion	Discussion and interpretation • 'Academic communitarianism' versus radical feminism • Development of self-efficacy among younger scholars • De-gendered expertise; gendered people skills • Social dimensions and the erosion of public–private boundaries • Public–private boundaries, feminism and German political culture • Meritocracy and diversity	Discussion
After the conclusion	Appendix References	Acknowledgements Notes References Appendix	References

the sample of women in the two countries, as well as the collection and analysis of the qualitative data based on interviews with the women. The results are described under three subheadings, each of which presents a set of important findings. The findings are documented, or illustrated, by quotations from the interviews. The discussion and interpretation of the findings are presented in the conclusion part of the article, where six subheadings are used to emphasize the major patterns that were revealed by the study. Each of these patterns are discussed in relation to previous research, and to the British and German context. After the conclusion, the article includes acknowledgements of the funding source, the respondents, and one of the author's colleagues. Furthermore, some end notes, the list of references, and a brief appendix are included at the end of the article. The appendix presents the six main questions in the interview guide.

The article by Crosnoe and Muller (2014), on family socioeconomic status, peers, and the path to college, presents a mixed methods study, based on both quantitative and qualitative data. The article starts with an abstract and acknowledgements of various kinds of support from institutions and persons. In the introduction part of the article, the authors discuss their research question in relation to relevant literature. One part of the research question deals with 'how socioeconomic disparities in course work play out over time and across peer contexts' (Crosnoe and Muller, 2014: 605), and the other part is focused on 'the instrumental resources that students receive and elicit from their parents and peers' (Crosnoe and Muller, 2014: 606). Different subheadings are used for the description of the two parts of the research question. The methodology part of the article describes the quantitative data, which were made available from a nationally representative data set on high school students, and the qualitative data, which were based on fieldwork at one high school, including observation, interviews and use of various types of documents. Furthermore, the quantitative measurement as well as the quantitative and qualitative analyses are described. It is pointed out that the quantitative data are used to examine different kinds of effects, whereas the qualitative data are used to identify mechanisms underlying the effects. In the results part of the article, the quantitative analyses are presented, focusing on course work trajectories and relationships between parents, course mates and course work, and the qualitative analyses are described, with emphasis on instrumental support from parents and peers. Findings based on the quantitative analyses are documented by tables and figures, while figures are also used to document findings from the qualitative analyses. In the conclusion part of the article, the authors discuss the major findings and contributions of the study in relation to previous research, and they present a suggestion for further research. The article ends with the list of references.

In sum, although the three journal articles compared in Table 26.4 are based on different types of studies, including quantitative, qualitative and mixed methods studies, they are organized and structured in similar ways. There are differences between the articles as to how results and findings are documented or illustrated. Whereas findings from quantitative analyses are documented by tables and figures, quotations and figures are used to document and illustrate findings based on qualitative analyses. Furthermore, there are some differences between articles in the extent to which subheadings are used to clarify the substantial content of various parts or elements of the article. However, despite these differences, there seem to be small variations in the basic structure of journal articles, regardless of the type of research they are based on. Compared to articles on quantitative research, articles about qualitative research may be characterized by more emphasis on narrative perspectives and storytelling (Golden-Biddle and Locke, 2007). This is mainly a difference in style rather than structure.

Publishing research

As pointed out above, there are several ways of publishing research reports. A major report may be published as a book. A report written in article format is typically published in an academic journal, but it may also be published as a chapter in a book, or it may be presented at an academic conference and then published in the conference proceedings. Furthermore, a paper that is presented at a conference may later be revised and published as a journal article or a book chapter. When a thesis is written as a coherent major report, the whole thesis may be used as the basis for a book, or parts of the thesis may be selected for one or more articles.

For publishing an article, it is important to identify a journal, a conference or a book where the article is likely to fit in. There are different types of journals. Some journals are specific to one discipline, for example the *British Journal of Sociology*, *American Journal of Psychology*, *Australian Journal of Anthropology* and *Journal of Geography*. Other journals are multidisciplinary, covering for example social science or social research in general, such as the *International Social Science Journal* and *Nordic Journal of Social Research*. Furthermore, a number of journals are oriented towards particular topical areas or special research fields, for example the *International Journal of Urban and Regional Research*, *British Journal of Social Work* and *International Journal of Nursing Studies*.

There are differences among journals as to how prestigious they are. Typically, journals using external referees to evaluate manuscripts are more prestigious than journals where only the editor makes the decisions regarding acceptance or rejection of manuscripts. Furthermore, the prestige of journals is high if a large proportion of the manuscripts received are rejected, and if the articles in the journal are frequently cited in other publications. It gives more prestige for the author to publish in a prestigious journal than to publish in other journals, but it may be very difficult to get a manuscript accepted for publication in the most prestigious journals.

Having identified a few potential journals for an article, it is a good idea to examine the profile of each journal more closely to select one particular journal as the most relevant and interesting place for publishing the article. This journal's guidelines to authors should be examined to see how the manuscript should be written, edited and prepared for publishing. When the manuscript have been adapted to these guidelines, it may be sent to the journal editor and submitted for publication.

The manuscript is then reviewed by the editor and most often also by external referees. The main purpose of the review process is to ensure that the academic quality of the manuscript is high enough to be accepted as an article in the journal. The reviewers give a written evaluation of the manuscript and conclude with a recommendation to the editor. The conclusion may be that the paper should be accepted for publication as it is, or accepted for publication after some specified changes, or rejected. This review process may take several weeks and sometimes several months.

If the manuscript is accepted, it will be published. If it is accepted with revision, the author can change the manuscript according to the comments and then send it to the editor again for publication. It is advisable to follow up the comments very carefully, since the final manuscript will be examined thoroughly by the journal editor. The publishing process also takes a long time, from several weeks to several months.

If the manuscript is rejected, the usual strategy is to improve the paper and submit it for publication in another journal. The comments from the reviewers are useful, both for improving the paper, and for selecting an alternative journal.

An alternative to publishing in a journal is to submit the manuscript as a paper for presentation at an academic conference and subsequent publication in the conference proceedings. Then the first step is to identify a conference which is relevant for the particular paper. Like journals, conferences may be disciplinary or multidisciplinary, or they may be oriented towards particular topical areas or special research fields. Examples are the *British Sociological Association Annual Conference*, the *International Congress of Psychology*, the *International Conference on Interdisciplinary Social Science*, the *Association for Consumer Research Conference* and the *European Conference on Gender Equality in Higher Education*.

When a number of potential conferences have been identified, the profile and organization of each conference should be examined, in order to select a particular conference for presenting the paper. In due time before a conference, the conference organizers publish a 'call for papers', inviting scholars to submit abstracts or manuscripts for presentation at the conference. The call for papers specifies details on the conference, such as time, location, and instructions for submitting papers, including deadline, as well as length, format and style of the abstract and manuscript. The manuscript should be adapted to these instructions and sent to the organizer of the conference within the deadline. Sometimes there is a separate deadline for submitting only an abstract, and then a later deadline for submitting the full manuscript.

Conferences may have various kinds of review processes for accepting or rejecting papers that have been submitted for presentation. If the paper is accepted, a presentation of the paper is included in the conference programme with a specified time slot. Usually this time slot is not long enough to read the manuscript, so the presentation has to be limited to a brief overview of the main points. For this purpose it is useful to use some visualizations. How to make visualizations was described in Chapter 25.

If a paper is accepted for presentation at a conference, the full paper may be published in the conference proceedings, either before or after the conference. Sometimes, only the best papers at the conference are included in the published proceedings. This means that there is a special review process for the proceedings, in addition to the review process for the presentations.

A paper may be accepted with some required or recommended changes. Then the manuscript has to be revised according to these comments and resubmitted for presentation. If the paper is rejected, it is always possible to improve the paper and submit it for presentation at another conference.

The process of publishing an article as a book chapter in an anthology differs from the publishing process for journal articles and conference papers. First of all, there are fewer possibilities for publishing a book chapter than there are for publishing a journal article or for presenting a conference paper. It may be difficult to find a relevant book that is being planned. The most common procedure is that book editors select scholars whose research and qualifications they know, and invite these scholars to contribute chapters. Scholars who do not receive an invitation may, for example, use their networks, social media or other communication channels to distribute information about their potential contributions for anthologies, so that book editors become aware of these possibilities. Another alternative is to initiate and edit a whole anthology, where the particular manuscript may be included, in addition to contributions from colleagues or other scholars. Students who are writing theses about related topics, or different aspects of a more general social problem, may collaborate on editing an anthology, where parts of all their theses are collected and published.

Furthermore, networks and other communication channels as well as enquiries to publishers may be used to find information about anthologies that are being planned. If relevant book plans are identified, the editors may be contacted about the possibilities of including a particular manuscript in their books. If one or more editors are interested, a particular book may be selected for publishing of the manuscript. Based on further communication with the editor, the manuscript is adapted to the purpose and format of the book, and the manuscript is sent to the editor, who may reject it, accept it as it is, or accept it with some revisions.

If the paper is not rejected, it will be published in the book, either without revisions, or with the revisions that are required or recommended by the editor. If the paper is not accepted, alternative strategies for publishing should be considered.

Selecting and rewriting parts of a major report for journal articles, conference papers or book chapters may be a demanding task. However, it may be even more demanding to write a book based on the whole report. Nevertheless, using a thesis or other major report as a basis for a monograph may be a reasonable publishing strategy. The first step in the process of publishing a book is to identify potential publishers. The book catalogues of different publishers may be useful information about the types of books that are published by each publisher, and thus a good basis for considering where the manuscript is most likely to fit in.

The next step is to examine more thoroughly the profiles and guidelines of the potential publishers that have been identified, in order to select one of them as the most relevant and interesting publisher for the manuscript.

Most publishers want a proposal for the book before they decide whether or not they are interested in publishing. Typically, a proposal describes the purpose and content of the book, as well as considerations regarding the primary audience, the market potential, and the strengths of the planned book compared to similar and competing books in the market. Moreover, a typical proposal includes a working title of the book, a table of contents, a brief description of each chapter, a brief version of the author's curriculum vitae, and a plan for

delivery of the manuscript. Sometimes, drafts of a few chapters are attached to the proposal. However, each publisher has its own specific guidelines for proposals. It is important to write a proposal that is well adapted to the particular guidelines of the selected publisher.

When the proposal has been sent to the publisher, it is reviewed by one of the editors. It may also be sent to external referees, who are asked to evaluate the proposal. Compared to evaluations of manuscripts for journal articles, the evaluation of book proposals is usually based on a larger set of criteria. The proposal is evaluated according to criteria regarding the market potential of the book, readability of the text, and attractiveness to a wider audience, in addition to the criteria related to academic quality.

In order to meet all these criteria, a book that is based on a thesis or another major research report may differ significantly from the original thesis or report. For the book it may be necessary to exclude or rewrite some parts of the original text, and it may be appropriate to add some new chapters.

If the proposal is accepted with some required changes, it should be revised according to the specific requirements and resubmitted to the publisher. If it is accepted as it is, a contract for the book may be signed by the author and the publisher, and the major work with the manuscript can start. A usual procedure is to submit a draft of each chapter, to receive comments on the draft from the publisher, and to revise all chapters as well as the complete manuscript based on these comments.

If the proposal is rejected, it may be improved and sent to another publisher. Another alternative would be to publish parts of the thesis or report as one or more articles instead of publishing a book based on the whole report.

An overview of typical publishing processes for different types of manuscripts and different types of publications is presented in Table 26.5.

Table 26.5 Typical publishing processes for different types of manuscripts and different types of publications

Format of manuscript	Article (part of major report)			Major report
Type of publication	Journal article	Conference paper	Chapter in book (anthology)	Book (monograph)
Deciding how and where to publish	Identify potential journals	Identify potential conferences	Identify relevant books that are being planned	Identify potential publishers
	Examine profile and guidelines of journals	Examine 'call for papers' of the conferences	Contact editors of the books about possible inclusion of your manuscript	Examine publishers' profiles and guidelines
	Select a journal	Select a conference	Select a book	Select a publisher
Adapting to publication requirements	(Re)write the manuscript, adapted to journal guidelines	(Re)write abstract and manuscript, adapted to the call for papers	(Re)write the manuscript, adapted to the editor's instructions	Write a proposal, adapted to publisher guidelines
Submitting for evaluation	Send the manuscript to the journal editor	Send the abstract and/or the manuscript to the organizer of the conference	Send the manuscript to the book editor	Send the proposal to the publisher
Revising and resubmitting	If the manuscript is accepted with revisions, revise and resubmit it	If the manuscript is accepted with revisions, revise and resubmit it	If the manuscript is accepted with revisions, revise and resubmit it	If the proposal is accepted with revisions, revise and resubmit it
Submitting and publishing the final manuscript	If the manuscript is fully accepted, it will be published	If the manuscript is fully accepted, it may be presented at the conference and published in the conference proceedings	If the manuscript is fully accepted, it will be published	If the proposal is fully accepted, sign a contract, (re)write and submit the final manuscript, which will be published (perhaps after evaluation and revision of each chapter)

CHAPTER HIGHLIGHTS

- There are different reasons for writing about research, including scientific, societal and personal reasons.
- Students may have to write various kinds of essays as a basis for their learning, and as a part of their exams. The writing should be adapted to the conditions for the essay, and the students are advised to work carefully with the understanding and specification of the topic, the selection of sources, and the development of the message, ideas and arguments of the essay.

- In general, there are two basic formats for writing about research:
  - The *major report* format, including master's and doctoral theses
  - The *article* format, including journal articles, conference papers and book chapters.
- Writing about research is called academic writing.
- Features of the writing process include:

- o Starting the writing early in a research project, with a main writing process concentrated at the end of the project
- o Establishing good working conditions for the writing process
- o Planning the writing process well, with a realistic time schedule
- o Presenting an overall story or message in the report
- o Developing an outline before writing the full text
- o Dividing the text logically into paragraphs, sections, chapters and larger parts
- o Inserting references and documenting findings where it is appropriate
- o Revising drafts of the text, based on your own reading and comments from others.

- The style of academic texts is characterized by

  - o clarity, precision, formality, and consistency
  - o formal rules and common conventions in language, grammar, spelling and punctuation
  - o caution in the writing, such as using non-discriminatory language, balancing confidence and tentativeness, justifying assumptions and arguments, documenting assertions and findings, using correct references, and avoiding plagiarism.

- A typical research report is divided into four major parts:

  - o Introduction, including background, research question, and literature review
  - o Methodology, including research design, data, and methods for collection and analysis of data
  - o Results, including data analysis and findings
  - o Conclusion, including discussion of findings, major conclusions, limitations

of the study, and recommendations for further research.

- This basic structure is common for quantitative, qualitative and mixed methods research. However, reports on qualitative research are characterized by special emphasis on narrative perspectives, based on storytelling, with the researcher as storyteller. Reports on mixed methods research pay particular attention to the complementarity and integration of results based on different data and methods.
- Although this basic structure is focused on empirical reports, it is also relevant for theoretical and conceptual reports, with some adjustments.
- A thesis is based on research and written for a master's degree or PhD. Typically it is a coherent major report, but it may also consist of a set of articles and an introduction that relates the articles to each other and to the thesis as a whole.
- A PhD thesis is longer and more advanced than a master's thesis.
- Different universities and different degree programmes may have their own specific requirements regarding length, content, style and structure of theses.
- Articles are shorter, more focused and more concise than major reports. An article may be focused on a part of a thesis or another major report.
- A report written in the article format may be published in a journal, presented at a conference and included in conference proceedings, or included as a chapter in a book (anthology).
- A major report may be published as a book (monograph).
- The process of publishing includes deciding how and where to publish, adapting to publication requirements, submitting for evaluation, revising and resubmitting.

I recommend that you read the articles that are compared in Table 26.4:

Beckfield, Jason (2006) 'European integration and income inequality', *American Sociological Review* 71, 964–985.

Pritchard, Rosalind (2010b) 'Gender inequalities among staff in British and German universities: a qualitative study', *Compare* 40(4), 515–532.

Crosnoe, Robert, and Chandra Muller (2014) 'Family socioeconomic status, peers, and the path to college', *Social Problems* 61(4), 602–604.

All three articles deal with inequality. The article by Beckfield (2006) is based on a quantitative study of income inequality in European countries. Pritchard (2010b) writes about a qualitative study of gender inequality among university staff members in two European countries. The article by Crosnoe and Muller (2014) deals with educational inequality among high school students, based on a mixed methods study in the USA. The comparison of these articles shows that they are organized and structured in similar ways. There are differences between the articles as to how results and findings are documented or illustrated, and there are some differences in the extent to which subheadings are used to clarify the substantial content of various parts or elements of the article.

Furthermore, it is recommended to look at master's or PhD theses, to examine how they are written and organized. Those who are going to write a thesis for a degree at a particular university should read some previous theses within the same degree programme. Three examples of master's theses, and two examples of PhD theses are described here:

Weir, Roisin (2014) *Gender roles in leadership and management: A narrative enquiry based in the U.K.* Master's thesis, Umeå University, Sweden.

This master's thesis in management is focused on a qualitative study of gender roles among middle managers in the UK. It is based on an interpretivist approach, using hermeneutics combined with a constructionist view. The study is a narrative inquiry, using semi-structured interviews, where the respondents were asked to tell stories about their experiences with managers and being a manager themselves. In the thesis, men and women are compared as to their leadership styles. One of the conclusions is that men do not always have a masculine leadership style and women do not always have a feminine leadership style.

Schmid, Claudia Theresia (2016) *Germany's 'open-door' policy in light of the recent refugee crisis: An interpretive thematic content analysis of possible reasons and underlying motivations.* Master's thesis, Linköping University, Sweden.

This is a master's thesis in social science, which is based on a qualitative study of the refugee policy in Germany, related to the most recent refugee crisis in Europe. In order to understand the reason for this policy, a content analysis of national and international media as well as parliamentary debates is presented. The themes identified in the media and debates were further analysed within constructivist and structural realist perspectives. The thesis concludes that because Germany's highly internal-moral-driven identity aligned well with its capabilities and national interests, Germany was able to continuously pursue its 'open-door' refugee policy despite resistance from a vocal opposition.

Johnson, Lorraine M. (2001) *Factors that determine hospitalization of older adults.* Master's thesis, California State University, Long Beach. ProQuest Dissertations Publishing, 1404433.

This is a master's thesis in social work, which presents a quantitative study of why older adults are hospitalized. Survey data were collected from older adults participating in congregate nutrition programmes at senior centres. The empirical analysis is focused on the impact on hospitalization by different factors, including caregiving, hospitalization history, functional ability and demographics. The study confirms findings from previous research and supports arguments for further research on how to manage long-term care needs of older adults.

Liu, Lisha (2013) *A qualitative study of international students' experiences of engaging in learning on UK full-time taught masters programmes.* PhD thesis, Institute of Education, University of London. ProQuest Dissertations Publishing, 10022078.

This PhD thesis in education describes a qualitative study of learning engagement among international students, which is a large postgraduate student group in the UK. In-depth interviews were carried out among international students at three UK universities. Based on the empirical findings, the thesis presents a conceptual framework to describe the international students' experiences of engagement in learning. The students' time input and emotional involvement in learning are emphasized as components in this framework.

Algwil, Kamila (2016) *Learning experiences of Libyan master's students at a UK university: Intercultural adaptation and identity.* PhD thesis, University of Huddersfield. ProQuest Dissertations Publishing, 10293787.

This PhD thesis in education is based on a qualitative and interpretive study, which examines Libyan students' expectations, perceptions, perspectives, experiences and aspirations regarding the UK higher education system. Semi-structured interviews and observation were carried out among Libyan students who came to the UK after the civil war and ongoing conflict in Libya. The findings show a number of challenges for Libyan students in their new learning environment. Some challenges are common to all international students, whereas other challenges might be specific to this group of Libyan students, related to the consequences of civil war and ongoing conflict.

STUDENT EXERCISES AND QUESTIONS

1 Why is it important to write about research?
2 Describe the typical structure of a research report.
3 What are the main differences between a major report and an article?
4 How are findings documented in reports on quantitative research, and in reports on qualitative research?
5 Describe the typical steps in the process of publishing a major report as a book.
6 Select two articles in a social science journal, one based on quantitative research and one based on qualitative research. Identify differences between the two articles as to documentation of findings, and style and structure of the articles.
7 Find a master's thesis in social science that has been approved at your university. Clarify the structure of the thesis, and describe the main research contribution of the thesis. Discuss how this contribution is presented and emphasized in different parts of the thesis.

Becker, Lucinda (2014)P *Writing Successful Reports and Dissertations*. London: Sage.

This book provides advice and tips for the different stages of writing a report or a thesis, from the first questions, decisions and choices, through the preparations and planning of the writing process, to the writing of the text and the completion of the report or thesis.

Bui, Yvonne N. (2014) *How to Write a Master's Thesis*. London: Sage.

This book is a systematic and detailed guide to writing a thesis for a master's degree. It starts with an overview of the degree and the thesis. Then it discusses how to select a research topic, how to use the literature from previous research, and how to make sure that the research is ethical. Furthermore, the book describes how to write each chapter and to do the final formatting of the thesis.

Craswell, Gail, and Megan Poore (2012): *Writing for Academic Success* (2nd edn). London: Sage.

This book describes the process of academic writing and the features of academic texts in general, and it discusses the writing of different types of texts, including research essays, book reviews, online texts, coursework exams, literature reviews, research proposals, research reports, theses, and conference presentations. The book also includes a chapter on publishing.

Joyner, Randy L., William A. Rouse, and Allan A. Glatthorn (2013): *Writing the Winning Thesis or Dissertation: A Step-by-Step Guide* (3rd edn). London: Sage.

This book deals with the whole process of writing a thesis, including how to prepare the research and the writing process, how to develop a proposal for the thesis, how to conduct the research, how to write each part of the thesis, and how to publish results from the thesis.

GLOSSARY

Absolute frequency   The number of units registered with a certain value on a variable.

Action research   Research based on collaboration between the researcher and special (usually weak) groups, partly for studying these groups' conditions, partly for developing actions for improving these conditions. Action research implies a continuous switching between research and action.

Actor   Acting social unit. An actor may be an individual or a group of individuals, for example a family, an organization, a company, a municipality or a nation. In social science studies actors are common as units of analysis. Actors are also one of three main types of sources in social research.

Additive index   A special type of index that is constructed by adding up the values of all the variables (indicators) included in the index, so that a unit's value on the index equals the sum of the values of the indicators.

Aggregated variable   A variable in multi-level analysis that is constructed based on units at one level and used in the analysis to describe features of units at a *higher* level.

Analysis of variance   A set of methods for decomposing variance within and between different groups, for analysing differences between the groups. Analysis of variance is the basis for the *F*-test, which is used in significance testing, for example in regression analysis. This is also called ANOVA.

Analytical induction   Method for generating theory based on analysis of qualitative data.

ANOVA   Abbreviation for *analysis of variance*.

Applied research   Research carried out with the intention of using the results for particular purposes in society.

Asymmetrical relation   A relation between two actors which has a different significance for the two actors. The actors have different value or strength in the relation, or one actor has power or influence over the other actor.

Atomistic fallacy   Conclusions drawn about conditions at a certain level, based on data about conditions at a *lower* level.

Automated content analysis   Using computers and special computer programs for the coding in quantitative content analysis. Automated content analysis may be used for content analysis of big data, such as data based on social media.

Bar chart   Visual presentation of a distribution, where each value of the variable is represented by a horizontal or vertical line (bar or column), and where the length of these lines shows the proportion of the units for each value.

Basic research   Research conducted for developing theories, methods and researcher qualifications. Such research is often initiated by the researchers themselves and motivated by their curiosity. Basic research is justified by challenges for scientific advancements rather than particular needs in society.

Betweenness   Measure of an actor's centrality in a network. Actors are central if their position in the network is between many other actors.

Big data   Data characterized by large volume, high velocity and great variety, including, for example, data from social media, large registers, or various forms of digital sources.

Big data study   Study based on big data.

Biographical study   Study of the life histories of individuals, typically based on qualitative data and focused on important or critical events in the individuals' lives.

Bivariate relationship   Relationship between two variables.

Case study   Intensive study of only one unit of analysis (case), or a few units (cases) that are compared.

Categorical data   Non-metric data expressed in numbers, typically data based on nominal or ordinal level of measurement.

Categorization   Dividing a set of data into different categories. The term is especially relevant in qualitative analysis.

Category   A class of phenomena with certain common features. A category includes all the units that have a particular position on a dimension.

Causal analysis   Analysis of causal relationships.

Causal hypothesis   Hypothesis about causal relations between two or more phenomena.

Causal model   Conceptual model where the causal variables and effect variables are presented as boxes, and where the causal relationships are presented as arrows from the causal variables to the effect variables.

Causal relationship   Relationship between two phenomena where one of the phenomena (the cause) with a high probability leads to the other phenomenon (the effect). The relationship requires an empirical non-spurious covariation between the two phenomena. Furthermore, the assumed cause must occur or exist before the assumed effect, and there must be sufficient proximity in time between the two phenomena.

Central tendency   Statistical measure showing which value on a variable is most central in the distribution of unit on this variable. The central tendency can be expressed as mode, median or mean.

Centrality   Statistical measure for a feature of an actor's position in a network. Centrality can be expressed in different ways, for example as degree, normalized degree centrality, or betweenness.

Centralization   Statistical measure of a feature of social networks. Centralization refers to centrality differences between the actors in the network.

Chart   A typical form of data visualization.

Chi-square test   Method for hypothesis testing, used in table analysis.

Closed-ended question   Question in a questionnaire with fixed response options.

Cluster sampling   Probability sampling where all units in the universe are divided into clusters, based on physical or geographical proximity of units within each cluster. Then clusters of units, rather than individual units, are randomly sampled.

Codebook   Overview of all the variables and values in a quantitative data set, including the criteria and rules for completing the data matrix. The codebook shows which numbers should be entered into the data matrix for different values of the different variables.

Coding schedule   Schedule for data recording in quantitative studies. Coding schedules are especially important in quantitative content analysis.

Cognitive question   Question (in a questionnaire) about facts or actual circumstances.

Cohort analysis   Analysis of time series data with reference to the respondents' age at the different times. The purpose is to examine changes within each birth cohort. A birth cohort consists of the people born at the same time.

Communicative validity   A type of validity in qualitative research, based on dialogue and discussion between the researcher and others about whether the data are good and appropriate for the research questions addressed in the study. Communicative validity may be based on collegial validation or actor validation.

Comparative study   Study of similarities and differences between social conditions at different places or in different contexts, such as two or more organizations, local communities or countries. Such studies require equivalent or comparable data on the conditions within the communities or contexts that are compared.

Competence validity   A type of validity in qualitative research, based on the researcher's competence for collecting and analysing qualitative data in the research area for the study.

Computational social science   A subfield of social research, which is focused on using computers and big data for analysing social networks, social geographic systems, as well as content of social media and traditional media.

Concept   Name given to a particular type of phenomena, or those phenomena that are included in a particular category.

Conceptual equivalence   Equivalence as to the meaning of social science concepts in societies that are compared in comparative research.

Condensation   Method in qualitative analysis for presenting the content of the data in an abbreviated or condensed form. The purpose is to develop a holistic understanding by means of a concentrated description of the essential meaning in the original data.

Conditional distribution   The distribution on a variable of those units that have a particular value on another variable, or a particular combination of values on two or more other variables.

Confidence interval   Term in estimation referring to the distance between the estimated minimum value and the estimated maximum value in the universe for a particular feature of the units in the sample.

Constant comparative method   A special method for analysing qualitative data, based on coding and categorization, often with the aim of developing grounded theory.

Construct validity   A type of definitional validity that shows the extent to which the relationship between indicators for different concepts corresponds to the known relationship between these concepts.

Content validity   A type of definitional validity that shows how adequate the operational definition of a concept is for the theoretical content of the concept.

Context effect   Effect of previous questions on the response to a particular question in a questionnaire. This is also called the sequence effect.

Context unit   The part of the text in a quantitative content analysis which has to be read through to assess which category should be selected when a particular variable is mentioned.

Contextual analysis   A type of multi-level analysis where phenomena at one level in society are examined in light of phenomena at higher levels. The phenomena at higher levels are regarded as contextual conditions for the phenomena at lower levels.

Contextual equivalence   Equivalence with regard to the contextual meaning of particular phenomena or conditions in those communities which are compared in a comparative study.

Contextual variable   A variable in a multi-level study that is constructed with reference to units at one level and used in the analysis as an expression of features of units at a lower level.

Contract research   Applied research that is ordered and financed by resourceful and powerful organizations or institutions in public administration, business or other sectors in society. The typical intention of those who order such research is to obtain a better basis for their decisions and activity in business and society.

Control effect   Effect of actors' reactions to being involved in a study, which means that actors' behaviour in the research situation is different from their usual behaviour. Thus, the data about the behaviour may be biased. This is also called *reactivity*.

Control group   A group of units in an experiment which is not exposed to the assumed causal variable but compared with the experimental group.

Correlation analysis   Quantitative analysis intended to calculate one statistical measure (correlation coefficient) as an expression of the relationship (correlation) between two variables.

Correlation coefficient   Statistical measure that expresses the relationship (correlation) between two variables. The coefficient varies between –1 and +1.

Correspondence analysis   Multivariate statistical technique that summarizes the information in cross tables for presentation in graphical visualizations.

Covariance   Statistical measure of dispersion of units that is common for different variables.

Criterion validity   A type of definitional validity that refers to the consistency between different indicators for the same concept.

Critical test   Empirical test of two theories used as alternative and contradicting explanations of particular phenomena in society. At least one of the theories has to be rejected by the empirical analysis of these phenomena.

Cross-level fallacy   A conclusion about conditions at one level based on data about conditions at a different level.

Data   Information, or empirical evidence, that is systematically collected and recorded in a particular form and for the purpose of particular analyses. There are different types of data. The distinction between qualitative and quantitative data is particularly important.

Data matrix   Large matrix or table for organizing the whole data set in a quantitative study. The matrix includes one row for each unit and one or more columns for each variable. The units' values on the variables are shown as numbers (codes) in the cells of the matrix.

Data scraping   Using search engines and programs to find online sources and data for social science studies.

Data visualization   Illustration of selected data or empirical findings by means of images or figures, in order to create accurate, clear and effective presentations to an audience of readers or viewers. Data visualizations may also be used in data analysis, especially for analysing big data.

Deductive research   Studies focusing on formulation of research questions and theory testing. Specific research questions are deduced or derived from the theory to be tested. In many cases, these research questions are formulated as hypotheses. Then the design is considered to be hypothetico-deductive.

Definitional validity   The consistency between the theoretical definition and the operational definition of a concept. Definitional validity can be specified in three ways: content validity, criterion validity and construct validity.

Degree   Measure of the centrality of actors in a social network, defined as the number of direct relations between this actor and other actors in the network.

Density   Statistical measure of a feature of social networks. Density shows the number of relations in the network as a proportion of the theoretically possible number of relations between all actors in the network.

Dependent variable   The variable included in an analysis of relationships which is assumed to be influenced by one or more other (independent) variables.

Descriptive statistics   Statistical methods used to identify, describe and characterize actual patterns or trends in the data being analysed.

Diachronic data   Data about the same phenomena or conditions at multiple times.

Dimension   A particular component of a concept, or a particular property of social units.

Discourse analysis   A special form of qualitative content analysis for developing holistic understanding of communication processes. A constructionist approach focusing on understanding of discourses as systems of ideas, beliefs, assumptions and concepts about social conditions and social reality.

Dispersion   Statistical measure of variation in a univariate distribution showing the extent to which the units are spread across different values, or the extent to which they are clustered around the mode, median or mean. The dispersion can be expressed as standardized modal percentage, quartile deviation, variance or standard deviation.

Distribution   Overview of the frequencies for all values on a variable.

Document   One of three main types of sources in social research. Documents include written texts, audio recordings, visual materials, audio-visual presentations, as well as digital texts, sounds, images and videos.

Drop-out   The units in an original sample that are not included in the final data set.

Ecological fallacy   Conclusions drawn about conditions at a certain level, based on data about conditions at a *higher* level. This is also called aggregative fallacy.

Empirical evidence   Information, facts or data about actual conditions in society, based on our experiences of these social conditions.

Epistemology   The study of knowledge, focusing on how knowledge is developed, the sources of knowledge and the conditions for knowledge development.

Equivalence problem   Problem related to comparability or equivalence between societies that are compared in comparative research.

Estimation   Method of statistical generalization. The starting point for estimation is a particular finding regarding a characteristic of the sample, such as the percentage of EU opponents or the mean income in the sample. The estimation is based on calculating a probable minimum value and a probable maximum value (the confidence interval) for the corresponding feature in the universe. The estimated confidence interval depends on the level of confidence that is chosen for the estimation.

Evaluative question   Question in a questionnaire about the respondent's values or evaluations.

Experiment   Research design for analyses of causal relationships under strictly controlled conditions. In the simplest form of an experiment, the units of analysis are randomly divided in two groups: an experimental group, which is exposed to an assumed causal variable, and a control group, which is not exposed to this variable. The two groups are compared before and after the experimental group's exposure to the causal variable. If the two groups have become more different, this change is regarded as an effect of the causal variable.

Experimental group   Group of units in an experiment that is exposed to the assumed causal varable.

Explained variance   The proportion of the total dispersion (variance) of the dependent variable that is explained by the independent variables in a regression analysis.

Exploratory study   Preliminary study, sometimes called a pilot study, which may be conducted before a more systematic study, often in areas with little previous research.

External validity   A type of validity that is especially relevant for experimental studies. External validity means that the results of the experiment are realistic and can be generalized to situations and conditions in society, so that a conclusion about a causal relationship is valid not only under the strictly controlled experimental conditions, but also in real social circumstances.

Factor analysis   Quantitative analysis of relationships between several variables at the interval or ratio level. The purpose is to identify different groups of variables (factors) where there are strong relationships between the variables within each group and weak relationships between variables in different groups.

Field   Area where the data collection in a study takes place. The term is most common in ethnography, participant observation and field research.

Field note   Note or memo used for recording and analysing data in participant observation. We distinguish between three types of field notes: observation notes, analytical notes and methodological notes.

Field observation   Structured observation of actors in their natural environment.

Field relation   The researcher's relation to different actors in participant observation.

Field research   Research based on combinations of different sources, data and methods, with particular emphasis on participant observation.

Focus group   Group of persons who participate together in unstructured interviewing. The interviewing is conducted as a discussion in the group, which is moderated by the researcher. The purpose is to utilize this group dynamics to obtain a variety of views, opinions and creative reflections on a number of selected topics.

Frequency   The number of units that are registered with a particular value on a variable.

F-test   Method of testing statistical significance, based on analysis of variance (ANOVA). The *F*-test is used, for example in regression analysis, for testing the significance for a whole group of regression coefficients or for the whole regression equation.

Gamma   Correlation coefficient for the relationship between two variables at the ordinal level. Gamma shows the extent to which the units in a study are rank-ordered similarly or differently on the two variables that are analysed.

Generation effect   Change over time shown as differences between cohorts. Such change is also called the cohort effect.

Global variable   Variable referring to only one level in a in a multi-level analysis.

Graphical scale   Scale where the differences between the categories are visually illustrated, for example in the form of temperature scales or other analogies. Graphical scales are often used in questionnaires, especially for examining attitudes or evaluations. Then the scale is called a graphical rating scale.

Gross sample   The (original) sample in a study, for example a probability sample drawn for a survey.

Grounded theory   A type of empirically based theory that may be developed in analysis of qualitative data, often based on analytical induction.

Haphazard sampling   Strategic sampling of units that happen to be available in a particular place at a particular time.

Hermeneutical study   Study based on interpretation and understanding of the meaning of different actions. Such studies are conducted in many research fields within social science. Hermeneutical analyses assume that all understanding is based on various types of preconception, and that no phenomena can be understood independently of the greater whole of which they are a part.

Historical-comparative study   Study focusing on comprehensive and complex research questions, often with emphasis on stability and change at different levels in different societies. Such studies combine the perspectives of time, space and level in the same analysis.

Hypothesis   Statement about social phenomena that can be examined and tested empirically. Typically, the hypothesis is formulated as an expected relationship between two or more variables.

Hypothesis testing   Method of statistical generalization. The purpose is to test whether a particular relationship in a probability sample of units is strong enough to be regarded as valid for the whole universe of these units.

Ideal type   Representation of a particular phenomenon, where the most important and most typical features of the phenomenon are isolated, highlighted and described in an idealized or pure form. An ideal type therefore functions roughly like a model. Weber's description of the bureaucracy as an ideal type is an example.

Idiographic study   Study focusing on individual phenomena or social conditions that are clearly defined in time and space. The purpose is to identify and understand the distinctive and unique characteristics of the specific conditions studied. This knowledge is believed to be valid only for the circumstances that are actually studied.

Independent variable   A variable in an analysis of relationships that is assumed to influence one or more other variables (dependent variables).

Index   Combination of two or more variables. The variables included in the index are called *indicators*.

Indicator   A variable that is included in an index.

Indigenous research   Research about and for indigenous peoples, such as the Aborigines in Australia, the Inuit and Native Americans in North America, and the Sámi people in the Nordic countries.

Inductive research   Studies focusing on interpretation of empirical findings for generating new theory. A particular theoretical understanding is induced or constructed based on the empirical analyses that are conducted.

Inductive statistics   Statistical methods for generalizing from a probability sample of units to the whole universe of these units.

Internal validity   A type of validity that is especially relevant for experimental studies. Internal validity refers to the validity of the experiment itself, so that a conclusion about a causal relationship is valid under the strictly controlled experimental conditions.

Inter-subjectivity method   Method for assessing the reliability, especially in quantitative studies. The method entails comparisons of data on the same phenomenon collected by different persons using the same instrument for the data collection.

Interval level   Level of measurement for variables or indexes that provide information about distances between values.

Interview guide   Description of how an unstructured interview is to be implemented, with emphasis on a list of general topics to be covered in the interview.

Laboratory observation   A type of structured observation, conducted under controlled conditions.

Latent content   The content of a text as it can be understood in light of a larger context. The latent content of a part of a text has to be understood in the context of a larger part of the text or the whole text.

Leading question   Question in a questionnaire where the formulation of the question or the construction of the response options leads the respondents towards particular response options.

Level of measurement   Feature of variables and indexes, referring to how nuanced and detailed the information provided by the variable or index is, and which methods can be used to analyse this information. We distinguish between four levels of measurement: nominal, ordinal, interval and ratio level.

Level of significance   In hypothesis testing, the probability of being wrong when we reject the null hypothesis. Usually we choose a level of significance of 0.05 ($p<0.05$).

Life phase effect   Change over time (between life phases) within each cohort. This is also called the age effect.

Likert scale   A type of composite scale in questionnaires where the respondent is asked to express degrees of agreement or disagreement with statements about a particular phenomenon.

Line chart   A type of visualization, used for presenting distributions on interval- or ratio-level varibles, relationships between variables, or trends over time.

Linguistic equivalence   Equivalence with regard to whether the same words and expressions have the same meaning across the societies that are compared in a comparative analysis.

Literature search   Search for literature at libraries or on the Internet, especially for writing literature reviews, developing new research questions, or discussing new research findings. The purpose is to systematize and present overviews of previous research in a particular area.

Logistic regression   A special type of regression analysis where the dependent variable is a dichotomy (variable with the values 0 and 1).

Longitudinal study   Study of processes, changes or development over time. Such studies require collection and analysis of comparable data at different time points or continuous observation of phenomena during a certain time period.

Manifest content   Content of a text as it appears directly of the formulation of the text. Particular words or phrases express the same manifest content whenever they are used in the text.

Macro level   Level of analysis referring to large and complex units, for example countries or states.

Margin of error   Estimated size of the random error in a probability sample for a certain level of confidence.

Meso level   Level of analysis, between micro and macro level, referring to units with varying size and complexity, for example organizations.

Methodological collectivism   A position in the theory of science arguing that the entirety that comprises society is different and more than the sum of the parts that make up that society, and that information about individuals is not sufficient as a basis for knowledge about social contexts or society at large.

Methodological equivalence   Equivalence with regard to how methods function in the different communities or contexts that are compared in a comparative study.

Methodological individualism   A position in the theory of science arguing that all social science knowledge must be based on knowledge about individuals and those situations, activities and attitudes which are related to individuals.

Methodological relationism   A position in the theory of science arguing that knowledge about social conditions cannot be based solely on the characteristics of individuals or of structures, but rather on relations between these levels and their distinctive characteristics.

Methodological situationalism   A position in the theory of science arguing that broader institutional and structural patterns in society cannot be understood only by examining individuals' actions or only by observing the institutions or structures as separate units of analysis. Knowledge of such patterns should be based on information about the specific interaction involved in the patterns and the specific social situations in which the interaction takes place.

Methodological triangulation   Combination of different data and methods, typically combination of qualitative and quantitative data, within one study. This is also called *mixed methods research*.

Methodology   The fundamental approaches or ways of thinking and understanding that underlie the development and utilization of different methods. Methodology refers to the fundamental approaches or ways of thinking and understanding that underlie the development and utilization of different methods.

Micro level   Level of analysis referring to small and simple units, for example individuals.

Mixed methods research   Combination of different data and methods, typically combination of qualitative and quantitative data, within one study. This is also called *methodological triangulation*.

Metric data   Quantitative data based on variables with interval or ratio level of measurement.

Model   A simplified and streamlined presentation of selected societal phenomena, highlighting the key features of these phenomena, while omitting other aspects of the phenomena.

Multi-level study   Study that includes units at two or more levels in society, with emphasis on analyses of the relationship between different levels.

Multiplex relation   Relation between two actors, which includes two or more types of content.

Narrative analysis A type of qualitative analysis implying that the text being analysed is organized or systematized with reference to typical elements in a story or narrative. This type of analysis is particularly suitable for establishing a comprehensive understanding of specific sequences or processes.

Narrative review A type of literature review typically used for developing research questions for new studies. There are four types of narrative reviews: general reviews, theoretical reviews, methodological reviews, and historical reviews.

Netnography Online fieldwork in ethnography.

Net sample The sample that remains after adjustments of the gross sample. Adjusting the gross sample means removing the units which are no longer in the universe, for example persons who have moved or passed away.

Network component A part of a network where all actors have direct or indirect relations to each other, but no relations to other actors in the network.

Nominal level Level of measurement for variables or indexes referring to differences between units.

Nomothetic study Study focusing on general relationships and patterns which are not limited to particular historical periods or particular geographical areas. The purpose is to develop general theories about conditions and relationships that are common to larger classes or categories of phenomena in society.

Normal distribution Symmetrical distribution with the highest frequency on the mean value. The frequencies are gradually reduced with both increasing and decreasing values from the mean value of the variable. This is also called a bell curve.

Normative study Study based on particular values, examining questions about how conditions in society should be (according to the particular values).

Null hypothesis Hypothesis formulated in hypothesis testing. To test a hypothesis on a particular relationship between variables, we formulate a null hypothesis stating that there is no relationship between the variables.

Observation schedule Schedule used for data recording in structured observation.

Online fieldwork Fieldwork conducted on the Internet, typically for online participant observation. The researcher participates in communication in online forums or groups while observing the activities in these forums or groups. Online fieldwork in ethnography is called *netnography*.

Online focus group Focus group discussion conducted by e-mail or on the Internet.

Online interview Unstructured interview conducted by means of e-mail or on the Internet.

Ontology The study of being, existence and reality. In social science, ontological discussions include considerations on the existence of different social phenomena.

Open-ended question   Question in a questionnaire without fixed response options.

Operationalization   Formulation of operational definitions, in terms of criteria for how units, concepts or relationships will be represented by empirical data.

Ordinal level   Level of measurement for variables with a particular order between the values.

Panel data   Survey data based on the same questionnaire and the same respondents at different time points.

Path analysis   Quantitative analysis of direct and indirect causal relationships in complex causal models.

Participant observation   Qualitative study based on direct observation of actors. The researcher participates in the social processes that are examined, and this participation is combined with observation of the other actors and the relations among them.

Pearson's *r*   Correlation coefficient showing to what extent there is a linear relationship between two variables at interval or ratio level.

Percentage difference   Measure of the strength of the relationship between the variables in a table analysis. The percentage difference shows the difference between the conditional distributions in a table.

Person-centred analysis   Qualitative analysis for holistic understanding of each person included in the study.

Phenomenological study   Study based on interpretation and understanding of the meaning of different actions. Such studies are mainly focused on actions and experiences in people's everyday lives and assume that reality is defined by the actors' own perceptions of what is real.

Pie chart   Visualization of distributions. The pie chart is a circle divided into sectors, where each sector represents a value on a variable. The proportion of all units having this value on the variable is equal to the sector's proportion of the whole circle.

Plagiarism   Copying and publishing texts written by other authors.

Population   All units included in or covered by a research question. This is also called a *universe*.

Population study   Study including all units in the population.

Positivism   A position in the theory of science, arguing that social scientific knowledge is developed through systematic studies of 'positively given' empirical facts about existing phenomena in society. It is assumed that these phenomena exist as observable and objective facts, that they cannot be influenced or changed by being observed and examined, and that the same methods can be used in both social science and natural science.

Postmodernism   A position in the theory of science arguing that conditions in society are fragmented, heterogeneous and diverse, and that there are no consistent, comprehensive or holistic patterns that can be defined unanimously as reality or social facts. It is assumed that there is not one, but many realities, and that there is no reality apart from those texts or stories that attempt to describe reality in different ways.

Pragmatic validity   A type of validity, especially in qualitative research, showing the extent to which the data and the results of a study form the basis for particular actions.

Pretest   A test of the instrument for data collection before the data collection starts. Pretests are especially common in quantitative studies.

Probability sample   Sample where all units in the universe have a known probability (higher than 0 and lower than 1) of being included.

Qualitative content analysis   Qualitative study based on documents as data source. Selected documents, such as texts, images, audio recordings, videos or digital materials, are systematized for examining particular research questions.

Qualitative data   Data that are usually expressed as text.

Quantitative content analysis   Quantitative study based on documents as data source. The content of selected documents, such as texts, images, audio recordings, videos or digital materials, is systematically examined and recorded in a structured coding schedule.

Quantitative data   Data expressed as numbers or other terms of quantities, such as many – few, more – less, or high – low.

Quota sampling   Strategic sampling based on dividing the units into different categories and sampling a certain number of units (quota) within each category.

Random error   Difference between a probability sample and the universe, which is result of only the sampling.

Ratio level   Level of measurement for variables or indexes that has a meaningful or natural zero value and provides information about proportion between values, for example age or income.

Reactivity   Effect of actors' reactions to being involved in a study, which means that actors' behaviour in the research situation is different from their usual behaviour. Thus, the data about the behaviour may be biased. This is also called the *control effect*.

Recall data   Qualitative or quantitative data based on questioning respondents about previous actions, opinions, events or conditions.

Recoding   Merging or grouping of two or more values on a variable.

Reflexivity   Effect of the researcher's background, experiences, frame of reference and way of thinking on the results of a study and the knowledge obtained in social research.

Regression analysis   Quantitative analysis of relationships between one dependent variable and one or more independent variables.

Regression coefficient   Statistical measure in regression analysis. The regression coefficient shows how steeply the regression line rises or falls in the scattergram. The coefficient is a measure of the relationship between the dependent variable and a particular independent variable.

Regression line   Visual representation of the relationship between variables in a regression analysis. The regression line is the straight line in the scattergram that best fits all the units in the data set.

Relation   Connection or tie between two actors.

Relative frequency   Frequency shown as a proportion, usually percentage, of all units in the distribution.

Reliability   Term referring to the accuracy or trustworthiness of the data. The reliability is high if the research design and data collection provide accurate data. Reliability manifests itself by the fact that we get identical data if we use the same design and methods for different collections of data about the same phenomena.

Research ethics   A set of norms and rules that ensures that research is based on acceptable moral standards.

Research question   A question about conditions in society to be examined and answered in a study. A research question can be formulated as a topic, a question, or a hypothesis.

Respondent   A person who answers questions in a questionnaire or in unstructured interviewing.

Response rate   The percentage of the net sample in a survey which is included in the final data set.

Sampling frame   Concrete overview of the units contained in the universe, typically a list of all the units, and in some cases also an overview of location or certain characteristics for each unit in the universe.

Scale   A set of categories, for example response options in a questionnaire, that are arranged in relation to each other in such a way that they form a variable at the ordinal, interval or ratio level.

Scattergram   Graph illustrating the dispersion of the units in a study in relation to two variables.

Secondary analysis   New analysis (reuse) of available data.

Self-selection sampling   Strategic sample based on selection of actors (persons) who volunteer to participate in the study.

Simple random sampling   Probability sampling based on random selection of units from a list of the units in the universe.

Snowball sampling Strategic sampling where the first actor selected is asked to propose a number of other actors who can also be included in the sample. These are in turn asked to propose additional actors for the sample, and so on in several steps.

Social network A pattern of relations between individuals or other actors, for example organizations.

Social structure A relatively stable pattern of relations between social positions. Social networks may be regarded as social structures.

Sociogram Visual representation of a social network, where the actors are shown as points, and the relations between the actors are illustrated as lines between the points.

Sociomatrix Representation of a social network, where the relations between the actors are expressed as numbers in the cells of a matrix.

Source Basis for information or data about phenomena and conditions in society. We distinguish between three main types of sources in social science: actors, respondents and documents.

Source-critical assessment Systematic assessment of whether, and how, data sources can be used in a study, emphasizing the sources' availability, relevance, authenticity,= and credibility.

Split-half method Method for assessing reliability, especially in quantitative studies. The method entails comparisons of data based on different indicators in the same index.

Spurious relationship Statistical relationship between two variables that is actually due to relationships between each of the two variables and a third variable. The statistical relationship between the two original variables will disappear when we control for the third variable.

Statistical generalization Conclusion about phenomena and conditions in a universe based on empirical studies about these phenomena and conditions in a probability sample of units from the universe. Statistical generalization is used in quantitative studies, often for testing hypotheses or theories.

Statistical relationship Relationship between two (or more) variables shown as a probability that units with particular values on one of the variables will have particular values also on the other variable(s). This is also called statistical covariation or statistical correlation.

Strategic sampling Sampling based on systematic or strategic considerations of which units are most relevant and most interesting to include in a particular study. The strategic considerations are related to the research questions as well as theoretical and analytical purposes of the study.

Stratified sampling Probability sampling where all units in the universe are divided into categories (strata), based on particular characteristics of the units. Then individual units are (proportionally or disproportionally) randomly sampled from each of these strata.

Structured observation   Quantitative study based on direct observation of actors, with emphasis on selected types of activities, opinion statements or events, which are recorded in a structured observation schedule. Structured observation may be used in field observation, field experiments or laboratory experiments.

Structured questioning   Quantitative study based on questioning of respondents, typically as a survey with a probability sample. The questioning is based on a questionnaire where the questions and most of the response options are fixed.

Survey   Study using a questionnaire for structured questioning of a probability sample of respondents, typically to obtain representative overviews of general conditions in society.

Survey experiment   Survey conducted as an experiment. The sample is randomly divided into different groups (experimental and control groups), which are exposed to different information or different attempts at persuasion in the questionnaire. Such information is typically presented in various types of vignette questions. By comparing the groups' answers we can identify possible effects of the particular information given to each experimental group.

Symmetrical relation   A relation between two actors which is equally significant for both actors, or reflects equivalence between the two actors.

Synchronic data   Data about phenomena and conditions at one time point.

Systematic review   A type of literature review, often presented as a stand-alone study. There are three types of systematic reviews: meta-analysis of quantitative studies, meta-synthesis of qualitative studies, and mixed methods research synthesis of both qualitative and quantitative studies as well as mixed methods studies.

Systematic sampling   Probability sampling that includes every nth unit on a list of all the units in the universe, where the first unit is randomly drawn from among the n first units on the list.

Table analysis   Quantitative analysis of relationships between two or more variables in contingency tables (cross tables).

Temporal chart   Visual presentation of trends and development over time, for example a line chart showing lines for different phenomena based on time series data.

Temporal fallacy   Conclusions drawn about development or change, based on data for only one time point (synchronous data).

Test–retest method   Method for assessing reliability, especially in quantitative studies. The method entails comparisons of data on the same phenomenon collected at different times using the same instrument for the data collection.

Time series data   Comparable data about particular phenomena or conditions at different times.

Split-half method Method for assessing reliability, especially in quantitative studies. The method entails comparisons of data based on different indicators in the same index.

Theme-centred analysis Qualitative analysis for obtaining an overall understanding of what characterizes each theme included in the study.

Theoretical generalization Assumption that results of a qualitative study based on a strategic sample are valid in a more general context and for a larger universe of units. This assumption is based on assessments of the empirical findings in connection with previous research and established theories, as well as discussions of the empirical patterns in light of the strategic selection of units and types of information in the study.

Theory Systematic reflection on social conditions. A set or system of concepts and relationships that are in a mutual relationship with each other, and which summarize and arrange preconditions, assumptions and knowledge about society.

***t*-test** Method for testing statistical significance in correlation analysis or regression analysis.

Type I error Rejecting a null hypothesis that is correct. In hypothesis testing it is important to avoid too large a Type I error.

Type II error Accepting a null hypothesis that is not correct. In hypothesis testing Type II error is regarded as less important than Type I error.

Typology A set of types that are arranged in a logical relationship to each other, and in relation to one or more general dimensions.

Typology-based index A special type of index where the selection of variables and value combinations for the index are based on logical and theoretical considerations.

Uniplex relation Relation between two actors which includes only one type of content.

Unit of analysis The social unit, or element in society, which is the focus of a social science study.

Unit of observation The unit that is directly examined in a study. The unit of observation and the unit of analysis in a study may be identical or different.

Universe All units included in or covered by a research question. This is also called a *population*.

Unstructured interviewing Qualitative study based on questioning of respondents. The questioning is conducted in a conversation between the interviewer (typically the researcher) and each respondent. The conversation is based on an interview guide, with emphasis on a list of general topics that are to be covered in the interview.

Validity   The adequacy or relevance of the data for the research questions and the phenomena to be examined. Validity is high if the research design and the data collection result in data that are relevant to the research questions. Validity is an expression of how well the actual data correspond to the researcher's intentions with the research design and data collection.

Variable   Characteristic or property of units in a quantitative analysis. Differences between units with regard to a particular variable are expressed as different values on this variable.

Web survey   Survey where the respondents receive, complete and return the questionnaire online, by e-mail or on the Internet.

REFERENCES

Ackland, Robert (2013) *Web Social Science: Concepts, Data and Tools for Social Scientists in the Digital Age*. London: Sage.

Algwil, Kamila (2016) *Learning experiences of Libyan master's students at a UK university: Intercultural adaptation and identity*. PhD thesis, University of Huddersfield. ProQuest Dissertations Publishing, 10293787.

Alver, Bente Gullveig, Tove Ingebjørg Fjell, and Ørjar Øyen (eds) (2007) *Research Ethics in Studies of Culture and Social Life*. Helsinki: Suomalainen Tiedeakatemia.

Andreassen, Cecilie Schou, Mark D. Griffiths, Jørn Hetland, Luca Kravina, Fredrik Jensen, and Ståle Pallesen (2014) 'The prevalence of workaholism: A survey study in a nationally representative sample of Norwegian employees', *PLoS One 9*(8), e102446.

Armsworth, Mary Witham (1989) 'Therapy of incest survivors: Abuse or support?', *Child Abuse & Neglect 13*, 549–562.

Atzmüller, Christiane, and Peter M. Steiner (2010) 'Experimental vignette studies in survey research', *Methodology 6*(3), 128–138.

Bales, Robert F. (1952) 'Some uniformities in behavior in small social systems', in Guy E. Swanson, Theodore M. Newcomb, and Eugene L. Hartley (eds), *Readings in Social Psychology* (rev. edn). New York: Holt, Rinehart and Winston, pp. 146–159.

Balderrama, Rafael, and Hilario Molina II (2009) 'How good are networks for migrant job seekers? Ethnographic evidence from North Carolina farm labor camps', *Sociological Inquiry 79*(2), 190–218.

Barnes, John (1954) 'Class and committee in a Norwegian island parish', *Human Relations 7*, 39–58.

Barthes, Roland (1977) 'The rhetoric of the image', in Roland Barthes, *Image – Music – Text. Essays Selected and Translated by Stephen Heath*. London: Collins, pp. 32–51.

Becker, Howard S. (2007) *Writing for Social Scientists: How to Start and Finish your Thesis, Book, or Article* (2nd edn, with a chapter by Pamela Richards). Chicago: University of Chicago Press.

Beckert, Jens, and Mark Lutter (2012) 'Why the poor play the lottery: Sociological approaches to explaining class-based lottery play', *Sociology 47*(6), 1152–1170.

Beckfield, Jason (2005) *The consequences of regional political and economic integration for inequality and the welfare state in Western Europe*. PhD thesis, Indiana University, Bloomington.

Beckfield, Jason (2006) 'European integration and income inequality', *American Sociological Review 71*, 964–985.

Berger, Peter L., and Thomas Luckmann (1967) *The Social Construction of Reality: A Treatise in the Sociology of Knowledge*. Garden City, NY: Doubleday.

Bergland, Adel, Marit Kirkevold, Per-Olof Sandman, Dag Hofoss, and David Edvardsson (2015) 'The thriving of older people assessment scale: Validity and reliability assessments', *Journal of Advanced Nursing 71*(4), 942–951.

Bernardi, Laura (2011) 'A mixed-methods social networks study design for research on transnational families', *Journal of Marriage and Family 73*, 788–803.

Blau, Peter M. (1963) *The Dynamics of Bureaucracy: A Study of Interpersonal Relationships in Two Government Agencies* (rev. edn). Chicago: University of Chicago Press.

Boland, Angela, M. Gemma Cherry, and Rumona Dickson (2017) *Doing a Systematic Review: A Student's Guide* (2nd edn). London: Sage.

Booth, Andrew, Anthea Sutton, and Diana Papaioannou (2016) *Systematic Approaches to a Successful Literature Review* (2nd edn). London: Sage.

Born, Andreas, Pieter van Eck, and Magnus Johannesson (2018) 'An experimental investigation of election promises', *Political Psychology 39*(3), 685–705.

Bourdieu, Pierre, and Loïc Wacquant (1992) *An Invitation to Reflexive Sociology*. Chicago: University of Chicago Press.

Brady, David, Andrew S. Fullerton, and Jennifer Moren Cross (2009) 'Putting poverty in political context: A multi-level analysis of adult poverty across 18 affluent democracies', *Social Forces 88*(1), 271–299.

Brotsky, Sarah R., and David Giles (2007) 'Inside the "pro-ana" community: A covert online participant observation', *Eating Disorders, 15*(2), 93–109.

Callinicos, Alex (1989) *Against Postmodernism: A Marxist Critique*. Cambridge: Polity Press.

Chan, Zenobya C. Y., Wun San Tam, Maggie K. Y. Lung, Wing Yan Wong, and Ching Wa Chau (2013) 'A systematic literature review of nurse shortage and the intention to leave', *Journal of Nursing Management 21*, 605–613.

Chaiyapa, Warathida, Miguel Esteban, and Yasuko Kameyama (2018) 'Why go green? Discourse analysis of motivations for Thailand's oil and gas companies to invest in renewable energy', *Energy Policy 120*, 448–459.

Coleman, James (1990) *Foundations of Social Theory*. Cambridge, MA: Harvard University Press.

Collins, Randall (1975) *Conflict Sociology: Toward an Explanatory Science* (with a contribution by Joan Annett). New York: Academic Press.

Crosnoe, Robert, and Chandra Muller (2014) 'Family socioeconomic status, peers, and the path to college', *Social Problems 61*(4), 602–604.

Desforges, Luke, and Rhys Jones (2001) 'Bilingualism and geographical knowledge: A case study of students at the University of Wales, Aberystwyth', *Social & Cultural Geography 2*(3), 333–346.

Dickes, Lori A., and Elizabeth Crouch (2015) 'Policy effectiveness of U.S. governors: The role of gender and changing institutional powers', *Women's Studies International Forum 53*, 90–98.

Dobermann, Darja, and Ian S. Hamilton (2017) 'Publication patterns in developmental psychology: Trends and social networks', *International Journal of Psychology 52*(4), 336–347.

Durkheim, Emile (1897) *Le suicide*. Paris: Alcan.

Durkheim, Emile (1964) *The Rules of Sociological Method*. New York: Free Press. (Original edition (1894): *Les règles de la méthode sociologique*. Paris: Alcan.)

Duxbury, Joy A., Karen Margaret Wright, Anna Hart, Diane Bradley, Pamela Roach, Neil Harris, and Bernie Carter (2010) 'A structured observation of the interaction between nurses and patients during the administration of medication in an acute mental health unit', *Journal of Clinical Nursing 19*(17–18), 2481–2492.

Elias, Norbert (1978) *What Is Sociology?* London: Hutchinson.

Elliott, Mark A., Christopher J. Armitage, and Christopher J. Baughan (2005) 'Exploring the beliefs underpinning drivers' intentions to comply with speed limits', *Transportation Research Part F: Psychology and Behaviour 8*(6), 459–479.

Enders, Walter, and Gary A. Hoover (2004) 'Whose line is it? Plagiarism in economics', *Journal of Economic Literature 42*(3), 487–493.

Eriksson, Elisabeth, Lisa Björklund Boistrup, and Robert Thornberg (2017) 'A categorisation of teacher feedback in the classroom: A field study on feedback based on routine classroom assessment in primary school', *Research Papers in Education 32*(3), 316–332.

Etain, Bruno, Lydia Guittet, Nicolas Weiss, Vincent Gajdos, and Sandrine Katsahian (2014) 'Attitudes of medical students towards conflict of interest: A national survey in France', *PLoS One 9*(3), e92858.

Eurofound (2012) *Third European Quality of Life Survey – Quality of Life in Europe: Impacts of the Crisis.* Luxembourg: Publications Office of the European Union.

Eurofound (2016) *Fourth European Quality of Life Survey: Source Questionnaire.* Luxembourg: Publications Office of the European Union.

Eurostat (2018) *Living Conditions in Europe: 2018 Edition.* Luxembourg: Publications Office of the European Union.

Evergreen, Stephanie D. H. (2017) *Effective Data Visualization: The Right Chart for the Right Data.* London: Sage.

Fink, Arlene (2014) *Conducting Research Literature Reviews: From the Internet to Paper* (4th edn). London: Sage.

Flood, John (1991) 'Doing business: The management of uncertainty in lawyers' work', *Law & Society Review 25*(1), 41–71.

Folkeson, Lennart, Hans Antonson, and J. O. Helldin (2013) 'Planners' views on cumulative effects: A focus-group study concerning transport infrastructure planning in Sweden', *Land Use Policy 30*(1), 243–253.

Franzen, Axel (2003) 'Environmental attitudes in international comparison: An analysis of the ISSP Surveys 1993 and 2000', *Social Science Quarterly 84*(2), 297–308.

Fredrickson, George (1981) *White Supremacy.* New York: Oxford University Press.

Friedman, George (2016) '3 reasons Brits voted for Brexit', *Forbes*, 5 July (https://www.forbes.com/sites/johnmauldin/2016/07/05/3-reasons-brits-voted-for-brexit/#2d6350341f9d).

Fung, Cadi Y., and Ellis Adjei Adams (2017) 'What motivates student environmental activists on college campuses? An in-depth qualitative study', *Social Sciences 6*(4), art. 134.

Gadamer, Hans-Georg (2008) *Philosophical Hermeneutics.* Berkeley: University of California Press.

Gardner, Glenn, Christine Duffield, Anna Doubrovsky, and Margaret Adams (2016) 'Identifying advanced practice: A national survey of a nursing workforce', *International Journal of Nursing Studies 55*, 60–70.

Geertz, Clifford (2000) *The Interpretation of Cultures: Selected Essays.* New York: Basic Books.

Giddens, Anthony (1984) *The Constitution of Society: Outline of the Theory of Structuration.* Cambridge: Polity Press.

Glaser, Barney G., and Anselm L. Strauss (1967) *The Discovery of Grounded Theory: Strategies for Qualitative Research.* Chicago: Aldine.

Goffman, Erving (1959) *The Presentation of Self in Everyday Life.* London: Penguin.

Goffman, Erving (1964) 'The neglected situation', *American Anthropologist 66*, 133–136.

Golden-Biddle, Karen, and Karen Locke (2007) *Composing Qualitative Research* (2nd edn). London: Sage.

Gorton, William A. (2010) 'The philosophy of social science', *Internet Encyclopedia of Philosophy* (http://www.iep.utm.edu/soc-sci/).

Gould, Dinah, and Marina Fontenla (2006) 'Commitment to nursing: Results of a qualitative interview study', *Journal of Nursing Management 14*, 213–221.

Granovetter, Mark (1973) 'The strength of weak ties', *American Journal of Sociology 78*, 1360–1380.

Greene, Jennifer C., Valerie J. Caracelli, and Wendy F. Graham (1989) 'Toward a conceptual framework for mixed-method evaluation design', *Educational Evaluation and Policy Analysis 11*, 255–274.

Grønmo, Sigmund, and Trond Løyning (2003) *Sosiale nettverk og økonomisk makt: Overlappende styremedlemskap mellom norske bedrifter 1970–2000* [Social Networks and Economic Power: Interlocking Directorates among Norwegian Companies, 1970–2000]. Bergen: Fagbokforlaget.

Hakoköngäs, Eemeli, and Inari Sakki (2016) 'Visualized collective memories: Social representations of history in images found in Finnish history textbooks', *Journal of Community & Applied Social Psychology 26*(6), 496–517.

Halikoupoulou, Daphne, and Tim Vlandas (2016) 'Risks, costs and labour markets: Explaining cross-national patterns of far right party success in European Parliament elections', *Journal of Common Market Studies 54*, 636–655.

Hansen, Hans-Tore, Olaf Jürgens, Anne Hege H. Strand, and Wolfgang Voges (2006) 'Poverty among households with children: A comparative study of Norway and Germany', *International Journal of Social Welfare 15*(4), 269–279.

Harmsen, Irene A., Liesbeth Mollema, Robert A. C. Ruiter, Theo G. W. Paulussen, Hester E. de Melker, and Gerjo Kok (2013) 'Why parents refuse childhood vaccination: A qualitative study using online focus groups', *BMC Public Health 13*, 1183.

Heemskerk, Eelke M. (2011) 'The social field of the European corporate elite: A network analysis of interlocking directorates among Europe's largest corporate boards', *Global Networks 11*(4), 440–460.

Heyvaert, Mieke, Karin Hannes, and Patrick Onghena (2017) *Using Mixed Methods Research Synthesis for Literature Reviews*. London: Sage.

Hjellbrekke, Johs (2019) *Multiple Correspondence Analysis for the Social Sciences*. New York: Routledge.

Holsti, Ole R. (1969) *Content Analysis for the Social Sciences and Humanities*. Reading, MA: Addison-Wesley.

Hultén, Bertil M. L. (2015) 'The impact of sound experiences on the shopping behavior of children and their parents', *Marketing Intelligence & Planning 33*(2), 197–215.

Hum, Noelle J., Perrin E. Chamberlin, Brittany L. Hambright, Anne C. Portwood, Amanda C. Schat, and Jennifer L. Bevan (2011) 'A picture is worth a thousand words: A content analysis of Facebook profile photographs', *Computers in Human Behavior 27*, 1828–1833.

Humphreys, Lee, Phillippa Gill, Balachander Krishnamurthy, and Elisabeth Newbury (2013) 'Historicizing new media: A content analysis of Twitter', *Journal of Communication 63*(3), 413–431.

Iskhakova, Lilia, Stefan Hoffmann, and Andreas Hilbert (2017) 'Alumni loyalty: Systematic literature review', *Journal of Nonprofit & Public Sector Marketing 29*(3), 274–316.

Jackson, Kristi, and Patricia Bazeley (2019) *Qualitative Data Analysis with NVivo* (3rd edn). London: Sage.

Jacoby, William G. (1998) *Statistical Graphics for Visualizing Multivariate Data*. London: Sage.

Jang, S. Mo, Tieming Geng, Jo-Yun Queenie Li, Ruofan Xia, Chin-Ter Huang, Hwalbin Kim, and Jijun Tang (2018) 'A computational approach for examining the roots and spreading patterns of fake news: Evolution tree analysis', *Computers in Human Behavior 84*, 103–113.

Jick, Todd D. (1979) 'Mixing qualitative and quantitative methods: Triangulation in action', *Administrative Science Quarterly 24*, 602–611.

Jirata, Tadesse Jaleta (2012); 'Learning through play: An ethnographic study of children's riddling in Ethiopia', *Africa 82*(2), 272–286.

Johnson, Daniel K. N., and Ayfer Ali (2004) 'A tale of two seasons: Participation and medal counts at the Summer and Winter Olympic Games', *Social Science Quarterly 85*(4), 974–993.

Johnson, Lorraine M. (2001) *Factors that determine hospitalization of older adults*. Master's thesis, California State University, Long Beach. ProQuest Dissertations Publishing, 1404433.

Jones, Cindy D'On (2015) 'Effects of writing instruction on kindergarten students' writing achievement: An experimental study', *Journal of Educational Research 108*(1), 35–44.

Joyner, Randy L., William A. Rouse, and Allan A. Glatthorn (2013) *Writing the Winning Thesis or Dissertation: A Step-by-Step Guide* (3rd edn). London: Sage.

Jungherr, Andreas, Harald Schoen, and Pascal Jürgens (2016) 'The mediation of politics through Twitter: An analysis of messages posted during the campaign for the German federal election 2013', *Journal of Computer-Mediated Communication 21*(1), 50–68.

Kaefer, Florian, Juliet Roper, and Paresha Sinha (2015) 'A software-assisted qualitative content analysis of news articles: Example and reflections', *Forum: Qualitative Social Research 16*(2), art. 8.

Kallio, Tomi J., Kirsi-Mari Kallio, and Annika Johanna Blomberg (2015) 'Physical space, culture and organisational creativity: A longitudinal study', *Facilities 33*(5–6), 389–411.

Kamano, Saori (2009) 'Housework and lesbian couples in Japan: Division, negotiation and interpretation', *Women's Studies International Forum 32*, 130–141.

Karlsson, Martin (2012) 'Understanding divergent patterns of political discussion in online forums – Evidence from the European Citizens' Consultations', *Journal of Information Technology & Politics 9*, 64–81.

Katona, George (1964) *The Mass Consumption Society*. New York: McGraw Hill.

Keefer, Lucas A., Chris Goode, and Laura Van Berkel (2015) 'Toward a psychological study of class consciousness: Development and validation of a social psychological model', *Journal of Social and Political Psychology 3*(2), 253–290.

Kelle, Udo (ed.) (1995) *Computer-Aided Qualitative Data Analysis: Theory, Methods and Practice*. London: Sage.

Kemp, Sharon, and Larry Dwyer (2003) 'Mission statements of international airlines: A content analysis', *Tourism Management 24*, 635–653.

Kerlinger, Fred N. (1999) *Foundations of Behavioral Sciences: Educational and Psychological Enquiry* (4th edn). New York: Holt, Rinehart & Winston.

Kirk, Andy (2016) *Data Visualisation: A Handbook for Data Driven Design*. London: Sage.

Kitchin, Rob (2014) *The Data Revolution: Big Data, Open Data, Data Infrastructures and Their Consequences*. London: Sage.

Knorr-Cetina, Karin (1981) 'The micro-sociological challenge of macro-sociology: Towards a reconstruction of social theory and methodology', in Karin Knorr-Cetina and Aaron D. Cicourel (eds), *Advances in Social Theory and Methodology*. London: Routledge and Kegan Paul, pp. 1–47.

Kogut, Bruce, Jordi Colomer, and Mariano Belinky (2014) 'Structural equality at the top of the corporation: Mandated quotas for women directors', *Strategic Management Journal 35*(6), 891–902.

Kozinets, Robert V. (2015) *Netnography: Redefined* (2nd edn). London: Sage.

Kramer, Adam D. I., Jamie E. Guillory, and Jeffrey T. Hancock (2014) 'Experimental evidence of massive-scale emotional contagion through social networks', *Proceedings of the National Academy of Sciences of the USA 111*(24), 8788–8790.

Krippendorff, Klaus (1970) 'Estimating the reliability, systematic error, and random error of interval data', *Educational and Psychological Measurement 30*(1), 61–70.

Krippendorff, Klaus (2018) *Content Analysis: An Introduction to its Methodology* (4th edn). London: Sage.

Kuhn, Thomas (1970) *The Structure of Scientific Revolutions*. Chicago: University of Chicago Press.

Lavik, Randi (1979) *Holdning til handling: Hvordan kvinner og menn legger vekt på ulike sider ved dagligvareinnkjøp* [Attitudes to Shopping: How Women and Men Emphasize Different Aspects of Grocery Shopping]. Oslo: Norwegian Fund for Market and Distribution Research.

Lawson, Katie M., Laura Y. Kooiman, and Olyvia Kuchta (2018) 'Professors' behaviors and attributes that promote U.S. women's success in male-dominated academic majors: Results from a mixed methods study', *Sex Roles 78*(7–8), 542–560.

Lazer, David, and Jason Radford (2017) 'Data ex machina: Introduction to big data', *Annual Review of Sociology 43*, 19–39.

Lee, Barbara, Esme Fuller-Thomson, Barbara Fallon, Nico Trocmé, and Tara Black (2017) 'Asian-Canadian children and families involved in the child welfare system in Canada: A mixed methods study', *Child Abuse & Neglect 70*, 342–355.

Levin, Noam, Ali Saleem, and David Crandall (2018) 'Utilizing remote sensing and big data to quantify conflict intensity: The Arab Spring as a case study', *Applied Geography 94*, 1–17.

Li, Liuchuang, Gaoliang Tian, and Wenjia Yan (2013) 'The network of interlocking directorates and firm performance in transition economies: Evidence from China', *Journal of Applied Business Research 29*(2), 607–620.

Liu, Lisha (2013) *A qualitative study of international students' experiences of engaging in learning on UK full-time taught masters programmes*. PhD thesis, Institute of Education, University of London. ProQuest Dissertations Publishing, 10022078.

Lonkila, Markku, and Timo Harmo (1999) 'Toward computer-assisted qualitative network analysis', *Connections 22*, 52–61.

Maddox, Bryan (2015) 'The neglected situation: Assessment performance and interaction in context', *Assessment in Education: Principles, Policy & Practice 22*(4), 427–443.

Malterud, Kirsti (2012) 'Systematic text condensation: A strategy for qualitative analysis', *Scandinavian Journal of Public Health 40*(8), 795–805.

Mann, Chris, and Fiona Stewart (2000) *Internet Communication and Qualitative Research: A Handbook for Researching Online*. London: Sage.

Marshall, Catherine, and Gretchen B. Rossman (2015) *Designing Qualitative Research* (6th edn). Beverly Hills, CA: Sage.

Martinson, Brian C., Melissa S. Anderson, and Raymond De Vries (2005) 'Scientists behaving badly', *Nature 435*, 737–738.

Mason, Jennifer (2006) *Six Strategies for Mixing Methods and Linking Data in Social Science Research*. ESRC National Centre for Research Methods, Manchester: NCRM Working Paper Series 4/06.

Mayring, Philipp (2014) *Qualitative Content Analysis: Theoretical Foundation, Basic Procedures and Software Solution*. Klagenfurt (http://nbn-resolving.de/urn:nbn:de:0168-ssoar-395173).

McDaniel, Brenda L., and James W. Grice (2008) 'Predicting psychological well-being from self-discrepancies: A comparison of idiographic and nomothetic measures', *Self and Identity 7*, 243–261.

Merton, Robert K. (1957) *Social Theory and Social Structure* (rev. enl. edn). New York: Free Press.

Merton, Robert K. (1959) 'Notes on problem-finding in sociology', in Robert K. Merton, Leonard Broom, and Leonard S. Cottrell, Jr. (eds), *Sociology Today: Problems and Prospects*. New York: Basic Books, pp. ix–xxxiv.

Merton, Robert K. (1973) *The Sociology of Science: Theoretical and Empirical Investigations*. Chicago: University of Chicago Press.

Miles, Matthew B., A. Michael Huberman, and Johnny Saldaña (2019) *Qualitative Data Analysis – International Student Edition: A Methods Sourcebook* (4th edn). London: Sage.

Miller, James D. (2017) *Big Data Visualization*. Birmingham: Packt Books.

Mintz, Beth, and Michael Schwartz (1985) *The Power Structure of American Business*. Chicago: The University of Chicago Press.

Moreno, Jacob (1934) *Who Shall Survive?* New York: Beacon Press.

Morse, Janice M. (ed.) (1994) *Critical Issues in Qualitative Research Methods*. Thousand Oaks, CA: Sage.

Munzert, Simon, Christian Rubba, Peter Meissner, and Dominic Nyhuis (2014) *Automated Data Collection with R: A Practical Guide to Web Scraping and Text Mining*. Chichester: Wiley.

Muro, Diego, and Martijn C. Vlaskamp (2016) 'How do prospects of EU membership influence support for secession? A survey experiment in Catalonia and Scotland', *West European Politics 39*(6), 1115–1138.

Mutz, Diana C. (2011) *Population-Based Survey Experiments*. Princeton, NJ: Princeton University Press.

Nasrabadi, Alireza Nikbakht, Ali Montazeri, Hasan Eftekhar Ardebili, Setareh Homami, Yousef Karimi, Saharnaz Nedjat, Mahdi Moshki, and Ali Akbar Mansourian (2016) 'Exploring gender-based sibling roles: A qualitative study on contemporary Iranian families', *Journal of Family Issues 37*(5), 692–716.

Nielsen, Rasmus Kleis (2012) *Ground Wars: Personalized Communication in Political Campaigns*. Princeton, NJ: Princeton University Press.

Noh, Jin-Won, Jinseok Kim, Jumin Park, Hyun-jung Kim, and Young Dae Kwon (2015) 'Gender difference in relationship between health-related quality of life and work status', *PLoS One 10*(12), e0143579.

Novák, Jakub, and Luděk Sýkora (2007) 'A city in motion: Time–space activity and mobility patterns of suburban inhabitants and the structuration of the spatial organization of the Prague metropolitan area', *Geografiska Annaler: Series B, Human Geography 89*(2), 147–168.

Oliver, Paul (2014) *Writing Your Thesis* (3rd edn). London: Sage.

Onwuegbusie, Anthony, R. Burke Johnson, and Kathleen M. T. Collins (2009) 'Call for mixed analysis: A philosophical framework for combining qualitative and quantitative approaches', *International Journal of Multiple Research Approaches 3*, 114–139.

Onwuegbuzie, Anthony J., and Rebecca Frels (2016) *Seven Steps to a Comprehensive Literature Review: A Multimodal and Cultural Approach*. London: Sage.

Oosthuizen, Martha J. (2012) 'The portrayal of nursing in South-African newspapers: A qualitative content analysis', *Africa Journal of Nursing and Midwifery 14*(1), 49–62.

Parsons, Talcott (1951) *The Social System*. New York: Free Press.

Parsons, Talcott, and Robert F. Bales (1953) 'The dimensions of action-space', in Talcott Parsons, Robert F. Bales, and Edward A. Shils, *Working Papers in the Theory of Action*. Glencoe, IL: Free Press.

Pawson, Ray, Trisha Greenhalgh, Gill Harvey, and Kieran Walshe (2005) 'Realist review – A new method of systematic review designed for complex policy interventions', *Journal of Health Services Research & Policy*, *10*, 21–34.

Perrin-Wallqvist, Renée, and Josephine Lindblom (2015) 'Coming out as gay: A phenomenological study about adolescents disclosing their homosexuality to their parents', *Social Behavior and Personality 43*(3), 467–480.

Persson, Nils Bertil Gerhard (2014) 'A study of personality and family- and school environment and possible interactional effects in 244 Swedish children – A multiple regression analysis', *Psychology 5*, 886–895.

Pflug, Verena, and Silvia Schneider (2016) 'School absenteeism: An online survey via social networks', *Child Psychiatry & Human Development 47*(3), 417–429.

Pritchard, Rosalind (2007) 'Gender inequality in British and German universities', *Compare 37*, 651–659.

Pritchard, Rosalind (2010a) 'Attitudes to gender equality issues in British and German academia', *Higher Education Management and Policy 22*(2), 37–60.

Pritchard, Rosalind (2010b) 'Gender inequalities among staff in British and German universities: A qualitative study', *Compare 40* (4), 515–532.

Ragin, Charles C. (1987) *The Comparative Method: Moving beyond Qualitative and Quantitative Strategies.* Berkeley: University of California Press.

Rahmqvist, Johanna, Michael B. Wells, and Anna Sarkadi (2014) Conscious parenting: A qualitative study on Swedish parents' motives to participate in a parenting program', *Journal of Child and Family Studies 23*, 934–944.

Rath, Jessica M., Eva Sharma, and Kenneth H. Beck (2013) 'Reliability and validity of the Glover-Nilsson smoking behavioral questionnaire', *American Journal of Health Behavior 37*(3), 310–317.

Rich, Timothy S. (2012) 'Deciphering North Korea's nuclear rhetoric: An automated content analysis of KCNA News', *Asian Affairs: An American Review 39*(2), 73–89.

Ritzer, George (1980) *Sociology: A Multiple Paradigm Science.* Boston: Allyn & Bacon.

Ruitenberg, Justine (2014) 'A typology of Dutch mothers' employment narratives: Drifters, privilegeds, balancers, ambitious', *Gender Issues 31*(1), 58–82.

Russell, Marie, Rachel Price, Louise Signal, James Stanley, Zachery Gerring, and Jacqueline Cumming (2011) 'What do passengers do during travel time? Structured observations on buses and trains', *Journal of Public Transportation 14*(3), 123–146.

Sasson, Hagit, and Gustavo Mesch (2016) 'Gender differences in the factors explaining risky behavior online', *Journal of Youth and Adolescence 45*(5), 973–985.

Schmid, Claudia Theresia (2016) *Germany's 'open-door' policy in light of the recent refugee crisis: An interpretive thematic content analysis of possible reasons and underlying motivations.* Master's thesis, Linköping University, Sweden.

Schütz, Alfred (1967) *The Phenomenology of the Social World.* Evanston, IL: Northwestern University Press.

Scott, John (1990) *A Matter of Record: Documentary Sources in Social Research.* Cambridge: Polity Press.

Shah, Dhavan, Joseph Cappella, and W. Russell Neuman, W (2015) 'Big data, digital media, and computational social science: Possibilities and perils', *Annals of the American Academy of Political and Social Science 659*, 6–13.

Skocpol, Theda (1979) *States and Social Revolutions: A Comparative Analysis of France, Russia and China.* Cambridge: Cambridge University Press.

Spanemberg, Lucas, Giovanni Abrahão Salum, Marco Antonio Caldieraro, Edgar Arrua Vares, Ricardo Dahmer Tiecher, Neusa Sica Da Rocha, Gordon Parker, and Marcelo P. Fleck (2014) 'Personality styles in depression: Testing reliability and validity of hierarchically organized constructs', *Personality and Individual Differences 70*, 72–79.

Stacey, Anthony (2016) 'Mitigating against data fabrication and falsification: A protocol of trias politica for business research', *Electronic Journal of Business Research Methods 14*(2), 72–82.

Steyrer, Johannes, Michael Schiffinger, and Reinhard Lang (2008) 'Organizational commitment – A missing link between leadership behavior and organizational performance?', *Scandinavian Journal of Management* 24, 364–374.

Stier, Haga, and Meir Yaish (2014) 'Occupational segregation and gender inequality in job quality: A multi-level approach', *Work, Employment and Society* 28(2), 225–246.

Stitzel, Brandli, Gary A. Hoover, and William Clark (2018) 'More on plagiarism in the social sciences', *Social Science Quarterly* 99(3), 1075–1088.

Stokman, Frans N., Ralf Ziegler, and John Scott (eds) (1985) *Networks of Corporate Power: A Comparative Analysis of Ten Countries*. Cambridge: Polity Press.

Sue, Valerie M., and Matthew T. Griffin (2016) *Data Visualization & Presentation with Microsoft Office*. London: Sage.

Sun, Ivan Y., Mingyue Su, and Yuning Wu (2011) 'Attitudes toward police response to domestic violence: A comparison of Chinese and American college students', *Journal of Interpersonal Violence* 26(16), 3289–3315.

Szalai, Alexander (ed.) (1972) *The Use of Time: Daily Activities of Urban and Suburban Populations in Twelve Countries*. The Hague: Mouton.

Tay, Louis, Vincent Ng, Abish Malik, Jiawei Zhang, Junghoon Chae, David S. Ebert, Yiqing Ding, Jieqiong Zhao, and Margaret Kern (2018) 'Big data visualizations in organizational science', *Organizational Research Methods* 21(3), 660–688.

te Grotenhuis, Manfred, and Anneke Matthijssen (2016) *Basic SPSS Tutorial*. London: Sage.

Tight, Malcolm (2017) *Understanding Case Study Research*. London: Sage.

Tourangeau, Roger, Frederick Conrad, and Mick P. Couper (2013) *The Science of Web Surveys*. Oxford: Oxford University Press.

Turcan, Romeo V., and Norman M. Fraser (2016) 'An ethnographic study of new venture and new sector legitimation. Evidence from Moldova', *International Journal of Emerging Markets* 11(1), 72–88.

Van Der Wildt, Anouk, Piet Van Avermaet, and Mieke Van Houtte (2015) 'Do birds singing the same song flock together? A mixed-method study on language as a tool for changing social homophily in primary schools in Flanders (Belgium)', *International Journal of Intercultural Relations* 49, 168–182.

Vu, Mary, Scott T. Leatherdale, and Rashid Ahmed (2011) 'Examining correlates of different cigarette access behaviours among Canadian youth: Data from the Canadian Youth Smoking Survey (2006)', *Addictive Behaviors* 36(12), 1313–1316.

Wadel, Cato (1973) *Now, Whose Fault Is That? The Struggle for Self-Esteem in the Face of Chronic Unemployment*. Toronto: University of Toronto Press.

Webb, Jeff, and Ann Engar (2016) 'Exploring classroom community: A social network study of Reacting to the Past', *Teaching & Learning Inquiry* 4(1).

Weber, Max (2013) *Economy and Society*. Berkeley: University of California Press. (Original edition (1922) *Wirtschaft und Gesellscahft*. Tübingen: Mohr.)

Weir, Roisin (2014) *Gender roles in leadership and management: A narrative enquiry based in the U.K.* Master's thesis, Umeå University, Sweden.

Welles, Brooke Foucault (2014) 'On minorities and outliers: The case for making Big Data small', *Big Data & Society* 1(1), 1–2.

Whyte, William Foot (1943) *Street Corner Society: The Social Structure of an Italian Slum*. Chicago: University of Chicago Press.

Williams, Matthew L., and Pete Burnap (2016) 'Cyberhate on social media in the aftermath of Woolwich: A case study in computational criminology and big data', *British Journal of Criminology 56*(2), 211–238.

Windelband, Wilhelm (1904) *Geschichte und Naturwissenschaft*. Strassbourg: Heitz.

Yanchus, Nancy J., Lindsey Ohler, Emily Crowe, Robert Teclaw, and Katerine Osatuke (2017) '"You just can't do it all": A secondary analysis of nurses' perceptions of teamwork, staffing and workload', *Journal of Research in Nursing 22*(4), 313–325.

Yang, Tingzhong, Ian R. H. Rockett, Qiaohong Lv, and Randall R. Cottrell (2012) 'Stress status and related characteristics among urban residents: A six-province capital cities study in China', *PLoS One 7*(1), e30521.

Yates, Luke, and Alan Warde (2015) 'The evolving content of meals in Great Britain. Results of a survey in 2012 in comparison with the 1950s', *Appetite 84*, 299–308.

Zerubavel, Eviatar (1999) *The Clockwork Muse: A Practical Guide to Writing Theses, Dissertations, and Books*. Cambridge, MA: Harvard University Press.

INDEX

Terms in italic can also be found in the glossary